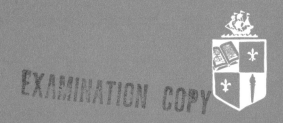

To

Mildred R. Kramer

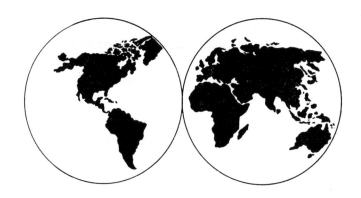

International Marketing

Second Edition

by **ROLAND L. KRAMER,** PH. D.
Professor of Commerce and Transportation
Wharton School of Finance and Commerce
University of Pennsylvania

SOUTH-WESTERN
Burlingame, Calif.
S81 Cincinnati

Chicago

PUBLISHING COMPANY
New Rochelle, N. Y.
Dallas

Preface

International Marketing, revised, is a rearrangement and, in some measure, a rewriting of its antecedent. Every effort has been made to update the book. In addition, new developments have been added such as the antitrust policy of the European Economic Community, new international banking and financing facilities, and foreign credit insurance in the United States. A new chapter on overseas manufacturing has been added.

The revision is also an acknowledgment of its reception that has been impressive and for which the author expresses his gratitude.

The present volume is divided into five parts — the nature and promotion of international marketing; international marketing organizations and methods, essentially home based; international marketing organizations and methods, essentially foreign based; technical and legal features of international marketing; and, financial features of international marketing — compared with three parts in its predecessor.

Part I provides a framework in which the actual organization and operations in international marketing fit. The economic principles that are applicable are treated in general. The international marketing position of the United States, foreign market surveys, and trade promotion activities of governments and of private United States agencies complete Part I.

The presentation in Part II is believed to be unique, since the marketing organizations and methods are presented from the standpoint of international marketing in such a manner as to avoid the confusion that results from treating exports and imports as separate topics. An aid to this treatment is presented in the opening pages of Chapters 9 and 10 by means of an outline.

Part III deals with foreign operations, dealer cooperation, international advertising, and cooperative exporting.

Part IV treats the major technical and legal features of international marketing. Part V presents the vital subject of financial features of international marketing. This is presented from the standpoint of the business enterprise and explains how and why these features should be thoroughly understood. International banking facilities and their use, foreign credit extension, foreign credit insurance, and foreign exchange problems are covered.

In addition to the privilege of having worked with the late Professor Grover G. Huebner for thirty-five years and having taught foreign trade and related fields for that period of time, the author has had the privilege of serving the Foreign Traders Association of Philadelphia, Inc., as Executive Secretary from 1934 to 1964. This affiliation has been richly rewarding, since the members of that fine group have always been helpful.

There are many who have aided, advised, criticized, and instructed in the completion of this book. These are Charles W. Applegate, deceased, former Export Manager of The Esterbrook Pen Company; Henry W. Farnum, Vice-President, Insurance Company of North America; William H. Lukens, retired Vice-President (Export) of the R. M. Hollingshead Corporation; Thomas C. Ballagh, President, Ballagh and Thrall, combination export managers; C. Robert Haines, Vice-President, Girard Trust Corn Exchange Bank; George W. Tomlinson, Assistant Vice-President, The First Pennsylvania Banking and Trust Company; William J. Martin, President, F. B. Vandergrift & Company; Joseph V. McGuire, Regional Manager, American Cable and Radio Corporation; and the foreign commerce staff of the Philadelphia Regional Office of the United States Department of Commerce.

Finally, two recent developments in the international marketing area indicate the serious and deep educational interest that has been evoked. The first of these is the Association for Education in International Business dating from 1959. This is an association of the teachers and researchers in the field of international business. Two meetings are held each year. The first is in connection with the National Foreign Trade Convention in November each year. The other is in connection with the Christmas meetings of the Allied Social Science Associations.

The other fascinating and thrilling development is the American Society of International Executives dating from April, 1964. This is a professional society, the aims of which are to raise the levels of those who are engaged in the international business field. Certain classes of membership are available only upon passing qualifying examinations; other classes of membership are open to experienced, senior, corporate, contributing, and cooperating applicants. This is the first attempt to professionalize the field of international business and, after five months, the robust baby gives every indication of growing to healthy maturity.

Roland L. Kramer

Contents

PART I THE NATURE AND PROMOTION OF INTERNATIONAL MARKETING

Chapter 1 • page 1 • The Nature of International Marketing

Chapter 2 • page 19 • The International Marketing Position of the United States

Chapter 3 • page 47 • Foreign Market Surveys

Chapter 4 • page 66 • Promotion by the United States Government

Chapter 5 • page 97 • Promotion by Foreign Governments and the United Nations

Chapter 6 • page 106 • Promotion by Private United States Agencies

Chapter 7 • page 120 • The Scope of International Marketing

Contents

PART IV TECHNICAL AND LEGAL FEATURES OF INTERNATIONAL MARKETING

PART V FINANCIAL FEATURES OF INTERNATIONAL MARKETING

PART I

THE NATURE AND PROMOTION
OF INTERNATIONAL MARKETING

Part I serves to impart a modest presentation of the *why* of international marketing. The reasons explaining the conduct of business with other countries and in other countries are examined. Then follows an analysis of *what* the international business means to the United States, that is, to the nation, to the people, to the industries, to the farms, and to the other economic segments of the country.

In the knowledge that it is wise to look before leaping, the nature and development of foreign market surveys is presented as a step preliminary to the conduct of international business. Such surveys seek to analyze the feasibility of the contemplated international marketing effort or the significance of changes affecting existing efforts. In order to undertake a foreign market survey of any nature, it is necessary not only to know *what* to look for but also to know *where* to look. Three chapters are devoted to an analysis of the sources of information and the nature of those sources that are available to the firm engaged in international marketing.

Part I concludes with a discussion of the scope of international marketing. This philosophical presentation will serve to draw together the *why*, the *what*, the *where*, and the *how* to formulate a business policy geared to international marketing.

CHAPTER 1

THE NATURE OF INTERNATIONAL MARKETING

International Marketing differs from domestic marketing for one basic reason, viz., it involves doing business with individuals, firms, organizations, and/or government entities in other countries. Accepting this as the truth, the reader may ask, "If this is all of the difference between domestic and international marketing, why such a large book and so much literature?"

This question has been raised for many decades. Even today, there are those who declare that domestic and international business are essentially the same — people must eat and find shelter and work, etc. Of course, this is perfectly true, but it completely overlooks the fact that international marketing has to do with business as well as physical conditions of peoples.

The Breadth of International Marketing

While international marketing deals with the conduct of business, it cannot ignore the circumstances and conditions under which this business can be conducted. If a business firm manufactures and seeks to export food, medicine, or clothing, it has a very direct interest in the basic physical conditions of peoples of other countries. The same may be said of any other product or service for which a market overeseas is sought. If books are to be exported, there must be people who can understand these books and also able to pay for them. If automobiles are exported, there must be roads and service facilities, as well as purchasing power. If industrial machinery is exported, there must be some industry that can make effective use of such machinery.

Therefore, as will be pointed out in Chapter 3, international marketing embraces a wide field of collateral studies, all of which have a direct bearing on the international marketing effort. Some of these will be pointed out later in this chapter.

The conduction of international business, however, is quite apart from this wide field of collateral studies. There are differences in attitudes and intensity with which business firms engage in this business. There is a necessity to develop a knowledge of international marketing conditions and of their frequent changes; this requires a knowledge of sources of information and of how to evaluate and use them.

The various methods of engaging in international marketing must be fully understood, because it is conceivable that practically all of these channels would be used at certain times and under certain circumstances by a given firm.

The financial conditions relating to the conduct of international marketing are quite different in most respects from those employed in financing domestic trade. The matter of credit extension and methods of financing are extremely important. Legal considerations are, in many respects, different from those found in domestic business.

Finally, there is the entire field of government control and restriction exercised by every sovereignty. In this discussion of the nature of international marketing, the assumption is that competition is open and free. Unfortunately, competition is generally not open and free; laws, restrictions, taxes, tariffs, and controls are all part of the expressed sovereignty of all countries. These devices are constantly changing, and they must be followed closely in any international marketing venture.

Differences in Resources and Skills

If someone wishes to obtain a product or service, he will normally and naturally seek it from the most convenient and least expensive source. Taken in order, these sources would be next door, in the neighborhood, downtown, next town, next county, nearest state, national market, and, finally, foreign market.

International marketing exists because of the differences in resources and skills throughout the world. The economic terminology for this condition is the international division of labor.

Climatic conditions or the existence of special national resources may cause certain nations or some sections of the world to produce particular commodities for domestic consumption and also for exportation to other countries that are not so favored. Since bananas are not commercially produced in the United States because of climatic and other factors, they are imported. The United States possesses no commercial deposits of tin; thus, all tin is imported into the United States. Many other articles of international commerce, however, are of such a character that they might be produced in all or most of the countries of the commercial world. International division of labor in their production depends essentially upon cost considerations.

Now, the fact that a country or a region possesses a certain product or skill does not mean that the product or skill will flow into international marketing. When competition is open and free, the matter of cost is of prime importance.

It stands to reason that if a given country is able to produce a certain product or service more cheaply than any other country can produce and deliver, there will be no point in importing such product or service into the first country. This is assuming, of course, that such product or service is being produced in sufficient volume to meet all of the needs of the first country.

However, there are different levels of costs and also of profits. Suppose a country were able to produce every product and service at a lower cost than any other country. The assumption would be that such country would import nothing but would export everything. As will be pointed out later, this is impossible because countries that purchase from the low cost country would have no means of paying for the products or services that they import.

Quite apart from this consideration, there is still another factor that would apply. There would naturally be a difference in the profit margins of the goods and services that are all produced at low cost. It would, therefore, be advantageous for such a country to devote its resources and skills to the products and services that provide the highest profit, and to import products and services that provide the least profit. In so doing, such a country would be in a better profit position because it would be exchanging its highest profit goods and services for those of other countries in which it has a lower profit position.

Many familiar examples may be cited to illustrate these points. The United States exports machinery because importing countries are unable to produce the same machinery at as low a price. Swiss watches are imported, despite tariff imposed by the United States, because these watches undersell similar (not necessarily identical) watches made in the United States. Foreign sports cars are being imported in increasing numbers because they continue to meet a certain type of demand for a small sports car that had traditionally not been produced in this country by United States automobile manufacturers.

Moreover, the international division of labor is less specific than national boundary lines. It does not provide each nation with exclusive industries and compel all other nations to import from them; rather, it results in agricultural nations or larger regions of the world and sections producing mainly raw materials, in contrast with industrial nations or regions. The former produce a heavy surplus of farm products or raw materials for exportation to industrial nations, and the latter produce a large surplus of manufactures for exportation to nonindustrial regions. A nation such as the United States, of course, may produce certain farm products and raw materials as well as certain manufactures for export, for international division of labor is regional rather than national in scope. The cost advantages of producing commodities in different regions of the world are not sufficiently divergent that they would prevent several countries from producing them for export. The problem of most American export industries is not only to develop a foreign market demand for commodities of the kind produced by them but also to meet the competition of rival export industries located in other regions, as well as rival American companies.

International marketing is by no means limited to trade between industrial regions and regions producing agricultural products or raw materials. There is much interchange of manufactures between the several industrial nations. Some of this is directly in accord with the division of labor principle, the interchange consisting of entirely unlike manufactured products, or of like products of substantially different quality. Although the United States, for example, has a large cotton textile industry that produces both for domestic consumption and for export, substantial quantities of distinctive cotton textiles of high grade continue to be imported. Some of the interchange of manufactures between industrial nations, moreover, consists of competitive products. Too, not all industries are established on the basis of favorable comparative costs or on the basis of patents or exclusive industrial information. The protective tariff and nontariff policies of many nations encourage industries, some of which do not have the advantage of favorable costs. If in such instances the restrictive wall is not prohibitive, low-cost foreign nations may find a limited market.

Were it not for international marketing, the continued development of the range of industries best adapted to the conditions prevailing in the

United States or any other country would obviously be impossible. Unless these industries regularly exported their surplus output, their growth in the future would be limited by the requirements of the domestic market, and the tendency of labor and capital would be to spill over into industries having a smaller comparative cost advantage. Were it not for the import trade, the development of industries having a smaller comparative cost advantage would become necessary, and domestic requirements would also compel the production of an increasing range of other commodities, regardless of unfavorable production costs.

Now we turn to another consideration that determines the extent to which countries with cost advantages engage in international marketing. Although many of the industries of any particular nation producing exportable commodities are determined largely by the division of labor and comparative cost principles, it does not follow that every industry having favorable comparative costs is actively engaged in the export trade. Nor does it follow that all of the industries due to particular climatic conditions or possession of certain natural resources promptly engage in the export trade from the moment of their establishment.

The principles discussed above determine the establishment of the industries producing exportable products, but they do not determine the point at which they will begin to export their commodities in appreciable quantities. An industry may be of the type that has the greatest comparative advantage in cost of production, and yet it may undergo many years of development before it will regularly export a substantial part of its output. Experience has shown that no industry ordinarily will produce largely for export so long as the domestic market readily absorbs its gradually increasing output.

An exception to this principle was revealed in the years following World War II when some countries, chiefly those of the United Kingdom, pushed exports and deliberately reduced domestic consumption. This was done because of the United Kingdom's desperate foreign trading position.

When the domestic market is saturated to the extent that further growth is retarded, or price demoralization, due to lack of an adequate domestic market, is imminent, an industry (provided it produces exportable products) begins to produce a permanent surplus for exportation. This point of surplus production determines the time when an industry having a comparative cost advantage enters the export trade in a permanent way. Many of the industries of the United States — iron and steel, farm machinery, automotive, petroleum, cotton textiles, etc., — are now regularly producing a surplus for export; some have reached the point of exportation sooner than others. Still other industries are not yet interested in the export trade, but they may attain the point of surplus production at some later date in their development. A number of American industries producing exportable products may never export an appreciable part of their output because of their inability to produce a surplus over and above domestic requirements. It is quite conceivable that certain of our exporting industries may in the future produce a smaller surplus and ultimately withdraw from the export markets.

The principle of surplus production does not imply that no products whatever are exported by an industry until it produces a permanent surplus. An industry may at times attempt to export a temporary surplus; or prices in domestic and foreign markets may temporarily be out of alignment so as to encourage exports; and there have long been export commission houses and other middlemen who will fill any foreign orders that they may obtain. For example, seasonal or style merchandise may be in surplus in the sense that the domestic market is no longer currently interested in purchasing such goods. They are then often sold outside of the United States. Prices fall out of alignment when, for example, foreign exchange rates change suddenly. If country A devalues its currency, prices of country A's goods will be temporarily less in foreign countries. A commodity may also lose its competitive position because of a government price stabilization policy. For many years, raw cotton was known as "King Cotton" because it was the United States export with the greatest single value. When prices were raised during the 1930's to help cotton farmers, the price of United States cotton was generally higher than competitive cotton offered in world markets. In the summer of 1956, the United States Government announced an intention to offer cotton for export at competitive prices, as a result of which cotton exports expanded greatly.

Finally, professional international middlemen, as export commission houses, act as buying agents in the United States and purchase anything their principals request, regardless of whether a surplus is technically available for export. But the quantities exported are usually small and irregular until a permanent surplus available for exportation is produced, and the producing industry usually does not become directly and keenly interested in export trade promotion until the point of surplus production has been reached or is imminent. An industry may, of course, discount the time when it will be producing a substantial export surplus, so as to place itself in a favorable position for exportation in the near future when it anticipates the production of a permanent surplus. The United States automobile, cash register, and sewing machine industries are examples of this policy. Long before the saturation of the domestic market is approached, these products (and others) are established in foreign markets. In such instances, the foreign and domestic markets are expected to grow together.

Sovereignty and Its Ramifications

Every national political entity is sovereign with respect to its own policies and the ways in which it deals with other sovereignties. It may pass laws governing the rights and privileges of citizens of other sovereignties residing or doing business within its jurisdiction. It may impose taxes and regulations on imported merchandise, bank deposits, investments, insurance underwriting, or any other activity that citizens of other sovereignties seek to perform within its jurisdiction.

Likewise, a citizen of any sovereignty can have relations of every nature with citizens of other sovereignties only to the extent provided by his own. For example, an American citizen can travel abroad only to the extent that his own sovereignty authorizes his passport. This may forbid his visiting certain other sovereign states.

Thus, the laws and policies of the governments of the markets of the world are determined by those governments; and the rights that any given citizen possesses depend upon the provision that his own country has made in negotiation (or without negotiation) with other sovereignties. Strictly speaking, when John Jones, United States citizen, travels abroad, he is not only John Jones — the more significant fact is that he is a citizen of the United States.

In all cases in which sovereign states deal with each other at the political level, agreements and treaties are negotiated, setting forth the conditions under which the citizens of the respective sovereignties may deal with each other.

Sovereignty lays the foundation for several other factors that are basic to international marketing. One of these is the right to establish its own monetary system.

The currency used in the United States is the United States dollar. The currency used in France is the French franc. Nearly every sovereignty has its own monetary system. When engaging in international marketing these different monetary systems provide peculiar conditions unknown in domestic trade.

The trading operation that involves the purchase and sale of the currency of one state (franc) with the currency of another state (United States dollar) is called *foreign exchange*. The units that one United States dollar will purchase in francs are expressed by the *foreign exchange rate* (price).

Sovereignty also provides the right to impose laws and regulations governing the conduct of international marketing. Nations in the contemporary period are more disposed to seek full employment and improved standards of living by forcing the rate of economic development. In such a situation, the cold economic facts are seldom measured and weighed. Emotion and pride may spawn work laws, minimum-wage laws, nationalistic twisting of foreign capitalists and business interests, building of factories, and other advanced concepts. Sometimes these concepts are further advanced than the countries that advance them.

In the case of more advanced nations, the policy of survival in face of external threats to peace will cause the adoption of policies that serve these objectives. "National security" is a banner under which many uneconomic and otherwise unjustified policies may be mobilized.

Thus, the contemporary scene demands that political objectives, and not only pure economics, must be judged as accurately as possible and dealt with accordingly.

As a derivative of sovereignty, although not identified with it, is the matter of different languages and customs.

International marketing is generally identified with people whose language and customs are different. One of the requirements of international marketing is to learn the meaning of languages and customs and how to deal with them. If correspondence is conducted in German; if personal sales representation is in Spanish; if business houses close for three hours in the early afternoon; if Saturday is a holiday; if, in short, there are languages or customs that are different, the business enterprise engaging in international marketing must take cognizance of them. It cannot overrule them because it lacks authority. It cannot ignore them because this would be foolish and possibly insulting.

Languages and customs can and should be fascinating features of international marketing. They are vastly different in many respects from similar factors encountered in domestic marketing.

International Marketing and National Welfare

A basic consideration that must be emphasized is what is known as the balance of international payments. National welfare would presumably be advanced if a country succeeded in exporting without the necessity of importing. In that way, it would have the rest of the world at its mercy as it would be receiving tribute for the privilege of being so superior economically. However, as pointed out above, such country would have no means of collecting for the exports that it sold.

The most prevalent misconception is that the nation's gain from foreign commerce springs from its "favorable balance of trade," that is, from the excess of exported over imported commodities. This export balance of trade or mercantilist theory, which prevailed more generally during the sixteenth, seventeenth, and eighteenth centuries, has long since been discarded by economists and by enlightened statesmen and businessmen. Some mercantilists emphasized an export trade balance because of its possible bearing upon increased gold stocks for war purposes, reduced dependence upon foreign sources of supply under war conditions, or enhanced domestic employment of labor. Failing to realize that national wealth is derived basically from the production and distribution of commodities and the performance of services, many of the mercantilists, however, overemphasized the precious metals as the basis of wealth. They regarded the excess of exported over imported commodities as the main national gain derived from international commerce, because they believed that this excess would come to the nation in the form of gold. Many devices were employed to encourage exports and discourage imports.

A nation may, indeed, be so situated in its business relations with the rest of the world that its imports *must* exceed its exports. An excess of imports may provide the basis that makes possible the receipt of interest and dividends on foreign investments, of payments for services performed in international marketing, or of returns from other transactions that add to the aggregate gain arising from a nation's total international business relations. The United Kingdom, for example, for many years imported foreign commodities in excess of its export trade, the excess of imports being regarded as a necessary factor in the nation's balance of international payments and a source of financial gain. The commodity exports of the United States, on the contrary, have for many years exceeded its commodity imports. Both nations have gained from their international commerce.

Whether the exports or imports of a particular country show an excess has depended largely upon its position as a debtor or a creditor nation, the position of the service and capital movement items entering into its balance of international payments, and the stage of its economic development. A borrowing nation will usually at first have an excess of imports, the borrowed funds being received primarily not in the form of gold imports but in the form of imported commodities of commerce. Later, it usually will have an excess of exports, for during the period of interest remittance or of loan repayment, the borrowed funds will be returned mainly in the form of exported commodities. Conversely, a creditor nation will at first usually have an excess of exports; and later, during the period of repayment, an excess of imports. The change from an excess of exports to an excess of imports may occur even before the period of principal repayments is reached, for interest payments must be made to the creditor nation; and when they are no longer offset by new loans, the relationship between exports and imports may be revised. But the exact status of a nation's export or import balance of trade at any particular time in the future cannot be forecast, for all of the service and capital movement items of its balance of international payments are pertinent factors, and many of them may undergo drastic changes.

The mercantilists' balance-of-trade theory clearly does not agree with the experience of modern trading nations and the known interrelations of the items comprising the balance of international payments.

The gain resulting from international commerce does not result from the acquisition of precious metals; nor is it derived from commodity exports alone. Imports and exports are mutually advantageous and, indeed, necessary to modern economic life. Both are essential items in the total balance of international payments, both are related to the service and capital movement items of this balance, and they are also related to each other. Both are directly essential to a nation's well-being, for no nation is, or could advantageously be, self-sufficient.

Purchasing Power

Whereas the need for a balance of international payments is concerned with the existence of adequate foreign exchange for the transfer of funds between nations, purchasing power as used here is concerned with the ability of the purchasers of imported wares to make payment in the national currencies of their respective countries. It is, of course, part and parcel of the international division of labor and comparative cost principles that purchasing power tends to increase by reducing unit costs of producing and by raising the wages of large groups of workers. As an immediate direct trade factor, however, the purchasing power of foreign customers determines the market in particular countries, and concurrently limits the ability of each country to import merchandise from abroad. The ability of business firms or consumers to purchase and pay for large or small quantities of merchandise is a direct trade factor in domestic as well as in foreign commerce. In this connection, the current development programs of underdeveloped areas are to be evaluated especially as to their long-run implications.

The Business Enterpriser

The value of international marketing to individual producers, financial institutions, merchants, carriers, and other business concerns is not difficult to understand. They are interested in foreign trade because of the direct or indirect profits derived from it. Producers not only expect a profit on the commodities sold abroad, but they also look upon foreign markets as a basis upon which they can increase their production beyond the limits set by domestic commerce. Export markets enable many industries to keep their labor and capital employed more fully and continuously, to expand their plants more rapidly than domestic commerce alone would warrant, to realize the reduced costs so frequently resulting from mass production, to steady their prices, or to distribute their sales so widely that the effects of business depressions will be reduced to a minimum. Not all of these benefits have always been attained.

Some American industries regularly export a large proportion of their output. Approximately 27 percent of the nation's petroleum lubricants, 73 percent of its railroad locomotives, 66 percent of its other locomotives (industrial and mining), 58 percent of its track-laying type tractors, 28 percent of its textile machinery and parts, and 26 percent of its pulp mill products are sold abroad. Many important agricultural products — cotton, cotton linters, cottonseed, leaf tobacco, wheat, field peas, hops, lemons and limes, mohair, milled rice, dried and evaporated fruits, dry whole milk, oleo oil, and lard — have been exported on a pronounced scale, and the relationship between foreign trade and their production and distribution is clear. Finally, certain minerals — bauxite, molybdenum, phosphate rock, and sulfur — are exported extensively in relation to production.

Most manufacturing industries in the United States are less dependent upon foreign markets. Many of those now engaged in the export trade do not export more than from 5 to 15 percent of their output. In such industries the importance of the export trade is sometimes underestimated. The small percentage of total output sold abroad is not a true measure of the effect it may have upon an industry. A loss of 10 percent of an industry's market may spell the difference between prosperity and depression. The last small percentage of output and sales may have an important effect upon an industry's profits and upon its ability to operate its plants to capacity. If this 10 percent of additional market is provided by the export trade, it is readily discernible why an increasing range of industries is so keenly interested in foreign sales.

There is more misunderstanding concerning the importance of foreign commerce to the nation as a whole than with respect to its importance to individual foreign trading concerns. The enlightened businessman is interested in the national welfare as well as in the profits of his enterprise, and the government and general public, as well as the business community, are concerned with commercial policy.

Trade Promotion

All of the factors and considerations discussed thus far would remain inert were it not for the provision of trade promotion. It is too frequently assumed that the products of an industry having a comparative cost advantage and having reached the stage of surplus production will flow to foreign markets automatically without effort on the part of the nation's exporters. In this respect foreign and domestic commerce are alike. The amount that can be produced advantageously depends upon the ability of the industry to produce and also upon market demand. Unless foreign markets can be developed, an industry cannot produce a large and growing export surplus. Many exportable products may be wholly or largely dispensed with by potential importing countries, and the foreign demand, even for products that are commonly regarded as necessities, may be kept at a minimum in certain foreign countries because of low purchasing power. But the foreign market demand for many products is subject to stimulation by means of effective trade promotion and efficient sales methods. If left to itself, the market demand for many kinds of exportable products would, no doubt, seriously limit the production of an export surplus.

Competition for world trade in certain commodities may be chiefly or wholly limited to rival producers of a single exporting nation, but in such instances active competition may result from this rivalry. The automobile, or business machines, or other manufactures of the United States, for example, compete with each other in foreign markets; they also face competition on the part of foreign producers.

National Gain from International Marketing

The most positive gain derived by a nation from its export trade arises in those of its industries that have the greatest comparative cost advantage, for it is these industries that are best adapted to conditions as they exist in the nation. After the point of surplus production is reached, the continued growth and prosperity of these industries depend upon the development of export as well as domestic markets. There may also be a national gain in the case of other industries having a cost advantage, although it does not follow that a nation necessarily benefits by establishing all of them. The exportation of the surplus output produced by industries developed by a nation because of distinctive climatic conditions or the possession of natural resources may result in a clear national gain, for such industries may also be well adapted to prevailing conditions, and their continued growth may depend very directly upon exportation to available foreign markets. It does not, of course, follow that every industry favored by climatic conditions should or will be developed to the exclusion of industries not so largely dependent upon climatic conditions, or that a nation should deplete certain of its natural resources by exporting huge quantities that could advantageously be conserved for future use within the nation.

The petroleum industry is a case in point. In the United States, Texas imposes restrictions on production in order to conserve petroleum. On the other hand, Venezuela and Saudi Arabia permit foreign companies to develop and export their petroleum with no restrictions on production. Still another country, Brazil, is reluctant to permit foreign concerns to develop her petroleum resources. With her own efforts, Brazil thus far has been relatively unsuccessful.

The development of exporting industries having favorable comparative costs not only provides a nation with desirable sources for capital investment, but also enhances the standard of living of its people. The expansion of these exporting industries as a result of wider markets —

domestic plus export — moreover, spreads certain fixed costs over a large number of units of output and therefore reduces unit costs of production. This, in turn, makes possible lower domestic as well as lower export prices. These industries are best able to pay maximum wages to their employees, and, under competitive conditions, their favorable wage levels may well exert an influence upon the wages paid in other industries. Whenever the reduced unit costs are actually passed along to domestic consumers, their purchasing power is raised. The nation's standard of living is affected favorably, not only by wage levels maintained in the export industries having favorable comparative costs, and by their effect upon wages in nonexporting industries, but also by the increased purchasing power resulting from the influence exerted upon unit costs and domestic prices.[1]

The influence of a policy of economic self-sufficiency upon a nation's standard of living is in sharp contrast. Whereas the expansion of the exporting industries having favorable costs creates more and more employment of the most desirable kind, economic self-sufficiency would create employment in high-cost industries. It would at the same time reduce the amount of future employment in the low-cost exporting industries because of the important relationship existing between merchandise imports and exports in a nation's balance of international payments. It should be recalled that merchandise exports and imports each provide the other with an important part of the necessary foreign exchange, and each provides the ocean carriers, which transport overseas exports and imports, with the return cargoes that are such essential factors in maintaining efficient steamship operation and reasonable ocean freight rates.

The gains derived by a nation from its *import* trade are, however, not limited to the functions performed by merchandise imports in providing foreign exchange for the settlement of export bills and return cargoes for ocean carriers. The greatest direct national gain from the import trade arises from the acquisition, at favorable costs, of commodities that are advantageously produced abroad, and of many raw materials and foods the production of which is largely or wholly limited to foreign regions by climatic conditions or the location of national re-

---

[1]A significant demonstration of these principles is revealed in *Forbes* magazine of June 1, 1963. A special report on automation analyzed the changes that have taken place between 1957 and 1962 in 65 large United States manufacturing companies — 5 each in 13 different product lines. The results for these 65 companies show that assets employed in business were increased 34 percent, resulting in 22 percent more sales with 4 percent fewer employees, each of whom, on the average, received higher wages while prices to consumers have been held down or actually reduced.

sources. Imports of necessary or desired products that cannot be produced at home except at higher costs or, in some instances, only at wholly excessive costs, obviously affect the nation's standard of living favorably.

Wars and the threats of wars encourage and may virtually compel economic self-sufficiency to whatever extent it may be possible in particular countries, but nations forced into this position are concerned more with survival than with favorable living standards. Under peacetime conditions a policy of economic self-sufficiency cannot conceivably provide the national gains resulting from international marketing, based upon the general principles referred to above.

For "national defense," a nation may protect an iron and steel, chemical, precision machinery, or any other industry deemed to be essential for national defense or security. The question of comparative cost advantage is ignored. A product may also be restricted or even forbidden to be exported for the same reason. For example, scrap iron has frequently been restricted by the United States for export because of its importance in iron and steel manufacture.

Summary

1. International marketing is the conduct of business and related services with people in other countries. Businesses in the United States depend in varying degrees upon export markets for a portion of their sales. By means of export sales, the profit position of a business may be improved. Imports in many cases provide the basis for large domestic industries, for example, newspaper publishing, coffee market, and tin cans. In addition to manufacturing enterprises, farmers, miners, merchants, brokers, transportation, and many other activities participate in the conduct of export and import trade.
2. Fundamentally, international marketing depends upon differences in cost levels. One product or service is sold in export because its price is the most attractive, all things considered. When competition is open and free, price is the sole determinant of a trading position. However, it is not open and free due to restrictions imposed under the sovereignty of all nations.
3. The basic difference between domestic and international marketing is that in the latter business is transacted with persons, corporations, and/or government entities in other countries. Since every country possesses sovereignty, this means that each may establish its own monetary system, devise its own laws and regulations, and make its own economic development plans. In addition, language and customs are generally much different in foreign countries.

4. A country's international marketing is determined by a variety of principles, namely, international division of labor, comparative costs, surplus production, balance of international payments, purchasing power of importing country, and trade promotion.

5. National welfare of any country is advanced by exchanging the products and services in which it has a great cost advantage for the products and services of other countries in which it has little if any advantage. This means that both countries will obtain products and services thus exchanged at the lowest possible prices.

6. Purchasing power is a vital factor in international, as well as domestic, marketing. This not only means the ability of a customer to pay for a product or service in his own currency, but it also means the ability of the entire country to remit the foreign exchange necessary to pay for such products or services.

7. Trade promotion is the very essence of international marketing. All of the basic factors could be favorable, but if there were no trade promotion, business would not flow.

QUESTIONS

1. Cite the varied operations that are involved in an export and import transaction.

2. Discuss the implications of sovereignty as a factor peculiar to international marketing.

3. Explain the implications inherent in a situation where United States dollars cannot be remitted by another country.

4. Cite the varied ways in which government regulations constitute a factor peculiar to international marketing.

5. Speaking at the ninth (1957) annual meeting of the International Bank for Reconstruction and Development, President Eugene R. Black stated that an important "cause of imbalance in the development of the less developed countries today is simply the fact that some governments are trying to do too much."
   Evaluate this comment in terms of the economic development objectives of less developed countries.

6. How important is a knowledge of languages and customs to the international trader? Explain fully.

7. In what ways, if at all, is an excess of merchandise exports over merchandise imports considered to be favorable? To whom is such an excess favorable?

8. (a) Define the principal of the international division of labor.
   (b) Is it effective in domestic as well as in international trade?

9. Explain the principle of comparative costs as applied to international commerce.

10. Why does the exportation of a given product generally depend upon the occurrence of a surplus of production?
11. (a) Define the concept of the balance of international payments.
    (b) How does an imbalance in the international payments of any country affect its international trading position? Explain.
12. Define the gains and the sources of the gains that a country derives from international marketing.
13. Compare a national policy of self-sufficiency with a policy of international marketing from the standpoint of the economic welfare of a country.

PROBLEMS

1. Choose any country in the world and prepare a report upon its international marketing position. Seek to explain the reasons for any improvement or deterioration that you may discover.
2. Select any one item of export or of import and explain in terms of the application of economic principles why this item is exported or imported.
3. Prepare a report on the balance of payments of the United States, explaining the importance of the several items reported therein.

COLLATERAL READINGS

Heck, Harold J. *Foreign Commerce.* New York: McGraw-Hill Book Company, Inc., 1953. Chapters 11 and 12.

Hoover, Calvin B. *International Trade and Domestic Employment.* New York: McGraw-Hill Book Company, Inc., 1945. Chapter 1.

Horn, Paul V. *International Trade Principles and Practices,* Third Edition. New York: Prentice-Hall, Inc., 1951. Chapters 3, 4, and 8.

International Monetary Fund. *International Monetary Statistics.* Washington, D.C.: Government Printing Office, monthly.

Killough, H. B. and Lucy W. *Economics of International Trade.* New York: McGraw-Hill Book Company, Inc., 1948. Chapters 2, 3, 10, and 11.

Tarshis, Lorie. *Introduction to International Trade and Finance.* New York: John Wiley & Sons, Inc., 1955. Chapter 1, 4, and 8–12.

Towle, Lawrence W. *International Trade and Commercial Policy.* New York and London: Harper & Brothers, 1956. Chapter 1.

United Nations. *Economic Survey of Asia and the Far East.* New York: United Nations, annual.

—————————————. *Economic Survey of Europe.* New York: United Nations, annual.

—————————————. *Economic Survey of Latin America*. New York: United Nations, annual.

—————————————. *Monthly Bulletin of Statistics*. New York: United Nations.

United States Department of Commerce, Bureau of the Census. *Foreign Trade of the United States*. Washington, D.C.: Government Printing Office, various commodity and country series.

United States Department of Commerce, Bureau of International Commerce. *International Commerce*. Washington, D.C.: Government Printing Office.

—————————————. *Overseas Business Reports* (economic reports on foreign countries). Washington, D.C.: Government Printing Office, serial.

United States Department of Commerce, Office of Business Economics. *Survey of Current Business*. Washington, D.C.: Government Printing Office, monthly.

CHAPTER 2

THE INTERNATIONAL MARKETING POSITION OF THE UNITED STATES

Although the international marketing of the entire commercial world is governed by the general principles referred to in the preceding chapter, the importance of international marketing to the several nations necessarily varies. None of the countries that now so largely interchange their surplus commodities approach self-sufficiency, but it is well established that some of them are more largely dependent upon foreign imports than others, and that the industries of some countries are less dependent upon foreign markets than those of other countries.

Dependence Upon Foreign Markets

The United States is less dependent upon foreign sources of supply than are the industrial nations of Western Europe. Within the United States there is an exceptionally wide range of resources: agricultural, mineral, forest, and maritime. There is a wide range of climatic conditions, a large population with an unusually high purchasing power, a large and efficient supply of labor, a vast supply of capital, a high degree of managerial skill and energy, and efficient transportation services. These conditions have made possible the development of a wide range of industries.

The United States is both an agricultural and an industrial nation — the range of our manufacturing industries, indeed, is constantly widening — and the nation is also a substantial producer of forest, mineral, and marine products. Some of these industries were the direct result of existing natural resources; some of them found their origin in inventive genius, knowledge of productive processes, and patent rights;

19

others were established on the basis of favorable comparative costs, and the range of industries was influenced by the historic protective tariff policy of the United States.

None of the industrial countries of Western Europe can so largely depend upon home production to meet their consumption requirements. The United Kingdom is particularly dependent upon outside food supplies; and lack of natural resources compels that nation to import many commodities of major importance, such as petroleum, cotton, iron, copper, wool, tobacco, hides and skins, and lumber. Conversely, many other countries, such as the Latin American countries, Australia, and South Africa, in which manufacturing industries are not so largely developed and which produce mainly farm or mineral products, are compelled to depend far more generally upon imported manufactures than is the case in the United States.

American industries similarly are not so largely dependent upon foreign markets as are those of many other countries. Many of the industries of Western Europe and Japan must of necessity produce an export surplus in order to make possible the heavy importation of food supplies and raw materials. Their exports provide the principal basis of international settlement for the imports so essential to factory production and national welfare. The nonindustrial regions of the world similarly must produce a heavy export surplus of farm products and industrial materials in order to pay for their imports of manufactures. Even with the manufacturing industries they have, the home markets of many of these countries are too small to readily absorb so large a volume of their major industries as is absorbed in the United States.

The export trade is comparatively less important to the United States than to many other countries both because the nation is relatively more self-contained in its home production and because its industries are blessed with an immensely large home market. The nation's import trade, important though it undoubtedly is, is comparatively less compelling because of this same relatively high degree of self-sufficiency in production. However, the United States is by no means self-sufficient.

Importance of World Trade

The United States has become by far the world's leading exporter and importer of merchandise. Out of a total world export trade (including communist countries) in 1960 of $127.5 billion, the United States accounted for $20.3 billion or 16 percent, followed by Germany with $11.4 billion or 9 percent, and then the United Kingdom with $9.9 billion or 7.7 percent.

As the world's leading import nation, the United States in 1960 imported $14.7 billion or nearly 11 percent of world imports of $134.3 billion.[1] The United Kingdom was close behind with $12.3 billion or over 9 percent.

In 1960 world exports of $127.5 billion were divided in the ratio of two thirds for developed nations and one third for less developed nations. In terms of free nations and communist controlled nations, the free nations had 88 percent of world exports and the communist areas the smaller share of less than 12 percent. All of these figures include trade between and among all countries — free and communistic.

On still another basis of division, the European Common Market countries (six in number) accounted for 23.3 percent of the 1960 total and the European Free Trade Association (seven in number) accounted for nearly 14.3 percent. Thus, the European Common Market as a group has the greatest share of total world export trade. All of Latin America (20 republics) had exports of $8.6 billion or nearly 7 percent of the total; Japan's exports were $4 billion or slightly more than 3 percent; and the USSR's exports were $5.6 billion or a little more than 4 percent.

The comparatively greater dependence of a number of foreign nations upon exports and imports does not signify that foreign trade is unimportant to the United States. Our foreign trade has attained vast proportions. The division of labor, surplus production, comparative costs, balance of payments, and purchasing power principles are operative in the United States as elsewhere. It is only that our nation is comparatively more self-contained in the possession of an unusually large and expanding home market and a wide range of domestic resources. A general idea of the value of American merchandise exports as a whole from 1881 to 1962 in comparison with the value of imported merchandise can be obtained from Table 2-1.

Omitting the two World Wars and immediate postwar years when exports underwent sharp increases, our merchandise exports of the present century gradually increased during peacetime conditions until the worldwide business depression of the 1930's. In 1929, when the highest

---

[1]World imports exceed the value of world exports by approximately the cost of insurance and freight. Data from U.S. Bureau of the Census, *Statistical Abstract of the United States* (Washington, D.C., 1962).

Table 2–1

MERCHANDISE EXPORTS, IMPORTS, AND BALANCE OF TRADE

(Data Cover Period Beginning July 1, 1881, and Ending Dec. 31, 1962)
(Values in Millions of Dollars)

Yearly Average or Year (Fiscal Years, 1881–1915; Calendar Years Thereafter)	Merchandise			Excess of Exports (+) or Imports (−)	
	Exports		Total Imports	Percent Imports Are of Total Exports	Merchandise
	Total	Domestic			
1881–1890..........	765	750	692	90.4	+ 73
1891–1900..........	1,025	1,006	763	74.4	+ 262
1901–1910..........	1,616	1,589	1,159	71.7	+ 458
1911–1915..........	2,371	2,332	1,712	72.2	+ 658
1915–1920*.........	6,521	6,417	3,358	51.5	+3,163
1921–1925..........	4,397	4,310	3,450	78.5	+ 947
1926–1930..........	4,777	4,688	4,033	84.4	+ 744
1931–1935..........	2,025	1,989	1,713	84.6	+ 312
1936–1940..........	3,220	3,167	2,482	77.1	+ 738
1941–1945..........	10,051	9,922	3,514	35.0	+6,537
1946–1950..........	11,829	11,673	6,659	56.3	+5,170
1951...............	15,032	14,879	10,967	73.0	+4,065
1952...............	15,201	15,049	10,717	70.5	+4,483
1953...............	15,774	15,652	10,873	69.0	+4,900
1954...............	15,110	14,981	10,215	67.6	+4,894
1955...............	15,547	15,419	11,384	73.2	+4,163
1956...............	19,090	18,940	12,615	66.1	+6,475
1957...............	20,850	20,671	12,982	62.3	+7,868
1958...............	17,910	17,745	12,792	71.4	+5,118
1959...............	17,622	17,438	15,207	86.3	+2,414
1960...............	20,550	20,349	14,654	71.3	+5,896
1961...............	20,962	20,717	14,713	70.5	+6,249
1962...............	21,628	21,359	16,387	75.8	+5,241

*Period July 1, 1915 to Dec. 31, 1920.

Source: U.S. Bureau of the Census, *Statistical Abstract of the United States* (Washington, D.C., annual).

pre-World War II point was reached, our domestic industries as a whole added to their domestic market, foreign sales amounting to $5,157 million; and $84 million of foreign products were reexported. This represented an increase, in terms of value, of 142 percent over that of the pre-World War I period, 1910–1914. The 1929 figure, however, has been dwarfed by the export values of the 1950's. This period, it may be argued, cannot be called a normal peacetime period because extensive aid was still flowing to other countries as a result of World War II. The expansion continued with the 1960's with an important component known as military grant-aid and also a sizeable item called economic or developmental assistance. Moreover, prices had increased materially.

Measures of Exports and Imports.   Changes in price levels, of course, conceal the actual volume changes that have occurred in our foreign trade. On a value basis, uncorrected for price changes and using an index of 100 for 1957–59 average values, exports for the five-year period 1946–50 were 64, increasing to 82 for the 1951–55 period and to 102 for the 1956–60 period. For the year 1960, the index was 109.

On the basis of index numbers, the *quantity* of United States exports in 1946–50 was 76, rising to 87 in 1951–55, and to 103 in 1956–60, with 1960 at 108. On a basis of *unit values* of exports, the index for 1946–50 was 84; in 1951–55, 94; in 1956–60, 100; with 1960 at 101.

On the basis of an identical analysis, the import trade shows an increase in value, uncorrected for price changes; and with the base continuing as the 1957–59 average, the 1946–50 value index was 47, rising in 1951–55 to 78, in 1956–60 to 100, with 1960 at 108. On a basis of *quantity* of imports, comparable figures for 1946–50 are 60, in 1951–55 up to 76, in 1955–60 still higher to 99, and in 1960 continuing up to 109, after having declined from 113 for the year 1959. On a basis of *unit values* of imports, the changes are from 79 in 1946–50 to 103 in 1951–55 and to 100 in 1956–60. The figure was 99 in 1960, having declined from a high of 104 in 1957.[2]

GNP and International Marketing.   Efforts to measure the importance of international marketing to the total economy of a country lead to a comparison between international marketing and gross national product. Since GNP includes expenditures for services and non-movable products, for example, buildings and bridges, as well as the difference between exports and imports (the trade balance), it is much more inclusive than are exports and imports of merchandise. For such comparative value as it may be worth, exports since 1929 have comprised from 3 to 6.8 percent of GNP, having reached the higher figure in the year 1944. In the 1950's, the percentage changed little, namely, 3.6 to 4.6, and has so continued into the 1960's.

[2]U.S. Bureau of the Census, *Statistical Abstract of the United States* (Washington, D.C., annual).

Imports are a smaller value and therefore a smaller percentage than exports. In the 1950's, the percentage was around 3. In general, this is slightly higher than the percentages for the 1930's and 1940's. In 1960, it was 3.0 and in 1961, it was 2.8.[3]

Production of Movable Goods and International Marketing. Another measure of the importance of international marketing to the total economy may be secured by comparing it to the production of movable goods — agricultural products (cash receipts), manufacturing (value added), mining (mine value), and freight receipts (cost of moving these products to points of distribution or exportation).

The ratio of domestic exports to total production of movable commodities in the United States did not increase during the prosperous 1920's because production as a whole and domestic requirements also increased enormously. Aside from World War I and the immediate postwar period, this ratio was about 10 percent during the quarter century ending in 1929. Since then, the export ratio has been somewhat lower, amounting to 7.4 percent in 1937; 7.5 percent in 1939; 12.2 percent in 1947 but down to 9.0 percent in 1948; 7.0 percent in 1950; 9.0 percent in 1951; 8.5 percent in 1954; 9.9 percent in 1957; and between 7.6 and 8.8 percent in 1958–61.[4]

Unless this relationship between exports and total production is scrutinized with care, a gross understatement of the importance of the export trade and failure to appreciate the progress that has been made may result. Also, the reader may be confused in his conception of that ratio's highly important influence upon the profits of business enterprises and its advantageous effect upon production costs. An export ratio of but 7 or 10 percent may do much to steady employment, investment returns, and prices. Moreover, an average export ratio based upon all exportable commodities does not segregate exportable goods that are, in fact, exported on but a very small scale, or not at all, from those that are exported far in excess of 10 percent of current output.

The export trade of the United States has exerted an important effect upon the expansion of numerous American industries beyond the requirements of their domestic markets; and numerous industries would not continue to operate, at least as they do now, were it not for the imported materials they use.

---

[3]U.S. Department of Commerce, *Exports in Relation to United States Production 1961* (Overseas Business Reports 62-18 [December, 1962]).
    [4]*Ibid.*

Exports as a Share of Domestic Production

The United States Department of Commerce annually publishes compilations revealing the relation of exports to production of a long list of individual commodity groups and products. Compilations are also made to reveal the relation of imports to the total of domestic production plus imports, i.e., imports in relation to "new supply."

The compilations of the share of domestic production that is exported reveal a wide variation among the several commodity groups and specific commodities. Some examples will be presented for 1961.[5]

Parenthetically, it should be pointed out that changes in these percentages may be due to (1) an increase or a decrease in exports or (2) an increase or a decrease in production. The percentages do indicate, however, the extent to which the foreign markets are important, regardless of the volume of domestic production.

All percentages are on the basis of values rather than volume or quantity. The reason for selecting percentages of value is that this measure is always available, while measures of quantity are often lacking.

Commodity Exports of 30 plus Percentage Points of Production.
Commodities that in 1961 revealed an export percentage of 30 or more in relation to domestic production are listed in Table 2-2.

Table 2-2

Commodity Export	% of 1961 Production
Bauxite and other aluminum ores	88
Field peas, except cow peas	81
Mohair and other wool-like hair	65
Cyclic (coal tar) crudes	60
Hops	58
Tracklaying type tractors	58
Molybdenum	56
Grease and inedible tallow	53
Wheat	49
Parts and attachments for tracklaying type tractors	47
Certain clover seeds	40
Cottonseed oil, refined	39
Rye	38
Milled rice and by-products	38
Refined copper and alloys	38

[5]U.S. Bureau of the Census, *U.S. Commodity Exports and Imports As Related to Output, 1961 and 1960* (Washington, D.C.: 1963).

Table 2–2 (continued)

Commodity Export	% of 1961 Production
Raw cotton	37
Carbon blacks	34
Cottonseed	33
Lemons and limes	32
Leaf tobacco	30
Sulfur	30

Commodity Exports of 20–29 Percentage Points of Production. Commodities with 1961 exports of from 20 to 29 percent of domestic production are listed in Table 2-3.

Table 2–3

Commodity Export	% of 1961 Production
Oil field machinery and equipment	29
Small arms, including machine guns	29
Selected grass seeds	28
Phosphate rock	28
Textile machinery and parts	28
Gum and wood chemicals	27
Lubricating oils	27
Metal cutting machine tools and parts	27
(of which, gear cutting and finishing machines 72)	
Metal working machines, except tools	27
(of which, rolling mill machinery 47)	
Pulpmill products	26
Sewing machines and parts	26
Machine tools, metal forming, and parts	25
Broadcast systems and closed circuit systems	25
Manganese ores and concentrates	23
Synthetic rubber	23
Soybeans	22
Special industrial machinery	22
Land transportation motors, etc.	21
Aircraft and missile engine parts	21
Flaxseed	20
Pulp and paper machinery and parts	20

Commodity Exports of 10–19 Percentage Points of Production. The specific commodity and subcommodity exports in 1961 that fall into the 10–19 percentage group number about 60. These include crude agricultural products — barley, grain sorghums, dry beans, grapefruit, and pears. Mineral products included are chromium; anthracite, bituminous and lignite coal; magnesite; brucite; talc; soapstone;

pyrophyllite; and asbestos. Processed agricultural products are lard, canned poultry and other small game, condensed and evaporated milk, dry milk products, dry and dehydrated fruits and vegetables, wheat flour (not prepared), flavoring extracts and beverage bases, cottonseed oil and cotton linters. A long list of manufactured products completes the list, ending with pens and mechanical pencils.

From this analysis it appears clear that export markets for ten or more percentage points of total production exist for numerous industries and products today. It is not possible to evaluate the importance of such markets to these industries, but it must be substantial.

Milk — dry nonfat and dry whole — illustrates an increase in foreign markets for a product that is enjoying greater demand because of its nutritive value. Penicillin and DDT illustrate new products for which a ready foreign market is eager.

The principles of division of labor, comparative costs, surplus production, and ability of foreign countries to settle their international accounts are all reflected in these relationships.

Imports as a Share of Total "New Supply"[6]

An analysis of the importance of imports to the domestic economy of the United States is afforded by the studies made by the U.S. Department of Commerce. These studies relate imports to the domestic production plus imports of each product that can be identified. This calculation provides what is called "new supply."

Since domestic production does not exist for some products, the percentage of imports to "new supply" is obviously 100. Table 2-4 lists such products.

Table 2–4

Imports 100 Percent of "New Supply"

Castor, sesame, and poppyseed	Industrial diamonds
Jute	Cryolite
Brazil, chestnut, pignolia, pistachio, and cashew nuts	Gem diamonds
	Alpaca
Copra	Cashmere
Persian lamb and caracul	Camel wool
Tin ores	Aleppo wool

---

[6]*Ibid.*

Although percentages are not indicated for some products with the explanation that the relationship between imports and "new supply" is not applicable, it is obvious that such products as raw silk, coffee, tea, and cocoa beans should be included in the 100 percentage group.

Commodity Imports of 30 plus Percentage Points of "New Supply." Imported commodities that constitute 30 percent or more of "new supply," exclusive of the 100 percent commodities previously shown are listed in Table 2-5.

Table 2–5

Commodity Imports	30% or more of "New Supply"
Natural abrasives, except sand	98
Manganese ores and concentrates	94
Asbestos	93
Chromium	88
Bauxite and other aluminum ores	87
Newsprint	73
Peat	73
Raw cane sugar and by-products	69
Lapidary work	65
Cigar filler	62
Fluorspar	59
Magnesite and brucite	55
Scouring and combing mill products	50
Feathers, plumes, and artificial flowers	40
Wools	35
Titanium ores	33
Pulpmill products	32
Vitreous china table and kitchen ware	32
Vegetable oils	31
Lead ores and concentrates	31
Tree nuts, edible	30

Commodity Imports of 20–29 Percentage Points of "New Supply." The category of imports that comprise 20–29 percent of "new supply" are broken down in Table 2-6.

Table 2–6

Commodity Imports	20–29% of "New Supply"
Iron ores and concentrates	28
Motorcycles, bicycles, and parts	27
Mercury ores	24
Hops	23
Leather gloves	22

Table 2–6 (continued)

Commodity Imports	20–29% of "New Supply"
Steel nails and spikes	22
Sewing machines and parts	22
Gypsum	21
Canned and cured seafood	21
Wines and brandy	21
Other distilled, rectified, and blended liquors	21
Copper smelter products	21
Household and auto radios and radio phonograph combinations	20

Commodity Imports of 10–19 Percentage Points of "New Supply."

To complete the analysis of imports in relation to "new supply" in the United States, Table 2-7 lists the imports that comprised from 10–19 percent of "new supply" in 1961.

Table 2–7

Commodity Imports	10–19% of "New Supply"
Cordage and twine	19
Cyclic (coal tar) crudes	19
Rubber footwear	19
Refined lead	18
Watch cases	18
Canned meats	17
Tungsten ore and concentrates	16
Earthenware food utensils	16
Barite, crude, prepared	15
Mica, scrap sheet, ground	15
Potash, soda, and borate minerals	14
Residual (petroleum) fuel	14
Typewriters and parts	14
Optical instruments and lenses	14
Sulfur	13
Unfinished (petroleum) oils	13
Electric razors	13
Watches and clocks	13
Fishing tackle and equipment	13
Lace goods	12
Rough russet and crust leathers	12
Natural gas	11
Pickles and pickle products	11
Nonmetallic bonded abrasive products and artificial crude lump stone	11
Cutlery, scissors, shears, etc.	11
Printing presses	11
Carpets, rugs, and mats, n. e. c.	10
Sawmill products and hardwood dimension flooring	10
Ceramic wall and floor tile	10
Refined zinc	10
Motion picture equipment	10
Silverware and plated ware	10

Local Analysis of Importance of International Marketing

An analysis of the importance of international marketing to manufacturers in a local area will illustrate these points still further.[7] Using the year 1951 as a base, one factual survey found that 22 percent of all area manufacturing establishments were engaged in some degree in exporting, and a slightly higher percentage were engaged in importing. In one important classification — chemicals — exports comprised 4.7 percent of total sales of chemical manufacturers. That is not an impressive percentage. But, for drugs and medicines, a subgroup, the percentage was 19.5; and for printer's ink, it was 15.5. Now, for drugs and medicines, the portion of total sales that is exported varies for the different firms in this subgroup. These percentages ranged from 0 to 76. In printer's ink, the highest individual percentage reported was 17; for paints and varnishes, with a subgroup figure of 8.1 percent, the highest ratio reported by a single manufacturer was 24 percent.

The same evidence is derived from an analysis of the import trade. Taking chemicals again, the share of total purchases imported was 26.4 percent; but for individual firms the highest percentages for specific lines of production were 11 for printer's ink, 12 for mucilage and paste, 23 for toilet preparations, 40 for fertilizers, 86 for gasoline, 99 for paints and varnishes, and 100 for one drug and medicine firm.

The survey also revealed that, from the standpoint of employment, firms which neither export nor import were 63.5 percent of all manufacturing firms and they accounted for only 34.3 percent of total manufacturing employment.

Thus, it is particularly essential to note that any conclusion based solely upon an average of 10 or any other percent completely ignores the fact that many of the industries referred to above are directly dependent upon exports to a far greater degree. Exports have enabled these industries to expand well beyond the requirements of their domestic markets. The loss of their export markets would be serious not only to these industries and the employees who gain a livelihood from them, but also to the nation as a whole.

The expansion of various industries beyond the requirements of domestic commerce has occurred throughout the entire nation. Our exporting industries are located not only at the seaboard ports and the adjacent coastal states, but also throughout all of the interior states of the

---

[7]Philadelphia Committee for a National Trade Policy, *World Trade Survey of Philadelphia Area Manufacturers* (December, 1954).

Central West, the North and Southwest, the Southern states, and the Rocky Mountain areas. Everywhere this expansion has provided additional employment for labor and capital, and as many of the exporting industries have the advantage of favorable production costs warranting comparatively favorable wages, they have enhanced the standard of living of large groups of American workers. Their effect upon living standards has indeed not been limited to the workers employed in the exporting industries, for the demand for labor in these industries has influenced wages in nonexporting industries, and the expanded production resulting from the export trade has in some instances resulted in lower commodity prices within the United States by making possible the reduction of unit production costs. Our commodity exports have, of course, also performed a further necessary function by providing the principal basis for the financial settlement of import transactions.

To consider the field of agriculture, cotton exports may serve as a single important illustration. In the past, over one half of the cotton crop has normally been exported. Yet this crop governed the economic welfare of the cotton-growing states more largely than any other circumstance. Nor is the economic importance of the cotton export trade limited to the South and the Southwest. These states provided important markets for many industries located in other sections of the United States. The loss of purchasing power throughout the South and the Southwest that would be occasioned by a loss of our export markets for raw cotton would obviously affect the sales of all of these industries adversely, and to a greater or lesser degree would, at least temporarily, retard our economic prosperity.

Export Trade

The wide range of exportable commodities produced in the United States due to our abundance of natural resources, labor, capital, and other economic factors previously referred to, and in part also to the protective tariff policy, should not blind one to the constant operation of the international division of labor and comparative cost principles in the determination of American exports. Basic economic changes are gradually occurring in the United States and in foreign countries, and these changes are gradually resulting in a recasting of the world division of labor.

Crude Foodstuffs. Our food exports continue to be of great importance but they have been relegated to a secondary position. As may be seen in Table 2-8, crude foodstuffs, such as wheat, soybeans, and barley, comprised 18.0 percent of our merchandise exports during the period of 1881–1890; 10.6 percent during the period 1901–1910; less than 4 percent in the 1930's; and, with emergency food shipments in the post-World War II period, they increased to about 9 percent. In the 1950's and 1960's, the percentage has varied between a high of 9.4 in 1951 and 1962 and a low of 4.9 in 1954.

Table 2–8

PERCENTAGE OF EXPORTS OF MERCHANDISE FROM THE
UNITED STATES BY ECONOMIC CLASSES

(Data Cover Period Beginning July 1, 1881, and Ending Dec. 31, 1962)
(Values in Millions of Dollars)

Yearly Average or Year (Fiscal Years, 1881–1915; Calendar Years Thereafter)	Total Value Domestic Exports	Crude Materials %	Crude Foodstuffs %	Manufactured Foodstuffs %	Semimanufactures %	Finished Manufactures %
1881–1890..........	750	36.0	18.0	25.3	5.2	15.6
1891–1900..........	1,006	29.9	18.1	25.6	8.0	18.4
1901–1910..........	1,589	31.0	10.6	20.1	12.8	25.6
1911–1915..........	2,332	30.7	8.8	14.3	15.4	30.7
1915–1920*.........	6,417	18.2	9.2	17.7	15.4	39.6
1921–1925..........	4,310	27.5	9.7	13.9	12.4	36.3
1926–1930..........	4,688	24.4	6.4	9.7	14.1	45.4
1931–1935..........	1,989	30.2	3.8	8.8	14.5	42.6
1936–1940..........	3,167	19.0	3.8	5.5	19.3	52.4
1941–1945..........	9,922	5.8	1.7	11.9	9.4	71.3
1946–1950..........	11,673	14.0	8.3	10.3	11.1	56.3
1951..............	14,879	16.6	9.4	5.9	11.2	56.9
1952..............	15,049	13.2	9.1	4.9	10.8	62.1
1953..............	15,652	10.4	6.2	4.8	9.1	69.5
1954..............	14,981	12.7	4.9	5.6	12.1	64.7
1955..............	15,419	12.4	6.0	6.6	15.0	60.1
1956..............	18,940	13.3	7.0	6.7	14.6	58.4
1957..............	20,671	15.1	6.4	5.6	15.7	57.2
1958..............	17,745	12.1	7.2	6.2	12.8	61.6
1959..............	17,438	11.0	8.3	6.2	14.1	60.4
1960..............	20,349	12.7	8.1	5.5	17.3	56.4
1961..............	20,717	12.3	9.2	5.6	15.9	57.1
1962..............	21,359	10.5	9.4	6.4	14.3	59.5

*Period July 1, 1915 to Dec. 31, 1920.

Source: U.S. Bureau of the Census, *Statistical Abstract of the United States* (Washington, D.C., annual).

Manufactured Foodstuffs. Exports of manufactured foodstuffs, for example, meat products, fish products, and vegetables, during the same period declined from 25.3 percent during the first of these periods to 20.1 percent during the second, down to 5.5 percent in the 1936–1940 period, and continued at that ratio through 1954, except for the 1941–1950 decade of war and rehabilitation. In 1956, they increased to 6.7 percent and since that date, they have ranged between a high of 6.4 percent in 1962 and a low of 5.5 percent in 1960.

Crude Materials. Crude materials exported by the United States include anthracite, bituminous and lignite coal, phosphate rock, sulfur, and molybdenum. The percentage of crude material exports to total exports remained somewhat in excess of 30 percent throughout most of the period 1881–1935, the chief exception being from 1915 to 1930 when the ratio fell below 30 percent. In the 1940's and 1950's, the ratio of crude materials was between 5.8 percent and 16.6 percent, leveling off between 10.5 percent and 12.7 percent from 1958 to 1962.

Finished Manufactures. As indicated by the lower proportion of exports of crude materials, our manufacturing industries are consuming more of the nation's raw materials. Many of these industries have grown with astonishing rapidity, and their exports have attained leadership in the nation's export trade. Finished manufactures, such as tractors, buses, aircraft, and sewing machines, are now the largest group of exports; they grew from 15.6 percent of total merchandise exports in the period 1881–1890 to 30.7 percent in the period 1911–1915; to 45.4 percent in 1926–1930; to 52.4 percent in 1936–1940; and to a high of 69.5 percent in 1953. Since that year, the percentage has varied between 56.4 in 1960 and 60.4 in 1959.

Semimanufactures. Exports of semimanufactures, for example, vegetable oils and fertilizers, advanced from 5.2 percent during the first of these periods to 15.4 percent in the 1911–1915 period, then fluctuated within relatively narrow limits until the outbreak of World War II. During the period 1931–1935 they averaged 14.5 percent, and in the period 1936–1940, they accounted for 19.3 percent of total domestic exports. The sudden advance in 1940 was due directly to a war demand. In the 1940's and up to 1953, the ratio remained between 9 and 11 percent. The years 1954–1957 show an increase from 12.1 percent to 15.7 percent. Thereafter, the percentage has fluctuated between a low of 12.8 in 1958 and a high of 17.3 in 1960.

The Port of New York Authority

Finished manufactures make up the largest share of our export trade. Here is a 150-ton rolling-mill housing being loaded aboard the Mogomisan Maru at the Brooklyn Navy Yard.

Both because of the ability to produce and the prevalence of foreign demand, the dominant tendency is to export finished manufactures, particularly those requiring much fabrication and easily adaptable to mass-production methods. The effectiveness of mass production can, of course, be retarded both in the domestic and in the foreign market if the quality or design of the industry's products does not meet the requirements of its customers. There are many instances of mass production on the part of industrial concerns, however, that rank high in the quality of their product and in their endeavor to meet the demand for improvements and new designs or styles.

Agricultural Products. The United States is also an agricultural nation and agricultural exports, such as grains, meats, and leaf tobacco, are still an important part of the export picture. The role of agricultural exports has, of course, greatly diminished over the years, as population in the United States grew and consumed more of its own produce. At the same time many foreign countries expanded their own agricultural production. In the period as long ago as 1882–1886, agricultural exports were 75.9 percent of all domestic exports. By 1912–1916, the figure was reduced to 45.1 percent; by 1932–1936 to 36.4 percent; and by 1942–1946 to 18.9 percent. In 1947–1951, the percentage was up to 28 and in 1952–1956 it was back to 21. In 1960 and 1961, the figure was 24 and in 1962, 23.6.

On the other hand, imports of agricultural products have always constituted a large proportion of total imports. For a period of 100 years, the percentage of agricultural imports to the total was no lower than 30 and has been as high as 61.5 percent in the 1917–1921 period. From 1946 through 1953, the percentage fluctuated roughly between 40 and 50 percent but declined in 1952–1956 to 39%. The percentage continued to drop to 30 in 1957, to 29 in 1959 and to 26 in 1960 and 1961. It was down to 23.8 in 1962. This decline is due in part to lower prices of imported agricultural products and in part to the greater volume of total imports.

Export Markets. International division of labor is also largely responsible for the changing trend of our export markets. The shift from food and raw material exports to exports of finished manufactures naturally causes one to anticipate a change in the location of export markets. The industrial countries of Europe that have always been foremost as export markets for American foods and raw materials became important markets for industrial machinery, refined mineral oils, copper, lead, lumber, and a considerable list of finished manufactures, some of which are specialties or general manufactures of distinctive quality or price. But the principal demand for finished manufactures developed in the nonindustrial regions of the world. Between the industrial districts of the United States and the nonindustrial regions of the United States and of foreign countries there is a clean-cut division of labor that creates an interchange of products.

Although our total exports to Europe have increased, they comprised 64 percent of total merchandise exports during the prewar period 1911–1915, and 80.2 percent during the years 1881–1890. During the years

1931–1935, our European exports averaged 47.4 percent of total merchandise exports, declined in 1946–1950 to 34.8 percent, and through the 1950's declined from 26.9 to 18.2 percent in 1951–1953. From this low point in 1953, exports to Europe have expanded to a high point of 34.5 percent in 1960 and have remained close to that level through 1962. Since the beginning of the century when American exports of manufactures first began to be of substantial importance, the percentage of total

Table 2–9

PERCENTAGE OF EXPORTS BY CONTINENTS AND GREAT TRADE REGIONS

(Data Cover Period Beginning July 1, 1881, and Ending Dec. 31, 1962. Hawaiian Islands are included in Oceania prior to 1901; the Philippine Islands are included in Asia for all years; Turkey in Europe is included in Asia beginning 1928.)

Yearly Average or Year (Fiscal Years, 1881–1915; Calendar Years Thereafter)	North America		South America	Europe	Asia	Australia and Oceania	Africa
	Northern %	Southern %	%	%	%	%	%
1881–1890	5.3	5.7	3.9	80.2	2.5	1.8	.5
1891–1900	6.3	6.2	3.4	77.9	3.2	2.0	1.1
1901–1910	9.4	7.8	4.0	70.0	5.4	1.9	1.4
1911–1915	14.2	7.7	5.2	64.0	5.6	2.2	1.1
1915–1920*	12.0	7.7	5.5	63.2	8.6	1.7	1.3
1921–1925	14.3	10.1	6.8	52.7	11.3	3.2	1.6
1926–1930	17.4	8.4	9.4	46.8	12.0	3.7	2.3
1931–1935	14.8	8.0	7.0	47.4	17.3	2.4	3.1
1936–1940	16.2	9.0	9.9	41.4	16.6	2.7	4.2
1941–1945	12.9	5.7	5.0	56.4	8.0	3.6	8.4
1946–1950	16.0	11.8	14.1	34.8	15.4	1.6	5.2
1951	17.2	11.3	13.8	26.9	14.9	1.6	3.9
1952	18.4	11.2	12.1	22.0	13.9	1.5	3.7
1953	19.0	10.0	9.7	18.2	12.7	1.1	3.2
1954	18.4	10.7	12.0	22.6	13.0	1.6	3.9
1955	20.8	11.9	10.8	27.0	13.6	1.7	3.9
1956	20.9	10.5	10.4	27.1	14.6	1.3	3.1
1957	18.8	10.6	12.6	27.8	16.2	1.3	3.3
1958	21.6	13.2	14.0	29.1	16.7	1.6	3.8
1959	23.6	11.2	12.5	29.1	17.3	2.0	4.3
1960	19.6	8.8	11.1	34.5	19.3	2.5	4.1
1961	19.0	7.7	11.7	33.7	21.5	2.1	4.3
1962	19.7	8.0	10.3	33.4	21.2	2.4	5.0

*Period July 1, 1915 to Dec. 31, 1920.

Source: U.S. Bureau of the Census, *Statistical Abstract of the United States* (Washington, D.C., annual).

exports destined to the non-European markets has generally risen to a higher level. The relative percentages are shown in Table 2-9.

The percentage of total exports to Asia, to Australia and Oceania, and to Africa have expanded throughout the years, but exports to South America and Southern North America have shown a decline from the 1958 level. Exports to Northern North America (almost all to Canada) have also shown a reduced percentage from the 1959 figure.

In recent years, about 17–21 percent of total United States exports were destined for Asia; 18–20 percent for the northern countries of North America; 8–11 percent for the southern countries of North America; 10–12 percent for South America; around 4 percent for Africa; and about 2 percent for Australia and Oceania. When the Latin American markets of North and South America are combined, it will be noticed in Table 2-9 that the percentage of total exports destined for them advanced from an average of 9.6 percent in the years 1891–1900 to an average of 15 percent during the period 1931–1935, to 25.9 percent in 1946–1950, and slightly lower in the 1950's. In 1958, exports to Latin America showed an increased percentage level of 27.2 but declined rapidly through 1962 when the percentage was 18.3. The disappearance of Cuba as a market for United States exports accounts for most of this decline.

Import Trade

International division of labor has also in a large measure determined the nature of our imports, the sources from which they are obtained, and the changes that have occurred.

Finished Manufactures. Finished manufactures, which for many years comprised the largest group of imports, declined from over 30 percent of the total during the early 1880's to 22.4 percent during the prewar period 1911–1915. See Table 2–10. They increased slightly to 23.0 percent in 1931–1935, declined to 17.9 percent in 1946–1950, and began increasing each year in the 1950's and 1960's, reaching 36.6 percent in 1962. These percentages are higher than any shown in Table 2–10 that gives all of the years back to 1881. Chief commodities in the finished manufactures group are textiles, paper (chiefly newsprint), machinery and vehicles, and a miscellaneous group embracing clocks and watches, photographic goods, art works and antiques, etc. Many of the commodities compete directly with American industries, and their importa-

Table 2-10

PERCENTAGE OF IMPORTS OF MERCHANDISE INTO THE UNITED STATES BY ECONOMIC CLASSES

(Data Cover Period Beginning July 1, 1881, and Ending Dec. 31, 1962)
(Values in Millions of Dollars)

Yearly Average or Year (Fiscal Years, 1881–1915; Calendar Years Thereafter)	Total Imports for Consumption*	Crude Materials	Crud Foodstuffs	Manufactured Foodstuffs	Semimanufactures	Finished Manufactures
		%	%	%	%	%
1881–1890	692	21.4	15.4	17.8	14.8	30.7
1891–1900	763	26.4	16.9	17.0	13.9	25.8
1901–1910	1,159	34.1	11.8	12.0	17.3	24.8
1911–1915	1,712	34.9	12.8	12.6	17.4	22.4
1915–1920†	3,358	40.1	12.2	16.2	17.1	14.4
1921–1925	3,450	37.4	11.1	13.0	17.7	20.9
1926–1930	4,033	36.8	12.6	9.9	18.9	21.9
1931–1935	1,704	28.9	15.6	13.7	18.7	23.0
1936–1940	2,440	33.1	13.1	14.2	20.9	18.7
1941–1945	3,476	33.0	16.4	11.5	21.2	18.0
1946–1950	6,584	30.3	18.8	10.7	22.3	17.9
1951	10,817	31.1	19.2	9.4	22.7	17.5
1952	10,747	27.3	19.2	10.1	23.9	19.5
1953	10,779	24.2	20.3	10.3	24.8	20.4
1954	10,240	23.6	21.5	10.9	22.6	21.4
1955	11,337	25.1	17.6	9.9	24.5	22.9
1956	12,516	24.7	16.3	9.3	24.0	25.7
1957	12,951	24.8	15.6	9.8	22.6	27.2
1958	12,739	21.7	15.2	11.8	20.7	30.6
1959	14,994	20.7	12.1	10.7	22.1	34.5
1960	14,650	20.6	11.7	10.7	21.1	35.9
1961	14,657	21.5	11.7	10.9	21.2	34.7
1962	16,249	20.6	10.9	11.1	20.9	36.6

*"General imports" through 1932, "imports for consumption" thereafter.
†Period July 1, 1915 to Dec. 31, 1920.
Source: U.S. Bureau of the Census, *Statistical Abstract of the United States* (Washington, D.C., annual).

tion is restricted somewhat by protective import duties as well as by the efforts of the nation's growing industries to dominate the domestic market. Their nature, moreover, has in many instances changed with the rise of domestic industries. As the cotton and wool textile industries of the United States increased their output, imports of foreign textiles gradually changed from ordinary textile products to high-class fabrics not produced on such a large scale in domestic mills. Steel rails and many standard iron and steel products were imported from abroad before the American iron and steel industry was established and also during its infancy, but during later years the importation of ordinary iron and steel products declined and in many instances was discontinued. Machinery and vehicles have shown marked increases in recent years.

Semimanufactures. Imports of foreign semimanufactures as a whole are also increasing in value and their relative position in the import trade has advanced somewhat because many of them are utilized by American industries in the production of finished manufactures. During the early 1880's, semimanufactures comprised about 14 percent of the total value of imports. During the years 1911–1915, they were 17.4 percent; during 1931–1935, 18.7 percent; in 1946–1950, 22.3 percent; and around the same figure in the 1950's and 1960's. Chemicals, refined copper, vegetable oils, tin, wood pulp, prepared fibers, leather, pig iron, and other foreign wares that have undergone partial manufacture, are imported for use in American industries and are influenced by an increasing demand for industrial materials. Some of them compete directly with American semimanufactures and industrial materials and are subject to protective tariff duties, but many of them differ from imported finished manufactures in that their importation is encouraged by American producers of finished manufactures.

Crude Foodstuffs. A third group of imports consists of crude foodstuffs for most of which there is a ready demand in the United States, and many of which are clearly the result of an international division of labor. Many foodstuffs are imported from foreign regions possessing favorable climatic conditions, tropical and subtropical foods being exchanged for manufactures produced in the industrial regions of the United States, and to a smaller extent for American flour, prepared meat products, condensed milk, and other foods not produced on an adequate scale in the specialized agricultural regions of the tropics. Imports of coffee, tropical fruits, nuts and vegetables, tea, cocoa beans, etc., find a ready market in the United States, and division of labor fortunately makes it possible to export sufficient American products to assist greatly in providing a basis for settlement. Crude foodstuffs as a group have for many years played an increasingly important role in the import trade. They comprised about 15 percent of the total during the early 1880's, about 13 percent during the prewar period 1911–1915, increased to 18.8 percent in 1946–1950, and continued to increase to 21.5 percent in 1954. The share of crude foodstuffs imports has declined from that level and reached a low point of 10.9 percent in 1962. Lower prices rather than reduced volume account for these declines.

Manufactured Foodstuffs. Additional foreign foods are imported after being manufactured or prepared for consumption or for further manufacture in American plants, for example, meat, dairy, and fish products. Raw cane sugar, a semirefined product, competes with the American beet and cane sugar, but it is imported on an enormous scale, for it is the basic raw material of most of our cane sugar refining industry. Other manufactured or partly manufactured foods are included in this group. Their relative position in the import trade declined from about 18 percent during the period 1881–1890 to 12.6 percent during the years 1911–1915 and to 10.7 percent in 1946–1950. They continued to decline from 1954 through 1957 but have expanded beginning with 1958 and comprise now 10–11 percent of total imports.

Crude Materials. The outstanding feature of the import trade has been the importance of foreign raw materials. Many manufacturing industries have outgrown the domestic production of raw materials. Some of them are dependent almost entirely upon foreign raw materials; others find it necessary to supplement the domestic supply with substantial quantities of foreign raw materials; and still others, because of geographical location and transportation costs, price or quality considerations, are induced to import industrial raw materials from abroad. Raw silk, crude rubber, furs, crude petroleum, hides and skins, wool and mohair, leaf tobacco, crude chemicals, oil seeds, uncut diamonds, long-staple cotton fibers and textile grasses, iron ore, manganese ore, and other crude materials as a group advanced from 20 percent of all merchandise imports during the early 1880's to about 35 percent during the period 1911–1915, declined to around 29 percent in 1931–1935, rose slightly in 1946–1950, but declined again in the 1950's and 1960's to the 20 percent level.

Sources of Imports. International division of labor as the primary basis for this import trade is clearly in evidence. Crude materials and foodstuffs are imported mainly from non-European regions; finished manufactures, mainly from Europe, Canada, and Japan. American supplies of raw materials and foods, on the contrary, are exported to Europe, and American finished manufactures mainly to nonindustrial regions located in other continents. Semimanufactures, imports as well as exports, are rather widely distributed; they are naturally exported to the industrial regions of Europe and the United States from regions

The Firestone Tire and Rubber Company

Crude materials, such as latex, oftentimes enjoy an insatiable market in the United States. If it were not for synthetics, rubber product manufacturers would be wholly dependent on foreign raw materials. Here a rubber tapper on a Liberian plantation makes an incision in a rubber tree.

Table 2–11

PERCENTAGE OF IMPORTS BY CONTINENTS AND GREAT TRADE REGIONS

(Data Cover Period Beginning July 1, 1881, and Ending Dec. 31, 1962)

Yearly Average or Year (Fiscal Years, 1881–1915; Calendar Years Thereafter)	North America		South America	Europe	Asia	Australia and Oceania	Africa
	North-ern %	South-ern %	%	%	%	%	%
1881–1890.......	5.9	14.1	11.4	55.6	10.4	2.0	.5
1891–1900.......	4.8	13.4	14.1	51.6	12.7	2.6	1.0
1901–1910.......	5.7	13.4	12.0	51.3	15.3	1.1	1.2
1911–1915.......	7.7	14.5	12.8	46.6	15.8	1.1	1.4
1915–1920*.....	12.7	17.5	17.6	20.3	27.1	2.1	2.7
1921–1925.......	11.5	14.9	12.2	30.4	27.3	1.6	2.1
1926–1930.......	11.9	11.4	13.5	29.9	29.7	1.3	2.3
1931–1935.......	13.8	10.3	14.3	30.1	28.7	.9	1.9
1936–1940.......	14.8	9.9	13.6	25.3	31.6	1.5	3.3
1941–1945.......	27.1	16.8	22.8	8.2	13.6	5.3	6.2
1946–1950.......	21.5	14.3	22.2	15.2	18.7	2.5	5.6
1951...........	20.8	11.1	21.2	18.6	18.8	4.1	5.4
1952...........	22.3	12.6	21.3	18.9	16.9	2.3	5.7
1953...........	22.7	11.7	21.9	21.5	15.0	1.9	5.5
1954...........	23.3	12.3	22.1	20.4	14.4	1.6	5.9
1955...........	23.3	12.1	19.5	21.6	16.5	1.5	5.4
1956...........	22.9	11.4	20.0	23.5	15.8	1.6	4.7
1957...........	22.4	12.1	19.8	24.2	15.3	1.7	4.5
1958...........	22.6	13.1	17.4	25.4	15.0	1.5	5.0
1959...........	21.6	10.2	15.5	29.4	16.8	2.2	4.3
1960...........	21.0	10.2	16.3	28.4	18.1	1.7	4.2
1961...........	22.3	9.3	16.0	28.2	17.5	2.1	4.6
1962...........	22.4	9.0	15.0	28.2	18.1	2.7	4.6

*Period July 1, 1915 to Dec. 31, 1920.

Source: U.S. Bureau of the Census, *Statistical Abstract of the United States* (Washington, D.C., annual).

located in Europe, in the United States, or elsewhere that are equipped with the necessary processing facilities, and which produce a surplus for exportation. The sources of American imports as a whole by continents and great trade regions are shown statistically in Table 2–11.

Sources of imports into the United States reveal the same general trends as in the case of export markets. Although in the 1880's Europe was the source of over 50 percent of imports, this share had declined to 30 percent in the 1931–1935 period, to 15 percent in the 1946–1950 period (adversely affected by the war), and remained around 20 percent in the 1950's, with a marked increase from 18.6 percent in 1951 to 24.2 percent in 1957 to 29.4 percent in 1959. The ratio decreased in 1961 and 1962 to 28.2 percent.

Imports from Latin America (southern North America and South America combined) started in the 1880's at around 25 percent, and this same ratio was maintained rather consistently for the next 50 years, except for the 1915–1920 period when the ratio was over 35 percent. Again, in the 1941–1945 war period, Latin America registered a high ratio of nearly 40 percent. Throughout the 1950's, Latin America provided about one third of total imports until 1958 after which date the percentage has declined to about 25.

As a source of imports, Asia revealed a rapid rise from 1880 to 1940. During the 1936–1940 period, Asia was the leading continental source of imports, with 31.6 percent of the total. This figure declined greatly in the postwar period to 15.0 percent in 1958, and improved to 18.1 percent in 1962.

Africa, while a minor source of imports, shows the greatest proportionate increase over the years. In the 1880's Africa provided less than 1 percent of total United States imports. By 1911–1915, the ratio was up to 1.4 percent; in 1931–1935, it was 1.9 percent; in 1936–1940, it was 3.3 percent; and throughout the early 1950's, it remained just below 6 percent. Since 1956 and 1958, however, the ratio has fallen below 5 percent.

Imports from Australia and Oceania show little relative change since the 1880's except during the World War II period and 1951.

The nature of a heavy proportion of our imports and the way so many of them fit directly into our economic life as materials for American industries or foods for public consumption comprise a major aspect of the import trade. Economic self-sufficiency would obviously affect the nation's standard of living unfavorably, for some of the imported products could not be produced here and many could be produced only at a level of substantially higher costs. Another effect is that American exports are dependent upon these imports and upon the import trade as a whole. The United States must export in order to obtain necessary imports, and the nation must similarly import commodities in order to create a basis for its exports. Merchandise imports and exports have normally always comprised the largest items in the international balance of payments of the United States, even though the service and capital movements have also become of great importance. Commodity imports, except during wholly abnormal conditions, are the largest single offset to the vast sums due on commodity exports; they normally do much to keep exchange rates in alignment, and they provide substantial return cargoes for the ocean carriers upon which all exporters depend for necessary transportation services.

Summary

1. Although the United States is less dependent upon international marketing for its economic well-being than probably any other country in the free world, it is the world's leading exporting and importing nation.
2. Merchandise exports of the United States, on a basis of current values, have increased sevenfold since the 1936–1940 prewar period; and even from such a recent time basis as 1957–1959, they have increased 15 percent. There has also been a quantitative increase in exports.
3. Merchandise imports have also increased sevenfold on a basis of current values since the pre-World War II period and from the 1957–1959 base period, they have shown a 20 percent increase. The quantity of imports also has increased.
4. Although exports of the United States comprise a small percentage of GNP or any other measure of total national economic activity, the importance of the export and import trade is best demonstrated in relation to specific products, lines of business, and individual firms.
5. The leading commodity group of exports is manufactures, representing nearly 60 percent of the total exports. The leading geographical markets are Europe, accounting for one third of exports, followed by Asia, Canada, and Latin America, each with about one fifth of the total.
6. Merchandise imports are led by finished manufactures with over one third of total imports. This group is followed by semimanufactures with over one fifth and crude materials with about one fifth. Crude materials imported show a declining proportional trend and manufactures an increasing trend. Foodstuffs, both raw and manufactured, and semimanufactures comprise about one fourth of the import total each.
7. Geographical sources of imports show that Europe has become the leading area with over one fourth of total imports. Europe is followed by Latin America with about one fourth, then Canada with over one fifth, and Asia with a little less than one fifth.

QUESTIONS

1. Discuss the relative dependence of the United States and of the United Kingdom upon international marketing.

2. Which country contemporaneously is the leading world exporter and which is the leading world importer?
3. Evaluate the meaning of the different index numbers indicating changes in value, quantity, and unit value of exports and imports.
4. Evaluate the foreign trade of the United States in terms of GNP and of the value of the production of movable goods.
5. Criticize a literal application of the evaluation revealed in the answer to Question 4.
6. Cite examples of the importance of exports and imports to specific industries and to specific firms.
7. Discuss the place of food exports (both raw and manufactured) in United States total exports and explain the reasons for the changes that have occurred over time.
8. Discuss the place of crude materials in United States total exports, explaining the changes that have occurred over time.
9. In terms of the commodity characteristics of the export trade of the United States, which commodity group leads and why?
10. Evaluate the place and the changes that have occurred in the position of agricultural products in the export and import trade of the United States.
11. Explain the changes that have taken place in the geographical distribution of United States exports of merchandise.
12. Discuss the position and the changes that have occurred in the finished manufactured imports of the United States.
13. Discuss the place of food imports (both raw and manufactured) in United States total imports and explain the reasons for changes that have occurred over time.
14. Evaluate the place and the changes that have occurred in the position of crude materials in the import trade of the United States.
15. Explain the changes that have taken place in the geographical distribution of United States imports of merchandise.

PROBLEM

Investigate and report upon one of the following topics:
(a) Changes since 1900 in the importance and position of any single export or import of any country.
(b) Changes since 1900 in the importance of any single country in the export and import trade.
In both cases the report should reveal reasons for the changes.

COLLATERAL READINGS

Dewhurst, J. Frederic and Associates. *America's Needs and Resources.* New York: Twentieth Century Fund, 1955.

Heck, Harold J. *Foreign Commerce.* New York: McGraw-Hill Book Company, Inc., 1953. Chapter 3.

Hoover, Calvin B. *International Trade and Domestic Employment.* New York: McGraw-Hill Book Company, Inc., 1945. Chapter 9.

Horn, Paul V. *International Trade Principles and Practices,* Third Edition. New York: Prentice-Hall, Inc., 1951. Chapter 2.

General Agreement on Tariffs and Trade (GATT). *International Trade.* Geneva: annual.

International Monetary Fund. *International Financial Statistics.* Washington, D.C.: Government Printing Office, monthly.

Pratt, E. E. *Modern International Commerce.* New York: Allyn and Bacon, Inc., 1956. Chapter 1.

President's Materials Policy Commission. *Resources for Freedom.* Washington, D.C.: 1951.

Tarshis, Lorie. *Introduction to International Trade and Finance.* New York: John Wiley & Sons, Inc., 1955. Chapters 5 and 6.

United Nations. *Commodity Trade Statistics.* New York: United Nations, monthly.

——————————. *Direction of International Trade.* New York: United Nations, monthly.

——————————. *Monthly Bulletin of Statistics.* New York: United Nations.

United States Department of Agriculture. *Trading in Competitive Markets.* Washington, D.C.: Government Printing Office, 1949.

——————————. *Yearbook of Agriculture.* Washington, D.C.: Government Printing Office, annual.

United States Department of Commerce. Bureau of the Census. *Foreign Trade (F.T. Series) of the United States.* Washington, D.C.: Government Printing Office, monthly.

——————————. *Historical Statistics of the United States, Colonial Times to 1957.* Washington, D.C.: Government Printing Office, 1960.

——————————. *Quarterly Summary of Foreign Commerce of the United States.* Washington, D.C.: Government Printing Office.

——————————. *Statistical Abstract of the United States.* Washington, D.C.: Government Printing Office, annual.

Woytinsky, W. S. and E. S. *World Commerce and Governments.* New York: Twentieth Century Fund, 1955. Chapters 1–4.

CHAPTER **3**

FOREIGN MARKET SURVEYS

The making of market surveys seems to be as essential a part of international marketing as the mechanism through which foreign markets are promoted and sales are accomplished and financed. No exporter — whether producer or middleman — will establish an extensive trade organization or set aside substantial funds for advertising or other promotional work without considering carefully the future possibilities of the foreign markets in which such steps are contemplated. In one way or another he will endeavor to ascertain the facts needed as a basis for intelligent judgment. This is the essence of a market survey.

The exporter is interested primarily in a survey that discloses market possibilities for a particular commodity or group of commodities. The government, too, has made surveys of this character; but as its interests are broader, it has also prepared market handbooks containing general surveys covering a wider range of commodities or market studies that are of value to all exporters.[1]

Nature and Purpose of Foreign Market Surveys

Foreign market surveys are continuous in nature. The many factors to be considered, compared, and analyzed bear directly upon the security of the foreign enterprise.

Their timely study and analysis — ahead of major happenings — keeps a trader abreast of the markets, teaches him when to launch a campaign, when to push collections with greater vigor, when to alter

[1]For a complete description of the promotional activities of the Government, see Chapter 4.

his terms. It also keeps him diversified, i.e., on many markets; from these indicators, the exporter can deduce how to adjust his planning.

Our leading corporations do *not* disregard the dry statistics, the seemingly "secondary" or "general" data. To them, commercial intelligence means over-all knowledge in the greatest possible detail. They have research departments, coordinators, special investigators, chief economists, networks of regularly reporting overseas agents, sources of confidential information reaching into foreign governments, "correspondents," statisticians, and several "friendly banking connections," who provide rumors and facts and present evaluations and projections.

Big business takes no chance. Big business, as experience has shown, never foregoes an opportunity of obtaining yet another morsel of intelligence, yet another compilation of facts, one more survey or interpretation of developments on foreign markets. Big business is willing to spend money in order not to miss a single detail, a single straw in the wind which may safeguard current transactions and investments or avoid losses in time to come.

Big Firms Get Bigger. It is usually the smaller merchant, the "average" exporter, and the "medium-sized" manufacturer who saves a few dollars and quite illogically seems to feel that "such fancy figures are above my head." And this attitude appears to be what causes the smaller outfit to stay small, while the big concerns got big and get bigger because they "don't miss a trick."

If one analyzes who missed a chance when a new overseas market opened up, who got stuck when a currency dropped, when a country "suddenly" delayed payments, when an inflation "struck without warning," one discovers that it is usually a large group of smaller firms.

The big concerns usually got wind of what was around the bend, long before it happened. They "visualize" possibilities, "project" their sales into the future on the basis of hard if minute facts, minor developments which spell trends, and protect themselves before the dark shadows are cast ahead by everyone to see.

Or, the smaller firms depend on *one* bank report, one or two informants, rather than on carefully screened and evaluated compendia from all available sources. Reliance on a limited number of indicators can be dangerous. Unreliability, lack of objectivity and selectivity, rumors "fed" by design, and intentionally "released" misinformation can slant the news to the point where a caricature emerges instead of a true picture. The careful investigator finds that single reports can contain mistakes which may be fatal.

Trade Statistics. A recent survey proved that statistics on Japan's over-all trade are full of holes. Those of the Tokyo Trade Ministry, those of at least two major New York banks, those published in two leading publications, were all divergent by millions of dollars! Such discrepancies can be caused partly by different "standards of comparison" and "bases of calculation and assembly," partly by "various adjustments," weighting of sorts and, lastly, they can result from plain misinformation systematically floated abroad.

The practical analyst will compare, cull, and recompare. To check into German-Indonesian commerce bearing on United States sales, he will obtain reports from Frankfurt, Hamburg, and Bonn, as well as from Jakarta. Then he will check against United States Department of Commerce figures. In addition, he will consult private bank bulletins issued here and abroad. [2]

Sources of Market Information

Much of the data needed by an exporter in preparing a specific market survey may be obtained from sources available in the United States — from the publications and files of the government agencies that are discussed in Chapters 4 and 5; from the nongovernment trade promotion organizations that are referred to in Chapter 6; from the foreign departments of banks; from the statistical reports and other publications of United Nations sources, the larger foreign trading banks, international marketing organizations; and from other libraries. Data not available in the United States and the very specific market data desired in a foreign market survey are obtained "on the ground," but time and expense can be saved by making a careful preliminary study on the basis of information readily to be had within the United States.

In this connection, a most informative survey was undertaken by the Bureau of International Commerce (formerly Bureau of Foreign Commerce) to determine the value that businessmen attribute to the extensive published data of the Bureau. The story of this survey appeared in the *Journal of Commerce* in an article entitled, "World Traders Pass Up Profit Potentials." [3]

The survey indicated that *basic* information (balance of payments, national income, foreign government budgets, agricultural developments, and employment and retail trade trends) was not considered to be valuable by over three fourths of the firms participating in the survey. [4] This finding was not influenced in any appreciable manner by the size or the location of firms surveyed.

---

[2]S. J. Rundt, "Know the Market," *Export Trade and Shipper* (subsequently entitled *Export Trade*, and in May, 1964, changed to *Business Abroad and Export Trade*) (February 28, 1955), p. 23.

[3]*Journal of Commerce* (November 6, 1958), p. 1.

[4]Bureau of Foreign Commerce, "Use of Foreign Economic and Commercial Information by the United States International Business Community" (1958).

Importance of Basic Market Information

As indicated by S. J. Rundt in the quotation cited a few pages earlier, the large companies are supposed to use information that is either ignored or considered to be of no value by smaller firms.[5]

It is often stated in international business circles that small firms cannot expect to afford the expense of making foreign market surveys. With such a wealth of basic information available in the United States, this is a misguided and startling assertion. The difficulty probably goes much deeper in this respect — many companies engaged in international marketing or seeking to engage in it do not understand the importance of basic information in making their plans.

The vice-president in charge of the international business of a manufacturing company once addressed a class in international marketing. He glowingly reported the success of his operations in Mexico. The students inquired about the possible changes in Mexico's ability to pay for his machines because of a declining export market for Mexico's products at that time. The vice-president completely ignored the questions and continued to praise his Mexican operations. In the opinion of the students, the vice-president was short-sighted and their opinion was verified not long afterward when Mexico devalued the peso, making the vice-president's machines more expensive to Mexican buyers. The fact is that the vice-president had no concept of the importance of basic economic information and of its relationship to foreign market potentials. This weakness on the part of international business executives is still present, according to the Bureau of International Commerce survey.

The small firm cannot properly plead inability to pay the cost of foreign market surveys. True, it may not be able to pay the cost of a field survey, but the particular problems that affect its operations may not call for a field survey. If the firm, whether large or small, believes in the value of foreign market research, there is a great deal that can be done right here in the United States. If this awareness is present, there are ways to provide and evaluate market information economically.

Proper analysis of the company's position in international marketing will often disclose that certain parts of a market survey may be contracted for by research firms that have facilities in foreign markets for conducting research. Paul F. Bellins cites such a quotation by a research firm, in that

---

[5]The Bureau of Foreign Commerce survey does not appear to support Mr. Rundt's assertion. The large as well as the small firms professed no value in basic information.

for $3,000 "they would conduct an on-the-spot market research job which would include information on size and characteristics of the market, potential for the product, public tastes and preferences, nature and extent of competition, buying power of the population, product design and packaging, pricing and discount practices, wholesale and retail distribution, and anticipated sales volume."[6]

Different Types of Foreign Market Surveys

Every foreign market research undertaking does not represent an initial attempt to appraise, enter, and develop a foreign market. Firms that are presently engaged in international marketing must continuously make surveys. This is just another way of saying that international business managers must be alert. If they are presently established in a market and they find that their participation in the market is falling off, some explanation must be found. This involves a survey which may reveal that domestic or foreign competition has increased, or that adverse import duties or allocations have caused the decline, or that the distribution pattern has declined in effectiveness, or that the market has fallen off because of some other factor.

Let us now consider the case of a company that is already engaged in international marketing and it offers a new product. The company has an established business in other lines and the survey would be directed solely to the possibility of marketing the new line. The expectation would be that the present distribution channels would be satisfactory for this new line.

Finally, a company that is new to international marketing and, to a lesser extent, a company that has been in international marketing, but now seeks to enter a market hitherto not included in its international business, must undertake a broader foreign market survey. Both of these companies must comprehend the basic factors affecting the market as well as the adaptability of their products to the market.

A foreign market survey can properly be divided into four main parts:

1. The market itself entirely apart from the product.
2. General factors of the market that relate to the product.
3. Specific factors that affect that market for the product.

---

[6]Paul F. Bellins, "Increasing Overseas Sales from Marketing Research," *Exporters' Digest and International Trade Review*, Vol. XXXI, No. 12 (December, 1957), p. 30.

4. Specific factors that influence the operations of the particular company for which the survey is being undertaken. This final part of the survey would include the policy of the company in relation to international business.

For illustration, let us set up a foreign market survey for a manufacturer of flashlights.

Foreign Market Survey for a Manufacturer of Flashlights

In this illustration, let us assume that the manufacturer makes the light bulbs and the batteries as well as the casings for the flashlights. The company does not engage in international marketing at present. The executives of the company believe that international business is important to the expansion of the company's business and they indicate complete backing for any plan that is feasible for their purposes.

The Market. Information concerning the prospective country of import would be compiled to serve as an introduction to the market. The main subjects to be included would be resources and production, transportation and location, climate, population, standard of living, government, foreign trade, and per capita income.

Resources and Production. *Resources and production* bear upon the survey since they provide the means of economic wealth and development of the country. Thus, the wealth may be chiefly in agriculture, in minerals, in manufacturing, or in fishing. The stability of the market may therefore depend upon the vagaries of these activities in light of changes in domestic and international factors. For example, if the wealth is of an agricultural nature and is secured from the raising of coffee or sugar, it may indicate an unstable market economically because of sudden changes in the world price for such agricultural products. The same may be true of mineral countries, although for countries whose main export is a mineral, the employment of the population is usually, if not always, in agriculture because mineral operations provide little employment.

If the country is a manufacturing country, then a first item of inquiry is whether flashlights are now produced in the market. This is also a matter of first importance when analyzing agricultural and mineral countries, because manufacturing in its infancy may include the production of flashlights. They are not so complicated to manufacture as many chemical products, for example.

Transportation and Location. Another aspect of the resources of the market is *transportation.* The existence of ocean routes, seaports, port facilities, railroads, highways, waterways, and airways is of prime importance. Even for flashlights, transportation facilities must be available to distribute them to the market centers and outlets. Transportation conditions also bear upon the packing of the goods, including flashlights, as explained in Chapter 22.

Finally, *location,* especially in its relation to transportation and communications services and charges, may be an important factor in the choice of markets. It is significant to note that the relative position of American products is highest in the nearby Latin American republics and lowest in those countries further removed. In the year 1962, of the total imports of Argentina, 29.0 percent were obtained from the United States; and the American percentage in Brazil was 31.0. In Venezuela, on the contrary, 54 percent of total imports were received from the United States in 1961; in Colombia, 55.8 percent in 1962; and in Mexico, 68.5 percent in 1962.[7]

Other factors, of course, are also operative, and the total export trade flowing from the United States to Argentina, the most distant of these markets, is normally heavy; but the favorable location of the nearby markets has undoubtedly been a primary factor in the comparative position of American exports. About 60 percent of Canadian imports were normally obtained from the United States before the outbreak of World War II, even though British merchandise has been entitled to preferential customs duties and Canada is politically a part of the British Commonwealth. In the postwar years, the United States share of Canadian imports has been approximately 70 percent.

Geographical location similarly operates against the American exporter in many instances. The American manufacturer of competitive products is handicapped to a greater or less extent in all European markets by the favorable location of British and continental producers and exporters. The European Economic Community (Common Market) and the European Free Trade Association both provide for preferential tariff rates on imports from countries that are members of these arrangements. The same may become true in the future with other regional agreements, such as the Latin American Free Trade Association, the Central American Community, etc. Japan, similarly, has a geographical advantage in the Far Eastern markets, which are considered distant overseas markets

[7]U.S. Department of Commerce, *United States Foreign Trade, December 1962 and Calendar Years 1956–1962* (Overseas Business Reports 63–101 [April, 1963]).

so far as European and American exporters are concerned. There are many regions in which geographical location neither handicaps nor favors the American exporter decisively.

TRANSPORTATION CHARGES AND SERVICES. Geographical location is translated into a dynamic trade factor primarily in terms of transportation charges and services. Ocean freight rates from American and European ports to the more distant overseas markets have usually been maintained at a reasonable parity, although not on the basis of exact equality, so as not to bar either group of competitors from them. Very substantial differences in distance are ignored in the long-distance trades. This international rate parity, however, is not maintained to nearby markets, and ocean rates may operate there as a cost advantage or handicap.

Rate parity, moreover, does not denote a parity of ocean services. In the past there were too many instances of unfavorable service differences in the long-distance trades. Slow-moving steamers, infrequent sailings, forced transshipments, triangular routes, and an inadequate number of regular steamship lines too often gave the European exporter a real advantage in delivery time and in the assurance with which deliveries could be promised. This competitive handicap has been largely remedied in the many overseas trades that are far removed both from the United States and Europe. In nearby and adjacent markets there necessarily continue to be service differences that materially affect the delivery of American exports, either favorably or unfavorably. Exporters of manufactures particularly are interested in regular, frequent, and fast steamship services. It should be noted, of course, that their interest is not solely in the competitive aspects of ocean transportation. Ocean rates and services in any case may affect delivery costs and delivery arrangements, and may materially influence the volume of sales in the market that is being surveyed.

INLAND TRANSPORTATION. Geographical location is also related to railroad and other forms of inland transportation. Direct rail services are an advantage to many American exporters in Canada and Mexico. The Great Lakes and improved motor highways afford additional trade routes to Canada. Inland exporters are always concerned with inland rates and services to the ocean and Great Lakes ports as well as with ocean steamship rates and services. Railroads and motor lines connect with ocean carriers at the ports, and both exporters and importers are keenly interested in the domestic or special railroad rates applicable to different ports; in the absorption of port handling costs; in railroad storage and demurrage charges at the ports; in storage facilities, free lighterage, and switching; in railroad wharfage facilities and charges; in ocean freight-forwarding arrangements; and in any other services, charges, or regulations that may affect the delivery of shipments to the ocean carrier.

Inland transportation may also be an important consideration abroad when deliveries are contemplated at inland points within an underdeveloped market. To many inland destinations the only available means of transportation are rivers, unimproved highways, and mountain or desert trails. The use of primitive river craft, road carts, or pack animals may not only limit sales, but may also largely govern the prices and the packing of the exported wares.

Improved freight, passenger, and mail transportation services exert a very direct influence over the geographical location of a market. Speed, frequency, and regularity may, in effect, largely overcome the unfavorable location of a distant foreign market. Improved cable, telephone, and radio services affect international commerce in much the same manner. The progress that has been made in the speed and certainty with which messages are conveyed is discussed in Chapter 20.

Climate. *Climate* is a factor of importance because it not only relates to the resources and their use, but it also has a bearing on the health of the population and, therefore, its productivity.

Population. For obvious reasons *population* is a basic factor in a foreign market survey. The number of people in a market, however, is of little importance unless they are considered in terms of their standard of living. What use would 5 or 50 million people be as customers if they had no interest in buying or had no income with which to purchase flashlights? Therefore, the population in the foreign market must be interpreted in terms of its purchasing power. Before proceeding further along that line, however, it is well to indicate that for some products, such as men's goods, the distribution of the population on a basis of sex is necessary; for children's goods, on a basis of age groups; and for household items, on a basis of family units. Regardless of how the population is divided, however, the important point is its purchasing power — whether as men, children, families, or the entire population.

Standard of Living. Data bearing upon the *standard of living* are not satisfactorily available from all markets, but such data as are available should be utilized to the fullest possible extent. Average income figures provide a guide, but that is all. For a product such as flashlights, the average income figure would be useful, since it is a product that is sold on a family and possibly on an individual basis.

Moreover, since the price of a flashlight is low, it would find a market in large numbers where electrical refrigerators and automobiles might sell only in very small numbers. In the latter case, it is important to note the extremes of income because in even the poorer, underdeveloped countries, an economic factor of great importance is the existence of two economic strata of society — upper and lower. In many cases, the upper strata possesses a purchasing power comparable to that of highly developed and wealthy markets.

On the other hand, if a large segment of the population is at a mere subsistence level, the market for any product that calls for payment in money is distinctly limited or does not exist at all.

Government. One of the basic factors to be considered in a foreign market survey is the type of *government* that has been established in the country. While businessmen have found it desirable to avoid politics in international business, they cannot ignore the role of the government because of its bearing on many phases of business enterprise. The government may be friendly to business, but exacting in levying heavy taxes upon business. This is unusual, however, because the tax structure of nearly all of the underdeveloped markets is based upon real estate and consumption rather than upon business or income. The right to do business and the extent of foreign investment that is permitted are determined by government policy.

Foreign Trade. The amount of and the nature of the *foreign trade* of a market is important because of its direct bearing upon the market for flashlights. The reader may ask "If a country exports coffee, what has this to do with the market for imported flashlights?" As explained in Chapter 1, a country literally earns the capacity to import by exporting its products and its services. Therefore, in a very direct sense, the payment for such flashlights as the company may be able to sell will come from the earnings derived from the exportation of coffee. Whether or not the market will automatically purchase flashlights does not follow; there are many other factors to be considered.

The foreign trade of a market not only tells the story of the goods exported and imported but it also discloses the markets with which trading is conducted. The position of the United States and of competing countries is revealed from a country analysis. But what has this to do with the market for flashlights? Suppose the United States is a small supplier or a large supplier in the market. If the United States is a small supplier and a large buyer, the indications are that dollar exchange for the payment of imports from the United States is readily available and will continue to be available. On the other hand, if the United States is a large supplier and a small buyer, the availability of dollar exchange may be greatly strained. All of this presupposes no control over the use of foreign exchange. When foreign exchange is controlled, as pointed out in Chapter 33, the relation between exporting and importing with a given country will probably have a bearing upon the allocation of exchange by the financial authorities of the market in question.

Per Capita Income. Another aspect of the foreign trade of the market that is often overlooked by international marketing executives is the *per capita income* of the market. An analysis for 1962 — based upon a similar study for 1957 — reveals the following interesting per capita standings of foreign markets for United States products:

Table 3–1

PER CAPITA PURCHASES OF UNITED STATES PRODUCTS [8]

1962

Country	Per capita	Total (Millions of Dollars)
Bermuda	1590.00	37.5
Bahamas	501.85	54.2
Canal Zone	453.49	19.5
Netherlands Antilles	388.66	75.4
Kuwait	213.00	63.9
Canada	210.42	3829.7
Panama	95.18	104.7
Israel	79.50	174.9
Netherlands	64.84	752.2
Venezuela	61.62	468.3
Switzerland	54.33	298.8
Liberia	40.00	51.0
Australia	39.99	399.9

[8]*Ibid.* Population data from *United Nations Statistical Yearbook 1962* (New York: United Nations).

It will be noted from a study of Table 3-1 that only countries such as Canada, Netherlands, Venezuela, and Australia would be thought of as prime markets for United States products. All of the others appear in the table by reason of special circumstances that might be overlooked unless a per capita analysis such as this were undertaken.

Bermuda heads the list because of the heavy volume of United States tourist trade in that country. It is followed by the Bahamas for much the same reason. The Canal Zone is high in the list because of the expenditures in connection with the Canal; and some of this largesse spills over into the Panama Republic. The oil-rich countries are represented in the table by the Netherlands Antilles, Kuwait, and, of course, Venezuela. Israel appears in the table because of the flow of loans and gifts from American Jewry. Switzerland's position is accounted for in part because of the tourist income; and Liberia's per capita imports from the United States are influenced by the dominant position of a large American rubber company in that country.

Returning to the four countries mentioned above (but excluding Venezuela) as being natural rather than influenced by special circumstances, Canada is generally not considered as a foreign market by American firms, but this country is our leading foreign market. The Netherlands and Australia are high because of their dependence upon international trade. The Netherlands consistently has been a liberal trading nation; and Australia exports wool that is in great demand in the United States. In addition, both countries enjoy a high standard of living, and the same is true of Canada.

Per capita purchases from the world and from the United States are of no importance in a survey of certain markets, as, for example, the marketing of industrial raw materials or of capital goods; but data concerning per capita purchasing are of great importance in the matter of foodstuffs and other consumer products, including flashlights.

General Market Factors Relating to the Product. In this part of the survey, the research comes closer to the flashlight problem itself. In this section, we shall discuss matters pertaining to the trade policy of the country and its foreign exchange situation and policies

Foreign Trade Policy. The foreign trade policy of the market may reveal that flashlights are considered to be luxuries and thus would be assessed high import duties — so high, in fact, as to price imported flashlights out of the market. On the other hand, the import duties may be low, indicating that foreign flashlights can be profitably marketed.

Foreign Exchange Policy. The same factors mentioned above will enter into a consideration of the foreign exchange policy of the market. Whether flashlights are considered to be essential or nonessential will be reflected in the allocation of exchange (provided foreign exchange is controlled). This is a most important factor to be considered in the foreign market surveys for nearly all countries during the post-World War II period.

Specific Market Factors Relating to the Product. Here we come still closer to the market for flashlights. In this section of the survey, subjects that will be included are domestic production of flashlights, imports of flashlights, countries from which imported, the public and private illumination available in the market, and competitive means of illumination.

Domestic Production. If flashlights are produced domestically, it might appear at first that the market is closed for any imported variety. Upon a closer examination, however, it may be revealed that the domestic product is not satisfactory to the consumer. It may be too expensive, batteries and bulbs may be unreliable, or the color of the cases may be unattractive. Domestic production of a proposed import must be thoroughly examined before concluding that imports are not possible.

Imports. Imports must be studied closely to determine not only the volume and price of imports, but also the countries that supply the imports. Sometimes, the average price of imports can be determined by dividing the number of units imported into the reported value of imports. Perhaps this works out to 50 cents (United States dollars). Next, the basis of valuation must be determined, for example, foreign market value or imported value. The value thus determined probably will differ among the several countries from which the imports come. An analysis of country sources will therefore provide knowledge as to the different prices quoted by the several supplying countries. This information thus provides a basis for comparative pricing. As stated in connection with domestic production, the quality of the flashlights and other characteristics, however, cannot be revealed from import statistics alone. This is a matter that can only be determined from a field survey.

Illumination Conditions. To ascertain the importance of flashlights as a means of illumination, such conditions must be examined. If there is ample power installed in the market, the assumption could be made that the market for flashlights is limited. This does not necessarily follow, however, because (1) illumination may not be evenly distributed and this would be particularly true in the case of countries dominated by rural conditions, for example, India; and (2) supplemental and emergency illumination may be needed, as in the case of metropolitan centers with suburban areas and homes that have basements.

Specific conditions such as these may call for the use of flashlights, despite the existence of adequately installed power units. In the United States, for example, with its extensive power installations, flashlights are still widely sold. Even the number of automobiles in operation would be a factor influencing the sale of flashlights because every motorist can testify to the value of a flashlight.

Alternate sources of illumination must also be examined. Perhaps it may be found that oil lamps or candles are commonly used, particularly in the rural areas. The flashlight, however, does possess the advantages of being safe and fully portable, which is not true of oil lamps and candles. Therefore, the known existing market for flashlights can be determined by an analysis of the specific factors that are in operation.

Specific Factors Influencing the Operations of the Company. This last part of the survey is applicable only to the firm in whose interests the foreign market survey is undertaken. The topics that would be included in this phase of the survey are: (1) the policy of the company with respect to international business,[9] and the adaptability of the flashlights for foreign marketing; (2) the price at which flashlights can be profitably sold; (3) the channels of distribution in the market; and (4) terms of sale, and similar matters.

Policy of the Company. If the executives of the firm have seriously decided to go into international marketing and to abide by their decision through all conditions, if possible, a first and extremely important step has been taken. Furthermore, if the adaptability of the product to foreign market requirements is assured, then the company can proceed to make plans for foreign distribution.

---

[9]The need for developing a philosophy of doing business abroad is further explored in Chapter 7.

Price. The price of imported flashlights, as determined by the analysis mentioned earlier, will give an idea of the price competition to be met from imported flashlights. The competing price of domestically produced flashlights may be obtained by requesting the Bureau of International Commerce to obtain this information from a foreign service officer stationed in the market under study. If it appears feasible to meet or beat the prices at which competitive flashlights are being offered in the market, the next step would be to determine the method by which the market is to be developed.

Channels of Distribution. This step of the survey would involve an analysis of the distribution methods used by competing firms. Information along this line can often be obtained from friendly American firms engaged in exporting similar goods. Editors of foreign trade and international business magazines, who make frequent trips to foreign markets, may also be helpful.

It is generally desirable, and even necessary, to offer a product for sale in a foreign market in the same channels as competitors do. This does not mean, however, that the newcomer to the market will use the same representatives that his competitors do. In the case of flashlights, it is likely that the distribution in a market is performed by wholesalers of hardware or of electrical lines. Some of these wholesalers will doubtless be importers; and one or several of them may be eager to add a line of flashlights because they do not have a line, or they may wish to eliminate a line that they have been handling. The types of arrangements that may be made with the representative are discussed in Chapter 10.[10]

Terms of Sale and Similar Matters. While the price at which the flashlights can be sold may be satisfactory, the terms of sale may be an obstacle to export sales. In many countries, the terms of sale are considered to be as important as the price. If the custom in the flashlight trade is to sell on credit terms, a newcomer to the market would be introducing unnecessary obstacles by insisting on cash payments.

The price quotation, whether it is based on some shipping point in the exporting country or in the importing country, will also be an important factor. The representative who agrees to handle the new line of flashlights may not be willing to keep a stock of bulbs, batteries, and other

---

[10]The names of possible representatives can be obtained from *Trade Lists*, published by the Bureau of International Commerce. See Chapter 4.

parts; and if this is so, another representative should be selected. For such a product as flashlights, it would be essential to maintain a ready stock of these items. Finally, such matters as advertising, trademark registration, taxes, and many other conditions that affect the market must be considered and these will be discussed in other chapters.

Finding and Recommendations. From the data compiled in conducting this foreign market survey, the possible findings may be as follows:

1. The market is one that is subject to severe economic fluctuations, due to a narrow base for its international transactions. It has a one-crop economy, for example, sugar or coffee.

2. When the price of the basic export commodity is high, the market for all imports is good.

3. Transportation facilities are satisfactory, although rural areas are not served adequately.

4. The number of motor vehicles in operation is a factor favorable to the sale of flashlights.

5. The market is close to the United States, thus favoring American export sales.

6. Per capita imports from the United States are high.

7. The population is large enough and has sufficient purchasing power to buy a considerable number of flashlights.

8. Flashlights can be sold to all classes of the population, except possibly those at a subsistence level.

9. The government is relatively stable and is traditionally friendly to the United States.

10. Foreign flashlights are currently being imported and sold, indicating that such domestic production as there is does not prevent importation.

11. Chief foreign competition comes from Canada, United Kingdom, Germany, and Japan.

12. The flashlights from Japan are cheapest, those from Germany are next, while the Canadian and British flashlights are sold at about the same price as those of the company for which the survey is being undertaken.

13. There are no exchange restrictions adverse to the importation of foreign flashlights.

14. Import duties on flashlights are not high and they are the same for all supplying countries.

15. Since illumination facilities are not fully developed, there is a need for flashlights to provide light in areas where no satisfactory alternate means of illumination is available. Where candles and oil lamps may be used, the evident superiority of flashlights can be easily demonstrated. This superiority may have been shown before by the fact that domestic production and imports of flashlights continue.

16. An importing wholesaler with exclusive distribution rights is indicated as the best outlet for the company. Three names, obtained from the Bureau of International Commerce, are being considered. They are now being checked with other international marketing executives who do business with these firms.

The concluding remarks and recommendations in the survey report might be stated as:

The market for flashlights exists in the country. If an aggressive importing wholesaler can be obtained to handle the line on an exclusive basis, the company should enjoy a good market for its product.

Summary

1. A foreign market survey is essential before a major step in the direction of exporting is taken. It constitutes a method of "looking before leaping."
2. Information must be sought from every available and reliable source. To do this requires both a knowledge of the sources and the value to be obtained from them.
3. Small, as well as large, companies interested in international marketing can do a great deal in the direction of compiling a useful foreign market survey. Considerable information is available in the United States for this purpose.
4. Foreign market surveys are necessary to explain changes in the position of a firm presently engaged in international marketing; or to investigate the market for a new line offered by an existing international marketing company; or to provide the basis for determining whether a company that has not previously engaged in international marketing is justified in doing so.
5. A foreign market survey may be divided into four major parts: (a) the market itself; (b) general market factors relating to the sale of the product under consideration; (c) specific market factors relating to the product; and, (d) specific factors influencing the operations of the company.
6. The factors that exert an influence upon the market itself are: resources and production, transportation, location, climate, population, standard of living, government, foreign trade, and per capita income.
7. The general market factors relating to the product include the foreign trade policy and the foreign exchange policy of the market.

8. The specific market factors relating to the product include domestic production, imports, and alternate sources for illumination.
9. The specific factors that influence the operations of the company concerned with the survey include the policy of the company and the adaptability of the product, the price of the product, the channels of distribution, and the terms of sale.
10. The survey would conclude with a summary of findings and the recommendations.

QUESTIONS

1. What are the purposes of foreign market surveys?
2. Is there any difference between small and large firms with respect to the thoroughness of foreign market surveys? Explain.
3. Who undertakes foreign market surveys?
4. What are the main divisions of a complete foreign market survey? Explain the contribution of each division to the complete survey.
5. Is there any purpose in making a survey of Belgium as a market for United States machinery? Explain.
6. Is there any purpose in making a survey of a country as a market for lumber if it has within its borders large tracts of untapped lumber? Explain.
7. How would you deal with population in a foreign market survey?
8. Why should a market be surveyed if statistics reveal that its needs are being amply supplied?
9. How does geographical location influence the interest in a foreign market survey?
10. Discuss transportation, both inland and international, as a factor included in a foreign market survey.
11. Discuss the relation between political control and foreign market possibilities.
12. Discuss the relation between price and quality as a foreign market survey factor.
13. Is a foreign market survey ever completed? Comment.

PROBLEMS

1. Select a single commodity export and the country to which you would like to export it.
   Prepare a foreign market survey report dealing with this subject and draw valid conclusions.
2. Select a single commodity import and the country from which you would like to import it.
   Prepare a market survey report dealing with this subject and draw valid conclusions.

COLLATERAL READINGS

Dartnell International Trade Handbook, The. Chicago: The Dartnell Corporation, 1963.

de Haas, J. A. *The Practice of Foreign Trade.* New York: McGraw-Hill Book Company, Inc., 1935. Chapter 10.

Heck, Harold J. *Foreign Commerce.* New York: McGraw-Hill Book Company, Inc., 1953. Chapter 19.

Horn, Paul V. *International Trade Principles and Practices,* Third Edition. New York: Prentice-Hall, Inc., 1951. Chapter 25.

MacDonald, Philip. *Practical Exporting.* New York: Ronald Press Company, 1949. Chapter 4.

Pratt, E. E. *Modern International Commerce.* New York: Allyn and Bacon, Inc., 1956. Chapter 4.

Tosdal, H. R. *Problems in Export Sales Management.* New York: McGraw-Hill Book Company, Inc., 1922. Chapter 3.

In addition to the United Nations and United States references listed in the collateral readings for Chapter 1, the following references are helpful in preparing foreign market surveys as they contain information especially useful for that purpose:

American Management Association, Inc., International Management Division. *Market Research in International Operations* (AMA Management Report No. 53). New York: 1960.

Export Trade. New York: Thomas Ashwell and Co., Inc., weekly. Note: Beginning with the 1959 issues, the words "*and Shipper*" were dropped from the title of this publication, and in May, 1964, it was changed to *Business Abroad and Export Trade.*

International Markets. New York: Dun & Bradstreet, Inc., monthly.

United States Chamber of Commerce. *Foreign Commerce Handbook,* Thirteenth Edition. Washington, D.C.: 1959.

United States Department of Commerce, Bureau of International Commerce. *Investments in (name of country).* Washington, D.C.: Government Printing Office, a series of handbooks that constitute foreign market surveys of the respective countries treated in this series.

CHAPTER 4

PROMOTION BY THE UNITED STATES GOVERNMENT

Since the beginning of the United States, the State Department (called "Foreign Office" in most foreign countries) has played the primary role in conducting foreign relations, including those of a commercial nature. During the present century, as the interests of the United States were drawn increasingly into world affairs, additional agencies of the United States Government sought to promote international marketing. Some of these agencies are new, such as the Bureau of International Commerce (originally [1912] called the Bureau of Foreign and Domestic Commerce); many of them, such as the Departments of Agriculture, Treasury, and Interior, however, were established agencies that found a need to deal with international marketing matters in order to represent properly the interests for which they were founded.

This chapter will explain briefly the international marketing promotion functions of the several United States Government agencies.

Department of State

The principal responsibility for the determination of the policy of the Government in relation to international problems devolves upon the Department of State. Some of the more vital decisions on questions of foreign affairs are made by the President, but the day-to-day negotiations with foreign countries, the specific measures for the protection of American interests and the promotion of friendly relations between the United States and other countries, and the conduct of the voluminous correspondence with the diplomatic and consular representatives of the United States, as well as with representatives of foreign powers accredited to the United States, are delegated to the Department of State. [1]

---

[1] "The Department of State of the United States — Functions, Organization and Recruitment of Personnel" (undated mimeographed brochure of the Department).

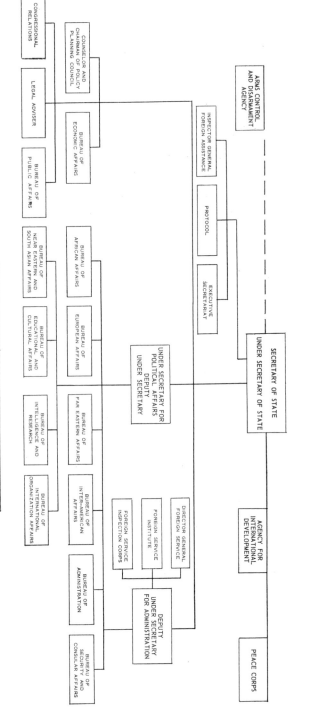

Chart 4-1

DEPARTMENT OF STATE

Basic Organization. The work of the Department is directed by the Secretary of State, who is the highest ranking member of the Cabinet. He is at the head not only of the home establishment in Washington but also of the Foreign Service of the United States in lands abroad.[2] Chart 4-1 on page 67 depicts the organization of the Department.

The Foreign Service of the United States forms the field force through which the Department of State establishes and maintains the necessary contacts with foreign governments. The Foreign Service, which includes all ambassadors and ministers, counselors of embassy or legation, diplomatic secretaries, consuls, consuls general, vice-consuls, and subordinate personnel, deals with every political, commercial, administrative, or social problem that enters into the relations of the United States with foreign countries. Through the Foreign Service, the Department protects American citizens in foreign countries, American shipping and seamen, and American interests in general. The officers of the Foreign Service carry on negotiations in conformity with instructions from the Department, report on political and economic conditions and trends of significance to the United States, and strive to create goodwill and common understanding for enhancing international confidence and cooperation among governments and peoples.[3]

Basic Changes Due to Global Interests. In considering the international trade promotion work of the Department of State, it is well to bear in mind the striking changes in the international position of the United States and the sharp increase in our global responsibilities that have transpired during the past twenty-five years. Vast expansion in the organization and functions of the Department has occurred over this period of time.

Basic changes occurred during the postwar period in both multilateral and regional policy activities. A separate staff was set up in the Department to deal with United Nations affairs. Also, on the basis of congressional legislation, the Department carried out the suggestion of the Hoover Commission that it set up geographic bureaus to deal with all aspects of our relations with major areas of the world. Specialists in economics, intelligence, administration, and public affairs were associated with the political officers in the bureaus in order to coordinate all relevant considerations as a basis of policy determination with respect to particular countries and regions.[4]

---

[2] *Ibid.*
[3] *Ibid.*
[4] *The Department of State 1930–1955*, pamphlet, pp. 16 and 17.

Present Economic Activities. The present regional bureaus are those of European Affairs; Near Eastern and South Asian Affairs; African Affairs; Far Eastern Affairs; and Inter-American Affairs. Each is headed by an Assistant Secretary of State, who functions as an operating vice-president, making all decisions for his area except those requiring the approval of the Secretary or the Under Secretary, or of the President. Each regional bureau is responsible for the general conduct of foreign relations with the countries within their particular area by applying overall political, security, economic, public affairs, social, consular, administrative, and other policies and practices.

A Bureau of United Nations Affairs was created at the same time that the geographic bureaus were established. It has since become the Bureau of International Organization Affairs.[5]

Also as a result of these changed conditions, the economic activities of the Department of State extend over a number of important fields:

1. Economic assistance policy, involving the use of foreign aid, in conjunction with other foreign economic measures, to stimulate production abroad and to improve economic conditions in underdeveloped areas so as to strengthen the ability of free nations to resist aggression from without and subversion from within.

2. International trade policies, including the promotion of prosperity through commercial interchange; the furthering of the international exchange of technology and related data; the application of export controls and other security measures; and the conduct of activities with reference to specific commodities, including not only strategic commodities traded on world markets but also those commodities of which the United States is, or may be, a competing exporter and which bulk large in the total trade of friendly foreign countries.

3. Financial and development policy, relating to the protection and encouragement of United States investment abroad and the investment and development programs and policies of foreign governments; foreign loans and grants, and other international financial matters, including the convertibility of sterling and other currencies, the balance of payments, the relaxation of exchange restrictions, and exchange rate adjustments.

4. International transportation and communications policy, relating to ocean shipping; preferences and discriminations in this field; safety of life at sea; international aspects of inland surface transport; and the facilitation of travel, of international civil aviation, and of international wire and radio communications.

All these are integral parts of the total foreign policy problem of the United States, and they will continue to require the allotment of

---

[5] *U.S. Government Organization Manual, 1962–63*, p. 79.

Department resources to deal with them in the context of our overall foreign policy. [6]

A Bureau of Economic Affairs is responsible for the development of economic aspects of overall United States foreign policy, assuring consistency among the various components of economic policy. Embraced within this operation is an Office of International Trade and Finance, which, among other things, is responsible for developing policy recommendations relating to international trade, restrictive business practices affecting American interests abroad, and international aspects of industrial property rights.

Agency for International Development (AID). AID has the responsibility of carrying out nonmilitary United States foreign assistance programs and for continuous supervision and general direction of all assistance programs. It also functions with respect to Latin American development and Chilean reconstruction, as well as functions concerning agricultural trade development.

The office of Inspector General, Foreign Assistance, was established in 1961 chiefly to review the effectiveness of the inspection systems of the Foreign Assistance operating agencies and of the Peace Corps.

The Foreign Service of the United States. The Foreign Service of the United States has always been a primary source of information on foreign countries. In 1957, the Foreign Service operated through 81 diplomatic missions and 190 consulates in countries recognized diplomatically by the United States Government.

At the close of World War II, certain intelligence branches of the Office of Strategic Services (OSS) were transferred to the Department of State. Moreover, in 1939, the foreign service of the Department of Commerce (purely commercial representation) and of the Department of Agriculture (purely agricultural interests) were consolidated with the Foreign Service of the United States.

At the close of World War II, the Foreign Service was found to be deficient in terms of qualified personnel. Temporary arrangements were adopted to build up the Service, but with meager results. A task force of the first Hoover Commission on government reorganization in 1949 offered recommendations to improve the situation. Finally, in 1954,

---

[6] *The Department of State, op. cit.,* pp. 35 and 36.

a special Secretary's Public Committee on Personnel conducted an intensive study and presented its recommendations.[7]

One basic difficulty lay in the fact that the Foreign Service had become a disjointed, disintegrated, and essentially expatriated service.

> Not only is the Service far too small for the tasks devolving upon it; it is also critically deficient in various technical specialties — notably economic, labor, agricultural, commercial promotion, area-language, and administrative — that have become indispensable to the successful practice of diplomacy in its vastly broadened, mid-twentieth century meaning. [8]

In addition to the Foreign Service Officers Corps, there are also Foreign Service Reserve Officers and a Foreign Service Staff. The Reserve is a branch composed of specialists on temporary assignment. The Staff includes officers, clerical, and custodial personnel. Finally, numerous aliens are employed overseas by the Foreign Service.

As stated by the late Secretary of State Dulles:

> The national interest urgently requires a stronger and more versatile Foreign Service. I agree with the Committee that the way to achieve this objective is to bring into the Foreign Service Officers Corps many of those civil servants now in the Washington headquarters, Foreign Service Reserve Officers, and higher-level Foreign Service Staff. The members of the expanded Service will be obligated to serve at home and abroad and will staff not only posts in the field but the majority of officer positions in the Department as well. [9]

The functions of the three present categories of the Foreign Service, as modified, are as follows:

> 1. The Foreign Service Officer Corps will be expanded to staff substantially all officer positions abroad and all "Foreign Service positions" in the home office. The Committee estimated that there will eventually be approximately 3,900 Foreign Service officers based on current budget resources.

> 2. The Foreign Service Reserve will continue for the purpose of making temporary appointments or appointments of persons not yet eligible for lateral entry to the Foreign Service Officers Corps.

> 3. The Foreign Service Staff will be essentially limited to technical, clerical, and custodial personnel in the lower and middle grades.[10]

---

[7]"Toward a Stronger Foreign Service," Department of State Publication 5458 (June, 1954). See also Charles E. Saltzman, Under Secretary of State for Administration, "The Reorganization of the American Foreign Service," *Department of State Bulletin* (September 27, 1954).

[8]"Toward a Stronger Foreign Service," *op. cit.*, pp. 7–8.

[9]*Department of State Bulletin* (September 27, 1954), p. 444.

[10]*Ibid.*, pp. 445–446.

Trade Promotion. As far as commercial activity is concerned, the Foreign Service is engaged in the promotion and the protection of the foreign trade of the United States. The functions of trade promotion are summarized below.

1. Keep constantly on the alert for and submit immediate reports on concrete trade opportunities for the benefit of American importers and exporters as well as the employment of American techniques, engineering, and production skills, and other professional skills and services.

2. Carefully study and report on the potentialities of overseas areas and districts as a market for American products, as a competitor of American products in other countries, and as a source of supply to the American economy.

3. Endeavor to create, within the scope of the duties to which they are assigned, a demand for American products within their districts.

4. Investigate and report on factors affecting the production and exportation to the United States of local products that might be desirable for import, as well as any such products concerning which United States firms and individuals express an interest.

5. Investigate and submit World Trade Directory Reports on the general standing and distributing capacity of foreign firms within their districts. World Trade Directory Reports provide data to American businessmen on firms and individuals engaged in business — selling or buying. The WTD reports make this possible by describing the foreign firms' organization, capital, turnover, method of operation, nationality of principals, territory covered, products handled, location of headquarters, branches, names of firms represented, which in turn constitute reference data of the most valuable type, since they enable the American firm to develop other first-hand data on prospective connections and to judge whether the foreign firm is handling competitive products and should possibly, therefore, be avoided.

6. Upon request, prepare and submit trade lists of commercial firms within their districts.

7. Facilitate and report in advance on proposed visits of alien professional and businessmen to the United States so that

interested firms and agencies may have the opportunity to meet them.

8. Maintain commercial reading room for use of local businessmen and see that it is supplied with current copies of American daily newspapers, trade journals, and catalogs, and especially with those that are of special interest in particular districts around the world.

9. Lend direct assistance by supplying all proper information to American citizens traveling abroad on business and to salesmen, buyers, and other representatives of American manufacturers and exporters and importers abroad, and by facilitating in every proper way their legitimate business in connection with American trade interests.

10. Answer trade inquiries received from firms and individuals.

11. Encourage the establishment and support of American Chambers of Commerce.

12. Prepare for, and upon instructions perform, trade conference work when in the United States, not only for the Department of State and other agencies of the government, but also for Chambers of Commerce, foreign trade associations, exporters, importers, farmers, bankers, and professional and business organizations having trade problems or interest in conditions abroad.

Trade Protection. The functions of trade protection that are performed by the Foreign Service are listed below.

1. Protect the national commercial reputation of the United States.

2. Observe, report on, and whenever possible endeavor to remove discriminations against American agricultural, commercial, labor, and industrial interests in other countries.

3. Guard against the infringement of rights of American citizens in matters relating to commerce and navigation, based on custom, international law or treaty; officers keep currently informed on and report concerning enactment of laws relating to patents, trademarks, and other branches of local industrial property law and intellectual property, including copyrights; officers report promptly, with recommendations, concerning cases of infringement or piracy, after supplying such information

as the officer can to enable the owner to take legal proceedings to protect his rights.

4. Appraise and evaluate for the information of the Department and citizens of the United States the effect on the industrial, agricultural, and commercial interests of the United States of treaties, trade agreements, quota control laws and decrees, exchange-control mechanisms, and barter and compensation arrangements to which the country of assignment is a party.

5. Furnish information regarding national and local laws and administrative regulations, governmental and private monopolies operating in restraint of trade.

6. Investigate and report on restrictions upon commercial travelers.

7. Exert influence to prevent discrimination against American interests by seeing that specifications for construction or other work abroad are drawn to give American manufacturers equal opportunity to compete for all public and private contracts to be let under a system of open bidding.

8. Endeavor to adjust and obtain settlement of trade complaints filed against American exporters.

9. Use their good offices in connection with appointments of boards of survey to examine and report on the condition of American merchandise imported into foreign countries of which complaint has been made by the importers.

10. Aid in the arbitration of trade disputes by submitting names of individuals considered competent to act as arbitrators (but may not themselves act as such arbitrators).

Department of Commerce

The Department of Commerce,[11] the "businessman's department," was established under the organic act of 1903 "to foster, promote, and develop the foreign and domestic commerce, the mining, manufacturing, shipping, and fishing industries, and the transportation facilities of the United States." Several important changes have occurred from time to time in the effectuation of these functions by means of separately organized bureaus. Chart 4-2 on page 75 gives the organization of the Department of Commerce.

---

[11] Valuable assistance in preparing this section was rendered by the Philadelphia Regional Office the Department and the Field Office in Cincinnati.

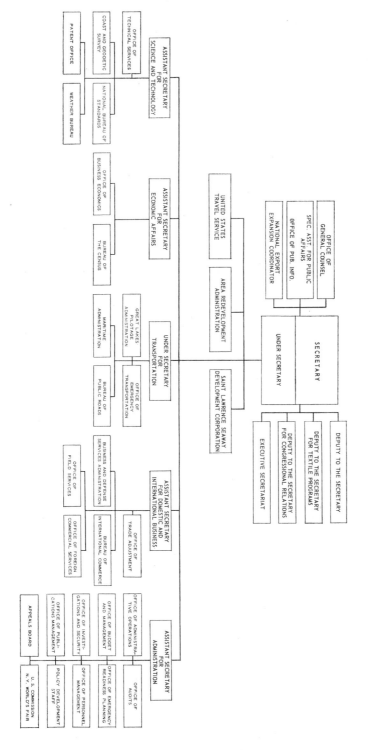

Chart 4-2

DEPARTMENT OF COMMERCE

75

Chart 4-3

BUREAU OF INTERNATIONAL COMMERCE

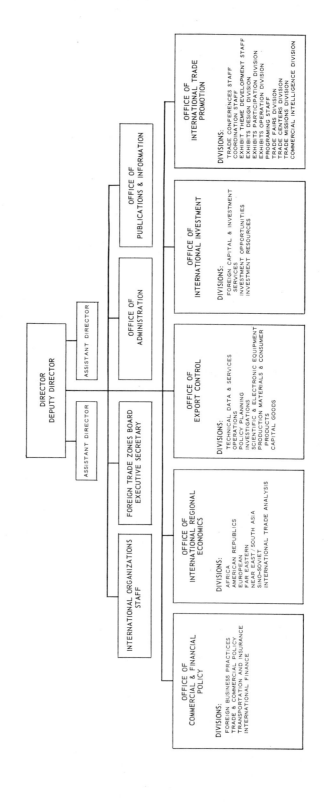

DIRECTOR
DEPUTY DIRECTOR

ASSISTANT DIRECTOR

ASSISTANT DIRECTOR

INTERNATIONAL ORGANIZATIONS STAFF

FOREIGN TRADE ZONES BOARD EXECUTIVE SECRETARY

OFFICE OF ADMINISTRATION

OFFICE OF PUBLICATIONS & INFORMATION

OFFICE OF COMMERCIAL & FINANCIAL POLICY

DIVISIONS:
FOREIGN BUSINESS PRACTICES
TRADE & COMMERCIAL POLICY
TRANSPORTATION AND INSURANCE
INTERNATIONAL FINANCE

OFFICE OF INTERNATIONAL REGIONAL ECONOMICS

DIVISIONS:
AFRICA
AMERICAN REPUBLICS
EUROPEAN
FAR EASTERN
NEAR EAST/ SOUTH ASIA
SINO-SOVIET
INTERNATIONAL TRADE ANALYSIS

OFFICE OF EXPORT CONTROL

DIVISIONS:
TECHNICAL DATA & SERVICES
OPERATIONS
POLICY PLANNING
INVESTIGATIONS
SCIENTIFIC & ELECTRONIC EQUIPMENT
PRODUCTION MATERIALS & CONSUMER PRODUCTS
CAPITAL GOODS

OFFICE OF INTERNATIONAL INVESTMENT

DIVISIONS:
FOREIGN CAPITAL & INVESTMENT SERVICES
INVESTMENT OPPORTUNITIES
INVESTMENT RESOURCES

OFFICE OF INTERNATIONAL TRADE PROMOTION

DIVISIONS:
TRADE CONFERENCES STAFF
COORDINATION STAFF
EXHIBIT THEME DEVELOPMENT STAFF
EXHIBITS DESIGN DIVISION
EXHIBITS PARTICIPATION DIVISION
EXHIBITS OPERATION DIVISION
PROGRAMING STAFF
TRADE FAIRS DIVISION
TRADE CENTERS DIVISION
TRADE MISSIONS DIVISION
COMMERCIAL INTELLIGENCE DIVISION

The Department now embraces a number of units related in one way or another with international marketing. Chief among these, for our study, are the ones that deal directly with the foreign trader and help him in the practical conduct of his business. Reference is made to the Bureau of International Commerce, (the name adopted in 1962); the Business and Defense Services Administration; and the Bureau of the Census. Chart 4-3 on page 76 gives the organization of the Bureau of International Commerce

Under the reorganization of 1962, an Assistant Secretary for Domestic and International Business supervises the Business and Defense Services Administration, the new Bureau of International Commerce, the Commerce Department field offices throughout the United States, and the overseas commercial service.

Field Offices. Each of the 39 Department of Commerce Field Offices is a small Department of Commerce in its own area.

Whether the visitor to a Field Office is experienced in international commerce or is a beginner, he will find a wealth of information.

Here are a few specific types of information available from the Field Office international trade specialist:

How to get started in world trade, step by step;

Marketing and economic reports;

Foreign business regulations;

International trade statistics;

Information on foreign transportation, insurance, credit sources, patents, trademarks, copyrights;

Directories of foreign advertising agencies, market research organizations, international trade development organizations;

Publications on every phase of international commerce; and

Trade and investment opportunities abroad.

Commerce Field Offices work with the Regional Export Expansion Councils, trade associations, chambers of commerce, local offices of the Small Business Administration, and other groups interested in selling overseas.[12]

Bureau of International Commerce. The Bureau of International Commerce performs its services through the following offices:

---

[12]U.S. Department of Commerce, *Selling Around the World* (Washington, D.C., 1963), p. 26.

Office of International Trade Promotion. This office administers Commercial Intelligence, Trade Centers, Trade Fairs, Trade Missions and Trade Conferences. Commercial Intelligence deals chiefly with trade lists and World Trade Directory Reports (see page 575). The Office of Trade Fairs has to do with United States exhibits at trade fairs conducted all over the world. The purposes of these exhibits are to tell the story of American free enterprise and also to sell United States goods.

Although the United States is a latecomer to this type of marketing, by the end of 1962 official U.S. Exhibitions will have been staged 127 times in 39 countries around the world. More than 80 million people on both sides of the Iron Curtain will have seen displays and demonstrations of American products and technology.

Beginning in 1963, an augmented international trade fairs program will provide for staging U.S. Exhibitions in areas selected entirely for their sales potential. These new showcases for U.S. products will reinforce the export expansion campaign to sell American goods abroad. While helping to reduce the deficit in the U.S. balance of payments, these commercial exhibitions will continue to demonstrate the results of free enterprise.

The Bureau of International Commerce trade fairs program depends entirely upon the cooperation of American industry. Many of the more than 4,000 companies which have participated in U.S. Exhibitions had never before exported their products and made their first overseas sales at international trade fairs.

The cost of participating is, in most cases, nominal. In almost all U.S. Exhibitions, display space for American products is free. In a few locations, market conditions are so favorable — and consequent sales opportunities so promising — that American firms are asked to help defray costs of construction and installation.[13]

TRADE CENTERS. U. S. Trade Centers provide a most convenient and inexpensive way for a small businessman to display his products overseas. The Trade Center is not only a commercial showroom. It also enables a firm to test its products in markets where the demand for U.S. goods is combined with the dollar resources to pay for them.

Unlike trade fairs, Trade Centers are permanent installations where the products of different industries are displayed for a few days to about three weeks.

Each showing is based on the collective marketing experience of specialists from the Commerce Department, industry, and trade associations. This team initiates a new display when its research discloses that a certain line of products — machine tools, for example, or toys, or men's wear — has a good chance for profitable sales in the area served by the Center.

---

[13]Ibid., pp. 17–18.

Each Trade Center has a trade promotion staff to work closely with Commercial Officers from the American Embassy in the country where the Center is located. They conduct an extensive promotional campaign to attract buyers and prospective agents for the exhibited products.

Trade Centers were established primarily to increase U.S. exports, so emphasis is placed on displaying American products not yet sold in the area or in helping manufacturers not yet represented by an agent.

Centers are "All American" activities. Only goods made in the United States can be displayed. Trade Centers are established to help improve the U.S. balance-of-payments picture by sales of U.S.-made goods.[14]

[U.S. Trade Centers are operating in Bangkok, Frankfurt, London, Milan, and Tokyo.]

TRADE MISSIONS. A trade mission is a selected group of business specialists who have volunteered to carry specific U.S. business proposals to international markets. These men do not represent themselves or their companies; they represent the whole U.S. business community.

Each Mission takes with it a commercial library of more than 1,000 business and trade publications, directories, and reference books donated by the American publishing industry. When the Mission leaves the host country, this library is left at the American Embassy or Consulate for use by local businessmen.

Trade Missions are organized to talk business. By doing simply this, the Missions create favorable impressions of the United States.

Although Trade Missions travel under U.S. Government auspices and are accompanied by a Commerce Department international trade expert, the Government does not become a party to any of the transactions discussed or concluded.

During the Mission's 3 to 5 weeks abroad, many conferences with individual businessmen, business groups, public officials, the press, and trade associations result in solid sales of U.S. products.

Business proposals for trade in certain items, for licensing, or for joint ventures, are submitted by businessmen anywhere in the United States in advance of the Trade Mission's departure. Details of the qualifications for Trade Mission participation are available from any Field Office.

Opportunities for trade or investment brought back by the Missions are published in *International Commerce*, discussed in special end-of-mission conferences, and released to the daily and trade press. Any U.S. businessman can then deal directly with his overseas counterpart.

Besides the businessmen who travel overseas with Trade Missions or under other sponsorship, thousands of Americans go abroad each year independently for business reasons.

---

[14]*Ibid.*, pp. 16–17.

The Commerce Department's business travel service helps smooth the way for them, too. Travel service is available at any of the 39 Field Offices or in Washington. In either case, the businessman planning a trip overseas will be brought up-to-date on the areas he will visit.

Briefings are by specialists abreast of economic situations and trade development activities in each country and region overseas. They are familiar with the problems bearing on international trade within these areas. They not only know the problems, they can propose possible solutions.

At the business traveler's request, appropriate Foreign Service posts are notified of his itinerary and his particular requirements for certain information.

Industry Organized Trade Missions are a newer concept of privately initiated Missions but recognized officially by the U.S. Government.

Unlike traditional U.S. Trade Missions, these groups are selected by an industry or industry association. Members pay all of their own expenses including travel, meals, and lodging.

These Mission members are encouraged to conclude business on the spot.

Like Government-financed Missions, the Do-It-Yourself groups receive a scheduled briefing in Washington before departure. A Commerce Department specialist precedes the Mission to set up appointments.

The international trade resources of the entire Department of Commerce are at the disposal of any business group interested in new international sales through a Do-It-Yourself Trade Mission.[15]

Office of International Regional Economics. This office in the Bureau of International Commerce has an International Trade Analysis staff and separate Divisions dealing with Africa, the American Republics, British Commonwealth, European, Far Eastern, Near East/South Asia, and Sino-Soviet areas. These units specialize in the geographical areas indicated, dealing with every aspect of the economic, financial, and commercial situation in each area.

Office of International Investment. This office has divisions covering Foreign Capital and Investment, Investment Opportunities, and Investment Resources. The Office encourages and promotes increased participation by private enterprisers in all kinds of aid and investment, with special emphasis on the developing countries. To do this, the Office provides information to United States business firms with regard to joint

---

[15]*Ibid.*, pp. 20–21.

ventures abroad; collaborates with the Area Development Administration in assisting state industrial development authorities seeking foreign enterprise investment; stimulates development of new approaches and new organization arrangements in United States industry to gain wider participation in development activities abroad, especially small and medium-sized United States business firms; and encourages private enterprise in developing countries.

Office of Commercial and Financial Policy. This office has divisions dealing with Foreign Business Practices, Trade and Commercial Policy, Transportation and Insurance, and International Finance. This is the central office of the Department of Commerce with respect to planning and development of the Department's international economic policies and programs. The experience of American businessmen is sought.

The National and Regional Export Expansion Councils. These councils represent attempts to promote United States export trade, particularly by firms not yet engaged in export, by bringing to the attention of management the opportunities and assistance available through the local Field Offices of the Department of Commerce.

The National Export Expansion Council (NEEC) consists of American business leaders appointed by the Secretary of Commerce to work with the Department of Commerce in promoting world trade.

Each of these men — all of whom have volunteered to serve without pay — has had long experience in U.S. industry. As individuals and as a group, they give advice and guidance to fellow businessmen interested in foreign markets but not yet exporting.

The scope of export opportunities is shown by the more than 6,500 leads to overseas sales developed last year by Commercial Officers at American Embassies and Consulates and made available to businessmen here.

Vital to export expansion is the need for these inquiries from abroad to reach all U.S. companies.

Helping to effectively direct these export trade opportunities — and other timely marketing information — to U.S. business is one of the most important functions of the Regional Export Expansion Councils (REEC's).

These Regional Export Expansion Councils are established in the same areas served by the Department of Commerce Field Offices, thus they carry out the NEEC's programs across the country.

More than 1,000 volunteer businessmen:

•Assist in organizing industry participation in international Trade Fairs and Trade Centers;

•Provide both the encouragement and the know-how to trade organizations interested in forming their own groups for export expansion;

•Obtain speakers for meetings of business organizations interested in world trade;

•Publicize international trade through business publications, trade and association journals, and the daily press; and

•Cooperate in operating conferences, seminars, and workshops on world trade.

With guidance from the REEC's, these conferences, seminars, and workshops are stimulating hundreds of businessmen — who have not previously sold their products overseas — to get into world trade.[16]

Office of Export Control. This office issues licenses for such products for such destinations as may be under U.S. Government control.

The Security of the United States and other free world nations requires control over the export of strategic materials and industrial technical data which could help the Sino-Soviet Bloc.

But since export expansion is vital to economic growth in the United States, the Bureau of International Commerce administers export controls on a highly selective basis.

All exports from the United States, its territories, and its possessions are subject to export controls. However, the great majority of U.S. exports are made under general licenses which may be used without specific authority from the Government. Owners of industrial technical data concerned with the release of these data may request an opinion from the Bureau about the desirability of exporting such information.

For the newcomer to world trade, it is important to know that complete information and help with export licenses is available from any Field Office or from the Bureau of International Commerce.

Three findings are involved in determining whether a validated export license is required: (1) what is being shipped; (2) where it is going; (3) how it will be used.

If a validated export license *is* necessary, applications are filed with the Bureau of International Commerce.[17]

Business and Defense Services Administration. The Business and Defense Services Administration, through its industry and commodity divisions, advises U.S. businessmen of the international sales potential of specific commodities. BDSA commodity specialists hold daily discus-

[16]*Ibid.*, pp. 22–23.
[17]*Ibid.*, p. 25.

sions with trade association executives, manufacturers, and other businessmen — all of whom contribute to a pool of commodity information, from raw materials to finished products.

Foreign Services. These major marketing units — BIC and BDSA — obtain information for the international businessman principally through the Commercial Officers in the Foreign Service of the United States, located in 300 posts in 107 countries. Daily, about 500 dispatches concerning business conditions or trade and investment opportunities are analyzed and made available, almost immediately, to the U.S. businessman. Unfortunately but a small fraction of available information can be published. Foreign Service dispatches can be reviewed in the Department when information in depth is required.[18]

Marketing Service. Various direct promotional services are performed for the use of the international marketing firm. In addition to the information obtained through the Foreign Service, a wealth of statistics is regularly examined and evaluated, and newspapers and magazines in dozens of languages are studied for significant data. Regular visits from overseas businessmen and official guests often add significant information.

> *Trade Lists* help you find customers, agents, distributors, licensees, and sources of supply abroad. Each list gives names and addresses of firms handling a specific commodity in one foreign country. . . . Each list also contains a summary of basic trade and industry data, including a brief analysis of foreign trade in the commodity covered, Government regulations affecting trade, and other useful market data. Lists of importers and dealers [in over 70 standard categories] indicate relative size of each firm, method of operation, products handled, territory covered, and size of sales force. Lists of exporters and manufacturers show relative size or production capacity of each firm, and the products handled.
>
> *World Trade Directory Reports* supply the detailed information you need on specific foreign firms to determine their competence and reliability before you do business with them. These reports, which complement the Trade List service and supplement Trade Contact Surveys, are prepared by the U.S. Foreign Service and represent a consensus of reliable sources of information.
>
> *Trade Contact Surveys* are offered as a special service to help you find agents, distributors, or licensees abroad. A local canvass in a par-

---

[18]*Ibid.*, pp. 10–11.

ticular foreign country is made by a U.S. Foreign Service officer to locate several firms which meet your individual requirements and which
express an interest in your proposal. A survey is usually completed in
about 60 days. The report covering results includes pertinent marketing data as well as names, addresses, and brief descriptions of the
prospects recommended. Individual WTD reports on the prospects are
also supplied.

The Agency Index is designed to put prospective foreign buyers in
prompt touch with local sources of supply of your products. It is a
facility for maintaining at U.S. Foreign Service posts throughout the
world the names and addresses of the foreign representatives of American firms. The Index enables commercial officers abroad to direct in-
quirers quickly to your local oversea agents, distributors, or licensees.[19]

Bureau of the Census. The Bureau of the Census is engaged in fact
finding. It produces statistical material basic to production and marketing studies; and it compiles the official foreign trade statistics of the
United States.

Maritime Administration. The development of the American merchant marine operating in foreign trade is placed in the hands of the
Maritime Administration in the Department of Commerce. Under the
terms of the Merchant Marine Act of 1936, the declared policy of the
United States Government is to possess a merchant marine sufficient to
carry its domestic water-borne commerce and a substantial portion of its
water-borne export and import foreign commerce. Further, the merchant marine should be sufficient to operate on all routes essential for
maintaining the flow of that commerce at all times. It should be "capable of serving as a naval and military auxiliary in time of war or national emergency; owned and operated under the United States flag
by citizens of the United States insofar as may be practicable; composed
of the best-equipped, safest, and most suitable types of vessels, constructed in the United States and manned with a trained and efficient
citizen personnel."[20]

This ambitious program to serve the foreign trade interests of the
country was initiated in 1936–1937 with a realignment of American
flag services operating under subsidy in the several world trade routes.
Under the law, construction-differential subsidies are paid, and when

---

[19]U.S. Department of Commerce, *Low Cost Marketing Aids for Higher Export Profits* (Washington, D.C., 1963).

[20]Merchant Marine Act 1936, Title I.

built, the private operators of these vessels, under certain conditions, receive payment of operating-differential subsidies. The training of licensed and unlicensed personnel for service on American merchant vessels is conducted by the Administration.

Other Department of Commerce Agencies. Several other units in the Department of Commerce are also useful to the world trader.

The Office of Business Economics is engaged in research, collation, and analysis of data having to do with the balance of international payments of the United States, national income, current business, and national economics. The publications of the OBE are useful in systematic business planning.

The National Bureau of Standards has benefited not only the government but also private commerce and industry by its research activities in connection with standards of practice and standards of performance. It has played an active role in increasing the durability and usefulness of many of the commodities of commerce; and has aided in the establishment of standard grades, types, and sizes of commodities and nomenclature applicable thereto.

The Coast and Geodetic Survey is charged with surveying and charting the coasts of the United States and its possessions. It compiles technical data useful in constructing maps and aeronautical charts and in aerial as well as in sea navigation.

The Patent Office issues letters of patent, and registers trademarks, prints, and labels used in foreign trade and interstate commerce.

The Foreign Trade Zones Board[21] administers the Foreign Trade Zones Act under which customs-free areas may be established at United States ports.

The Weather Bureau functions for international as well as for national interests.

The Civil Aeronautics Administrator reports to the Congress and the President through the Secretary of Commerce.

Publications. The Department of Commerce publishes a vast amount of material that is valuable to the international trader and to the student of international economic subjects. Of broad, general interest is *International Commerce*, a weekly dealing with up-to-date market, commodity, policy, and other conditions, and offering opportunities for

---

[21]See Chapter 23 for a discussion of the establishment of free ports.

international transactions. The *Survey of Current Business*, monthly, is a wealth of statistical and analytical data, including foreign trade and balance of payments data. The *Statistical Abstract of the United States*, annual, is a mine of statistical and historical data on every conceivable subject, including foreign trade. Official foreign trade statistics, monthly, are published in a variety of *"FT"* series, and *Quarterly Summary of Foreign Commerce* is a more readily available statistical presentation.

The Department also publishes supplements to *International Commerce*, dealing with some specific subject, e.g., "Africa Sales Frontier for U.S. Business," which happens to be the title of the first supplement issued. *Overseas Business Reports* are issued throughout the year and deal with economic conditions of foreign countries, basic data on the economy of specific countries, foreign trade, living and business costs abroad, licensing and other restrictions, etc.

Objectives. As expressed in an article explaining the reorganization, the following objectives were stated:

> For the Department of Commerce to play its full role in helping speed the growth of American industry, we must increase the scope, the competence, and efficiency of the commodity activities lodged in the Business and Defense Services Administration and relate them properly to our domestic and overseas field services and to the specialized programs of the Bureau of International Commerce.
>
> The reorganization is also directed at implementing specific parts of the Trade Expansion Act. Under the Act, there will, of course, be a Special Representative appointed by the President who will have direct negotiating responsibilities. Nevertheless, it will be the continuing job of the Commerce Department to provide the negotiator with detailed industry information on the potential benefits from opening markets abroad and the potential impact on domestic industry of reducing tariffs here at home.
>
> We will also provide the President's Representative with information about non-tariff barriers abroad, so that their correction can proceed along with the work of lowering tariffs.
>
> The Secretary of Commerce has responsibilities, too, in granting trade adjustment assistance to industries that may be injured by imports. These will be exercised, in large part, through the facilities of the reorganized Business And Defense Services Administration. In this way, decisions will be based on a thorough knowledge of the conditions of the relevant industries and the types of technical and other assistance that can be most effective.
>
> In the past year and a half we have greatly improved the services of the Department of Commerce for promoting American products

abroad, for bringing export opportunities to the attention of American companies, and for helping the companies, new at export, go after the sales that are possible overseas.

The new organization should make our promotion techniques even more effective. Trade missions, trade fairs, trade centers — all will be channeled into markets that have been examined by BDSA industry specialists and by BIC country specialists.

With the Field Service and overseas commercial service linked more closely, it should also be easier to get companies to participate in overseas missions and fairs. We should have better follow-up, too.[22]

Department of Agriculture

The Department of Agriculture is concerned with foreign trade in several direct and indirect ways. The Agricultural Research Service performs the work that aims to improve the farm products that move to market, including overseas markets. The Forest Service manages the national forest resources, including those in Alaska and Puerto Rico, for orderly and continuous use and for the maintenance of stable economic conditions in national forest communities.

The Agricultural Marketing Service aids the orderly and efficient marketing of farm products. A marketing research program seeks to improve the handling, storage, processing, transportation, and distribution of farm products. This program includes the dissemination of market news; standardization, inspection, grading, and classifying of farm products; and surplus sales to domestic and foreign buyers.

The Commodity Exchange Authority supervises trading on commodity exchanges designated as contract markets. There are 17 of these, dealing with farm products such as corn and wool. Under the Commodity Exchange Act, price manipulation and corners are to be prevented and market operations are to be free of misleading information or fraudulent acts.

The Foreign Agricultural Service develops foreign markets for the production of our farms. This includes continual appraisal of marketing opportunities abroad and of competition and trade barriers. It also includes efforts to improve international trade conditions for United States agricultural products and by administering foreign trade programs, including the export sale of United States farm surpluses for foreign currencies. The Service is able to operate as a source of current informa-

---

[22]U.S. Department of Commerce, *International Commerce* (February 5, 1962), pp. 4–5.

tion on world agricultural commodity and trade policy by means of agricultural officers stationed in all principal countries, in addition to agricultural marketing specialists who make special investigations abroad.

The Commodity Credit Corporation is charged with price support of agricultural products as specified in legislative enactments.[23] The CCC also may purchase abroad commodities to meet both foreign and domestic requirements; it procures agricultural products for relief programs abroad; it may export, at competitive world prices, any commodity that is not in short supply. The Commodity Credit Corporation administers United States participation in the International Wheat Agreement, together with the Agricultural Stabilization and Conservation Service. The latter also administers the quota provisions of the Sugar Act and the National Wool Act.

The Federal Crop Insurance Corporation provides farmers a means of insuring crop investments against such risks as weather, insects, and disease. It does not insure profits; it only covers the cash outlay of the farmer up to the date of loss.

Other Government Departments and Agencies

While the United States Departments of State, Commerce, and Agriculture deal fully or more directly with international marketing matters than other departments, nevertheless, a number of these other departments, in specialized ways, are useful to the international marketing firm. Such departments will be considered briefly in this section.

Treasury Department. The Treasury Department, through the Customs Service, administers all customs regulations; imposes import duties; provides the basis for the Government's import, export, and vessel entrance and clearance statistics that are published by the Department of Commerce through the Bureau of the Census; administers the entrance and clearance of vessels and cargoes at American ports; inspects all export declarations to assure compliance with export license regulations; and applies a number of the federal navigation laws. The Bureau of Customs also performs vessel admeasuring functions.

An Office of International Finance is concerned with the various world agencies, such as International Monetary Fund, International

---

[23]At time of writing, price support is mandatory on so-called basic crops, namely, corn, wheat, rice, tobacco, and cotton. Price support is permissive for other commodities. These items are changed from time to time.

Bank for Reconstruction and Development, International Finance Corporation, Inter-American Development Bank, etc. with the (United States) National Advisory Council on International Monetary and Financial Problems; with international loans and assistance programs; with the United States Exchange Stabilization Fund; with gold, exchange, trade agreements, countervailing duties; and with financial and monetary problems in foreign areas under United States control. A Division of Foreign Assets Control administers regulations concerning trade and foreign exchange with designated unfriendly areas.

The Office of International Tax Affairs analyzes activities concerning international tax matters and negotiates international tax agreements at a technical level. It also may participate in the negotiation of tax agreements with other countries, along with the Department of State.

In peacetime the United States Coast Guard is in the Treasury Department. It provides the maintenance of lighthouses and other aids for protection of life and property and for navigational aids. It enforces the vessel inspection laws and a variety of laws that can be effectively enforced through the ship and air arms of the Coast Guard. The narcotic laws, including the permissive features of the Narcotics Drug Import and Export Act, are administered by a Commissioner of Narcotics.

Army Department. The Corps of Engineers of the Army Department spends the appropriations of Congress for river and harbor improvements; constructs breakwaters; excavates channels; dredges harbors; and makes ports and channel surveys and investigations and recommendations to Congress. Extensive surveys covering the ports of the United States and its possessions and territories are published by the Engineers. The Corps of Engineers also defines the pier head limit beyond which piers and wharves may not be constructed in harbors, and exercises police power relative to the pollution of navigable waters. The civil administration of the Panama Canal is vested in the Army Department. The Panama Canal Company operates the Panama Canal and all equipment, facilities, and supplies connected therewith, including a steamship line.

Navy Department. The Navy Department, apart from the protection afforded to commerce and shipping during wartime, aids shipping through two operations in the office of the Chief of Naval Operations. One operation is the publication of nautical charts, manuals of instruction, bulletins, and sailing directions, and broadcasts of urgent information to vessels. The Naval Observatory aids shipping by publishing valuable astronomical data, testing navigation instruments, and establishing standard time and differences of longitude.

Interior Department. The Department of the Interior supervises the administration of the Virgin Islands and other miscellaneous island areas including the Trust Territory of the Pacific Islands (comprises an area north of New Guinea and includes the Mariana, Caroline, and Marshall Islands). For many years the Department has played a part in the production and distribution of the mineral products of the United States through the efforts of the Geological Survey. The Bureau of Mines conducts economic analyses pertaining to world production, distribution, and consumption of all mineral commodities; and it has charge of the production and sale of helium for medical, scientific, and commercial use, under regulations approved by the President. The Fish and Wildlife Service regulates and protects the salmon and other fisheries of Alaska and administers the fur-seal herd of the North Pacific. It also administers the laws pertaining to the protection of fish and wildlife everywhere under the Department's jurisdiction.

The Office of Oil and Gas carries out functions under the Defense Production Act of 1950, which aims to provide adequate supplies and facilities of petroleum to fulfill both civilian and military requirements. The Oil Import Administration allocates imports of petroleum products and issues licenses on the basis of these allocations.

The Bureau of Commercial Fisheries not only deals with the protection and maintenance of marine and inland fisheries but also is concerned with commercial aspects. The Bureau conducts activities concerning international agreements pertaining to fishery resources such as the Northwest Atlantic Fisheries Convention, North Pacific Fisheries Convention, and the Whaling Convention.

The economic and social development of the Virgin Islands is charged to the Virgin Island Corporation. The Office of Territories seeks to protect the economic, social, and political development of the territorial areas such as Canton, Palmyra, and Enderbury Islands; and Jarvis, Baker, and Howland Islands; and the Trust Territory of the Pacific Islands.

United States Tariff Commission. The Tariff Commission is very directly identified with the conduct of the import trade of the United States. It is charged with investigating the administration of United States customs laws and their fiscal and industrial effects, and studying foreign trade policies. Numerous publications have appeared, including *Summary of Tariff Information*. Under the Tariff Act of 1930, the Tariff Commission is charged with the administration of the flexible provisions whereby tariff rates may be changed.[24]

It also investigates charges of unfair competition in the import trade. Under the trade agreements acts, the Commission has always been an important participant in negotiations. Under the present act, the Commission is also called upon to certify the limits to which concessions can be granted without doing injury to a domestic industry. Under certain circumstances, the President would be required to reserve from negotiations any article with respect to which the Tariff Commission found that imports of such article were seriously injuring or threatening injury to the domestic industry concerned. These articles would be reserved for a four-year period. It also is charged with hearing appeals from allegedly injured producers claiming excessive imports under reduced tariffs.

Department of Labor. In the Department of Labor, the Bureau of International Labor Affairs deals with international labor developments in relation to United States foreign and domestic policy, analyzes the impact of domestic policy and developments on the labor aspects of foreign affairs, etc. It represents the United States in the International Labor Organization (ILO). In the field of technical cooperation and exchange of persons, the Office supplies consultants for foreign assignment, furnishes materials for use abroad, and conducts training programs for foreign nationals. The Department stations its own labor attachés in foreign countries.

Post Office Department. The Post Office Department aids international marketing by providing the international mail service, including airmail service, through negotiating (subject to the approval of the President) postal treaties with and postal conventions among foreign countries.

---

[24]Tariff rates are further discussed in Chapter 23.

Financial Agencies. A number of agencies, some of long standing and others of comparatively recent origin, are concerned in various ways with financial matters pertaining to foreign trade. The Federal Reserve System opened the financial resources of the United States to the needs of foreign commerce.[25] Moreover, foreign exchange matters command the attention of the Federal Reserve System. The monthly *Federal Reserve Bulletin* carries material bearing on international trade and on financial conditions of foreign countries.

The Export-Import Bank of Washington serves specific financial requirements of foreign trade and territorial trade as a means of facilitating exports, imports, and the exchange of commodities. The Securities and Exchange Commission supervises registration of new security issues offered in the American financial market and engages in research along related lines.

Health and Educational Services. In preventing the introduction of disease from abroad, the Public Health Service of the Department of Health, Education, and Welfare conducts the national maritime quarantine activities, makes physical examination of immigrants, and inspects passengers and crews of vessels and airplanes arriving from foreign ports. The Food and Drug Administration, among other acts, enforces the Food, Drug, and Cosmetic Act, Tea Importation Act, and Import Milk Act. Provision is made for exclusion from the United States of imports of products which are in violation of these statutes.

The Office of Education participates in the international educational relations field by advising and assisting in evaluating foreign credentials in connection with overseas technical assistance programs; administering student and teacher exchange; etc.

Justice Department. The Department of Justice is charged with protecting the interest of the government in matters of reappraisement and classification of imported goods, and all litigation incident thereto. The Immigration and Naturalization Service of the Justice Department deals with aliens and administers laws pertaining to naturalization. It also patrols the borders in an attempt to prevent illegal entry.

Transportation and Communication. The Federal Communications Commission is charged with the regulation of interstate and foreign

---

[25]See Chapter 26 for further details of the role played by the Federal Reserve System in providing for international banking facilities.

communication by wire (telephone, telegraph, and cable service) or radio (broadcasting), centralizing these duties and responsibilities with a view to more effective communications service.

The Interstate Commerce Commission, in its regulation of rates and services of railroads, supervises the establishment of special rates and regulations governing export and import freight traffic; and provides regulations governing the safe transportation of explosives by common carriers in interstate or foreign commerce.

Jurisdiction over waterpower projects on navigable streams affecting the interests of interstate or foreign commerce is vested in the Federal Power Commission.

The Civil Aeronautics Board, CAB, regulates the economic aspects of domestic and international United States air carrier operations and of the common carriers of foreign air carriers to and from the United States. It also participates in the establishment and development of international air transportation.

Federal Trade Commission. Supervision over the Export Trade Act providing for the organization and functioning in export trade of cooperative associations of competing American firms under certain exemptions from the antitrust acts, is vested in the Federal Trade Commission.[26] The Commission is also charged with the enforcement of the unfair trade provisions of the Federal Trade Commission Act applicable to practices in export as well as in domestic trade.

International Agencies. The adjustment of boundary questions with our neighbors is left to the International Boundary Commission, United States and Canada; and to the International Boundary and Water Commission, United States and Mexico. The St. Lawrence Seaway Development Corporation in the U.S. Department of Commerce is charged with constructing the United States portion of the St. Lawrence Seaway and with making the necessary arrangements to coordinate with other United States and Canadian bodies.

There are numerous joint, regional, and global groups in which the United States participates. Most of them relate to matters of understanding among nations, as in trade terms and conditions, weights and measures, and telecommunications. Others deal with specific commodities, such as tin, wheat, cotton, fisheries, and wool.

---

[26]The nature of cooperative export associations is further described in Chapter 17.

One intergovernmental agency in which the United States is a participating member is the Organization of American States (OAS), the General Secretariat of which is the Pan American Union. It is a regional agency within the United Nations. The scope of its activities has expanded in every field of international cooperation, including the economic and social fields.

Finally, the United Nations and specialized agencies of which the United States is a member seek to provide the physical and economic conditions that will cause markets to be expanded all over the world. They also publish a vast amount of valuable data in the international marketing area.[27] Annual regional economic surveys are excellent analyses of economic conditions abroad. Foreign trade statistical publications, which deal with all countries in a given volume, include *Direction of International Trade* and *Commodity Trade Statistics*. The International Monetary Fund publishes *International Monetary Statistics* (monthly).

Summary

1. The United States Government actively seeks to promote the foreign (chiefly export) trade of the country. The Department of State is the "official" representative of the United States in foreign matters. In addition, through the Foreign Service Officers considerable information is made available to United States international traders.

2. This information becomes available through the United States Department of Commerce, which publishes a vast number and variety of books, pamphlets, and magazines. Agricultural information is made available through the United States Department of Agriculture, and mineral data through the United States Department of the Interior.

3. Numerous other United States Government departments and agencies materially help international marketing and many of them deal with certain specific interests, for example, Tariff Commission and Maritime Commission (Administration); or indirectly provide assistance, for example, Corps of Engineers and Federal Reserve Board.

4. Various international agencies interest themselves in adjusting boundary questions, in gaining international understanding in trade terms and conditions, and in making available international marketing statistics.

---

[27]*See also* Chapters 5 and 6 for a more detailed discussion of these matters.

QUESTIONS

1. Define the function of the United States Department of State in the international relations field.

2. How have recent basic changes brought about changes in the operation of the Department of State?

3. Discuss the several fields in which the economic activities of the Department of State are conducted.

4. (a) Define the Foreign Service of the Department of State.
   (b) Explain its functions.
   (c) Discuss its shortcomings as revealed in a 1954 evaluation.
   (d) Define the present three categories of the Foreign Service.

5. Comment on the trade promotion activities of the Foreign Service.

6. Describe briefly the organization of the Bureau of International Commerce.

7. Define the purposes and uses of World Trade Directory (WTD) reports and trade lists.

8. Comment critically on the trade fairs and trade mission programs.

9. Evaluate the foreign trade publications of the Department of Commerce of the United States.

10. Define the functions of each of the following United States Government agencies:
    (a) Foreign Trade Zones Board.
    (b) Maritime Administration.
    (c) Customs Service.
    (d) Tariff Commission.
    (e) Federal Trade Commission.

11. Explain the foreign trade functions of the United States Department of Agriculture.

PROBLEM

Select any one of the United States Government agencies cited in this chapter (or any new agencies that may later have come into existence) and investigate and prepare a report on:
   (a) Its legal authority to operate.
   (b) Its organization structure.
   (c) Its services.
   (d) Its budget allowance.

COLLATERAL READINGS

Dartnell International Trade Handbook, The. Chicago: The Dartnell Corporation, 1963.

Exporters' Encyclopaedia. New York: Thomas Ashwell and Co., Inc., annual.

Heck, Harold J. *Foreign Commerce.* New York: McGraw-Hill Book Company, Inc., 1953. Chapters 7 and 19.

Horn, Paul V. *International Trade Principles and Practices,* Third Edition. New York: Prentice-Hall, Inc., 1951. Chapters 1 and 25.

United States Chamber of Commerce. *Foreign Commerce Handbook,* Thirteenth Edition. Washington, D.C.: 1959.

United States, Executive Office of the President, Office of Government Reports. *United States Government Manual.* Washington, D.C.: Government Printing Office, annual.

United States General Services Administration, National Archives and Records Service, Office of the Federal Register, *United States Government Organization Manual.* Washington, D.C.: Government Printing Office, annual.

CHAPTER 5

PROMOTION BY FOREIGN GOVERNMENTS
AND THE UNITED NATIONS

The entire international marketing program of any nation is embraced in what is termed its foreign commercial policy. The purpose of this discussion is to describe briefly the methods employed in the promotion of international marketing by the countries themselves as well as the United Nations.

Promotion by Foreign Governments

Every commercial nation has adopted a program of promotion of international marketing, ranging from the collection and dissemination of information beneficial to exporters to outright subsidy of exports or government monopoly of international marketing. Emphasis is invariably placed upon the export trade, although the basic program of some countries such as Germany, Japan, and the United Kingdom is designed to assure adequate supplies of foreign merchandise by providing exports sufficient to pay for them.

International Agreements. The raw material producing nations, most of which fall into the underdeveloped category, seek to promote their exports by means of international commodity agreements, under which the prices of primary products may be stabilized, with special emphasis on the higher price side.[1]

Subsidies. Subsidies to promote exports have been practised for many years. If the country that is using this device happens to have a monopoly in the production and sale of the product that is subsidized,

---

[1]See Chapter 18.

the plan is likely to be successful. In such a situation, the only difficulty is the possibility of competition from newly discovered or established supplies of the subsidized product or from synthetic production. At one time, Japan had a monopoly on camphor produced in Formosa (now Taiwan or Free China), and Chile had a monopoly in nitrate of soda. Chile decided that, to maintain the monopoly, it would be wise to keep the world price of nitrate of soda at a decreasing level by means of exchange depreciation. This plan was very successful until synthetic nitrates became available and Chile's economy was rocked. Japan's camphor monopoly also disappeared when synthetic chemical products successfully kept moths out of woolen products.

Subsidy of exports is an appealing approach to the problem of export promotion. Many countries have done this by various means, such as lower taxes on profits from export sales, lower transportation rates for exported merchandise, and exchange rate advantages. West Germany has decreased income taxes on profits from export sales. The President's 1963 Export Promotion Conference recommended similar attractions for American export trade. Germany and South Africa are countries that have allowed lower transportation rates for exported merchandise. In multiple-exchange rate systems, practised by many countries,[2] rates are frequently established in order to permit financial incentives to export products that are more difficult to sell abroad. Korea enlarged its export subsidy program on August 1, 1961. The subsidies averaged 200 hwan per United States dollar for export receipts from that date to the end of the year. Since the then current rate was 1300 hwan per United States dollar, exporters from Korea received 1500 hwan. With an original goal of $50 million of exports for 1961, Korea exported only $19 million in the first half of 1961. Therefore, the additional inducement was offered.

Under the provisions of the General Agreement on Tariffs and Trade (GATT), Article XVI declares that any Contracting Party's export subsidy that bears directly or indirectly to reduce imports of any product into its territory is to be notified in writing to the other Contracting Parties. This notification is to reveal the nature and extent of the subsidy, the circumstances making it necessary, and the estimated effect on the trade in this product. If any Party is damaged or threatened with injury by reason of this subsidy, discussions are to follow to determine the possibility of limiting the subsidy.

---

[2]See Chapter 33, p. 618.

It would now appear that one of the sentences at the beginning of the chapter must be modified to assert that practically every nation does something in order to promote its foreign trade, particularly exports. Even the "Soviet Bloc spends millions on multicolored advertising of exports to the Free World," announces an article in *International Commerce* of July 15, 1963, page 2. The article claims that this export drive has two objectives: "(1) persuade the world of the benefits and advantages of the communist economy; and (2) enter markets traditionally served by countries of the Free World in a vigorous quest for more trade."

Administration of Trade Promotion. This leads to the question of the administration and control of foreign trade promotion by governments. In the Soviet Bloc, all control is obviously exercised by the state; and, whether it be export promotion or sports or the arts, political overtones are inevitable.

As to the countries of the Free World, the question relates to the respective duties and responsibilities of the political arm of the government (State Department in the United States; Foreign Office in other countries) as against the commercial arm of the government (Department of Commerce in the United States and many countries; Board of Trade in the United Kingdom; MITI —Ministry of Trade and Industry in Japan).

The basis for this question may be simply stated as: Should foreign trade promotion be controlled by the political respresentatives abroad or by the commercial representatives? This is not solely a matter of departmental pride or a matter of the adequacy of the promotion effort. Foreign Service Officers of all countries are identified with the political arm of the respective countries. They are trained in diplomacy, foreign languages, customs, history, and possibly some economics; but there is no requirement that they be trained in business or that they shall have had any business experience. Thus, the export promotion and foreign market reporting of the political foreign service officers may not deal with subjects in a manner that can be understood and acted upon by business firms. On the other hand, if the commercial branch of a government had the right to select, train, and station representatives abroad, it is quite likely that they would be capable of promotion and of reporting in ways that the business firm will be able to utilize.

This discussion is by no means purely theoretical. Most of the countries of the world conduct their export promotion through the officers of the consular service. These are political officers and there is no assurance that they will find either time or inclination to promote export trade. The more active commercial nations assign officers to foreign posts bearing such titles as commercial counselor, commercial secretary, commercial attaché, economics officer, and trade commissioner. These officials have no political work to do and their entire effort is devoted to commercial and/or economic representation.

The best way to explain this question is to describe the present procedure followed by the United States Government. This question was thoroughly discussed during the President's Conference on Export Promotion held in September, 1963 in Washington, D.C. One of the recommendations of this conference was that the commercial attaché service be placed under the jurisdication of the Department of Commerce rather than the Department of State, where it has been lodged for thirty years. The gist of the argument is that if the Department of Commerce selects and controls the commercial attachés, the reporting will be more usable by business firms. United States commercial attachés are assigned to the Embassy or Legation in each country. Their reports are submitted to the State Department which edits them and passes them along to the Department of Commerce. This obviously delays the receipt and publication of these reports. There was also some complaint at the Conference of the time it takes to receive replies to inquiries addressed to commercial attachés directly or to the Department of State.

Thirty years ago, commercial attachés and trade commissioners were selected, trained, and assigned by the Department of Commerce. They reported to the Department of Commerce. This was changed when the Department of State claimed successfully that export trade promotion and foreign market reporting involved political matters or related to political affairs. Thereupon, these services were taken over by the Department of State, despite the pleas of the international trading fraternity. Although the Department of Commerce regained some right to nominate commercial officers to be assigned abroad, they lost control of them and, of even greater importance, they lost supervision and direction of what they are expected to do.[3]

In 1917 the British Government wrestled with this problem and established a Department of Overseas Trade, on the recognition of the fact that the Foreign Office (State Department) and the Board of Trade

---

[3]Interestingly enough, during all of these thirty years, the Departments of Agriculture, Treasury, Labor, the several armed services, and some other departments maintained their own representatives abroad under their own supervision.

(Commerce Department) each performed a distinctive foreign service. Since one could not absorb the other, a joint organization was created, viz., the DOT. In 1919, the consular service was attached to the DOT.

This system was later abandoned and the Board of Trade now supervises United Kingdom commerce, industry, overseas trade, including commercial relations with other countries, import and export trade, the protective tariff, industrial development, and consumer protection. Their commercial officers abroad, designated by different titles, report direct to the Board of Trade.

Promotion by the United Nations

While individual countries seek to promote their own export trade, the United Nations does extensive work bearing on the international marketing possibilities of all countries. It is true that the United Nations is not interested in the export trade of any particular country, but it is interested in the development of the international trade of all countries.

Economic and Social Council and Commission on International Commodity Trade. The Economic and Social Council of the UN — the agency concerned with matters pertaining to economic development and trade — is "convinced that trade between nations is a paramount means of fostering international cooperation and is indispensable to efforts by governments throughout the world to raise the living standards of their peoples."[4]

Based upon the cited quotation, the UN is greatly interested in establishing conditions in all countries conducive to raising their standards of living. If such standards are to rise, international trade is indispensable. This is merely restating an economic truism, viz., that no country can live unto itself without impairing its standard of living. The Soviet Union initially tried to do this, but it found that it is impossible if — and this is a big if — economic development is to be achieved.

The Economic and Social Council, at its 32nd Session in mid 1961 observed that long-term development of trade, particularly for the less developed countries, depends upon their ability to export and also upon the trends in the policies of the industrial nations. Commenting on the lot of the less developed countries, the Council declares that raw material exports alone will not afford the necessary foreign exchange to promote

---

[4]United Nations, *Yearbook* (1962), p. 190.

economic development; some manufactures of the less developed countries must be exported to the developed countries; and, with great wisdom, the report adds "this is not easy." The Council concludes that foreign capital is still the most important factor to close the trade gap of the less developed countries.

The Commission on International Commodity Trade is concerned with the stability of international trade in primary products. Through the Interim Coordinating Committee for International Commodity Arrangements, study groups are established, conferences are called, and efforts are coordinated. The Committee considered a report on compensatory financing to deal with fluctuations in the export proceeds of primary producing countries. Efforts of this kind, if successful, will improve the international marketing conditions of all countries.

Commenting on the necessity to reduce barriers to international trade, which is the objective of the GATT, the Economic and Social Council offers the advice that developed countries should be willing to grant tariff concessions to less developed countries without asking reciprocal concessions. In such ways, the UN, through the Economic and Social Council, pleads for unselfish consideration for the welfare of the less developed countries.

Technical Assistance Board and Regional Economic Commissions. The UN does not stop at the preaching level; it does something about the matters previously mentioned. In order to promote economic development, funds are made available to make surveys, to perform research, and to provide training. A Technical Assistance Board also functions in cooperation with the economic development programs. In 1961, the chief avenues in which the efforts of this Board were devoted were natural resources development, social activities, industrial development, economic planning programs and services, and public administration. In the African area, the work takes the form of assistance and economic and educational development. For rural areas everywhere, there is training for community development and land reform.

The regional Economic Commissions are concerned with specific geographical areas. These are the Economic Commission for Europe (ECE), for Asia and the Far East (ECAFE), for Latin America (ECLA), and for Africa (ECA). These commissions study the economic conditions of the several areas, recommend improvements and changes, and publish both periodical and annual reports. In addition, the UN publishes the *World Economic Survey* (annual). As stated elsewhere, the UN also publishes *Direction of International Trade* and *Commodity Trade Statistics.* These are the only publications which give the entire world trade situation in a single volume, first, by country and, second, by commodity and country. In order to make the commodity statistics more useful, the UN sponsored a study of commodity descriptions and classifications, as a result of which Standard International Trade Classification (SITC) was approved by the Economic and Social Council in 1960. This is now the commodity and trade classification used in *Commodity Trade Statistics.* It is also used by the United States Bureau of the Census which compiles and publishes foreign trade statistics for the United States. By means of this development, the use of a single classification for both statistical purposes and for customs nomenclature will be possible. If this works, international traders will benefit greatly by the comparability of trade descriptions and by the ease of determining the import duty applicable by reason of the commodity trade description.

In the field of transportation and communications, the UN is considering a conference on international travel and frontier formalities. A Convention on Road Traffic, 1949, superseding a League of Nations Convention of 1926, deals with customs regulations and registration. A separate protocol relates to traffic signals, but this has not gone very far. Work is being done on a convention concerning the international transport of dangerous goods.

In the fiscal and financial field, the UN held workshops in the matter of national budgeting and budget classification; studied tax reform; provided technical experts and fellowships; and published several important books such as UN *Statistical Yearbook, International Tax Agreements, World Guide to International Tax Agreements,* and *World Tax Series.*

Summary

1. Every commercial nation has adopted a program of export promotion and countries not generally classified as commercial have done likewise.
2. The raw material producing nations seek to improve their terms of trade by means of international commodity agreements.
3. Subsidies in various forms are sometimes granted to encourage export trade.
4. Under GATT, export subsidies must be made known and defended by the exporter or exporting nation.
5. Whether the control of export promotion should be in the political branch of a government or in the commercial branch is a matter of constant concern. Representatives of the political arm may have no knowledge of business and, therefore, not be effective in export promotion. This ordinarily

would not be true of the representatives of the commercial branch of the government.

6. The UN, through the Economic and Social Council particularly, does a great amount of work to facilitate the conduct of international marketing and to improve the economic conditions of countries so that they will become better markets in the future. Statistical classification has been improved and standardized; regulations of international transport have been unified to some extent; improvements have been made in budgeting, taxation, land distribution, and social and educational development.

7. The Economic and Social Council calls for the adoption of trade policies that will facilitate the improvement of living and trade conditions throughout the world. Part of this call is for sacrifices on the part of the developed countries in favor of the less developed countries.

8. The UN promotes efforts to provide international commodity agreements beneficial to the raw material producing countries.

9. The several regional commissions are concerned with the economic situation and economic development in the several geographical areas of the world. Each commission publishes periodical and annual reports and the UN publishes the *World Economic Survey* annually.

QUESTIONS

1. Why do commercial nations try to promote their export trade?

2. Why do noncommercial nations do likewise? How do they seek to accomplish this purpose?

3. Explain the purpose and results of export subsidy programs.

4. Why does the Soviet Bloc advertise lavishly to promote exports to the Free nations?

5. Cite several kinds of export incentives of a financial nature that have been practised by some countries.

6. Why is the matter of control over foreign trade promotion, as between the political and commercial arms of a government, of such importance?

7. How does the UN, through the Economic and Social Council,
    (a) Improve the market conditions of the less developed countries?
    (b) Improve the circumstances and arrangements under which international marketing is conducted?
    (c) Improve the ability to undertake foreign market surveys?

PROBLEM

A discussion of international marketing promotion by governments and the UN is presented in this chapter. Select a country or UN agency and prepare a report on the international marketing promotion program of that country or agency. Include in your report a description of the organization for international marketing promotion; the services rendered; and the budgetary allowance, if available.

COLLATERAL READINGS

Dartnell International Trade Handbook, The. Chicago: The Dartnell Corporation, 1963.

Dominion of Canada, Department of Trade and Commerce. *Foreign Trade.* Ottawa: biweekly.

United Kingdom, Board of Trade. *Board of Trade Journal.* London: weekly.

United Nations, *Yearbook.* New York: annual.

United States Department of Commerce, Bureau of International Commerce. *International Commerce* (weekly). Washington, D.C.: Government Printing Office.

CHAPTER 6

PROMOTION BY PRIVATE UNITED STATES AGENCIES

In addition to the general trade promotion activities performed by the United States Government, American foreign traders are also aided by many private organizations.   Most of these organizations perform general promotion functions either independently or through government channels, and some of them are particularly interested in government policies relating to international marketing. Some of them, however, in addition to the general matters to which they devote their attention, perform personal services for the exclusive benefit of members or subscribers.

International Marketing Associations and Clubs

In this section we shall examine the role played by the following international marketing associations and clubs in rendering trade promotion services: the National Foreign Trade Council, Inc., the National Council of American Importers, Inc., the National Association of Manufacturers, and various regional and local international trade associations.

National Foreign Trade Council, Inc. Many associations and clubs have been organized directly or exclusively within the field of international marketing. The National Foreign Trade Council, Inc., which was created in 1914, may be regarded as the businessman's spokesman for American foreign trade generally.   The Council provides "effective coordination of industrial, commercial, transportation and financial interests of the United States for the purpose of developing American foreign trade and investment policies on a sound basis."[1]

---

[1] *Exporters' Encyclopaedia* (1963), p. 1553.

The Council functions through a board of directors that elects the officers and engages a full-time staff. Committees of members are appointed in all technical foreign trade fields and also as representing specific area interests. Current matters of concern to the various committees are studied and action is recommended. Perhaps the Law Committee concludes that a new type of commercial treaty is desirable for American international trade interests. The committee may arrange to testify at hearings of the Senate Committee on Foreign Relations where such matters would come up. The various working committees represent the whole range of foreign commercial interests — legal, financial, governmental, and economic. The Council conducts an annual foreign trade convention that is attended by an average of two thousand delegates. Current international marketing problems are discussed in general and group sessions, recommendations are agreed upon and issued as "Final Declarations," and trade advisers are made available for consultation by individual delegates. The Council staff also makes investigations and surveys and provides trade information for members, prepares and publishes bulletins and pamphlets, and is available for consultations.

National Council of American Importers, Inc. There are other international marketing groups interested primarily in the foreign trade of particular American regions or localities or in particular segments of international trade. The National Council of American Importers, Inc., was formed in 1921 for the purpose of bringing about an equitable adjustment of the laws and regulations governing the entry of imported merchandise into the country. Its activities include tariff and customs questions, transportation and insurance problems, financial questions, and support of the import trade in face of threats of undue protection. The principal direct service rendered to its members is to supply them promptly with accurate information concerning all major developments affecting the import trade. This is done in various mimeographed bulletins.

National Association of Manufacturers. The National Association of Manufacturers, a major national organization of United States manufacturers, exercises international leadership and support of international activities and objectives in various ways. Among its many activities are those relating to regional and United Nations organizations. It deals with industrial relations, taxation, government problems, and international economic affairs as they affect domestic industry. It has a membership of approximately 18,000 representing all types of industry.

Regional and Local International Trade Associations. In addition to these national associations, there are also a number of regional international trade organizations that have at times conducted regional conventions or otherwise engaged in general international marketing promotion activities. The most numerous of the several types of international trade associations are the many local foreign trade clubs, the membership of which consists of the international marketing interests of particular cities or local areas.

American foreign traders have organized over fifty foreign trade clubs located in cities scattered throughout the country — inland as well as seaboard. Many of these clubs are operated in conjunction with chambers of commerce or other civic bodies; a few represent industrial interests.

All of these clubs function in the specific interests of the respective members. Regular business meetings are addressed by prominent speakers on phases of international marketing. At business and occasional social meetings good fellowship is promoted, which induces members to contribute willingly of their own experiences in foreign trade. By this means, members are mutually helpful in such practical ways as interchange of experience with relation to sales and credit terms, sales representation, packing, shipping, insuring, government regulations, and many other matters.

Foreign trade clubs also seek to represent the opinions and the desires of their members in matters of public policy by means of resolutions and personal appeals to public authorities. A few of these clubs annually convene regional foreign trade conferences that emulate, on a less pretentious scale, the annual convention of the National Foreign Trade Council, Inc.

Commerce and Industry Association of New York, Inc. Special mention in this connection should be made of such groups as the Commerce and Industry Association of New York, Inc., which supports an active World Trade Department. This department is divided into export, import, and trade opportunity divisions, and provides a letter of introduction service. The services performed are personal on behalf of the members; a weekly *World Trade Bulletin,* as well as directories and miscellaneous world trade reports, is published. Meetings are held to hear competent speakers including United States government officials in connection with current world trade problems.

Chicago Association of Commerce and Industry. This organization operates a World Trade Council and performs the services usually provided by such agencies. In addition, it sponsors the Chicago International Trade Fair, in connection with which the Chicago World Marketing and Economic Development Conference is a feature. In this function, it cooperates with the International Trade Club of Chicago.

Mississippi Valley World Trade Council. In New Orleans, a Mississippi Valley World Trade Council has been organized, representing the international trade interests of states in the Mississippi Valley area. The Council holds an annual world trade conference.

International House and International Trade Mart. Mention should also be made of the unique New Orleans development of an International House (1945) and, later, an International Trade Mart (1948). International House is "a home away from home" where foreign businessmen of all nationalities meet in a friendly atmosphere. Through its World Trade Development Department, services of translation, making appointments, arranging details of business inquiries, etc., are freely offered to all. The International Trade Mart is a display building containing merchandise from the United States and many foreign countries. These goods are available for inspection and orders may be placed.

Chambers of Commerce

Various chambers of commerce represent another group of private international marketing promotion agencies that are quite anxious to establish a favorable climate in which international marketing can be effectively conducted.

Chamber of Commerce of the United States. The Chamber of Commerce of the United States, within which are federated 3,800 local chambers of commerce and trade associations, representing over 3,000,000 individual businessmen and an individual or firm membership of over 27,000, has long been engaged in general international trade promotion activities. The Foreign Commerce Department carries on activities in this field.

Policy Declarations. Any member of the Chamber may suggest subjects for policy consideration. Each suggestion is referred to an appropriate committee for study. Chamber committees are appointed annually by the President of the Chamber and are selected to represent a geographical cross section of American business and industry. If the committee believes the matter is one on which the Chamber should take a stand, it prepares and presents to the board of directors a proposed declaration of policy, asking that it be referred to the Committee on Policy. Policies frequently originate with the committees themselves, with the board of directors, or with the Committee on Policy.

After approval by the board and the Policy Committee, the proposals are distributed for the full consideration and suggestions of the membership, and then brought before the annual meeting. There delegates representing the member chambers of commerce and trade associations may approve with or without amendments, disapprove, or vote to submit them to referendum vote by direct action of the board of directors. In emergencies, the board is authorized to adopt a declaration of policy on an urgent matter, its action to be reported, with the reasons, to the Chamber members.

The National Chamber has always been interested in international questions, both commercial and political. At its first annual meeting in 1913, for instance, it adopted a resolution on uniform bills of lading in foreign trade and another on recognizing the (then) new Republic of China. Other resolutions of this first meeting dealt with the Consular Service and the establishment of the Bureau of Foreign and Domestic Commerce (now Bureau of International Commerce).

The Chamber has supported the policy of the Trade Agreements Act continuously since 1933, the year before the Act itself became effective. In fact, as early as 1913, by referendum vote it advocated a permanent Tariff Commission, and in 1921 it accepted the principle of adjustment of tariff rates by administrative authority within limits set by Congress.

In the early years of the Chamber, exports were emphasized. Conditions prevailing since World War II have led to emphasis on the vital role played by imports in the United States economy. Timely, too, are policies stressing the importance of private enterprise in international economic relations. Leadership in the international field has been further demonstrated by the positive stand taken by the Chamber on the establishment of an international organization to settle postwar problems. This position was taken even before plans for the United Nations had been developed. The Chamber believes that long-term defense objectives will have general priority. These objectives include the promotion of an expanding world economy by reducing barriers to trade and by stimulating economic development through private endeavor.

Collaboration with Other Organizations. The Chamber also maintains national and international contacts with other organizations interested in international marketing. The "revised American foreign trade definitions — 1941,"[2] for example, were adopted by a joint committee representing the National Foreign Trade Council, Inc., the National Council of American Importers, Inc., and the Chamber of Commerce of the United States. A Canada-United States Committee, maintained jointly with the Canadian Chamber of Commerce considers subjects related to trade and communications between the two nations. The Chamber also maintains contact with chambers of commerce in foreign countries, including American chambers abroad. Along with its official organ, the *Nation's Business*, it issues other publications, some at regular intervals and others when a special study or report has been completed.

International Chamber of Commerce. The International Chamber of Commerce was organized in 1919, successor of the International Congress of Chambers of Commerce and Industrial and Commercial Organizations, which had assembled in 1905 and held biennial meetings from 1906 to 1914. The United States Council is the American national affiliate.

The ICC is the businessman's international body. It is his spokesman through public opinion on world economic affairs, his forum for international discussion and contact. The ICC can be considered a world parliament where manufacturers, bankers, industrialists, merchants, and traders meet to pool their views and information and to forge a common policy. The ICC in turn brings this policy to bear on individual governments, on the United Nations, and on world public opinion. Basically, the ICC's purpose is to be broadly representative of and to encourage better understanding among businessmen and business organizations of the world and to secure effective and constant action in improving world economic conditions.

Membership. The membership of the ICC is composed of thousands of businesses and associations in fifty-odd countries. Its recommendations on economic matters provide guidance for the governments of the world, either directly or through the United Nations, for the ICC as an organi-

---

[2]See Chapter 21 for a breakdown of the responsibility and the charges between buyer and seller under the revised foreign trade definitions.

zation of businessmen has been awarded top consultative status with the Economic and Social Council of the United Nations.

United States Council. The United States Council as a national affiliate of the ICC cooperates with the parent organization by expressing American views on international economic questions. The United States Council has taken vigorous action in stimulating support for (1) the increased flow of private capital investments; (2) the emphasis of world trade as a two-way street — imports as well as exports; and (3) the need for expansion of multilateral trade as the best means of insuring world progress.

The elimination of exchange controls, the return to free convertibility of currencies, the reduction of trade barriers, and the expansion of foreign investments in underdeveloped and semideveloped areas were the immediate concern of the ICC. Directly or indirectly this work assisted in the operation of business whether in international trade or not.

Working Commissions and Committees. The work of the ICC is carried out by working commissions composed of representative leading businessmen from many nations. The United States Council has its own committees and study groups composed of experts in various fields, which transmit to the international commissions the American thinking, or work on policy statements for purely American consumption. These commissions, committees, and study groups deal with economic matters both on a policy and on a technical level. Once a policy receives the full endorsement of the entire ICC or the United States Council alone, an extensive program of implementation aiming to make these business policies public policies is carried on.

Inter-American Council of Commerce and Production. In the spring of 1941 the first "Conference of American Associations of Commerce and Production" took place at Montevideo, Uruguay. This, in contrast with the various Pan-American commercial and financial conferences which have been part of the mechanism of governmental cooperation within the framework of the Pan American Union, was distinctly a businessmen's conference.

The Inter-American Council of Commerce and Production was then organized and today with headquarters in Montevideo represents over 400 associations and corporations in all 22 Western Hemisphere countries. The United States Inter-American Council is the American section, and every member country likewise has a national council. The

American Section maintains an Advisory Board, composed of Americans engaged in business in other American republics. This body has attacked fundamental problems, such as dollar shortage, state intervention, and Charter of Social Guarantees, and a biennial Inter-American conference is held.

American Chambers of Commerce Abroad. Occupying a singular position in the field of international marketing promotion are the 30 or more American chambers of commerce located abroad in foreign countries. These organizations are composed primarily of Americans engaged in business in foreign countries. As such they consist of a small group of aliens in a foreign land, possessing wide powers for good or evil. They are taken as representing the American public and as its spokesmen. Their interests are primarily commercial and their relationships are personal. They are thus unofficial Americans on the "firing line" of foreign commerce. In addition to Americans resident abroad, membership privileges are usually extended also to foreigners and nonresident Americans interested in United States trade with the country in which the chamber is located. Their outstanding activities are summarized:[3]

> 1. They protect American interests by taking legal steps to oppose discriminatory legislation or practices of the foreign country; by arbitrating trade disputes and obtaining settlements out of court; by assisting American travelers abroad; and by performing other services.
> 2. As organs of publicity for American ideals, institutions, and policies, foreign chambers of commerce endeavor to remove irritations and to bring about better understanding.
> 3. They promote American foreign trade. Various individual services are rendered in this connection.... Close cooperation is maintained with United States government representatives in the country where located, and many of them are members of the Chamber of Commerce of the United States. Some of them publish a periodical, and all issue bulletins from time to time.

Foreign Chambers of Commerce in the United States. Mention should also be made of the foreign chambers of commerce located in the United States of which there are nearly 50, with some countries being represented by two or more chambers in different cities. Their membership consists principally of nationals of the particular foreign country

---

[3]Edward F. Feely, "How the American Chamber of Commerce Abroad Helps the American Foreign Trade," *American Chambers of Commerce Abroad* (Washington, D.C.: Chamber of Commerce of the United States).

resident in the United States and Americans interested or engaged in trade with that country. In many instances, the latter comprise the bulk of the membership. Their major purpose is to promote commercial and cultural relations and understanding with the United States. Trade promotion is conducted in the same manner as in the case of American chambers of commerce abroad. Aside from the direct promotion of trade (for example, preparing market reports, lists of customers, letters of introduction, and soliciting agencies), other services are in some instances performed, such as credit investigations, translation services, exhibitions of foreign merchandise, legal guidance, and arbitration of trade disputes. Some of these chambers of commerce issue publications at regular intervals or special bulletins or reports and annual directories or yearbooks.

Local Chambers of Commerce. Many local chambers of commerce are interested in international marketing and, since about 3,800 local chambers as well as trade associations are members of the Chamber of Commerce of the United States, they were necessarily referred to in connection with the foreign trade interests of that organization. Some of the local chambers, however, maintain foreign trade bureaus or departments of their own, and the local chambers generally are especially interested in the foreign trade of the cities or local areas within which they are located. Such bureaus or departments are established to foster the export and import business of the members and constituents of the chamber, to keep them advised as to international marketing developments, to arouse interest in those not yet engaged in international commerce, and to perform specific international marketing services. Many local chambers of commerce have stressed port and harbor facilities, shipping routes and rates, steamship services, and other transportation matters.

Other Trade Promotion Agencies

Some of the many trade associations — national, regional, state, and local — have also become interested in the promotion of international marketing. A trade association, indeed, is in a particularly favorable position to promote international marketing along the commodity lines which it represents. Many trade associations maintain contact with the Bureau of International Commerce and the BDSA (Business and Defense Services Administration), particularly with their commodity sections or units. Some of them are engaged in foreign publicity work, and considerable attention has been directed to import problems by trade associations whose membership is dependent upon foreign sources of supply or who face import competition.

More specifically, various trade associations have concerned themselves with legislation, tariff and consular regulations, and other government relations here and abroad; credit information and collections; packing and transportation; arbitration of trade disputes; registration of trademarks; terms and other conditions of sale; the publication of lists of members, issued in various foreign languages, for distribution to interested trade contacts abroad and for use in replying to foreign inquiries; the maintenance of libraries containing the more important foreign books and periodicals published in their particular trades; the publication of trade journals containing export and import statistics, trade opportunities, and foreign trade notices.[4] Some trade associations also conduct conventions at which both the domestic and foreign trade problems of their particular trades are considered.

In addition to foreign trade associations and clubs and chambers of commerce, there are many private promotion agencies that render services for international traders in the United States. Several of these organizations are described in the following paragraphs.

The Philadelphia Trade and Convention Center. The Center operates an Inter-American Center, a Council for International Visitors, a Commercial Library containing thousands of trade publications, directories, yearbooks, foreign office reports, books of travel, reference books, trade reports, pamphlets and other sources containing statistics, and information as to tariffs, commercial laws, and other aspects of international trade.

Credit Agencies. Dun & Bradstreet, Inc., the National Association of Credit Management, and other credit agencies perform important services in the field of export credit information, and some of them also perform other services for American exporters. Dun & Bradstreet, Inc., through its foreign sales division, furnishes market as well as credit reports on business firms everywhere through 62 foreign offices. They

---

[4]Temporary National Economic Committee, Monograph #18, *Trade Association Survey;* Foreign Commerce Department, Chamber of Commerce of the United States, *Foreign Trade Promotion by Chambers of Commerce and Trade Associations.*

publish a *Latin American Sales Index* and a monthly magazine, *International Markets*. The National Association of Credit Management, through its Foreign Credit Administrative Committee, seeks to promote sound principles of credit in international trade and cooperates with credit agencies in other countries. It operates the Foreign Credit Interchange Bureau (exchange of ledger experience) and is concerned with all financial matters affecting foreign commerce, such as collections and exchange.

Banks. In the general field of international marketing finance are the banks and other financial institutions discussed in Chapter 26; and in the adjustment of trade disputes, foreign traders are assisted by the Inter-American Commercial Arbitration Commission and the American Arbitration Association and other more general organizations discussed in Chapter 25. Certain banks, moreover, promote foreign trade not only through their financial services, but also by providing credit reports, general market information, and specific advice as to a customer's foreign business. They may also assist their clients in obtaining foreign agency affiliations. Some of them maintain foreign trade departments or bureaus.

The Bankers Association for Foreign Trade promotes and fosters international banking and foreign trade by stimulating public interest and improving practices and techniques.

Advertising Associations. The International Advertising Association, Inc. provides opportunity for the interchange of information regarding international advertising and, thus, to promote United States trade. Its 1600 members are scattered through 60 countries. The Association of International Advertising Agencies is composed of seven of the leading agencies in this field with the objective of promoting efficiency and standardizing practices.

Miscellaneous Organizations. Steamship lines and international airlines are also sources of trade information. Export and import journals variously provide their advertisers with trade lists of foreign buyers; information as to specific sales contacts, trade opportunities, or trade leads; personalized letters to prospective customers or direct-mail campaigns; multigraphing services; translations of correspondence, circulars, etc., in particular foreign languages; market analyses and market information services; selected lists of foreign agents or representatives and aids in their selection; general international marketing information; introductions for American salesmen abroad and foreign buyers in the United States; and counsel as to general or specific international marketing problems.

Wide Variety of Published Sources. We are indebted to S. J. Rundt, Export and Foreign Exchange Consultant, for a listing of sources not commonly known in the United States. Writing on the subject "Know the Market,"[5] Mr. Rundt refers to what he calls "usually dependable and rather specialized publications" such as: the *Journal of Commerce*, the *Neue Zürcher Zeitung*, The (London) *Economist*, *Børsen* of Copenhagen, *El Mercurio* of Santiago, *Le Commerce du Levant* of Beirut, the *International Financial News Survey* of IMF, *Handelsblatt* of Düsseldorf, the bulletin of the *Agence Economique et Financière* of Brussels, the *Financial Post* of Toronto, *Het Financieele Dagblad* of Amsterdam, *Dawn* of Karachi, *24 Ore* of Milan, *The Bangkok Post*, *Indeks* of Belgrade, *Norges Handels og Sjøfartstidene* of Oslo, and the *Financial Times* of London.

Continuing, Mr. Rundt listed American and foreign dailies such as: *The New York Times*, *Le Monde* of Paris, *O Correio da Manha* of Rio, the *Manchester Guardian*, the *Rotterdamsche Courant*, *ABC* of Madrid, and many more. They contain valuable commercial and financial intelligence, internal economic affairs and world trade sections, with interpretive columns by outstanding economic theorists and leaders of industry and commerce.

Finally, states Mr. Rundt: "Last, but far from least, there are the many special area studies, special situation reports and spot bulletins by such important banks as Schroeder's, the Crédit Suisse, the Kredietbank of Brussels-Antwerp, Barclay's of London, the Royal Bank of Canada, The First National of Boston, the First National City of New York, the Export-Import Bank of Washington, the Bank deutscher Länder of Frankfurt, the Chartered Bank of India, Australia, and China in Hong Kong, the Morgan-Guaranty Trust Company of New York, 'Chase' of New York, and the various branches of the Bank of London and South America, to mention but a few."

Summary

1. International and national agencies seek to provide favorable circumstances and conditions under which international marketing can be effectively conducted. These groups include the National Foreign Trade Council, Inc.,

---

[5]S. J. Rundt, "Know the Market," *Export Trade and Shipper* (February 28, 1955), p. 23.

National Association of Manufacturers, Chamber of Commerce of the United States, and the United States Council of the International Chamber of Commerce.

2. Many private trade promotion agencies render services for United States international traders. Most of them perform direct promotional work, such as conducting foreign market surveys, developing trade lists of prospective representatives abroad, rendering credit reports, and providing translations. Prominent in this line of activity are the National Association of Credit Management, various trade and local associations or clubs, banks, publications, and steamship lines.

3. With this array of agencies ready and able to furnish information, the United States international trader appears to be very well equipped with sources for carrying on his work.

QUESTIONS

1. Define the purposes and functions of the National Foreign Trade Council, Inc.

2. What is the function of the National Council of American Importers, Inc.?

3. In what ways does the National Association of Manufacturers express interest in international marketing?

4. How are foreign traders assisted through membership in "foreign trade clubs?"

5. Cite one unique international marketing organization in either New York, New Orleans, or Chicago. State its functions.

6. In what ways does the Chamber of Commerce of the United States express interest in international marketing?

7. Define the functions of the International Chamber of Commerce.

8. Explain the kind of information that can be obtained from United States chambers of commerce abroad and from foreign chambers of commerce in the United States.

9. Define the international marketing role of local chambers of commerce in the United States.

10. How do trade journals seek to promote international marketing?

11. How can banks and steamship lines be helpful, from the standpoint of information, to international traders?

PROBLEMS

1. Visit a meeting of a local (regional or national) foreign trade club and write a report of the meeting.
2. Visit the local chamber of commerce in your community and prepare a report on its international marketing work. If it is not engaged in such work, study the local situation and prepare your report from the standpoint of the reasons why the chamber should perform services in this field.

COLLATERAL READINGS

Dartnell International Trade Handbook, The. Chicago: The Dartnell Corporation, 1963.

Exporters' Encyclopaedia. New York: Thomas Ashwell and Co., Inc., annual.

Horn, Paul V. *International Trade Principles and Practices,* Third Edition. New York: Prentice-Hall, Inc., 1951. Chapters 1 and 25.

United States Chamber of Commerce. *Activities of American Chambers of Commerce Abroad.* Washington, D.C.: 1961.

————————————. *Guide to Foreign Information Services.* Washington, D.C.: 1961.

————————————. *Introduction to Doing Import and Export Business,* Sixth Edition. Washington, D.C.: 1963.

CHAPTER 7

THE SCOPE OF INTERNATIONAL MARKETING

In view of the recognized rationale of international marketing, as described in Chapter 1; of the expanded and expanding international marketing position of the United States, as surveyed in Chapter 2; and of the extensive help available to the international trader through the various public and private international trade promotion agencies, surveyed in Chapters 4, 5, and 6, the next logical step in our analysis is to consider the international marketing organizations and marketing channels. As an introduction to a consideration of these channels, we shall first examine several subjects germane to the field, and group them together under the heading of "scope."

A Philosophy of Doing Business Abroad

This is the provocative title of the address given by Stanley C. Allyn, Chairman of the Board, The National Cash Register Company, at the 1958 National Foreign Trade Convention. In this presentation, Mr. Allyn speaks for an American company that has had nearly seventy-five years of experience in world marketing. For this reason, the views that he expressed at that meeting warrant close attention and comprehension. By way of introduction, Mr. Allyn stated:

> Every company which has been engaged in foreign trade for any length of time has, of necessity, developed a certain philosophy of doing business abroad. It has been hammered out on the anvil of experience, shaped by disappointment as well as success, tailored to meet a myriad of fast-changing situations around the world. In detail, probably no two of those philosophies are exactly alike. But in their basic elements and objectives, I think you will find certain principles common to all.

For whatever value it may be to others, I should like to discuss nine principles of overseas operation which we have found effective over a long period of time. These constitute our "Philosophy of Doing Business Abroad."

Out company has been in overseas trade for almost 75 years. More than 40 percent of our volume is represented by overseas sales.

Except for refinements which are inevitable in a rapidly changing world, the pattern has been substantially the same for many years. Here, then, are the basic principles of our foreign operations:

1. When we go into any foreign country, we go in for keeps.

2. We believe in staffing our overseas operations with nationals of the countries concerned.

3. We consistently invest part of our profits in the countries where those profits are earned.

4. We do not treat overseas employees as stepchildren. We treat them exactly as we treat our people at home.

5. We try to give the foreign market the product which the market wants . . . not the product which we think the market ought to have.

6. We have learned that . . . for us at least . . . service or maintenance of the product comes ahead of sales.

7. We believe in company operation overseas instead of general agencies.

8. We believe in first-hand contacts with our foreign markets, and that means we are constantly traveling.

9. Finally, we are extremely careful to respect the customs, traditions, religions, and sensitivities of foreign people.

These points will be briefly explored in this chapter.

Decision to Enter the Market. "When we go into any foreign market, we go in for keeps," is the first point listed by the speaker. An examination of this statement indicates that the "fly-by-night" in international marketing is not headed for success. Whether a firm goes into international marketing to stay or as a merely temporary expedient depends entirely upon the executive attitude.

Need for Executive Interest and Backing. Executive interest in the international operations is essential if any real progress in the development of that business is to be expected. On numerous occasions, export executives have been heard to complain privately that executive backing of the international business is lacking. One such executive declared at a recent foreign trade convention that his company expected him to select a firm to represent them in South Africa but would not consider permitting him to take a trip to South Africa to make such a selection. One vice-president of the company was favorable to this suggestion, but the president, who dominated the company, was opposed.

Another company, the largest in its line of operation, organized an export department following World War II. This development was a personal decision of the Chairman of the Board, who took great interest in the international side of the business. Sales overseas grew and the department expanded. The Chairman retired and his successor made a contrary decision — the company was not justified in engaging in international marketing since the products they offered for sale were almost entirely made under contract by independent manufacturers. Very suddenly, and without warning, word came that the international marketing effort was to be liquidated.

There are numerous instances of this nature that could be recited to indicate that (1) executive backing was not provided for the international marketing effort, or (2) the executive had changed or retired and as a result of this, a drastic change occurred in the operation of the international business.

This is not a new problem, by any means. As long ago as World War I, James H. Collins wrote a book entitled "Straight Business with South America."[1] This book spells the melancholy tale of a company that was enthusiastic about the prospect of engaging in international business with South America. They started off with a banquet and a company rally. Due to the errors committed by the company in the management of the international business, however, the attempt to export to South America was a failure.

One of the main reasons this particular company allowed the international business to atrophy was that the domestic business picked up handsomely. It may be difficult to understand but the domestic United States business is both a help and a hindrance to the international business of American enterprises. As a help, the economies of scale that the huge domestic market permit place our enterprisers in a position to sell their products abroad at competitive prices. This same condition has spawned sales promotion of a versatility that is strictly American. These are, of course, very desirable influences of the domestic market.

On the other hand, a hindrance so often occurs in that the magnitude of the domestic business is such as to cause a firm to lose interest in the international business. Very often, a company is satisfied with its volume of domestic business and does not seek to expand to world markets. In many other cases, companies that have tapped international

---

[1] James H. Collins, *Straight Business with South America* (New York and London: D. Appleton and Company, 1920).

markets decide to withdraw when domestic markets pick up and provide a sufficient volume of business to satisfy the company. As expressed by the president of a pharmaceutical company that has actively engaged in international business — "they (the company) could not understand why rivals allowed themselves to be so enchanted by the home market that they tended to overlook even greater opportunities abroad."[2]

The Family Concept. Experience has shown that a great obstacle to the expansion of many American companies into international markets is the "family concept." In a survey of the manufacturers in a geographical area to determine the importance of international business to their sales and purchases, very many of the small family-type manufacturers refused to reply to a questionnaire. Not infrequently, upon investigation, the reason for this refusal was that father and grandfather had successfully built up the business without answering such questionnaires, and, anyway, their interest in international marketing was nobody's business!

Therefore, it is firmly established that unless executive direction and backing are provided, the international marketing effort will probably languish and dry up.

Staffing Overseas Operations. Points 2 and 4 in Mr. Allyn's presentation bear upon the matter of securing the necessary personnel for doing business abroad. Many young graduates of courses in international marketing express an interest in finding employment with a company that will send them abroad — not for keeps but for a few months at a time. Experienced export executives look upon such ambitions as typical of the tourist. What alert and interested person — young or old — would not wish to travel abroad for a few months each year?

A challenge in today's international marketing is to find competent young people willing, if necessary, to stay abroad for an indeterminate period. This has always been difficult for American companies because young Americans have shown slight inclination to pack up and go abroad for an indefinite length of time.

This challenge is mitigated somewhat, and increasingly so, as restrictive laws are adopted in foreign markets, chiefly the underdeveloped

---

[2] John McKeen, President, Charles Pfizer and Co., declared by *Forbes* (December 15, 1962) as a "successful upstart." A subheading states: "You don't come up fast from nowhere without stepping on toes. So it is with Pfizer, which got to be the biggest U.S.-based drug company by methods which were not always gentle and seldom conventional." Quoted by permission of *Forbes.*

and ambitious markets. International Harvester in 1957 had 24,170 employees engaged abroad, of whom 111 were Americans.[3] Mr. Allyn declared that with an organization of almost 22,000 employees in National Cash Register's overseas operations, only *six* are Americans! While conceding that this company probably leans over backward on this score, he observed that experience leads the company to believe that it pays. Continuing, Mr. Allyn states:

> This policy has a most important by-product. When my associates and I visit an overseas operation, we are not insulated from the nationals by layers of Americans who might or might not have adjusted themselves to an understanding of the local scene.
>
> We are able to talk directly with the nationals because there is no one else to talk to. It is almost that simple and we propose to keep it that way.
>
> In these complicated times, this policy of avoiding insulation is even more important than it used to be. While the United States has been growing more internationally minded, many other countries are growing more nationalistic.
>
> It has been our experience that nationals acquire the necessary knowledge of our business with the same facility as Americans. More importantly, they know their own people . . . and the problems of their own country . . . far better than outsiders.
>
> By having so few Americans in our overseas organization, I do not want anyone to think we do not furnish our skills and techniques. An American who knows how to increase production can often be a more valuable ambassador than a lecturer on the fine points of democratic philosophy.

Reinvestment of Profits. The third principle of foreign operations presented in Mr. Allyn's talk related to the investment of profits in those countries where the profits are earned. As will be explained later,[4] such reinvestment of profits may be more involuntary than the international trader would like. When earnings abroad in foreign currencies cannot be brought back to the United States in dollars, reinvestment is one way to make use of such idle funds. But to state this procedure as a basic principle indicates that a company so committed is determined to build and expand its foreign operations for the long pull. This is further proof that a company goes into overseas business for keeps.

---

[3]*Export Trade and Shipper* (February 18, 1957), pp. 9 and 26.
[4]The subject of foreign exchange control is treated in Chapter 33.

Clearly, this conclusion would not apply to many companies that do not operate overseas. Many companies derive their earnings from their export and import transactions and they have no occasion to plow profits back into foreign operations.

Adaptability of the Product. Whether or not a product will find acceptance in international markets is an important question in any foreign marketing plan. One criticism of American manufacturers is that they seek to push their product abroad without considering the utility of the product to foreign buyers. Their philosophy seems to be "if the product is good enough for the American market, it is good enough for the foreign market." However, this does not necessarily follow. In the port of Manila following World War II, an up-to-date concrete pier was constructed. This pier put to shame the bamboo piers constructed by the Philippinos. A severe typhoon struck and the bamboo piers and also the concrete pier were demolished. The bamboo piers were replaced within twenty-four hours; the concrete pier, however, lay wrecked for over two years. There was evident common sense on the part of the Philippinos in building a pier that could be so quickly replaced.

Some international marketing executives declare that what they seek to sell is a service, that is, that while they offer a product to the market, their interest is in the service or utility that the product will render in the environment of the international market. This is true of any product, but it is particularly true of machinery and all kinds of technical equipment. Mr. Allyn, cited above, made this observation in explaining the fifth and sixth principles in his address:

> We would consider it foolishness to try to force an American product into situations for which it is not suitable.
> To implement this principle, we have established product development committees in every sector of the globe where we do business. The job of these committees is to appraise and reappraise the market and keep a close check on its requirements.
> Not all of our workable ideas originate in our United States headquarters. . . . not by any means. Manufacturing and selling to a foreign market is not a one-way street. A man who is stationed half the way around the globe is likely to develop a strong knack of resourcefulness. The result is that a number of important developments which were subsequently adopted for the business as a whole have originated abroad.

Stories, true or not, are often told of manufacturers of rain gear trying to sell this line of merchandise in northern Chile where it never rains, or of offering bacon slicers for sale in Israel or Arab countries, or of promoting the sale of refrigerators to Eskimos. The lesson to be learned with respect to the product is to be certain that the product will find acceptance in the international markets to which it is offered for sale.

If particular markets require changes in a product in order to render it acceptable, such changes must be made if success is to be expected. It does no good to believe, as many American companies seem to think, that the American product is good enough for the buyer in international markets. The changes required in a product may be due to a matter of taste, such as color; or of measurements, as electrical capacities and metric units; or of rearrangement, as placing the steering wheel of a motor vehicle to the right side to accommodate markets where traffic moves on the left side.

All of this sounds simple, but, for a company that is not committed to international marketing, the obstacles that are created by such changes may be sufficient to dissuade it from trying to enter the market at all. Moreover, any changes that relate to matters such as packing and shipping may cause resentment by a traffic department that has worked out packing arrangements for domestic trade and cannot see any justification for changing them for international markets.

Service or Maintenance of the Product. Service is a keynote of the merchandising program of many American companies. In some respects, this is a distinctly American discovery. The reason for this is that the industrial revolution brought about mass production by means of assembly-line operation, resulting in a flood of merchandise at the loading platforms of the manufacturers. The next important step was to mass-distribute this flood of products, leading to the development of improved merchandising. One of the attributes of improved merchandising is the servicing of products. Gone are the days when the manufacturer cared only for stocking his products on the shelves of his customers. It has become apparent that some effort must be exerted to help the customers move the goods and thus make room for additional orders — and further production.

Part of this development was the offering of service. How many manufacturers in the United States inculcate confidence in their products as well as in the company itself by publicizing the availability of factory-trained technicians for installation and servicing of a machine?

This same concept has been extended to world markets where it is appreciated at least as much as it is in the United States. Mr. Allyn expresses this phase of the philosophy of international marketing in the following statement:

> In many sectors of the globe, the salesman for American equipment is first asked about the kind of service he can provide and then asked what machine he has to sell . . . all of which makes sense. The customer is only interested in the work the machine will perform. If it breaks down, and there are no repair facilities at hand, the machine is just so many pounds of useless metal.
>
> In times of stress, service has kept our business going when there were no machines to sell and when we would otherwise have had to close our doors.

One United States manufacturer, as a means of teaching United States merchandising methods to his sales staffs abroad, has prepared a three-volume, 600-page sales training course translated into 10 languages, including Japanese. In 94 countries the company operates a sales training school with a nine-week program of full-time study.[5]

Overseas Operation Through Company Installations. In Mr. Allyn's presentation, he stated as another principle of foreign operations that his company believes in company operations overseas instead of general agencies. He explains the reason for this policy of his company is that agencies abroad (1) did not invest a sufficient amount of their profits to assure an expansion of the scope of their operations; (2) did not develop a feeling for the cash register business; and (3) did not give undivided attention to the line because they held other lines.

The experience of this company, however, does not necessarily apply to any other company — and Mr. Allyn also makes this point. The important thing to observe in respect to the philosophy of international marketing is that the company has a well-conceived and fully backed-up plan of overseas operations. This would be a corollary of the point expressed earlier, that when National Cash Register goes into a foreign market, it goes in for keeps. With its own foreign branches, it gives every indication of being in business abroad for keeps. And all of this operation, it may be recalled, is conducted with only six out of 22,000 employees abroad being American.

Probably there are not many companies that could decide with finality that this or that method of operation in international marketing

---

[5]*Journal of Commerce* (February 26, 1957), p. 24.

is a basic principle for them. Conditions vary so greatly among the several world markets that a standard method of operation may not be feasible.[6] But the point to be stressed is the willingness of the firm to embrace and pursue whatever method or technique of international marketing seems to be best suited to its needs. This requires continuing executive interest in overseas operations, determination to stay in overseas operations, and flexibility and adaptability. As stated by Mr. Allyn, the company in overseas operations must learn to "roll with the punches."

Contact with Foreign Markets. Mr. Allyn was quite clear in expressing his views that management must have first-hand contacts with foreign countries and for that reason considerable traveling is essential.

> We cannot sit on the banks of the Miami River in Dayton and get a world viewpoint. It is too easy to say "No" to ideas and suggestions from foreign managers when your operations are regulated by remote control. You can read reams of reports and statistics and still not know the most important element in any situation . . . which is simply people . . . the people in your own organization and the people who are your customers.
>
> That is why our executives travel thousands of miles a year in visits overseas. Included in this group are men responsible for sales, engineering, product development, research, finance, and manufacturing, as well as several of us from the Executive Office.
>
> We in Dayton are not the only ones who travel. We bring many of our overseas people to the United States. That is still another factor in our working equation of frequent personal contacts between people at the management and those at the supervisory level.
>
> My trips abroad have instilled in me the definite conviction that in their basic reactions, people are much the same the world over. Their outlook may result from differences in tradition, language, religion, standards of living, and geography. But they all have one common denominator . . . the desire to be treated like human beings. And they all have their sensitivities . . . and so do we.
>
> I have asked myself more than once on a trip abroad "Why is it that business finds a way to survive and grow in the face of the same obstacles that seem to stifle understanding among nations?"
>
> In my opinion, the basic reason is that business is *forced* to acquire an understanding of the customs of a country and the traditions and preferences of its people and to conduct itself accordingly.
>
> You either establish a common meeting ground, or you do not do business. . . .

---

[6]The more common methods of operation that are followed in establishing a foreign trade department are presented in Chapter 8.

Respect for Foreign People. The last point in Mr. Allyn's nine principles of overseas business philosophy pertains to the care with which the National Cash Register Company respects the customs, traditions, religions, and sensitivities of foreign people. In explaining this principle, Mr. Allyn reveals the stature of a business statesman.

> It is something of a paradox that while American products are universally popular, by no means the same thing can be said of American ideas. Perhaps we should examine the methods we are using to sell freedom to the rest of the world. That is the most important sale we have to make, and I sincerely believe that world trade . . . conducted with satisfaction to both sides . . . can be as important a factor as any in making that sale.
>
> I do know . . . as a fact . . . that business relations among men of different nationalities sometimes serve to take the edge off belligerency. And I can testify to that with a little anecdote from World War II.
>
> Our office in Paris was on the line of march when Hitler's Wehrmacht rumbled into town along the Champs Élysées.
>
> One of the tanks swerved out of line and headed straight for the office. The tank came to a halt and disgorged a German soldier who thundered on the door and made it plain that he wanted to come in. And in he came, and there he stood in that enemy uniform, with a gun on his hip and a grim look on his face.
>
> Our French employees had a bad moment, and then the German soldier suddenly smiled and said:
>
> "I'm from the National Cash Register Company in Berlin. I'm sorry I can't stay very long, but I was wondering if you made your quota last year."

Vocational Aspects of International Marketing

At this point, it is appropriate that we make several observations regarding the vocational aspects of international marketing. What are the job opportunities in this field and how does one find them?

For the experienced person, there are good employment opportunities in the international marketing field, provided of course that the candidate possesses those qualifications that a prospective employer is seeking. For the recent graduate, however, qualifications based upon experience are often lacking. The graduate with training in international marketing and also with some business experience and knowledge of a foreign language can sometimes find employment with companies engaged in international marketing. The first position the graduate takes will probably be for indoctrination purposes and may include correspondence work and possibly dealing with price quotations. After the indoctrination program is over, and if the candidate shows real adaptability and promise, he will probably move to a more responsible position and soon may find himself on his first trip abroad. Although this trip is not likely to be for any lengthy period of time, he is really started in the international marketing field.

There are many fields of service in international marketing — not only is there the sale and purchase of commodities but there is also the technical work inherent in these operations. There is the matter of advertising and sales promotion; settlement of trade disputes; helping to make decisions on the manner in which the international marketing will be conducted in a particular area, and other matters. Or, credit, financing, and collections may be the line of work in which the candidate finds himself best adapted. Or, perhaps he may choose a bank, insurance company, motion picture company, freight forwarder, steamship company, or any of the many lines found in international marketing that are of a service nature.

In most instances, however, openings along the lines indicated are not available to recent graduates of foreign marketing courses. If these lines are not available, the next best thing is to try to obtain a position with a company that is engaged in international marketing, planning as time goes on to shift to that branch of the company's operations. This method of finding a career in international marketing has much to recommend it. One executive of a large worldwide American company declared that whenever a person is needed in the international division, the company first looks over its domestic employees to find a suitable candidate. From the company standpoint, this is desirable because such a candidate has already been trained in company products and philosophy; and he may have an interest in, as well as an adaptability for, the international business. Recent graduates sometimes fail to realize that before they can be of any great value to an employer, they must first be educated as to the company's product or service and its philosophy.

While the emphasis in the conduct of overseas business appears to be on licensing and branch operations abroad, sight must not be lost of the fact that nearly $22 billion of United States exports and over $16 billion of United States imports must be handled by the staffs of firms located essentially in the United States. There is always a great deal of work to be performed by an international marketing organization right here in the United States, in addition to the functions performed by connections and facilities abroad.

Summary

1. Every company that has been engaged in international marketing for any length of time has, of necessity, developed a certain philosophy of doing business abroad.
2. The decision to enter the market calls for executive determination. The best chances of success for any company, after the decision has been made, lie in continued executive backing.
3. The large domestic United States market is both a hindrance and a help to the international marketing plans of an American company.
4. American youth, generally speaking, are not interested in going abroad for a protracted period of time. As nationalistic policies of countries, generally the new and relatively underdeveloped countries, tend to insist on the employment of nationals, the need for sending Americans abroad for long periods of time is obviated.
5. The product that is offered for sale in international marketing must be acceptable to the customers in the respective markets. This may require changes in the product, package, style, design, or any facet of the product and/or its presentation to the customers.
6. Service is the keynote of the international marketing effort of companies that are seriously engaged in that trade. This is merely another way of stating that a product is good only for rendering a service.
7. One basic principle of international marketing is to have respect for all peoples, regardless of national origin, religion, or race.
8. Opportunities for employment in international marketing are open to those who are qualified by both training and experience. The recent graduate must first acquire some experience, and one way to do so is to find a position with a company engaged in international marketing, although the first position may not be in the international division.

QUESTIONS

1. Explain why "every company which has been engaged in foreign trade for any length of time has, of necessity, developed a certain philosophy of doing business abroad."
2. Why is a decision to enter a foreign market so important? What factors bear most cogently on the making of this decision?
3. For a company initially engaging in international marketing, in what ways does the extent of its domestic market bear upon its prospects of success?
4. For companies long established in international marketing, in what ways does the extent of its domestic markets affect its overseas operations?
5. Why do young Americans prefer not to go abroad for long periods of time?
6. Why do many countries require the employment of nationals to a great extent?

7. Cite instances of the adaptability and of the inadaptability of products for international marketing.
8. When adapting a product to international marketing, why is it sometimes difficult to make any changes in the product or in anything pertaining to the product?
9. Why is service the keynote of the international marketing program?
10. Why is it necessary for a successful international trader to have respect for all peoples?
11. What are the difficulties of trying to find a position in international marketing?

PROBLEMS

1. Examine the case history of a company engaged in international marketing and prepare a report upon it. Such case histories appear from time to time in the *Journal of Commerce* (New York), *New York Times, Fortune,* and in publications of the National Planning Association, Washington, D.C.
2. Visit a retail establishment and note an imported product that is being offered for sale. Examine it closely and determine the differences in the product as compared with an American product with which it competes. Write your findings.

COLLATERAL READINGS

Fayerweather, John. *Management of International Operations, Text and Cases.* New York: McGraw-Hill Book Company, Inc., 1960. Chapters 1 and 8.

Grabbe, E. M. "Automation Expert Discusses Attitudes of Management in Europe, United States," *International Commerce.* Washington, D.C.: Government Printing Office, November 19, 1962, p. 7.

Horn, Paul V. *International Trade Principles and Practices,* Third Edition. New York: Prentice-Hall, Inc., 1951. Chapter 1.

National Foreign Trade Council. *Proceedings of National Foreign Trade Convention.* New York: annual.

Pratt, E. E. *Foreign Trade Handbook,* Third Edition. Chicago: The Dartnell Corporation, 1952. Part I, Chapter 2.

———————————— *Modern International Commerce.* New York: Allyn and Bacon, Inc., 1956. Chapter 4.

Van Cleef, Eugene. *Getting into Foreign Trade.* New York: Ronald Press Company, 1946. Chapters 2 and 8.

PART II

INTERNATIONAL MARKETING ORGANIZATIONS

Having acquired some knowledge as to why international marketing is desirable, what to look for as part of a foreign market survey, and where to look for the various sources of information, the business firm is now ready to consider the specific ways in which it can participate in international business.

Part II of the text examines the several marketing channels and facilities that can be readily controlled from the home base. These include the administration of international marketing, the channels available in the home market, the producers and commercial firms abroad, export salesmen and import buyers, and advertising methods and policies.

Part II stresses throughout the absolute necessity of incorporating administrative and executive support for every operation. This particular emphasis cannot be repeated too often, because the success of an international marketing venture is dependent entirely upon executive interest and backing.

International advertising and promotion are treated at the conclusion of Part II. This subject is closely identified with the marketing organizations included in this part.

CHAPTER 8

THE ADMINISTRATION OF INTERNATIONAL MARKETING

In light of the discussion of "The Scope of International Marketing" in the preceding chapter, the administration of international marketing is clearly a matter for executive decision and concern. An interesting example of the importance of executive backing is shown by the following statement: ". . . a weak export department which was riding along as an unprofitable appendage to domestic sales was dramatically strengthened when the same manager, who had been reporting to the sales manager, was required to report directly to the president."[1]

The present chapter will attempt to develop and explain this concept into its several ramifications.

A Global Concept

Ideally, the administration of international marketing would be fully integrated into the entire business operations of a firm. The entire organization would be just as much aware of developments and problems the company faces in India as in Indiana.

Commenting on the subject of organization, the management firm of Booz, Allen, and Hamilton, Inc., declares that about two thirds of the organization problems of a business are to be found in the top management structure. Continuing, their report states:

> In the majority of cases, organization difficulties emanate from appending the international business to the domestic business instead of integrating the two parts into a world business. Typically, the organ-

---

[1] Cited from *Search By Research* (Spencer Stuart and Associates, Inc., December, 1962), quoted by permission.

ization structure just evolves rather than being carefully planned. For example, most businesses tend to be organized along a product or functional line. Where the foreign business is added, it is usually geographically oriented at the first two organizational levels. If the basic organization rationale of the business is either product or functional, an immediate organizational divergence results. This creates problems starting with the chief executive, who must supervise and coordinate a geographical international organization with a product or functional domestic organization. Also, the transfer of know-how and technical competence is more difficult between these two diverse organizational entities and so catalyzes other problems. . . .

The major internal management problem is orientation — getting the top management team to think, act and operate in terms of a single integrated world business instead of a domestic business with an international arm. . . . Present management functions tend to be keyed to the domestic business; the foreign business is clearly appended, and a separate management approach is clearly evident in the domestic versus international end of the business.[2]

The presentation of the subject of organization of international marketing in this book is from the standpoint of the usual manner in which business is organized. This does not mean, however, that there are not companies that have adopted a truly global or international concept in business organization and operation. This broader approach is increasing as more business firms learn the advantages of the global concept because of their worldwide enterprise. It is obvious that as a company expands abroad by means of exports, foreign branch houses and factories, licensees, etc., a complex structure is developed that can become unwieldy. This problem is generally handled by turning all of the foreign business over to a separate division or company. On the other hand, the global concept permits such a far ranging organization to operate on the basis of the best utilization of company resources, wherever located.

An interesting comparison of these two approaches is afforded by Charts 8-1 and 8-2. These charts

> . . . typify the structural differences that . . . often exist at upper-management levels between a domestically oriented company and an internationally oriented one.
>
> These examples are real. Company A is a large, diversified, decentralized company with corporate headquarters in the United States. Company B is equally large, diversified, and decentralized, but has its

---

[2]Booz, Allen, and Hamilton, Inc., *The Emerging World Enterprise*, pp. 14–15. Copyright 1962 by Booz, Allen, and Hamilton, Inc., quoted by permission.

corporate headquarters in a European country. Both are in the same general industry, have similar product lines, have annual sales of nearly $1 billion, and seek to operate in all important world markets. Within this frame of reference, let us consider their respective organizational readiness to deal with strategic business problems and opportunities throughout the world:

Company A has assigned responsibility for all its overseas activities to an "international division." Currently, the division accounts for more than 25% of the corporation's sales and investment, and is growing on both these counts more rapidly than almost any domestic unit. To this extent, the chief executive has "delegated" ("abdicated"?) more than a fourth of his responsibility to one man.

Since a chief executive is charged with protecting the total investment made by his stockholders, he is implicitly responsible for distributing his own effort so that he is personally and directly exposed to all of his company's major investment opportunities and situations — and this should mean by country as well as by kind of business. Keeping this is mind, look now at the organizational team that shares responsibility for Company A's interests within the United States. In line management, reporting directly to the president, are three executive vice presidents (each responsible for a group of "autonomous" operating divisions), the presidents of two subsidiary companies (headquartered in the United States), and an executive vice president (in charge of the company's extensive research laboratories in this country). We might ask here, why is it appropriate for the president of Subsidiary B to report on operations directly to the president, but apparently inappropriate for the managing director of an equally large and important European subsidiary so to report?

On the staff, eight functional vice presidents report directly to the chief executive. With the exception of certain legal and financial services provided for the International Division, these executives devote their attention almost exclusively to providing functional management for the U.S. operating groups. Could not the corporation benefit as a whole if the functional-management responsibility (e.g., services, advice, coordination, cross-fertilization) were exercised on a world-wide basis? In such functions as research or manufacturing, is it not logical to provide an organizational device that facilitates the reviewing of techniques used overseas for possible profitable applicability within the United States, and vice versa?

Or consider the ability of Company A's organization to resolve, in the company's best over-all interests, such frequently asked questions as these:

•Can our company expand its business in the United States by importing a line of products from an overseas production source?

Chart 8-1

ORGANIZATION STRUCTURE OF COMPANY A — DOMESTICALLY ORIENTED

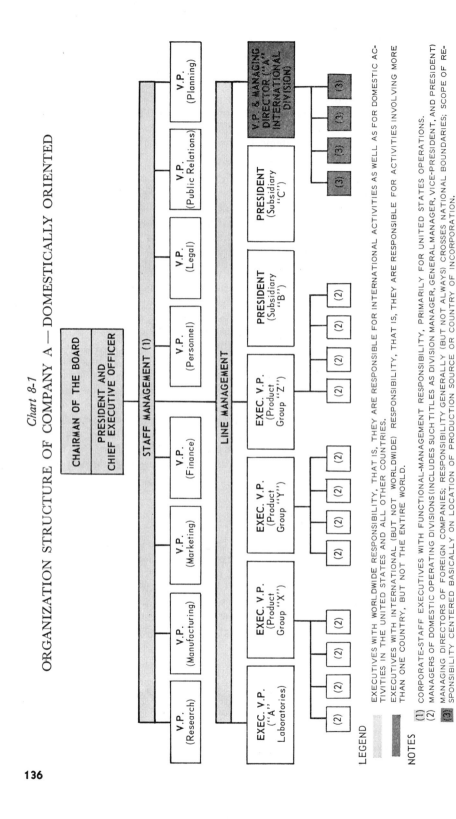

LEGEND

NOTES

EXECUTIVES WITH WORLDWIDE RESPONSIBILITY, THAT IS, THEY ARE RESPONSIBLE FOR INTERNATIONAL ACTIVITIES AS WELL AS FOR DOMESTIC ACTIVITIES IN THE UNITED STATES AND ALL OTHER COUNTRIES.

EXECUTIVES WITH INTERNATIONAL (BUT NOT WORLDWIDE) RESPONSIBILITY, THAT IS, THEY ARE RESPONSIBLE FOR ACTIVITIES INVOLVING MORE THAN ONE COUNTRY, BUT NOT THE ENTIRE WORLD.

(1) CORPORATE-STAFF EXECUTIVES WITH FUNCTIONAL-MANAGEMENT RESPONSIBILITY, PRIMARILY FOR UNITED STATES OPERATIONS.

(2) MANAGERS OF DOMESTIC OPERATING DIVISIONS (INCLUDES SUCH TITLES AS DIVISION MANAGER, GENERAL MANAGER, VICE-PRESIDENT, AND PRESIDENT)

(3) MANAGING DIRECTORS OF FOREIGN COMPANIES; RESPONSIBILITY GENERALLY (BUT NOT ALWAYS) CROSSES NATIONAL BOUNDARIES; SCOPE OF RESPONSIBILITY CENTERED BASICALLY ON LOCATION OF PRODUCTION SOURCE OR COUNTRY OF INCORPORATION.

Chart 8-2

ORGANIZATION STRUCTURE OF COMPANY B — INTERNATIONALLY ORIENTED

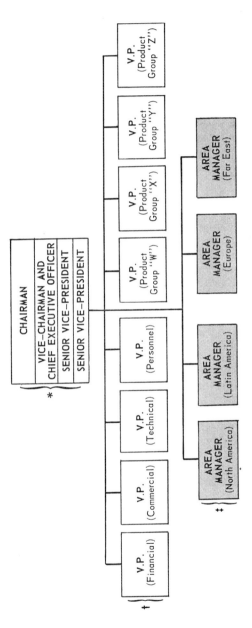

LEGEND

☐ EXECUTIVES WITH WORLDWIDE RESPONSIBILITY, THAT IS, THEY ARE RESPONSIBLE FOR INTERNATIONAL ACTIVITIES AS WELL AS FOR DOMESTIC AC-
TIVITIES IN ALL COUNTRIES.

▓ EXECUTIVES WITH INTERNATIONAL (BUT NOT WORLDWIDE) RESPONSIBILITY, THAT IS, THEY ARE RESPONSIBLE FOR ACTIVITIES INVOLVING MORE
THAN ONE COUNTRY, BUT NOT THE ENTIRE WORLD.

NOTES * FUNCTIONS AS ONE TOP-MANAGEMENT ENTITY, ALTHOUGH CHIEF EXECUTIVE OFFICER HAS FINAL AUTHORITY AND RESPONSIBILITY FOR THE COR-
PORATION'S PERFORMANCE WORLDWIDE; CHAIRMAN'S POSITION IS ADVISORY IN NATURE; SENIOR VICE-PRESIDENTS, WHEN DIRECTED, ACT AS DEPU-
TIES OF THE CHIEF EXECUTIVE OFFICER AND ARE SELECTED TO BRING SUPPLEMENTARY AND ESSENTIAL MANAGEMENT SKILLS TO THE TOP-MAN-
AGEMENT ENTITY ON A DAY-TO-DAY BASIS.

† COMPRISES THE "STRATEGIC MANAGEMENT BOARD" FOR THE CORPORATION WORLDWIDE, THESE EXECUTIVES, ALL BASED AT HEADQUARTERS, EX-
ERCISE STRATEGIC PLANNING, DECISION MAKING, COORDINATION, AND CONTROL FOR ALL FUNCTIONS AND ALL MAJOR PRODUCT LINES.

‡ INDICATES EXECUTIVES RESPONSIBLE FOR A GEOGRAPHICAL AREA OF THE WORLD, THE RESPONSIBILITY IN EACH CASE CROSSES NATIONAL BOUNDA-
RIES AND IS CENTERED ON A MANAGEABLE AREA OF GEOGRAPHY, OFFERING A PRACTICAL SPAN OF CONTROL FOR THE CHIEF EXECUTIVE THEREOF.
WHEN OVERALL STRATEGIC PLANS ARE APPROVED AT HEADQUARTERS, THIS "AREA MANAGER" (WHO MAY HAVE A TITLE OF PRESIDENT, VICE-
PRESIDENT, MANAGING DIRECTOR, OR THE LIKE) BECOMES FULLY RESPONSIBLE FOR EXECUTING THE PLANS, MANAGING COMPANY RESOURCES AND
FACILITIES WITHIN THE GEOGRAPHICAL AREA, AND ACHIEVING OPERATING TARGETS SPELLED OUT BY THE STRATEGIC MANAGEMENT BOARD.

●How can our production bases around the world be utilized so that we maximize market penetration and minimize costs?

●Should we acquire in the United States, in Europe, or elsewhere a company that makes products which we desire to add to our line?

Company B, in contrast, is organized as a true world enterprise. It has marshaled its management resources so that the company's prime executive skills are regularly brought to bear on business questions and problems, wherever in the world they occur.

The chief executive officer (vice chairman) has chosen in this case to appoint two senior vice presidents. These two men, along with the chairman, share the chief executive's top-management burden and act as "deputy chief executives" when it is appropriate to do so. The final authority for their actions, however, remains clearly and unquestionably in the hands of the vice chairman.

The members of the management board are based at headquarters. They provide the chief executive with a nucleus of top-notch executives whose sole responsibility it is to exercise strategic planning and control (for an assigned field of activity) on a world-wide basis.

Thus, the criterion of centralized strategic planning and control is met by this plan of organization. To our knowledge, all truly international companies have such a "strategic management board," but it takes many different names and forms. In Company B, the board consists of representatives of key functions and of key product lines. In other companies, these kinds of positions are supplemented (or to some extent replaced) by executive or group vice presidents responsible, on a line basis, for company interests in some quarter of the globe. The organizational relationships, within the board and external to it, also vary from company to company.[3]

A Matter of Jurisdiction

In a service bulletin of the International Executives Association (formerly the Export Managers Club of New York, Inc.), a question was raised relating to "sales destined for export received by domestic department." The questioner observed that, if the United States (domestic) sales organization handles the business,

> We get into such problems as having a customer getting equipment with English instruction plates instead of the foreign language instructions, forgetting to quote export packing, documentation difficulties, commission problems with our foreign representatives, etc.

---

[3]Gilbert H. Clee and Alfred di Scipio, "Creating a World Enterprise," *Harvard Business Review* (November–December, 1959). Reprinted by permission of the publishers.

The whole problem stems from these purchases being made where the buying offices are in the States, and the domestic organization claiming the sale is made here. We, in export, contend that these sales are due to requisitions originating overseas and due to the efforts of the representative.[4]

Export Sales: International Division or Domestic Sales Department? The comments received from the members of the International Executives Association who replied to this question varied somewhat, although most of them declared that the policy of their respective companies was to channel all export sales through the international division — *if*, at the time of the sale, it was known to be an export transaction. However, it is not always so easy to determine whether a given domestic sale is in fact an export sale. For example, a large domestic company that operates extensively abroad purchases equipment for its own use abroad, but the company purchases it from its United States headquarters. When the order is received, there may be no indication that it is for export. Moreover, companies that produce components purchased by other manufacturers do not know whether the finished product will be exported or not.

The replies referred to indicate that every effort is made to channel all export sales through the international division, even when sales are made by the domestic sales organization. Most of the companies report that split commissions are paid between the domestic sales department and the foreign representative of the company located in the territory to which the domestic purchase is destined. In most instances, moreover, credit for the sale goes to the international division, and this is important when bonuses are based upon sales reports.

The question appears to indicate that the international division of a company must be alert to prevent unwarranted usurpation of its territory by domestic sales departments.

Sales to Canada, Hawaii, and Puerto Rico. Another matter of jurisdiction relates to the question of trade with Canada, Hawaii, Alaska, and Puerto Rico. Since Alaska is a state and not disconnected from the mainland by a body of water, trade with that area is considered to be domestic.

Canada. While Canada is a foreign country that reflects problems of tariffs and exchange rates, it is so closely identified with the United States

---

[4]Export Managers Club of New York, Inc., *Service Bulletin 2199* (June 23, 1958).

that domestic sales departments very often supervise trade with the Dominion. One of the reasons for this is the ease of covering the markets of Canada, located as they are in the southern part of the country. Domestic salesmen covering the northern tier of states of the Union can move over into Canada and include that area in their sales territory. Moreover, transportation between the United States and Canada is often by rail or truck, thus avoiding the complications of ocean transportation. This is true despite the extent of Great Lakes shipping in United States–Canadian trade.

Hawaii. On the other hand, Hawaii, although a state, presents a different situation. The reasons for handling sales to Hawaii through the international division include: (1) Hawaii is located outside the continental United States; (2) goods are packed for and shipped by ocean transportation; (3) prices, in some cases, are based on export discount schedules; and (4) the state is covered by travelers to and from the Far East.

Firms that consider Hawaii a domestic market cite these considerations: (1) it has become the fiftieth state; (2) there are a few important Hawaiian factors[5] and they are well schooled in United States domestic operations; (3) the market is supplied from stocks on the west coast of the United States; (4) the state is subject to federal excise tax; (5) there are no export declarations, special invoices, export prices, or foreign regulations; and (6) Hawaiian shipments are considered to be domestic for parcel post and insurance.

From a questionnaire the Export Managers Club of New York found that, of the firms that commented on the question of Hawaii, 48 classified sales to Hawaii as export; 32, domestic; with 3 more firms changing from export to domestic. It is important to stress the fact that the views recorded and the votes counted refer only to those who responded to the questionnaire. The analysis also reveals a certain amount of contradiction, indicating that one company's policy is drastically different from another company's.

Puerto Rico. Puerto Rico has always been and continues to be considered an export market. Another questionnaire of the Export Managers Club of New York revealed that Puerto Rico was considered an export market by a vote of 95 to 1 — and the one vote represented a special situation where the exporter was in Florida. Puerto Rico is a foreign market because: (1) it is a country in which Spanish is spoken;

---

[5]See Chapter 10, page 188, for a discussion of *factors*.

(2) it is part of the Caribbean and Latin American area; (3) export declarations are required; (4) shipments are identical with export shipments; (5) taxes must be paid; (6) Puerto Rico is in the Western Hemisphere Corporation area; and (7) it is a Commonwealth, not a territory.

Allied Company Arrangement (Mother Hen)

Before considering the several types of administrative departments used by firms engaged in international business, mention should be made of what is perhaps the simplest way to engage in foreign business, the *allied company arrangement* or, as frequently referred to today, the Mother Hen concept.

When one manufacturer, *A*, with an export department and foreign distribution, contracts for the export sales rights for the products of another manufacturer, *B*, we have an effective and simple method of administering the foreign business. This method is employed in competitive (but related) as well as complementary lines. In such cases, manufacturer *A* merely adds the products of manufacturer *B* to his own line and offers them for sale under arrangements mutually agreed upon. Manufacturer *B* sells to *A* at agreed prices or discounts, and that is all *B* is obliged to do in order to have his goods sold in foreign markets.

There are many reasons for employing this method of departmental arrangement. Manufacturer *B* does not wish to bother with export sales, but he is willing to accept foreign business developed by manufacturer *A*. Or, *B* may handle export sales of his own products in certain markets and arrange with *A*, and possible *C* and *D*, for handling his products in other markets. While some firms engage in worldwide business, this does not mean that they conduct business through the same channels and under the same arrangements in all areas.

B finds an established export department and foreign distribution channels suited perfectly to his needs, and the net receipts from such sales may be quite satisfactory to *B*; that is, this arrangement may be more profitable on export sales than any other method of exporting that *B* could consider.

From the standpoint of manufacturer *A* (and possibly *C* and *D*), the products of *B* may fill out a line of tools, machinery, electrical goods, pharmaceuticals, or any other line produced and exported by *A* and others. In such cases, *B* products would be complementary. There are cases in which the same arrangements are made for competitive lines that are different in style, design, price, etc., or that may be fully competitive. If fully competitive, the advantage to manufacturer *A* in handling the competing line is to satisfy all or most demands for such products in certain foreign markets, and thus keep a measure of control over the entire market. Such additional sales of competing lines yield him a profit, and *B* also profits.[6]

The Built-In Department

Another simple manner in which the international business of a concern may be administered at headquarters is by distributing the work on a functional basis among the personnel already engaged in the same type of domestic work. In such a plan, called *built-in*, the minimum additional assistance required is that of the manager. The built-in organization utilizes the personnel setup as it exists and attempts through the instrumentality of a manager to give international marketing its proper balance and attention.

Built-In Export Departments. For export trade, sales may be supervised by the sales manager in cooperation with the export manager, or they may be entirely under the export manager. The treasurer or cashier handles all of the financial arrangements and the credit manager devotes part of his time to foreign credits. No special setup is created for placing orders, handling documents, packing merchandise, advertising, or any other functions.

Responsibilities of the Export Manager. The flexibility, economy, and simplicity of this plan may be readily grasped, although the efficiency with which the foreign work is conducted, particularly in the case of exports, is not always so marked. The responsibility is placed upon the export manager to instill an interest in, and an enthusiasm for, the foreign work. With no superior executive standing, the degree of tact and persuasion he possesses alone determines the extent to which he will be successful in obtaining cooperation.

The difficulties of the manager in such an organization may be readily seen. He must suggest to capable, experienced fellow officers in

---

[6]See *Export Trade* (February 21, 1963), p. 9, for a description of the operations of AMF International (American Machine and Foundry Company). In addition to its own products, AMF handles the overseas business of some 75 smaller United States manufacturers.

the company precisely how and what changes should be made in product or procedure in order to meet the needs of the international trade, as the export manager sees them. Perhaps he seeks to induce the credit manager to be more liberal in granting terms. The traffic manager, who may have worked out to a science the methods of packing merchandise for safe and economical movement in domestic trade, is advised to begin anew in the preparation of overseas shipments. Production methods which, after tedious efforts, may have been fully standardized, may have to be altered to provide a different make-up or assortment for foreign customers.

The success of this plan of organization is dependent upon the ability of the export manager in persuading his colleagues to recognize the peculiarities of and to make changes as are necessary in international marketing. The success of the built-in department is best assured by proper executive control over the international business. The manager is not left entirely to his own resources when the president or the vice-president is vitally interested in the international business.

Characteristics of the Built-In Export Department. The built-in plan is comparatively simple and is employed by a large number of concerns, particularly the smaller firms. Not only is the feature of economy attractive, but in some instances the feeling also prevails that international and domestic business are identical and specialization is therefore unnecessary. One manufacturer of hats, for example, who holds to this belief, trains nearly all his employees so that they are capable of handling both export and domestic orders. He believes that greater efficiency results from this interchange of functions than from the employment of separate international marketing personnel. Moreover, there is more even employment of time since a slump in one line may have no serious effects upon personnel.

The Export Committee. The built-in idea, however, begins to give way when certain functions are assigned exclusively to international marketing work. This may be done without setting up a distinct and complete foreign department. For example, the control over international marketing may be centralized in a committee of department heads or officials, as shown in Chart 8-3. The export committee may consist of the president of the company, *ex officio;* the director of exports, who is also chairman of the export committee; the export manager, who also is secretary of the committee; the advertising manager; the treasurer; and the wholesale manager. This committee would determine all policies relating to the international business of the company. In this type of built-in or-

Chart 8-3

ORGANIZATION OF A BUILT-IN EXPORT DEPARTMENT

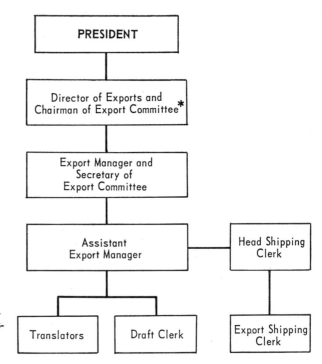

*EXPORT COMMITTEE ALSO INCLUDES PRESIDENT (EX OFFICIO), EXPORT MANAGER, ADVERTISING MANAGER, TREASURER, AND WHOLESALE MANAGER.

ganization, the director of exports and the export manager instill the foreign trade spirit, engender cooperation, and actively conduct the program. Moreover, they maintain direct contact, as may the other officials, with overseas distributors and managers.

Built-In Import Departments. Import departments of the built-in type are common. Indeed, among importing manufacturers the import department is generally identical with the purchasing division.

The same general scheme is also followed by large importing establishments, particularly those engaged in retail business, with an import manager coordinating the import functions of the several departments. The merchandise department, for example, would assemble data for the use of commodity buyers, maintain all records relating to imported merchandise, work in cooperation with the advertising manager, and in other ways concentrate on the service associated with the importation of merchandise. The accounting department would keep the accounts relating to imports, issue vouchers, and pay all bills. The accounting or comptroller department would break down costs. Customs work would be handled by a customhouse broker. Foreign offices and agents, supervised by the import manager, would assist traveling buyers, handle and expedite orders, and possibly pay bills.

The Separate Department

The separate department performs all of the functions relating to the export or the import trade, with the exception (generally) of production. The number of divisions and the size of the personnel are entirely dependent upon the volume of business. The department may be a functional unit within a company or it may be organized as a distinct corporate entity apart from the parent company.

Separate Export Departments. For export trade, a foreign trade or export manager supervises the department, although not infrequently a vice-president is in charge of a separate export or international department. Some departments are organized on a functional basis, others on a regional basis or an industrial basis, or a combination of several bases.

A separate export department is graphically presented in Chart 8-4 on page 146. This department is organized on a functional basis, which is the usual form of organization for medium-size concerns.

The export manager supervises all foreign sales and selects and trains the salesmen who cooperate with distributors abroad. He also selects and controls distributors as well as foreign branch managers, and he makes periodic visits to the field. Moreover, in cooperation with the advertising manager, the export manager processes the publicity plans for the foreign business. The assistant export manager in this plan is the office manager. The pricing department calculates price quotations, discounts, etc.; and orders are transcribed by the order department, copies being sent to the various interested divisions. All correspondence and advertising requiring translation are handled by a staff of translators. Orders are filled, packed, and shipped by the export shipper from the stocks maintained expressly for the foreign business. All accounts of the export department, as well as records with branches and distributors, are kept by the export credit department.

Credits are controlled by a special credit committee, consisting of the export manager, the assistant export manager, the treasurer, the

Chart 8-4

ORGANIZATION OF A SEPARATE EXPORT OR INTERNATIONAL DEPARTMENT
OF A MEDIUM-SIZE BUSINESS

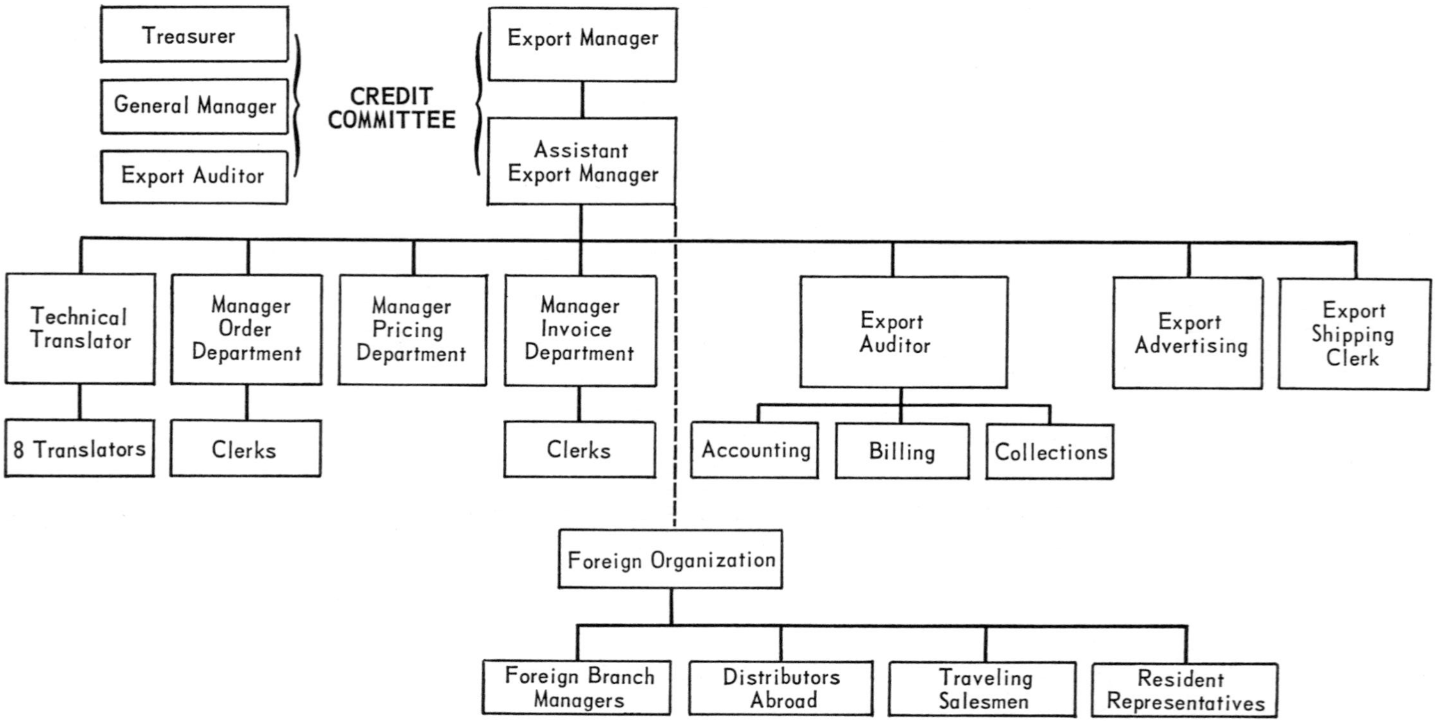

Chart 8-5

ORGANIZATION OF A SEPARATE EXPORT OR INTERNATIONAL DEPARTMENT
OF A LARGE MANUFACTURER

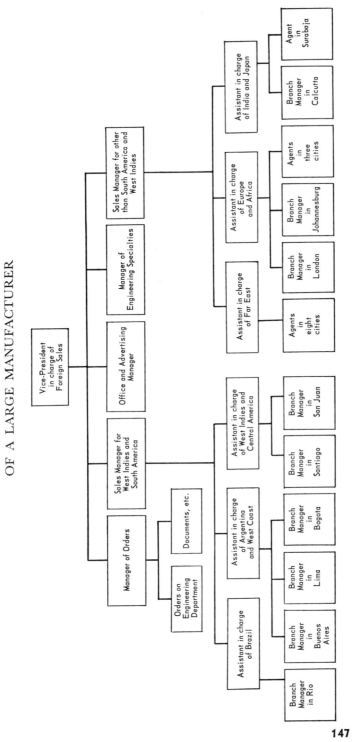

general manager, and the export auditor. Except for this one important phase of the business, the export department is autonomous.

Another setup that is particularly adapted to the needs of a large company is shown in Chart 8-5 on page 147. This plan is largely territorial or geographical in character. Some functional managers are also employed and, in addition, a manager for one commodity line. In this illustration, the export department organization emphasizes territorial specialization. The product in question is an expensive engineering machine, and buyers are frequently foreign government officials. Close contact with responsible purchasers is therefore required.

In charge of the export department is a vice-president of foreign sales. Two sales managers are each in charge of a broad territory. All of the details relating to the business are handled in the respective geographical departments. A separate office and advertising manager is employed, and requisitions on the engineering (manufacturing) division, as required to fill export orders, are transmitted through a separate manager. Credits and financing are especially important in this concern due to the large sums of money involved in individual orders. This work is handled principally by the finance department in collaboration with the vice-president in charge of foreign sales and the particular sales managers concerned. Whenever orders for products that are not manufactured by this company are received in connection with large construction projects abroad, the manager of engineering specialties communicates with American producers of such articles to place orders with them.

The separate export or international department, in some cases, is either split into two parts or two departments. This may occur as a firm establishes an increasing number of plants and/or licensees and continues to export from the home plant. The administration of the foreign plant or licensee operations may be placed under an executive with some such title as vice-president or director of foreign operations, while export sales would be under a vice-president or export manager.

Moreover, a given firm may have several separate export departments if the diversity of products that are produced justifies this kind of administration. Among the large chemical companies, this plan is sometimes followed, while in other lines also produced in wide variety, such as electrical and food products, this plan is generally not used.

Separate Import Departments. Separate import departments are not established so frequently as are separate export departments. The reasons for this were stated previously. Perhaps the greatest need for a separate import department is felt by large department stores and retail specialty shops. The ramifications of their business are so great that centralization of their import business may be highly desirable. Moreover, the technical details of customs clearance may in themselves be sufficient to warrant the establishment of a special import department.

The foreign (import) organization of one large department store is placed under the supervision of a vice-president. This officer is specifically charged with three major responsibilities, namely, (1) coordination of the entire activity of the foreign organization, (2) promotion of merchandise sales, and (3) supervision of the administration and finances of the foreign organization. The general manager of the headquarters office (New York) reports to this vice-president.

The functions of the foreign organization are divided into two main branches, one headed by a sales manager and the other headed by an administrative manager.

The specific duties of the sales manager are: (1) to process all samples received; (2) to assist in merchandise creation and development; (3) to schedule, develop, and hold sales meetings; and (4) to prepare for buyers' foreign trips, itineraries, budgets, etc.

Through the sales division, contact is promoted between foreign buying offices (of which this firm has seven) and the merchandise (selling) departments, enabling foreign channels to be informed regarding current demands for merchandise in the United States. The sales division transmits purchase orders and attends to correspondence and cables.

Promotion of import business may be performed in the foreign office by means of sampling. Supplementing the work of the traveling buyers, the foreign offices in Europe forward samples of goods that they believe to be marketable here. With each sample is transmitted the name of the manufacturer, price, delivery, terms, and style data. These samples are set up in a sample room to be inspected by interested buyers (merchandise department heads). Requests for further information or suggestions as to change in style, make-up, etc., are transmitted to the foreign office.

A recent innovation of import business promotion by department stores is a special display and sale of unique articles imported from a particular country. Such a display may be named "Italian Fair" or "Holland Fair." Every effort is exerted to embody the spirit and atmosphere of the country concerned. In this delightful exotic environment, customers throng to examine and purchase these imported articles.

The administrative manager performs the duties of: (1) processing imports through customs; (2) keeping foreign offices informed about customs matters, packing, shipping, and routing of merchandise purchased; (3) supervising the accounting, transfer of funds, and expenditures, which he controls for the entire organization, foreign and domestic; and (4) booking passage, controlling the financing, and checking of the buyers themselves.

Customs classification of an article determines the applicable rate and duty, and consequently enters into the determination of laid-down costs in this country. Every effort is made to keep correctly posted on United States customs matters. The administrative division also seeks to expedite the release of imported merchandise from steamship piers and customs appraisers' stores.

Advantages of a Separate Department. By thus segregating the foreign (export or import) work of a manufacturing or a merchandising concern, greater specialization and concentration may be achieved. When a large volume of export or import business is transacted, the separate department may be a more efficient plan of operation. The foreign business of the company and the profits derived therefrom may be more accurately measured. Errors are not so likely to creep in as when the built-in type is employed. One export manager who was restrained from properly expanding his built-in department because of the shortsightedness of conservative executives, declared that the errors in billing, packing, and documenting were appalling. Another export manager, on the other hand, was heartily in favor of his built-in department because he recognized no distinction between the domestic and the export functions and the work was being performed satisfactorily.

The separate department may also afford greater aggressiveness in the promotion and conduct of the foreign work. In the built-in type the manager may be hindered by lack of proper cooperation on the part of other department heads. The question becomes largely one of personalities, and if they do not harmonize, aggressiveness may cause difficulty.

International Marketing Subsidiary

The second way in which the foreign work of a company may be entirely separated from domestic operations is to organize an international marketing subsidiary. The parent concern then goes about its own affairs, doing business with the subsidiary in much the same manner as it transacts business with other firms. This plan is followed by some of the large exporting manufacturers, but in the import trade it is negligible. Often the selling company uses the name of the parent concern, for example, Westinghouse Electric International Company, Bethlehem Steel Export Corporation, and IBM World Trade Corporation.

Operations of the Subsidiary. The entire international trade of a company is taken over and supervised by this subsidiary. It handles the selling, credits, collections, advertising, shipping, accounting — the entire gamut of business operation. The subsidiary is billed at prices agreed on with the parent concern, pays the latter for these purchases, and endeavors to show a profit. The prices may be at cost or they may include a profit for the parent company. If they include a profit, the subsidiary is viewed as a middleman instead of a department in the business, and an undue handicap is at once imposed upon it. The practices of different companies vary in this respect.

Advantages of the Subsidiary. The reasons for the adoption of this plan of operation are various. First of all, there is the concentration of executive control in responsible, experienced officials. The executives of the subsidiary possess greater authority and responsibility than under any other plan. The business is supervised by a president and an entire staff of subordinate executives and clerks. In addition, all possibility of conflict between domestic and export (or import) interests or personnel is eliminated. Furthermore, one of the leading advantages of the subsidiary is the facility thereby provided of accurately determining the profit or loss from the foreign business. Overhead that was charged against the entire business, but which was not properly attributable directly to international trade, may be eliminated, showing possibly a greater profit on foreign business than was formerly realized.

The subsidiary, moreover, may have a tax advantage, such as when the income tax laws of foreign countries in which business is transacted consider the entire capital or profits of a company for tax purposes. Tax advantages under United States income tax provisions, when qualifying as a Western Hemisphere Trade Corporation or as an Export Trade Corporation, may provide compelling reasons for establishing an international marketing subsidiary.

Western Hemisphere Trade Corporation. As a Western Hemisphere Trade Corporation, the criteria to be met are:

1. It must be an American corporation, which bars incorporation abroad.

2. It must transact all of its business in the Western Hemisphere, including the West Indies and Puerto Rico, but excluding Hawaii.

3. Ninety percent of its gross income must come from the active conduct of a trade or business, computed over a three-year period.

4. Ninety-five percent of the gross income over a three-year period must be derived from sources outside of the United States.

The fourth criterion is complicated and final qualifying decisions are made by the District Director of Internal Revenue. If such criteria can be met and a Western Hemisphere Trade Corporation is established, a saving in normal tax and surtax could be effected, depending upon the amount of the incurred tax and the current rates of taxation.[7]

Export Trade Corporation. The Revenue Act of 1962 made provision for an entirely new type of corporation. The Export Trade Corporation is intended by the act to be a means of encouraging exports from the United States by exempting from United States taxation, subject to limitations, the "export trade income" of such corporations. Export trade income is defined as net income from the sale of property produced in the United States for use outside of the United States and sold to unrelated persons. It may include commissions and fees for the use of patents, secret processes, and related material owned by the manufacturer of the United States produced property.

While United States taxation is levied under the 1962 Revenue Act on foreign income if the amount of taxable income exceeds 30 percent of the foreign firm's total income, such taxation may be avoided by qualifying as an Export Trade Corporation. The definition is rather simple, namely, 90 percent of income, for a prior three-year period, must be obtained from foreign sources and at least 75 percent of its *total* income from such sources. Moreover, the amount exempt from tax is subject, as a maximum, to the smallest of three amounts:

---

[7]For example, in 1963, a corporation with a normal tax net income of $25,000 would pay about $7,200 in normal tax (there would be no surtax) while a Western Hemisphere Trade Corporation would pay $5,200, a saving of 8 percent of normal tax net income and of nearly 28 percent in taxes. If the normal tax net income is $100,000, the regular tax *and* surtax would be $45,200, but for the Western Hemisphere Trade Corporation, $31,000 — savings of 14¼ percent of normal tax net income and of about 30 percent in taxes. Finally, at $500,000 normal tax net income, the normal and surtaxes would be $248,200 against $177,000 — savings of 14¼ percent and 28 percent respectively. Excess profits taxes are not considered in these illustrations, but under present (1962) law, Western Hemisphere Trade Corporations are exempt from excess profits taxes; so are *any* companies doing 95 percent of their business abroad with 50 percent of gross income coming from the active conduct of a business. The Western Hemisphere Trade Corporation, however, may be called upon to pay income taxes in the countries with which it transacts business. The subject is somewhat complicated tax-wise.

1. One and one half times the Export Trade Corporation's export promotion expenses incurred in earning the export trade income, of which 90 percent must be paid outside of the United States.

2. Ten percent of gross receipts from export trade.

3. Increase in investment in export trade assets for the year. Such assets are defined as working capital, inventory, and handling facilities used to earn the export trade income.

Combination and Cooperative Methods

Instead of utilizing one of the foregoing arrangements to administer its international business, a company may become party to some combination or cooperative arrangement. When a Webb-Pomerene cooperative association[8] is formed by a group of manufacturers or merchandising concerns, the association may act for each member as a cooperative export department. Cooperation is also practised in importing when a group of department stores or retail specialty shops forms an association to facilitate placing import orders.

Combination Export Manager (CEM). An arrangement may be made with a combination export manager that may be an individual or an organization of combined export departments representing several lines, or the export department of a related but noncompeting manufacturer.

The CEM, generally speaking, appeals to firms when first contemplating entrance into export trade. They have available a trained export department capable of performing the studies, analyses, and operations expected of an export department.

The CEM conducts business in the name of the manufacturer that he represents. All correspondence and contracts are negotiated in the name of the manufacturer. All quotations and orders are subject to the approval of the manufacturer. The usual method of compensation for the CEM is by commission so that it is to his advantage to develop the export business as rapidly as possible. For certain kinds of work performed, such as negotiating abroad for a licensee or a site for a foreign operation, a fee plus expense basis may be used.

---

[8]The nature of cooperative associations engaged in exporting from the United States is described in Chapter 17.

According to one spokesman in the field, an export department for a given manufacturer is not justified unless there is a volume of foreign business of over $300–$400 thousand annually.[9]

The CEM devotes his entire attention to export work:

> This is better than using domestic people part time on export. It avoids costly mistakes from unfamiliarity with export details. Overseas customers and representatives get better cooperation. Sales increase. Responsibility is concentrated in an experienced export man. Costs are easily segregated; they are often lower than when scattered among domestic employees doing unfamiliar work involving disproportionately more time.
>
> . . . Domestic employees tend to treat export as a "step-child," less important than domestic sales, with secondary attention and temporary expedients. This loses business. Export customers go where their needs are met with efficiency, promptness, and understanding.[10]

A Shortcoming of the CEM Plan. One shortcoming of the CEM plan lies in the fact that a high degree of specialization may not be possible; extensive rather than intensive efforts may result, owing to the number of lines handled. If the lines are few in number, and if they are related, this feature might not be a hindrance; but most combination export managers are naturally anxious to add new lines. They feel that they can do so to advantage because their organization is already set up and, of course, the larger clientele will yield greater compensation. If closely related but noncompetitive lines are handled, additional orders may be readily obtained through established outlets. For inland manufacturers, the combination export manager might be especially advantageous as he may also supervise at the seaboard all matters relating to foreign shipment.

Management of International Business

In international marketing circles, the title of *export manager* refers to one who actually manages the export business of a company and who may range from a clerk to a top-level executive. The international business of a company may be under the direct supervision of a vice-president and, when selling companies are organized, under the president of that incorporated concern.

---

[9]Henry M. Sweeney, V. P., Smith, Kirkpatrick & Company, Inc., cited in *Journal of Commerce* (December 5, 1962).

[10]Thomas C. Ballagh, President, Ballagh, and Thrall, Inc., in *Export Trade and Shipper* (October 8, 1956), p. 7, and (August 1, 1960), p. 7. See also A. H. Fleck in *Export Trade* (November 19, 1962), p. 14.

The Expanding Role of the Export Manager. From a survey conducted jointly by the International Executives Association and the weekly magazine *Export Trade*, it was revealed that export managers of small, medium, and large companies are responsible not only for sales and advertising but they are also frequently responsible for credit and traffic. In addition, the survey revealed that nearly one third of the export managers who replied to the questionnaire were responsible for supervision of foreign branches and subsidiaries and/or licensees. When these last-named activities are placed under the supervision of the export manager, he has stepped beyond the conduct of export sales; he is also charged with supervising foreign operations. When this situation arises, it would appear that his title might more properly be Manager of International Operations, rather than Export Manager. The survey referred to also noted that nearly one half of the individuals replying to the questionnaire used the title of export manager; ten percent, export sales manager; and the balance, a wide variety of titles, with no more than two or three duplicates each.[11]

Increasing evidence of change in the role of the export manager is to be seen in the way that business groups that are not ordinarily identified with international business have begun to operate in this field. For example, the American Management Association has sponsored the International Management Association that holds seminars on the varied aspects of the management of foreign operations. They are not interested in exporting or importing as such. The American Marketing Association has been expanding its interest in the direction of what it calls *foreign marketing*. By this term, export and import are not intended, but rather the conduct of marketing *in* foreign countries. Moreover, for the first time in its history, the International Chamber of Commerce at its biennial Congress in 1959 held a general meeting on the subject of "World Marketing: A Top Management Responsibility." This marketing meeting, according to *Export Trade*, "is an indication of a vastly increased concern with modern marketing concepts by businessmen abroad."[12] The Export Managers Club of New York, Inc., changed its name to International Executives Association and the Export Managers Club of Chicago changed its name to International Operations Club of Chicago. Changes have also been made in the names of the local "export" clubs located throughout the country.

---

[11]*Export Trade and Shipper* (November 5, 1956), pp. 6 and 7.
[12]*Export Trade* (January 19, 1959), p. 11.

All of these developments are significant for the business executive who heretofore has been called the export manager. His role has grown, in many cases, into a far broader concept than indicated by that time-honored title. This statement does not apply to every business firm that conducts international business because many of them do not have foreign operations under their control. As expressed by one consultant on marketing and sales management, located in Mexico City:

> The export manager as we knew him years ago is obsolete. Today the export manager is an internationally minded business builder fully aware of market trends, problems and potential of the company overseas.
>
> Instead of working exclusively with dealers, distributors and representatives, the export manager now works closely with foreign licensees and company-owned subsidiaries and with overseas firms in which his company may have only a minority interest. This shift in the export manager's role has made it necessary for him to become an effective consultant on marketing, management and personnel and forces him to spend more time "in the field" than ever before. Further, the export manager now must have a much better understanding of his company's role and profit picture in international business. Often he must become active in the internal affairs of the country in which his products are being sold.[13]

Qualifications of the Executive in Charge of International Business. The qualifications of a manager or of an executive who is in charge of the international business of a concern have been elaborately expounded in international marketing literature. According to one old-time authority, an export manager should be:

> ... a man who has a broad and practical knowledge of international commerce gained from personal experience in the many important markets of the world; who is thoroughly familiar with banking methods and exchange; who can correspond and converse intelligently in at least the four principal commercial languages; whose knowledge of geography affords him a vivid picture of every prospective or established market; who not only knows intimately his own products but is an enthusiastic believer in their merits, and above all, is a one hundred per cent salesman.[14]

Mr. B. Olney Hough,[15] on the other hand, looks more to the man's ability to appreciate the point of view of foreigners with whom he deals,

---

[13]Martin Lowe, *ibid.* (August 12, 1963), p. 21.
[14]A Schoonmaker, *Proceedings, Thirteenth National Foreign Trade Convention* (1926), p. 355.
[15]*Op. cit.*, p. 7.

while conceding that his language and travel credentials are important. Furthermore, the export executive, like the head of any business department or organization, should be a capable executive. He must be able to establish and administer an effective export organization and be capable of selecting effective business policies. If in charge of a built-in department, he must be able to obtain cooperation on the part of other departments of his firm's business organization.

The literature in international marketing has never stressed the qualifications of an import manager. This is understandable because purchasing departments of manufacturers often include overseas purchasing or, at least, purchase of foreign products. The knowledge called for here is knowledge of the product, the trading terms and techniques, etc. Moreover, import managers for wool, hides, coffee, metal, paper, and other firms engaged in business in which foreign products play an important part are known as *commodity experts.*

In the merchandise lines — department and specialty stores — the import manager may be an administrative officer entirely, since the actual buying would be conducted through overseas channels or by traveling buyers who are merchandise (sales) managers of the establishment. These traveling buyers must know their products, but the import manager knows the arrangements and procedures required to facilitate import purchasing. Indeed, the import manager (or manager of the foreign department) of a retail store may be a cost and customs tariff expert only. In this connection it is well to be reminded that some export managers may come no closer to international markets than the local post office. The question depends upon the nature of the business and upon the scope of the import or export trade of a given firm.

Location of the Foreign Trade Department

Considerable discussion has taken place at times with respect to the location of the foreign trade department — the seaboard v. the factory. The most logical place seems to be at the seaboard since international marketing activities and facilities are concentrated there.

It is clear that a built-in department can be situated at no other place than at the factory. With separate departments or selling companies, it becomes physically possible to establish the export organization at a seaboard location. In those organizations stressing the cooperative keynote of the built-in type, the factory location seems to be best. Some companies realize the principal advantages of both schemes by establishing an office at seaboard and leaving the bulk of the department at the factory. In this case, the manager makes frequent trips between the factory and seaboard.

The decision in the question of where to locate depends upon the product sold as well as upon the policy of a particular company. If, for example, staple lines are handled and it appears to be advisable to maintain spot stocks for prompt shipment at seaboard, then the seaboard location is undoubtedly preferable. When import departments are established by manufacturers, they may primarily handle shipping and customshouse work at the port. Seaboard location is also desirable for import buying activities that function through import organizations at seaboard, as in the case of certain raw materials. If a merchandising company establishes an import department, there is an essential tie-in with selling division heads, who often are the firm's buyers, and store location would undoubtedly be essential. Each individual case must be decided upon its own merits.

Summary

1. The international division of a company must be alert to assure that it has control of all the international business of the company, regardless of whether an order comes from a domestic or a foreign source.
2. The export or import department of a trading or manufacturing firm provides the focus for the conduct of its international business. This is not always true, however, with regard to importing, for a manufacturing company may handle its imports by means of a (domestic) purchasing department.
3. The allied company arrangement provides a ready-made marketing organization for international trade.
4. The built-in department depends upon the domestic organization for international trade work, except for direction by an export manager.
5. The separate department provides specialized attention to certain or all of the international marketing functions.
6. The international marketing subsidiary is a further separation of domestic from foreign marketing; and in the case of branch factories, foreign plantations, and mines, etc., production is also separated from the domestic marketing activities.
7. Tax provisions may exert determining influence on the international marketing operation.
8. Other forms of headquarters organization include cooperative methods with competing firms or placing the conduct of international marketing in the hands of combination export managers. A CEM offers many advan-

tages to companies that are not initially prepared to go into foreign markets through their own efforts.

9. The responsibilities of the export manager vary widely and extend, in many instances, to supervision of foreign branches and licensees. In this respect, the export manager also is actually a director of foreign operations because he does more than supervise exports from the United States.

10. The qualifications of an export executive are extensive and somewhat unique. Basically, administrative ability is not to be overlooked when emphasizing the unique characteristics.

QUESTIONS

1. Why should the foreign trade department complain if orders destined for overseas are obtained through the efforts of the domestic sales organization? After all, is not the company more important than any part of it?

2. Why is it that export departments virtually, without exception, supervise trade with Puerto Rico while they infrequently supervise trade with Canada, and presumably about one half of the shipments to Hawaii?

3. Give some examples of arrangements under which an American manufacturing exporter sells the products of other manufacturers. Explain the advantages of these arrangements to the parties involved. Explain also the possible disadvantages.

4. Why is it desirable for exporting and importing enterprises to establish export and import departments, respectively?

5. Define a built-in department; a separate export department; an international marketing subsidiary; a combination export manager. From the standpoint of recognized business functions, compare these types.

6. Evaluate the elements of strength and of weakness in the built-in type of department.

7. How would an export order be handled through the several units of a separate export department? How would an overseas inquiry be handled?

8. Trace the functional movement of an import transaction through a department store to the retail counter.

9. Comment on the reasons for establishing an international marketing subsidiary by a manufacturer.

10. Evaluate the elements of strength and of weakness of the combination export manager.

11. Discuss the qualifications of an export manager for each of the types of organization discussed in this chapter.

12. Comment on the changing role of the traditional export manager.

13. How does the U.S. tax structure influence the method of organization for international marketing?

PROBLEMS

1. The Enterprise Textile Company has received inquiries over several years from business firms in Latin American countries. The inquiries relate to the textile yarns manufactured by the company. All of the letters are in a foreign language. Since domestic business has been good, these inquiries have been ignored.

   The management now decides that something should be done about these inquiries. From the standpoint of foreign trade departments, suggest ways of acting upon these inquiries.

2. The Prime Pump Company is seeking an export manager to replace Mr. Sloan who is resigning. Two candidates are under consideration. Mr. Thomas is a young man with some export experience with a drug company. He speaks Spanish, is married, and would like the opportunity to move up from a clerkship to the position of export manager.

   Mr. Applegate is also a young man with a degree in business administration, having specialized in foreign commerce. He has a smattering of Spanish and French, is unmarried, and his experience has been in domestic sales work with an insurance company.

   Evaluate the qualifications of these two candidates for the position of export manager. Which candidate would you recommend for the position?

3. Jones and MacMullen is the name of a firm of combination export managers. They handle accounts of twenty different manufacturers. Although the lines handled vary somewhat as to type, they feel that this is no disadvantage because the staff is large enough to assign a competent person to handle one or more accounts.

   One risk in this type of business operation is that clients withdraw in favor of setting up their own export sales organization. Jones and MacMullen have been losing accounts at an alarming rate. They seek your advice as to what can be done to remedy this situation.

COLLATERAL READINGS

Chamber of Commerce of the United States. *An Introduction to Doing Import and Export Business*, Sixth Revised Edition. Washington, D.C.: 1963.

Clee, Gilbert H. and Alfred di Scipio, "Creating a World Enterprise," *Harvard Business Review*, Vol. 37, No. 6 (November–December, 1959), pp. 77–89.

Collins, V. D. *World Marketing*. Philadelphia: J. B. Lippincott Company, 1935. Chapter 6.

Dartnell International Trade Handbook, The. Chicago: The Dartnell Corporation, 1963. Part 1, Chapter 2; Part 4, Chapters 1, 2, and 3; Part 6, Chapters 3 and 4; Part 9 ,Chapter 1.

de Haas, J. A. *The Practice of Foreign Trade*. New York: McGraw-Hill Book Company, Inc., 1935. Chapter 10.

Economic Cooperation Administration, Office of Small Business. *Guide for the Prospective Exporter.* Washington, D.C.: Government Printing Office, 1949.

Fayerweather, John. *Management of International Operations,* Text and Cases. New York: McGraw-Hill Book Company, Inc., 1960. Chapters 6 and 8.

Heck, Harold J. *Foreign Commerce.* New York: McGraw-Hill Book Company, Inc., 1953. Chapter 5.

Horn, Paul V. *International Trade Principles and Practices,* Third Edition. New York: Prentice-Hall, Inc., 1951. Chapter 25.

MacDonald, Philip. *Practical Exporting.* New York: Ronald Press Company, 1949. Chapter 1.

Martyn, Howe. *International Business.* London: Collier-Macmillan Limited, 1964. Chapters 10 and 11.

National Foreign Trade Council, Inc. *Report of National Foreign Trade Convention.* New York: annual.

Pratt, E. E. *Modern International Commerce.* New York: Allyn and Bacon, Inc., 1956. Chapter 2.

Roorbach, G. B. *Import Purchasing: Principles and Problems.* Chicago and New York: A. W. Shaw Company, 1927. Chapters 3 and 4.

United States Department of Commerce. *Export and Import Practice.* Washington, D.C.: Government Printing Office, 1944.

Van Cleef, Eugene. *Getting Into Foreign Trade.* New York: Ronald Press Company, 1946. Chapter 3.

CHAPTER 9

INTERNATIONAL MARKETING CHANNELS IN THE HOME MARKET

The international marketing organization of a particular business firm refers not only to the administrative organization for directing the international business, but also involves the various marketing channels that are utilized by the firm. In order to facilitate an understanding of the characteristics and features of international marketing channels, the discussion of channels is divided into: (1) international marketing channels in the home market and (2) international marketing channels abroad. Thus the distinction is made on the basis of the *location* of each particular channel, not on the *nationality* of those traders utilizing it.

A newcomer in international marketing may well ask himself, "Can I engage in international marketing through facilities at home, or must I inevitably utilize marketing facilities abroad?" It must be remembered that every business enterprise at one time was a newcomer. This question might also arise for any manager responsible for his firm's international marketing activities; as it applies to certain areas of the world, his knowledge of available facilities may be unsurpassed. But, his knowledge of the facilities for areas heretofore untapped may leave much to be desired. It should make no difference to the business firm whether its buyer or its supplier is an American or a person of some other nationality. What *does* count is where the buyer or supplier can be reached and what he can do.

Some texts deal with the subject of marketing channels on a basis of "direct" and "indirect" international marketing. By "indirect" is generally meant the employment of international trade middlemen located in the home market. By "direct," on the other hand, the employment of channels abroad is intended. But these channels abroad include many middlemen, and confusion may arise by calling a method of distribution "direct" when middlemen are used.

This text does not refer to "direct" and "indirect" channels, as such. The presentation offered here is based upon the location of the channel, whether at home or abroad. There can be middlemen of all types as well as branches, agents, salesmen, etc., in *both* geographical designations. Moreover, this text, in dealing with the channels of international marketing, considers import and export organizations simultaneously. A commission house can be an export or it can be an import commission house; an agent abroad for a domestic manufacturer is a foreign agent, and the agent in the domestic market for a foreign manufacturer is, to such a manufacturer, also a foreign agent. There appears to be no point in treating agents that are foreign to domestic manufacturers in one chapter, and then to deal with domestic agents for foreign manufacturers in another chapter.

This text deals exactly with what the title states — *international marketing* — not just foreign trade as such. Therefore, each channel, insofar as it is applicable, is treated in both its export and its import functions. Needless repetition is not only obviated by this treatment, but the reader also learns about a marketing channel in its full ramifications at the same time.

Despite the statements just made, the treatment in this chapter will be from the standpoint of the United States. This is done only to facilitate and simplify the discussion of the topic, international marketing channels in the home market.

Types of International Marketing Channels in the Home Market

A firm may sell its products in foreign countries, or it may sell imported products and yet, as far as the firm is concerned, the business is essentially domestic. There are many international marketing channels located in the home country, and the firm that desires export sales or import purchases may deal with these channels instead of engaging in actual conduct of international marketing.

This chapter will be devoted to a discussion of these channels, which include the following:

1. Foreign firms' connections in the home market, e.g., the United States, such as:
   a. Salesmen from abroad.
   b. Agents and distributors.

    c. Branches.

    d. Licensees.

2. Resident buyers in the home market, e.g., the United States, for

    a. Private firms, large contractors, mines, plantations, and utilities located abroad.

    b. Foreign (government) purchasing missions.

3. Home market (American) international marketing middlemen, classified as follows:

    a. Export and/or import commission houses.

    b. Export and/or import merchants.

    c. Manufacturer's export agents.

    d. Export and import brokers.

    e. Export houses or trading firms.

Foreign Firms' Connections in the Home Market (United States)

Export sales can be made in the home market to buyers representing foreign firms, as, for example, sales at tobacco auctions and raw cotton markets. Import purchases may be made from traveling salesmen from abroad who solicit prospective domestic buyers; from agents and distributors who secure orders for the principals that they represent; from branch offices and storage facilities operated in the home country by foreign interests; and from licensees — home country manufacturers licensed by foreign manufacturers to produce the latter's line of merchandise.

Salesmen from Abroad. Just as domestic salesmen travel abroad, salesmen for foreign companies come to the domestic market to sell specialized lines of merchandise. They may represent a manufacturer or an exporter of style goods, jewelry, or machinery and equipment. They commonly carry samples and specifications and call upon buyers in the chief buying markets of the home country. For style goods and jewelry, the chief buying market in the United States, for example, is New York City, while machinery and equipment would be sold either to dealers in such products or to producers who have use for them.

Agents and Distributors. Many foreign companies are represented in the home market by agents or distributors, whose function is to obtain orders for and to sell foreign merchandise. These marketing channels will be treated in some detail in the next chapter. They are mentioned here because the literature in international marketing invariably deals with only foreign agents for United States companies. Since this text is devoted to international marketing, it is appropriate to include agents and distributors of foreign companies as channels for international marketing located right here in the United States or in any other domestic market.

Many of the foreign products that find a market in the domestic home market are manufactured, and they are satisfactorily and effectively marketed by agents and distributors — home market representatives of foreign manufacturers. For example, one such representative at one time had the entire United States market for the imported liquors that he handled. An Italian manufacturer of business machines (Olivetti)[1] exports small- to medium-sized calculating machines to the United States market, while at the same time United States manufacturers of business machines are expanding their markets abroad. This apparent contradiction is explained by differences in the products, prices, service, or promotion by the companies.

Other agents or distributors have a portion of the United States market, such as is seen in the market here for imported automobiles.[2] (The United States is also a great exporter of motor vehicles.)

Agents and distributors are located all over the free world. They provide international marketing channels for all kinds of products, chiefly manufactured. The producer relies upon these agents and distributors to market his products in the area designated.

Branches. As will be described in more detail in Chapter 14, branches may be offices, branch houses, assembly plants, or factories. Just as United States companies have established these facilities abroad, foreign companies have established them in the American market. Indeed, if we were to go back to the time of World War I, we would find many more instances of foreign companies operating in this country than there are at present. Some of the branches that foreign companies established here have long since been acquired by United States investors. Chemical and machinery companies may be cited in this connection.

---

[1] Olivetti now owns Underwood Typewriter Company, an American manufacturer.

[2] One of these foreign producers (Fiat of Italy) ships its cars to the United States in its own converted 10,000-ton Liberty ship; it is now a 1,000-car ferry.

The United States branch of Rohm and Haas, a German company, is now owned and controlled by interests in the United States. SKF ball-bearings, Swedish owned, and certain textile companies, British owned, have also been acquired, at least to the extent of their United States facilities, by American owners.

Nevertheless, there are still some foreign companies operating branches in the United States that yet remain under foreign control. Did you smokers ever visit the Dunhill shop in Radio City, New York? or the famous Jansen (Danish) silver store on Fifth Avenue? or one of the French cosmetic and perfume establishments in this country? Did you ever hear of Lux soap? That is a product of the British Unilever combine. A famous Czech shoe manufacturer — Bata — readjusted to the drastic changes induced by World War II and now has headquarters in Canada and in Switzerland. The company has its factories in the United States and the shoes are distributed under the name of Bata and the brand names of retailers.

Just as in the case of foreign branches of United States companies, these branches are established in the United States market to supply that market. It is not likely that a foreign company could profitably set up a factory in the United States for purposes of exporting from this country; the cost factors would probably forbid such an operation. Therefore, the production of these items or the distribution of the foreign products that have been imported by the overseas company are for the purpose of meeting requirements of the domestic United States market.

Licensees. Foreign manufacturers also license United States manufacturers to produce their lines of merchandise in this country for domestic consumption. This is one of the subjects that has created so much interest in United States international marketing circles. In this case, however, the interest is in licensing foreign companies to produce United States products for sale abroad.[3]

There are many instances of licensing of United States manufacturers by foreign manufacturers for the production of foreign-designed merchandise that will be offered for sale in the American market. Some of these arrangements have been based upon patents, as in the case of petroleum, rubber, and chemical industries. Other licenses have been granted in machinery and equipment lines. The point is that licensing

---

[3]The subject of licensing for foreign operations is treated in detail in Chapter 16.

works both ways — American companies license foreign companies and vice versa.

Resident Buyers in the Home Market (United States)

International marketing is conducted through resident buyers in the home market that represent either private or governmental interests abroad. Such foreign-situated interests may be mines, plantations, or utilities that are owned by Americans as well as by foreigners.

Large operators abroad, whether American or foreign, frequently have a resident buyer or an office in the United States. This buyer (or office) will purchase supplies and equipment from American manufacturers (or their export organizations). For example, an American contractor is engaged by a foreign municipality to construct a sewerage system. The contractor will be in the market for such equipment as he will need from the United States.

One of the problems mentioned in Chapter 8 referred to that of purchases made in the United States for export shipment. In light of the extensive operations in foreign countries, many of them conducted by American companies, it is evident that a sizable share of the exports from the United States arises from orders placed in this country by firms operating abroad. A petroleum company, a mining company, a plantation company, and a manufacturing company, with headquarters in the United States, will place orders for much of their equipment, at least such as is purchased in the United States, through the headquarters organization in this country.

In the past, allied governments have established purchasing missions whose function was to undertake all war and other necessary purchases abroad. After World War II, moreover, many of these missions continued to function, representing foreign governments in this country in connection with Economic Cooperation Administration (ECA) procurement. While ECA business generally was conducted through private trading channels both in this and beneficiary countries, certain products, such as food, fuel, and fertilizer, were frequently purchased by these missions. Foreign countries whose governments are committed to state-trading also conduct the bulk of their trade with other countries through purchasing and sales missions located in this country. For example, the Soviet Union purchases most of its American products and sells some Soviet products in this market through Amtorg Trading Corporation — a New York corporation.

Home Market (American) International Marketing Middlemen[4]

These middlemen are among the direct successors of nineteenth century merchant shippers. In the early days of sailing vessels, the merchant owned and operated his own boats for conducting his overseas business. Selling and buying were part and parcel with the shipping business; a supercargo on board ship took charge of the buying and selling. With the development of steam navigation and the consequent increase in cost of an ocean-going vessel, some of the merchant shippers went into the common carrier shipping business and others engaged in merchandising, while a few continued in both. The early commission houses had their origin in this setting.

Home market international marketing middlemen are now generally divided functionally into the following categories:

1. Export and/or import commission houses.
2. Export and/or import merchants.
3. Manufacturer's export agents.
4. Export and import brokers.
5. Export houses or trading firms.

For actual business firms, there may be no clear line of demarcation between these various types, but each type represents a distinctive function that must be understood in an analysis of home market international marketing middlemen.

According to the interests they represent and the mode of compensation, home market international marketing middlemen may be distinguished functionally in the following manner:

1. The commission house acts in the interests of the buyer, receiving a purchasing commission from the buyer.

2. The merchant acts in his own interests, depending upon a profit.

3. The manufacturer's export agent acts in the interests of producers or manufacturers, receiving a sales commission from these principals.

---

[4]A unique attempt to evaluate the importance of middlemen in world trade was made by Robert M. Lichtenberg. He used data for 1952 and identified middlemen as employed when foreign trade statistics indicated trade between supplying and consuming countries and *handled by a trader in a third country.* His study revealed that middlemen in a world trade sense are located primarily in a few industrial nations of Western Europe, in the United States, and in outlying entrepôts as Hong Kong. These middlemen are found to be primarily active in the trade in such products as fuels, rubber, minerals, sugar, tobacco, and fodder. See Robert M. Lichtenberg, *The Role of Middleman Transactions in World Trade* (Occasional Paper No. 64 [New York: National Bureau of Economic Research, 1959]).

4. Brokers may represent either buyer or seller and usually trade in staple articles that are often sold in organized commodity markets. Brokers receive a commission from the party they represent.

5. Export houses or trading firms may engage in both export and import business and may perform many, or all, of the functions of the middlemen listed above.

Export and/or Import Commission Houses. An export commission house places orders with home market manufacturers for the account of foreign buyers, while the import commission house places orders with foreign producers for the account of home market buyers.

Export Commission Houses. The export commission house is the resident representative in the United States of foreign buyers. It receives orders or "indents"[5] from these buyers and acts as purchasing agent for them in the United States. In case standard goods are ordered, the commission house merely places the order with the designated manufacturer and attends to all details of exporting. In many instances, however, a foreign buyer designates in a general way the merchandise he wants and stipulates the price he is willing to pay. It then becomes the duty of the commission house to "shop around."

It is not to be inferred that a commission house sits idly by and waits for business to come in. On the contrary, foreign agencies and branches are often established for the purpose of developing new business as well as for holding established customers. The interests of the buyer are protected throughout, and a buying commission is commonly charged for this service.

The export commission house was a pioneer in establishing foreign trade, and it is estimated that these concerns handled the bulk of United States exports about the middle of the nineteenth century. With a decline in the share of foreign trade conducted by American middlemen, the commission house, as such, has largely disappeared; but the function still remains.

Import Commission Houses. The import commission house is the resident representative in the United States for *American* buyers. For ex-

---

[5]Technically, *indents* are offers to purchase at prices and under other conditions stipulated by the prospective purchaser. In practice (trans-Pacific trades), indents are often synonymous with orders.

ample, an American firm that is not engaged in international marketing desires to obtain a particular kind of material or piece of equipment abroad, say, Brazilian overshoes, Chilean wine, or African masks. For this purpose, the American firm can make arrangements with an import commission house with offices in the United States and the commission house will undertake to purchase the product or products required. Likewise, a business firm in another country, for example, Peru, may wish to purchase a product from the United States, but does not know from whom to purchase it, and the product is not available in Peru. The import commission house in Peru will take care of the purchase for him. Raw and semimanufactured materials, however, are so important in the import trade of the United States and transactions in these lines are so large in the aggregate that specialized brokers are commonly used.

Sometimes import commission houses receive consignments from foreign producers by whom they are paid a selling commission. In this case, they are more akin to foreign agents or brokers. In the department store trade, buying agents sometimes place orders abroad for a group of stores, receiving a commission for so doing. They maintain showrooms for the display of samples and take care of the interests of their clients.

Quite often, a commission house combines exporting and importing. Chart 9-1 shows the organization of an old-line commission house, while

Chart 9-1

ORGANIZATION OF AN OLD-LINE COMMISSION HOUSE

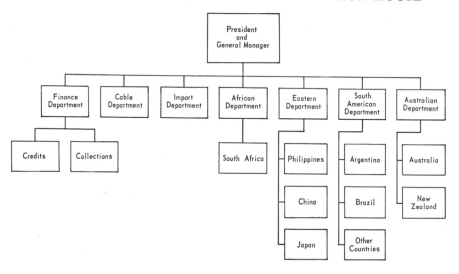

Chart 9-2

ORGANIZATION OF A LARGE EXPORT AND IMPORT COMMISSION HOUSE

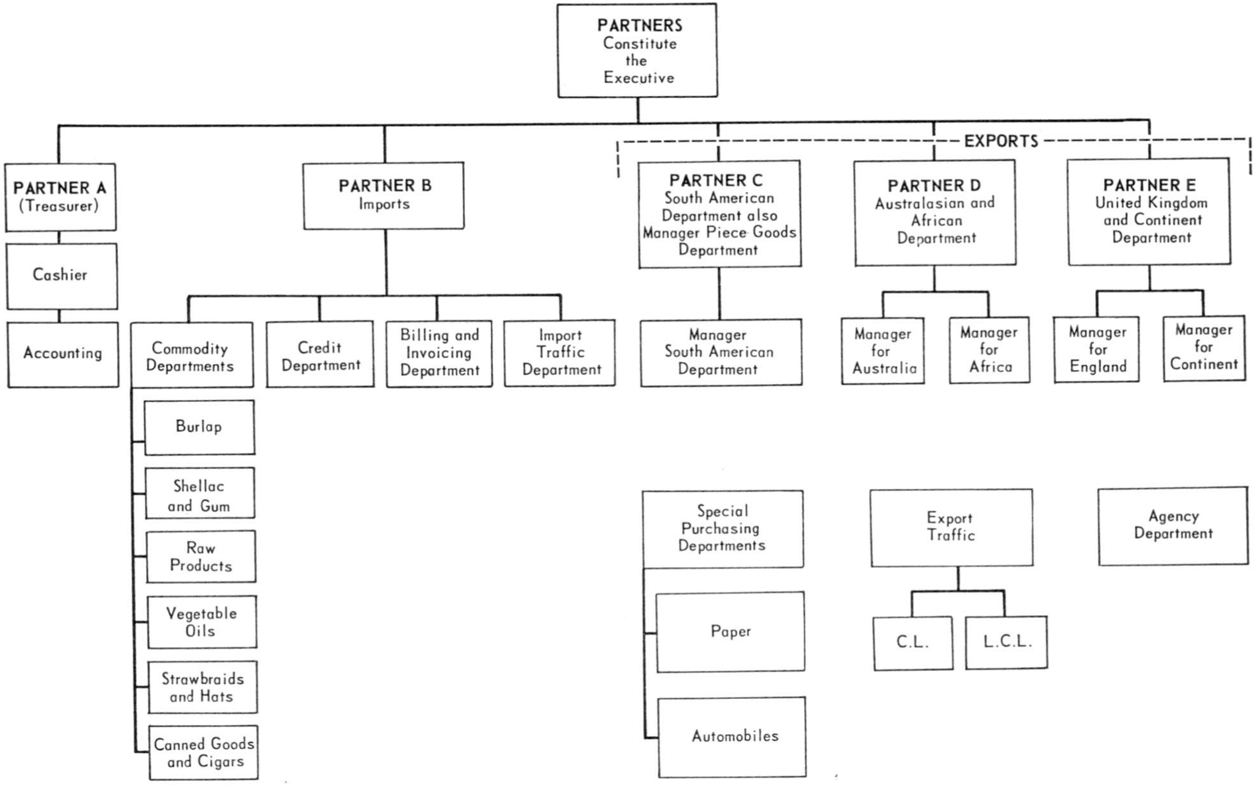

171

Chart 9-2 outlines the more complex forms that this type of international marketing agency may represent.

Export and/or Import Merchants. The merchant buys outright for his own account and sells, if possible, at a profit. The merchandise that is exported is usually selected by the merchant, although at times it may be ordered in advance by a buyer. The merchant sells goods, as distinguished from the commission house that essentially performs a buying function. Ordinarily, stocks of merchandise are maintained at home or abroad in order that prompt deliveries may be made.

Except in the case of companies that have developed a high degree of commodity specialization, it has become increasingly hazardous to carry stocks of merchandise to fill anticipated demands in international commerce. Competition, price changes, tariff revisions, and foreign exchange and import restrictions have combined to make this practice highly speculative.

Import merchants are particularly important in certain American import trades; they are found in many lines, but especially in food products, in certain raw materials such as wool and silk, and in specialty manufactures such as linens, chinaware, gloves, toys, and laces.

As in the case of the commission house, merchant trading, particularly from the export standpoint, exists today mainly as a function and has in many instances been merged with the commission and export agency operation, as well as with manufacturing. The import merchant, however, continues to operate as a distinct type of import agency, either exclusively as an importer or as a department store or specialty line.

Manufacturer's Export Agents. The manufacturer's export agent enters into contract with a manufacturer whereby he undertakes to sell the manufacturer's merchandise in foreign countries.[6] For this service, a sales commission is paid, as distinguished from a buying commission or a profit, which is the basis of compensation for the commission house and the merchant respectively.

A typical sales arrangement indicates the terms of the relationship established between the manufacturer and the export agent. The agent acts as the export department of the manufacturer, carrying on corre-

---

[6]This agent may be a manufacturer of complementary or even competitive lines, who has a complete export organization for his own line of merchandise, or he may be a combination export manager. See page 153 of the preceding chapter.

Chart 9-3

ORGANIZATION OF A MANUFACTURER'S EXPORT AGENT

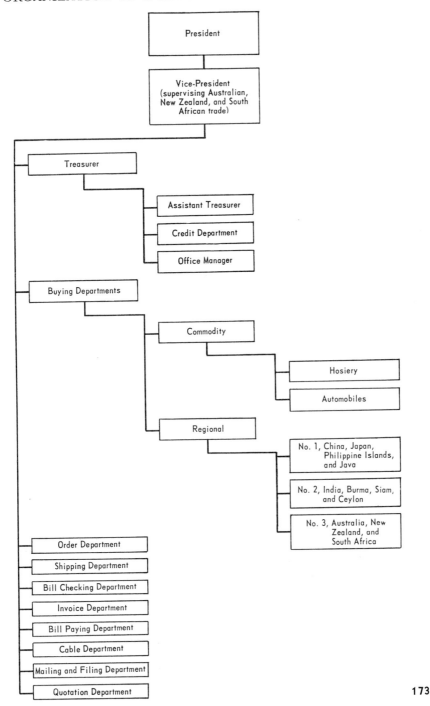

173

spondence and sales as the export division of the manufacturer. Although the manufacturer's export agent undertakes to develop new foreign business, he may, but usually does not, assume foreign credit risks.

When export orders are received, the merchandise is shipped by the manufacturer, and generally consigned to the export agent. The manufacturer's bills are checked. Delivery of the merchandise is handled by foreign branches or agencies of the manufacturer's export agent, unless direct shipment to the customer is made. At times, a special sales force may also be employed by the foreign branch of the export agent to push certain articles.

To conduct such a business as this, both commodity and regional divisions may be necessary. A number of manufacturers' lines will be handled, usually falling into related lines; competitive lines are not ordinarily handled.[7]

Chart 9-3 on page 173 depicts the organization of a manufacturer's export agent, showing the regional, commodity, and functional divisions. The commodity units pertain to purchasing only. The functional units perform for all of the regional units.

Export and Import Brokers. *Brokers,* by definition, bring buyers and sellers together. The term broker is often applied in a broad manner, however, and so-called brokerage concerns may conduct business in several other ways. They are more often to be found in the trade of staple articles, many of which are bought and sold on organized markets or exchanges. Examples are grain, cotton, wool, sugar, and coffee. Moreover, merchandise that is consigned to a market, United States or foreign, is frequently disposed of through brokers. This particular business is exceptionally important in American import trade.

Export Houses. *Export (trading) house* is a term that today is more accurately descriptive of many international marketing middlemen than are any of the separate terms already mentioned, except brokers and import merchants. Frequently an export house is loosely referred to as a commission house, but this terminology is misleading because an export house does not operate entirely on a commission basis. In the sense dis-

---

[7]An interesting example of a case in which a large manufacturer, with its own plants and connections all over the world, utilizes the services of a manufacturer's export agent is evident from the following news report: "Appointment of Transaero, Inc. (Mineola, N.Y.) as its authorized export representative has been announced by the General Electric Co.'s Lamp Division. Transaero will handle G.E.'s complete line of aircraft lamps." Quoted from "Business Briefs" in *Export Trade* (August 19, 1963), p. 17.

cussed here, moreover, *export* refers to international trade as a whole rather than to the outward movement of merchandise from a given country. Many so-called export houses engage also in the import trade.

With the exception of brokers and import merchants, there is practically no independent existence of individual types of American international marketing middlemen. A concern beginning as a commission house soon discovers that certain products of home manufacture offer lucrative export sales possibilities, and it might then add a merchant business. With its established foreign connections, it may then be attracted by an export sales agency proposition of some manufacturer. Or the concern may have started as a manufacturer's export agent and then have been induced to conduct a commission business on casual orders placed by regular customers or by new concerns. This business is often unattractive; but if sales connections are to be developed, it is necessary to accommodate customers to the greatest possible extent.

The addition of import business may come about as naturally as do the other functions; or the house may have started as an importer and added the export business later. Through branches and agencies located abroad, the house becomes generally interested in certain foreign countries. A market may be noted in a given country, e.g., the United States, for certain products available abroad and, with no appreciable increase in overhead, import lines are added.

With export and import trade thus developed between the United States and certain foreign countries, further ramifications may follow. One of America's largest foreign trading houses owns and operates sugar estates, cotton mills, woolen mills, nitrate plants, and its own port facilities at some of the ports where it does business. This concern owns its own bank, owns and operates a line of steamships, and operates an airline in South America. Such a house is known as an export house since it is impossible to define correctly its activities with any of the standard functional terms. It is all of these and more. The term export (trading) house, therefore, has come into being as a professional mercantile concern engaged in international business.

Many more export houses or trading firms are to be found headquartered in European countries and in Japan. They have branches in areas where they do business abroad and this includes the United States. They have been in the international trading business for as long as a century or more. One might be inclined to imagine that they are the successors of the fifteenth and sixteenth century London East India Company, Hudson's Bay Company, Dutch East India Company, etc.

While some of them do business with the United States and have offices there, they generally operate in what is called today the developing markets. These are in Asia, Latin America, and Africa. Many of the British houses specialize even today in trade with the Commonwealth countries.

The newly-independent countries of Africa south of the Sahara provide a good example. Practically all of the foreign business of these countries is with industrial countries, and trading firms headquartered in these countries carry on the business. If an American exporter wishes to sell a product to one of these countries, he is advised to go to Europe, because orders for foreign merchandise imported to these countries must be approved by the head offices in Europe — London, Amsterdam, Brussels, Hamburg, etc. If a direct contact is made in Africa, the American exporter is advised to send a copy of all correspondence to the head office in Europe of the African company.

The greatest of these firms is United Africa Company (UAC) which is part of the Unilever interests. UAC operates wholesale and some retail stores all over west Africa. Palm oil comes from Unilever's plantations in Nigeria and elsewhere; we know the results in the United States as Palmolive soap.

Japan is the best example of a country where trading houses dominate the international business of the country. The factories, banks, and trading houses in Japan are *all* tied together, and the trading houses conduct most of the international business of the country. There are many of these firms in Japan, the most outstanding being Mitsui and Company, the largest trading house in the world.

Organization and Operation. Most of the export houses or trading firms operating today were originally organized on a partnership basis, even though a private corporation may be formed to separate the several financial interests. Most of the general business departments are likewise to be found. There is a financial department that may also handle credits, an accounting department, a billing and invoicing department, and a cables, mail, and shipping or traffic department. Some companies do not have a central shipping department, each commodity or regional division performing its own forwarding. When imports are heavy, a customs department may be established. An agency department may be maintained to look into new export agency possibilities.

Many export houses or trading firms have also established foreign branches, agencies, or affiliated companies in the territories where they have their principal interests.

Commodity and Regional Specialization. Export and import houses generally tend to specialize according to commodities and/or regions. Many have established special export commodity departments for textiles, hardware, foodstuffs, automotive products, and machinery; and import specialization knows no limit.

If the export house leans toward commission business, the work of the department is confined largely to buying. For import merchant business, the manager of each commodity department maintains contact abroad and disposes of imported products. As a manufacturer's export agent affiliated by contract with certain manufacturers, the work of the commodity divisions of the export house is of a sales character.

Miscellaneous Services. Financing is an important element in the work of export or trading firms. These houses are generally prepared to pay cash when they buy, and they extend whatever credits may be necessary when they sell. In the import trade, advances may be made to foreign producers of commodities that are shipped to the home market.

In the export trade, practically all export houses pay cash against shipping documents for merchandise purchased from manufacturers, and then extend credit to their foreign customers. When acting as a manufacturer's export agent, however, the middleman usually receives credit from the manufacturer.

Export houses often perform their own freight fowarding service. The export house is in a position to combine several smaller shipments and thereby economize on ocean freight charges.[8] This service is particularly attractive to a foreign buyer who has submitted an order or indent covering a group of miscellaneous articles to be obtained from different sources of supply.

With regard to import trade, users of foreign products, importing directly, may sometimes find themselves without the needed merchandise when market conditions become such as to make it unprofitable or impossible for the foreign exporter to make shipment. There may also be difficult problems of quality, packing, financing, and insuring. These difficulties, however, can be shifted to a third party, the import middleman or trading firm, when the users of foreign products make their purchases through him.

As stated above, an export house or trading firm may maintain its own steamship line and operate an airline overseas. A few export houses have acquired an interest in, or own outright, some banking concern.

---

[8]By avoiding payment of minimum bill of lading charges.

This affords an added facility for handling international financial transactions, for dealing in foreign exchange, and even for acting as a fiscal agent for foreign governments.

The Future of International Marketing Middlemen

The commission house, whether a separate firm or a function, will continue to occupy an important position for some traders. There are and probably will continue to be importers in foreign countries who will depend on the commission house to procure needed merchandise from other countries. Many small importers are financially, as well as technically, unable to conduct their own importing. Moreover, there are larger foreign dealers, usually in commercial districts of secondary importance, who are required to handle a wide range of merchandise and who experience a slow turnover. These can obtain valuable service from a commission house; services in connection with shipping and financing may be sufficient to commend them to such dealers.

Too, there will always be many small as well as irregular exporters. In both cases, there is no desire to build up direct foreign sales connections, and the middleman is an alternative. If conditions should change and these concerns should develop into strong exporters, they may outgrow the middleman, but other small manufacturers will undoubtedly take their place.

When an experienced export house or trading firm acts as a manufacturer's export agent, there is ample evidence of its success. Many large American manufacturers who possess their own export sales channels find a useful place for the export house. An exporter may be unable to maintain his own sales connections in every market of the world. Many out-of-the-way places will not support an agent, a distributor, or a branch. It is noteworthy that in some parts of the world where credit is an unknown factor and where the market itself is extremely difficult, export houses are frequently relied upon.

Staple products in both export and import trade have long benefited from the specialized attention of middlemen. Exports of grains, cotton, and other farm products have passed through the hands of brokers, merchants, and commission firms; and imports of numerous crude materials and foodstuffs that loom so large in the import trade of the United States have similarly been handled by these middlemen. The continuance of trade in these types of products in the future will doubtless find these middlemen functioning the same as they have in the past.

Summary

1. There are many marketing channels located in the home market, e.g. the United States, by means of which international marketing can be conducted.
2. Importers may purchase through sales facilities established in the home country by foreign firms — salesmen, agents and distributors, branches, and licensees.
3. Exporters may obtain sales contracts with representatives of private or government purchasers located in the home market.
4. One type of international marketing facility found in the home market specializes in this business for the benefit of its clients and customers. It generally produces nothing for sale. This agency is the old-line export and import commission house, which technically is a purchasing representative for a foreign buyer.
5. The export and/or import merchant buys and sells on his own account.
6. The manufacturer's export agent assumes contractual obligations to represent a manufacturer in export transactions.
7. The broker is a commodity specialist functioning usually in raw material trades, both export and import, and operating on a commission basis.
8. Although the agencies described above are considered as separately existing organizations, some large firms perform two or more of these types of services. Such firms may be called export houses.
9. There is both regional and commodity specialization in the operation of international marketing firms.

QUESTIONS

1. Cite and describe examples of foreign firms' connections in the United States. In what ways do their functions differ?
2. Name one product that is sold in the United States and that is made in this country by a foreign company.
3. Describe the operations of purchasing and sales missions.
4. Define each of the following middlemen:
    (a) Export commission house.
    (b) Import merchant.
    (c) Manufacturer's export agent.
    (d) Export broker.
5. Why would a plantation operator in Africa purchase supplies from the United States through an export commission house?
6. Trace an export order from its inception to its shipment through a manufacturer's export agent.
7. Explain this statement: "With the exception of brokers and import merchants, there is practically no independent existence of individual types of American international marketing middlemen."

8. Describe the evolution of the export house to the present time, indicating the various ramifications of its operation.
9. Describe briefly the organization and operation of export houses.
10. What kinds of financial services do export houses commonly offer to their clientele?
11. Debate the following statement: "In view of the increase in direct business and the consequent reduction in the position of certain middlemen, the export middleman is headed for oblivion."

PROBLEMS

1. Assume that you are employed by a British manufacturer of bicycles who has never sold his product in the United States. Your assignment is to study the United States market for these bicycles. All reasonable assumptions should be made, for example, that the bicycles are competitively priced, well styled, etc. Prepare a report of the potential market for the British-made bicycles, and incorporate within the report your recommendations as to which marketing channel(s) should be utilized by this manufacturer.
2. If it is possible for you to do so, visit the office of an export or an import broker (grain, cotton, coffee, sugar, etc.). Write a report on the manner in which this business is conducted as you observe it.
3. A missionary group in Africa orders all of its supplies from an export commission house. In so doing, they know that they are charged a buying commission of about 5 percent. Nevertheless, the group has used this commission house since before World War I. Why is the missionary group justified in purchasing in this manner? Explain.
4. Many foreign governments maintain buying missions in the United States and some of them maintain more than one such office. From the nearest foreign consular office or United States Bureau of International Commerce office — or even from the foreign country embassy in Washington, D.C. — obtain the name and address of such a buying office or offices. If possible, make a personal visit to the office of the buying mission; but if that is not possible, address a letter to the head of the mission inquiring as to exactly how the operation is conducted. Ask for figures on the nature and value of the United States products purchased, and the interests in the foreign country on whose behalf the purchases are made. Prepare a written report on the results of your study.
5. From your library obtain a copy of the National Planning Association report entitled "Casa Grace." This is a study of the operations of one of the most important so-called export houses in business today. Digest the study and prepare a written report on it.
6. The importation of foreign passenger automobiles has attracted wide attention in recent years. Doubtless, one or more of the various makes of foreign

cars is offered for sale in your community or in one that is close by. Visit the place of business of this foreign car dealer and discuss with him the market in the United States for these cars and the terms and conditions under which he operates (whether upon direct appointment by the foreign manufacturer or upon appointment by a distributor in a large distribution center). Gather all of the pertinent information that you can on the way in which the business is established and conducted and prepare a written report of your findings.

COLLATERAL READINGS

Collins, V. D. *World Marketing*. Philadelphia: J. B. Lippincott Company, 1935. Chapter 6.

Dartnell International Trade Handbook, The. Chicago: The Dartnell Corporation, 1963. Part I, Chapter 2.

de Haas, J. A. *The Practice of Foreign Trade*. New York: McGraw-Hill Book Company, Inc., 1935. Chapter 11.

Heck, Harold J. *Foreign Commerce*. New York: McGraw-Hill Book Company, Inc., 1953. Chapter 5.

Horn, Paul V. *International Trade Principles and Practices*, Third Edition. New York: Prentice-Hall, Inc., 1951. Chapter 25.

MacDonald, Philip. *Practical Exporting*. New York: Ronald Press Company, 1949. Chapter 2.

Pratt, E. E. *Foreign Trade Handbook*, Third Edition. Chicago: The Dartnell Corporation, 1952. Part I, Section 4.

——————————. *Modern International Commerce*. New York: Allyn and Bacon, Inc., 1956. Chapters 2 and 13.

Roorbach, G. B. *Import Purchasing: Principles and Problems*. Chicago and New York: A. W. Shaw Company, 1927. Chapters 3, 4, 9, and 10.

——————————. *Problems in Foreign Trade*. New York: McGraw-Hill Book Company, Inc., 1933, Part II.

Tosdal, H. R. *Problems in Export Sales Management*. New York: McGraw-Hill Book Company, Inc., 1922. Chapters 2 and 5.

Wyman, Walter F. *Export Merchandising*. New York: McGraw-Hill Book Company, Inc., 1922. Chapters 9 and 17.

CHAPTER 10

PRODUCERS AND COMMERCIAL FIRMS ABROAD

From the management standpoint, we now treat channels of international marketing that are dealt with at long range. In the previous chapter, the international business was handled by various types of trading firms located in the home (exporting or importing) country. None of the problems of international trading were encountered; they were all assumed by the trading firms.

Now, the management must deal with the international trading problems itself. It must locate its customers or representatives; determine their reliability; negotiate contracts for sale or purchase; pack and ship; deal in international payments; deal with governments, etc. These problems are sufficient to indicate the necessity for assigning this work to employees capable of solving such problems.

While the international business of many, if not most, of the developing countries is carried on by trading firms and facilities foreign to these countries, the reverse is generally true of the industrial countries; they conduct their own international business through their own or contracted facilities. For example, the bulk of United States international marketing is conducted through channels located and operated abroad rather than through channels located in this country. Some of these channels are under the control of American exporters, importers, manufacturers, mining concerns, etc.; others are entirely independent; still others represent joint control between American and foreign interests.

Producers and commercial firms abroad comprise those listed below. A description of these channels will be taken up in this and succeeding chapters. The present chapter deals with independent producers and independent commercial firms.

1. Independent producers and independent commercial firms:
   a. Producers:
      (1) Licensees.
      (2) Contract manufacturing.
   b. Import and export houses.
   c. Wholesalers and retailers.
   d. Brokers.
   e. Factors.
   f. Resident salesmen and buyers.
   g. Lessees.
   h. Agents.
   i. Distributors.
   j. Commercial gatherings.
2. Outlets and contacts controlled by exporting and importing firms:
   a. Traveling export salesmen and import buyers.
   b. Raw material production facilities — mines, plantations, etc.
   c. Mail order.
   d. Foreign operations:
      (1) Branches — offices, houses, warehouses.
      (2) Assembly branches.
      (3) Manufacturing branches.
3. Facilitating channels and services:
   a. Advertising and trade promotion.
   b. Correspondence.
   c. Communications — radio, cable, telephone.

Independent Producers

Producers located in foreign countries may be factories, mines, or plantations; and they may be foreign-owned, United States-owned, or jointly owned. For example, a foreign automobile manufacturer is represented in the United States by an American distributor; a mine located abroad sells ore to American importing wholesalers; and a cacao plantation abroad sells its crop to a British import merchant with a branch office operating in the United States, to which the cacao is shipped for sale in the United States.

A considerable volume of import business of the United States consists of ore and agricultural products, and a portion of that trade moves through various channels. Foreign manufacturers, however, handle a part of their sales to this country through American commercial firms (distributors and agents).

American exports move directly to producers in foreign countries when orders for their supplies and equipment come directly from these producers abroad. A tea estate in Ceylon, for example, may purchase certain kinds of iron pipe through an American manufacturer's export department, conducting negotiations through such facilitating channels and services as correspondence, cable, and possibly telephone. A factory in Mexico may purchase directly from a St. Louis manufacturer certain parts required in manufacturing its products.

Licensees. Producers also enter into licensing agreements with foreign manufacturers, whereby the producer uses the processes, patents, trademarks, designs, or other know-how of the foreign manufacturer. While generally considered to be a type of foreign operation akin to foreign branches, the producers under license are not, as is the case of a foreign branch, under the control of the foreign manufacturer. Licensing has received so much attention in the international business field that a separate chapter is devoted to that subject.[1]

Contract Manufacturing. A manufacturing company engaged in international marketing may decide to market its products in foreign markets, and to contract for the manufacture of those products by a competent manufacturer established in such markets.

This plan of operation is *not* a branch; it is *not* a licensing agreement; it is a *contract manufacturing* operation. For example, let us assume that American Publishing Company produces and sells its own books in the United States. The British Publishing Company is asked to print, publish, and distribute a British edition of a book that American Publishing has brought out in America and for which the British copyright has been obtained. The books are thus produced and distributed by the British Publishing Company through its own sales outlets in the British Isles — or elsewhere, if the agreement so provides.

Under this arrangement, American Publishing makes no investment, provides no technical assistance, and commits itself to nothing as to future developments. British Publishing has a contract to manufacture a book according to the specifications established by American Publishing.

---

[1]See Chapter 16.

The contract will probably call upon American Publishing to pay the cost of publication and allot a given share of profits to British Publishing.

A great majority of manufactured exports, however, are handled through sales channels abroad, sometimes branch offices and houses, but more often through commercial firms.

Independent Commercial Firms

Every country, foreign or domestic, has a number of and generally a variety of commercial firms that are free to purchase or to represent the lines of any company. These same firms may become parties to sales, distributor, or agency contracts, but they are considered under the heading of "independent" because they are free to act as they choose.

Import and Export Houses. Import houses form an important contact point in foreign markets. Generally import houses handle a wide variety of products. They are found in all countries, and sometimes are large firms, often with branch offices and warehouses in various important distribution centers. They send out a corps of salesmen; advertise, display, and service their products; take care of local hauling and shipping problems; extend credit; and perform many other necessary distributive functions.

Exporters and export houses are often general export and import concerns, while in other instances they specialize in one commodity. In the coffee trade of Brazil, for example, the coffee often passes from planters through commissarios to export merchants who sell to United States import merchants. Rubber from the eastern plantations, gathered at Singapore, may reach the United States through general export and import houses.

Wholesalers and Retailers. Wholesalers are integral parts of the distribution systems of most countries. The larger ones often import goods direct instead of depending upon import houses. Smaller wholesalers, especially those located at secondary interior distributive centers, may do no importing themselves but may purchase foreign goods from other importers or wholesalers. Insofar as the wholesalers perform the exporting and importing functions, they differ only in small degree from export and import houses.

Wholesale-retail concerns conduct both a wholesale and a retail business. They are more important in many foreign markets, for example, Latin American countries, than in the United States. Such firms are usually located in the larger cities and handle a wide variety of products. In his own city the owner may operate retail stores of his own and sell to such other retailers there as well. He also sends salesmen to outlying points where they visit retail dealers.

Retailers of some kind or other are numerous in all countries, being indispensable in the distribution of personal consumption goods. There is infinite variation in the types of retailers. In western Europe the variation is much the same as in the United States, except that consumer cooperative stores are more important there and chain and mail-order stores less important. The same is true of metropolitan centers in South America and even, to some extent, in the Far East, except that the consumer cooperatives are of negligible importance. Flashy specialty shops, palatial department stores, chains in less numbers, general stores, supermarkets, small shops, vendors, peddlers — all are present. The outlying districts are served by smaller, often poorly equipped retailers who know little or nothing of modern merchandising methods. But even here there is considerable variety — the Western European rural districts offering many reliable and efficient stores in contrast with the female traders' shacks of the West Coast of Africa, and the dingy small huts of South American agricultural and mining districts.

Only in comparatively few instances does international trade flow at the retail level and then almost always with the metropolitan and larger urban retailers. Department stores and large consumer cooperatives, by virtue of the size of their purchases, will endeavor to make direct contact with foreign exporters in order to gain every possible buying economy. Specialty and other unit retailers in larger cities must be solicited by salesmen, by advertising, by catalog, by letter, etc.

Large individual and institutional buyers sometimes purchase foreign products directly from producers or middlemen. For example, a hospital may import certain equipment directly from foreign manufacturers or supply houses.

In considering these clearly defined units in the distribution chain abroad, it should be borne in mind that such precision is often difficult to find in practice. As the volume of business declines, the functions begin to telescope, and the import and export house may also do the wholesaling. It will be noted, moreover, that the jobber is not mentioned among these wholesale channels. As a distinctive entity the jobber is

The Procter & Gamble Company

Retail store in London, England. Fairy Snow is formulated by an American firm especially for the British market; local water conditions and washing methods are given consideration in its manufacture.

rarely found in foreign countries except where the volume in one line is great, and even then the jobbing function, in many instances, would probably be performed by the import or export house or by the wholesaler. Finally, different channels may be used for the same product as determined by factors affecting conditions in the various markets.

Brokers. Brokers are important distributive agencies for many commodities in numerous markets, especially where goods are sold on exchanges or at auctions. The European grain exchanges offer facilities for trading in American as well as in other grains. American copper is bought and sold on the floor of the London Metal Exchange; likewise, raw cotton of American growth, in the pits of the Liverpool Cotton Exchange. Such exchanges ordinarily provide for future as well as spot trading. There are also many brokers who act as intermediaries between exporters and their customers or between a local foreign house and its customers. They are paid brokerage fees of various amounts, depending upon the services rendered.

Brokers are, in many instances, associated with the operation of auctions. While auctions are of only minor importance in distributing American products abroad, they are exceedingly important for disposing of many staple exports of all countries. Auctions are particularly prominent in the trade of raw products. Some auctions are held at primary collecting points contiguous to foreign producing areas, but most of them are located at European centers that for years have occupied a position of prime importance in the grading, sorting, and selling of the products of their colonial possessions. The United Kingdom and Holland are particularly prominent in this respect.

Import auctions for goods entering the American import trade are the tea auctions at Calcutta and Colombo (in the countries of production) and in London (in the marketing country). Plantation rubber is often sold at auctions situated in Singapore and Colombo. Australian wool may be auctioned in Sydney or in Liverpool and London.

Although there is a general tendency toward the location of these markets in the areas of production, the established European centers will probably continue to be of some importance. By collecting the wool, spices, and tea from all producing centers and assembling them in the European market, a greater variety of grades is displayed and standardization of grades is possible. These features are attractive to buyers. Moreover, the superior merchandising, shipping, and financing facilities available at the older European markets comprise a competitive advantage of considerable importance not likely to be entirely overcome for a long time.

Factors. *Factors*, sometimes known as *del credere agents*, are middlemen whose functions have always included the financing of transactions. In the United States, factors are essentially financial institutions, equipped to buy accounts receivables from manufacturers obliged to sell on credit. They are active in the textile industry, and they have also operated in the leather and lumber export trade with Europe. Their role is essentially to carry the financing burden in lines in which a large number of manufacturers, from small to large, are to be found. Usually, they not only advance funds, if needed, to manufacturers, but also to customers of the manufacturer whose credit standing factors are known to be particularly well informed.

In the United States, from the standpoint of import trade, factoring is important, especially for European manufacturers who do not know the American market well. They are not informed on financing laws of the United States and turn to factors.

Another type of broker is typified by the *Oriental comprador* who was found only in the distribution systems of the Far East, particularly China. Language difficulties, the impossibility of foreigners obtaining reliable credit data, and the lack of long-established world trading houses compelled even the foreign (owned and staffed by Britons, Germans, etc.) import houses, let alone the exporters, to use the native comprador. The comprador assumed the burden of getting dealers to handle products and partially guaranteed their credit. In the same way he collected national goods for export.

Resident Salesmen and Buyers. *Resident salesmen* are individuals who have agreements with manufacturers whereby they are to sell their products, the goods to be shipped directly from the manufacturer to the buyer and billed to the latter by the manufacturer. *Resident buyers* are engaged by importers to place orders for them in the foreign market. They may be entrusted with selecting such merchandise as they might locate and which appears to them to offer a good opportunity for profit on the part of the principal.

Lessees. In some lines, products are not sold to customers but are leased, and in some companies, the customer has a choice to buy or to rent the product. In the case of renting or leasing, title to the product remains with the exporting firm or manufacturer, and the lessee must return the product or have it available for return or exchange at the conclusion of the lease agreement. This method of marketing is to be found in the case of expensive business machines such as computer-calculators, etc.; sporting equipment as pin spotting machines for bowling alleys; some industrial machinery lines; automobiles; and other products.

Agents. *Agents* are commercial firms appointed to promote the sale of an exporter's product in some defined territory. An agent solicits orders for the products that he represents and sends these orders to the exporter (principal) whom he represents.[2] If accepted, the order is shipped directly to the buyer (not the agent) and payment is usually, but not always, made by the buyer directly to the exporter. For these services, the agent receives a commission on all sales in his territory.

In the import trade, foreign agents are sometimes appointed for the purpose of placing orders abroad for specified merchandise and of performing other functions in connection with buying. Agents, called *commissionaires*, are sometimes employed by importers of finished products. In this case, where selection is paramount, order placing is restricted generally to repeat orders. They also provide market data, arrange itineraries and appointments for visiting buyers, and take care of shipments of merchandise. Buying agents usually operate on a commission basis, although sometimes they may operate on a salary and expense method.

Distributors. *Distributors* are also commercial firms appointed to promote the sale of an exporter's product in some defined territory. Operating as a distributor, a firm purchases samples and stocks of goods at list prices less discount. Samples are used for demonstration purposes and the stock is shipped out to customers. In addition, the distributor services the material or equipment that he handles, maintains a supply of repair parts, advertises, and conducts the business for the manufacturer under the terms of the agreement governing his operations. For example, an American machinery manufacturer has a representative in Mexico City who acts, under contract, as his distributor. He purchases the machinery from the manufacturer and resells it at a profit.

Commercial Gatherings. *Commercial gatherings* provide facilities through which sales or purchases may be made, either by means of a number of trading methods or by direct contact.

Foreign fairs, exhibits, and expositions[3] provide a means for exhibiting and/or buying and selling products foreign to the country, as well as domestically made products. These fairs are very important in Europe. The permanent exhibits are largely of purely advertising value, but fairs and expositions are used for buying and selling large aggregate quantities of foreign wares. The fair or exposition corporation provides only the space and primary facilities and does no trading on its own.

---

[2]This method of operation is often referred to as "indent" business.

[3]For additional discussion of this subject, see page 78 of Chapter 4.

Under a program designed in early 1955, the United States Government through the Department of Commerce is seeking to arouse greater interest in international trade fairs on the part of American businessmen. In addition, the program aims at telling "the story of our free enterprise system and to provide effective international trade promotion cooperation."[4]

As an identifying insignia for American exhibits at trade fairs abroad, the Statue of Liberty has been adopted. The Department of Commerce states that the advantages of international trade fairs to American importers include: (1) increasing business, (2) promoting markets, (3) testing buyer and consumer reaction, (4) aiding in consummation of dealerships and agencies, and (5) increasing investment opportunity. For American exporters, the trade fair is considered to be a major selling tool for developing foreign markets with a minimum of cost for the benefits obtained. To some of these trade fairs, the United States Government, through the Department of Commerce, sends so-called, "Trade Missions." These missions are composed of American businessmen knowledgeable in a given field. After a briefing session in Washington, D.C., the "Trade Mission" sets up headquarters at a trade fair abroad. Advice is offered to foreign businessmen, inquiries for United States products and investment opportunities are solicited, and travel in the general area of the fair is also conducted. This is part of the export expansion program of the United States Government.[5]

The several international trade fairs offer exhibitors certain inducements such as: (1) reduced railroad fares and freight rates, (2) storage and erection facilities, (3) translation and stenographic services, and (4) special import regulations for products to be exhibited.

Bazaars also fall in this group of commercial gatherings, and the very name breathes the atmosphere of the Orient. These are counterparts of the market place in European and American countries. A bazaar usually consists of a group of tiny retail shops nestled together in one locality. Each shop is usually owned and operated by the proprietor who squats on the doorstep within reach of the merchandise. Often the shops handling competing lines occupy the same section. In large population centers the bazaars are operated daily, while in smaller centers they are held at more widely separated periods of time, in which case they are considered to be more like fairs.

---

[4]From President Eisenhower's January 10, 1955, message to Congress.
[5]See Chapter 4. Note particularly the discussion of United States Trade Centers abroad.

Marketing Through Agents and Distributors

Most of the sales outlets discussed previously in this chapter are in a position to act as agent or distributor for a particular exporting firm. Before considering the technical and legal matters concerning these sales outlets, it would be well to discuss certain matters of definition.

While the terms "agent" and "distributor" are often used interchangeably, there is a valid distinction between them. An *agent* is one who acts on behalf of a principal within the expressed or implied authority of the agreement. A *distributor* is an independent customer. The agent does *not* purchase goods; he places orders; the title to such merchandise does not pass to the agent. The distributor *does* purchase goods, acquires title, and disposes of the merchandise to the best of his ability.

Types of Agents and Distributors. Agents and distributors may be classified in many ways and in considerable detail. Classed according to selling rights, they may be exclusive, semiexclusive, general, or lessee.

Exclusive. An exclusive agent or distributor is one who has the sole rights in all sales of goods in the territory covered by the agreement, thus assuring the agent his commissions and the distributor his discounts on all sales in the territory. Under such circumstances, even though the order for goods should come without the agent's mediation or effort, the agent would nevertheless receive a full or split commission on the order. Where the agency agreement permits, such a commission is paid an exclusive agent even on orders that are solicited directly in the agent's territory by the exporter.

There is one essential difference in the services given when exclusive representation is held. In this instance, agents are ready to exert extraordinary efforts to obtain orders for the sale of the goods, since they are assured that the returns thereon will all accrue to them. Hence, they frequently instruct their salesmen to stress the product. Distributors have established service departments, use more advertising, and are ready to carry larger and better assorted stocks. In short, the exporter can normally expect better sales and supplementary services from concerns holding exclusive rights than if such a monopoly were not granted.

An example of a clause dealing with this matter is this — "Our company considers your company our exclusive distributor for the territory and products mentioned. It is agreed by you that neither your company, any associated or affiliate company, or company with whom you are connected will handle or sell in any way any product which we consider similar, or competitive to those manufactured by us. Noncompliance would justify immediate cancellation."

Semiexclusive. Certain agents or distributors, however, do not have exclusive selling rights on all sales of goods in their territories. Their rights are modified in various respects. For example, it is frequently found that sales to governments — in some cases only federal governments, in other instances all governmental bodies, including federal, state, and municipal, and their various departments — are reserved to the exporter, and the agent receives no commission, nor has he any claim for commission on such sales. The semiexclusive agent or distributor, furthermore, may have no claim to commissions where the exporter directly solicits large-quantity purchasers in his territory, and competition compels the exporter to cut his price to such a point that he cannot afford to pay a commission to the agent or distributor on this business.

General. The *general agent* is an exclusive agent of a peculiar type. Where an exclusive agent is appointed, the exporter agrees to appoint no other agents or subagents in that territory without the consent of the exclusive agent. If the agent is, however, a general agent, the exporter has the right to appoint any and as many other agents in that territory as he may choose. A split commission, however, must be paid the general agent on all sales to or through the other agents in his territory. Thus it is seen that he has exclusive sales rights. The difference between the two types of agents lies in their control over the appointment of other agents in their territory.

Lessee. At times the product is not sold at all but is merely leased to the agent, who in turn leases it to his customers. Here there is no sale as the title is never transferred.

Services Rendered by Agents and Distributors. The services rendered by foreign agents and distributors vary greatly. Much depends upon the type of product involved, the market conditions, the kind of concern chosen, and the attitude and situation of the manufacturer. Mechanical products, such as automobiles, cash registers, and typewriters, require the distributor to render extensive service in supplying spare parts and repairing, and also well-equipped demonstration and display facilities. Tank and storage systems and light and power plants must be installed by engineers sometimes sent directly from the plant of the manufacturer, but often supplied from the distributor's staff. Where markets contain many buyers of poor credit standing, or where their credit status cannot be satisfactorily ascertained, the agent may assume or guarantee credits. If the distributor is a large import house, he carries a heavy distributive burden in larger stocks, extensive credits, and local hauling and shipping. Then, too, some exporters prefer to handle their advertising themselves, others desire the agent or distributor to do this, granting him financial aid, while still others divide the burden between the agents and themselves.[6] Even for the same product and similar markets, services rendered by different agents will vary with their capital, organization, and policies.

Selection of Agents and Distributors. Proper selection of agents and distributors is the most critical problem involved in this method of distribution. Much of the burden of effective selling must necessarily rest upon them. If they fail to do their duty, the manufacturer cannot possibly hope to obtain satisfactory distribution; hence, vital importance is attached to selecting the best houses.

From many of the sources mentioned in earlier chapters, especially the Bureau of International Commerce, Dun & Bradstreet, Inc., banks, foreign trade journals, brother exporters, and others, names of foreign (and, from some of them, domestic) concerns and information relating to them can be obtained.

While there are many concerns in foreign lands soliciting agencies and distributorships for American products, these are likely to be the less desirable ones. Ordinarily, the better the foreign houses the more they are sought as representatives. They are in a position to choose from many companies in countries seeking agencies and distributorships. Therefore, it becomes necessary to convince them of the desirability of accepting the appointment. Being certain of the fairness of the offer, the exporter should proceed to convince the prospective agent or distributor of the merits of his organization, products, services, and policies. Here the manufacturer can adduce his financial strength, ability to export well, enthusiasm for export markets, success in other markets, the basic qualities of the product, its attractive packaging, the superior merchandising methods used, dealer cooperation, and the liberality of the terms of the agreement such as the amount of commissions or margins allowed, price protection, and sales quotas.

The main factors to be considered in sifting a list of candidates are their character, ability, financial status, reputation and standing with the

---

[6]A complete discussion of how the exporter cooperates with the agent or distributor in developing international advertising policies is presented in Chapter 13.

trade, the lines of product handled, sales policy, location, trade group affiliation, nationality, and political influence. All of these considerations must be analyzed not only from the point of view of the present but also of the future.

Character. Character is a primary consideration in selecting an agent or distributor. The agent's inherent capacity, his favorable trade standing, and every other good qualification he has is brought to naught when he chooses to tie up a line, offers rebates, accepts two commissions, speculates with the manufacturer's goods at the latter's expense, misappropriates advertising and other funds and allowances, or where he simply refuses to live up to the spirit of the agreement by failing to apply his initiative and intelligence.

Ability. The agent or distributor must have a thorough knowledge of his market. He must have the requisite sales organization to handle the product. This may require branch offices at certain points in the territory. Some commodities call for expert technicians on the staff of the agent, or for service facilities, or for storage, or for intensive distribution by the distributor.

Financial Status. The financial status of the agent or distributor should be carefully scrutinized when sifting representation possibilities. Where the distributor is expected to purchase from the manufacturer and particularly where, in such instances, the individual units represent a considerable investment and must be kept in stock in fair quantities, the financial resources of the distributor must be considerable. Furthermore, here the accounts of the manufacturer are all with the distributor. It concentrates the former's risks in one party and thus increases the risk. Not only must the distributor have adequate financial resources for normal times, but his ability to meet the problems of business depression and financial crises must also be considered.

Reputation. The personal element — the human equation — figures largely in foreign business as well as in domestic trade. The manufacturer should analyze his list of agents and distributors with respect to their trade standing, contacts, and reputation. Much may also depend upon the social status of the proprietors of the firm.

Lines Handled. Due consideration should also be given to the lines already being handled by prospective agents and distributors. As a rule, it is undesirable to appoint a firm that handles a competitive product. Some foreign houses, moreover, have overextended themselves by taking on too many or too great a variety of lines. As a result, they are unable to give proper attention to any one line. Such representatives should ordinarily be avoided. Other foreign concerns handle only a small group of related products or perhaps only one line of goods. Such specialization in selling is often highly desirable and makes for more effective representation of the one product.

Sales Policy. The manufacturer has, no doubt, built up certain traditions regarding the selling of his products. He has certain distribution "beliefs." Is the prospective agent or distributor reported as being highly progressive — a "live wire" organization — or is it termed a conservative house? Is it a young or an old concern? What do the data show about the personality of the heads of the firm? Do they make use of advertising, novel sales methods, etc.? These and many other pertinent statements may give some clue to the sales temperament of the agent or distributor. If it is in harmony with that of the manufacturer, there will be little danger of splitting upon fundamental issues.

Location. The location of the agent or distributor is a factor of importance in sifting the prospect list. It is desirable that he be so located that he can readily render assistance in receiving shipments. Location at certain points may incur the necessity of transshipment of the goods. He should be situated at a point that has the most adequate transportation facilities with the remainder of the territory. In the case of Colombia, for instance, exporters have found that an agent or distributor located at, say, Barranquilla cannot adequately cover the entire country owing to poor transportation and communication facilities; and hence additional representatives have been placed at Medellín, Bogotá, Cali, Cúcuta, and Manizales.

Trade Group Affiliation. As is the case within the United States, foreign distribution systems exhibit more or less definite trade cleavages between the various middlemen involved. There is usually a wholesale middleman group and a retail middleman group. In certain countries hybrid wholesale-retail houses are prevalent. In many other countries pure importing houses exist as a distinct and separate group. This makes it imperative for the manufacturer to determine the trade group to which the agent or distributor actually belongs. This is not easy to determine because firms at times represent themselves as being importers or wholesalers where, as a matter of fact, the trade does not recognize them as such. Should the contract be granted to a retail house, other retailers and all wholesalers may refuse to deal with the firm. The same principle holds true where a wholesale firm is given the representation; other wholesalers may be loath to buy from or through it.

Nationality. The nationality of the agent or distributor must likewise be considered. This factor bears upon the problem of adequate representation in two ways: first, the attitude of the agent or distributor toward the manufacturer, and, secondly, the attitude of the trade toward the agent or distributor. A third factor in times of national emergency is the attitude of the exporter's country. On July 17, 1941, "The Proclaimed List of Certain Blocked Nationals" was released by the United States Government and was supplemented several times in succeeding months. With the entrance of the United States into the war in December, 1941, all dealings with parties named in the "black list" were prohibited. Under postwar export control regulations, export licenses may not be approved for shipment of some goods to certain foreign firms located in particular countries.

The fact that English, German, French, or Dutch houses have proved satisfactory to exporters of those respective countries does not necessarily guarantee the American manufacturer adequate representation. There are many exporters who sincerely believe that there is little hope of getting such foreign houses to stand behind American goods and push them with all their energy and skill. But it is certainly true that there are numerous instances where American manufacturers are receiving the best representation from these foreign houses. Everything depends upon the individual house.

With regard to the second part of the problem, it is maintained that in certain markets and lines the trade is prejudiced against nationals of a third country and will not buy from them when they can get what they want from other houses, whether national or American. In the Philippine Republic, for example, laws have been enacted seeking to bar Chinese business firms from participating in Philippine marketing.

Political Influence. Where government business forms an important part of sales, the political influence of the house becomes an important element in selecting the agent or distributor.

Agency and Distributive Contracts and Agreements

In this discussion, agency contracts will be treated in detail and distributor contracts will be analyzed.

The Need for a Written Agency Contract. The terms of the agency as finally agreed upon constitute the *agency contract.* Ordinarily these terms are reduced to writing in order to make a permanent record of the rights, duties, and liabilities of the exporter and his agent. Some exporters, more particularly the older ones who have agency arrangements of long standing, have not used what could properly be termed a written contract, but have merely confirmed the grant of the agency by letter stating a few particulars such as territory and commissions or discounts. Other agency problems have been decided mutually as they arose. And yet such exporters have enjoyed unsurpassed success with their agents. The attitude of one large manufacturer whose products are sold throughout the world is expressed in these words: "Our agreement is quite short and rather informal. We point out to most of our people that the agreement is no better than the intent of both parties."

But now it is considered better practice to prepare a written contract covering all of the important phases of the agency relationship. Sometimes a formal contract with legal terminology is used, but an informal presentation of terms, often on the exporter's letterhead, is much more frequently found. Casting the terms of the agency into the form of a complete and clearly written document helps to avoid misunderstanding and consequent ill feeling later on, constitutes better legal protection to the exporter where large credits are extended to the agent and where the rights of third parties might be involved, and is often helpful and necessary to the agent in obtaining foreign government business or getting credit from banks.

Basic Provisions in the Agency Contract.[7]   All the essential provisions that should be placed in agency contracts cannot be outlined, as they will vary radically with the manufacturer, the product, the agent, and the market. There are, however, certain basic provisions that are found in one form or another in almost all well-drawn contracts. Some of these provisions represent concessions granted and obligations assumed by the manufacturer; others relate to concessions granted and obligations assumed by the agent; and still a third group relate to mutual concessions and obligations.

The Manufacturer's Concessions and Obligations. Regarding the provisions included in the first class dealing with concessions and obligations of the manufacturer, there would be the enabling clause, the territory

---

[7]See Chapter 18 for antitrust aspects of agency and distributor contracts.

clause, the duration clause, the compensation clause, and the advertising clause. The contract should fully describe the nature of the agency granted the agent. Is it in every respect an exclusive agency? May the agent represent competing lines? In whose name are sales to be made? These and other matters make up the fundamental character of the representation granted the agent. The territory granted the agent must also be specified in the agreement. Care should be taken to see that this is accurately done. The duration of the grant of agency should be long enough to allow a thorough test of the market and of the desirability of the agency connection. The agent's compensation, which is usually in the form of commissions, should be definitely stated. Where the manufacturer is ready to carry some of the advertising burden, a definite statement of what he will do should also be included.

The Agent's Concessions and Obligations. The basic provisions covering the agent's concessions and obligations would include a competitive-goods clause, an efforts clause, an advertising clause, a security clause, and, possibly, a trademarks clause. If the agent is to be prohibited from handling any competitive line, this should be inserted in the contract. Where he is already handling a competitive line, he should be given reasonable time to dispose of such stocks as he may have. The efforts clause should state that the agent agrees to use his best efforts to sell the goods. Whatever advertising activities and expenses the agent agrees to assume are also a basic part of every contract.

An agent is likely to post security for certain financial privileges and obligations he has in favor of the principal. Such security should be clearly defined — whether property, deposit, or bond — and the use of such security, interest earned, and similar matters should be clarified.

The trademarks clause would forbid the agent to register the trademark of the goods he represents, all registration rights remaining in the name of the principal. Instances may be cited of agents in certain countries who have registered trademarks in their own name. Under the laws of such countries, an agent thereby obtains legal ownership of a trademark, which entails exclusive right to its use. Should occasion sometime require the removal of that agent, the principal would obviously be faced with a difficult situation.[8]

Mutual Concessions and Obligations. Certain mutual concessions and obligations form a basic part of every agency contract. These relate to

---

[8]Various aspects of foreign commercial law are discussed in Chapter 24.

the duration of the contract. They should make clear the circumstances that shall enable either party to cancel the contract, the exact nature of the notice of cancellation that must be given, and how and when cancellation is to become effective.

In the case of an agency, as distinguished from a distributor arrangement, the manufacturer reclaims certain rights to property and goodwill that legally belong to him as principal.

Other Common Provisions in the Agency Contract. Along with the basic provisions described above, one frequently finds most of the following: a direct sales clause, an indirect sales clause, an extraterritorial sales clause, a quota clause, a stock clause, a price-change clause, a damaged-goods clause, a settlement-of-payments clause, an Acts-of-God clause, an approval-of-order clause, an assignability clause, and a jurisdiction clause.

Direct Sales Clause. It may be highly desirable that the manufacturer retain the right to solicit orders and sell direct to the trade, for example, governmental bodies. Therefore, the direct sales clause should state the conditions, if any, under which the manufacturer may solicit orders direct from the trade of the agent's territory, and what rights and compensation the agent is to have under such circumstances.

Indirect Sales Clause. The indirect sales clause should set forth the protection that the manufacturer agrees to give the agent on sales made by the former to commission houses and other middlemen shipping his products into the agent's territory. An exclusive agency implies exclusive selling rights in the territory of the agent, and, therefore, he usually wants as much protection as possible from sales made in his territory through such third parties. This is only reasonable.

Extraterritorial Sales Clause. The extraterritorial sales clause, frequently found in agency contracts, governs the agent's selling the manufacturer's product outside the agent's territory. With certain lines of goods this raises some very fine points of distinction.

Quota Clause. The quota clause found in many contracts sets certain sales or purchase quotas that the agent is expected to meet. They may be expressed in physical units of the goods or in monetary terms. They may be yearly, semiannual, "for the season," or some other period of time. The quotas are often set up on a graduated basis beginning with the first year and increasing thereafter, and are subject to change at certain specified times. It has been found that by giving the agent a definite goal to work for, he is stimulated to greater effort. The establishment of such quotas, however, assumes a thorough knowledge of foreign market possibilities. From the manufacturer's standpoint, the quota affords some basis for determining and controlling the production schedule. It should also consider the manufacturer's ability to meet the quota (impending shortages, national defense priorities, etc.).

Whether quota shipments are to be made by purchase or by actual sales to final purchasers must be brought out. This is a very important difference. If the agency contract calls for payment for goods that are received — which it rarely does — the remaining quota will be shipped and the agent would be obliged to pay. Generally, the agent obtains an order and therefore the quota would not be shipped until the order is received. No order — no quota.

When shipments are made, many matters must be decided, such as the selection and nature of storage cities and facilities, cost of warehousing and possible revenues therefrom, insurance, inspection of inventory by principal, and taking inventory and installing inventory control methods. When an agent holds several contracts with various manufacturers, the segregation of the property of the several principals is extremely important, especially in the event of termination of a contract.

Stock Clause. The question of parts and maintenance of stocks of both parts and complete products are also matters on which definite understanding should be reached. When stocks are maintained, agreement must be reached concerning deliveries to buyers, namely, whether from stock or by reorder from the manufacturer. Generally, however, agents do not carry stocks.

Price-Change Clause. A majority of contracts have some sort of price-change clause. It governs the rights of both parties when price changes are made by the manufacturer, giving greater or less price protection to the agent and his clients, or perhaps no protection whatsoever. In any event, it specifies that the manufacturer has the right to change prices.

Price control is also a matter for agreement. The manufacturer may insist on controlling the prices that will be quoted by his agent. This may become particularly important in event of currency devaluation, import tariff increases, import quotas, or similar matters.

Damaged-Goods Clause. In the event shipments arrive in damaged conditions, agreement should determine the procedure to be followed in claiming adjustment, against whom, within what time limit, etc., and also the disposition of damaged or substandard merchandise, payment of commissions thereon, and similar matters.

Settlement-of-Payments Clause. Agreement is also necessary to determine terms and methods of payment. The frequency of settlement of accounts, the question of overdue accounts, the possibility of exchange control or depreciation, and other financial considerations of this nature are so important during periods of uncertain currency conditions.

Acts-of-God Clause. An Acts-of-God clause is often found in the general run of agency contracts. Its purpose is to exempt the manufacturer from liability for failure to comply with the other terms of the contract or for delay in shipments owing to certain enumerated causes.

Approval-of-Order Clause. Most contracts have an approval-of-order clause, particularly where the agent is acting solely as a commission agent. Such a clause may be expressed this way: "It is mutually agreed that the authority of the Sales Representative is limited to the solicitation of orders for the Company's products, and that no representation, agreement, or warranty shall be binding on the Company unless in writing and signed by the duly authorized official of the Company." The effect of such clauses is to subject the filling of all orders forwarded by the agent to the proper approval of the manufacturer. This provision will apply to capital goods. The manufacturer can thus control such credit risks as he may assume, and he also can prevent illegal or undesirable sale of his products by the agent.[9]

Assignability Clause. The assignability clause occurs again and again and its growing prevalence is a good sign, for the matter it covers is of much importance. Such clauses state whether the contract is assignable or nonassignable. Most of such clauses relate only to the agent's ability to assign the contract; nothing is stated regarding the manufacturer's right of assigning the agreement. No doubt the latter is much less likely to desire to assign the contract. It does no harm, however, to protect the agent likewise by making its provisions cover both parties.

Jurisdiction Clause. Occurring frequently enough to be classed with these usual clauses is the jurisdiction clause. It designates the country whose law shall be followed in all legal questions relating to the contract.

---

[9]Export control regulations of the United States Government embody control over final purchasers and end-use of exported products.

When the manufacturer designates an American jurisdiction, it affords him additional legal protection. Arbitration and specific rules to govern in case of dispute may be provided.

Such a clause may be worded as follows: "It is agreed that this agreement is considered to have been entered into in ------- but any dispute arising under the agreement will be settled in accord with the laws of the State of Wisconsin, United States of America, Wisconsin being the state of incorporation of ------ , renouncing any benefits of law in other countries, and submitting to the jurisdiction of the courts of the State of Wisconsin, United States of America."

Although these clauses are usually found in agency contracts, they vary radically with each contract. Nor can any general rule be laid down as to what the contents of such clauses should be — for the very reason that individual circumstances vary widely and call for all sorts and shades of treatment. A great variety of minor or special clauses occur now and then in agency agreements. While necessary and desirable for the agency to which they may apply, they are, on the whole, quite uncommon.

Once the agency contract has been carefully drawn up and properly executed and signed, the manufacturer must not think that, so far as the contract goes, the problem is solved once and for all. The conditions surrounding the agency undergo a continuous process of change. Certain provisions of the contract become antiquated, others become inadequate, and new matters arise that should be made a matter of written agreement. This requires a periodic check and revision of agency contracts.

Basic Provisions in the Distributor Contract. Distributor contracts differ from agency contracts because of the difference in the position of the agent and of the distributor. Practically all of the provisions of the agency contract will apply also to the distributor contract, while certain provisions of distributors' contracts have no place in agency contracts. The following clauses represent the principal conditions that are found in distributor contracts but not in agency contracts.

Purchase Clause. The distributor undertakes to purchase (not merely order for the account of some other customer) his requirements for the product or products that he handles. There may be a quota statement of such purchases.

Advertising Clause. The manufacturer may agree to establish an advertising appropriation to be devoted to the promotion of the products in the territory assigned; and, usually, he also promises to provide advertising materials for use by the distributor. Finally, the distributor may be expected to agree *not* to advertise the products concerned *without* the prior approval of the manufacturer.

Sales Expense Clause. The expenses of selling are paid for entirely by the distributor, and while this is also true of the agent, a distributor may be called upon to incur more sales expense than an agent. In one contract, for example, if a sales or product conference is called at the manufacturer's home office or at some foreign city other than the one in which the distributor is situated, the latter nevertheless is obligated to attend and to pay all of his expenses. In some cases, when the conference is held in the United States, the living expenses while in the United States are paid by the manufacturer.

Stock Clause. The distributor is often called upon to maintain a stock of products that he handles. Current orders are then filled from this stock that is then replenished by further purchases.

Service Clause. This clause is particularly important in the contract of the distributor who handles equipment and machinery of every kind. The clause may call upon the distributor to retain in his employ a suitable number of mechanics or servicemen and to provide adequate facilities for the maintenance, repair, and servicing of all equipment located in the distributor's territory.

Approval-of-Order Clause. Since the distributor purchases the products for resale, it would appear that he would have authority to sell to any customer. However, such is not the case. In many distributor contracts, orders obtained by the distributor must be approved by the manufacturer. This is an interesting example of the extent to which some manufacturers of trademarked goods, in particular, go to control the ultimate distribution of their merchandise.

Disavowal of Agency Arrangement Clause. In order to make certain that a distributor's contract can not be construed as conferring any agency rights to the distributor, a clause is sometimes inserted declaring that the representative (distributor) is not in any way an agent of the principal (manufacturer) and has no right or authority to assume any obligation of any kind, express or implied, on behalf of the principal, or to act for him or to bind the principal in any respect, nor can he pledge the principal's credit.

Such a clause is this: "It is agreed that the Representative will represent ------ in the capacity of an exclusive sales representative, but not as agent or legal representative, in the sale and distribution of products in the territory."

Interestingly enough, and at the same time confusing, such disavowal of agency authority is sometimes found in contracts in which the representative is called the agent!

Desirability of the Agency and Distributor Methods. Where the possibilities of the market give promise of only a moderate volume of sales for some time to come, the agency method is very effective. Since the agent handles a number of lines, only moderate sales of each will enable him to earn substantial total commissions. On the other hand, where repair service, spare parts, and a stock of commodities must always be at hand, or where the supervision of these must be close and continuous, the distributor plan is effective. When the product requires constant, intensive sales efforts, and especially when this condition is combined with the necessity of selling small units through many dealers, both the agency and distributor methods are found effective.

The agent's or distributor's intimate knowledge of local sources of credit information, his access to certain sources that the manufacturer's branch house or subsidiary might not be able to reach, and his personal knowledge of the past practices of dealers make him probably the most effective local medium for obtaining credit information.

When foreign governments are large buyers of the product, the laws governing bidding on such business may make it imperative to use an agent who is a resident or a citizen of that country. His political influence, in any event, can be used to advantage in getting such business — and this by no means implies unscrupulous business practice. There is a proper as well as an improper use of such connections. Where the trade is particularly hostile to the establishment of branch houses or subsidiaries of American manufacturers in their country, the agency and distributor methods afford a way to avoid this early antagonism. Much also depends upon whether the manufacturer can obtain a representative of the caliber that he desires.

Summary

1. Foreign marketing channels located abroad embrace three main groups, namely, (1) independent producers and commercial firms; (2) outlets and contacts controlled by United States exporting and importing firms; and (3) facilitating channels and services.

2. Independent producers and commercial firms include foreign producers (manufacturers, plantation operators, mining companies, public utilities, etc.) regardless of the nationality of the owner. Every country has international marketing firms (exporters and importers) as well as wholesalers, retailers, brokers, auctions, and public institutions. Factors are found in some trades and in some markets. Other foreign agencies include resident sales representatives and engineering concerns.

3. Since many United States firms market abroad through agents and distributors located in foreign markets, it is important to distinguish between these two types of representatives and between exclusive and semiexclusive arrangements. An exclusive agent or distributor has the sole rights in all sales of goods in the territory covered by the agreement, while the rights of a semiexclusive agent or distributor are modified in certain respects.

4. An agent is a representative who possesses certain legal rights emanating from the agency relationship. The agent generally stocks no merchandise but submits orders taken on the basis of samples or description. The distributor, on the other hand, purchases merchandise for stock, sells, delivers, services, and stocks spare parts. The agent receives a sales commission, while the distributor may also receive a commission or purchase at list price less trade discount.

5. In selecting agents and distributors the main factors to be considered are: character, ability, financial status, reputation, lines handled, sales policy, location, trade group, nationality, and political influence.

6. A contract with an agent or distributor may be a formal document or it may be evidenced by an informal understanding. The points on which understanding is to be reached include whether competing lines may be handled, duties to be performed, compensation, advertising arrangements, security, records to be kept, audit of records, price changes, trademark protection, and cancellation of contract.

7. The agency or distributor contract should be checked and revised periodically, since the conditions under which an agency or distributorship operates are continually changing.

8. The agency and distributor methods are very effective trading channels when the market gives promise of only a moderate volume of sales for some time to come, and when the sales potential is identified by close local contact with political or national interests.

QUESTIONS

1. Explain the concept of a systematic study of international marketing channels based upon their independent status. Can you add any channels to the listing presented in this chapter?

2. Explain the concept of "foreign" as used in this chapter to refer to trading channels. Criticize this concept.

3. Define the following international marketing channels:
   (a) Agent.
   (b) Distributor.
   (c) Import house.
   (d) Auction.
   (e) Factor.
   (f) Comprador.
4. Evaluate the following independent producers and commercial firms in terms of their usefulness for conducting United States export and import trade.
   (a) Agent.
   (b) Wholesaler.
   (c) Retailer.
   (d) Broker.
   (e) Resident buyer.
5. Of what value are fairs and exhibitions as international marketing channels?
6. Distinguish between agents and distributors when classified as exclusive, semiexclusive, general, and lessee.
7. Discuss the factors to be considered in selecting agents and distributors abroad. Attempt to rate these factors according to their relative importance.
8. Define and justify the following clauses commonly found in agency contracts:
   (a) Territory.
   (b) Efforts.
   (c) Financial security.
   (d) Direct sales.
   (e) Extraterritorial sales.
   (f) Quota.
   (g) Approval of order.
   (h) Cancellation.
9. Define and justify the following clauses commonly found in distributor contracts:
   (a) Advertising.
   (b) Stock.
   (c) Service.
   (d) Disavowal of agency arrangement.

PROBLEMS

1. An exclusive distributor in a foreign country has become aware of the sale of merchandise for which he has the exclusive contract, but which he does not handle. Upon investigation, he found that this merchandise is coming into his country through the branch office of an export commission house situated in the country of his supplier. How can this situation be remedied?

2. An American export sales manager has been traveling throughout the Far East studying the position of his company's distributors and agents. In such countries as the Philippine Republic, Indonesia, Thailand, India, and Pakistan, the representatives have been functioning for many years. They are Europeans and Chinese. The sales manager has noted during his trip, however, that nationalism is making it increasingly difficult for these European and Chinese firms to continue in business. At the same time, the sales manager realizes that there is little choice of competent native (indigenous) firms to replace these representatives. Suggest a solution to this problem.

COLLATERAL READINGS

Collins, V. D. *World Marketing*. Philadelphia: J. B. Lippincott Company, 1935. Chapter 7.

Dartnell International Trade Handbook, The. Chicago: The Dartnell Corporation, 1963.

de Haas, J. A. *The Practice of Foreign Trade*. New York: McGraw-Hill Book Company, Inc., 1935. Chapters 7, 8, and 13.

Horn, Paul V. *International Trade Principles and Practices*, Third Edition. New York: Prentice-Hall, Inc., 1951. Chapter 26.

MacDonald, Philip. *Practical Exporting*. New York: Ronald Press Company, 1949. Chapter 3.

Pratt, E. E. *Modern International Commerce*. New York: Allyn and Bacon, Inc., 1956. Chapters 3 and 5.

Roorbach, G. B. *Problems in Foreign Trade*. New York: McGraw-Hill Book Company, Inc., 1933. Part III.

Tosdal, H. R. *Problems in Export Sales Management*. New York: McGraw-Hill Book Company, Inc., 1922. Chapter 7.

United States Department of Commerce. *Exclusive Sales Agreements in Foreign Trade*. Washington, D.C.: Government Printing Office, 1927.

Wyman, Walter F. *Export Merchandising*. New York: McGraw-Hill Book Company, Inc., 1922. Chapters 28–30.

CHAPTER 11

EXPORT SALESMEN AND IMPORT BUYERS

Of all of the methods of conducting international marketing, none is as old or as significant as the use of the foreign traveler. The personal contact with the export salesman and the import buyer transmits confidence to the foreign country representatives with whom they deal. Having been thoroughly trained before being sent on a foreign mission, these men can speak of their business with knowledge and authority. The customers and suppliers with whom they deal are aware of the responsible position that they fill and can have full confidence in the negotiations to be conducted.

Types of Export Salesmen and Import Buyers

In this section we shall examine the characteristics of three types of export salesmen and import buyers: (1) traveling representatives, (2) resident salesmen and buyers, and (3) combination salesmen and buyers.

Traveling Representatives. Some export salesmen and import buyers leave the United States for a certain period of time, travel to and through foreign countries to sell or buy, and return to the United States upon completion of the merchandising trip. These may be referred to as *traveling representatives*.

Export salesmen and import buyers of this type assume the entire responsibility of making sales or purchases; no other method of doing business need be carried on. They are the sole foreign representatives of their employers; they are "on their own," far away from the home base.

The Demonstrator or Tutor. One type of traveling representative works in conjunction with agents, distributors, or commissionaires already representing the exporter or importer. In export selling, such a salesman may be sent abroad to visit the firm's agencies and instill energy, enthusiasm, and loyalty. He may also instruct agents as to new products or new sales and publicity methods, straighten out difficult problems, or tackle stubborn customers. The salesman is thus a *demonstrator* or *tutor*. Such salesmen represent a highly developed type of selling, whether at home or abroad. Their work is to keep an organization running, as well as to build one up.

The Technical Expert. A second type of traveling representative is the *technical expert* sent to visit foreign connections. In technical and mechanical lines it is difficult in many countries to find local representatives adequately trained in technical matters. These experts demonstrate and install complicated machinery and equipment, and when assembly or production facilities are established abroad, they perform essential work in connection with these activities.

In the import trade, buyers are sometimes sent abroad to cooperate with established buying offices or connections. Questions concerning selection of merchandise, supply sources, inspection, packing and shipping, and other matters may require the presence of a traveling buying representative. Usually the buying office or connection is prepared to assist buyers whenever they find it desirable to go abroad.

Resident Salesmen and Buyers. A *resident salesman* or *buyer* is one who is sent out from the United States to reside for a length of time in a certain territory and to maintain headquarters there, which is in reality a branch. His work will be discussed in Chapter 14.

When American exporters establish branches abroad, salesmen are usually employed by the branch. Such salesmen are often not Americans, but nationals of the country in which the branch is located. These salesmen do not require the peculiar qualifications of traveling representatives, as they are usually of local origin. The same may be said of foreign branch organizations established by American importers. The manager is in charge and supervises the work of the buyers employed.

Combination Salesmen and Buyers. Many concerns deal in products that are best represented by personal contact, but in which the volume of business transacted is insufficient to warrant the expense of engaging an exclusive salesman or buyer. In such instances, a combination representative may be desirable.

In the importing business, for example, specialty and novelty lines that are best purchased by direct buyers may be small in volume so far as one particular item is concerned. A *combination buyer* may, therefore, be sent abroad to purchase a group of articles — that may or may not be related — in the countries that he visits. This is a common practice of department stores and certain other retail establishments.

When the same plan is used as a sales method, however, the problem is somewhat different. If a salesman should handle a range of products manufactured by one particular concern, he would not be known as the combination salesman. A *combination export salesman* carries two or more lines from *different* producers; instead of one employer's interest to represent, he has two or more.

Combination salesmen naturally carry noncompeting lines of goods and preferably related lines, such as a group of automobile accessories: one brand each of spark plugs, windshield wipers, warning signals, and cigar lighters. It is obvious that a combination salesman cannot give the same care and attention to a line of merchandise as a salesman representing only one line. But if the lines are as analogous as those indicated, each may receive a fair share of attention, since a sales prospect for any one of the lines is a prospect for the others.

A combination salesman may gather together his merchandise lines by personal contact, by advertising, or by introduction. The proposition is laid before all of the interested concerns and agreement is reached as to the apportionment of salary and expense, as well as other matters.

Although this plan of selling may be successful in many lines where combination is feasible, there are two chief difficulties. First, there is the natural tendency to push the lines that move most easily and which, therefore, do not require excessive sales effort. This risk exists whenever a salesman's compensation is on the straight salary basis. In attempting to obviate this tendency, a second difficulty may be encountered. If compensation is on the basis of commission, the natural tendency will be to concentrate on the most lucrative lines. In either case, there is considerable probability that all lines will not receive the same attention.

Qualifications of Export Salesmen and Import Buyers

It is generally conceded that when an exporter contemplates sending abroad a salesman, or an importer a buyer, the person selected should embody the highest qualifications. The American businessman who goes abroad bears a threefold responsibility in regard to the reputation of his country, his firm, and himself. Whether he realizes it or not, he will be accepted as a sample of his countrymen and of his company.

Some indication of the qualifications that export salesmen and import buyers should possess in order to enable them to measure fully up to their position will manifest the care to be exercised in their selection.

Personal Qualifications. The personal qualifications that should be embodied within the export salesman and import buyer include a good personality, reliability, sociability, tact and courtesy, tenacity, and accuracy.

Personality. A foreign representative should have a good personality. This embraces a wider connotation than mere appearance; it refers also to character. Self-control is stressed because the restraint imposed by home ties or convention is absent. Habits at all times must be moderate. Vexations, delays, and conditions should not result in ill temper.

Reliability. The export salesman and the import buyer, of course, should be reliable and should have sound judgment. Often thousands of miles away from the home office, the foreign representative must be capable of standing "on his own." Decisions must be his responsibility.

Sociability. He should possess good social qualities. Export salesmen and import buyers, as is generally true of all business representatives, should be good "mixers." The man who draws a close line of color, race, or creed is at once handicapped in exemplifying this quality. In other countries there are people who are often essentially different in many respects from ourselves. A foreign representative should be capable of associating with these people as his equals. A superiority complex is apt to cause resentment and to result in failure.

Tact and Courtesy. He should be tactful and courteous, and this implies a willingness to consider the point of view and feelings of other people. This comment applies particularly to the sales representative. Much has been said about the courtesy that custom decrees in foreign countries, while at the same time too little stress has been placed upon the importance of tact. An overzealousness in courtesy is quite conceivable, but the tactful person is at all times in a comfortable and even enviable position. Social customs that engender the display of courtesy on the part of foreigners may be gradually acquired by the tactful visitor from alien shores. An overeagerness to acquire and conform to the requirements of foreign social usage has at times led to submerged ridicule.

Tenacity. The exporter's or importer's choice frequently goes to the tenacious individual rather than to the temperamental one. Particularly in export selling, results are often long in coming and without that courage and tenacity of purpose to be found in the "plugger," there is bound to be discouragement.

Accuracy. Accuracy in the many details of business is essential everywhere, and it is particularly important in export selling and import purchasing. Errors, even though slight, are bound to cause irritation and misunderstanding. An appreciation of the importance of this characteristic will make the sales representative exacting in the transmission of orders, in making promises, and in other activities that call for accuracy. Care taken at this contact point between an exporter and his overseas customers will assuredly facilitate the maintenance of goodwill. Accuracy is equally as important for the import buyer. His ability to size up a situation affecting the supply of an article that he seeks, to get at prices and at the delivered costs of goods, bear a decided relation to the profitability of purchasing the articles in question.

Professional Qualifications. Another group of qualifications may be noted as indicating what foreign representatives should *know*, rather than what they should *be*.

Knowledge of Product. It is obviously important that any salesman should possess a thorough knowledge of his product. Because of the distance that an export salesman may travel, it is particularly important that he be thoroughly conversant with every aspect of the product he is selling — its technical description, its utility, its assembly, and its operation. Frequently it is found advisable to train such men in the production branch of the business, in order that they may acquire this information.

If knowledge of product is essential for a salesman, it is at least as important for a buyer. A buyer must be capable of judging the quality and marketability of products. This examination will not stop with one line or one brand but may extend over many. Whereas the salesman already possesses the product and goes out to get business, the buyer's task is to procure a product that will in turn result in business for his firm. One is inclined to say that, proportionately, knowledge of merchandise is even more essential for import buyers than for export salesmen.

Knowledge of Country. Knowledge of the country to be visited is an important asset. Preference is given by many exporters and importers to persons who have previously traveled abroad, especially in the countries to which they are to be sent. The salesman or the buyer who has not made such trips, however, is not barred, as other qualifications are of equal or greater importance. Considerable knowledge of a foreign country may be obtained through study, although this cannot be considered the equivalent of actual experience.

Knowledge of Languages. Knowledge of the language of the country to be visited is often a prime qualification for business travelers. It is highly desirable for a representative who is going abroad to be able to converse in the language of the country. The employment of interpreters is a practice now frowned upon. Especially in selling, the sales appeal frequently loses its effectiveness when translated and delivered by an interpreter. Buyers connected with importing firms in many countries, however, may pride themselves on their knowledge of English and, therefore, prefer to converse in that language.

English is widely employed in trading circles all over the world. It is spoken in the United Kingdom and all British colonies and dominions, including such vast areas as Canada, Australia, New Zealand, and South Africa. Furthermore, English is the language used in Far Eastern trade generally, and it is widely employed in countries of northern Europe. French, Spanish, and German are usually considered as the balance of the commercial languages of the world, except that Portuguese is necessary in the case of Brazil and Portugal.

Americans have in the past been considered unwilling to acquire the knowledge of a foreign language, but this attitude has been changing. A strong impetus to the study of Spanish and Portuguese was initiated by conditions arising from World War II.

Knowledge of Current Events. When buying or selling in foreign lands where the approach is tedious and slow, conversation is likely to shift to any subject except the business on which the representative is bent. Many topics that come up for discussion relate to problems and conditions existing in the home country of the traveler. The Free World's industrial, commercial, and financial organization and development are closely followed by foreign businessmen. Political and international problems are likewise of interest. It becomes evident, therefore, that the purchase or sales representative who is traveling in foreign lands should be fully informed on such matters. His presentation of the pertinent facts involved in questions such as these may have a decided bearing upon the esteem in which his country, as a nation, is to be held by foreigners. When abroad, the traveler represents his nation as well as his house. Obviously, the education, experience, reading, breadth of interest, and knowledge of the export salesman or import buyer are of importance in surveying his qualifications.

Differences Between Buying and Selling

Although previous qualifications have been discussed broadly for salesmen and for buyers alike, the essential differences between buying and selling should be noted. In the usual run of business, the salesman is on the offensive while the buyer is on the defensive. The former endeavors to persuade the buyer to purchase his particular brand or quality of merchandise. It is only in instances of restricted supply that we find buyers competing for the purchase of goods. For this reason, it is borne out in practice that salesmen require more of these qualifications than do buyers. Salesmen, in a sense, are intruding while buyers are more genuinely welcome. Any shortcomings the buyer may possess do not loom so large as those of the salesman.

Moreover, a difference based upon trade practice may be pointed out. While the export salesman usually devotes his entire time to this type of work, usually the traveling buyer is also engaged in work at home. Buying trips are made periodically and for shorter periods than are most sales trips. For example, in the department store business, the buyers are also the heads of particular merchandise (sales) departments. For this reason, it is important that they be capable domestic sales executives as well as successful import buyers. Exporting concerns frequently engage men to be trained as export salesmen, but a buyer is selected only after he has demonstrated ability in the managerial and technical phases of a business.

Collateral Duties of Export Salesmen and Import Buyers

The duties of the various types of salesmen and buyers are in many respects broader than those brought out in the preceding discussion. Buyers are called upon to represent the interests of their principals in every matter affecting the business, in style and price changes, in production conditions, inspection of merchandise, etc., as well as in the purchase of merchandise.

Similarly, the export salesman who serves his firm to the fullest extent is more than a salesman. He is, among other things, a direct source of credit information. The export salesman is in a position to forward valuable data concerning a customer's credit standing abroad. The export salesman frequently takes a more or less active part in advertising and trade promotion campaigns. Not only may his advice as to methods be worthy of consideration, but his location abroad may also permit him to provide necessary data concerning publicity media and channels. Being the firm's only direct foreign representative, the salesman may be able to assist the export advertising manager locally after a campaign is under way.

When trade disputes arise, the foreign traveler is expected to take an active interest in bringing about satisfactory adjustment. Should foreign customs, quarantine regulations, or legal difficulties interfere with a market or a source of supply, he is expected to make a study of the situation and to take steps to untangle the difficulty, if possible.

Both the salesman and the buyer should be able to advise, or at least to provide information concerning the probable future of the market. If a change in trade methods is decided upon, they may be able to assist in making preliminary, if not final, arrangements. They may, indeed, be able to make valuable suggestions involving changes in commodities themselves, where circumstances warrant some alteration.

Cooperation with Export Salesmen and Import Buyers

An exporter or an importer has no justification for assuming that as soon as his foreign traveler has departed, the success or failure of the venture lies entirely within the province of the latter. Although these travelers are essentially placed upon their own responsibility, there is a great deal that the principal may do in order to assure success of the sales or buying trip.

Cooperation begins before the departure of the representative. The way must be prepared in order that time will not be lost in gaining a foothold or in seeking contacts. Letters may be sent in advance to United States Government representatives, chambers of commerce (especially American), or other public bodies abroad. Correspondence may also be directed to agents, distributors, or prospective customers, and to commissionaires and producing companies, announcing the proposed trip.

The itinerary of the traveler will include the places deemed best to visit, and as much detail as possible is to be previously arranged. Itineraries are naturally subject to change. Letters of encouragement, sales helps, testimonials, data on the product being sold or bought, changes in supply or demand, and other matters of information all prove to the foreign traveler that the home base has not forgotten him.

An important phase of cooperation consists in backing up the judgment of the traveler. Under the qualifications of salesmen and buyers to be noted are the essentials of reliability and good judgment. If an error has been committed in selecting the individual who goes abroad, the fault lies with the principal; the assumption is that these desirable qualifications are present. Commitments that the salesman or buyer has made in the name of his principals, and in good faith on the basis of the authority entrusted to him, should be rigidly backed. It is easy to understand that no greater discouragement could come to a salesman than that occasioned by the cancellation of orders after strenuous efforts have finally yielded success. Instances may be cited where the export concern has refused to meet the salesman's commitments on such matters as quality, style, or makeup. Often such alterations from standard forms are essentially unimportant from the production angle, but they may be decidedly significant to the foreign customer. Similarly, the judgment of the buyer is to be supported after he has done the best he could under the circumstances that he faced.

The importance of close cooperation with the buyer or salesman in the foreign field does not mean that he is to be allowed a completely free rein without any semblance of control or authority. Whatever specific instructions may be given him are necessarily binding upon his actions.

Finally, good business demands that certain records be periodically submitted by the traveler. These include expense accounts, reports on customers or suppliers, credit data, and orders taken or placed.

Foreign Regulations Affecting Commercial Travelers

It is important that a buyer or salesman be fully informed with respect to foreign regulations with which he will be obliged to comply. Certain regulations involve the expenditure of funds and others the preparation and carrying of certain documents.

License Fees and Taxes. In some countries, export salesmen may find themselves confronted with the necessity of paying license fees for the privilege of visiting the trade. These fees, in some instances, may apply throughout the country; but there are often provincial and even municipal fees also to be paid. The most satisfactory way to avoid payment of onerous license fees is for the traveler to affiliate temporarily with a local concern that already has complied with the license requirements. In this way the foreign traveler is considered a member of the staff of the local house. If agents or branches of the exporter are located in the foreign country, this arrangement may be made quite easily.

Miscellaneous taxes, such as those based upon income or those levied on advertising matter, may also be levied.

Import Duties. Import duty may be levied by foreign governments on salesmen's samples.[1] Generally speaking, such duty is not levied in case the samples are of no commercial value. Thus, efforts may be made to deprive commodities of such value while still preserving their utility as samples. This may be accomplished by mutilating the merchandise in an immaterial manner such as punching a hole or splitting. At times such mutilation might serve to demonstrate more effectively the construction and quality of a sample. Usually a bond may be posted to guarantee payment of duties that are levied, in case samples are not reexported within a certain time limit prescribed by the foreign law.

Documents. As to the documents that travelers must possess in order to enjoy certain privileges, passports are required by most foreign countries; and occasionally a health certificate is required in addition to or in lieu of the passport. A power of attorney is required by the law of some countries as evidence of the authority of the traveler to act for his principal. Without such authority, the salesman or the buyer would be unable to sign a contract. He is what has been called a "legal nobody." In many countries the document is scrutinized with extreme care in order to determine the precise limits of the authority conferred.

Foreign travelers should also possess some evidence of personal identification. Although not legally necessary, it is highly desirable that letters of introduction be carried. Such letters not only are prepared by the principal for whom the traveler is acting but also may be written by brother exporting or importing concerns or personal acquaintances.

---

[1]In 1956, the Customs Cooperation Council, which is a multigovernmental organization, adopted a convention providing for the free importation of commercial samples of value, models, and certain advertising films. Seventeen countries have adopted this convention. In 1961, this Council, in cooperation with the International Chamber of Commerce and GATT, adopted two conventions extending the range of commodities eligible for temporary free admission. In 1961, still another convention was adopted providing for an international customer's document permitting temporary free admission of the categories of merchandise previously named.

Conditions Favoring the Employment of Salesmen and Buyers

Although ironclad rules may not be laid down to demonstrate precisely the desirability of employing salesmen and buyers in preference to other methods of conducting international marketing, there are certain conditions that are generally most favorable to their employment.

Line of Merchandise. There are lines of merchandise, both export and import, that may be satisfactorily handled only by direct personal supervision and attention. Individuals alone will provide this. Technical products entering largely into the export trade require explanation and demonstration. Sales of machinery and mechanical appliances of various kinds are often made through salesmen. When stocks or repair parts are required to be kept on hand, however, or when servicing facilities are required, traveling salesmen are not as effective as branches or agents and distributors.

The same may be said of specialties that enter both the import and the export trades. Specialties and novelties are imported to a large extent through the medium of buyers. Indeed, such articles afford a real test of the purchasing and merchandising ability of a buyer.

For quality goods, the same acumen for selection is demanded and a skilled buyer should be employed. He purchases for a particular clientele, and to do his work successfully, he must be fully acquainted with their tastes. In the export trade, quality goods consist largely of trade-marked articles; and export salesmen are often, but not exclusively, employed.

Volume of Trade. Another factor favorable to the use of export salesmen and import buyers is an adequate volume of trade. As a buying or a selling trip may involve the outlay of relatively large sums of money, a sufficient volume of business must be anticipated to make the venture very profitable.

Articles that move in international commerce during distinct seasons of the year are often best handled by personal representatives, especially when the type of product also recommends this method. The volume of business to be transacted during this restricted period of time may be sufficient to warrant the expenditure, whereas if spread over an entire year the trip might be unprofitable.

Territory to Be Covered. Among other conditions, volume is affected by the foreign territory to be covered. If a single product may be procured only in one locality, the expense of a buyer is generally less than if a wider territory is covered. Foreign markets that are well organized or products that are fairly standardized may recommend selection of an import buyer in preference to establishing a purchase office or branch. Furs sold on European auctions, Australian wool, Indian hides and skins and other products have been purchased in the past by traveling buyers. On the other hand, unstandardized products demand the selection of a buyer or some adequate substitute, as in the purchase of toys. In the case of export salesmen, the territory to be covered is more flexible, because no definite limitation is imposed as by production. Sales trips extending over many months or even more than a year may be arranged, and during this time sufficient territory may be covered to make the sales venture profitable in the aggregate.

Distance from the United States. The actual distance of a foreign country from the United States is a factor in considering the advisability of sending a personal representative. Great distance militates against close contact with foreign markets and sources of supply. While cable and airmail letter reports are in many instances depended upon as a means of closer contact, adequate contact is at times possible only by means of personal representation. Traveling salesmen are commonly employed in trade with nearby foreign markets.

Summary

1. The personal representative (salesman or buyer) has always been important in all trade, both domestic and foreign. When abroad, a sales or purchase representative bears a threefold responsibility — to his country, to his company, and to himself.
2. Traveling representatives may be travelers from the United States for a relatively short period of time, or they may be stationed in posts abroad for long periods of time. Another type being increasingly used is the technical expert, who may, in fact, not be a sales representative of any sort.
3. Some salesmen and many buyers handle a variety of lines of merchandise. They are known as combination salesmen or buyers.
4. Sales representatives are expected to do more than get orders. They study and report on conditions and on the standing of customers, and they try to settle disputes.
5. Full cooperation with the traveling representatives will assist greatly in making the trip successful.
6. The salesman in particular is expected to meet certain personal qualifications since he is in the position of the "aggressor" in business transactions.

These qualifications include personality, reliability, sociability, tact and courtesy, tenacity, and accuracy.

7. The foreign representative must possess certain professional qualifications — he must have a knowledge of his product, country, languages, and current events.

8. Foreign representatives face regulations imposed by foreign authorities, such as customs clearance of and possible duty payment for samples, payment of license fees, and sundry taxes. Various documents are also required. A power of attorney may be absolutely essential.

QUESTIONS

1. Distinguish among the several recognized types of export salesmen and import buyers.
2. Contrast the function of selling with the function of buying.
3. Discuss the advantages and the disadvantage of
   (a) Combination import buyers.
   (b) Combination export salesmen.
4. Why should a buyer be more fully informed as to a product than a salesman?
5. Would you expect an export salesman to prepare an acceptable credit report on a buyer to whom he has sold a large order on commission? Explain.
6. Outline a procedure to prepare the way and to cooperate with:
   (a) An export salesman.
   (b) An import buyer when the trips involved are extensive and time-consuming.
7. Compare the essential qualifications for the buyer or seller in each of the following situations:
   (a) An American food company sends a buyer to purchase coffee in Hamburg, Germany.
   (b) An American manufacturer of writing instruments sends a salesman to confer with distributors and customers abroad.
   (c) An American merchandising firm sends a buyer to the Cologne, Germany, trade fair to purchase toys for a group of retail stores.
   (d) An American manufacturer of earth-moving equipment sends a salesman to a country where a large construction project is under way. The manufacturer has a competent distributor located in the country in question.
8. Contrast the regulations faced by an American commercial traveler in the United States with the regulations faced by American (and all alien) commercial travelers in other countries.
9. Evaluate the circumstances and conditions under which export salesmen and import buyers are likely to be employed at the present time and in the future.

PROBLEMS

1. An American cosmetics manufacturer seeks to introduce his line of products into foreign markets by means of export salesmen.

    One candidate under consideration is Mr. Brown, who has successfully sold the company's products domestically for ten years. The only time Mr. Brown has been abroad was on his honeymoon in Canada. He studied Spanish in high school.

    Another candidate is Mr. White, who has traveled abroad for five years for a tool manufacturer. He seeks a change in the product he is handling. Which candidate would you select and why?

2. A novelty retailer-importer considers the desirability of sending a buyer to Mexico to seek novelty merchandise to be offered for sale in the "Mexican Shop," which is to be opened in the large retail store.

    If you were the head of this establishment, what qualifications would you seek in this buyer? Why?

COLLATERAL READINGS

Collins, V. D. *World Marketing*. Philadelphia: J. B. Lippincott Company, 1935. Chapter 7.

Dartnell International Trade Handbook, The. Chicago: The Dartnell Corporation, 1963. Part 6, Chapters 4, 5, and 6; Part 7.

de Haas, J. A. *The Practice of Foreign Trade*. New York: McGraw-Hill Book Company, Inc., 1935. Chapters 12 and 13.

Horn, Paul V. *International Trade Principles and Practices*, Third Edition. New York: Prentice-Hall, Inc., 1951. Chapter 26.

MacDonald, Philip. *Practical Exporting*. New York: Ronald Press Company, 1949. Chapter 3.

Pratt, E. E. *Modern International Commerce*. New York: Allyn and Bacon, Inc., 1956. Chapter 4.

Roorbach, G. B. *Problems in Foreign Trade*. New York: McGraw-Hill Book Company, Inc., 1933. Part III.

Tosdal, H. R. *Problems in Export Sales Management*. New York: McGraw-Hill Book Company, Inc., 1922. Chapter 8.

Wyman, Walter F. *Export Merchandising*. New York: McGraw-Hill Book Company, Inc., 1922. Chapters 10–14.

CHAPTER 12

INTERNATIONAL ADVERTISING MEDIA

In the keen competition encountered in world markets, the American foreign trader is aided, as perhaps are the businessmen of no other nation, by the sales-producing force of advertising.

Skillfully planned and directed publicity not only at home but also abroad will overcome prejudice, combat foreign competition, establish new habits, satisfy wants, build goodwill, and thus multiply sales and lay a foundation for permanent and profitable business.

This is not to say that the businessmen of other industrial nations do not utilize advertising to good advantage. However, mass production in the United States poured such a mountain of products on the market that, in line with the purchasing power of this market, it was necessary to develop mass distribution. Thus, advertising, in all of its branches, was rapidly developed as an integral part of mass distribution.

The subject of advertising in all of its ramifications is extremely complex; and when its usefulness and application in foreign countries are considered, the most that can be attempted in chapters of this nature is to outline the highlights and sketch the principles. Details relating to the use of any one channel of advertising for any one product or service in any one country are exacting. Witness the veritable libraries of books bearing on advertising in the United States market alone.[1]

While advertising is used as a sales method in itself as in the mail-order business, its use has stimulating effects when it is also coordinated with appropriate sales efforts. During a condition of scarcity, such as in

---

[1] This chapter will not deal with advertising in the United States market, whether for domestically made or imported products. It deals exclusively with the conditions of advertising abroad, whether goods are made in the United States and exported or whether they are made and sold in foreign countries.

wars or in emergencies, when supplies are exhausted, sales managers may use retentive advertising to keep the name of the product before the public. Often in this type of advertisement, the supply shortage is explained.[2] This is especially important where distant markets are involved. Advertising efforts are also sometimes geared toward the general welfare of the people. For example, "during World War II, American advertisers working in conjunction with our State Department and more directly with the Office of War Information contributed immeasurably toward winning the public opinion of nations which at the start were borderline cases."[3]

Finally, in times of national awareness of actual or potential enmity from foreign sources, "international advertising should overlook no opportunity to make friends for America."[4] In line with this state of world politics, an editorial in *Export Trade and Shipper*[5] declares:

> The impact of world developments on American business has become so direct and so obvious, even on companies whose operations are purely domestic, that every broad-gauge senior executive is inevitably and deeply concerned with international relations and world trade trends. Never was this more clearly shown than by the heavy attendance by top management, of many of our largest corporations, at the meeting of the United States Council of the International Chamber of Commerce two weeks ago. Particularly heavy is the responsibility of the top executives of those enterprises which serve foreign markets, whether by direct exports from this country, or through foreign branch factories or subsidiaries, or a combination of methods. In the minds of millions of individual foreigners American business and American products are our most ubiquitous ambassadors and most effective messengers of goodwill.

With statements of this nature expressed in the early 1950's, how much more significant are these views today, considering the impact of the Cold War and the efforts of the protagonists to influence favorably the uncommitted nations of the world.

---

[2]George F. Zealand, Publisher, Pan American Publishing Co., Inc., in *Export Trade and Shipper* (January 22, 1951), p. 36.

[3]N. DeFilippes, the N. DeFilippes Company, *ibid.*, p. 22.

[4]Stated by James F. Curtis, President, Coca-Cola Export Corporation, at the Second International Advertising Convention, 1950. See also William S. Honneus, Advertising Director, *Time International*, in *Export Trade and Shipper* (January 22, 1951), lead article entitled "More Than Selling Goods Required of Advertising in 1951 — Cultivation of Good Will for America Is Good Business and Civic Obligation"; and issue of October 2, 1950, where his lead article bears the subtitle "Case Histories Showing How Leading Firms are Winning Good-will for Themselves and the U.S."

[5]October 22, 1950, p. 22.

Fundamentals of Advertising Abroad

At the Ninth International Advertising Convention held in 1957 in New York, Arthur "Red" Motley observed the following four fundamentals of advertising abroad:

1. Create a *climate* at home on the part of top management. Try to have them think in terms of the domestic market and to take the same broad vision with regard to international operations. This is probably the most basic of all fundamentals as this same factor was emphasized in Chapter 7.

2. Do not think of the overseas market as a poor market. Despite the fact that a certain market may be underdeveloped, there is a market with money and it is interested in quality.

3. News is of prime importance so do not overdo prestige or age of company or establishment of a trade name or even the number of gold medals won at trade fairs since 1890 or 1870.

4. People are interested in real people, real situations, and in the use of a product. One of the great fundamentals is that people wish to believe that many other people just like themselves are doing the same thing; use the same equipment, the same product, the same service; have the same fine complexion, the same chic look; and can command the same means of traveling — by automobile.

"How much is the calling card of your company worth?" asks Harry E. Maynard, U.S. Advertising Manager, *Life International* editions. Dealing with this question, he continues . . . "in addition to advertising its products in all its overseas markets, a corporation must also introduce itself to the overseas market through corporate image advertising . . . ."[6]

Pointed out in this presentation is the attitude of people in other countries. In the United States we are inclined to say, "If the proposition is all right, the people behind it are all right." In older civilizations, for example, Europe, the attitude is the reverse — "If the people are all right, the proposition is all right."

For the long-term program of an international marketing firm, the importance of establishing a company and a brand image cannot be over-emphasized.

This leads into the public relations concept as compared with advertising. Public relations is usually defined as the art of influencing others to look upon you as you would have them look. It is an approach that seeks to promote the prestige or reputation of the business firm as a firm rather than as a producer of this particular soap or machine.

---

[6]In *Export Trade* (May 25, 1959), p. 11.

While all channels of advertising may be used to promote a good corporate image by skillful public relations, there is basically the essential that the company, from top management down, is worthy of the image that is portrayed. This means top management backing and high ethical standards. The phrase "corporate image advertising" is commonly used. It refers to publicity of any and all sorts that will serve to give a good impression of the company that makes the products. In the view of Mr. Maynard, this is preliminary to advertising products. In general, business firms do both simultaneously; for instance, "The world-famous manufacturer of X product invites your consideration of its offerings."

International Advertising Copy. Domestic advertising copy, particularly for use in the publications field, is often found to be unsatisfactory for international advertising purposes. The form in which a story is to be told is said to depend upon the temperament and psychology of the people for whom it is intended. The "snappy" or jocular copy, which appeals to the American public, would not be satisfactory in a more conservative part of the world. Tradition, religion, and economic conditions may dictate the necessity of wording an appeal in such manner as to meet particular situations.

> The Frenchman has quite definite ideas about advertising. He prefers a slogan. He will not be bothered with discursive texts (as in more disciplined countries like Germany). Loquaciousness is lost on him. He wants to be captivated and amused at the same time.
> And he often gets what he wants. French advertising is original, sometimes brilliant. Despite this there is still a tendency to lose harmony between a brilliant conception and the final ad.
> Another failing is the tendency, especially in women's magazines, to pack too many trade names into an ad. This brings about the pretense of its being a consumer ad when in reality it is a dealer's ad.[7]

With respect to Germany, the following observation is made:

> Advertising here, generally considered, is still about five years behind the U.S. The VW [Volkswagon] campaign may pave the way for more originality in the usual dead-serious German approach to advertising.[8]

Concerning Japan the comment is:

---

[7]*Advertising Age*, Vol. 34, No. 21 (May 20, 1963), p. 56. Reprinted by permission of the publisher.
[8]*Ibid.*

Commercials are generally couched in very polite terms and never come right out and say, "Buy Brand X Today." Such approach is offensive to delicate Japanese sensitivities. Rather the message will attempt an interesting explanation of [the] product and at the end suggest mildly that you try the product once. The most direct ads will say "XYZ Brand Please."[9]

Finally with respect to the Arab world:

Advertising to the 30,000,000 people living in seven Arab lands was almost an unknown commodity ten years ago.

But today, it's estimated that ad budgets for the seven countries are somewhere in the neighborhood of $10,000,000 annually—with most of the money going to Arab and English-language newspapers, local radio and television, cinemas and outdoor.[10]

Illustrations. The use of illustrations in international advertising calls for a knowledge of local conditions in order that they may fit required circumstances. A picture tells a story that is understood everywhere and, particularly in countries where literacy is not high, illustrations may be of greater proportionate value then copy. Color preferences are also to be found and superstitions may sometimes eliminate entirely or may strongly recommend the use of certain subjects for copy purposes. These factors are especially significant in connection with outdoor advertising, window display cards, or other illustrations that appear before the transient public, as well as packages, magazines, and catalogs.

Certain taboos are important and the successful advertiser will take note of them. A few examples will serve to illustrate this fact. Illustrations to be used for advertising in India, for example, should never show a cow — it is a sacred animal. Advertisers in Moslem countries should not forget that the purdah (a screen hiding women from the sight of men or strangers) is not extinct. An advertiser in the Sudan showed a camel in his illustration, knowing that camels are to be found there. Unfortunately he showed a Bactrian (two-humped) camel—and Sudanese camels have but one hump! Animals used to illustrate humans are not attractive or even understandable to Arabs. Allah states that a beast is a beast and a man is a man.

The symbol of three is lucky in West Africa. In the Far East white is the color of mourning among the Chinese and blue is not very lucky, but in the Far and Middle East and Africa red is a very lucky color.

---

[9]*Ibid.*, p. 78.
[10]*Ibid.*, p. 96.

Color plays an important role in the lives of these people and all films should be produced in bright colors. In Greece and Cyprus, houses should be white with blue shutters, the national colors of Greece.[11]

Many a sale has been lost which may have taken years of build-up through polite correspondence — only to be thrown to the winds during a personal meeting when one of the parties violates a customs taboo.

The well-meaning American custom of patting a child on the head . . . is one example of a strong Oriental taboo where the head is held sacred. A careless flick of a cigarette into a hearth is also commonplace here in the United States but in Japan the hearth is regarded as sacred.

Our Hong Kong adviser tells that the Chinese do not, as a rule, send clocks as presents. Giving clocks as gifts is strictly taboo . . . since to the Chinese, clocks can be taken as a bad omen. An overseas advertiser should think twice before using a gift-giving angle in his clock promotions.

Perhaps because religion is a more all-pervading life force in the Orient than in the Occident, it is good business sense not to choose an advertising symbol which might offend the religious sensibilities of Eastern peoples.[12]

With regard to the emerging African markets, it is declared that "the African is a sedulous imitator of European taste and custom. . . ." Symbols rather than colors have a greater impact on the African mind. However, certain symbols such as serpents and chameleons are anathema to many Africans. The white press reaches only a small group of educated Africans. The Africans have their own newspapers. Radio and television are powerful for advertising purposes as literacy is not necessary. Nevertheless, television advertisements are slanted to the white population. Bus advertising is useful with tapes of recorded music supplying the advertising spots. For motion pictures, mobile projection vans are used for rural areas and advertising films are also shown.[13]

Since this discussion relates to the advertising of consumer goods, it is well to emphasize that in the sale of capital goods and other industrial items these problems are not so likely to arise. The buyer in the latter cases purchases on the basis of facts and performance.

---

[11]Bruno Kiwi, Director, Pearl and Dean Overseas Company, London, in *Export Trade* (January 26, 1959), p. 74.

[12]Noble de Roin, President, International Advertising Company, Denver, Colorado, in *Export Trade and Shipper* (May 12, 1958), p. 55. Mr. de Roin also quoted Elma Kelly, Managing Director, Cathay Limited, Hong Kong.

[13]*Export Trade* (January 28, 1963), pp. 13–14.

Translation. A common problem in copy work for international marketing is translation. If it is intended for a British public, it is important to render the copy in the King's English and to recognize differences in American and British spellings and colloquialisms. A more difficult problem is translating copy into a foreign tongue. Particularly in technical translations, as in export catalogs, there may be a complete absence of foreign synonyms for certain English words. Perhaps new words may be coined or a description may be phrased that will correctly convey the idea in the foreign language. Moreover, there is sometimes the question of a number of languages or dialects in a particular market. In India, for example, there are 14 languages and any nation-wide campaign — be it visual or audio — must be planned very carefully.

It is obvious that expert assistance is needed to render technical expressions intelligible in foreign tongues. A successful translation formula is often a combination of one who knows the article and one who knows the foreign language. For nontechnical translations, a common plan is to submit copy to branches or dealers abroad, thus assuring observance of local language requirements. Some large foreign advertisers follow the plan of setting up the basic pattern of advertisements in this country and sending out this material to distributors and branch managers abroad who take care of translations to suit their respective markets. Others do the original writing of an advertisement in the language of the country. From a survey of many advertisements prepared abroad in Europe, Latin America, Middle East, and South Asia, the conclusion was drawn that "foreign copy writers follow closely the themes and techniques familiar to us, and originally developed largely by American ad men. Artwork and layout are marked by a sound simplicity of technique, reflecting the foreign atmosphere in varying degrees."[14]

An interesting example of an illustration that works in the opposite direction, that is, copy for use in the United States market, demonstrates the futility of literal translations. One concern in Europe was preparing a booklet for distribution in the United States. One page made reference to the tourist attractions of a certain area. One sentence, in the original, stated "fresh fruits are enjoyed by gourmets throughout the year." When translated literally into English, this read "all year long the fruits are enjoying the gastronomists."[15] As one professional group of language interpretors states — to kill a sales message, translate it!

---

[14]*Export Trade and Shipper* (January 23, 1950), p. 16, with illustrations.

[15]David Penn, Director, Hill and Knowlton International, at the Tenth International Advertising Association Convention, 1958.

Trademarks and Trade Names. Trademarks and trade names are used extensively by manufacturers of consumer and industrial goods entering export markets. As a distinctive symbol of a common origin and quality of all merchandise on which or in reference to which they are used, trademarks and trade names are without equal. In conjunction with advanced methods of advertising and merchandising, these symbols have played an important part in the export program of numerous international marketing firms. Frequently, the same trademark or trade name used in domestic sales will meet the requirements of the foreign market. There is, indeed, believed to be value attached to the application of the same symbol for a certain line of merchandise marketed all over the world. The protection of rights inherent in the advertising value

Campbell Soup Company

The same trade name that is used in domestic sales is found prominently displayed in this Stockholm market.

of these symbols is often a matter of concern due to diversity of laws throughout the world.[16]

Since advertising depends so heavily on symbolism to achieve its ends, care should be exercised in choosing a symbol for international advertising.

> Identification, the function of the trade-mark, is the passport link between our manufacturers and products and the overseas customers. And in the past 15 years, identification has not kept pace with the rapid expansion of our international business; and our problems will multiply in the years ahead with the trends for common markets in several world areas. . . .
>
> The handling of identification problems at home and abroad can easily be streamlined by sound and logical cooperation of the management team. We (International Harvester) have an Executive Product Identification Committee comprised of top management representatives of sales, advertising, engineering, manufacturing, industrial design, Foreign Operations, and the legal trade-mark responsibilities. This committee discusses, reviews, and approves all recommendations for identification which include trade-marks, trade names, product model designation, painting, and decoration. Each representative considers his share of responsibility in the over-all recommendation, and adjustments or modifications are made when needed to form a compromise that will be satisfactory to all interests of the management.[17]

As an essential element in advertising programs, trademarks and trade names command the same attention overseas as they do at home and probably more. In areas in which literacy is low and consumer trade is sought, these symbols may constitute the heart of the merchandising plan.

Fields of International Advertising Media

A survey of international advertising media can be only general in character, since the specific conditions that currently affect any particular method or locality are constantly changing.

International advertising media may be divided into three fields:

1. Trade or industrial.   3. Professional or ethical.
2. Consumer.

---

[16]The subject of trademarks, along with various other aspects of foreign commercial law, is presented in Chapter 24.

[17]Fitzhugh Granger, Manager of Merchandising Services, International Harvester Foreign Operations, at the United States Trademark Association meeting, April 11, 1958, Atlantic City, New Jersey. Reported in *Export Trade and Shipper* (May 12, 1958), p. 20.

As recognized in domestic practice, *trade* or *industrial* advertising aims to reach distributors, seeking to induce them to stock the merchandise advertised, and commission sales representatives who solicit indent orders. *Consumer* advertising, on the other hand, seeks to induce consumers to purchase advertised products by name or brand from the store or outlet that serves the consumer. *Professional* or *ethical* advertising attempts to influence professional people to prescribe or to advise the use of the publicized products. Medical and dental publications come to mind in this connection. Some advertising media serve exclusively the aims of one field, but in many instances the media may be useful in more than one field.

Many factors, depending upon the nature of the product and a company's sales objectives, affect the advertising program, even within one or another of these broad groupings.

> For example, certain consumer goods, such as patent medicines, foodstuffs, etc., would be handled on a country-by-country basis with slam-bang explosive promotional programs. In such cases it is common to arbitrarily face the distribution, even through consignment or sale-or-return methods, and depend upon the sheer weight of advertising to dispose of merchandise and create a continuing demand. Other consumer goods would be handled on a slower and less hazardous basis in which sales distribution and advertising would go hand in hand.[18]

Publication Advertising. In this section we shall first examine the characteristics of United States publications that circulate chiefly abroad. Then, we shall discuss the role played by foreign publications in international advertising and inquire into some of the problems that face the export advertiser who uses foreign publications.

United States Publications Circulating Chiefly Abroad. Among the media useful in international advertising are the various magazines and papers issued in the United States for circulation in foreign countries. They are read by businessmen abroad, reaching prospective importers and dealers. They provide knowledge of the scientific developments affecting technical operations and modern methods of distribution and advertising fields where information is not usually available abroad, for example, drugs, medicine, engineering, automotive, and chemical. "In a specialized field, a business magazine groups together the buying power of many countries, none of which would be sufficient standing alone to make pos-

---

[18]Charles W. Applegate, the late Director of Foreign Sales, The Esterbrook Pen Company, Camden, New Jersey, in a letter to the author, dated January 27, 1956. Mr Applegate kindly reviewed this and the following chapter.

sible the publication of a generous, profusely illustrated, technically live, and editorially advanced magazine."[19]

These publications may be general or specialized. Some of them, such as *American Exporter*, *American Exporter-Industrial* (both English and Spanish), and *Importers Guide*, are general in appeal but maintain departments for special lines of goods — hardware, textiles, automotive, electrical, etc. Others are class or technical journals, such as *El Automovil Americano*, *Ingenieria Internacional* (2 editions), *El Farmaceutico*, *Oral Hygiene*, *Vision* (2 editions), and many others. These journals are leaders in their respective fields in international trade. "Industrial advertisers . . . depend solely on trade papers for they carry the prestige-building influence of United States origin."[20]

Journals especially designed to reach the consumer class of trade in foreign markets include *La Hacienda*, *Readers Digest* (with twelve separate foreign editions), *Time* (with four foreign editions) *Newsweek* (international editions), *Life International*, and several others. These journals are read in the homes, clubs, and farms in foreign countries and carry advertisements largely of branded consumer goods or services.

There is another type of United States publication for international distribution, published from time to time by firms of international merchants and circulated widely in those areas where these concerns have special interests.

These United States journals that circulate abroad will produce inquiries for goods and initiate trade relations which may subsequently develop into sales or dealer connections. Moreover, there is an advertising value in the continuity of keeping the trademark or name of the manufacturer before the readers of these journals. The popular journals, of course, reach the consumer market.

The publications also often perform auxiliary services for the concerns that advertise in their columns. Translation of correspondence arising from advertisements, credit reports on foreign buyers, lists of prospective customers, point-of-sale items supplied free, and advice on international marketing problems may all be included in the services offered gratuitously, depending upon the advertising contract.

Foreign Publications. Daily newspapers are among the most effective methods of reaching the buying public in any land. There is no civilized part of the world that does not boast of its newspaper, and the effective-

---

[19]James L. Gilbert, *Export Trade and Shipper* (January 20, 1941), p. 12.
[20]Thomas W. Hughes, at the First International Advertising Convention, 1949.

ness of this medium for advertising purposes may be compared favorably with its position in the United States. Indeed, newspapers may afford a greater relative value for advertising purposes abroad than in this country. When the literacy of a people is low, the consuming population for most goods is confined largely to those highest in the economic and social scale. These are generally literate and read the dailies that are published locally. It therefore follows that an advertisement in the newspapers will reach almost the entire effective buying public.

Magazines, weekly or monthly, published abroad are also to be considered by the international advertiser. These may have a wide circulation throughout a country, and in some instances, as in the case of feminine interests, they may provide the only means of special appeal. The use of magazines is important to make United States trademarks and United States products known and to reach distributors or sales representatives who may not be covered by United States trade magazines. Generally, however, magazines in foreign countries are confined in their circulation to a certain locality where they may be of considerable, although restricted, advertising value. One or two examples will serve to illustrate these problems.

With respect to the number of readers for one newspaper in an underdeveloped country, Jagan Nath Jaini of National Advertising Service observed that in India there are 330 dailies with a total circulation of more than 3 million. While conceding that this is not an impressive standing, he declared, "But each copy is read by several people and circulations are growing day by day."[21]

Advertising in the Benelux countries introduces problems that are not likely to be anticipated by the uninformed. According to a Belgian, Dan E. G. Rosseels, Advertising Manager of the Belgian editions of *Libelle, Goed Nieuws-Bonnes Nouvelles*, and *Panorama*, a common mistake in advertising in Belgium is to consider that country as French-speaking, whereas 55 percent of the population speaks Flemish.

A news dispatch to the *Philadelphia Inquirer* of July 3, 1963, from Brussels, Belgium, stated:

> Premier Theo Lefevre called on King Baudouin to ask him to accept the resignation of his Government. . . . The issue that brought down the Government — the language status of Brussels suburbs — is symbolic of the problem that has split the 9 million people of Belgium and led to clashes between the two language groups. North Belgians

---

[21]*Proceedings, Ninth International Advertising Association, 1957.*

are Flemings. They speak Flemish, a form of Dutch. South Belgians are Walloons. They speak French. Brussels, in the Flemish area, is essentially a two language city.

With more and more French speaking people moving to Flemish suburbs, the Government proposed to make the suburbs bi-lingual. The Flemings said, "No."

In a Reuter's despatch of July 12, 1963, the lower house of Parliament had passed a reform bill following extensive debate, which "aroused new activity by Flemish extremists, who were blamed for Thursday's explosion of a bomb at the tomb of Belgium's unknown soldier."

With respect to the press in the Netherlands, political parties and religion have a very important influence on readership, circulation, and geographical distribution of newspapers and other periodicals.

> The political system is mainly based on religious concepts; so are the trade unions, libraries, youth movements, clubs, and welfare organizations. As a result, readership of newspapers and other periodicals is only rarely determined by social or income groups. Roman Catholics will read one or more Catholic papers; Protestants read Protestant papers; members of the Dutch labor party may prefer a socialist paper; and still others will choose a "neutral" paper. . . .
>
> The advertising message thus benefits by the often tremendous goodwill (and reader influence) of the medium. The publications realize this too and apply high standards to their advertising, for the editors realize that they would be blamed for unethical advertising.[22]
>
> Magazines collectively in Latin America lag behind their contemporaries in other parts of the globe. By and large, magazines have not caught the tempo and editorial know-how so well developed in other world areas. They lack production polish, quality printing and fine paper. Few have captured the imaginations or fancies of local audiences.
>
> Yet, magazines perhaps are the most effective and economical vehicle through which to direct advertising messages. The reason is simple: They selectively pinpoint the literate, high income people and permit the advertiser to concentrate sales power where it does the most good.
>
> Mexico's magazines suffer the same ills as Mexico's newspapers, and more besides. Poor quality paper and ink offer advertisers little. Between 25 and 30 general interest domestic magazines are published.[23]

In the African (Rhodesia and Nyasaland) markets, the white press reaches only a small group of educated Africans.

---

[22]Dan E. G. Rosseels, as quoted in *Export Trade and Shipper* (January 28, 1957), p. 18.
[23]*Advertising Age, op. cit.,* pp. 91, 93.

The advertising value of foreign newspapers and magazines depends, in large measure, on the nature of the product that is advertised. From this standpoint, these advertising media must be carefully studied in order to prevent unnecessary waste of funds.

Problems in Using Foreign Publications. Several serious difficulties may confront advertisers in most foreign publications. It is generally considered that in many foreign countries advertising is behind in its development, when compared with American advertising. This is not true of all publications or of all countries, but the export advertiser is likely to find a different appreciation of advertising abroad from that at home.

Some of the difficult problems that may be encountered are:

1. Difficulty of ascertaining circulation figures. There is seldom to be found abroad any complement of the ABC (Audit Bureau of Circulation) in the United States. Reliable circulation figures for all or a certain number of publications are obtained through ABC or a foreign equivalent in the United Kingdom and the Dominions (Canada, Australia, New Zealand, South Africa, India), Norway, Sweden, Denmark, Argentina, Puerto Rico, Mexico, Venezuela, and Dominican Republic. There is a slow growth abroad in appreciating the value of independent audits of circulation. For example, India's ABC began in 1948 and Puerto Rico's in 1949.[24] Therefore, the circulation claims of foreign newspapers and magazines may or may not be accurate.

2. Ascertaining class and sex of readers.

3. Accurate analysis of the purchasing power of readers may also be difficult.

4. Political views of newspapers in foreign countries are often pronounced and the class of readers, for example, liberal, radical, progressive, and labor, may be determined from this attitude. The editorial views of some newspapers may eliminate them from consideration for advertising purposes by American exporters, particularly when these views are un-American or anti-American. In times when the national interest of the United States may not be concerned, however, anti-American editorials may not necessarily be taken seriously.

Although legally there is complete press freedom in Mexico, newspapers are heavily dependent on the government. With an estimated

---

[24]Thomas W. Hughes, *loc. cit.*

50% of all economic activity directly controlled by federal corporations and agencies, the government is one of the largest display advertisers. Aside from that, it also buys space in the news columns.

This is a customary form of advertising in Mexico. Federal officials pay to have their press releases published. State governors will buy full pages so that their annual addresses to the legislatures — or any other activities they feel warrant it — will be given what they consider sufficient space in the capital's dailies.

The news columns are for sale not only to the government, but to anyone who has the price. Since there is no indication what space is paid for, it is impossible to tell exactly how much advertising appears in a given newspaper.

The government, along with private industry, helps publishers pay reporters, handing out a monthly stipend to newsmen on a given "beat."[25]

5. Ascertaining rates and space. The one-price system is an American institution and has yet to win approval throughout the world. There may be alternate haggling and bargaining in dealing with publishers abroad. Sometimes so-called "American" advertising rates are higher than for local advertisers. The higher American rate is claimed to be due to the inclusion of an allowance for the publisher representative's commission, in addition to an advertising agency commission. The United States representatives of international publications advertising and foreign editors should be considered part of overhead.

Much must be done in the area of media rates, which are not firm and often subject to negotiation. There is no universal adherence to established agency commission systems. Many media allow agency commission discounts to advertisers placing business direct. In Brazil, where the agency commission is 20%, agencies normally charge a service fee of 17.65% on the net which, in effect, amounts to lowering card rates almost 6%. This, in turn, makes it difficult for many Brazilian agencies to operate at a fair profit.[26]

6. Lack of uniformity of column width and page size, which results in greater production expense for the advertiser.[27]

---

[25]*Advertising Age, op. cit.*, p. 91.

[26]*Ibid.*, p. 94.

[27]Difficulties and peculiarities of international publications' advertising have been given serious attention by the Association of International Publishers' Representatives, an organization formed in 1933 and organized in 1935 by American representatives of newspapers and magazines published in foreign countries.

In addition to the national press, there are newspapers and magazines of other nationalities published in foreign countries. Some United States papers are published abroad, for example, *European Herald Tribune*. Such media may possess a wide appeal when it is considered that publications in English are read by the British, by the Americans, and by many educated local residents.

Direct-Mail Advertising. Direct-mail advertising, in its accepted sense, consists of all forms of publicity sent by an advertiser to prospective customers with the intention and hope of influencing or consummating a sale. In its most extended use by an exporting manufacturer or export house, it provides a flexible counterpart of publication advertising.

Direct-mail advertising is most effective when purchases may be made locally or where inquiries may be addressed to a local dealer or sales office. Direct-mail advertising consists principally of various forms of printed matter transmitted through the mails, for example, letters, catalogs, house organs,[28] booklets, and a large number of miscellaneous forms such as calendars and blotters, which are so well-known in the United States.

Circularization. Circular letters, either individual or in series, are used extensively in international marketing as part of the advertising program.

The first step in circularization is the preparation of a mailing list. Assistance in preparing this list may be obtained from the international trade-promoting organizations and agencies described in Chapter 6 and from the Bureau of International Commerce. Limited lists may be obtained directly from officers of the Foreign Service. Various directories may also be consulted, some of which are worldwide in coverage. *Kelly's Directory of Merchants, Manufacturers and Shippers of the World* (annual) is particularly well-known, as are *Annuaire du Commerce Didot-Botin* and *International Register of Telegraphic and Trade Addresses*. In addition, a number of American directories, such as *Buyers for Export* (Thomas Ashwell and Company, Inc.) and *Latin American Sales Index* (Dun & Bradstreet, Inc.), are published.

---

[28]A house organ may actually be a magazine designed to build goodwill for the exporting company, for example, International Harvester Co.'s quarterly *Horizons*. "Studebaker's *Overseas News* (also quarterly) serves its world-wide dealer organization three ways: as a newspaper; as a sales promotion piece; and as a public relations tool." A British company, Imperial Chemical Industries, Ltd., publishes *Endeavor* (quarterly) that is mailed all over the world to scientists and educators.

Telephone directories and local directories, both general and classified, are widely available. Care is to be exercised, however, in the use of lists obtained from these sources. Unless classification is complete, serious errors may occur so as to confuse retailers with importers or wholesalers, for example.

The chief weakness of circularization in international as in domestic trade is the absence of individual appeal. Methods of duplication, however, have been so improved that simulated individualized letters may be distributed.

Export Catalogs. Another direct-mail piece of advertising is the export catalog. An export catalog should provide the sales force necessary to sway a prospect into attention, then consideration, conviction, and finally action. It has to tell its own story and answer all manner of questions or objections that might be raised and otherwise go unchallenged. The catalog cannot argue and convince as does the salesman — it tells its story and then closes its cover.

Although the preparation of catalogs presents some peculiar export problems, their value is well recognized. The export catalog should be attractive in appearance and have illustrations throughout, since many countries have not developed industrially and therefore word descriptions of technical products cannot be readily grasped. Action illustrations are more convincing, both at home and abroad. Telegraphic code words should be printed in connection with the articles and parts of articles carried in an export catalog in order to facilitate the sending of cable or radio communications.

Prices. Export catalogs may indicate the price of each article, particularly if the catalog is intended for trade use rather than for consumer distribution. If the catalog is intended for consumer advertising, however, prices may be omitted by an exporter and inserted, if at all, by overseas representatives.

Such price lists should contain specific information as to weights and measurements, shipping terms, and possibly terms of payment. A covering letter may also be used to give the terms of payment and the exporter's banking references.

When prices are shown, it is preferable to indicate list prices in United States currency.[29] The use of the dollar sign ($) should be accompanied by a clear indication in the catalog that United States currency is intended, since many other nations employ the dollar sign as a

---

[29]For a discussion of international pricing procedures, see Chapter 21.

currency symbol. In some cases it may be advisable to quote prices in a foreign currency. When, in view of local distribution, prices in local currency are to appear in print, they generally are to be inserted by representatives or branches abroad. Another alternative is provided by showing in the price list the foreign equivalent acceptable in lieu of dollars. Only with currencies of reasonable stability, however, may this practice be safely adopted.

DISCOUNTS. Discounts should be omitted from the export catalog. They are generally shown on a separate sheet, which may also indicate such data as shipping weights and measurements, freight rates, and other matters for ready reference. The necessity of carefully guarding the secrecy of discounts is enhanced when the distribution of catalogs to more than one class of foreign distributor is contemplated. It is decidedly unwise to allow the retailer to know what the wholesaler pays, and to let the wholesaler know the cost of goods to the importer (if there is a separate importer).

SPECIFICATIONS. An accurate and clear description of product specifications is also essential in an export catalog. The catalog, in anticipating every sort of question that may arise, should specify weights, measurements, capacities, ratings, packing, equipment, description, and all other essential data. Moreover, a reader of the export catalog is most likely to be familiar with the metric system, rather than American units of weight and measure.

OTHER INFORMATION. Other information carried in a catalog relates to the standing, age, reputation, etc., of the manufacturing or merchandising concern issuing the catalog. Cuts of the factory or office building may be used and the general tone and quality of a catalog may be expected to bespeak the corporate image.

It is rather naive to state that a catalog should be printed in a language that is understood by prospective readers. Moreover, an export catalog is not always merely a translation of a domestic catalog. The large amount of additional data appearing exclusively in an export catalog indicates the necessity of recomposing, if not rewriting, the domestic catalog for overseas distribution. This decision, of course, will depend upon the extent of revision entailed.

DISTRIBUTION. Due to the host of professional and amateur catalog collectors throughout the world, it is highly advisable to adopt a cautious policy of distribution. Free distribution to a carefully selected mailing list is one means of placing a catalog in the hands of proper persons. It is also advisable to place copies of catalogs in the hands of American Foreign Service Officers abroad, chambers of commerce, and other similar organizations to which prospective buyers may be expected to direct inquiries.

Motion Pictures (Cinema). International theater screen advertising is gaining increased recognition as a major, effective and growing medium.[30]

In countries too small to support quality magazines and newspapers, cinema advertising enjoys considerable success. Many theaters in small countries sell commercial film time. In certain areas, however, audiences have grumbled about the quality of cinema advertising, and some governments (Brazil for example) have issued decrees banning them.[31]

It is often thought that theater advertising is restricted only to the showing of "spot" commercials on the theater screen. However, in many world markets, in addition to showing spot commercials we find that they are also running soft-sell short subjects, and newsreels containing paid-for news items such as the opening of a client's store or similar promotional activity. Ever growing in importance is the use of theatres for merchandising. This includes giving out samples, distributing redeemable coupons and also lobby displays. The last three activities are generally tied in with conventional spot commercials on the screen.

Cinema advertising is world-wide. The latest estimate is that there are 140 markets in which theater advertising plays an important role. As such markets grow in importance, an organization devoted exclusively to handling cinema advertising usually is formed. These theater advertising factors are grouped together into two world-wide organizations. The oldest is the *International Screen Advertising Services* with headquarters in London, England. This organization has more than 21 large theater advertising concerns as members and through them theater commercials can be booked in more than 100 world markets.

The second world organization is the *International Screen Publicity Association*. These two organizations cooperate each year in holding the International Advertising Film Festival. Films are designed to take advantage of the large screen and generally tend toward a softer sell with emphasis on amusement values. This is out of respect to the "captive" nature of their audiences.

---

[30]International Advertising Association, *International Advertiser*, Vol. 1, No. 1 (June, 1960), p. 10.

[31]*Advertising Age, op. cit.*, p. 93.

There are two main types of theater advertising: individual placement and package plans. Individual placement means that one orders a *specific* commercial exhibited in a specific theater for a specific time period. Package purchases involve either a number of theaters on a set circuit or the use of an entertainment vehicle such as a sportsreel, newsreel or revista short subject to encapsulate the commercial. Once spliced into such a short subject, the advertising film remains part of it during all its bookings.

One must evaluate the audiences reached by both systems in relation to the *product being advertised*. Generally speaking, package plans tend to reach more people at a lower cost-per-thousand than does individual placement. The cost per thousand for some packages is remarkably low. For example, the Cine Mundial revista circuit plays 336 theaters throughout Colombia at a cost per thousand of (US) $1.15 for a one-minute film.

It is frequently misleading to make overall generalizations, but the tendency is to advertise high-ticket or luxury items through specific cinema placements and widely sold consumer products through package plans, especially those in which the commercial is encapsulated in a sportsreel or a revista.

It is generally conceded that theater advertising has many "plus" values in terms of its *quality* of impact. To mention a few, there are the advantages of the large screen size, the vivid colors which do so much for package and product identification, the complete absence of messages for competing products, the relatively few other commercials shown on the program, and the power of movement, product demonstration and sound.

Unfortunately, when media comparisons are put in recommendations for client consideration, the comparative cost-per-thousand figures assume major importance.

One major factor of theater advertising which does not always receive the notice that it deserves is the essentially "captive" nature of the audience. A very accurate determination of the "readership" of a given ad is possible if the theater attendance is known. And, in most markets, this figure is available and reasonably accurate.

Professional theater advertising organizations have come to recognize that only through furnishing detailed audience data and accurate attendance figures will advertisers continue to invest their advertising budgets in cinemas. Information — *accurate* information — is a prime factor in the growth of the whole medium.

In most markets accurate attendance figures *are* available either from government tax records or from the confidential files of theatrical film distributors who book their films on a percentage basis.

International Screen Advertising Services members have taken the lead throughout the world in upgrading the quantity and quality of theater information. Markets, for which two years ago the data consisted of only the name of the theater and the rate, are now supplying complete information on individual theaters. . . .

Turning to the question of program control and verification, we can report significant strides to reduce problems in this area. The professional theater advertising companies are fully aware that failure to perform can severely discourage advertisers. Companies all over the world are actively undertaking programs designed to show theater owners and managers the importance of accurate performance and reporting. Liaison with the theatrical checking organizations has provided control heretofore unavailable to theater advertising.

One of the major strengths of theater advertising is the ability to select the proper theaters which attract the type of patrons the advertiser is specifically trying to reach. To make these selections the media buyer depends on accurate information. It is the basic working material from which the conscientious buyer fashions a campaign recommendation.[32]

The use of cinema firms or of slides is highly effective in the hands of salesmen agents, distributors, and branch managers.

Commercial Fairs and Exhibits. Commercial fairs and exhibits, held at regular intervals in many foreign cities, afford the exporter a novel method of publicity. Such events are more common and are more largely attended than are those in the United States, and in many instances they have attained a high reputation.[33] By engaging space at a fair, distributing literature, and providing demonstrations, it may be possible to obtain good distribution connections abroad.

Among the various private and old established fairs are the Leipzig sample fairs that date from the Middle Ages. The International Sample Fair at Lyon, first held in 1419, annually attracts worldwide attention, and the same is true of the sample fair that has been held at Frankfort-on-Main since the year 1219. Of recent origin is the British Industries Fair that is held annually at London, Birmingham, and Glasgow. The Canadian National Exhibition held each year at Toronto is also wide in scope.

In recent years, as sales efforts have become more direct, American concerns have taken more interest in these events as exhibitors. Formerly they were visited almost exclusively by import buyers who found a wide display of foreign products.[34]

---

[32]International Advertising Association, *op. cit.*, pp. 10–11.

[33]Probably the first United States international commercial fair, as distinguished from an exhibition, was the Chicago Fair, first held in 1950. San Francisco, however, has held a World Trade Fair annually since 1948, with exhibits from home and abroad, and provides facilities to discuss business and travel. A World Trade Fair, held in New York in 1957, has also been repeated annually.

[34]See also Chapter 4.

Outdoor Advertising. "Outdoor advertising is one of the major advertising media throughout the world. The tremendous increase in the daily use of the automobile in many countries found corresponding increases in the importance of the outdoor medium."[35]

Outdoor advertising relates to billboards, electric or illuminated signs, and posters. As is true of every method of advertising when used abroad, it will be found that conditions vary widely throughout the world

> Aside from billboards, which are growing in number and effectiveness, located at heavily traveled points and in sporting areas, in a few countries some stores have painted advertisements which are colorful and attractive on walls, doors, or metal store front closures.
>
> A new type of display made from thousands of oversized, varicolored sequins has made its appearance in a few countries. Usually this sign is limited to trade-marks, trade names, or simple designs. If properly located, this display has a glittering, live brilliance which attracts the eye even from a distance.
>
> Some companies have made good use of small, permanent, all-weather enameled metal signs. Sometimes the product trademark or company name could be illustrated without the need for text matter; thus the sign was purchased in bulk for universal distribution. Frequently such signs were purchased and distributed from abroad at a considerable saving. However, companies and their foreign representatives were unanimous in their opinion that the placing of the sign must be done by the manufacturer or his own representative. . . .
>
> The judicious distribution at sporting events of eye shades and fans with advertising messages is effective for some products, as are wall or wallet calendars. However, these are so acceptable that the advertiser must be prepared to meet a demand of astronomical proportions.
>
> Bus cards are good, especially for products usually bought by the bus riders. However, most buses are overcrowded; therefore interior cards are of doubtful value. The outside cards are more visible and the preferred position, those on the back of the bus.[36]

Specific consideration should be given to permanent metal signs in areas where heat, humidity, or other severe weather conditions would make other types of outdoor signs impractical. Under the most favorable conditions, outdoor advertising is managed with the same ease and it produces the same results as in the United States. In many places, however, centralized ownership of outdoor advertising facilities is lacking,

---

[35]International Advertising Association, *Code of Standards of Advertising Practice* (New York, 1961), p. 103.
[36]Applegate, *op. cit.*, p. 21.

rates are not fixed, and municipal ordinances may hinder their employment. Long-range home office supervision is out of the question and
branch house, dealer, or agency control over outdoor advertising of all
kinds is essential.

The Coca-Cola Export Corporation

A permanent metal sign, which incorporates a domestic trademark, hangs above
the entrance to this dealer's store in Baalbek, Lebanon.

Light standards are also equipped in some countries for carrying
advertisements. It is true, however, that electric signs, including neon,
are nowhere as widely to be found as in the United States; and it is
generally admitted that no country has succeeded quite so well in effectively concealing landscapes behind billboards. One American company
is fortunate in having a name that lends itself to ingenious Spanish advertising by means of illuminated electric signs. Admiral uses a step by
step flashing message in Spanish. The first flash reveals MIRA (Spanish
for look!); then follows ADMIRA (Spanish for admire!); finally, the
complete name is shown ADMIRAL.

Samples and Demonstrations. *Sample distribution* is probably the oldest form of advertising. What form of promotion can be more effective than by offering a free sample of the product? Such an offer suggests that the producer is so certain of the appeal of his product that a sample will be sufficient to create a customer.

This method of publicity is extended chiefly to consumer type merchandise. It is perfectly feasible to give away samples of chewing gum, cigarettes, beverages, etc. However, there are certain problems that arise in connection with the use of samples in international advertising. These are:

1. The method of distribution must be closely controlled to make certain that the samples will serve the purpose intended.

2. Import duties may be a controlling factor in determining the economic desirability of sample distribution abroad.

3. Availability of the product in the appropriate sales channels must be assured. It makes no sense to distribute samples and then have no arrangements for convinced customers to purchase the product! In many instances, it should be noted, sample distribution would be handled by the representative in a foreign country and would thus constitute a dealer help, which will be discussed in the succeeding chapter.

4. Care must be exercised to make certain that the sample distribution is effective. There are people in many countries who believe (for very good reasons) that anything given away free is worth nothing. Free sample distribution under such circumstances would be useless.

Product demonstrations apply generally to industrial goods. An automobile distributor or dealer, for example, takes a prospective customer for a ride and thereby demonstrates the performance of the product. Demonstrations are also made at places where prospective buyers are likely to gather, as at a trade or sample fair. One of the outstanding commercial features of the American exhibit at the Brussels Fair (1957) was the display and demonstration of American products.

Radio. In recent years, radio advertising has attracted wide and increasing attention and American advertisers have been prompt in investigating possibilities of the radio for promoting foreign sales.

Radio advertising in international marketing is conducted almost entirely through local broadcasting stations abroad. These stations are either government owned and controlled (generally accepting no advertising) or they are independent. Many of them broadcast both long- and shortwave. Radio chains have been slow in developing in the various countries.

Radio advertising has shown vast drawing power, particularly for promoting the sale of consumer goods. This is of special value in advertising in countries with low literacy ratios, but with purchasing power for the advertised product. The number of radio listeners in an overseas area, such as Latin America, cannot be accurately determined from the estimated number of radio-receiving sets because of the installation of loud speakers at public squares, markets, cafes, drug and department stores, beaches, hotels, and amusement resorts.

In many countries, radio actually "is the most important medium only because the situation is somewhat worse from a factual and accurate measurement point of view. Costs have little bearing on coverage and are based mainly on how well the station can substantiate its claim of being the 'leading station.' "[37]

In other words, radio has pulling power for the mass of consumers, although statistics to measure its effect accurately are not available. Continuing, Mr. Hughes asserts that "stations cannot be judged by the printed information on power, frequency, and programming because it is not necessary to emit 5,000 watts from a 5,000-watt transmitter — it will operate on less, and often does — frequencies both long- and short-wave are seldom clear channel. . . . And if you will investigate program titles, in an effort to locate your new show in a good time bracket, you will find too many titles to be nothing but platter sessions with numerous spot commercials interrupting every recording. Even station logs are tough things to get from many stations."[38]

There appears to be gradual improvement in the quality of radio advertising service available abroad as competition has forced foreign radio stations to schedule better programs.[39] United States exporters who utilize local radio broadcasting overseas previously confined their attention to "spot" announcements, although the use of live talent is increasing as station facilities improve.

An Association of Representatives for Foreign Broadcasting Stations was formed in 1939 to standardize and broaden their services to export

[37]Hughes, *loc. cit.*

[38]Hughes, *loc. cit.*

[39]Eugene Bernald, Vice-President, Pan-American Broadcasting Co., *Export Trade and Shipper* (January 23, 1950), p. 80.

advertisers and agencies. The association has endeavored to secure reliable station data, listener habits, and program preferences; and it has succeeded in stabilizing the rates of many stations. It seeks to assist local

Table 12-1
HOW TELEVISION STACKS UP OVERSEAS[40]
Transmitting Stations 1951–1962*

	12/51	12/52	12/53	12/54	12/55	12/56	12/57	12/58	12/59	12/60	12/61	12/6
Non-Bloc Countries**	22	33	56	88	133	212	371	617	899	1,224	1,666	2,09
Communist Bloc	6	9	16	18	31	48	76	122	189	264	381	5
WORLD TOTAL	28	42	72	106	164	260	447	739	1,088	1,488	2,047	2,6

TV RECEIVERS (rounded in thousands)

	12/51	12/52	12/53	12/54	12/55	12/56	12/57	12/58	12/59	12/60	12/61	12/6
Non-Bloc Countries**	1,117	2,153	3,297	5,009	6,905	10,051	14,045	19,565	26,796	35,535	44,401	64,1
Communist Bloc	40	80	254	479	1,061	1,478	2,345	3,314	5,294	7,407	9,359	11,31
WORLD TOTAL	1,157	2,233	3,551	5,488	7,966	11,529	16,390	22,879	32,090	42,942	53,760	65,50

*Exclusive of the United States, Canada, and Armed Forces stations abroad.   **Includes Yugoslavi

TRANSMITTING STATIONS AND RECEIVERS BY AREAS
January 1–December 31, 1962

	TRANSMITTING STATIONS		RECEIVERS	
	Jan. 1 1962	Dec. 31 1962	In Use Jan. 1, 1962	In Use Dec. 31, 1962
Western Europe*............	1,324	1,503	29,256,000	33,695,700
Latin America & Caribbean...	137	154	4,522,000	5,182,700
Near East & South Asia (including Arab World).......	24	37	368,000	485,400
Africa (non-Arab)...........	6	10	34,000	51,300
Far East....................	175	388	10,221,000	14,776,800
NON-BLOC TOTAL**.....	1,666	2,092	44,401,000	54,191,900
Communist Bloc.............	381	549	9,359,000	11,310,000
WORLD WIDE TOTAL**	2,047	2,641	53,760,000	65,501,900

* Includes Yugoslavia. ** Except U.S., Canada and Armed Forces stations abroad.

---

[40]*Advertising Age, op. cit.,* p. 74.

stations to build better programs and to offer a more varied form of entertainment.

Television. Television, the newcomer to the advertising media field (having been introduced in the United States as recently as 1947), is arousing the same interest abroad that it has in this country. Progress of installing television transmitting stations in foreign countries was slow due to the great expense of the equipment.

Attention is called to Table 12-1, showing the number of television transmitting stations in the world from 1951 to 1962, and transmitting stations and receivers for 1961 and 1962, divided geographically.

The increases revealed in this table are nothing short of fantastic. As of December, 1959, world total of transmitting stations crossed the 1,000 mark and in three years had risen to over 2.5 thousand stations. While 80 percent of these stations are located in non-Soviet Bloc countries, both sections of the world have shown marked increases.

The distribution of stations and receivers geographically shows that three fourths of the stations in the non-Bloc area are located in Western Europe (the United States, Canada, and Armed Forces stations abroad are not included in this tabulation). With nearly 20 percent of the stations, the Far East is the second geographical area, followed by Latin America and the Caribbean with about 8 percent. The Near East, South Asia, and Africa, including the Arab world, is far behind, with slightly more than 2 percent. The distribution of receivers follows the same general pattern, although Western Europe accounts for about 62 percent of the total number of receivers, the Far East 25 percent, Latin America and the Caribbean, 10 percent and the small balance going to the rest of the non-Bloc world.

Three systems of controlling television are in effect throughout the world today:

1. The multiple enterprise system used in the United States and in Latin America.
2. The monopolistic system used, for example, in Belgium and France.
3. The combination system such as used in Italy and Great Britain.

Multiple Enterprise System. Under this system numerous broadcasting stations are permitted to operate; and they operate for commercial profit. This system is the plan used in the United States.

Monopolistic System. No commercial broadcasting is permitted under the monopolistic system. In France, for example, television is controlled by Radiodiffusion Television Francais (RTF). "General programs are varied in scope and content, including drama, films, newsreels, sports, panel shows, and Eurovision." The last named, Eurovision, was pioneered by RTF and BBC (British Broadcasting Company) television and consists of a network linking eight European countries — the United Kingdom, Switzerland, the Netherlands, Italy, German Federal Republic, France, Denmark, and Belgium.

Combination System. Under this system, used in Great Britain and in Italy, "prior to 1955, British TV viewers on a particular night were treated to a one and one-half hour program called, 'The Development of the Lung Fish.' Viewers were either left gasping for breath or irrevocably opposed to 'culture' in such large doses." In 1955, the Independent Television Authority (ITA) was formed and was placed under the control of the Postmaster General. All television facilities are owned, in the name of the government, by the Postmaster General who grants concessions to four private program contractors. These contractors now command 70 to 90 percent of the television audience and obtain revenue from commercials. Advertisers do not control nor sponsor programs. The commercials are sold adjacent to or within the programs.

Italy permits no live commercials; but film commercials are permitted for two and one-fourth minutes, of which only 20 seconds may be used for actual selling. The remaining one minute and fifty-five seconds must show anything considered to be quality entertainment.[41]

International Advertising Expenditures

A very interesting and potentially significant statistical survey of the division of the international advertising dollar among the several chief media was inaugurated in 1949 (covering the year 1948) by *Export Trade and Shipper* hereafter referred to as *Export Trade* (changed to *Business Abroad and Export Trade* as of May, 1964). This survey appears in the Annual Export Advertising number, beginning with the thirteenth, of that valuable export management weekly.

The data cover "agency handled" accounts of United States exporters. In other words, the data do not include export advertising ex-

---

[41]Most of the information on television is taken from an address given by James von Brunn at the Ninth International Advertising Convention, 1957, and published in *Proceedings, Ninth Annual Advertising Convention, 1957*

penditures handled otherwise than through an agency. Additional factual data are prepared by the International Advertising Association, which was established in 1938 as the Export Advertising Association. Its members are associated with manufacturing and service businesses, media representatives, and advertising agencies throughout the United States and in over 60 countries. Its objectives are to raise the standards of international advertising and to help members to increase their knowledge of the use of up-to-date advertising methods and policies.

Insofar as these annual surveys indicate the use of the several international advertising media by various industrial classifications, no valid conclusions can be drawn.

Summary

1. Advertising (and sales promotion) are primarily designed to develop business, and in some instances they may be used to maintain national prestige.
2. The fundamentals of advertising abroad stress the development of a proper climate, a proper concept of the market, an awareness of the value of news, and an appreciation of real people and their attitudes.
3. The development of international advertising copy, particularly in languages other than English, calls for very close attention. This is especially true of consumer advertising where color and pattern likes and dislikes must be considered. Translation into a language other than English calls for something more than a mere literal translation.
4. For trademarked goods, the protection received from the use of, as well as the utility of, the trademark is important.
5. International advertising media fall into three fields: (1) trade or industrial, (2) consumer, and (3) professional or ethical.
6. Channels of international advertising embrace publications — United States publications circulating chiefly abroad and foreign publications. The use of the latter may raise some interesting and sometimes baffling questions.
7. Another channel is direct-mail advertising by correspondence and by the use of export catalogs. The compilation of a mailing list and the distribution of letters and catalogs call for a knowledge of sources and methods. The catalog should be different in many respects from the domestic catalog.
8. Motion pictures (cinema) can be used to good advantage in advertising abroad. This applies to public as well as private showing of films.
9. Commercial fairs and exhibits have become increasingly important in advertising in international markets.
10. Outdoor advertising is far advanced in many countries and some methods are used that are unique in those markets.
11. Sample distribution is an effective international advertising medium for some types of consumer goods, while product demonstrations are generally applied to the advertising of industrial goods.

12. Radio and, in the last several years, television have expanded rapidly abroad. However, these facilities are generally not so freely available for advertising as is true in the United States.

QUESTIONS

1. Explain the unique status of advertising abroad in time of national emergency.
2. Critically evaluate the stated fundamentals of international advertising.
3. In the preparation of copy for use abroad, explain the problems of
   (a) Illustrations.
   (b) Translation.
4. Explain the significance of the use of trademarks in selling abroad. Does this significance apply equally to the sale of grain, leaf tobacco, lumber, radios, cigarettes, automobiles, and machinery?
5. Define the several fields into which international advertising may be divided.
6. Of what advertising value are United States publications that circulate abroad? Give several examples of the different kinds of United States publications that circulate chiefly abroad.
7. Comment on the auxiliary services performed for advertisers by some United States publications.
8. Is it correct to assume that daily newspapers, weekly and monthly news, fiction, and special-interest magazines circulate in other countries the same as they do in the United States? Explain.
9. Comment on the so-called problems likely to be encountered in the use of foreign publications for United States advertising purposes. How serious are these problems, and how may they possibly be overcome?
10. Explain the use of direct mail for advertising abroad.
11. What sources are available for compiling mailing lists of prospects abroad?
12. In what ways and for what reasons does an export catalog differ from a domestic catalog?
13. Explain the use of motion pictures and slides for international advertising purposes.
14. Of what advertising value to United States firms are the fairs and exhibitions that are held in other countries?
15. Discuss the peculiarities of using outdoor advertising in other countries to publicize United States products.
16. How effective do you believe sample distribution is as a medium of international advertising?
17. Of what advertising value to United States firms is the use of radio and television for export sales purposes?

PROBLEMS

1. Obtain the names of several exporting manufacturers who are engaged in the same line of manufacturing. You can obtain the names of the companies and the name or names of officers of the company from the National Foreign Trade Council, *Proceedings*, Annual Foreign Trade Convention. A list of all delegates is published in the *Proceedings*. For addresses, you can use *Thomas' Register of Manufacturers of the United States*.

   Write to the officials of these companies for samples of the advertising that they use in foreign markets. If your efforts are fruitful, you can then prepare an exhibit on which the advertisements of the several companies are mounted for comparative purposes.

2. Examine a report of the Annual Convention of the International Advertising Association. The Convention is covered in considerable detail by *Export Trade*, the export manager's weekly journal (now called *Business Abroad and Export Trade*). The Convention is usually held in May of each year. From these *Proceedings*, prepare a report on such subjects as the following (based on the 1958 Convention):

   (a) Advertising as affected by politico-economic changes, that is, European Common Market, the Far East, Latin America, etc.

   (b) Advertising channels
       (1) Publications.
       (2) Radio.
       (3) Television.
       (4) Other.

   (c) Case studies of the international advertising program of individual companies, such as Quaker Oats International or Kodak; or for individual products, such as electrical appliances, industrial equipment and machine tools, cosmetics and toiletries.

3. Visit a library in your area and examine the advertising carried in the foreign newspapers and magazines. Select the advertisements of United States products.

   Compare these advertisements with the advertisements of the same company covering the same products that appear in United States domestic newspapers and magazines.

   Prepare a report on the similarities and/or differences that you are able to detect between the domestic and the foreign advertising.

COLLATERAL READINGS

See the list of readings given at the end of Chapter 13 on page 271.

DEALER COOPERATION AND INTERNATIONAL ADVERTISING POLICY

Having completed a survey of international advertising media, our attention will now be directed to the subjects of dealer cooperation and the determination of international advertising policy.

Dealer Cooperation

Of special significance in international advertising methods comes the whole range of publicity methods included in the term *dealer cooperation*. American ingenuity, recognized as paramount in the field of advertising, is constantly devising new advertising methods in accordance with the distinctly American merchandising formula of helping the dealer dispose of his goods. Time was when the sale to the distributor or storekeeper terminated the interest of the seller until the next buying season. Modern merchandising practice, however, does not allow the seller to consider his work completed until dealers have received assistance in their sales efforts. The entire purpose of dealer cooperation is to help the dealers to sell; and this is guided and controlled by the four fundamental factors of good retail merchandising applicable all over the world:

1. Attractive store front and window display.
2. Proper inside arrangement of advertisements and goods to establish immediate sales appeal.
3. Teaching (or creating enthusiasm in) the dealer to back up the product on every possible occasion.
4. Teaching the dealer to engage in publicity work of his own for the purpose of drawing customers who might otherwise be entirely missed.

Dealer cooperation is generally considered as comprising two distinct classes: (1) those efforts that focus directly upon the distributor himself, known as *sales promotion,* and (2) those that are used directly on the distributor's customers, termed *dealers' helps.*

Sales Promotion. All efforts to make the distributor himself a better dealer come under the heading of sales promotion. Much of this work is done by means of letters, bulletins, or folders. These may contain suggestions on salesmanship, demonstration or display, methods of stock-keeping, or accounting systems, and other such matters. The foreign salesmen or missionary salesmen who work with the distributors' salesmen can help the dealer solve many of his distribution problems, and, at times, members of the dealer's staff may come to the producer's headquarters and spend some time in the manufacturer's plant and on the road, learning at first hand about the product and its sales problems.

Other methods of sales promotion include dealer conventions, which have been tried at times with success. Although house organs are not widely employed, they do serve as a good method of sales promotion.

Dealers' Helps. One of the most valuable forms of dealers' helps is that of letters for the use of dealers. Frequently the exporter will make up quantities of these and send them to his dealers for local addressing and mailing. Samples have given exceptionally good results, although careful safeguards are to be observed in distributing free samples. Store and window displays are an effective form of dealers' helps. Metal and painted signs and electros featuring the dealer's name along with the exporter's product are also extensively used. Booklets, pamphlets, folders, blotters, souvenirs, and the like, as well as lantern slides and films, are supplied to foreign distributors to be distributed or shown to their customers.

Printed or lithographed material in color, such as brochures, instruction sheets, catalogs, and "point-of-sale" display cards are always needed in markets abroad. Distributors and dealers naturally want and need — in the language of their country — the same beautifully reproduced material used so effectively in the United States.

To do this from scratch in each country is rarely practical or even possible, but a little cooperation with the domestic advertising department will often help solve this. First, explain your needs to the artists and layout men so they can produce colorful domestic material and still confine the text matter to black or one color.

Thus when brochures, etc., are produced, a proportion for export would be printed only in colors. The plate with copy would be omitted.

These flat color sheets may then be sent to foreign countries for over-printing in the language of the country. For example, in the Union of South Africa the text could be overprinted in Bantu, Afrikaans, or English.

As regards show cards, since some countries have facilities for mounting and attaching easels and others do not, an advance decision is required as to the quantity to be overprinted or lithographed in flat sheets and another quantity mounted. These mounted or unmounted sheets may be overprinted or silkscreened according to the type of card. Easels may be attached locally when available or may be shipped separately.

If the original artwork and layouts are planned properly in advance, then in countries where the importation of printed material — including show cards — is prohibited, the electrotypes or photofilms may be sent and the text plate would be sent with the copy of the plate routed out. This could be inserted locally and the printing completed in perfect register.

At all times the foreign language translations should be referred to the home office for checking.[1]

In general, dealers overseas are not convinced in advance of the necessity for dealer cooperation, and the international firm must then "sell" the program.[2] Often it pays to consult foreign dealers when setting up plans, thus giving greater assurance of meeting market considerations. Export salesmen can be very effective in emphasizing the value of dealer cooperation and sales promotion devices. Ordinarily, expensive dealers' helps are charged to the dealer at cost price, or perhaps less; inexpensive ones are distributed free.

International Advertising Policy

After the fundamentals of international advertising have been grasped and put into practice, the chief policy matter to be determined is the extent to which control over advertising will be vested in representatives abroad, whether they be agents, distributors, dealers, salesmen, or branch managers. Basically, the question is: Can the company safely relinquish any aspect of control over the international advertising program?

---

[1]Charles W. Applegate in *Export Trade and Shipper* (January 28, 1957), pp. 21 and 76.

[2]Thomas W. Hughes, quoted in the preceding chapter, declared that dealer promotion abroad is neglected because dealers are not geared to the merchandising angles as we know them in this country.

This is a matter of prime importance to firms whose advertising is a vital part of their international marketing program. This would be true of trademarked goods and, to a surprising extent, it would also be true of nearly all manufactured products that depend upon a name as a symbol of quality.

An early policy of administering international advertising consisted of making an *advertising allowance* to the representative abroad. This allowance would be in addition to the commission or discount that he received on sales. The purpose of this allowance was to provide financial assistance and thus encourage local advertising abroad by representatives located there. Usually the representative was expected to match the allowance made by the supplier.

This policy makes a great deal of sense when it is recognized that a representative in Sao Paulo, for example, may be expected to know more about advertising in Brazil than the exporting firm located in the United States. The premise may be false, however, in that a successful sales representative may know nothing about advertising. If this is the case, as it often is, the so-called advertising allowance becomes an extra sales commission or discount. Under this condition, the exporting firm is being fooled and no advertising is bought with these funds.

As conducted in the present era, the control over international advertising policy may be classified as:

1. Centralized — keeping headquarters control over the advertising program.

2. Cooperative — full cooperation with representatives abroad, along with divided responsibility.

3. Decentralized — complete control of all international advertising is surrendered to the representatives in the respective markets.

Centralized Control. The basic reason for centralized control was stated succinctly by Joshua B. Powers, foreign periodical representative in the United States:

> To Americans, advertising is a calculated part of the merchandising problem. To many foreigners, advertising is just publicity. Advertising is a function of management and cannot be safely delegated. Many foreigners believe in the principle of small scale and large profits. Americans believe in the principle of large sales and small profits. This being true, we can state it as a principle that American manufacturers

cannot turn over to foreign distributors their advertising funds and expect them to be invested to their satisfaction.[3]

Commenting on the centralized control concept, Harry E. Maynard of International Editions of *Life* declares, "Only headquarters from its vast overall view of dealing with the history of diversified products, many countries, and markets can plan the longer term strategy and corporate advertising."[4]

This is the attitude of the soft drink industry. When the companies commence operations abroad, they insist on the same rigid control of quality that they do in the United States. Since service is the main product that they sell, they insist on maintaining advertising standards. However, it is not always possible to control standards from headquarters in the United States as will be shown later.

Like many companies engaged in international marketing, the California Texas Oil Company maintains headquarters in the United States (New York). From this spot, every phase of the business is managed, including advertising and sales promotion.

Such statements as these indicate a basic policy of controlling advertising and sales promotion from headquarters. This is centralized control. Nevertheless, in the practical world of this era, it is not always feasible or even possible to control international advertising from headquarters, despite policy statements or declarations to the contrary.

One thing is certain and that is if the international marketing firm controls the entire international advertising program and expenditures in connection therewith, the representatives abroad will not be encouraged to promote sales by advertising of their own.

Cooperative Control. The cooperative method of control is a means of eliciting advice and cooperation from representatives abroad in connection with the international advertising program. At many international advertising meetings, this method is frequently referred to as the "50–50 method," suggesting that there is an even division of responsibility and expenses between the international marketing firm and the representatives abroad, including branch managers. When "50–50" is cited, it refers in most cases, if not all, to the use of space advertising media (publications) only.

---

[3]Quoted by Robert H. Otto, President, Robert Otto and Company, international advertising agency, at the First International Advertising Convention, 1949.

[4]Cited in *Export Trade* (January 30, 1961), p. 28.

A clear statement of the implementation of the cooperative method was cited by Benjamin Donaldson, Director, International Advertising, Ford International Division.[5] This Division at Dearborn "is responsible for advertising that is worldwide or hemispherewide or in the areas covered by leading international publications. At the same time, advertising within a given market is the special concern of the company facility and dealer body responsible for sales within that market." Of course, Mr. Donaldson observes, assistance is provided in the form of copy, plates, mats, etc.; but actual decisions regarding the copy platforms, artwork, and media are left to the facility and dealers involved.

As expounded in 1963 by Donald E. McKellar, then Advertising Manager of the International Division of Ford Motor Company, the same philosophy pertains. However, advertising agencies have been selected to such an extent that the company facility and dealer body have been largely relieved of the responsibility for local advertising, although they are expected to cooperate fully and advise the local advertising agencies.[6]

Decentralized Control. In theory, this method would place complete control of advertising in the hands of representatives abroad. In practice, however, decentralization places control of only certain aspects of the advertising program under representatives abroad.

To go back to the soft drink and the petroleum businesses mentioned above, Pepsi-Cola International found, for example, that in many markets, advertising materials cannot be imported; but sometimes the company can get negatives into a country from which advertising materials are produced or local printers and lithographers are instructed. In many cases they do a most satisfactory job. In the case of Mexico, for instance, the advertising output is so typically Latin American, that the advertising materials are sent to other countries in this hemisphere. They operate as a local company within every country in which the product is sold, and they work with local advertising agencies as a rule. These agencies are instructed by the company representatives.[7]

In the petroleum business, Caltex, while managing every phase of the international business from headquarters, operates abroad through 90 corporations scattered in 77 countries of the Eastern Hemisphere.

---

[5]Tenth International Advertising Association Convention, 1958.

[6]In *Export Trade* (January 30, 1961), p. 28. *Ibid.* (May 27, 1963), pp. 11, 23–26.

[7]Frederick Fleischman, Advertising Manager, Pepsi-Cola International, at the Foreign Traders Association of Philadelphia, Inc., meeting, March 19, 1957.

These corporations are set up under local law and staffed almost entirely by nationals. In South Africa there is a South African company, and they think like South Africans and use a South African agency. While headquarters manages all phases of the business, in the field the company does a job as a Dutchman or as an Australian.[8]

Pros and Cons of Cooperative and Decentralized Control Methods.

Any discussion of cooperative and decentralized methods of controlling international advertising is certain to bring out differences of opinion. Advertising agencies, generally speaking, are not favorably disposed toward these methods, and this is quite understandable. They have developed specialized services for the purposes of international advertising, and when foreign sales representatives participate in the execution of policy, they are inclined to think that the program is not being given proper consideration. One agency spokesman summarizes his analysis of the weaknesses of cooperative and decentralized methods of control in the following five statements:[9]

1. There is no proper check to determine if the distributor actually spends the money turned over to him as an advertising allowance.
2. The advertisements that the distributor does provide are often below the standard of the company.
3. Many times, the distributor places emphasis on *his* business rather than on the manufacturer's product.
4. There is often a general lack of planning.
5. Media selection is often too big a problem.

To these five statements, we may add a sixth that was stated by Bill Ely, New York Manager, *European Herald Tribune.*[10]

6. The corporate image, central in nearly all international advertising campaigns today cannot be adequately mirrored.

In a foreign trade meeting at which the subject of international advertising was discussed, one thoroughly experienced vice-president in charge of foreign sales for a manufacturer of industrial and consumer automotive products exclaimed:

I know a lot of you do not agree with it and I am not so sure I agree 100 percent myself, but there is such a thing as cooperative ad-

---

[8]E. Edson Poler, Export Advertising Manager, Caltex, at the Foreign Traders Association of Philadelphia, Inc., meeting, March 19, 1957.
[9]H. I. Orwig, Buchen Company, at the Midwest Advertising Conference, as reported in *Export Trade and Shipper* (May 12, 1958), p. 50.
[10]*Export Trade* (January 26, 1959), p. 21.

vertising with your overseas distributors. It works for some people. It has many advantages, a few disadvantages.[11]

The views of those who favor the use of cooperative methods of controlling international advertising, and some degree of decentralization, are:

1. The representative abroad knows the language, people, customs, and everything pertaining to the market.

2. He is likely to be quite capable in handling advertising, particularly local radio, television, movie slides, and point-of-sale material.

3. Checking the expenditure of advertising allowances granted to the representative abroad is easily controlled. No allowance is granted until receipted vouchers and copies of the advertisements are presented.

4. Cooperation has a distinct merit in that the representative abroad contributes an additional or equal amount.

5. Media selection is not a problem for local advertising; the international marketing company can still conduct advertising at the regional or national level. There can very easily be a tie-in between these two advertising approaches and there could be an overall plan. This all depends upon the attitude of the international marketing company and the ability of and relations with the representative abroad.

6. Cooperative advertising can be arranged through advertising agencies in the United States and agencies abroad.

Advertising Agencies

The advertising agency is so integral a part of the advertising business in the United States that a consideration of international advertising would not be complete without discussing these agencies.

The advertising agency functions include the following:

1. In the field of marketing to collaborate closely with the appropriate departments of the advertiser, to study the product and its markets and distribution.

2. In the field of advertising to conceive, conduct and interpret copy testing media, research and study of competitive advertising.

---

[11]William H. Lukens, Vice-President, Export, R. M. Hollingshead Corporation, at the Foreign Traders Association of Philadelphia, Inc., meeting March 19, 1957.

Also, in other research or studies necessary to provide a solid foundation upon which the advertising plan can be created; and subsequently check for the efficiency of the methods employed.

3. To draw up the advertising campaign plan with an assessment and allocation of expenditures within the agreed appropriation; and to help coordinate the campaign with other sales promotion activities.

4. To supervise and implement the advertising campaign.

5. To ensure good coordination between advertising, sales promotion and other publicity.

The advertiser is responsible for product and product development as well as for the general market situation in the countries where he desires to promote his product.[12]

There are four different types of advertising agencies now recognized in the international field:

1. The established domestic advertising agency that has organized an export or international division or department and operates abroad through branches, but chiefly by means of affiliate and associate agencies.

2. The export advertising agency that is based in the home country, e.g., the United States, but does business exclusively outside of the home country.

3. The so-called international agency that has regular domestic accounts in the country where it is headquartered. This type has branches and correspondent agencies abroad which serve both domestic and foreign clients. The international agency is identical with or an extension of the first type listed, if, of course, it is a domestic United States agency.

4. The foreign advertising agency that is located and operates abroad, although it is in a position to handle advertising in the home country where it is headquartered.

Domestic Advertising Agencies. Many United States companies when first entering international markets naturally turned to the advertising agency or agencies that had taken care of their domestic advertising. In many cases, however, the domestic advertising agency is just as uninformed concerning the subject of advertising abroad as the reader was before he undertook to read Chapters 12 and 13. As a means of taking care of international advertising, some domestic agencies choose

---

[12]International Advertising Association, "Standards and Practices," *Code of Standards of Advertising Practice* (New York, 1961), p. 25.

to set up a separate department that deals with the international advertising requirements of their clients. Some of them have established their own branch offices abroad or have a group of associates engaged in advertising in foreign markets, that is, advertising agencies abroad.

Export Advertising Agency. This type of agency, while based in the home country, transacts all of its advertising business abroad. This may be accomplished through foreign branches and also by affiliation with advertising agencies abroad.

International Advertising Agencies. When the agency devotes its full activities to the international field and operates abroad through associated agencies, it is known as an *international advertising agency*. These are staffed in all departments of agency operation and specialize in foreign advertising, handling accounts for both foreign and domestic (national) advertisers. They generally do not handle domestic accounts.

These United States overseas, export, or international agencies function through local independent advertising agencies with whom they have formed an association. In some cases, the United States agency may utilize more than one local associate in a particular country because of a competitive product situation or because of an agency specialization.

Advantages of the International Advertising Agency. The international advertising agency claims the following advantages:

1. Their artwork is better than that available in foreign countries and offers more appeal.

2. They assist in locating distributive agents abroad.

3. They offer close contact with the advertiser, thus affording a means of familiarizing the agency with new ideas concerning the marketing of the product.

4. They afford centralization and uniformity in a worldwide campaign.

5. Their practices are the result of experience based on market analysis, trade advertising, etc.

6. They offer economy in some respects, as the same artwork and production can be used over a wide area.

7. They are able to control truthfulness in advertising.

8. They undertake to handle all detail work, thereby reducing the necessary size of the export advertising department.

9. They offer translation facilities and foreign copywriters.

10. They prepare radio and television programs, commercials, shorts, and movie trailers, both in the United States and abroad.

Commenting on the role that the advertising agency should be expected to play in the decade of the sixties, Braxton Pollard declares that

Unquestionably, a new and more efficient agency plan of operations must be provided.

Conceding that market and advertising know-how are fully executed in countless local agencies and offices of international advertising agencies all over the world, he declares that

The key problem and the greatest void are at home. In the drive to participate in this global market, who in the parent agency will have the international know-how to successfully guide and manage the overseas advertising operation and advise the U.S. client at headquarters? U.S. agencies would be wise to concentrate on strengthening their own centralized international staffing rather than on overseas mergers.

Continuing, Mr. Pollard states:

Today's need is for more U.S. agencies, with management oriented to international operations and dedicated to global business, who can advise the client at home, help determine advertising policy, strategy, provide advertisement ideas and even prototype advertisements when advisable and then direct the effort to get the advertising executed and presented through capable well-run local agencies who know the market and the people.[13]

Compensation and Expenses. The accepted method of compensating advertising agencies is by means of a flat service fee (15 to 20 percent), with all discounts and commissions received from media credited to the account of the advertiser. Certain additional expense items, such as production costs, may also be charged to the advertiser.

While advertising agencies are highly competitive with each other, there is also much of common interest that draws them together. The Association of International Advertising Agencies was organized for the "interchange of ideas and experiences in order to promote the efficiency and scope of its members and to standardize the practice of the profession of export advertising."[14] One of its asserted achievements has been

---

[13]Braxton Pollard, in *Export Trade* (January 29, 1962), p. 10.
[14]Daniel C. Kaufherr, President, Association of Export Advertising Agencies and Vice-President, Irwin Vladimir & Co., Inc., in *Export Trade and Shipper* (January 23, 1950), p. 15.

the holding down of advertising rates of certain foreign publications and radio stations.

With regard to the matter of paying invoices in local currency, using blocked funds of advertisers rather than paying in United States dollars as the advertising media desired, Mr. Kaufherr observes that "the members' first duty was to their clients and their frozen or blocked accounts."[15]

Foreign Advertising Agency. It might be supposed that the advertising agency established and operating in the various foreign countries would be best equipped to handle advertising not only for national but also for foreign advertisers. One would be inclined to think that they are thoroughly familiar with each particular foreign market and, of course, face no language or empathy barriers.

To reach this conclusion, it would be necessary to believe that the art of advertising and, indeed, all aspects of marketing, are equally developed all over the world. This is by no means true, as witnessed by the following comments.

> An air almost of secrecy pervades French companies in their relations with the public and even, more surprisingly, with advertising agencies. It is virtually impossible to obtain advertising budget figures or get any true indication of company profits in any sector. This may be due to a tradition of "tax dodging" inherent among the French, where the penalties are not so steep as in the U.S. A kind of excessive individualism permeates France, with everyone playing his cards close to his vest.
>
> This is a perfectly human and understandable trait, but in advertising it makes for a considerable lack of communication between advertiser, agency and consequently the public.
>
> One of the main factors behind the debate on the agency system is that much agency work here [Sweden] has been done more to meet the clients' demands rather than to perform what the agency believes is the best sales and marketing strategy. Agencies too frequently are merely "servants," taking orders.
>
> The ideal situation, in which agency and client work together for the main purpose of selling, is rare here.
>
> One problem every form of media contends with is the tendency of advertisers to pay for space with the product advertised, rather than with cash. In face of strong competition, almost every newspaper and radio station in Mexico has had to go along with this barter system, known as *intercambio* (interchange). Space and time salesmen, once they have sold a client, are faced with the prospect of peddling the product before they can collect their commissions.

---

[15] *Ibid.*

The advertising agency picture in Athens is cloudy at best, typical of most developing markets where advertising is barely understood and the function of agencies completely confusing to most business men and to the public. The several hundred one-man-office space brokers and art shops which service clients directly help to keep the issue murky.

There are about a dozen agencies which conform to the generally-accepted pattern of marketing companies. Hellenic, Alector, Greca, Minos, Gnomi, Dits are among the leaders. New foreign accounts seeking Greek markets have put a squeeze on the profits of the local agencies handling them. The clients want services not usually supplied by Greek agencies, some of whom provide them virtually free in the hope that larger future billings will result.

Confounding the monetary picture is the fact that most Greek agencies work on a so-called 20% commission, and then slide about 10% of that back under the counter to the client. Advertisers price-shop for agencies depending on the size of the kickback they're promised. Offering a fatter rebate than the competition is one cut-throat, but very successful, way for an agency to get new billing in Athens.[16]

International Advertising Department

In the case of a built-in export department, the domestic advertising department would be responsible for international advertising. In a separate export department and certainly in an export selling subsidiary, there would be an international advertising assignment and possibly a department. Some international marketing companies handle advertising by means of a so-called *house agency*, which is an advertising agency owned by the manufacturer to handle all advertising, domestic and foreign, for the company and its subsidiaries. If an advertiser expects to do all the work of the advertising agencies, obviously he must add competent personnel and increase his budget.

Operations. Whether composed of one-man or full-scale operation with media, production, checking, art, accounting, and research departments, the advertising department should perform the following operations when an advertising agency is used:

1. With the sales department, establish sales objectives and, therefore, the budget.

2. Determine advertising strategy.

---

[16]*Advertising Age*, op. cit.

3. Analyze ideas of agencies, as submitted.
4. Check on the agency.
5. Administer expenses.
6. Sell the program to the company as well as customers.
7. Handle media that the agency is not prepared to handle, such as catalogs, booklets, leaflets, direct-mail letters and literature, and displays.[17]

The International Advertising Budget. A vital part of international advertising policy is a determination of the amount to be appropriated for this purpose. There are numerous considerations bearing on this matter, but in recent years emphasis has been increasing on, first of all, establishing the objectives that are sought and then fixing the amount needed or the amount that can be justified budget-wise to meet those objectives.

Basically, the size of the international advertising budget should be the same as the domestic budget per dollar of sale. Because of many factors, it costs more per dollar of sale to create the impulses to buy in foreign markets than in the United States. The principal problem is, by means of evaluating available international markets, to establish a safe sales forecast. On a basis of this forecast, the domestic advertising percentage, or more, should be applied for the amount of international advertising necessary to attain the desired goal.

Too great emphasis cannot be laid on this point, and the determination of objectives is a very searching quest. The keynote is to "rethink" or "reexamine" constantly. Take nothing for granted. For example, you may be selling baking powder in 4-ounce cans. The grocer makes a profit from each sale. The chemist thinks of the product as a cream of tartar compound that exerts a leavening action by the release of carbon dioxide in a certain set of conditions. Actually, you are selling a group of intangibles — the desire of the woman to gain the approval of the family or of her friends and neighbors, etc. Exactly what, then, are you selling? And to whom? An importer? A distributor? A plantation owner? A contractor? Male customers? Under 40 years of age? Living in such and such sections of a city or a country? Having such and such standard of living? Examine and reexamine your problem, the

---

[17]International Advertising Association, "Standards and Practices," *Code of Standards of Advertising Practice* (New York, 1961), pp. 20–21.

experts declare, so that you will know where you are headed — what your advertising objectives are.[18]

After having determined the true objectives to be sought in international advertising, the stage is set for determining the sum to be budgeted. There are several ways to establish the international advertising budget, each of which offers some merit to certain concerns handling certain products, under certain circumstances and conditions, in certain countries or areas of countries, and at certain periods of time.[19]

1. Guesswork, by which a given amount is set by hunch — or by what the company feels it can afford — or by the amount spent by a competitor.

2. Distributors' requests, in which the amount appropriated is based upon the requests for advertising allowances submitted by foreign representatives. These sums are usually based on past year's sales and they are to be spent in local advertising. This method has so many things wrong with it I often wonder why the practice is used at all. People thousands of miles away cannot possibly know or understand broad company experience. How can they plan a budget that will fit over-all policy and meet long-range objectives?

3. Past performance, by means of a given proportion of gross sales or net profit for a prior year. This is probably the method most widely used. "This is an excellent way to eliminate guesswork — and a wonderful way to ride the caboose but forget to look ahead to your goal."[20]

4. Quota of forecast of sales; thus, the method is no better than the forecast.

5. Accumulated reserves,[21] which is a long-range financial viewpoint. Under this method, funds would presumably be set aside in good times for use in bad times.

6. Objectives or "task" plan by which the budget is set at an amount necessary to do a certain job, that is, reach the desired objectives. The task or steps toward the objective may be altered to fit the funds available.

In international marketing, with the greater lack of research facilities and facts, this method is even more difficult to employ than in domestic trade. "But some courageous firms are doing it."[22]

"The 'task method' is particularly effective in overseas selling because it necessitates the study of each individual area and directs the

[18]From Ben Holdsworth, Export Advertising Counselor, J. Walter Thompson Company, speaking before the December 13, 1950, meeting of the Foreign Traders Association of Philadelphia, Inc.
[19]From Braxton Pollard, Manager, International Advertising, Monsanto Chemical Company, speaking at the First International Advertising Convention, 1949; and reprinted in *Export Trade and Shipper* (January 28, 1957).
[20]Holdsworth, *op. cit.*
[21]Suggested by Ben Holdsworth.
[22]Holdsworth, *op. cit.*

application of effort where it will do the greatest good. With well-defined objectives, and data on markets, costs, and effectiveness of media, along with information on local conditions, the advertiser is likely to get more for his advertising money and do a more effective job than by any of the other commonly used methods of determining budgets."[23]

Summary

1. Sales promotion is provided through dealer cooperation — helping the dealer to dispose of his goods. It takes two forms, namely, (1) helping the dealer directly and (2) directing the effort to the consumer to induce him to purchase from the dealer.
2. International advertising policy is basically a matter of overall merchandising policy. As such, it stems from executive determination. The international advertiser may control all advertising abroad, in which case it is known as centralized control. In most instances, however, there is a cooperative arrangement with some division of responsibilities and expenses between the advertiser and his foreign representatives. Complete decentralization — surrendering all rights to international advertising policy — is rarely, if ever, practiced.
3. International advertising may be placed through a domestic advertising agency, with or without an international affiliation or department; international advertising agencies that specialize in advertising abroad; or with foreign advertising agencies.
4. An international advertising department may be operated at headquarters. The personnel for such a department must perform certain operations.
5. The international advertising budget may be determined in several ways, extending from sheer guesswork to an objective-seeking appropriation — and anything in between these extremes.

QUESTIONS

1. Explain briefly the fundamental factors of good retail merchandising.
2. Cite several instances of sales promotion in international trade.
3. Describe several forms of dealers' helps that are used in international trade.
4. (a) Describe the several methods by which international advertising may be controlled.
   (b) Explain the advantages and disadvantages of each of these methods.
5. Discuss the value of cooperative international advertising.
6. Describe the various ways in which domestic advertising agencies may handle the international advertising requirements of their clients.

---

[23]Pollard, *op. cit.*, p. 73.

7. Explain the operations of an international advertising agency.

8. Evaluate the several operating advantages that are claimed by the international advertising agency.

9. (a) Describe the operations of a foreign advertising agency.

(b) What are the advantages of staffing foreign advertising agencies with nationals?

10. What is a *house agency?*

11. (a) How may the amount of the international advertising budget be determined?

(b) Define the several ways in which it may be determined.

(c) Which method do you believe is more successful? Why?

PROBLEMS

1. With the growth of its international business (23 new overseas bottlers in 1956 and 28 in 1957) Pepsi-Cola International, Ltd., is considering the desirability of decentralizing its operations.

The company operates by licensing bottlers to whom the company sells its concentrate. Donald M. Kendall, President, states that "our chief export is merchandising and marketing know-how."

Strict quality control is exercised over the bottlers by means of an audit system and by a staff of quality checkers or "traveling laboratories."

Under the decentralization plan, six divisions will be established to replace the present eleven regional offices. The regions are (1) Europe, (2) Middle East — North Africa — India, (3) Southern Africa, (4) Far East, (5) Mexico — Caribbean, and (6) South America. Each division would be supervised by a vice-president.

By this change it is hoped to provide for greater liaison with the New York headquarters. Better service to bottlers is also to be anticipated and advertising and merchandising techniques will be expanded. Local requirements will be more correctly met by this type of organization, it is claimed. For example, in the Belgian Congo, bongo drums are effective merchandising techniques, while sun caps perform the same function in Manila, and kites, in Thailand.

Do you favor the proposed decentralization plan? Explain.

2. Advertising and promotion are the lifeblood of the detergent and toilet goods business in the United States and it is the same overseas. Colgate-Palmolive International, Inc., proves this statement to the tune of more than $30 million in foreign advertising — one of the largest foreign advertising budgets of any American company.

In light of the treatment of international advertising in this chapter, what policy or policies would you recommend for this company in connection with the following advertising methods?

(a) Radio programs.

(b) Television programs.

(c) Samples.

3. A well-known name in the dental cream and other household products is Squibb. At the end of World War II, this company faced the problem of introducing its full line of ethical products. The objective of a publicity program was to make the name of Squibb known to the government officials, industry, finance, and public health officials abroad; and the company needed the cooperation of the medical and pharmaceutical professions.

In seeking to devise an advertising program for international markets, the company faced the taboo of advertising pharmaceuticals to the public because of the opposition of the medical and pharmaceutical professions.

In view of this obstacle, the company decided upon institutional advertising and the problem concerned the type of institutional advertising to be used. In light of the ideas expressed in this chapter and the one preceding, what recommendations would you offer to the company as to the vehicle for this institutional advertising abroad and the control that would be exercised over it?

COLLATERAL READINGS

Collins, V. D. *World Marketing*. Philadelphia: J. B. Lippincott Company, 1935. Chapters 8 and 9.

Dartnell International Trade Handbook, The. Chicago: The Dartnell Corporation, 1963.

de Haas, J. A. *The Practice of Foreign Trade*. New York: McGraw-Hill Book Company, Inc., 1935. Chapter 13.

Heck, Harold J. *Foreign Commerce*. New York: McGraw-Hill Book Company, Inc., 1953. Chapter 19.

Horn, Paul V. *International Trade Principles and Practices*, Third Edition. New York: Prentice-Hall, Inc., 1951. Chapter 27.

International Advertising Association. *Proceedings — Annual Convention*. New York.

MacDonald, Philip. *Practical Exporting*. New York: Ronald Press Company, 1949. Chapter 7.

Pratt, E. E. *Modern International Commerce*. New York: Allyn and Bacon, Inc., 1956. Chapter 6.

Tosdal, H. R. *Problems in Export Sales Management*. New York: McGraw-Hill Book Company, Inc., 1922. Chapter 7.

Wyman, Walter F. *Export Merchandising*. New York: McGraw-Hill Book Company, Inc., 1922. Chapters 16, 19, 20–23.

PART III

FOREIGN OPERATIONS AND
INTERNATIONAL COOPERATIVE MARKETING

Part III deals chiefly with operations abroad that are not so readily controlled from the home base. The sequence of chapters is foreign operations, which are treated here as sales organizations; overseas manufacturing, which is a new chapter added to this revised edition; and, licensing for foreign operations. Then follow two chapters dealing with cooperative marketing arrangements in the international field, and most of these are to be found in foreign countries rather than the United States. A summary chapter concludes the treatment of international marketing organizations. It seeks to point out how the selection of international marketing policies is influenced by characteristics of the commodity, the market, and the policies of each individual firm. This is an important chapter intended to acquaint the student with the fact that the best laid plans of mice and men are influenced greatly by the commodity and the market; in other words, there is no one best way to engage in international marketing.

CHAPTER 14

FOREIGN OPERATIONS

Foreign operations is the term now used to embrace all kinds of business conducted in foreign countries by enterprises of a different nationality. From the standpoint of the United States, the term means the operation of businesses in foreign countries by American companies.

The industrial nations of western Europe were the first to engage in what we know as foreign operations. Such European business firms built railroads, canals, public utility facilities, water works, and factories. Likewise, plantation and mining operations were commenced by these firms. American companies came on the scene at a later date. In fact, it was not until almost the twentieth century that American companies began to engage in foreign operations. The earliest of these were the meat packers, petroleum companies, plantation companies, mining companies, and a few enterprising manufacturers. Among these was H. J. Heinz — "the pickle people" — whose first effort in foreign operations was the establishment of a factory in Scotland in 1867.

At the close of World War I, wider interest in foreign operations was reflected by the increase in the number of American companies that established manufacturing operations in foreign countries. This was a feature of the expanded international marketing of the United States and of the closer study of foreign markets by manufacturers and other enterprisers that are definitely committed to worldwide distribution. Buying branches and offices similarly have been established to purchase raw materials, foodstuffs, and finished manufactures (style merchandise).

Since the end of World War II, added emphasis has been given to the establishment of foreign operations. One reason for this emphasis is the increased volume and speed of transportation, whereby the world has become smaller and countries more quickly reached. Another element is the recovery of European countries and Japan from the ravages of the war. Concomitant with this recovery has been the establishment and operation of up-to-date production facilities. Technical knowledge and research activities have been developed to an advanced degree, and the exchange of such knowledge across national boundaries has been more common. With rising living standards in all of the industrial countries, markets have been expanded and competently qualified employees have become available in all of these countries. Finally, the emergence of the European Economic Community or Common Market has been a direct cause for the expansion of manufacturing operations within the Common Market. Regionalization in other parts of the world has not shown this same effect up to the present time.

Types of Foreign Operations

For purposes of discussion, the types of foreign operations found in international marketing may be indicated as:

1. Foreign purchase or sales branch (or office).
2. Foreign storage or warehouse branch.
3. Foreign assembly plant.
4. Foreign branch manufacturing plant.
5. Licensing.

Foreign Purchase or Sales Branch (or Office). The foreign purchase or sales branch performs a strictly merchandising function, and it is operated often in conjunction with storage or manufacturing facilities. The branch, however, may be the sole channel of foreign distribution or purchase. From the sales angle, it may be in reality a miniature of the parent organization, exclusive of production. Or, it may comprise only office space, or even desk space, in which event stocks are usually not carried; but samples, catalogs, and descriptive matter are kept on hand in the foreign purchase or sales branch.

In the case of a small branch office, the resident manager covers the territory assigned to him, visiting dealers to solicit orders, promote sales, and settle claims and disputes. He may also look after shipments and conduct credit investigations. Many concerns employ such offices in the principal trade centers. Similarly, a foreign buying office may be maintained. A manufacturer in the United States who uses foreign raw materials or a merchant who uses manufactures is thus in a position to keep in close touch with sources of supply, to keep advised of current and prospective market conditions, to arrange for handling and shipment of goods, and in other ways to obtain a valuable buying service. Moreover, there is at least one association composed of a number of department stores that maintains cooperative foreign (buying) offices in foreign countries. Through these offices, visiting buyers representing the several stores composing the association are assisted in making purchases. When buyers are not in the field, orders may be transmitted to these offices by letter or cable. By means of such an association, the combined purchasing power of all the members in several particular lines can be used to their advantage.

In a full-fledged foreign branch house, all of the functions of the branch office are performed, and, in addition, parts are supplied and usually orders are filled. Shipments, however, may be made from the parent company directly to customers, especially when purchases are large and represent high value. The branch manager will control all selling efforts of salesmen attached to the branch. Sales are usually made only through wholesale or retail channels, but in a few instances branch retail stores have been established. Certain camera, agricultural implements, machinery, general merchandise, and shoe companies provide an illustration of foreign branch retail selling; certain specialty shops have also established retail import branches.

Foreign Storage or Warehouse Branch. When stocks are maintained, the foreign storage or warehouse branch comes into play. It may be used entirely for filling orders or it may be coordinated with merchandising or manufacturing functions. Whenever prompt delivery is an important factor, or when repair, replacement, and supply parts are essential, storage becomes indispensable. One concern established foreign storage branches because foreign agents could not be induced to lay in a stock of parts sufficient to serve the trade satisfactorily. An importer may store merchandise abroad for many reasons, such as awaiting better price, storing at less expense than at home, and holding for favorable changes in exchange rates or in freight charges or in customs duties; he may also store while determining the best country in which to attempt selling the shipment.

Foreign Assembly Plant. The third type of foreign operations is the foreign assembly plant. Foreign assembly plants are established in order to save ocean freight, government fees, foreign customs duties, and other charges incurred in the exportation of merchandise. When merchandise is shipped in large quantities and in knocked-down condition, freight charges and official fees are relatively lower; and customs duties are frequently less for parts than for complete units of goods.

Since the imports of the United States are predominantly of a raw and bulky nature, the foreign assembly of imported merchandise is not so common as in the case of exports of manufactured goods. Nevertheless, importers of raw materials may find advantage in collecting, sorting, grading, and otherwise preparing commodities prior to shipment to the United States market.

Foreign Branch Manufacturing Plant. From the assembly function to a fully-equipped manufacturing establishment abroad is a long step, and yet a progressive one. The extent to which manufacturing processes may be economically transferred to a foreign country will be dictated by production costs, as well as by economy in such export expenses as mentioned above, and frequently by the tariff, taxation, or other policies of foreign governments. Importing firms, at times identified with financial groups, operate factories or other production units abroad. These facilities may function to supply foreign (not the United States) markets, as is largely the case with meat-packing firms in South America. Utilities operating in foreign countries confine their entire market to the countries in which they are situated. More often, however, as in metals, petroleum, sugar, rug-weaving, and many other lines, operation is for the supply of the home market. Plantations — bananas, coffee, and rubber — are also operated overseas by home-based companies.

Licensing. Foreign licensing as a method of operation has increased in importance since World War II. One reason is the emphasis on exchange of technical know-how. Another reason is the continued difficulty — due to foreign exchange allotment restrictions — of obtaining payment from certain countries for particular lines of merchandise. Moreover, increasing industrialization in the so-called underdeveloped countries has provided manufacturing facilities that may be utilized by licensing. In addition, some firms with patent holdings may not have personnel adequate for operating foreign branches, and they may decide to license.

Thus, rather than make direct investments abroad and acquire title to property located there, a manufacturer or other enterpriser interested in foreign markets may decide to operate under licensing agreements. In this way, another manufacturer or enterpriser previously established and operating in a given market will be licensed to produce the products or services of the first under a technical assistance or know-how, or trademark or patent procedure.

The subject of licensing is treated in Chapter 16.

Foreign Branch Operation

Problems of administration and operation of foreign branches are viewed by many firms with apprehension. This attitude undoubtedly springs from the difficulties that are likely to be encountered and from the expense and risk.

Extent of Foreign Branch Operation. Some indication of the extent of United States branch operation in foreign countries may be observed from the estimated value of those enterprises. As of the end of 1961, American distribution facilities abroad, both wholesale and retail, represented a value of over $2.6 billion.[1] American-owned manufacturing enterprises in foreign countries were estimated to be worth $11.9 billion. Other direct investments indicative of American participation in overseas operations included public utilities and transportation, $2.2 billion; petroleum properties, over $12.1 billion; and mining and smelting, $3.0 billion. These estimates speak eloquently of the scale on which American enterprise has participated in the development of resources abroad and has sought to bring closer together, by distributive outlets, the products of the United States and those of foreign nations.

According to studies conducted by the United States Department of Commerce, the production of goods in foreign countries by United States-controlled manufacturing companies reached a value of $25.5 billion in 1961. This was $2.0 billion more than the data for the year 1960 and, compared with the figures for the year 1957 when the information was first disseminated, represents a 40 percent increase.

The distribution of the $25.5 billion indicated Europe to be in the lead with $10.7 billion (70 percent above the 1957 figure); Canada $8.9 billion; Latin America $2.4 billion; and the balance of $3.5 billion embracing all other areas.[2]

---

[1] U.S. Department of Commerce, *Survey of Current Business* (August, 1962), Table 2, p. 22.

[2] U.S. Department of Commerce, *International Commerce* (October 1, 1962), p. 5.

Management of the Branch. The selection of the manager is a deciding factor in foreign branch operation. It is to be assumed that the manager will be selected with the greatest of care. If he is a man of unquestionable ability and integrity, there is no reason to doubt that proper administration will be provided. When selected, he is worthy of unstinted support in the prosecution of his work.

Desirable candidates for branch manager are to be found within the ranks of the company. When the work of the branch is to be largely technical in nature, then an expert along certain lines may be selected. When foreign factories are established, the importance of technical skill is readily seen. If sales and promotion work are paramount and yet the product is technical in nature, then mechanical knowledge plus sales ability are needed. If seeking a resident foreign manager for a buying branch, a man who knows products, markets, and techniques is sought.

It is often stated that a branch manager and, of course, the assistant manager, must be American citizens. Personnel ranking below the managerial staff level are rarely recruited from the United States, since efficient and economical help is available abroad. Moreover, labor laws in many countries rigidly limit the number of foreigners that may be employed, and the laws may also require the training of nationals to take over the duties of some or all of these foreigners within a stated number of years. On investigation, it is found that some foreign traders express no preference as to the nationality of a manager, while others employ nationals exclusively.

Companies that have developed a widespread branch house system sometimes provide direct foreign supervision in addition to a manager. When a certain trading area is well organized through a chain of branches, a supervisor may be placed in charge of a group of branches located in a given area. Many firms divide the world into trading regions with a supervisor in charge of each area.

In all matters involved in branch house operation, it is to be understood that the manager is given considerable voice in the determination of policies. Final decision does not rest with him in all matters; but if he is in a true sense the branch manager, his opinion, as guided by his dual knowledge of the market and the company, is of inestimable value. Close cooperation will, as in other plans of distribution or purchase, assure the greatest degree of success.

Finances. Financial control is provided by various means. Some concerns keep a duplicate set of books in the home office, so that an accurate picture of branch operation is at all times possible. Specified sums of money are provided periodically until the receipts of the branch make this unnecessary. All expenditures are, at stated intervals, to be supported by vouchers, and regular auditing of accounts is usually practiced. One large firm states that its own corps of accountants travels from branch to branch, adding significantly that "in every instance they are Scotchmen." Still other concerns exercise no detailed supervision but allow the manager almost complete discretion in the handling of funds.

Credits and Advertising. Closely associated with financial management is the credit problem. Close supervision over credits is often exercised by the home office. The same may be said of advertising, particularly of expenditures authorized for this purpose. In advertising it is usually found that the branch handles all the details of the program, engaging the space, supplying copy and cuts (which often may be made up in the home office), checking the insertions, and paying the bills. The home office may supervise expenditures, advertising policy, types of media, etc., but the operation of the plan is conducted by the branch.[3]

Quotas. Branches may or may not be placed on a quota basis, as is sometimes the case in agency operation. By adjusting the method of compensation, the same net result may be obtained and in a more judicious manner. In addition to the salary usually paid foreign branch managers, a sales commission provides the incentive to increase volume. Even without this attraction of immediate personal gain, the desirable manager is the type who strives to make a good showing for the work entrusted to him.

Since a manager is not synonymous with a salesman, there is a factor of economical and efficient operation also to be considered. The two go hand in hand in branch house management. Increased sales and accordingly commissions are urged, but efficient management is in no sense secondary in importance. One company insists that branch managers purchase 20 percent of the capital stock of the branch company. This is one way of guaranteeing a well-rounded interest in the business.

Prices. Prices are not so generally supervised by the home office as are some other matters. To exercise too rigid control over selling or buying prices would at once destroy a decided advantage of branch opera-

---

[3]See Chapter 12.

tion. Flexibility, if at all desired, is to be found to a large extent in the management of prices. Considerable discretion, therefore, as dictated by local conditions, is often placed in the hands of the branch manager. If price control is rigidly exercised by the home office, the cables and, perhaps, telephones are probably kept busy.

In this connection it is of interest to note the bases on which goods are billed to a branch. In some cases consignments are made and when the goods are sold, the branch remits. Another method often followed is to sell goods to the branch at wholesale or at a special discount.

Business Organization for Foreign Operations

From a legal point of view, branches may be considered as of two types: (1) branch of the home company or of a subsidiary of the home company, and (2) fully incorporated company under local (foreign) law. The legal requirements for domiciling a concern in foreign countries are the same for the branch of either a parent or a subsidiary (home) company. The latter may be organized specifically for the purpose of transacting business in a particular foreign country. For example, the Cross and Armstrong Company, Inc., may, for its Brazilian business, organize the Cross and Armstrong Company of Brazil, Inc.

Several questions enter the determination as to which business form or procedure will be best for a given enterprise. Such questions are:

1. Does the foreign government require use of a domestic entity as a prerequisite to (a) an investment permit or an exchange license, (b) ownership of certain types of property, (c) conduct of certain types of business, or (d) granting of financial or other concessions to a new enterprise?

2. Is local equity participation required? If so, what form is best suited to protection of the relative positions of the American and foreign investors?

3. Does discrimination exist between domestic and foreign entities, either in law or in administrative practice?

4. If either U.S. or foreign government sources of financing are to be used, is a particular form required?[4]

In determining the form of the foreign business enterprise, decisions must sometimes be made between the advantages to be obtained operating under foreign law and those that are lost by this procedure. For example, an American company that might find it advisable to utilize

---

[4]U.S. Department of Commerce, *Foreign Commerce Weekly* (May 21, 1962), p. 914.

one of the several financing agencies, as the Export-Import Bank, may lose this opportunity if it is not an American company.

A business engaged in foreign operations must set up some kind of business organization. One way in which it may operate is to consider the foreign operation a branch of the home company. In this case, a foreign company seeks to come into another country and engage in business. Whether it can do this and, if so, under what conditions are matters that are determined under international treaties and agreements, as well as the local law of the particular country.

A variation of the type presented above in which a company may organize is to establish a subsidiary that would administer all of the foreign business operations of the company within a given area or country. For example, there is IBM World Trade Corporation, which supervises all overseas business operations for the parent company and, also, a company like Cross and Armstrong, Inc., that for its Brazilian business organizes the Cross and Armstrong Company of Brazil, Inc. In either case, it is still a foreign corporation that is seeking to do business in all or in individual countries.

A second way in which the company may organize for foreign business is to establish a business in a foreign country under the laws of that foreign country. International treaties and agreements also determine the right of foreign companies to engage in business and to organize under local law. For example, under local law many countries will not permit foreigners to organize banks, insurance companies, or sometimes certain kinds of business, such as iron and steel production. However, foreign firms engaged in such businesses may establish branches of the parent company, but they are not permitted to organize a company under foreign law; such businesses are reserved for national companies.

A variation of the foreign company is a joint arrangement with capital and business enterprisers in the foreign country. Under this plan, the financing and control of the foreign operation is shared with others in the particular country. As indicated above, this may not be a matter of choice if the law of a particular country requires domestic participation in any foreign operation.

Steps to Follow in Establishing a Branch. In order that a concern may obtain legal footing in a foreign country, a defined procedure is to be followed and the following documents are generally required to be filed:

1. A certified copy of the articles of incorporation or charter and of the company's bylaws. Filing these papers will serve to guarantee that the concern is duly organized and operating at home, without which domestication abroad would not be permitted. Some countries require, in addition, a certificate attesting to the fact that the company is actually engaged in business and is in good standing. This may be accomplished in some instances by filing a copy of the latest balance sheet.

2. A certified copy of the resolution of the board of directors authorizing domestication in the foreign country. This resolution may contain a statement of the amount of capital to be devoted to the foreign branch.

3. A certified copy of the names and addresses of directors, officers, and stockholders. Some countries require also that this list indicate the amount of stock held by each.

4. A power of attorney in favor of a resident of the foreign country who is granted authority to petition or apply for domestication, and on whom all legal processes may be served. An additional power of attorney may also be required for the branch manager, setting forth the specific powers delegated including the right to sue and be sued, to maintain a bank account in the company's name, and to represent the company's interests in the foreign country.

Next, such fees, taxes, and deposits as may be required by law are to be paid. After all the steps have been complied with, it is generally required that a notice be published in the official gazette or daily press in the foreign country, announcing the intention of the company to open a branch there. Following this, an official decree in some countries grants final authorization to begin operations.

All of these formalities are not required by every country, but most of them are to be found in the laws of foreign countries governing the domestication of alien concerns. Particularly in countries where a strict code system of law prevails is there likely to be a maximum of qualifying steps and formalities.[5]

Prior to the enactment of the 1962 Revenue Act, many United States companies had set up foreign subsidiaries to provide a base for carrying on foreign business in so-called "tax havens." By means of this

---

[5]The nature of common law and code law is treated on page 454 of Chapter 24.

device, profits earned abroad were not subject to United States taxation until the earnings were remitted to the United States. However, the 1962 Revenue Act, in general, changed this by declaring that profits earned abroad were subject to United States taxation when *earned* and not when *remitted*, as before.

Exceptions to this provision are made in the case of operations in less developed countries when the earnings are reinvested in such countries; and, for some United States stockholders, some of the income of some foreign corporations. Under this provision, for example, stockholders with less than 10 percent of the stock of the corporation will not be taxed currently, and the corporation must be United States-controlled, that is, more than 50 percent of the voting stock owned by United States stockholders. The holdings of the stockholders with less than 10 percent of the voting power are not counted in computing control as more than 50 percent. Finally, if the foreign-controlled corporation is declared by the United States Treasury as not being used for substantial tax avoidance, there is no tax if the gross income of such corporation is less than 30 percent of gross income from all sources; if more than 70 percent of gross income, all of its net income, with certain deductions — dividends, interest, etc., and income from aircraft and vessels to the extent that these items represent a reinvestment in the less developed countries — is declared to be foreign-base income. If between 30 and 70 percent, only the items comprising that income are taken into account.

There are three components of foreign-base income: (1) foreign personal holding company income, such as rents, except when received from a trade or business; (2) foreign-base company sales income from purchases and sales of property produced and sold outside of the country in which the controlled foreign corporation is organized; and (3) foreign-base company services income from technical, managerial, and related services performed for a related person[6] outside of the country of organization of the controlled foreign corporation.

Foreign Incorporation v. Domestication Abroad. The question frequently arises as to the relative merits of branch organization by means of foreign incorporation as compared with domestication. While this problem is necessarily one to be considered for each particular country, certain general considerations may be presented.

---

[6] A "related person" is an individual, partnership, trust, estate, or corporation which controls the foreign corporation; subsidiaries of the controlled foreign corporation; or another foreign corporation controlled by the same person or persons.

Foreign Incorporation. In favor of foreign incorporation these conditions may be cited:

1. A foreign concern may be admitted only upon governmental consent, which may be withdrawn at any time; or provisions of the company's charter may have to be changed, according to the action of the government.

2. Foreign incorporation is preferable if foreign capital is to be solicited and if foreign management of the concern is required or desired.

3. Expense of incorporation is no greater and sometimes considerably less than for domestication.

4. The law may require a foreign company to appoint a resident of the country in which a branch is registered to act as the official agent of the company. Among his duties is the filing of an annual statement disclosing the entire business of the concern, which might be looked upon by the parent company as undesirable.

5. Taxation difficulties may arise because there may be no clear-cut segregation of the business of the branch from the entire overseas transactions of the parent company. The question arises, "How much was earned in the foreign country?" Unless the business of each country is segregated by means of separately incorporated companies, difficulty in answering the question is likely to occur.

6. In countries where foreigners are prevented by law from acquiring property, a locally incorporated company may do so.

Domestication Abroad. Certain factors favor domestication abroad.

1. The registered foreign branch is entirely controlled from the home office. If incorporated abroad, however, the law may require that annual meetings and directors' meetings be held there, with home control thereby being largely relinquished.

2. The powers and duties of the branch manager may be clearly set forth in the power of attorney granted him, while in local incorporation full control must pass to the officials of the foreign concern.

Factors Favoring Foreign Operations

In this concluding section we shall look at the following factors, each of which, when applicable to a particular company, will tend to favor the establishment of foreign operations.

1. Volume of business.
2. Nature of business.
3. Financial resources.
4. Nationalism.
5. Unsatisfactory agency possibilities.
6. Reduction of factory overhead.
7. Legal considerations.
8. Investment guarantee program.

Volume of Business. The volume of business is found to be the most common factor governing the advisability of establishing foreign operations. When the volume of business has approached a figure sufficiently large to offset increased selling expenses incurred in branch sales distribution, a most favorable factor is present. Potential volume of business may be set down in this connection, as the amount of existing business rarely is of sufficient magnitude to dictate the establishment of branches. Market possibilities may be so attractive, however, that the branch may be expected eventually to attain the necessary volume.

Volume alone, however, does not necessarily prove the advisability of establishing foreign operations. Many large exporters obtain highly satisfactory distribution through other channels. Conversely, in some lines, conditions other than volume are of a determining character.

Nature of Business. Some export wares are of a specialized, technical nature, and for this reason effective sales distribution is obtained principally through the foreign operations method. Articles that require demonstration, service facilities, and repair and replacement parts are especially adaptable to this plan of distribution. For example, several automobile companies have established assembly plants abroad, partly for the purpose of maintaining adequate repair and replacement facilities. Other lines of machinery are similarly distributed in the most effective manner when these necessary facilities are made available.

Another example in which the nature of the business influenced the sales distribution pattern is that of a world famous exporter of wearing apparel, a specialty product. This exporter established foreign branches in order to maintain accurate and up-to-date contact with current styles that were largely set in London and Paris. In another situation, a packing house reported that its branch managers obtained better foreign prices than commission agents were able to procure.

Financial Resources. Adequate financial resources are another prerequisite of foreign operations. The establishment of a foreign operations system of manufacturing or production may require a substantial initial outlay of funds. For this reason, it may be decided to license a manufacturer abroad.

Nationalism. Sentiment may be a factor in establishing foreign operations. The "Buy British" campaign in British Empire countries so affected the exports of one concern that it became necessary to locate branch factories in important British markets. Even in the absence of organized propaganda of this nature, a foreign operation affords a sense of permanency, and it is identified with the interests of the country in which it is established. Customers place more confidence in the company and in its product. Sentiment favoring local merchandise was strengthened in the wave of nationalism during the years following 1930 and continues unabated.

A "Buy Argentine" policy was announced by that country on July 1, 1963. This is designed to encourage purchases from domestic suppliers. All requests of public agencies to import supplies and equipment will be screened to determine if the same products can be purchased from domestic producers at a reasonable price. In order to put domestic suppliers on a more competitive footing in regard to credit terms, the Central Bank will finance up to 80 percent of the payments involved for a period of up to five years.[7]

Moreover, nationalism may be expressed in terms of incentives to investment of foreign capital. Many countries — not only the less developed countries — offer various kinds of financial inducements to encourage investment in, usually, specific kinds of business. Such incentives may be of the nature of tax concessions — exemption, reduction, postponement, etc. — or by exchange preferences, provided, of course, that exchange is handled in such manner.[8]

Unsatisfactory Agency Possibilities. The chief competitor of the foreign operation system is probably the foreign agency and distributor method. For various reasons a manufacturer may decide to adopt the foreign operation method because of unsatisfactory agency or distributor

---

[7] *The Review of the River Plata* (July 10, 1963); *Analisis* (Buenos Aires: July 15, 1963), published in *International Finance New Survey*, Vol. XV, No. 31 (August 9, 1963), p. 276.

[8] See U.S. Department of Commerce, *Foreign Commerce Weekly* (June 4, 1962), p. 994. One of a series entitled "A Management Checklist for Overseas Business."

possibilities. The territory may be too large for them to cover efficiently; the firm's present representatives may have been unsatisfactory, and all desirable and available candidates may already possess arrangements with other manufacturers, or cannot be attracted to the proposition.

Reduction of Factory Overhead. While foreign operations may return no profit, they may be maintained for the purpose of reducing factory overhead. This is accomplished by means of the increased production required by export sales made through the branch. One company reported that foreign branches are maintained principally to provide an outlet for inferior quality products. The presumption arises that these "seconds" are not attractive to other more economical channels of distribution, and that the branch is therefore necessary.

Legal Considerations. A frequent cause for the establishment of foreign operations is of legal origin. Import duties, as discussed earlier, are frequently so high on finished and assembled manufactures as to encourage the establishment of a foreign assembly plant or factory. Foreign exchange restrictions may bring about the same result. Taxes may impose a heavy burden on a business not established within a country. In many instances, official business with governmental units is impossible unless a foreign supplier is nationalized and maintains local goods.

Moreover, patent laws may require the presence in the country of manufacturing concerns holding foreign patent rights. The law may contain a so-called "working clause," requiring that patents actually be worked in order to maintain the validity of a patent right. This may be accomplished directly or through a licensing arrangement; but if control over foreign exploitation of a patent is desired, a branch plant will offer the best plan.

Investment Guarantee Program. Conditions may arise that necessitate or render advisable the withdrawal of foreign operations. Wars and civil commotion are responsible for closing many branches located in affected countries. It is apparent that unless the investment incident to the establishment of foreign operations is safeguarded, this means of distribution is unattractive. In some cases, foreign operations have also been closed because of exchange rate difficulties.

Under the investment guarantee program of the United States government, *new* investment in foreign operations may be guaranteed against currency inconvertibility, expropriation or confiscation, and loss by reason of war. These risks are not covered, however, in all countries.[9]

Summary

1. Foreign operations constitute the most direct method of international marketing. These are of several types, namely: (1) purchase or sales branch or office, (2) storage or warehouse branch, (3) assembly plant, (4) manufacturing plant, and (5) licensing agreement.
2. Some United States companies operate retail stores abroad (cameras, sewing machines, a certain so-called mail-order house, etc.). Most branches are operated by manufacturing establishments.
3. Three different types of license agreements are recognized, each of which is designed to meet certain conditions: patents, trademarks, and the provision of technical know-how.
4. The qualifications of a branch manager are very important considerations in operating a foreign branch. Labor laws may require the employment of nationals in jobs below the managerial staff level.
5. Administrative supervision of foreign operations is exercised in various ways, with emphasis in this respect being laid on financial matters. Credit policies and advertising expenditures are often controlled by headquarters.
6. Foreign legal requirements to authorize the establishment of foreign operations are exacting. The headquarters or parent company may seek domestication abroad, or a new corporation may be created and organized abroad.
7. Foreign operation is favored chiefly when the volume of present or prospective business is great. Other factors that exert a favorable influence toward the establishment of foreign operations are related to the nature of the business, financial resources, nationalism, unsatisfactory agency possibilities, reduction of factory overhead, legal considerations, and the investment guarantee program.

QUESTIONS

1. Why do business firms go in for foreign operations?
2. Distinguish among the several types of foreign operations that are recognized in international marketing.

---

[9]For further information about the investment guarantee program of the United States, see Chapter 31.

3. As the head of a company engaged in international marketing, outline the managerial responsibilities and authority you would delegate to the manager of:
   (a) A branch office.
   (b) A storage branch.
   (c) An assembly plant.
   (d) A manufacturing plant.
4. Why should some firms view the subject of foreign operations with apprehension?
5. As the president of a firm manufacturing electronic computing equipment, you have decided to establish several foreign branches throughout Europe. What qualifications would you look for in the selection of your branch managers?
6. Compare the merits and the demerits of foreign operation by means of (a) incorporation abroad and (b) domesticating the American company.
7. Discuss the circumstances and conditions under which the several types of foreign operation are favored.

PROBLEMS

1. Because of high import duties, an American manufacturer of cakes and cookies is suddenly shut out of a South American market. The import duties were raised to a prohibitive level in order to afford protection to a national baking firm that claimed it could satisfactorily meet the needs of the market. In so doing, domestic employment would be provided and foreign exchange, previously paid for imported cakes and cookies, would be saved.
   What steps should the American company take in an effort to hold that market? Evaluate the problems inherent in such steps.
2. From your library, find the most recent study of the United States Department of Commerce on foreign investments of the United States. Study the data from the standpoint of foreign operations of American companies. After comparing the data with those found in this chapter, write a report in which you show any significant changes that may have occurred.
3. An American manufacturer of business machines transacts 40 percent of his business abroad. Distribution abroad is by means of agents and distributors. The profits earned on these export sales are taxable at 52 percent in the United States.
   Explain how the company can change its method of conducting its export sales and thereby achieve a saving in taxes, including foreign as well as United States taxes.

COLLATERAL READINGS

Bryson, G. D. *American Management Abroad*. New York: Harper & Row, 1961.

Collins, V. D. *World Marketing*. Philadelphia: J. B. Lippincott Company, 1935. Chapter 7.

Dartnell International Trade Handbook, The. Chicago: The Dartnell Corporation, 1963. Part 1, Chapter 2; Parts 3, 4, and 5.

de Haas, J. A. *The Practice of Foreign Trade*. New York: McGraw-Hill Book Company, Inc., 1935. Chapter 13.

Fayerweather, John. *Management of International Operations*, Text and Cases. New York: McGraw-Hill Book Company, Inc., 1960. Chapter 4.

Horn, Paul V. *International Trade Principles and Practices*, Third Edition. New York: Prentice-Hall, Inc., 1951. Chapter 26.

International Management Association. *Proceedings, Conference on Foreign Operations*. New York: annual.

MacDonald, Philip. *Practical Exporting*. New York: Ronald Press Company, 1949. Chapter 3.

Pratt, E. E. *Modern International Commerce*. New York: Allyn and Bacon, Inc., 1956. Chapter 4.

Roorbach, G. B. *Problems in Foreign Trade*. New York: McGraw-Hill Book Company, Inc., 1933. Part IV.

Tosdal, H. R. *Problems in Export Sales Management*. New York: McGraw-Hill Book Company, Inc., 1922. Chapter 9.

United States Department of Commerce, Bureau of International Commerce. *Investments in (name of country)*. Washington, D.C.: Government Printing Office, a series of handbooks on different countries.

Case studies on United States business abroad:

Burgess, E. W., and F. H. Harbison. *Casa Grace in Peru*. Washington, D.C.: National Planning Association, 1954.

Lindeman, John. *The Philippine American Life Insurance Company*. Washington, D.C.: National Planning Association, 1955.

Taylor, Wayne C. *The Creole Petroleum Corporation in Venezuela*. Washington, D.C.: National Planning Association, 1955.

————————. *The Firestone Operations in Liberia*. Washington, D.C.: National Planning Association, 1956.

Wood, Richardson, and Virginia Keyes. *Sears Roebuck de Mexico, S. A.* Washington, D.C.: National Planning Association, 1953.

CHAPTER 15

OVERSEAS MANUFACTURING

As stated in the preceding chapter, manufacturing overseas is one of the ways to engage in foreign operations. Actually, manufacturing overseas is basically a production matter and secondarily a marketing matter. A top sales executive who might have been successful in the management of a foreign sales branch may be a dismal failure when it comes to managing a factory. It is for this reason that overseas manufacturing is approached cautiously, because personnel beyond the export sales level must be provided. As will be discussed in this chapter, manufacturing brings into the picture many problems that are not encountered in the sales area.

This subject will be discussed in terms of the extent of manufacturing overseas by American enterprisers; the extent of manufacturing in the United States by foreign enterprisers; and the reasons for and the problems encountered in overseas manufacturing.

Extent of United States Manufacturing Overseas

The establishment of factories abroad as an efficient and often necessary means of competing in foreign markets is a long-established practice of U.S. manufacturing concerns. Such foreign investment expanded with great rapidity during and after the first World War, primarily in Canada and Europe.

Major factors inducing these ventures are: cost advantages in producing closer to markets, especially when materials or components and trained labor are available; consumer preferences for locally produced goods; gains in expert knowledge of market conditions and access to patents and licenses to produce specialized items through joint operations with local entrepreneurs; mounting financial strength of U.S. companies, facilitating the purchase of existing foreign concerns, often as a relatively quick method of countering developing competition; pressures from tariffs, exchange controls, quotas, and patent laws that give major advantage to locally produced goods.[1]

The growth of United States investments in manufacturing abroad has been phenomenal, particularly since 1950. Table 15-1 shows the growth of United States direct investments in manufacturing overseas from 1929 to 1963.

Table 15-1

UNITED STATES INVESTMENTS IN MANUFACTURING OVERSEAS

Year	Value of Investments (In millions of $ U.S.)
1929	1813
1936	1710
1943	2276
1950	3831
1957	8009
1959	9692
1963	14890

Source: U.S. Department of Commerce, *U.S. Business Investments in Foreign Countries* (1929–1959), Table 5, p. 93.
U.S. Department of Commerce, *Survey of Current Business* (August, 1964), Table 2, p. 10.

Since 1946, and especially since 1950, there has been a vigorous, sustained growth of demand in many countries, combined with foreign exchange shortages at times limiting exports from the United States. Also, the recent emergence of new nations and regional economic blocs will probably tend to foster local production. Direct investments in manufacturing abroad doubled between 1940 and 1950, and more than doubled again by 1957, and doubled once more by 1963, despite some losses in value caused by exchange depreciations.[2]

The geographical distribution of these investments in manufacturing abroad is presented in Table 15-2.

Europe is currently the geographical area accounting for the largest share of United States manufacturing investments overseas. Canada, which heretofore had been the leading geographical area, was passed by Europe in 1961. These two geographical areas together account for over 70 percent of all of the foreign manufacturing investments by United States enterprisers. These areas are not the less developed countries, by any means.

---

[1]U.S. Department of Commerce, *U.S. Business Investments in Foreign Countries* (Washington, D.C.: Government Printing Office, 1960), p. 19.
[2]*Ibid.*, p. 20.

Table 15-2

UNITED STATES INVESTMENTS IN MANUFACTURING
ABROAD
BY GEOGRAPHICAL AREAS
1929–1963
(In millions of $ U.S.)

Area	1929	1936	1943	1950	1957	1959	1963
Total	1813	1710	2276	3831	8009	9692	14890
Canada	819	799	941	1897	3924	4558	5746
Latin America	231	192	325	781	1280	1426	2211
Europe	629	612	879	932	2195	2927	5610
Africa	7	10	13	55	106	120	176
Asia	76	54	68	60	190	248	420
Oceania	50	42	50	107	314	412	728

Source: U.S. Department of Commerce, *U.S. Business Investments in Foreign Countries* (1929–1959), Table 5, p. 93.

U.S. Department of Commerce, *Survey of Current Business* (August, 1964), Table 2, p. 10.

Manufacturing investments in Latin America occupy third place, and they, too, have shown a great increase since 1959. The other geographical areas are small, in comparison with the three leaders which, in 1963, accounted for over 90 percent of the total.

The major kinds of business represented by these American manufacturing establishments overseas are presented in Table 15-3.

Table 15-3

UNITED STATES MANUFACTURING INVESTMENTS ABROAD
BY COMMODITY GROUPS
1929–1963
(In millions of $ U.S.)

Commodity Group	1929	1936	1940	1950	1957	1959	1963
Total	1813	1710	1926	3831	8009	9692	14890
Food	222	220	245	483	723	821	1242
Paper and allied products	279	269	308	378	722	811	1053
Chemicals and allied products	138	205	221	512	1378	1657	2580
Rubber	60	63	64	182	401	460	623
Primary and fabricated metals	150	185	187	385	941	1161	1659
Machinery (except electrical)	185	159	193	420	927	1200	1805
Electrical machinery	259	183	214	387	731	834	1198
Transportation equipment	184	206	283	485	1204	1602	2941
All other	337	221	212	599	983	1147	1789

Source: U.S. Department of Commerce, *U.S. Business Investments in Foreign Countries* (1929–1957), Table 8, p. 96.

U.S. Department of Commerce, *Survey of Current Business* (August, 1964), Table 6, p. 13.

Transportation equipment is the largest single commodity group into which United States manufacturing investments abroad have gone. This group more than doubled from 1959 to 1963. The chief line of activity in this group is the assembly and manufacturing of motor vehicles — passenger cars, trucks, and buses. This group is relatively widespread in its geographical distribution around the world. Indeed, the American motor companies started manufacturing abroad early when they realized that the world was their market and that manufacturing was the most effective way, if other factors were favorable.

The chemicals and allied products group occupies the second spot in the commodity distribution of United States manufacturing investments abroad. This group scored an increase of 55 percent between 1959 and 1963.

> Foreign investments by the chemical industry are extremely varied, with products ranging from drugs to basic chemicals and fertilizers, and with operations ranging from packaging of finished products to processing of raw materials. Since the demand for these products is universal, and many can be produced with a relatively small plant, investments in this industry are somewhat more evenly distributed throughout the world than are other manufacturing operations.[3]

The production of machinery, other than electrical, occupies third place in the commodity grouping. The production of this equipment is largely established in the industrial countries and in such developing nations as Brazil, Mexico, and Australia.

The fourth commodity group is primary and fabricated metals. These activities are generally associated with Canada and the United Kingdom.

The fifth commodity group is food which is located chiefly in Canada, the United Kingdom, and some Latin American countries. Next in the commodity distribution is electrical machinery which is distributed geographically the same as described for primary and fabricated metals. Paper and allied products follow, and this manufacturing business is chiefly located in Canada, with some smaller operations extending to other countries in recent years.

The last of the specific commodity groups is rubber which is widely distributed, particularly with respect to the manufacture of automobile tires and tubes.

---

[3]*Ibid.*, p. 20.

As this analysis reveals, United States investments in manufacturing overseas have expanded rapidly in all lines of manufacturing into which the data are divided. Many of the factors influencing this expansion will be covered later in this chapter.

Foreign Manufacturing Investments in the United States

Another measure of the extent of manufacturing abroad is revealed by a study of foreign manufacturing investments in the United States. Foreign capital was invested early in the United States, and many of the foreign manufacturing companies have been bought out by American investors; or, separate American companies have been set up under American law with stock held by American investors.

According to information published by the United States Department of Commerce,[4] foreign manufacturing investments in the United States grew from $729 million in 1937 to $1138 million in 1950, to $2471 million in 1959, and to $2754 million in 1961. For the year 1961, foreign investments in United States manufacturing constituted nearly two fifths of total foreign direct investments in this country. However, the most complete breakdown of foreign investments in the United States is for the year 1959,[5] when the total manufacturing investments in the United States amounted to $2471 million.

Table 15-4 shows the country distribution for 1959 and also, in less detail, for 1960. Total distribution only is given for 1961 through 1963.

Table 15-4

FOREIGN MANUFACTURING INVESTMENTS IN THE
UNITED STATES BY COUNTRY
(In millions of $ U.S.)

Country	1959	1960	1961	1962	1963
Total	2471	2611	2754	2885	3018
Canada	907	932			
Europe	1501	1611			
Latin America	10				
Asia	49	68			
Africa	3				
All other	1				

Source: U.S. Department of Commerce, *Foreign Business Investments in the United States* (1962), p. 35. For 1960–63, from U.S. Department of Commerce, *Survey of Current Business* (August, 1964), Table 11, p. 14.

---

[4]*Foreign Business Investments in the United States* (1962), Table 1, p. 34.
[5]*Ibid.*

Canada was the country with the leading position in foreign manu-facturing investments in the United States in 1959. Canada was followed by the United Kingdom with $698 million, then Switzerland with $395 million. The Netherlands showed $197 million and Sweden $104 million. All other countries participated at an amount less than $100 million.

The commodity distribution of the foreign manufacturing invest-ments in the United States is shown in Table 15-5.

Table 15-5

FOREIGN DIRECT INVESTMENT IN UNITED STATES MANUFACTURING BY MAJOR COMMODITY GROUPS
1937 and 1959
(In millions of $ U.S.)

Commodity Group	1937		1959	
	Amount	Percent of Total	Amount	Percent of Total
Total	729		2471	
Food products, tobacco, and beverages	116	16	931	38
Chemicals and allied products	220	30	465	19
Primary and fabricated metals	43	6	125	5
Machinery, except electrical	32	4	275	11
Electrical machinery	12	2	83	3
Textiles	217	30	216	9
Other	89	12	376	15

Source: U.S. Department of Commerce, *Foreign Business Investments in the United States* (1962), p. 8.

Many foreign manufacturing companies, principally European and a few Canadian firms with a leading position in their industries through patents, production techniques, or extensive experience, long ago established production facilities in the United States. A wide range of commodities has been involved, including many chemicals, artificial fibres, specialty food products and beverages, textiles, paper products, and many types of machinery.

The contribution of foreign manufacturing enterprise to the United States economy has been mainly to widen the spectrum of prod-ucts available, occasionally introducing products of considerable im-portance. Foreign-controlled enterprises now do not weigh heavily, in the aggregate, in any major branch of United States manufacturing.

Over time, the commodity composition of the manufacturing in-vestments has changed considerably. Food products and beverages are now the largest group but ranked third in the 1930's, while textile prod-ucts, which were then the largest [sic] group, now account for under 10 per cent of the total. Chemicals and related products have been a major field for investment for many years, while the relative importance of investments in pulp and paper production has increased.[6]

[6]U.S. Department of Commerce, *Foreign Business Investments in the United States* (1962), p. 7.

Over one half of the total Canadian manufacturing investments in
the United States

> ...is in companies producing alcoholic beverages, with sizable invest-
> ments also in the production of machinery and fabricated metals,
> mainly nickel. Nearly all of the Canadian investments are in wholly
> owned subsidiaries. . . . [United Kingdom's] investments cover a rela-
> tively broad group of products, ranging from food and tobacco through
> various kinds of machinery, rubber products, and paper and pulp. . . .
> Manufacturing investments from Switzerland . . . are mainly in the
> production of chemicals and pharmaceuticals, as well as in several
> companies producing well known food specialities. The Netherlands
> investment in United States manufacturing is concentrated in a few
> companies producing electrical machinery, chemicals, artificial fibres,
> and foodstuffs. Sweden's manufacturing investment . . . is connected
> mainly with a few companies producing machinery. German manu-
> facturing investments are now comparatively small, with substantial
> investments — especially in the chemical industry — having been
> seized by the United States Government in both world wars.[7]

Why Manufacture Overseas?

There is only one basic reason for manufacturing overseas — or anywhere, for that matter — and that is to make a profit. Foreign manufacturing is rarely, if ever, the first international business venture undertaken by a company. No firm would dream of establishing a factory in
any market unless and until the market had already been tapped by one
or several of the marketing facilities and channels discussed in previous
chapters. Conceivably, a company that is new to an area might decide,
after a market survey had been completed, that manufacturing is the
only logical and profitable way to enter the market. Experience proves,
however, that the companies that are now manufacturing overseas had
first exported their products to the market in which they are now manufacturing. In other words, they were convinced by experience that the
market was there and certain circumstances and conditions had arisen
that made it desirable for them to manufacture. These circumstances
and conditions will now be analyzed.

Tariffs and Import Restrictions. One reason why a firm will manufacture in a given country is because the market has been closed as a
result of high tariffs or other import restrictions. High tariffs in the

---

[7]*Ibid.*, p. 9.

United States were certainly responsible in large part for the foreign manufacturing companies that established factories in the United States.

However, this and other matters that are discussed in this section are, by their very nature, *negative* factors, and it is not correct to twist them to a positive side. High tariffs and import restrictions in any market are adverse to importation; indeed, their very purpose is to discourage or shut out imports. An international business firm that is enjoying a market that is so threatened or destroyed may be able to save his market by manufacturing abroad. If the tariff or other restriction had not been imposed, this question might never have arisen; the firm might have been well content to export to this market and not manufacture in it.

Currency Restrictions. These are of the same general effect as tariffs and import restrictions, but they are generally temporary in nature. While exchange restrictions of all kinds are encountered in world trading,[8] they usually are temporary as countries find ways to improve the situation and to have more foreign exchange with which to continue international trading. Parenthetically, currency restrictions may adversely affect manufacturing operations as well as importing. If the manufacturing process requires equipment, raw materials, supplies, etc. to be imported, currency restrictions would probably prevent their importation and the manufacturing operation could not function.

Nationalism. This is a factor bearing on the subject of manufacturing abroad. It is expressed in terms of patriotic preference for products manufactured at home rather than imported. It is an expression of local or national pride. Empire Preference of the British Empire in the 1930's stressed this appeal. Why any one would prefer to purchase local or national products in preference to imported products, simply because they are produced locally, defies all rational explanations. Nevertheless, it is an important factor with which to deal.

When this philosophy takes hold, its expression does not depend upon mere sentiment. Rather, the philosophy finds expression in the very tariff, import, and currency restrictions mentioned above. It is particularly powerful in this era where developing nations are striving to become somewhat industrialized, and one way to obtain public backing for higher priced and lower quality manufactured goods that are domestically produced is to appeal to patriotic pride.

---

[8] See Chapter 33.

Nationalism has caused many manufacturers to consider seriously the desirability of manufacturing abroad, in order to derive some benefit from the very factor that might have closed their export market and now may appeal as a manufacturing location.

Competition. This is always a force to deal with in business, whether domestic or international. Shorn of the nationalistic, tariff, and currency restriction obstacles discussed above, the international business firm may find that it is losing out in competition with either or both domestic or foreign manufacturers in a given market. These competitors are taking a greater share of the market and an intensive market survey may reveal that the competitor's prices are lower, his quality better, his marketing strategy superior, or any one of a number of reasons.

In order to meet this competition, the desirability of manufacturing abroad must be considered. It is clear that it is no longer profitable to export products to this market, so that prospects for manufacturing in that market must be carefully analyzed. If the firm has sufficient capital, it may be able to buy out one of the competitors and thus present a stronger competitive position. Whatever the solution, the market is bound to disappear as an exporting market, as competitors increase their share of the trade.

Potentiality. Quite apart from competition, the potential outlook for business in a given area may be sufficient reason for manufacturing overseas. This is a positive factor. If the business firm is selling in the market by exporting its wares, it is in a position to determine the long-run potential; and, if it is promising, the firm may consider the desirability of manufacturing. In this case, there is no rush; the firm can take its time and gradually plan for the shift over to manufacturing. One reason for going into manufacturing is that the firm knows from experience that if the market has a good potential, sooner or later some other manufacturer, foreign or domestic, will begin producing the commodity. Many a foreign market has been saved for a wide-awake firm that established manufacturing at a time when it was advantageous. Companies establishing plants at later dates have lost this initial advantage and may never catch up.

This factor was probably paramount in inducing American manufacturers to set up factories in Europe when the Common Market was formed. Not only was there concern for the anticipated increase in tariff rates against imports coming from countries outside of the Common

Market, but there was as well a great appreciation of the potential market that was expected to arise from the welding of the Common Market into a more or less homogeneous market. Potential was undoubtedly a factor inducing foreign manufacturers to establish production facilities in the United States market.

Profit Possibilities. All of the above as well as many other factors must inevitably add up to the profit possibilities of the manufacturing operation. This does not mean that the operation must appear to be profitable from the very beginning. It is the potential that is important, and it may be several years before profits appear. However, if the potential is such as to offer promise of long-run profitability, the move may be made with more assurance.

In order to determine the profitability of the enterprise, whether in the long or short run, certain considerations must be weighed.

Financial considerations. In order to establish a manufacturing enterprise abroad or to buy out a manufacturer already in the market, the firm must have sufficient financial resources available for this purpose. It may be possible to attract foreign (indigenous) capital to go into the venture, and thus reduce the amount of capital required by the manufacturing company. In doing this, however, as will be pointed out later, some degree of control must be surrendered.

Not only must consideration be given to the initial investment required to begin the manufacturing operations, but funds must also be available to finance the company for as long a time as may be necessary before a profit can be earned. This may be a period of several years.

Government Considerations. Doubtless, the first item to be considered under this heading is stability of the government. Probably the main reason for the preponderance of American manufacturing investments in the European area and Canada is the government stability in these countries. Invested capital shuns unstable governments like a righteous person shuns sin. This offers a paradox in that the 1962 Revenue Act of the United States gives preference, taxwise, to investments made in developing countries.[9]

Stability of the government is reflected in several ways as far as the manufacturing enterprise is concerned. Stable governments are not likely to nationalize an industry; they keep their national finances in

---

[9]See Chapter 14.

balance; their exchange rates are relatively stable; there are few, if any, foreign exchange restrictions that will prevent a manufacturing company from remitting profits or acquiring necessary raw materials and other supplies from abroad. As brought out in Chapter 32, an American business firm operating in a foreign country must be able to remit its profits in United States dollars; profits in cruzeiros (Brazil) or rupees (Ceylon, Pakistan, and India) do not satisfy American stockholders. The same is true of any other country.

On the other hand, the foreign government may actually offer inducements to encourage foreign capital investments in manufacturing within its territory. Such inducements include the offer of free land, exemption from taxes for a period of time, financial assistance in building a structure, special lower transportation rates for imported raw materials and components, etc.[10]

Management. Management of the manufacturing operation abroad presents a number of difficult problems. If the facility is completely owned by the parent company, personnel must be available to take over the management function. Very often, the move to manufacture is the next step to a branch sales office, but the executive in charge of the sales office may not be qualified to manage a manufacturing operation. Therefore, new personnel may be necessary, and this may cause a strain on the company. Qualified manufacturing executives may not be willing to transfer to a foreign post.

If the operation is conducted on a joint basis in cooperation with a foreign manufacturer, it may be feasible to place foreign personnel in charge of manufacturing. Many companies are reluctant to do this on the theory that administrative control would be lost; they insist on placing their own executives in such positions. Other companies are less hesitant to give foreigners top positions in their foreign companies. Some companies follow a definite policy of what is called "50-50," which means that in all of their foreign operations, they seek foreign partners who will assume 50 percent of the investment and responsibility. Fortunately, we are in an era in which foreign executives are appreciated, and many companies are proud of the fact that their foreign manufacturing operations are supervised by foreigners.

In some countries and in some lines of manufacturing, it may not be possible to keep complete control of the operation. The laws of such

---

[10]These inducements are also offered by the states and lesser communities of the United States in order to attract new industry.

countries may require that foreign enterprises be jointly owned and controlled, because they do not wish to have their industries dominated by foreign interests. This is another expression of nationalism.

Supply of Raw Materials and Components. Another decision that must be made before the establishment of a manufacturing operation abroad relates to the availability of raw materials and components. One exporter explains that while many countries believe that they should otherwise manufacture everything, if possible, nevertheless find it necessary to import raw materials that are not available locally. This may result in high prices for such imports, and therefore the manufacturing operation may be 25–75 percent higher in cost than in the home country.

Moreover, the international financial position of many countries reaches such a stage when there is no foreign exchange available even for raw material imports. Local manufacturing plants have been closed down for weeks and months because of the unavailability of raw materials. The same factors are true of components that must be imported. Many manufacturing operations are in some measure an assembly of components. If they are not available from local sources, they must be imported and the same risks are run as in the case of raw materials. Such a situation is cited by one exporter when he points out that containers — tin cans, drums, and cartons — cost from two to six times as much when made by a local manufacturer rather than by someone in the home country. One company claims that lithographed tin cans cannot be made as cheaply in Canada as they can in the home country even after the cans are shipped into Canada and a duty of 17½ percent paid thereon. In another country, this exporter found that locally manufactured tin cans were made from an inferior quality of tin plate, and as a result the cans rusted and corroded.

Labor Situation. Any manufacturer contemplating the establishment of a factory in a new location is vitally concerned with the labor situation in that locality. The same is true of manufacturing abroad. It is often assumed that factories are established abroad in order to profit by reason of the lower wages paid to workers. This is not as simple as it sounds. Consider the following points:

> Each country, of course, has its own labor laws, labor conditions, and labor practices. The initial questions with respect to these matters are the same as those that arise in the U.S., but they must be supplemented with a number of additional questions:
> What are the minimum wage rates and the maximum-hour limitations?

What are the differentiations between skilled and unskilled workers and male and female workers?

What are the nature and extent of labor organizations and the legal status of organized labor?

What are the standard provisions of labor agreements, either required by law or by established practice in the particular industry?

In many countries, provisions normally left to collective bargaining in the U.S. are automatically fixed by law. Further investigation should include these questions:

Is profit sharing with workers compulsory or customary?

What are the provisions for hiring, seniority, severance pay, and discharge?

Are there any requirements for education of employees or their families?

Must housing or housing allowances be provided?

Are medical and maternity care necessary?

Determine, also, if a particular percentage of the work force must be nationals or if a particular percentage of payroll must be paid to nationals. Sometimes, exceptions can be obtained from such requirements, although the exceptions are often for a limited period. If residence or work permits are required of nonnationals, determine the conditions for granting them in advance, for issuance of these permits may involve considerable delay and impede establishment of the venture within a reasonable time.

If the law provides for equal pay to nationals and foreigners for comparable work, the standards for determining what is comparable work should be investigated.[11]

Japan is often cited as an instance of a manufacturing country with an abnormally low wage level. While wages have been rising in Japan, as labor unions gain more power, there are what we would call paternalistic practices built into the industrial system. According to a Japanese business executive, these include:

1. Monthly withholding.
   a. The company contributes the same amount as its employees.
      (1) Health insurance.
      (2) Old age pension.
      (3) Unemployment insurance.
   b. The company contributes the whole amount — worker's accident insurance.

---

[11]U.S. Department of Commerce, *Foreign Commerce Weekly* (June 11, 1962), inside front cover.

2. Minimum wage law — labor standard law.
3. Employee's fringe benefits.
   a. Midyear and year-end allowances (2–4 months salary per year).
   b. Commuting expense allowance.
   c. Lunch provided by the company.
   d. Housing accommodation (single house, apartment or dormitory provided by the company) at a nominal rate.
   e. Retirement allowance (lump sum or 3-year installment).
   f. Recreation facilities such as tennis, volley ball, baseball, swimming, skiing, and company employees' picnics twice each year.

Summary

1. Overseas manufacture may be an efficient and necessary means of competing in foreign markets. Many factors account for the expansion of manufacturing abroad.
2. Manufacturing operations overseas by United States companies are concentrated in Europe and Canada.
3. The commodity distribution of United States manufacturing investments abroad is more diffuse than is the geographical distribution. While transportation equipment is the leading commodity group, all other groups, with the single exception of rubber products, showed a value of more than $1 billion in 1963.
4. Foreign manufacturing investments in the United States again show that Europe and Canada are predominant; in fact, they have practically all of the foreign manufacturing investments.
5. Manufacturing overseas, like any other business operation in a private enterprise economy, is an effort to make a profit.
6. Tariffs and import restrictions may cause a foreign firm to undertake manufacturing in a given country.
7. Currency restrictions may also induce foreign manufacturers to come into a given country, but this may not necessarily follow.
8. Nationalism may provide an atmosphere encouraging to foreign manufacturing in a country where nationalism is present. This is a condition that is common in this era.
9. Competition and the potential of a foreign market are factors that attract foreign manufacturing investments.
10. Among the conditions involved in establishing a manufacturing operation overseas, the matter of finances is paramount. There are several ways to deal with this matter. Other factors are the government, the management, the availability of supplies, and the labor situation.

QUESTIONS

1. Comment on the reasons cited for the establishment of manufacturing operations abroad.
2. Why are United States manufacturing investments concentrated in Europe and Canada?
3. Explain why transportation equipment is the leading commodity group among United States manufacturing operations overseas.
4. Comment on the significance of foreign manufacturing investments in the United States.
5. Is it likely that a company new to the foreign market would conduct its first step by manufacturing? Explain.
6. Why may tariffs and import restrictions induce a foreign manufacturer to undertake manufacturing in a given country?
7. How may currency restrictions discourage foreign manufacturing in a given country?
8. Rationalize the meaning and objectives of nationalism as applied to manufacturing.
9. Discuss the several ways in which the matter of finances may be handled in manufacturing overseas.
10. In what ways do governments impede and in what ways do they encourage foreign manufacturing investments in their territory?
11. Why are many American manufacturers reluctant to place foreign executives in charge of manufacturing operations overseas? Do you agree with this policy?
12. Comment on the general assertion that manufacturing overseas is less expensive than in the home country.
13. Discuss the several angles that the labor situation may present in manufacturing abroad.

COLLATERAL READINGS

Bryson, G. D. *American Management Abroad.* New York: Harper & Row, 1961.
Case Studies in Foreign Operations. New York: American Management Association, 1956.
Dartnell International Trade Handbook, The. Chicago: The Dartnell Corporation, 1963.
Fayerweather, John. *Management of International Operations,* Text and Cases. New York: McGraw-Hill Book Company, Inc., 1960. Chapters 4 and 5.
Fenn, Dan J., Jr. *Management Guide to Overseas Operations.* New York: McGraw-Hill Book Company, Inc., 1957.
Gibbons, William J. *Tax Factors in Basing International Business Abroad.* Boston, Mass.: Little, Brown & Company, 1957.

International Management Association. *Proceedings, Conference on Foreign Operations.* New York: annual. Note: This association is now a division of American Management Association.

Taylor, Wayne C. *The Firestone Operations in Liberia.* Washington, D.C.: National Planning Association, 1956.

U.S. Department of Commerce. *Factors Limiting United States Investments Abroad.* Washington, D.C.: Government Printing Office, 1953 and 1954. Parts 1 and 2.

———————————— *Foreign Business Investments in the United States.* Washington, D.C.: Government Printing Office, 1962.

————————————*Investments in (name of country).* Washington, D.C.: Government Printing Office, various years.

———————————— *Survey of Current Business.* Washington, D.C.: Government Printing Office, monthly.

———————————— *U.S. Business Investments in Foreign Countries.* Washington, D.C.: Government Printing Office, 1960.

———————————— *United States Investments in the Latin American Economy.* Washington, D.C.: Government Printing Office, 1957.

CHAPTER 16

LICENSING FOR FOREIGN OPERATIONS[1]

Licensing is a method of foreign operation whereby a firm in one country (the *licensor*) agrees with a firm in another country (the *licensee*) for the licensee to use the manufacturing, processing, trademark, know-how, technical assistance, merchandising knowledge, or some other skill provided by the licensor. This is a simple definition that applies to an American company operating abroad and to foreign companies operating in the United States. It also applies to domestic operations, because some United States companies license other United States companies in the same manner.

Preliminary Considerations

Before any steps are taken, a survey of the market in which the operation is to be conducted must be made. The subjects to be included in such a survey are treated in Chapter 3.

If the survey indicates that foreign licensing can be expected to be successful, a further examination is necessary to determine what the licensor has to offer in order to induce a foreign company to enter into a licensing agreement. There may be a patent that would attract a licensee and that could be a valuable consideration. The same would apply to copyrights and trademarks. These devices could be turned over to the licensee and, if he possesses adequate knowledge, he could use them without any outside help from the licensor. This, however, would be an ideal situation that rarely exists.

---

[1]Grateful acknowledgment is made to Thomas C. Ballagh, President, Ballagh and Thrall, Inc., for assistance in writing this chapter.

If the license proposition calls for the offer of technical assistance or know-how, the question arises as to whether the licensor has sufficient personnel who can be spared for these purposes. Moreover, know-how is difficult to evaluate, and unless the company can definitely establish that what it has to offer is valuable and that it would be profitable to the licensee, a satisfactory agreement would probably not be reached.

Selecting a Licensee

There are several choices that may be considered by the firm that is seeking a satisfactory licensee in a particular country.[2] These candidates for licensee are listed below. We shall briefly examine the desirability of each of these choices.

1. The present sales representative.
2. A competing manufacturer.
3. A manufacturer making a similar but noncompeting product.
4. A manufacturer of a dissimilar product who is seeking diversification.
5. A capitalist looking for investment opportunity.

Present Sales Representative. If a company is presently engaged in marketing in the country where it is considering the possibility of a license arrangement, it is probably operating through a representative in that country. Very often, this representative becomes the first candidate for a licensee, because he is already acquainted with the company and with its products.

If it becomes necessary to set the representative up in production, this is quite another problem, as he may know nothing of production if he has devoted all his efforts to distribution. If it does appear that he would be successful in production, the question of capital must then be considered. One of the reasons for using the licensing method as compared with the establishment of direct branches is that a smaller amount of capital may be provided. Therefore, providing the necessary supply of capital would be an important consideration when a representative or distributor is deemed to be the ideal candidate for the licensee.

Moreover, a distributor-licensee may subcontract the manufacturing and he will then need to pass on the technical know-how to others,

---

[2]See Chapters 4 and 6 for the sources of names of prospective licensees.

which reduces the licensor's control. Since manufacturing and sales are to be handled in separate companies, there is divided responsibility for success. Yet the distributor-licensee should assume the licensee responsibilities for royalty payments, place firm orders with the local subcontractor, and probably be prepared to carry an inventory.

Competing Manufacturer. A competitor already has the manufacturing facilities, established sales outlets, reputation, experience, and judgment of the sales potential and probably profits. He is, however, more likely to be interested in only a part of the licensor's line, especially the newest developments, particularly if they are or may be patented in the licensee's country.

Manufacturer of a Similar Product. A manufacturer of a similar but noncompeting product may have most of the machinery and experience that will be required. He may or may not already be selling to the same class of customers. Usually he will be more willing to take on additional products in order to complete his line, and to pay more for the licensor's technical know-how, even without patents, than will a competing manufacturer.

Manufacturer of a Dissimilar Product. A manufacturer of a dissimilar product may have capital, general manufacturing and business experience, and some trained personnel. If he enters into a licensing agreement, however, he will need more specialized equipment, more training, and a new sales organization. Since he is less able to judge the potential market than the competing manufacturer and the manufacturer of a similar product, he is thus less sure of making a success of the venture.

Capitalist. A capitalist without an existing factory or sales force or experience must start largely from scratch, and with a larger investment than the other choices for licensee. Further, to be successful, the capitalist will need more assistance from the licensor.

As moneyed interests in the less developed countries come to depend less on real estate for investment and as they realize the opportunities for manufacturing under the development programs of most countries, the capitalist is likely to become a more important selection for licensee.

Scope of Licensing Abroad

Licensing may cover any number of operations, processes, rights, or skills that one firm can effectively pass along to another firm. Recently, the emphasis has been placed on patents, copyrights, trademarks, technical assistance, and know-how. Let us review briefly these areas of operation in which licensing is to be found.

Patents. Patents afford a valuable right that the patent holder may choose to license to another company. The patent generally is one that covers some part of a process rather than an entire product, as few patents today are basic.

Copyrights. Copyrights can likewise be licensed, and in this case the license would be granted to a publisher or printer. Copyrights, like patents, are protected under law and the licensee cannot duplicate anything that is copyrighted unless authority is granted by the owner of the patent or copyright.

Trademarks. As was explained in Chapter 12, trademarks play a key role in the international marketing plans of certain manufacturers. The license, therefore, may be for the use of the trademark of the licensor, and in this case there would be a production or marketing arrangement in connection with which the trademark would be used.

Technical Assistance. Technical assistance is a type of licensing under which instruction or demonstration is called for by the licensor. This instruction may be in relation to the use of the patent that may have been licensed, or it may relate to services that are extended in connection with marketing or management techniques, dramatic production, or any number of areas in which the licensor possesses knowledge that can be licensed and transmitted by means of technical assistance.

Know-how. Although know-how is closely related to technical assistance, it usually refers to the manufacturing techniques or other proprietary rights and skills that the licensor may have to offer. Know-how refers to knowledge and may or may not have anything to do with patents. Know-how would demonstrate or show how an inventory control system should be installed, or how a consumer financing operation should be established, or how a display could be effectively set up in a merchandising establishment. Technical assistance, however, would not merely demonstrate or show how to do these things, but would step in and help to do them and continue to help until the licensee had acquired sufficient proficiency.

Miscellaneous Areas of Operation. It should be understood that licensing does not apply only to the production or the marketing of products. It also refers to such knowledge as indicated above — how to operate a consumer finance system, how to plan and conduct a motion picture production, how to make the best use of the agricultural equipment or pesticides of a manufacturer, how to apply a certain treatment devised by a veterinarian or pharmaceutical firm, etc. There are limitless areas in which licensing agreements may be made.

There is also *cross licensing*, by means of which the licensee becomes the licensor. In other words, licensing works both ways. If the proper firm has been selected as a licensee, it is reasonable to suppose that it may know something or have some process that the licensor would be glad to have. Although this amounts to merely an exchange of knowledge and rights, two distinct agreements would be made because the two licensing arrangements are quite independent of each other.

Reasons for Increased Use of Licensing Abroad

In considering the reasons for the increased use of licensing abroad, reference must be made again to the reasons for foreign operations of any kind, namely, as a source of additional earnings. It is the profit motive that induces firms to go into business, whether it be domestic or international.

Another phase of the profitability angle is a marketing advantage that can be acquired by means of licensing. This marketing advantage may be in terms of meeting the needs of foreign customers, or overcoming trade barriers to the importation of finished goods, or building goodwill on which further market advances may be based, or protecting patents, trademarks, and copyrights by having a licensee utilize them and thus keep them alive.

These two conditions apply to all methods of operating abroad and, therefore, they account in part for the increased use of licensing. However, there are other factors that can be cited as having a direct influence on the increased use of licensing.

Nationalism. New countries are coming into being every year, and when we add to these countries those that have been politically independent for many years and still underdeveloped, the force of nationalism can be appreciated. The new and developing countries are ambitious and in a hurry, and, at the same time, they are varyingly suspicious of foreign industrial penetration. It is no longer possible for a firm to operate wherever it chooses in this world; it must consider nationalism.

Nationalism can be expressed in terms of willingness to permit foreign operations and the conditions under which they will be permitted. It is also expressed in terms of the degree to which financial control may be exercised over national enterprises. It may also refer to the nature of the operation and as to whether it will add to the productive or export potential of the country. Nationalism may be found in laws that govern the proportion of foreign personnel that is permitted in a given company operating abroad, and it is also expressed in "buy at home" policies. In the United States we are made quite aware of nationalism in the so-called "Buy American Act" in our federal statutes.

For these and many other reasons of a specific or subtle nature, nationalism is providing a force that induces enterprising firms to consider the desirability of licensing. In terms of the conditions mentioned here and as far as the policies of the foreign country are concerned, licensing is a more acceptable form of foreign operation than the foreign subsidiary or the joint-company arrangement.

Productive Ability. Productive ability is an economic rather than a political or emotional factor that induces licensing abroad to an increasing extent. There has always been considerable licensing between the United States and European countries and Canada. This is due to the degree of productive ability and development in these countries.

Licensing of patents, manufacturing processes, and technical assistance calls for a licensee who is already engaged in processing in some manner. An American firm with a patented product or a technical procedure would have no reason to seek a licensee in a country where no industry exists along the lines of the licensor's operations. While Europe has recovered rapidly from the physical destruction of the war, as has Japan, the economic development programs of less developed countries are showing results in the way of factories and other production facilities. The American licensor may now find profitable license opportunities in many countries heretofore not considered to be industrial — Mexico, Brazil, Argentina, Australia, South Africa, and many others who presently and in the future offer lucrative licensing opportunities.

Reciprocity. Because licensing often works both ways, reciprocity is another reason accounting for the increased use of licensing. If an American licensor signs an agreement with an industrial firm in another country, it is quite conceivable that this industrial firm has some patent or technical knowledge that could profitably be licensed to the American firm. This reciprocal arrangement has the unique advantage of making the licensing agreements doubly binding and reflects a condition of mutual interdependence.

Investment Considerations. As indicated in the preceding chapter, one of the major requirements for foreign operations is the provision of an adequate amount of capital. Licensing affords a method of foreign operation where the capital of the licensor may not be needed. Companies that seek to become established in foreign markets and do not have the necessary capital to set up their own operations can enter into a licensing agreement which, in effect, utilizes the capital of the licensee. This is not to say that the licensor may be called upon to furnish some equipment or machinery, but if so, the investment represented would be less than setting up his own establishment.

Personnel Considerations. With the establishment of foreign operations, one of the requisites is the provision of administrative and technical personnel to start and often to run the foreign operation. Companies do not always have sufficient personnel that can be sent overseas for extended periods of time. In such cases, the licensing procedure is again attractive because the administrative and technical personnel are probably in the employ of the licensee.

Provisions of Licensing Agreements

At the outset in the development of a licensing agreement, it is well to consider the necessity for the establishment of mutual confidence between the licensor and the licensee. This does not come naturally; it is something that must be consciously developed. It is undesirable to negotiate and conclude a licensing agreement entirely by correspondence. The parties need to meet face-to-face and get to know each other. They must make every effort to understand the point of view and the business philosophy of each other. As many firms that operate by means of licenses testify, the success of the arrangement depends, in the last analysis, on mutual confidence.

Role of the Foreign Government. The first matter to be considered in working out the terms of the licensing agreement is the policy of the government of the country in which the proposed licensee is located.

The government may require that the licensing agreement be submitted for official approval. This approval may be influenced by such considerations as the contribution that the proposed agreement will make to the economy or to the export potential of the country; or the import saving nature of the agreement.

Since the licensor expects some financial return from the license agreement, government approval may depend upon the amount of this return and the currency in which the return is to be paid. If United States dollars are short, a licensing agreement calling for payment of financial returns in United States dollars may be difficult to enforce.

Purpose of the Licensing Operation. The purpose of the licensing operation will determine the provisions to be incorporated in an agreement. A few of these purposes, previously mentioned as areas of licensing operation, will now be examined briefly from the standpoint of the provisions of the agreement.

Patents. If patents are involved in a licensing agreement, there must be provisions that recognize the legal requirements of the country of the licensee. The laws pertaining to patents may require that the patent that has been obtained in the licensee's country must be worked. In other words, the law may not permit the patent to be acquired and then locked up; it must be worked. To see that the patent is worked will be the function of the licensee.

Another matter that must be decided is the ownership of the patent. Despite the fact that the patent is obtained in the licensee's country and he has a license to work the patent, the ownership of the patent resides in the licensor. It would be shortsighted for any licensor to permit the ownership of the patent to pass from his possession.

The matter of changes or improvements in a process that would have a bearing on the existing or on future patents must also be considered. The agreement may provide for the licensor to furnish the licensee all specifications of improvements that he has made in his patented process. Should he be obligated to pass these along? The general consensus appears to be that one of the best ways to preserve the confidence and loyalty of the licensee is to keep "feeding" him improvements as they become available. From this standpoint, it is a question not of revealing the secrets of the licensor, but of expressing confidence in the licensee and thus assuring continued cooperation and understanding.

Trademarks. In terms of the licensing agreement, trademarks constitute a special kind of problem. There are legal requirements as in the case of patents to work a trademark; but a trademark that is not worked is of no use whatsoever. For products that are identified to the buyer by means of a trademark, this device is an important factor in marketing.

If the right to use a trademark is provided for in a licensing agreement, the prime consideration, as in the case of patents, is the ownership of the trademark. The American licensor will insist on registering the trademark in his own name and will never permit it to be registered in the licensees name. As explained in Chapter 12 the value of a trademark to companies whose products are marketed by means of such identification is literally priceless, and the ownership of this value must reside in the licensor. One spokesman on this point declares that the trademark should never be included in a licensing agreement that covers a patent or technical know-how. It is asserted that the trademark tends to become a public matter in many countries, and, therefore, it is unwise to combine the trademark provision in the general licensing agreement. It should be provided for in a special agreement.[3]

Technical Assistance. The nature of technical assistance must be clearly described in the licensing agreement. Perhaps equipment and supplies are necessary, and the nature and value of these must be determined. The use of personnel from the licensor's establishment is often required, and this must be spelled out — what skills are provided, how many, at what cost, in what currency, for how long, and where they are to be stationed.

Sometimes under the laws of the country of the licensee, technicians are expected to train nationals so that they will be competent to take over the operations. Upon completion of this training program, the technicians return home. Very often, a time limit is set for this program, for example, three years.

Know-how. As stated earlier, know-how refers to knowledge rather than to a process. It may relate to engineering or architectural drawings, marketing techniques, management techniques, and other areas of knowledge.

---

[3]Peter G. Schmitt, Director of Associated Companies Divisions, Westinghouse International Company, at the annual meeting of the United States Trade-Mark Association, 1958, Atlantic City, New Jersey, and reported in *Export Trade and Shipper* (May 12, 1958).

The provision of know-how must be set forth in the license agreement is specific terms. What drawings and what techniques are included? Who owns the drawings and designs? Supposing the agreement is canceled, what happens to such drawings and designs? All such matters must be provided for in the agreement. Of course, it is possible for the licensee to copy drawings or designs, and their return in the event of cancellation of the agreement may be useless. But this is an excellent example of where mutual confidence plays an important role, for an honest licensee will not copy the drawings or designs that have been furnished under an agreement.

Financial Considerations. This part of the licensing agreement refers to the nature of the financial considerations, the payment schedule, and foreign exchange problems.

Nature of the Financial Considerations. The basis of payment to a licensor under a licensing agreement is usually called a *royalty.* Most licensors, however, also insist on an initial payment to seal the agreement. In this case, the licensee agrees to pay an initial sum that will depend, in part, upon the extent and nature of the investment that both of the parties make in the venture. The initial payment also helps to cover the costs of negotiation, of preparing drawings, etc.

The royalty may be a percentage of the invoice value of products manufactured in accordance with the agreement; or, it may be a certain amount per unit of product, such as $100 per appliance. If the royalty or license fee is based upon volume or upon a percentage of the invoice value of products manufactured, provision may be made for a higher or a lower fee in the future if the volume expands. This would be designed to encourage the licensee and to show confidence in him.

There may be a fixed fee rather than a variable fee. The fixed fee would be more appropriate for certain operations in which the contribution of the knowledge cannot be quantitatively measured as, for example, a marketing procedure or a management technique.

There may be a minimum fee, regardless of the way in which the fee is calculated. If there is more than one product involved in the agreement, there should be a minimum fee stated for each separate product. This is considered to be good business since it serves to keep the licensee interested in the development of the enterprise. For a few years, the minimum fee may be set at a fraction of what may be expected from the operation of the agreement and then increased each year under the agreement to reflect and encourage the anticipated growth in volume.

Payment Schedule. Whether payment of such fees is to be in cash or in some other form must also be considered. The licensor may be interested in keeping in close touch with the market. One way to assure this is to acquire an interest in the licensee's enterprise. Therefore, fees may be payable, in part, in the stock of the licensee's company. Or, the licensor may acquire, as part of the arrangement, an option to purchase stock of the licensee.

Payments for improvements in processes or techniques must also be determined. Sometimes the licensor is called upon for more than had been anticipated when the agreement was negotiated. Payment is generally provided for in the case of improvements in the form of drawings or designs; but services provided by the licensor, even services that may result in such improvements, may be provided at no cost or else at a percentage of the research and development costs.

Foreign Exchange Problems. The frequency of payment of the royalty must be determined, but of greater importance is the matter of foreign exchange. If the agreement calls for cash payment of licensing fees, whether foreign exchange will be available for this purpose is a matter of government policy, as stated before. Where more than one exchange rate prevails, as is true in the case of some countries that control exchange, a decision must be made as to which of these exchange rates will be used to make the transfer. Here again the matter of mutual confidence is important because neither party should seek to take undue advantage of the other.

Term of the Agreement. The term of the licensing agreement must be determined. In view of the time and effort required to negotiate and conclude such an agreement, it would appear that a longer rather than a shorter period of time should be provided for. There are license agreements made for only 2, 3, or 5 years, but most of them run for 10 and for as many as 15 years.

Quality Control and Maintenance of Standards. If the licensing agreement provides for production of some nature according to the specifications and know-how of the licensor, there is the important matter of quality control and maintenance of standards that must be considered. Many licensing agreements provide for some means of checking quality, either by means of an independent audit or by representatives of the licensor. In the softdrink beverage industry, this checking is performed by what one spokesman referred to as "traveling laboratories." Quality control is also important to protect trademark validity and reputation.

Antitrust Considerations. If the licensing agreement were to restrict the sales of the licensee to his domestic market, such a provision might run afoul of the antitrust laws of the licensor's country. In light of the antitrust provisions of the Treaty of Rome that set up the European Economic Community, licensing agreements may contain provisions that are either declared to be null and void under Article 85 (1) of the Treaty or, that having been registered with the Commission of the Community under Regulation 17, are declared to be null and void.[4]

It is unwise and probably illegal to restrict the exports of the licensee negatively, as, for example, to state that he cannot export to this or to that market. In a positive sense, however, it is well to grant export sales rights in territories that the licensee can cover and that are not otherwise covered. If the licensee lives up to the agreement, he will not export to areas other than those specified in the agreement. Or, the licensor may have distribution facilities that can be supplied from the production of the licensee. In this way, the licensor controls the export distribution of the licensee.

Some firms claim that it is superfluous to control the distribution of the licensee's production and state that distribution is his problem. In other cases, companies announce the existence of licensees as well as foreign factories and invite customers to purchase from any of them according to their own convenience and currency situations.

Miscellaneous Provisions. Provisions of a miscellaneous nature relate to the settlement of disagreements — whether by direct negotiation, by means of mediation, or by arbitration — and under what legal concepts.[5] There may also be a provision calling for a minimum production. There may be an efforts provision, calling on the licensee to push the sales of the products that are produced under license. In this connection, there may be an advertising provision setting forth the advertising efforts and expenditures of both parties to the agreement. If the licensor is presently engaged in advertising in the country in which the licensee is located or in which he exports, this advertising would probably be continued, since it affords the licensor some control over this marketing facility. As explained in Chapters 12 and 13, American companies are usually jealous of the control of advertising.

---

[4]See Chapter 18.
[5]The settlement of commercial disputes is discussed in Chapter 25

Another miscellaneous provision relates to the possibility of the licensee being forced out of business because of government action or of his decision to enter some other line of business. Provision is also made for a momentum clause — a statement of the number of payments that are to be continued after the termination of the agreement, how long they are to continue, and how they are to be determined.

Negotiating the Agreement. Despite this discussion of the provisions of licensing agreements which suggests an element of rigidity about the contents of the latter, experience has shown that each licensing agreement is tailored to each situation, and is usually consummated only after protracted negotiations. Even with this much effort, it may be necessary to start the negotiation of another agreement after efforts on the first one have failed. And there is no assurance that the second or third effort will be any more successful. The first prospect may have been unable to produce a certain product satisfactorily; the second may have had no adequate sales organization to distribute the product; a third may have balked on the initial payment or the royalties.

The selection of a licensee and the negotiation of a satisfactory agreement are exceedingly complex, time consuming, and therefore expensive procedures. There is no magic formula to produce an ideal licensee. It is a question of seeking, selecting, negotiating, and negotiating still more.

An Evaluation of Licensing Abroad

Licensing has received increasing attention on the part of United States firms as a means of operating abroad. As stated at the beginning of this chapter, licensing abroad avoids the expenditure of relatively large sums of capital and the assignment of important personnel, as would be true in the case of a manufacturing subsidiary and, to a lesser extent, of a joint manufacturing operation abroad.

At the same time, the element of control of the foreign operation is largely, if not entirely, lost to the licensor. Such products as the licensee produces are sold in the market in which he is located and may also be sold in foreign markets. This is a matter of great concern to the licensor because it is conceivable that the licensee, with the aid that the license agreement has made available to him, may succeed in taking over the foreign sales markets of the licensor. If this occurs, the license agreement has provided a basis for putting the licensor out of the export market.

Several means of protecting against such an eventuality may be considered. Probably the most important is the establishment of a basis of mutual confidence between the licensor and the licensee. This is rather vague and not entirely reassuring. Therefore, the licensor feels impelled to keep improving his product, process, method, or technique; and by making such improvements available to the licensee, the latter is brought to believe that the licensor rightfully is entitled to the royalty payments.

> If you have created a demand for a product with your trade-mark and the licensee wants to or is willing to use your trade-mark, your control over the licensee and his desire to continue the agreement, even after its normal period has expired, is much greater. By building up a trade-mark, he knows that, should he sever his connections, you are in a position to license someone else to take advantage of the trade-mark or that you can enter as a competitor yourself using this trade-mark.[6]

The importance of the establishment of minimum royalties is reflected in the following situation:

> The situation may arise wherein the licensee is quite content to produce at a restricted level, maintaining that his profits are good and to expand would require additional investments which he is unwilling to make; and, in general, he may display an attitude of being quite content at his present level. The United States licensor, on the other hand, may feel that the licensee's competitors are making gains and that the licensee's percentage of the market is falling. Obviously, a licensee's failure to expand means the licensor's royalties are also failing to increase.[7]

The establishment of a license agreement is, at best, a complex matter. It will be recalled that it involves not only the position of the licensor and the licensee but also the government of the country of the licensee.

> A license agreement is like a marriage. Both parties should thoroughly understand each other's objectives, strengths, and weaknesses; and must be convinced that they can live longer together before signing a contract. The simile can be carried even further in that once the marriage ceremony has taken place, each party must maintain the flexibility necessary to adapt itself to the idiosyncrasies of the other in order to maintain the family life and protect the children, who in this case are represented by production and profits.[8]

---

[6]S. Wilson Clark, Manager of Export Sales, The Yale and Towne Manufacturing Company, at the 27th Annual Meeting, Foreign Traders Association of Philadelphia, Inc., 1958.
[7]*Ibid.*
[8]*Ibid.*

Summary

1. Three methods of manufacturing abroad are the establishment of a foreign subsidiary, a joint arrangement with a concern in the foreign market, and licensing. The avoidance of the need for large sums of capital and the assignment of important personnel to the foreign operation are two major reasons for an increased interest in licensing abroad.
2. Licensing is a means of making available the use of skills in manufacturing, processing, marketing, management, or any other operation.
3. Licensing must show evidence of being profitable both for the licensor and the licensee before any effort is made to enter into an agreement.
4. Candidates for licensee may be the present sales representative of the licensor; a competing manufacturer; a manufacturer of similar but noncompeting products; a manufacturer of a dissimilar product seeking diversification; or a capitalist.
5. Licensing may refer to patents, copyrights, trademarks, technical assistance, know-how, and other arrangements, such as cross licensing.
6. Among the factors that account for the increased interest in licensing abroad nationalism abroad, improved productive ability, reciprocity (cross licensing), the reduction of large capital expenditures, and the retention of important personnel may be mentioned.
7. The main provisions of licensing agreements must consider the role of the licensee's government, the purpose for which the license is granted, the financial considerations, the terms of the agreement, quality control and maintenance of standards, antitrust considerations, means of settling disagreements, the requirement on the part of the licensee to push the sale of products manufactured under license and to advertise, the consideration of what is to be done if the licensee cancels the agreement or engages in some other business, and the continuation of payments in the form of royalties in such event.
8. Every licensing agreement must be tailored to each particular situation. It is not uncommon for a licensor to negotiate with two, three, or more prospects before reaching a satisfactory agreement or before deciding to give up.
9. Every effort should be made to prevent the licensee from driving the licensor out of world markets. The best protection against this possibility is for the licensor to continue to improve his product or process or technique, and thus assure the licensee that it is to his advantage to continue under the agreement.

QUESTIONS

1. Discuss the preliminary considerations that are necessary before beginning licensing negotiations.
2. Define licensing for foreign operations.

3. What foreign companies are the most important candidates for licensee?
4. Enumerate five areas in which the operation of licensing agreements may be found.
5. (a) Define technical assistance.
   (b) How does technical assistance differ from know-how?
6. Why is there increased interest in licensing for foreign operations on the part of United States producers and processors?
7. Describe the role of the foreign government with respect to licensing agreements.
8. Why should the ownership of patents, copyrights, and trademarks remain with the licensor?
9. Explain the several ways in which the various kinds of payments to the licensor may be provided.
10. Why is it usually desirable to make provision in a licensing agreement for the payment of a minimum royalty?
11. How may the quality of a product be controlled under a licensing agreement?
12. Why should care be taken to avoid conflict with the antitrust laws of the United States in a licensing agreement with a firm in Brazil, for example?
13. Why is the negotiation of a licensing agreement generally so prolonged?
14. How may a licensor protect himself against the possibility of the licensee progressing by reason of the license and eventually forcing the licensor out of world markets?
15. How can mutual confidence between the licensor and the licensee be established and maintained?

PROBLEMS

1. Select any one country and examine its laws and regulations that would affect the desirability and nature of licensing by foreign firms. Write a report of your findings.
2. Select any one of the sample licensing agreements to be found in Lawrence J. Eckstrom's "Licensing in Foreign Operations" (see the Collateral Readings). Prepare a written report covering the provisions of this agreement.
3. The Dever Equipment Company, manufacturers of heavy drive unit components and torque converters, fork trucks, and construction machinery, indicates certain disadvantages of both licensing and investment abroad. Licensing, the company finds, is generally for a ten-, or at most, a fifteen-year period. At the termination of this period, the United States firm has provided all of the help needed to enable the licensee to strike out independently as a competitor.
   Investment in a plant, on the other hand, calls for large sums of capital, a waiting period of some duration before profits can be realized, and the provision of key personnel.

In order to overcome these disadvantages, the Dever Equipment Company is considering a composite arrangement. Under this plan, investment in the foreign licensee's plant would be built up during the life of the licensing agreement. At the end of ten or fifteen years, when the licensing agreement would expire, the company would have built up a sizable investment in the licensed foreign company.

Discuss the desirability of this proposal.

COLLATERAL READINGS

Bryson, G. D. *American Management Abroad.* New York: Harper & Row, 1961.

Cardinale, Joseph S. *Manual on the Foreign License and Technical Assistance Agreement.* New York: Thomas Ashwell and Co., Inc., 1958.

Case Studies in Foreign Operations. New York: American Management Association, 1956.

Dartnell International Trade Handbook, The. Chicago: The Dartnell Corporation, 1963.

Eckstrom, Lawrence J. *Licensing in Foreign Operations.* Essex, Conn.: Foreign Operations Service, Inc., 1958.

Fenn, Dan J., Jr. *Management Guide to Overseas Operations.* New York: McGraw-Hill Book Company, Inc., 1957.

Foreign Licensing Agreements. Studies in Business Policy Number 86. New York: National Industrial Conference Board, 1958.

Foreign Licensing: Questions and Answers. New York: Pegasus International Corporation (undated).

Gibbons, William J. *Tax Factors in Basing International Business Abroad.* Boston, Mass.: Little, Brown & Company, 1957.

Newgarden, Albert (ed.). *Taxation of Business Income from Foreign Corporations.* New York: American Management Association, 1958.

CHAPTER 17

COOPERATION IN EXPORTING FROM THE UNITED STATES

As discussed in this chapter, cooperation in exporting from the United States means the voluntary combination of *independent* and *competitive* business concerns, each of which retains its identity, for purposes of mutual development of foreign markets. While competing American enterprises contemplating such action are at once faced with the possibility of prosecution under the federal antitrust laws, this illegality, as far as *export* trade is concerned, was removed, under certain restrictions, by the Webb-Pomerene or Export Trade Act approved April 10, 1918. The prohibition continues, however, against cooperation among competitors engaged in the *domestic* or in the *import* trade.

The Desirability of Cooperation Among Exporters

The specific reasons why removal of the antitrust ban should prove beneficial in the promotion of American export trade were revealed in a survey conducted by the Federal Trade Commission. The report declares in part that "while the United States has been absorbed in domestic development, other nations have followed definite policies for the expansion of their foreign trade and have perfected efficient means for the purpose in view."[1] The Commission declares that "in seeking business abroad American manufacturers and producers must meet aggressive competition from powerful foreign combinations, often international in character."[2] Continuing, the Commission states:

If Americans are to enter the markets of the world on more nearly equal terms with their organized competitors and their organized cus-

[1] Federal Trade Commission, *Report on Cooperation in American Export Trade*, Part I (1916), p. 3.

[2] *Ibid.*, p. 4.

tomers, and if small American producers and manufacturers are to engage in export trade on profitable terms, they must be free to unite their efforts.

Without any export organization, foodstuffs and raw materials can readily be sold at some price but to avoid needless expense in distribution, to meet formidable foreign buying organizations, and to insure profitable export prices, cooperation among American producers of such commodities is desirable.

In the sale of factory products, cooperation is even more desirable. Such goods must be advertised, demonstrated, and a market created abroad, often in the face of the keenest competition from great combinations of foreign manufacturers. Obviously only strong organizations can undertake this contest.[3]

In conclusion the Commission finds:

1. That other nations have marked advantages in foreign trade from superior facilities and more effective organizations.

2. That doubt and fear as to legal restrictions prevent Americans from developing equally effective organizations for overseas business and that the foreign trade of American manufacturers and producers, particularly the smaller concerns, suffers in consequence.[4]

On the basis of this report of the Federal Trade Commission, the Webb-Pomerene Act was enacted by Congress.

The law was first used to facilitate the sale of goods to the Allies during World War I. It was of importance during the reconstruction period after that war when large quantities of materials were shipped abroad to rehabilitate Europe. The so-called "boom period" opened new markets for American goods in foreign countries, and when the depression followed, cooperation in export under the law aided many American exporters to continue in business in the face of very unfavorable trade conditions.

Later, the war in China closed many Oriental markets to American exporters, forcing the associations to develop other markets to take the place of that trade. And when war broke out again in Europe in 1939, the countries involved in that conflict were eliminated one by one as markets for American goods, so that trade was shifted again this time toward Latin America and Africa. . . . These shifts were readily made by a cooperative organization with agents abroad and knowledge of foreign conditions. . . . Since World War II, "the problems that have been presented to American exporters have increased in difficulty and complexity.

---

[3]*Ibid.*, p. 8.
[4]*Ibid.*, p. 3.

As a result of unsettled world trade conditions, cooperative effort under the Export Trade Act has assumed even greater importance than before."[5]

Provisions and Interpretation of the Webb-Pomerene Act

Export trade is defined in the Act as "solely trade or commerce in goods, wares, or merchandise exported, or in the course of being exported from the United States or any Territory thereof to any foreign nation." By its very nature, production is excluded from the meaning of "trade or commerce." The question as to what constitutes "in the course of being exported" depends upon the interpretation adopted by the Federal Trade Commission, where the administration of the Act has been vested. This phrase was defined by the Commission on July 31, 1924, in answer to questions on disputed points submitted for interpretation by the silver producers of the United States. In accordance with this opinion, it is now considered legal for export associations merely to allot export orders among their members or merely to fix "the prices at which their individual members shall sell in export trade."

The Commission further ruled that "there is nothing in the Act which prevents an association formed under it from entering into any cooperative relationship with a foreign corporation, for the sole purpose of operation in a foreign market." This view opens the door to international cooperation between American associations and foreign concerns.

On July 13, 1955, however, the Federal Trade Commission warned against the practice of price-fixing arrangements between Webb-Pomerene associations and foreign competitors, declaring that such practice is not necessarily exempt from the antitrust acts. In other words, this specific practice is not to be interpreted as coming within the meaning of the phrase "in the course of export trade." Sales made to export houses located in the United States are also authorized, "if the product sold is intended for, is actually marked for, and enters into export trade."

Geographical Area. The Act permits cooperation in exporting "from the United States or any Territory thereof to any foreign nation." The associations may, therefore, be organized in territories of the United States, and if formed in these territories, they may ship to foreign countries but not to the United States or to other American possessions or

---

[5]Federal Trade Commission, *Annual Report* (1948), pp. 66–67.

territories. Moreover, associations formed in the United States may not ship to any American possession or territory.

Application of Antitrust Dictum. Sections 2, 3, and 4 of the Act declare the precise extent of exemption from the antitrust laws. The general intent of the Act is to retain the long-established antitrust policy at home and to alter it only for purposes of the export trade.

Section 2 declares the Sherman Law to be inoperative against export associations formed under the Act, provided their activities cause (1) no "restraint of trade within the United States," (2) nor "restraint of the export trade of any domestic competitor of such association," (3) nor any artificial or intentional enhancement or depression of "prices within the United States of commodities of the class exported by such association," (4) nor any substantial lessening of competition within the United States, (5) nor any restraint of trade therein.

Under Section 3, the prohibition contained in the Clayton Act is removed in order that any corporation may acquire stock of export associations "unless the effect of such acquisition or ownership may be to restrain trade or substantially lessen competition within the United States."

Section 4, however, provides that the Federal Trade Commission Act, prohibiting unfair methods of competition, "shall be construed as extending to unfair methods of competition used in export trade against competitors engaged in export trade, even though acts constituting such unfair methods are done without the territorial jurisdiction of the United States."

This section obviously aims to enforce the same standard of commercial morality, whether American enterprises are engaged in trade at home or abroad. As interpreted by the Federal Trade Commission, unfair methods include, among other practices, the use of misleading labels, misrepresentation, full line forcing, and unfair discounts. In one instance, for example, the Commission brought about the discontinuance of misleading labels on condensed milk exported to Mexico. In addition, the Commission entertains complaints filed by foreign buyers of American products. It occasionally considers cases arising from the import trade, acting under the Federal Trade Commission and not the Webb-Pomerene Act.

This feature of the Act, in particular, is ample evidence of the intent of Congress to place American exporting combinations on a legal parity with foreigners, but not to lower the standards of American business practice. This position tended to allay the suspicions aroused in some foreign countries that discrimination against foreigners was authorized by permitting business practice abroad which the law prohibits at home.

Section 5 defines the procedure to be followed in (1) registering an export association at time of organization and (2) thereafter filing the annual report of an association.

Penalties. Failure on the part of an association to comply with any request of the Commission for information in the broad sense contemplated in the law removes from such association "the benefit of the provisions of section two and section three of this Act, and it shall also forfeit to the United States the sum of $100 for each and every day of the continuance of such failure." The enforcement of the Webb-Pomerene Act is effectively provided for in this simple manner.

The Commission is also required to investigate associations when it has reason to believe that the law, in one way or another, is being violated. If this proves to be true, recommendations are to be made "for the readjustment of its business, in order that it may thereafter maintain its organization and management and conduct its business in accordance with law." In case such recommendations are not obeyed, legal action is to be instituted.

In recent years, the Commission has been required to call upon a number of cooperative associations to change certain methods of operation. In a number of cases, associations were required to cease a practice of agreeing upon export sales prices and terms with American nonmembers. In one case, the association was also charged with agreeing on export market quotas with nonmembers. One association was advised not to hold stock in any companies in foreign countries engaged in the manufacture of the product in which the association dealt, and not to sell any products of non-American origin. In still another case, the accusation was the reverse, namely, that the association was seeking to keep nonmember competitors from entering export markets.

One case was heard by the Supreme Court in which the Court held the Federal Trade Commission to have primary jurisdiction. The case involved charges of efforts to eliminate competing imports by foreign members; restrictions or elimination of exports by domestic producers from the United States to many world markets; prevention of independent domestic producers from competing in export; restriction of United States production; and price fixing in the United States.[6]

---

[6] *United States Alkali Export Association* v. *United States*, 325 U.S. 196 (1945).

Activities Under the Webb-Pomerene Act

An association, as contemplated in the Act, is meant to include "any corporation or combination, by contract or otherwise, of two or more persons, partnerships, or corporations." Entire freedom to combine in any manner whatsoever is thereby authorized.

A study of the number of associations formed since the passage of the Webb-Pomerene Act indicates an initial impetus, followed by a slump, and then maintenance of a steady level. The number of associations has varied from 31 to 51 for the years 1934–1963, inclusive; with a declining level of 37 in 1957 to 31 in 1963. The reported value of products exported varied from a low of under $100 million to over or near $1 billion in the years 1947–1963.

The character of the export trade that appears to benefit most from the Act may be inferred from the annual reports of the Federal Trade Commission. These summary statements divide exports of Webb-Pomerene associations into five groups. Comparing 1937 and 1960, we find that metals and metal products constituted 47.5 percent of the total in 1937 and less than 2 percent in 1960. Products of mines and wells were 16.5 percent and less than 1 percent, respectively. Lumber and wood products were 3.7 percent and much less than 1 percent, respectively. The last specific grouping — foodstuffs — showed 10.1 percent in 1937 and 23.4 percent in 1960. The miscellaneous group was 22.2 percent in 1937 and approximately 66 percent in 1960.

This comparison would indicate that Webb-Pomerene associations have been formed in a much wider group of industries. No details of the miscellaneous group are given, except to state that it included abrasives, textiles, motion pictures, pencils, scientific instruments, typewriters, pulp, paper and paperboard, and rubber tires and tubes.

Organization and Operation. Three general types of organization that have been used are:

1. The association that serves as a central agent for the members, taking orders, negotiating sales, and handling shipment of the goods to foreign countries.

2. The association that directs the exports of the members and retains certain functions in export trade, but permits the members to take the orders through their already established agents abroad.

3. The export company formed for the purpose of buying the members' products and reselling them in foreign markets.

The first and second methods of operation may be combined, the members using their established agents for some markets and the association sales office for new markets or those in which the trade is not of sufficient volume to warrant the expense of individual agents.[7]

The particular form of organization may range from a loose agreement to a formally incorporated company. Most of the associations are incorporated. Some associations operate in a simple, easy manner, while others are complex and elaborate. Those formed to conduct certain of the advisory functions, for example, allocation of orders or territory and fixing prices, terms, and conditions, rather than to handle sales, may ordinarily be organized in a simple manner.

Export Trade Associations do not always engage in exporting to every part of the world; neither do they necessarily handle the export of an entire range of products in a given industry.

Classes of Membership. An association may have more than one class of members depending upon the service performed. One association has a "full" membership and a "limited" membership; another has a "packer" division and a "merchants" division.

In general, Export Trade Associations admit all members on the same basis, recognizing no classes or classifications whatsoever.

Capital Shares. The division of capital shares of Export Trade Associations may follow several plans, ranging from the equal division among all members on an equal basis to the assignment of shares on a proportionate basis, such as by volume of business. One way of distributing stock on a basis of volume is by means of quota production over a given period; or, according to the export shipping or producing capacity of the several members, etc.

Board of Directors. Usually, associations have a board of directors or trustees to manage their affairs. Different methods are followed to determine representation on the board, such as each member company being entitled to representation; or, the selection of directors on a basis of regional or functional qualification.

Profit Basis. Some Export Trade Associations operate on a profit basis, the profits being distributed among the members at certain intervals, and others (probably the majority) work on an expense basis resulting, of course, in no profit to be divided.

---

[7]United States Congress, Senate, 76th Congress, 3rd Session, Temporary National Economic Committee, *Export Prices and Export Cartels*, Monograph (November 6, 1941), p. 136.

Working Capital. Working capital is usually obtained from the sale of capital stock. Some associations assess "initiation dues" which may not be the same for all classes of members.

Expenses. One prominent lumber association distributes export orders to members at the full sales price and prorates monthly expenses. Another association (in the fertilizer business) distributes expenses on a basis of quotas assigned to the several members. Still another lumber firm charges a commission equal to the cost of transacting business as the exclusive sales agent for the members, plus the cost of developing new markets and building up a reserve fund exclusively for use in market development. Expenses are in some cases divided according to the relationship that the export shipments of each member bears to the total actual exports in a particular period. In still other instances, costs are assessed on a basis of holdings of capital stock.

Price Administration. As to the control of prices by Export Trade Associations, it is found that generally they establish minimum export prices, leaving to foreign agents the setting of actual prices as affected by conditions. Those associations that operate a central selling agency will generally export larger quantities of merchandise than any one of the members would be likely to ship at a given time. For this reason, it is often possible for the export association to fix export prices that will hold for a longer period of time than had been possible when each member was individually shipping smaller orders abroad. Some associations leave export price control to the respective members, while at least one association not only establishes the prices to be observed by foreign agents, but also supervises the operation of these agents by means of a traveling official of the association. Another plan is to place control over prices and terms of sale under the jurisdiction of a price committee of the export association.

Allocation of Orders. The allocation of orders among the several members of Export Trade Associations may be determined according to a quota arrangement embodied in the association agreement, or there may be no special plan for assigning orders. A number of export quota plans are predicated on capacity or production. This basis may be determined from the reports of the various members as to the quantity of merchandise that is expected to be available for export shipment. Some associations allocate orders according to a percentage distribution of the annual export business of the association. When several different classes of products are handled, quotas may be assigned on a basis of a given share of each particular class. Some of the lumber companies, furthermore, finding that different cuts of lumber are required by different foreign markets, may assign quotas on a complicated point system which reflects this important market quality factor. A still more finely drawn division is illustrated by a fruit export association that allocates quotas not only by commodities but also according to foreign ports of destination. Another basis of quota assignment is capital stock holdings.

Finally, there is a question as to adjustment for shipments in excess of quota assignment and also the reverse, namely, shipments below quota. Plans for the solution of these problems vary. In some agreements, each member is obliged to supply the market as orders come in. Failing to do so, he loses his turn, there being no carry-over from period to period. In other plans, some provision is made for adjusting these quota differences.

In order to enforce the provisions of association agreements, clauses are sometimes inserted stipulating certain penalties that will be suffered or forfeits required in case of violation.

Advantages Realized. Numerous advantages have been realized by associations operating under the Act. These include:

1. Stabilization of export prices.

2. Reduction of selling costs so that small concerns, unable individually to branch out into foreign markets, are well able to pay their share of expense.

3. Standardization of grades, contract terms, and sales conditions. (The Walnut Export Sales Company, for example, established a uniform brand "WESCO" and rigidly maintains quality by careful inspection).

4. Prompt and efficient filling of orders.

5. Elimination of hurtful practices.

6. Combating combinations of buyers that might be in position to play one exporter against another.

7. Storage of seasonal products, thus averting oversupply and consequent low prices.

8. Consolidation of cargoes and chartering of steamers for better service and lower transportation costs.

9. Joint advertising and exploitation work.

10. Adjustment of claims.

11. Bidding on and securing large orders for shipments over a long period of time.

12. Filling orders for a variety of grades, styles, and dimensions by allocating orders among the members.

13. Division of territory, not only among members but also with foreign competitors.

14. Utilization of direct exporting channels and methods.

Difficulties Experienced. The Webb-Pomerene Act has been shown to be particularly adapted to the needs of exporters of raw and bulky products; in the case of direct selling, however, the manufacturers of finished articles are less attracted to this cooperative plan. Such manufacturers stand to gain indirectly by means of agreements on price, sales terms, territorial allotment, and other matters permitted under the Act.

In the case of raw and bulky products, individual attention to particular brands or qualities is not required, since raw materials generally may be grouped together with a loss of identity without adversely affecting their marketability. In the case of goods sold on a basis of brand or trademark, however, cooperative export marketing is rarely successful.

An inherent difficulty of some associations lies in the fundamental inability to cooperate on the part of the members. Bickerings and competitive psychology, engendered in the domestic market, cannot always be successfully subjugated in the interest of cooperation for export. Sometimes the export business proves an excessively heavy burden. One association declares, for example, that early in its corporate life it was found "very difficult to represent a whole industry in exports." This difficulty, the association significantly reported, is "due solely to the individuals in the industry." Some associations suffered, on the other hand, from poor management and have gone out of business. Some began with a great deal of enthusiasm and optimism, and later, failing to attract a sufficient number of members into the organization, were dissolved. Still other associations encountered such keen competition abroad that, in spite of their combined front, they were practically driven from the foreign markets. Several pearl button export associations, for example, felt this pressure from Japan. Finally, many manufacturers of branded and trademarked goods who endeavored to engage in export trade on this cooperative basis found the inherent difficulties of adequately representing individual interests in such a program to be insurmountable.

Shortcomings of the Webb-Pomerene Act

Certain additional difficulties are traceable to shortcomings imposed by the Act that may be remedied by legislative action. It is generally felt that the elimination of all of our territorial possessions as markets for merchandise shipped by Webb associations is an unfortunate limitation. Some possessions of the United States are, from a practical angle, distinctly foreign markets. Undoubtedly, the greatest deficiency of the law, however, is the restriction of its provisions to the export trade. At first, the Federal Trade Commission's interpretation of the phrase "export trade" was narrow. The later expansion of this interpretation under the Silver letter of 1924 enabled cooperative associations to engage in important activities formerly believed to be forbidden. But the exclusion of the import trade from the application of the law remains.

Attempts have been made to amend the Webb-Pomerene Act in order to permit cooperative importing. Impetus in this direction was gained by the activities of selling combinations in foreign countries that had forced up the price of several raw materials imported into the United States. At one time the crude rubber situation was particularly annoying. Efforts to procure necessary legislative action in 1928 failed, when the House rejected an amendment which would have permitted import combinations and the Senate did not vote upon the measure.

Recent Developments

The provisions of the Revenue Act of 1962, whereby some foreign income is taxed as of the time it is earned rather than at the time it is remitted, may provide renewed interest in Webb-Pomerene Associations. This is because relief from these provisions is available in cases where the entire business, or a large percentage of it, is conducted outside of the United States.[8] The Webb-Pomerene Association must be engaged in trade or commerce "in the course of being exported." By deft arrangements, keeping in mind the limitations of both the Webb-Pomerene Act and the Revenue Act of 1962, renewed interest in Webb-Pomerene Associations is quite possible.[9]

Summary

1. Antitrust laws in the United States have been partially set aside to permit the organization of competitors, insofar as they are engaged in the conduct

---

[8]See Chapter 14.

[9]See Terry Nevel, "The Webb Association: Tax and Antitrust Vehicle for Exporters", *Export Trade* (July 29, 1963), p. 7, et. seq.

of the export trade, to agree on prices, terms, markets, etc. None of these practices, however, are permitted in the import trade.

2. The exemption from the antitrust laws, as far as export trade is concerned, was instigated because of the combinations that were permitted by competing nations.

3. In operating under the Webb-Pomerene Act, which grants exemption from the antitrust laws, nothing is permitted that will affect domestic commerce. Moreover, unfair methods of competition are forbidden, as they are in domestic trade.

4. Under the Webb-Pomerene Act, about 50 associations of exporters have been formed, mainly in lines of business where trademarked products are not handled.

5. Some of the cooperative export associations merely agree on terms and prices, while others go so far as to handle the actual export sales for all participants. There are various methods of business organization and operation.

6. Numerous advantages are cited as a result of the operation of the Webb-Pomerene Act. Difficulties are experienced, however, since the Act does not cover commerce with our territorial possessions nor does it cover the import trade of the United States.

QUESTIONS

1. Why does United States federal legislation prohibit "combinations in restraint of trade"?

2. Why should an exception be provided for combinations engaged in the *export* trade? Why is no exception provided for combinations engaged in *import* trade?

3. As provided in the Webb-Pomerene Act (Export Trade Act), define the following terms:
   (a) Export trade.
   (b) In the course of being exported.

4. Explain the restrictions under which exemption from the following acts is provided by the Webb-Pomerene Act:
   (a) Sherman Act.
   (b) Clayton Act.
   (c) Federal Trade Commission Act.

5. How is the Webb-Pomerene Act administered, by what agency, and under what penalties for violation?

6. Define the several recognized bases of operation of Webb-Pomerene associations.

7. How do export trade associations deal with the question of price?

8. How do export trade associations handle the problem of allocating orders among the individual members?

9. Comment on the specific advantages realized by export trade associations.
10. Explain some of the difficulties experienced by export trade associations.
11. Why are raw products more susceptible to cooperation in exporting than is true of manufactured, particularly branded, products?
12. Suggest improvements in the terms of the Webb-Pomerene Act. Can you think of any obstacles to the adoption of these improvements?

PROBLEMS

1. In view of the increased interest in economic, particularly industrial, development throughout the world, there is believed to be a bright future for exports of tools and equipment.

   A trade association was formed some years ago, the members of which are individual dealers in used machine tools. Many of these tools are heavy, complicated, and expensive. As in any used product line of business, the merchant must be flexible and sharp. Traditionally there has been much secrecy among the several firms engaged in this business.

   If this trade association should see good possibilities in export markets, how might it operate under the Webb-Pomerene Act? What difficulties is this particular association likely to encounter? Under what conditions do you believe the association would be successful?

2. Examine the decisions of the courts pertaining to the overseas business operations of United States companies. Some significant decisions are listed below. Write a critical report of your study of these and any other cases.

   United States v. *General Electric Co.*, 82 F. Supp. 753 (D.N.J.) 1949
   American Banana Co. v. *United States*, 213 U.S. 347 (1909)
   United States v. *Aluminum Co. of America*, 148 F. 2d 416 (2d Cir. 1945)
   Standard Oil Co. of N. J. v. *United States*, 221 U.S. 1 (1911)
   Timken Roller Bearing Co. v. *United States*, 341 U.S. 593 (1951)
   Steele et al. v. *Bulova Watch Co., Inc.*, 344 U.S. 280 (1952)
   United States v. *Minnesota Mining and Manufacturing Co. et al.*, 92 F. Supp. 947 (1950)

COLLATERAL READINGS

Beer, Henry W. *Federal Trade Law and Practice.* New York: Baker, Voorhis and Company, 1942.

Brewster, Kingman. *Anti-Trust and American Business Abroad.* New York: McGraw-Hill Book Company, Inc., 1958.

Dartnell International Trade Handbook, The. Chicago: The Dartnell Corporation, 1963.

Horn, Paul V. *International Trade Principles and Practices*, Third Edition. New York: Prentice-Hall, Inc., 1951. Chapter 2.

Hugin, Adolph Charles. *Private International Trade Regulating Arrangements and the Anti-Trust Laws*. Washington, D.C.: Catholic University Press, 1949. A dissertation.

Kirsh, Benjamin S. *Trade Associations in Law and Business*. New York: Central Book Company, 1938.

National Foreign Trade Council. *Report of National Foreign Trade Convention*. New York: annual.

Notz, W. F. and R. S. Harvey. *American Foreign Trade*. Indianapolis: Bobbs-Merrill, 1921.

Pratt, E. E. *Modern International Commerce*. New York: Allyn and Bacon, Inc., 1956. Chapter 2.

Roorbach, G. B. *Import Purchasing: Principles and Problems*. Chicago and New York: A. W. Shaw Company, 1927. Chapter 10 D.

——————————. *Problems in Foreign Trade*. New York: McGraw-Hill Book Company, Inc., 1933. Part III C.

Schwartz, Louis B. *Free Enterprise and Economic Organization — Legal and Related Materials*. Brooklyn: Foundation Press, 1952.

United States Congress, Senate, 76th Congress, 3rd Session, Temporary National Economic Committee, *Export Prices and Export Cartels*, Monograph No. 6. Washington, D.C.: 1941.

United States Federal Trade Commission. *Annual Report*. Washington, D.C.

——————————. *Cooperation in American Export Trade*, 2 Volumes. Washington, D.C.: 1916.

——————————. *Discussion of Practice and Procedure Under the Export Trade Act (Webb-Pomerene Law)*. Foreign Trade Series No. 1, 1919. Washington, D.C.

——————————. Foreign Trade Series No. 2, 1935. Washington, D.C.

Chapter 18

INTERNATIONAL MARKETING COMBINATIONS ABROAD

Cooperation among competitive independent economic enterprises has been more common in foreign countries than in the United States. The Federal Trade Commission's "Report on Cooperation in American Export Trade," referred to in the preceding chapter, indicated the extent to which, up to 1914, foreign producers were united for concerted action in commercial and industrial activity. Moreover, it will be recalled that this situation provided the basis for the adoption of the Webb-Pomerene Act.

Wars and economic depression cause great strain upon international combines. Such combinations of necessity are created out of national combines. When nationalism becomes dominant, international understandings are avoided. Nevertheless, the economic urgency to bring about stabilization in production, export, and price leads to national and international combinations insofar as national and multinational legislation tolerates, prohibits, or encourages such action.

It is generally known that Germany and Japan particularly favored combinations in industry and trade. World War II was expected to bring an end to these practices, since they are known to increase the war potential of these countries. Nevertheless, indications are that the tendency to combine as a means of controlling competition is again evident in those countries.

Legal Concepts Concerning Restraint of Trade

The attitude of many foreign countries toward combinations in industrial and commercial enterprises differs radically from the attitude of the United States. While we have pursued a policy of free competition, foreign governments have permitted the elimination of competition in varying degrees.

In Great Britain the common law limits freedom to combine by declaring null and void all contracts and agreements in restraint of trade. Such understandings, however, "are not actually illegal unless they involve an illegal act" . . . and "a contract which is technically in restraint of trade has long been regarded by the courts as valid and enforceable when it involves a particular restraint which is not larger than the protection of the party with whom the contract was made reasonably requires."[1] Apart from legal obstacles, however, the traditional individualistic attitude of British concerns has militated against the development of combinations. Following World War I, various government bodies pointed out the necessity for cooperation in British industry in order to engage effectively in the forthcoming world competition. The Balfour Committee on Industry and Trade recommended in 1929 that British industry be "rationalized" through voluntary action.

The present policy of the United Kingdom is expressed in the Restrictive Practices Act of 1948, revised in 1956. Under the revised act, restrictive trade practices agreements are required to be registered with a government official. A Restrictive Practices Court is set up with the status of the High Court and is charged with making judicial decisions. To guide the Court, criteria are set forth in an effort to determine whether the facts weigh against restrictive trade practices more heavily than they do in benefits that the public derives as a result of such restrictive trade practices. For example, the chemists (druggists in the United States) may agree on restrictive trade practices as a result of which the public would be protected. In the view of the Court this protection may outweigh the disadvantages of a restrictive trade practice. Every restrictive agreement found to be contrary to the public interest is void. In every case, the burden of proof is on the parties seeking to maintain the restrictive trade practice.

Resale price maintenance on a *collective* basis is unlawful under certain conditions, for example, enforcing conditions under which the price of the goods is set, or boycotts, or fines. As to *individual* price maintenance, the law upholds this principle, thus protecting a firm that fixes its own resale prices.

The Monopolies Commission deals with "agreements relating exclusively to exports and to single-firm monopolies — single firms which

---

[1]League of Nations, *Review of Legislation on Cartels and Trusts*, p. 8.

control at least one third of the market."[2] Exports were not included in the Restrictive Practices Act, but any restrictions relating to exports were to be registered with the Board of Trade which, if it chose, could refer the agreement to the Monopolies Commission.

The self-governing dominions of the British Commonwealth have generally followed the basic British policy, but in some instances they have preferred the more direct antitrust legislation of the United States. Canada, for example, enacted the Combines Investigation Act in 1923 for the purpose of inquiring into the operation of alleged combines and bringing action in cases where required.

In the Union of South Africa, a Distribution Costs Commission in 1947, with regard to price agreements and monopoly practices, declared that the Union should not "follow the example of the United States of America in its prohibitory legislation . . . it should not seek to disturb arrangements which, on investigation, prove to have effected savings, provided these savings accrue to the benefit of the buyers as well as sellers."[3]

In continental Europe the attitude toward combination in trade and industry has generally been favorable. Germany has always been a leader in concentration movements by encouraging and, occasionally, participating officially in restrictive agreements. However, the Treaty of Rome and the antitrust rules of the Common Market have changed this situation materially, as will be explained shortly.

Types of Combinations Abroad

Unhampered by legal obstructions, international marketing combinations in foreign countries have taken various forms. First to be considered is the cartel, a term generally associated with German industrial organization, but possessing a much wider application. A cartel aims to control the market; it tends to create a monopoly although it rarely succeeds in doing so.

Cartels. "A cartel may be defined as a combination in restraint of competition in industry and trade that is implemented through agreements among enterprises maintaining separate identities and separate

---

[2]See *Cartel*, October, 1956, pp. 127–129, article by Lord Meston, author of the Secretary's Guide to the Restrictive Practices Act, 1956. *Cartel* is a quarterly publication of the International Co-operative Alliance, London, England.

[3]United States Federal Trade Commission, *Annual Report 1948*, p. 73.

ownerships, stock controls and managements."[4]   The Federal Trade Commission declares that United States industries participating in cartels include producers of aluminum, alkalies, electrical equipment and appliances, fertilizer (phosphates and potash), petroleum products, steel products, and sulphur.

From the threat of overproduction in basic mass-production industries, the cartel form of organization has expanded into other fields of activity, so that a classification of cartels includes not only (1) those organized to limit output; but also (2) those established to maintain prices; or (3) to agree upon sales territories, foreign as well as national; or (4) to agree upon uniform documents, credits, and other collateral phases of merchandising; or (5) to undertake centralized selling.   There is also considerable overlapping in this classification.

Trading Companies.   The French phenomenon of commercial combination is the *comptoir*, which, by definition, is an incorporated trading company. A comptoir operates essentially through sales agreements and centralized selling agencies representing all of the members. The well-known Comptoir Métallurgique de Longwy, now out of existence, was established in 1876 for the purpose of advertising Lorraine pig iron. Occasionally comptoirs have found it necessary to restrict production, but generally their activities are confined to merchandising — sales quotas, price agreements, and territorial divisions. In these respects they are identical with several types of cartels.

National Combinations.   In the United Kingdom, combinations have been formed in certain lines, in spite of traditional individualism. Some of these, as in munitions, are of the closed type of merger or fusion as commonly practiced in the United States. Many others are distinct cartel agreements. In Japan, traditional combinations are largely along family lines, the undertakings of a firm like Mitsui and Co., for example, being widely ramified and often unrelated. Cartel-like associations formed among firms in given lines of business or in trade with given areas have been established under compulsory legislation in Japan. Despite the breakup of the large Japanese industrial combines at the close of World War II, these have since been reorganized and again represent vast commercial power.

---

[4]United States Federal Trade Commission, *Annual Report 1946*, p. 13.

International Combinations. In the international sphere, combinations have been the outgrowth of national combines. Indeed, the establishment of international control over production or distribution is predicated primarily upon extensive national control. Therefore, a favorable legal attitude on the part of the governments involved is most important for the development of international combinations. Cheapness and ease of transportation and communication over great distances have been cited as conditions favorable to international agreement.[5] Other factors are the existence of standard articles of mass production; high degree of mechanization of productive processes; limited sources of supply of materials, labor, or patents; large minimum and optimum size of plant.[6] These may be considered as normal factors, affecting the establishment of international combines even before 1914.

Characteristics of International Combinations

With few exceptions, as in electrical products, international combines are concerned chiefly with raw materials and basic manufactures, or, in other words, articles supplied in bulk or in a few recognized grades.[7] A list of international cartels and other industrial understandings that is definite, although incomplete, divides them into eight classifications: mining industries, metal industries, chemical industries, ceramic industries, electrical industries, textile industries, miscellaneous industries, and insurance and traffic.[8]

Insofar as details permit analysis, these combines attempted one or more of the following activities: allotment of sales territories; allotment of sales quotas; establishment of common sales agencies and common purchase agencies; price fixing; regulation of terms of sale; regulation of production; pooling of profits; and patent pooling and cross-licensing. Of increasing importance in the present era is the matter of international marketing agreements relating to raw materials. The new emphasis that is being placed in this direction derives from the pleas of the raw material producing countries. Many of these countries are in the less developed category; therefore, the stability of the economic conditions of such countries is directly related to the volume and price of their raw

---

[5]Alfred Plummer, *International Combines in Modern Industry* (2nd ed.; London: Sir I. Pitman and Sons, Ltd., 1938), p. 64.
[6]Theodore J. Kreps, *Hearings of Temporary National Economic Committee*, Part 25, p. 13082.
[7]Plummer, *op. cit.*, p. 64.
[8]Dr. Heinrich Friedlaender, quoted by Theodore J. Kreps, *op. cit.*, pp. 13368–13369

material exports. These exports are generally shipped to the developed countries, which are the markets for these exports of raw materials and raw foodstuffs. Fluctuations in the volume and prices of these products have adversely affected the economic stability of the exporting countries. Since one of the pressures of the present era is concern for the welfare of the less developed countries, efforts to stabilize their economic position will serve this objective.

A description of representative agreements will afford an understanding of the problems and objectives of international cartelization.

International Steel Cartel. The International Steel Cartel was initially formed in the fall of 1926 by steel producers in Belgium, France, Germany, Luxembourg, and the Saar, while producers of Czechoslovakia, Austria, Hungary, and Yugoslavia shortly joined.

An underlying cause for the formation of the cartel was the separation from Germany of Luxembourg and the Saar with their important steel production. German steel manufacturers were forced into some kind of accord in order to reestablish something of the former economic alignment. The original purpose of the cartel was control of production, although experience has shown that effective control could not be exercised without price agreement and efforts in this direction were made.

World War II caused a disruption of this cartel, but the pressing need for international agreement was clearly evident in the establishment of an official agency, namely, the European Coal and Steel Community. Under this intergovernmental agreement, typical cartel practices are evident, but in this case official national and international sanction has been provided.

Aluminum. International combination in the aluminum industry dates from 1901. When electrolytic patents expired in 1905, producers experienced severe competition, and later the International Aluminum Syndicate was formed. This was an attempt on the part of French, British, German, and Swiss companies to control competition and fix prices without restricting production or establishing quotas. The cartel was intended to provide interchange of information, promotion of sales, and stabilization of prices as well as reduction in costs of production. While controlling approximately one half of world production of raw aluminum, the cartel has invariably pursued a liberal price policy that has partially assured its continuance.

Electrical Goods. Several international cartels and agreements have been based essentially upon patent holding. The International Incadescent Electric Lamp Cartel was antedated by an electric bulb cartel formed as early as 1903; and exchange of patents and secrets has always been prominent in this field. Membership embraced European producers as well as those of Japan, the United States, Mexico, and Brazil. Under the terms of the agreements, the companies apportioned among themselves the principal world markets.

Rayon. Pooling of patents has been a prime purpose of cartels in the rayon industry. Many of the basic rayon patents have been held in European countries, and some of the largest American producers are either subsidiaries of European manufacturers or they are affiliated with them by stock control or by interchange of patents. The Rayon Cartel embraced both continental European producers and the British industry. In addition to patent pooling, the cartel functioned through common sales agencies in export trade.

Dyestuffs. The dyestuffs industry affords perhaps the best example of, first, national combination and, then, widespread and powerful international cartelization. The great German chemical combine, I. G. Farbenindustrie A. G. (known as I. G.), was first constituted in 1916 and a complete fusion of the many strong German chemical firms was effected in 1925. The industry in Switzerland was also powerful and strongly organized. Through patent control, licensing arrangements, branch plants, and marketing agreements, a widespread international control in dyestuffs was developed, embracing virtually all countries.

Diamonds. Doubtless, the most closely monopolized trade in the world is the diamond trade. De Beers Consolidated Mines, Ltd., exercises control through a group of companies affiliated with it. Probably 95 percent of the gem and industrial diamonds produced in the west are in the hands of this combine. It not only participates in production through its various company holdings, but it also purchases the output of companies that are not members of the combine. London is the wholesale market where two companies — Diamond Trading Company and Industrial Distributors, Ltd. — market gem and industrial diamonds, respectively. The De Beers diamond combine made the news in 1960 when it succeeded in negotiating a contract with the Soviet Union to purchase and market the diamonds produced in the Soviet Union that were to be exported.

Antitrust

The antitrust operations of the United States Department of Justice and of the Federal Trade Commission are familiar to all who know anything about the United States policy regarding competition and monopoly. These are legal principles that are applicable to American companies operating in the United States. The limit to which these American legal practices may be extended to foreign areas where American companies operate appears to be unsettled. Time and again the United States legal authorities have broken up arrangements in which American companies participate with foreign business interests, regardless of whether or not these arrangements directly affect the United States market.

The antitrust policy of the United States was derived from the old British common law as explained in Chapter 24. This same policy has not been followed in other industrial nations to any marked degree, but the European Economic Community appears, at least in principle, to be veering toward an antitrust policy for the six countries embraced in the Common Market. As pertaining to business practices that may affect contract arrangements with European agents, licensees, and distributors for American companies, as well as American companies operating in Europe, Article 85, paragraph 1 of the Rome Treaty describes as prohibited such practices as:

... (a) the direct or indirect fixing of purchase or selling prices or of any other trading conditions;

(b) the limitation or control of production, markets, technical development or investment;

(c) market-sharing or the sharing of sources of supply;

(d) the application of unequal conditions to parties undertaking equivalent engagements in commercial transactions, thereby placing them at a commercial disadvantage;

(e) the subjection of the conclusion of a contract to the acceptance of the parties to the contract of additional engagements which by their nature or in commercial usage have no connection with the subject of such contract.

However, Article 85, paragraph 3 appears to take much of the sting out of the prohibitions of paragraph 1. This paragraph declares that such practices outlawed in paragraph 1 will not be invalid if they

... contribute to the improvement of the production or distribution of goods or to the promotion of technical or economic progress, while reserving to users an equitable share in the profit resulting therefrom, and which do not:

(a) subject the concerns in question to any restrictions not indispensable to the achievement of the above objectives;

(b) enable such concerns to eliminate competition in respect of a substantial proportion of the goods concerned.

Article 86 refers specifically to monopolies or quasi-monopolies already in existence. These are declared to be incompatible with the Common Market if, by reason of their dominant position, they improperly exploit their position. Practices such as the following are specifically outlawed:

. . . (a) the imposition, direct or indirect, of any unfair purchase or selling prices or of any other unfair trading conditions;

(b) the limitation of production, markets or technical development to the prejudice of consumers;

(c) the application of unequal conditions to parties undertaking equivalent engagements in commercial transactions, thereby placing them at a commercial disadvantage;

(d) the same prohibition as listed under (e) above.

The Common Market Commission is issuing regulations pertaining to these and other conditions of the Rome Treaty.

A Consultative Committee on Cartels and Monopolies has been constituted. It is composed of representatives of the six member states. Agreements that appear to violate the above provisions must be filed with the Committee which will decide as to whether or not exemption is justified. Unless and until the Committee has made dispensation with respect to any agreement submitted to it for consideration, such restriction is considered to be prohibited and void.

The original deadline for filing copies of these agreements was November 1, 1962, and this was intended to apply to the presumably more important instances of restriction. Approximately 1000 registrations were filed with the Commission by that deadline. For bilateral agreements in general and presumably not so important, a later deadline of February 1, 1963, was set. In response to that requirement, about 30,000 registrations were filed, and the situation is such that action will be necessarily deferred on these registrations. Hanging over the firms that have filed these agreements are the heavy financial penalties that may be assessed.

Raw Materials — International Agreements to Stabilize Trade[9]

International commodity agreements at the government level have become more common in the post-World War II era. One main char-

---

[9]See also Chapter 21.

acteristic of such agreements is that they generally include countries that are consumers or buyers of the products to which the agreements pertain. This is not true of the industrial combines discussed above where the private producers alone have formed these combines for their own benefit.

Wheat. The outstanding raw material agreement in the post-war era is the International Wheat Agreement of 1949. This agreement has been hailed as a success in stabilizing the international *price* of wheat. As stated above, consuming as well as producing nations are members of the agreement. The consuming nations undertake to buy and the producing nations to supply certain quantities of wheat, with agreements for both a floor and a ceiling price. Perhaps the reason the International Wheat Agreement has been successful thus far is that the United States and Canada are members, and they enforce domestic measures to control production and to stabilize prices.

Coffee. Until 1963, the United States Government has refrained from joining other international agreements designed to stabilize world *trade* in raw materials. However, on May 21, 1963, the United States Senate approved the United States entry into the International Coffee Agreement, and on December 27, 1963, the agreement came into full force and effect. This agreement was initiated in 1959 and includes the major producing countries in Latin America and in Africa, but it excludes important producers in Asia and Africa. It attempts to stabilize trade by establishing export quotas. By and large, this method has not been successful and prices of coffee have not been stabilized. This is probably the reason that the United States, as the major world importer of coffee, decided to enter the agreement.

Sugar. While the United States controls the quantity of sugar to be allotted to domestic producers and foreign suppliers, it has not become a member of the International Sugar Council. Although the Council includes both producing and consuming nations, the absence of the United States, as the biggest consumer, has hindered the effectiveness of the agreement. The sugar agreement also operates on a basis of export quotas, supplemented by voluntary production restrictions. However, these production restrictions have not been effective and the international price of sugar has not been stabilized. The elimination of Cuba as a supplier of the United States market caused wide disturbances in the world sugar trade, because Cuba was forced to sell its surplus to Communist countries which, in turn, dumped some of their purchases on the world market at low prices.

Tin. A Tin Council embracing seven producing countries has been operating since 1956. Inherent in this scheme is the establishment of a central buffer stock with funds provided by the individual member nations. When a surplus of tin developed in 1958, the buffer stock method failed because the members did not have the funds to pay for the metal that would go into the buffer. Export quotas were then decreed, but world prices of tin continued to fall. With production curbs in effect, the supply was decreased and when demand increased in 1961, producers were unable to increase output rapidly. As a consequence, the price of tin rose to a high level.

Petroleum. Efforts to stabilize the price of crude petroleum and to regulate exports took form in 1960 after the major international oil companies reduced the price of crude petroleum. The producing countries in the Middle East plus Venezuela formed an organization at a meeting in Baghdad, Iraq, with the purpose of establishing export controls and of restoring the price of crude petroleum to the level it had been before the price reduction was instituted. Membership is to be open to all producing nations but, significantly, consuming countries are not invited to join.

Other Products. With the overriding urge to bring about stabilization of prices of raw materials entering international trade, producing nations seek to establish agreements that may be expected to achieve this objective. Agreement on cocoa beans has been far advanced, while plans for control over trade in copper, tea, jute, and copra are pushed. Under the guidance of the UN Lead and Zinc Study Group, the countries producing these metals are seeking price stabilization, possibly by means of production controls.

Benefits of Cartels

The benefits claimed for cartel agreements may be set forth in outline, as follows:[10]

Lower Costs of Production.

1. Methods of production are standardized through mutual agreement.
2. Rate of production is kept at a more uniform level.
3. Competitive overexpansion is reduced.
4. Risk premium is less. Less stock necessary to meet unexpected demands.
5. Cartel research institutes are established, patents and processes pooled.
6. Problems of management are solved in mutual conference.

Lower Marketing Costs.

1. Advertising is done by cartel (syndicate) rather than individual enterprise.
2. Terms of trade are made uniform, preventing unfair competition.
3. Transportation expenses to uneconomical markets are eliminated through allocation of markets.
4. Exploitation of seller or purchaser of cartel products is avoided through conclusion of intercartel agreements.

Smoothing Out Cyclical Ups and Downs.

1. Greater equilibrium between productive capacity, production, and consumption is obtained.
2. Rate of employment is less subject to severe fluctuations.
3. Prices are kept at a more stable level.

Obstacles to Success of Cartels

As a means of restraining competition, the cartel form of organization is subject to serious limitations.

Independence of Members. The independence enjoyed by the members gives rise to independent expression of opinion. With regard to Germany, it has been said that ". . . all these syndicates are riddled

---

[10]Kreps, *op. cit.*, pp. 13081–13082.

with internal dissensions and are constantly threatened with disintegration."[11] When extended to the international field, this condition is accentuated. The International Steel Cartel, for example, had to contend at times with continuous overproduction of German manufacturers. When quotas are established, it may be more profitable for a member to produce in excess of a quota allotment, because the fines thereby incurred may not be so burdensome as losses sustained through curtailment of production.

Incentive for Overproduction. Another obstacle is the incentive on the part of each member to produce in excess of allotments during one period in order to support a contention for a larger quota during a subsequent period. This difficulty is inherent in pooling arrangements. Unless effective disciplinary measures are adopted, a member may at any time violate an agreement and precipitate open competition. The International Zinc Cartel was forced to disband late in 1929 owing to "overproduction by the new plants in Norway, France, and Silesia and the announced intention of one of the American producers to change his Mexican shipments to Europe from 70,000 tons of concentrate to 30,000 tons of refined metal annually. . . ."[12] Reconstructed in 1931, the cartel was again dissolved in 1935 due to rising nationalism and monetary difficulties.

Diverse Economic Conditions. Difficulties of international agreements are further intensified by differences in economic conditions prevailing in the constituent countries. These difficulties may give rise not only to protracted negotiations leading to the formation of an agreement but also to continuous dissension, often resulting in dissolution.

Government Policies. Government policies sometimes present disturbing problems. These policies may relate to protective tariff and efforts to encourage the establishment of national industries untrammeled by foreign affiliation or control. Two examples are: (1) the participation of British interests in several international cartels and agreements has been hindered by the failure of the British Government to indicate its sanction, and (2) the absence of American producers from direct participation in some cartels is partially traceable to uncertainty caused by the antitrust laws in the United States.

---

[11]League of Nations, *Cartel and Combines* (1927), p. 13.
[12]*Commerce Reports* (March 3, 1930), p. 556.

Such difficulties as are inherent in loose forms of agreement have led to such close forms of combination in international commerce as communities of interest, and complete fusions or mergers. The highest development of the tendency toward combination is the fusion or merger, a phenomenon that is especially characteristic of the United States and that has been increasingly important in Great Britain and other industrial countries. The fusion or merger is not necessarily a monopoly, but it is a combination in which the merged companies lose their independent identity.

This survey is by no means complete, but it is an attempt to present the chief characteristics of trading combinations with which American traders must either compete in world markets or else collaborate. In the case of industrial raw materials, the United States and other industrial nations are the buyers of these products and are thus directly affected by any agreements to stabilize trade or prices.

As shown in this analysis, the strength of a given national industry, in terms of world competition, is dependent upon its strength within its own national sphere. The commercial and industrial strength of American firms, faced with national and international combines of the scope here described, derives partly from the powerful organizations that have developed in this country within the framework of antitrust legislation and from the facilities provided by the Webb-Pomerene Act.

Summary

1. Many foreign countries, chiefly the main industrial competitors of American exporters, have less rigid antitrust legislation than does the United States.
2. Even the United Kingdom, whose common law forbids combinations in restraint of trade, is tolerant of combines that benefit production or trade and lead to more efficient methods.
3. Germany's method of controlling competition has traditionally been the cartel. This method of controlling the market may extend control over production as well. The cartel form of organization is practiced in many countries, but usually there are restraints on the freedom to operate.
4. In Japan, industrial and commercial combines have been along family lines.
5. Antitrust rules of the Common Market appear to discourage cartelization in the prewar sense. The regulations seem to use a kind of rule of reason under which combinations in restraint of trade may be justified.
6. International combines have been an outgrowth of national combinations. They occur in industries characterized by many factors, such as homogeneity and mechanization of product, limited sources of supply of materials, and patents.

7. International commodity agreements dealing with raw materials are becoming more common. One reason for this development is the great interest in assisting the developing countries by this means.
8. International commodity agreements in the raw materials trade offer the possibility of stabilizing the economy of the less developed countries by seeking to maintain stable (higher?) world prices for such products.
9. Cartels offer many benefits, but they also reveal certain weaknesses.

QUESTIONS

1. Explain and compare the legal concepts concerning restraint of trade as observed in the United States, Great Britain, Germany, Japan, and the European Economic Community.
2. Define cartels, comptoirs, mergers, and stock control.
3. Explain the business phenomena conducive to control over international competition.
4. In comparing various cartels, cite differences in the objectives of specific cartels.
5. Why are international commodity agreements dealing with raw materials so important now?
6. From the information provided in this chapter, attempt to explain the circumstances, both favorable and unfavorable, to the successful operation of international commodity agreements.
7. Comment critically on the declared benefits of cartels.
8. Comment critically on the weaknesses of cartels.

PROBLEM

Obtain the most recent information on the antitrust or monopoly policy of any country of your choice, such as the United States, the United Kingdom, Germany, France, Italy, Canada, Japan, and the European Economic Community.

Prepare a report on the provisions of this policy and, insofar as possible, describe what has occurred as a result of this policy.

COLLATERAL READINGS

Brewster, Kingman. *Antitrust and American Business Abroad.* New York: Mc-Graw-Hill Book Company, Inc., 1958.

Dartnell International Trade Handbook, The. Chicago: The Dartnell Corporation, 1963.

International Cooperative Alliance. *Cartel.* London: quarterly.

League of Nations. *Cartels and Combines.* Geneva: 1927.

——————————. *Cartels and Trusts and Their Development.* Geneva: 1927.

Towle, Lawrence W. *International Trade and Commercial Policy.* New York and London: Harper & Brothers, 1956. Chapter 27.

United Nations, Economic and Social Council. *Restrictive Business Practices,* International Documents Service, 19th Session, Supplement No. 3A. New York: United Nations, 1955.

United States Congress, Hearings before the Temporary National Economic Committee. *Cartels, Part 25.* Washington, D.C.: 1940.

United States Congress, Senate. *A Study of the Anti-Trust Laws.* Hearings before the Sub-Committee on Antitrust and Monopoly, Committee on the Judiciary, 84th Congress, 1st Session. Washington, D.C.: 1955.

United States Federal Trade Commission. *Annual Report.* Washington, D.C.

——————————. *Cooperation in American Export Trade,* 2 volumes. Washington, D.C.: 1914.

——————————. *Copper Industry, The.* Part I, *The Copper Industry of the United States and International Copper Cartels.* Washington, D.C.: 1947.

——————————. *International Electrical Equipment Cartel.* Washington, D.C.: 1948.

——————————. *International Phosphate Cartels.* Washington, D.C.: 1946.

——————————. *International Steel Cartels.* Washington, D.C.: 1948.

——————————. *Sulphur Industry and International Cartels, The.* Washington, D.C.: 1947.

CHAPTER 19

SELECTION OF INTERNATIONAL MARKETING POLICIES

The success of an international marketing concern will be influenced by the skill with which it selects its foreign markets and sources; by subsequent conditions affecting production costs and prices; by changing considerations relating to the nature, reputation, and quality of its wares; by current business, financial, and political conditions; by the extent of national and foreign competition; by tariff, exchange, and other legislative enactments; by shipping services and costs; and by the effectiveness of its management and operation. Most of the market survey factors considered in Chapter 3 are subject to change after the original choice of markets has been made. Its success will naturally depend in part upon keeping well informed currently. Much will depend on the adoption of effective distribution and trade promotion methods and policies in the first instance and on their subsequent adaptation to changing requirements.

Decision as to which of the several available methods and policies will be adopted in particular instances is an important executive function confronting every international trader. Business judgment usually enters into the decision, because the conditions influencing it do not always point precisely to a particular method or policy to the exclusion of all others. The choice of methods and policies will, however, be influenced by varying conditions that may conveniently be subdivided as follows:

1. Characteristics of the commodity.
2. Characteristics of the market.
3. Characteristics and policies of particular firms.

Characteristics of the Commodity

The export and import middlemen through which many of the great staples of commerce are marketed are in some instances influenced by the fact that they are produced by large numbers of unorganized producers and by other characteristics of the industries from which they spring, but the inherent characteristics of these commodities are also important considerations in determining the marketing channel used.

Inherent Characteristics. Staple agricultural products, such as grain and cotton, coffee and sugar, which are nonperishable and readily graded and classified or standardized, are well adapted to sale on the basis of grade or sample, to storage on a large scale in public and private elevators or warehouses, to sale on organized exchanges, to the use of the cable and radio in quoting prices and in transmitting orders, and to utilization of so-called indirect trade channels. They are sold at world

The inherent characteristics of staple agricultural products, such as tea, determine in part the trade channels through which the product will be marketed. In this scene, Indian women, with rattan baskets slung over their backs and strapped to their heads, are picking tea leaves on a tea plantation in Serdang.

prices,[1] largely determined on the organized markets of the principal importing countries in accordance with international conditions of supply and demand. Further, their sale is not dependent upon direct personal salesmanship.

Some manufactures or semimanufactures, likewise, are more or less staple in character; but as other conditions also are important in determining international marketing methods and policies, and in particular instances may dominate the decisions, it does not follow that all such products will be distributed through middlemen. There can be no doubt, however, but that the staple characteristics of products such as lumber, cotton gray goods, woodpulp, and flour facilitate somewhat the use of middlemen by many producers in these industries. The relative ease with which certain manufactures lend themselves to standardization also facilitates the adoption and maintenance of cooperative exporting methods through middlemen.[2]

The inherent nature of many manufactured products, particularly of complicated machinery such as locomotives, automobiles, farm machinery, and mining machinery, points toward more direct exporting and importing methods. Expert knowledge of the commodity, demonstrations, and personal salesmanship may be necessary or highly desirable, and the exporter frequently decides that the organization through which this can best be accomplished is one that he himself provides. When the exporting country fails to provide such direct promotion, the importer seeking a desirable piece of foreign equipment or style merchandise may decide to travel to the country where such products are available and make his purchases there.

Less complicated wares are better suited to distribution through export and import middlemen, and the extent to which agents and distributors are utilized may also be influenced by the characteristics of the commodities. Market conditions, or the characteristics and policies of the international marketing firm, may cause it to deal through middlemen or agents or distributors, but it will at least give consideration to the employment of export salesmen and import buyers or the establishment of branch houses for the sale or purchase of complicated mechanical products.

The inherent nature of machinery and mechanical products, moreover — products prominent in American export trade — may make it essential that adequate provision be made for replacement parts, and in

---

[1]Some staple commodities move under marketing or price-control mechanisms.
[2]Cooperative exporting methods are discussed in Chapter 17.

many instances for efficient local service stations. The sale of products such as electrical machinery may depend upon installation by the exporter. The sale of farm implements and other products, the demand for which is seasonal, may make it desirable to carry large stocks from which prompt delivery can be made, even though this policy may tie up funds in the commodities and in warehousing facilities or arrangements. The successful promotion of a market for farm implements or automobiles may depend very directly upon their adaptation to local conditions and preferences or requirements. These commodity characteristics have frequently led to local representation by salesmen, mechanical experts, or branch houses. If other conditions warrant, there is usually a strong tendency in the direction of branch houses for the promotion and sale of such commodities.

Financial Characteristics. Commodities differ also as to their financial characteristics. The credit requirements in connection with the resale to farmers of the more expensive types of farm machinery are a marketing problem. As a single grain binder, for example, represents a substantial investment, the grower's ability to pay may depend upon the harvesting and sale of his crop. Long agricultural credits may be essential to the successful development of a market, and they may influence the credit and sales arrangements. This need for long-term credits is an additional inducement to the establishment of branch houses abroad.

The heavy investment represented by many other products, the sale of which is not so largely seasonal, also affects their credit terms and methods of distribution. The heavy machinery trades in which a single machine may represent an investment of thousands of dollars sometimes find this commodity characteristic an obstacle to the carrying of stocks by middlemen, agents, or distributors.

Perishable Characteristics. The perishable character of a commodity may affect not only its shipping and storage facilities and methods but also its channels of distribution and marketing methods. Speed and special care in handling and storage are especially desirable; and producers whose sales are sufficiently large to warrant the expense may, therefore, prefer to maintain their own direct marketing organization, as in the case of bananas. In the local distribution of perishable products, many trade channels may be welcomed as a means of prompt merchandising, but perishability provides an incentive for direct representation abroad and emphasizes special attention to rapid delivery and to careful packing and handling. The perishable character of products has also at times been responsible for the adoption of a cash or short-term credit policy by the international marketing organization.

Promotion Characteristics. Advertising and promotion methods and the aggregate amount of advertising appropriation are influenced by the nature of the wares. There is special need for advertising products that are eventually to be resold abroad to the general consuming public. Salesmanship designed to reach the wholesale or retail dealer is not sufficient. The retail market needs to be developed and the exporter frequently sets aside advertising funds for this purpose, even when he is represented by a foreign agent or distributor. The methods of advertising consumers' goods, moreover, are selected with a view to reaching the thousands of individuals comprising the general consuming public.

Exporters of industrial machinery, railroad equipment, mining machinery, and the many other products that are of interest to only a limited number of manufacturing industries, transportation companies, mining concerns, public utilities, or other business enterprises can depend more largely on personal salesmanship. The general advertising activities of exporters of such products are less extensive and are usually confined to the preparation and distribution of descriptive letters, circulars, booklets, or catalogs, advertising in trade journals and business publications, and other methods particularly effective in developing a specialized market.

Importers dealing with the domestic market, such as the United States, generally handle promotion and advertising of consumer goods along with the regular domestic advertising. There are few instances in which foreign producers of consumers' goods sold in the American market themselves undertake promotion such as American exporters do in overseas markets. This is because of the high degree of development of promotion techniques in the American economy.

Characteristics of the Market

Although commodity characteristics may cause the exporter to decide in favor of particular exporting methods or policies, his decision with reference to different foreign markets may vary. If his foreign trade is distributed over a wide range of markets, he virtually always pursues a variety of methods. One of the reasons for this is that market characteristics are also an important consideration. Some of these market characteristics are specific in that they affect only particular commodities, while others are so general in scope that all or a wide variety of wares exported to particular markets are influenced by them.

Competition. Among the specific characteristics, special mention should be made of the amount of competition encountered in the sale of a particular product in different parts of the world. Increased competition has frequently been an incentive to more direct exporting methods. American machine tools were for some years distributed by American producers in foreign industrial countries very largely through foreign agents; but later when the Western European countries offered keen competition in the production and sale of some types of machine tools, branch houses or affiliated companies were established in a number of foreign markets. The emergence of the Common Market was a signal for American manufacturers to establish their own offices and factories in that area or to buy into European firms or to license them.

The exportation of ready-mixed paints to Mexican, Central American, West Indian and other Caribbean, and Canadian markets was from the very beginning entrusted to export salesmen because competition was fully anticipated. It was necessary to combat the customary practice of purchasing white lead and other paint ingredients. The establishment of retail stores abroad and the sale of American shoes to foreign retailers by American salesmen in some markets was also due at least in part to keen competition. In markets that are less competitive, American shoes have been variously exported through export commission houses, export brokers, foreign agents, or foreign wholesale importers.

Nature of Trading Organization. A second market characteristic affecting particular commodities may be the well-established position of certain American or foreign middlemen. A particular American export house may be so firmly entrenched in a foreign market through connections with importers, control of shipping and dock facilities, etc., as seriously to deter producers of general merchandise and many kinds of manufactured products from making more direct sales arrangements in particular markets. In other markets an exporter selling through an exclusive foreign agent or distributor may find that he is so firmly established as to handicap more direct distribution through export salesmen or branch houses. He may, indeed, conclude in some instances that the export house or the foreign agent or distributor so situated is exceptionally efficient and reliable.

The purchasing organization and policy of the importer, too, may in particular instances affect trade channels. Some importing houses, as was stated in Chapter 9, send buyers abroad or establish permanent middlemen as purchasing agents or representatives. Large consumers sometimes make purchases directly at the plant of a manufacturer. Foreign buyers of industrial machinery, for example, frequently make thorough inspections at American plants before making a purchase. At times the ownership and financial control of an enterprise affects trade channels. In the exportation of mining machinery, for example, the local management does not always have complete purchasing authority when the mining property is owned by foreign capital. The exporter's salesmen may have direct contact with the mining companies' offices at London, New York, or elsewhere, as well as with their local managers in South Africa, Peru, Mexico, or other mining regions.

Importers of raw materials as well as finished manufactures may send buyers abroad because organized markets for the sale of such materials may not exist and therefore personal inspection is called for. Or, the practices of shippers in certain countries may be so unreliable that the selection of purchases and packing and shipping them may require personal representation.

Selling to Public Businesses. When attempting to sell products for use in business enterprises owned publicly, sales organizations may need to be modified so as to facilitate sales to governments. In a foreign market where government ownership of railroads prevails, American exporters of locomotives, iron and steel, etc., have not infrequently operated through a national importing or financial house, even though their own salesmen, technical representatives, or other company representatives were on the ground. The reason may be that the bank or importing house is influential with the government, or that its services are needed in financing the transaction. The foreign government may wish to sell bonds in order to raise construction and equipment funds. The exporter may, indeed, find it necessary to take part in making arrangements through American financial institutions for the funds necessary to finance the sale. If the credit terms requested are longer than the exporter is prepared to grant, he may be able to make satisfactory arrangements with a large national importing or financial house.

On the other hand, sales of capital goods to governments are frequently financed through financial institutions and facilities set up by the governments of the industrialized nations and also by the multigovernment agencies. In such cases, the sales procedure remains the same but the funds are provided by such government sources.

Credit Factors. Credit considerations in particular markets may similarly affect trade channels when selling to private customers. American lumber has been variously exported through American export agents, brokers, export merchants, joint or cooperative sales agencies, foreign sales offices, traveling representatives, and consignment to foreign importers abroad and foreign resident buyers in the United States. Requests in European lumber markets for long-term credits, however, have at times caused lumber exporters to utilize the so-called London factor as an additional European middleman because of financial services performed by him.

Government Policy. Tariff or other governmental obstacles and keen competition, it will be recalled, have caused manufacturers in some instances to change their policies in particular regions so far as to erect

Characteristics of the market, such as tariffs, governmental barriers, and competition, have caused some manufacturers to establish production plants abroad, as is the case of this manufacturer of batteries in Hong Kong.

or purchase production plants.[3] Not only have some foreign manufacturers established plants in the United States due to tariff protection and the magnitude of the domestic market, but also some former German producers have been obliged to relinquish their American factories.

Location. Certain market characteristics to a greater or less degree influence the methods and trade channels of a wide range of products sold in particular foreign countries. The adjacent location of Canada, for example, has undoubtedly influenced the methods and policies of many American firms trading with that very important foreign market, making them similar or identical in many instances to those pursued in domestic commerce. The Chinese comprador system was for many years an accepted part of the trading arrangements of most foreigners doing business in China.

State Trading. Where state trading is practiced, exporting and importing methods are decidedly affected. The state trading nation may establish a purchasing and sales commission in foreign countries so that business transacted through such a commission is essentially domestic. When the United States Government purchases tin or rubber, the normal importing channels for such products are altered. The importer, under such circumstances, may only handle the product on behalf of the United States Government, which negotiated the purchase and placed the order. When the United States Government, through the Commodity Credit Corporation, exports American agricultural surplus commodities at prices below world levels and, at least in part, in foreign currency rather than in United States dollars, the commercial firms engaged in this business again become functionaries for the Government, since the trading transaction is conducted by the Government.

Characteristics and Policies of Particular Firms

It is obvious that neither commodity nor market characteristics account fully for the trade organization and methods of particular firms. In a given industry the export policies pursued by different producers in a particular market may vary widely, and in some industries certain characteristics common to most producers greatly influence the trade channels through which their surplus products are exported.

---

[3]The establishment of foreign branches is described in Chapter 14.

Staple Commodities. The exportation of grain and cotton through middlemen is encouraged by the commodity characteristics previously mentioned, but it is due primarily to the production of these crops by thousands of unorganized growers, who for the most part are dependent upon middlemen for the distribution of their grain or cotton in domestic as well as in foreign commerce. Cooperative marketing has progressed and it has been an aid to many grain and cotton growers, but both of these trades remain essentially in the hands of middlemen.

Grain is exported by wholesale grain dealers of the great primary and seaboard grain markets and by specialized grain export firms and American branches of foreign importers who purchase grain in the cen-

Port of New Orleans

Grain, such as that in the Public Grain Elevator at the Port of New Orleans, is produced by many unorganized growers who are dependent upon middlemen to distribute their product in domestic and foreign commerce.

tral wholesale markets, chiefly from the grain dealers who operate there. Cotton is exported mainly by cotton brokerage firms who, as in the case of central market grain dealers, are engaged in domestic commerce as well as in the export trade. As the growers have produced an export surplus of wheat and cotton without effective private control over the marketing of the surplus, the United States Government has also become a factor in the production and marketing of these crops. Likewise, other countries whose primary products are marketed in the United States have from time to time attempted to help stabilize a market and fix a price. Coffee, crude rubber, tea, wheat, and several other products have been under national or international control.

Manufactures. Manufactures are produced by businessmen who are more apt to insist upon a voice in determining prices and to control the distribution of their wares. But in a particular manufacturing industry different exporters may pursue quite different export methods and policies in the same foreign markets. The exporting manufacturer's trade organization and methods are frequently influenced by the volume of his sales or prospective sales in particular markets, by the volume of his export business as a whole, and by his financial position. Total volume of export sales frequently has much to do with the type of export department maintained by a manufacturer and with the extent to which he will depend upon American middlemen. He may depend entirely upon middlemen so long as his foreign sales are small and his interest in the export trade has not been aroused. Subsequently, however, he may organize an export department and establish direct connections in all of his principal foreign markets. Another firm in the same industry may, because of preference or smaller volume of sales, dispense with an export department and depend entirely upon export houses or other middlemen, or it may content itself with membership in a cooperative export association.

Volume of sales in particular foreign markets may influence very directly the methods of different exporters or of a given exporter in different markets. Volume of sales in particular markets has a direct bearing upon the establishment of branch houses or licensees, or the employment of salesmen, and upon the expenditure of large sums in advertising and trade promotion. The financial position of different exporters may affect their readiness to take these steps in anticipation of heavy sales in particular markets and also influence their ability or willingness to extend long-term credits to their customers. The more direct methods of exporting involve additional expense, and their adoption depends largely upon volume of trade. Even the largest manufacturing corporations that export commodities well adapted to branch house selling have not established branch houses in all of their foreign markets. Some depend upon traveling export salesmen, others upon foreign agents or distributors, and those of least importance upon middlemen.

Although the United States market is the largest in the world, few foreign manufacturers have established direct sales outlets here. This is due to the high development of American distribution and frequently to the inability or unwillingness of the foreign manufacturer to produce a volume of merchandise sufficient to meet the mass market needs.

Knowledge and Experience of the Firm. The adoption of particular methods or policies by different exporters and importers in a given industry depends also upon their knowledge and experience. As a result of market surveys and experience, some of them may have gained an extensive knowledge of foreign markets, export selling and import purchasing methods, shipping practices, credit terms and methods of financing, price quotations, and other practices differing from those customary in domestic commerce. Such concerns are in a position to decide intelligently as to the methods and policies best adapted to their several markets, and where desirable, to establish an international marketing organization for the direct purchase or sale and distribution of their commodities.

There have been instances of direct exporting by manufacturers during the earliest stages of their interest in international marketing, but the more general practice has been a gradual development from one stage to another. Many manufacturers first depended entirely upon export middlemen, the valuable services of whom were discussed in Chapter 9. With increased knowledge of foreign markets and export trade methods, increased volume of foreign sales, or greater need for foreign orders, and perhaps because of more intense foreign competition, they later decided to trade directly in their more important foreign markets, and still later the number of such markets was increased. Their first direct foreign trade is usually, although not always, conducted through foreign agents and distributors. Later, a combination of commodity, market, and firm characteristics induces some of them to employ traveling salesmen or to establish their own branch houses in a growing number of foreign markets. There has, of course, been no uniform historical development on the part of all exporting manufacturers. Not only do the commodity, market, and firm characteristics referred to vary, but the extent to which they are permitted to govern the methods and policies of particular firms depends upon the personal judgment and views of their executives.

Although dominated by unmanufactured merchandise in the United States import trade, there has always been a great deal of direct importing by wholesalers, retailers, and manufacturers. This has been due to the absence of exporting channels in producing countries, thus requiring importers to go abroad to purchase such goods as they desired. As time goes on, there is no indication of any change in this situation. Perhaps this can be attributed to foreign hesitancy to tackle the complicated and enormous American market.

Summary

1. The principles and conditions governing the selection of export and import marketing policies fall under three headings: (1) the characteristics of the commodity; (2) the characteristics of the market; and, (3) the characteristics and policies of the exporting or importing firm.
2. Raw materials generally can be sold without the use of personal selling or sales promotion. Therefore, they usually are handled by various middlemen. The broker is particularly important where the product can be graded and traded on the basis of grades. Finished goods, on the other hand, usually require promotion, stimulation, and personal representation.
3. Markets that are highly developed can be reached through channels that are highly developed, while in less developed markets with lower volume, we are likely to find more professional middlemen. A market in which state trading is practiced will generally permit no other method of marketing.
4. Individual firms vary considerably in their characteristics and policies. For reasons that rest upon tradition, experience, objectives, and other intangibles, individual firms, although in the same line of business, pursue different marketing practices.

QUESTIONS

1. How do commodity characteristics influence the selection of international marketing channels? Cite examples.
2. Compare the export marketing of raw cotton with that of agricultural machinery. Explain the reasons for any differences in the marketing policies.
3. Compare the import marketing of coffee and of Paris gowns. Explain the reasons for any differences in the marketing policies.
4. How does competition influence the selection of international marketing channels? Give examples.
5. What factors would you consider in determining the channel or channels for selling equipment to a petroleum company operating oil wells and refining facilities in Peru?
6. What factors would you consider in determining the channel or channels for marketing locomotives in Brazil?

7. How may changes in the tariff cause changes in international marketing channels, both export and import? Explain.
8. What sales channels would you use for selling merchandise to the Soviet Union?
9. Why do you think it conceivable that two firms producing the same merchandise and selling at the same prices would export through entirely different channels, for example, one through distributors and branches and the other through American middlemen and export salesmen?

PROBLEM

Select one kind of imported consumer goods available for retail sale in the United States market. It may be a foodstuff, a beverage, a time piece, a toy, etc. Determine the marketing channels through which this product traveled on its way from the foreign country of shipment to the retail merchant in your locality.

COLLATERAL READINGS

Fayerweather, John. *Management of International Operations*, Text and Cases. New York: McGraw-Hill Book Company, Inc., 1960. Chapter 3.
Also, see the list of readings given at the end of Chapter 8 on page 160.

PART IV

TECHNICAL AND LEGAL FEATURES OF INTERNATIONAL MARKETING

Part IV, as the title indicates, deals with certain technical and legal features of international marketing. One of these is international communications. Another subject of prime importance is the matter of international pricing and price quotations; this is a subject that is either known or it is not known; there is no half-way point. Packing, shipping, and insurance are inherent in every international business transaction, and the student should have some awareness of the ways to use these facilities. Problems peculiar to importing — the United States is used as an example — inform the reader not only of the difficulties he would face if he were an importer but also of the difficulties that an exporter's customer faces when he imports shipments made by the exporter. Legal aspects of international marketing are then considered as a means of informing the reader of the several kinds of legal problems that are likely to be encountered in international marketing. The settlement of commercial disputes concludes this part, and it emphasizes that mediation, conciliation, and arbitration play a vital part in this area of international marketing.

CHAPTER 20

INTERNATIONAL COMMUNICATIONS

Facilitating channels and services to be considered in connection with international marketing methods include the several phases of international communications, namely, correspondence, parcel post, cable, radio, and telephone. Each of these facilities will be discussed briefly as to their nature and use in the international commercial field.

Correspondence for International Marketing

Correspondence may be employed as the sole method of conducting foreign as well as domestic trade. In addition to mail-order houses, many international traders conduct a certain volume of trade by correspondence; and a number of manufacturers of clothing, tobacco products, optical, stationery goods, and other wares conduct their entire foreign trade by means of parcel post. The exclusive use of correspondence in international marketing has been seriously restricted by distance and unfamiliarity.

As a method of international marketing supplemental to other methods, correspondence is a vital force. Business could scarcely be conducted without the use of letters, and who can tell what good may not be accomplished by a letter dispatched at a crucial period, or what additional incentive may not be afforded to attract attention, push the sale, accept the price, alter the terms?

In recent years, the advent and extension of international airmail has afforded a means of more rapid mail connection and has imparted greater importance to correspondence as a factor in international marketing. Airmail routes now connect the United States with all parts of the world as continents and oceans are spanned by fast flying planes. Time in transit for letters and parcels has been cut to a fraction of the time required for steamer transit on some routes. Indeed, international airmail service is, in some trades, a formidable competitor of cable and radio communication.

The same general classification of letters applies in both domestic and foreign trade; differences are mainly in technique. Form letters are employed to take care of routine matters, and circular letters may be used to stimulate interest in a product and to push sales.[1]

Principles of Correspondence. Despite the acceptance of brevity and terseness in business correspondence in the United States, greater stress is being laid upon the necessity of recognizing a difference in international business correspondence. Many foreign businessmen have not adopted the crisp American style but incline toward the same well-rounded and thoroughly phrased type of letter previously common in this country.

Although there are exceptions, certain principles are usually considered essential in writing correspondence designed for international marketing. It is contended that the typical American business letter is viewed with disfavor by foreigners because to them it may seem to be discourteous. Friendship and courtesy play a large part in business relations overseas, and it is essential that this spirit be appreciated by Americans who write letters to foreign business firms. The mere fact of distance enhances the need for avoiding misunderstanding or ill feeling.

Individual appeal is essential in foreign correspondence, even more so than in domestic. Catering to the language preference of the addressee is one example. This means not only the use of a foreign language in the case of non-English-speaking customers, but, according to some authorities, also the correct use of English peculiar to the part of the world to which a letter may be destined. For example, in British territory the use of British expressions and spellings is recommended, as petrol (for gasoline); lorry (for truck); tram (for streetcar); and lift (for elevator).

Appreciating the point of view of the foreigner is also suggested. This requires that the writer of a letter be familiar with the conditions confronting the person whom he is addressing. Even when serious differences of opinion arise, a letter may be worded in such a way as to convey this appreciation of the other side of the question.

---

[1]For a discussion of circularizing in international marketing, see Chapter 12.

Seeking advice of the addressee is also suggested as a means of providing an individual touch. Moreover, requests for opinion may be sincerely extended as a means of assisting in the solution of international marketing problems.

Finally, errors must at all costs be avoided, for accuracy and completeness are essential. Enclosures must not be forgotten. A second copy of a letter should be forwarded by next mail in certain cases, particularly when important documents are sent, when airmail is used, or when transshipments may be necessary. When a second copy is thus forwarded, the word "copy" or "copied" usually appears on the letter.

In all fairness it should be noted that an examination of letters coming to this country from foreign businessmen does not reveal complete observance of some of these conditions. All such letters do not breathe romance, by any means. An increasing number of foreigners are evidencing a growing appreciation of modern methods and are placing fewer flourishes in their correspondence. Perhaps in each instance the writer of correspondence should take his cue from the style that is observed by the foreign correspondent.

Mechanics of Correspondence. Experienced international traders have found it desirable to consider certain mechanical features of correspondence which, in many instances, possess no counterpart in domestic trade. In other cases their application may be different or may be of greater significance.

Promptness in answering letters is always desirable but is especially important in foreign trade. Failure to catch a certain steamer mail connection overseas may cause a delay of weeks, whereas in domestic trade the mails are constantly flowing in all directions. The post office in every city publishes the closing dates for foreign mails. International airmail has so shortened distances, however, that this factor is of minor importance when airmail is used.

In handling correspondence for international marketing, it is usually advisable to retain as part of the communication "the original envelope, postage stamp, and postmark. . . . The envelope should be pinned to the letter, at least until an answer has been dictated. Important foreign letters are often written on stationery printed for domestic use, sometimes not giving the name of the country. There is much duplication of town names in Latin America and Spain, and cases have been known where export managers could not determine whether letters were from Chile, or Cuba, or Spain. The postage stamp always indicates the writer's country, the postmark usually gives the date, and other information of value is often printed on front or back of the envelope."[2] This is still good advice today.

Special Stationery. Many firms consider it advisable to use special stationery for handling their international trade correspondence. Some of the advantages of using special stationery are:

1. Since the special stationery contains a coded cable address, a saving in cable charges is realized by addressing messages to a code address rather than to the full name and address of a firm.

2. Just as a sales, purchase, accounting, or other department has the department name printed on stationery, the export or import department may similarly benefit from such prestige.

3. Some concerns employ the "square" or "baronial" style of envelope for foreign trade, with stationery to match. "This has its practical advantages in that bundles of letters as tied up for delivery or rail routing in foreign post offices usually conform to the baronial size and the ordinary American envelopes, particularly the long No. 10 size, are often badly multilated in being 'made to fit' these bundles." Moreover, "it is highly desirable that the mailing department recognize such correspondence at once as foreign mail in order to avoid slips in the matter of correct postage."[3] "Short-paid" letters may incur penalty postage collected from the addressee, which does not build goodwill for the exporter.

4. Although any concern may provide itself with an aristocratic style of stationery, it is difficult to maintain a claim to stability unless it is founded upon fact. "Established in 1882" may mean much to foreign businessmen, and American firms frequently show the date of establishment on their special foreign trade stationery.

5. Light-weight (tissue) paper is often used for export and import correspondence, since international airmail rates are based on one-half ounce weight.

---

[2]The Fifth-Third National Bank of Cincinnati, *Hints on Export Translations* (1921), p. 5.
[3]"Handling Export Correspondence," *Dun's International Review*, pp. 4–5.

Filing. Filing of foreign trade correspondence and documents is based upon general filing principles, but certain features are unique. Because many foreign names may be unintelligible to the American, it is advisable to file correspondence geographically rather than by firm name. Thus, in the case of Argentina, all Argentine correspondence would be filed together, with the cities of Argentina arranged alphabetically and with the different firms listed alphabetically according to the cities in which they are located.

The difficulty of understanding foreign names arises principally from the unusual customs of some countries. For filing purposes, it probably makes no difference whether letters are filed under a man's correct name or not, so long as the same plan is followed consistently. In writing a letter to Arturo Pancho y Suarez, however, the fact that correspondence might be filed under "Suarez" does not excuse the ignorance of saluting him as "My dear Mr. Suarez." This name in Spanish construction represents the mother's name prior to her marriage and the gentleman in question is Mr. Pancho. Similarly, in many Oriental countries the given name is last and the surname first. Mr. Yew Shan Hwei of Manila, let us say, is known as Mr. Yew, and not as Mr. Hwei. Other constructions which seem peculiar to the American include an apparent disregard for sex in many Latin Christian names, unintelligible mailing directions, and strange street locations.

Translation. For translating letters from and into foreign languages, large concerns frequently have a translation department. In other situations the letters are translated by various foreign trade bureaus and translation offices. Some foreign trade journals translate correspondence arising from advertisements carried in their columns.[4]

The language in which letters to foreign countries are to be written is not always easy to decide. When answering incoming letters, a courteous procedure is to reply in the same language, but this is not always observed. The foreigner, for example, may write in English to please the American correspondent, but with evident effort. For commercial correspondence purposes, English, French, German, and Spanish are considered sufficient, with Portuguese for Brazil as well as for Portugal and her colonies.

English is used for the British Commonwealth and is also the commercial language of the Far East generally. Moreover, English is em-

---

[4]For technical problems of translation, see Chapter 12.

ployed for commercial purposes in Scandinavian countries. Either German or English is preferable for use in the Baltic countries, and may also be used in correspondence with Holland and Denmark. The French language, in addition to its application in France and her colonies, Belgium, Haiti, and western Switzerland, is the commercial language of the Near East countries. For commercial purposes French is also acceptable in Italy. German is used in Germany and central Europe, and it also predominates in Switzerland. Spanish, in addition to its use in Spain and her colonies, is the language of all Latin American republics except Haiti and Brazil.

International Mail Services and Rates

The necessity for international agreements to establish and regulate the international mails give rise to the Universal Postal Union. This organization, with headquarters at Berne, Switzerland, dates back to 1875. Congresses are held at approximately five-year intervals for adoption of revisions in the regulations.

A second general postal convention to which the United States is also a party is the Postal Union of the Americas and Spain, established in 1920. It was an outgrowth of the South American Postal Union that was founded in 1911. The First Pan American Postal Congress (earlier name) was held in 1921 in Buenos Aires and congresses have since been held at five-year intervals.

Ordinary Letter Rates. Ordinary letter rates under the Universal Postal Union are eleven cents for the first ounce and seven cents per additional ounce; for post cards the rate is generally seven cents. Under the Postal Union of the Americas and Spain, domestic rates are reciprocally extended to all countries that have signed the convention. United States domestic rates, both for regular and airmail, apply to Mexico and Canada as well.[5]

In addition to other regular mail services, samples may be shipped in foreign mails, but in order to qualify they must be samples of merchandise without salable value.

International reply coupons of United States issue may be purchased at post offices for 15 cents each. The reply coupon, which may be exchanged in any country for a stamp or stamps representing the inter-

---

[5]See the current issue of *United States Postal Manual*.

national postage on a single-rate surface letter, affords a means of eliciting a reply. In addition, international mail may be registered.

Airmail Rates. International airmail regulations, as far as the United States is concerned, are those embodied in the Universal Postal Union. International airmail rates are higher than those for ordinary mail and vary depending upon distance, as Western Hemisphere (except Mexico, Canada, and United States Territories, which enjoy domestic rates); Europe and North Africa, 15 cents per one-half ounce; rest of the world, 25 cents per one-half ounce.

Air letters, or *aerogrammes*, represent another type of special postal service. The air letter, which can be folded into the form of an envelope and sealed, may be sent by air to all countries at a uniform rate of 11 cents each. The air letter sheets, which bear imprinted postage, are sold at all post offices.

The yellow *International Parcel Post* sticker should be attached to every parcel that is mailed to another country, even to each parcel mailed under a group-ship arrangement. Alternative, disposition of the parcel must also be indicated in the event the parcel is undeliverable as addressed.

International Parcel Post. Parcel post provides a separate subject distinct from the "regular" mails with which international postal conventions have dealt. An international parcel post convention has been drawn up in connection with the Universal Postal Union, but the United States has never become a party. The United States is a signatory, however, to the Parcel Post Agreement of the Postal Union of the Americas and Spain. Apart from this Pan American agreement, the policy of the United States is to make separate parcel post arrangements with individual countries.

The general principle involved is the payment by the country of origin to the country of destination of a fixed rate per pound or per par-

---

P. O. Form 2972 Jan. 1957

UNITED STATES OF AMERICA

DISPATCH   NOTE
(Bulletin d'Expédition)

STAMP OF MAILING OFFICE
(*Timbre du Bureau d'Origine*)

Number of Customs Declarations................Weight.....................Postage Paid $...............
(*Nombre de déclarations en douane*)   (*Poids*)   (*Affranchissement perçu*)

CUSTOMS DUTIES
(*Droits de Douane*)

Insured No...
(*Numéro d'assurance*)

Insured Value (*Valeur déclarée*):

CUSTOMS STAMP
(*Timbre de la Douane*)

(This side is filled in
by the accepting clerk.)

INSTRUCTIONS GIVEN BY SENDER
Dispositions de l'expéditeur

Senders must provide for an alternative disposition, striking out the requests not employed, as follows:
IF UNDELIVERABLE AS ADDRESSED:
Au cas de non-livraison, le colis doit être:

(A) Deliver to
Livré à M.

(B) Abandon.
Abandonné.

(C) **Return to sender. Return charges guaranteed.**
Renvoyé à l'expéditeur, qui s'engage à payer les frais de retour.

Randall Kraft
(Signature of sender—*Signature de l'expéditeur*)

149 Main Street
(Address of sender—*Adresse de l'expéditeur*)

Washington, D. C., U. S. A.

To -

JOHN CONDORODIS
(Name of addressee—*Nom du destinataire*)

HARILAOU 35
(Street and number—*Rue et numéro*)

ATHENS
(City, Province, State, etc.—*Ville, Province, Département, etc.*)

GREECE
(Country—*Pays*)

RECEIPT OF THE ADDRESSEE
QUITTANCE DU DESTINATAIRE

The undersigned declares he has received
Le   soussigné   déclare   avoir   reçu
the parcel designated on this bulletin
le   colis   décrit   sur le présent bulletin

(Signature du destinataire)

A dispatch note must be completed to cover shipments to certain countries. The sender indicates the alternate disposition of the shipment and attaches the note to the parcel.

cel. Although arrangements vary with different countries, some general observations may be made. The maximum weight usually permitted for international parcel post varies from 11 to 44 pounds. There are two

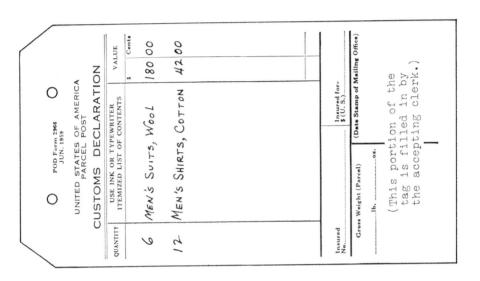

Customs declaration tags must be prepared and attached to international parcel-post shipments. Space is provided on the tag to indicate alternate disposition of the shipment and an itemized list of the contents.

parcel post rates in effect: $.90 for the first two pounds and $.35 for each additional pound to all countries, with the exception of Central America, the Caribbean, Mexico, and Canada, where the rates are $.80 for the first two pounds and $.30 for each additional pound.

Air parcel post is available to many countries. The unit of weight is 4 ounces or fraction thereof. The rate for the United Kingdom is $1.32; Japan, $1.39; West Germany, $1.34; and Colombia, $1.82.

For both regular and air parcel post, additional weight beyond the first unit is charged at lower rates. There are also limitations on the dimensions of parcels.

Registration of parcel post and provisions for payment of indemnity, in case of loss, damage, or rifling in international service are arranged with some countries. Insurance of parcel post is also provided by treaty with many countries, and c.o.d. service may likewise become available.[6]

Certain customs formalities are required in connection with international parcel post shipments, because import duty must be paid on incoming parcels the same as on other shipments of merchandise. Valuation and assessment, as well as collection of duty, are made at specified post offices in the United States where customs officials are located for that purpose.

Cable, Radio, and Telephone[7]

International communications afford a dramatic, almost instantaneous means of transmitting messages over long distances. In this field there are available the submarine cable, radiotelegraph (radio), and radiotelephone (international telephone).

Messages transmitted by these means are those requiring urgency or immediacy. They usually are brief, since the use of these facilities of transmission is expensive. Viewed in the light of the instantaneous nature of these services, however, charges may be quite reasonable, as when emergencies arise. Business conducted through these channels is of such a nature that it cannot wait for the mails — even airmail. Moreover, radiotelegraphy and radiotelephony afford the sole means of contact with ships at sea and with airplanes in flight.

As in the case of correspondence, international wire and radio communications provide a collateral method of conducting export and im-

---

[6]At the time of printing this textbook, no international c.o.d. service is available.
[7]Grateful acknowledgment is expressed to Joseph V. McGuire, Regional Manager, American Cable and Radio System, Philadelphia, for assistance in preparing this section.

port trade. In raw material trades, offer and acceptance of a contract of sale may be completed via cable, radio, or telephone. Generally, however, these facilities are used to complete arrangements already begun through some other trading channel, or to correct a misunderstanding, or to transmit information of immediate importance.

International Agreements. The international character of messages transmitted between the nations of the world early dictated the necessity of arriving at some uniform understanding, and an International Telegraph Convention was entered into in 1875 at St. Petersburg (Leningrad). Then, under the Washington Convention of 1927, questions of international use and allocation of wave frequencies were agreed upon.

International regulation of radio, telegraph, and telephone occurs under the aegis of the International Telecommunications Union, whose membership includes most of the countries of the world. The present agreement derives from the International Telecommunications Convention of Atlantic City, 1947. The regulations adopted at this Convention were later revised, as far as telegraph and telephone services are concerned, by a Conference held in 1949 in Paris.

Cable and Radio Languages. Three "languages" are recognized in cable and radio communication, namely, plain, code, and cipher.

Plain language is that which offers an intelligible meaning in any language that can be expressed in Roman letters. Plain language words are counted at the rate of fifteen letters per word.

Code language is composed of artificial words or bona fide words not having the meaning normally attributed to them and are counted at the rate of five letters per word.

Cipher language consists of messages that contain groups of ciphers, commercial marks, reference numbers, data in price lists and catalogs, etc. Each cipher "word" is counted at five characters to the word. Plain language words in messages containing code or cipher words or groups are still counted at fifteen letters to the word.

Classes of Service and Rates. Under the provisions of the 1949 Paris Conference of the Parties to the International Telecommunications Convention, significant changes in services and rates for international communications became effective July 1, 1950. As presently conducted, two classes of service are available for commercial users, full rate and letter telegram.

Full rate (symbol FR) is an expedited transmission and delivery service written in any of the three languages previously described or combinations thereof. The charges were reduced to approximately 75 percent of the full rate level applicable before July 1, 1950, with a minimum charge for seven words. An example of a cable message, full rate, is:

> BONARD Johannesburg (South Africa). Awaiting further advice concerning alleged misrepresentation of Item 467B in catalog 229S. (signed) Hercules

The chargeable number of words is eighteen (words in parentheses not included). "Misrepresentation" has seventeen letters and therefore counts as two words. The ciphers 467B and 229S (maximum of five characters to the word) and punctuation marks (periods) as used in their normal sense are counted as one word each.

Letter telegram (cable letter or radio letter, symbol LT) is an overnight service for plain language messages only, at 50% of the present full rate, with a minimum charge of 22 words.

Radiophoto is also available as a means of transmitting by radio to points overseas, from the gateway cities in the United States, exact reproductions of photographs, drawings, legal and commercial documents, signatures, chemical formulas, musical scores, and messages written in Arabic, Hebrew, and other non-English characters. The rates for radiophoto transmission are based on the area of the material transmitted, with a minimum charge of approximately $25 for an area of slightly more than 23 square inches.

International Telex service has become an important factor in international communications. This is a "direct" service between anyone having either Western Union Telex or Bell Teletype equipment in their offices for messages to anyone throughout the world having Telex equipment in their office. It costs either $2, $3, or $4 per minute, depending on where the message is being sent, with a minimum charge for three minutes in certain countries.

There has been a general downward trend in the rate levels for international cable, radio, and telephone communications, as a result of improvements and simplification in service. All destinations throughout the world have been divided into four rate groups; and in addition, the rates apply uniformly to all communications offices in the United States. Examples of these four levels of rates for cable and radio services are:

REPRESENTATIVE CABLE AND RADIO RATES BETWEEN ANY UNITED STATES COMMUNICATIONS OFFICE

and	Rates Per Word	
	Full Rate (Minimum 7 words)	Cable or Radio Letter (Minimum 22 words)
Great Britain..........	.21	.10½
Germany.............	.25	.12½
Colombia.............	.31	.15½
Japan...............	.34	.17

Radiotelephone rates between the United States and foreign countries have also been greatly reduced. When first opened to the public on January 7, 1927, the charge between New York and London was $75 for an initial period of three minutes and $25 for each succeeding minute. The rate has since been reduced to $12 and $4, respectively. Sunday and night rates are lower. Rates to ships at sea vary, depending upon the location of the ship equipped for telephone reception. The same variation in rate applies to airplanes in flight.

Cable and Radio Codes. Reference has been made several times to the use of codes. Cable and radio codes are lists of words that convey a secret meaning. Often a single code word will indicate an entire phrase or sentence. In addition to codes that are published in books and are widely used in commercial transactions, there are also private codes.

Regulations of the International Radio Telegraphic Convention prescribe the methods of approving codes, either for general commercial use or for private use. The Central Bureau at Berne passes on the acceptability of codes and publishes periodically a list of approved codes. In addition, there are many codes in use which have not been submitted to the Central Bureau for approval.

The ends sought by a cable or radio patron in the selection of a code for his use have been set forth as follows:

> Generally speaking a cable user demands of a code (a) adaptability to his correspondence, making it easy for him to code and decode his messages; (b) economy in cable charges; (c) conformity to conditions governing cabling so that there is a minimum liability to mutilation; and (d) acceptability on all communications systems, making it possible to use the code to or from any city in the world.[8]

---

[8]Bureau of International Commerce, *International Communications and the International Telegraph Convention*, Miscellaneous Series No. 121, p. 12.

Included among the commercial codes are those issued in different languages, some being in more than one language. Some codes are universal and some are phrase codes. Examples of general purpose cable codes are ABC Code, 5th, 6th, and 7th Editions; Acme Commodity and Phrase Code; Bentley's Complete Phrase Code; Bentley's Second Edition; Commercial Telegraph Code; Lieber's First; Lombard General Code; New Standard 3-Letter Code; Peterman's International, 3rd Edition; Rudolf Mosse (English) Universal Trade Code; and Western Union 5-Letter Code.

There is also a group of commodity or technical codes such as the Atlas Paper Code; Bunting Cotton Code; Codem Insurance Code; Lombard Shipping Code; Peerless Grain Code; Peterman's Banking Code, 2nd and 3rd; Stock and Bond Code; Universal Lumber Code, 2nd Edition; and many others.

Private codes may be worked out by a concern to fit certain peculiar problems or to meet all of its cable or radio requirements. For example, exporters devise code words to indicate the various products carried in export catalogs; and when salesmen or buyers or branches are employed, additional uses for private code words will be found. Owing to the complexity of the problem, it is advisable to seek advice of officials of the cable and radio companies.

As mentioned in the discussion of correspondence, foreign trading firms place on their stationery the names of codes that they are prepared to use. Moreover, as a means of economizing in the number of words required to indicate the address, it is customary to devise some word of ten letters or less as a cable address, which is also placed on stationery. The use of this word in conjunction with the city where located is sufficient description to permit delivery of a message. Such addresses are registered with the Western Union Telegraph Company in the city where the firm registering engages in business. A fee of $15 per year is charged for each address registered. In New York City, however, the Central Bureau for Registered Addresses takes care of registration for New York firms.

Competition Among Communications Facilities

The cable, wireless telegraph, and radiotelephone are complementary as well as competitive services; each is especially adapted to certain distinct types of service.

The cable transmits "record communications by means of the written message." It is a point-to-point, two-way service between individuals. Radiotelegraph, on the other hand, transmits the same signals in circumstances and to places that the cable does not reach. It is essentially a broadcasting one-way service. Not only does it reach across the seas in all directions, but it also spans great barriers and reaches the airplane and the ship at sea. Photographs, drawings, documents, and other pictorial material are transmitted by radio.

Radiotelephone provides rapid oral communication with all of the advantages this implies. It also reaches some ships at sea. However, both radiotelegraph and radiotelephone are affected by electrical disturbances or by static. Continued service cannot be guaranteed as readily as by submarine cables where breaks are seldom so severe as to cripple a line. The telephone service is also subject to fading and all radio broadcasting, whether telegraphic or telephonic, does not possess the secrecy of the cable. Science has, however, afforded a means whereby spoken messages are "scrambled" in order to render them unintelligible en route; and by the use of radio beams, point-to-point service is partially provided. On the other hand, wireless cannot be interrupted by cutting or breaking as is the case with cables.

Summary

1. Correspondence in international marketing may be used as a method of doing business (mail order), but it is chiefly employed to facilitate business transactions.
2. Correspondence with business firms overseas is expected to be conducted in a more leisurely and thorough manner than is common in domestic correspondence. There should be individual appeal, courtesy, and accuracy throughout.
3. Correspondence should be promptly taken care of. Special stationery may be used. Filing may be a problem due to the peculiar names of firms and places.
4. Translations may be made by the trading company's staff or by professionals. While English is used extensively, other languages, chiefly Spanish, French, and German, are also used.
5. International postal agreements provide for the flow of international correspondence and parcel post.
6. Cables, radio, and telephone are additional means of rapid communication, even instantaneous (in both directions) in the case of the telephone. Regulations governing the international use of these communications facilities are provided by intergovernment agreement.
7. Cable and radio recognize the use of three languages — plain, code, and cipher. Code books are available to facilitate economy in cable and radio communication. Many of these are commercial codes that are offered for sale. While cable, radio, and telephone appear to compete, each offers its respective advantages to the user.

QUESTIONS

1. As the export manager for a firm manufacturing trademarked hand tools, develop a manual of instructions for use by the correspondents employed in your office. Divide your manual into the following parts:
   (a) Courtesy.
   (b) Choice of language and words.
   (c) Length of letters.
   (d) "Copy" or "copied" principle.
   (e) Use of special stationery.
   (f) Filing.
2. From the standpoint of an international trader, explain the differences between airmailed letters, cable messages, radio messages, and telephone conversations.
3. Define the several languages authorized for international cable and radio communication.
4. Describe the classes of service offered by international cable and radio companies.

PROBLEMS

1. If it is possible for you to do so, examine some correspondence files of an exporting firm. Check your findings with the correspondence principles discussed in this chapter. Do the same with the correspondence files of an importing concern. Now compare your observations as between the exporter's and the importer's correspondence.
2. Locate a cable code book in a library or the office of an international trading company. From this book, code the following full-rate message in the shortest possible number of chargeable code "words."
   Mendeco, Barranquilla (Colombia) Expect to arrive July thirteenth with full details of proposition submitted by Foster. Do not leave until I have a chance to discuss the matter personally with you. (Your name).
3. From the offices of the telegraph and telephone companies, compile the basic rates for the different services offered to Santiago, Chile; Manila, Philippine Republic; Cairo, Egypt; and Oslo, Norway.

COLLATERAL READINGS

Dartnell International Trade Handbook, The. Chicago: The Dartnell Corporation, 1963.

Exporters' Encyclopaedia. New York: Thomas Ashwell and Co., Inc., annual.

Heck, Harold J. *Foreign Commerce.* New York: McGraw-Hill Book Company, Inc., 1953. Chapter 6.

Horn, Paul V. *International Trade Principles and Practices,* Third Edition. New York: Prentice-Hall, Inc., 1951. Chapter 17.

MacDonald, Philip. *Practical Exporting.* New York: Ronald Press Company, 1949. Chapters 6 and 7.

Pratt, E. E. *Modern International Commerce.* New York: Allyn and Bacon, Inc., 1956. Chapter 7.

Rosenthal, Morris. *Techniques of International Trade.* New York: McGraw-Hill Book Company, Inc., 1950. Part IX.

United States Post Office Department. *The Postal Manual.* Washington, D.C.: Government Printing Office, annual.

Wyman, Walter F. *Export Merchandising.* New York: McGraw-Hill Book Company, Inc., 1922. Chapter 15.

CHAPTER 21

INTERNATIONAL PRICING AND PRICE QUOTATIONS

Several important aspects of merchandise prices and price levels have necessarily been discussed in connection with other phases of the export and import trade. The general relationship between foreign price levels and trade balances was referred to in Chapter 2; price and quality considerations as market survey factors, in Chapter 3; while the relationship between prices and foreign exchange will be discussed in Chapter 32. The purpose at this point is to define the several types of prices and of price quotations used in international marketing.

United States Dollar and Foreign Currency Quotations

International marketing price quotations may be made in terms of the currency of the exporting country or that of the importing country or of a third country. Price quotations in United States dollars were more prevalent after the World War I period than formerly because the dollar was well known and was a relatively stable currency in comparison with the currencies of many foreign countries, and because American international banking facilities were improved. The direct exchange of commercial bills between the United States and many sections of the world became prevalent. In the years during and immediately following World War II, the United States dollar, along with a few other currencies (Swiss franc, Canadian dollar, Swedish kroner) were the only international currencies sufficiently stable to be used in American international marketing quotations. Now that foreign currencies have reached a stage of stability, the pound sterling has resumed its former position as a major international currency, and, with the United States dollar, accounts for a large proportion of pricing in international trade.

Price quotations in terms of the currency of the exporting country are advantageous to the exporter because they reduce his foreign exchange risks, facilitate the prompt determination of his profits, and, if his own currency is stable, reduce the necessity of frequent price changes. His exchange risks, when quoting in foreign currency, may in many instances be minimized by hedging in the foreign exchange market or by taking the other precautions discussed in Chapter 32. Hedging may be impossible, however, because of the absence of an open exchange market, and other precautions may be unreliable or difficult to execute.

The importer may favor price quotations in the currency of the exporting country if he foresees an additional speculative profit due to an expected exchange fluctuation before settlement, or because he believes that the assumption of exchange risks by him will affect the price quotation favorably. He frequently prefers purchasing at prices quoted in his own national currency, however, and in order to promote sales, the exporter may grant his request. Quotations in the currency of the importing country shift the risk of exchange fluctuations to the exporter. They enable the importer to compute his profits, to announce his resale prices promptly, and also more readily to compare price quotations received from the competitive exporters of different foreign countries. Custom, moreover, may largely determine the prevailing practice in particular trades, and the danger of nonpayment of bills due to unfortunate exchange speculation by importers may at times cause the exporter to favor foreign currency price quotations.

The practice of quoting prices in the currency of a third country is at times dictated by custom originally based upon sound reasons; and, in some instances, these reasons may be operative at the present time. When the currencies of both the exporting and the importing country are unstable, or when the banking facilities of a third country are depended upon for financial settlement, it may be desirable to quote prices in the currency of a third country. Pounds sterling, for example, were widely used by all countries prior to World War I, and United States dollars immediately following World War II.

Quoted Prices. Quoted prices in international marketing are generally based upon the established domestic price. There is no normal reason for quoting a higher or a lower price to a foreign customer simply because he is foreign.

If prices to foreign customers are lowered, there may be several good reasons for doing this. One of these may be the price level in the foreign country. If the market is one in which purchasing power is low, it may be necessary or desirable to reduce the quoted price in order to sell. Or, competition may be such that prices must be reduced in order to be able to compete. Finally, an exporting firm may have calculated that the cost of producing exported products is lower than for domestic products on the theory that overhead costs have already been absorbed in domestic prices; and, the export market is a kind of added or extra market that does not have the domestic overhead to bear. On this basis, the export price may be profitable to the company, even though it is lower than the domestic price.

Quoting export prices at levels lower than domestic prices is technically known as dumping. Generally speaking, only the industrial nations of the world penalize imports that are sold at dumped prices.

On the other hand, the export price may be higher than the domestic price on the theory that the export market is special and unreliable. This is a somewhat opportunistic attitude whereby the foreign customer pays more as a privilege to buy the imported product. In times of shortage and of war, export prices may be much higher than domestic prices due to the operation of the law of supply and demand.

International Price Quotations and Terms. Many of the technical terms used in international marketing are different from those prevailing in domestic commerce, and lack of uniformity still prevails to such a degree that confusion and misunderstanding sometimes result in trade disputes. Some export and import price quotations are not defined uniformly, even though American international marketing organizations, the International Chamber of Commerce, and the International Law Association have endeavored to standardize or clarify them.

International marketing price quotations and terms indicate the place of delivery, or more specifically, define:

> 1. The transportation and related charges and cost items included in the price.
> 2. The respective duties of seller and buyer.
> 3. Their respective liability in case of loss or damage.

As the several most commonly quoted prices are defined below, the reader will be able to distinguish between them as to the costs included in each and the respective duties and liabilities of the exporter and importer; but it should be obvious that no one of the quotations can be held up as preferable under all conditions. Under normal competitive conditions, few exporters can insist upon a particular quotation to the exclusion of others that may be requested by their customers. Importers may also be influenced greatly by their knowledge of costs, by the business arrangements that they maintain in the exporting countries in which they make their purchases, by customs, and by other considerations.

In December, 1919, a group of influential American international marketing organizations[1] recommended to manufacturers and exporters that the "use of abbreviated forms of export price quotations be abandoned, and that such terms be written out in full." Recognizing that this practice would probably not be accepted generally, however, they recommended the use of certain standardized abbreviated terms and definitions in the hope that they would be so generally adopted as to greatly reduce the danger of confusion and controversy. These terms and definitions became known as standard, even though they were not universally accepted.

On July 30, 1941, a joint committee of the Chamber of Commerce of the United States, the National Council of American Importers, and the National Foreign Trade Council changed and clarified the "American Foreign Trade Definitions" of 1919 in various respects by adopting the so-called "Revised American Foreign Trade Definitions — 1941." As these definitions have "no legal status at law unless there is specific legislation providing for them, or unless they are confirmed by court decisions,"[2] the joint committee suggests "that sellers and buyers agree to their acceptance as part of the contract of sale. These revised definitions will then become legally binding upon all parties." The definitions are similar to those published by the International Chamber of Commerce[3] but differ from them in some respects, and the terminology used also differs somewhat.

Price quotations, however, may still be interpreted variously by American manufacturers, exporters, and importers. Further confusion results from interpretations placed upon them by foreign exporters, importers, and by requests on the part of foreign exporters and importers that prices be quoted in abbreviated terminology not used in the United

---

[1]National Foreign Trade Council, Chamber of Commerce of United States of America, National Association of Manufacturers, American Manufacturers' Export Association, Philadelphia Commercial Museum, American Exporters' and Importers' Association, Chamber of Commerce of the State of New York, New York Produce Exchange, and New York Merchants Association.

[2] *Revised American Foreign Trade Definitions — 1941.* This source has been used throughout the chapter for all quoted references to price quotations, unless otherwise indicated.

[3]International Chamber of Commerce, *Trade Terms* (1929); *International Rules for the Interpretation of Trade Terms* (1936).

States. In the import trade, except on the part of experienced importers, the likelihood of confusion resulting from the use of foreign interpretations is particularly great because import prices are quoted by foreign manufacturers and exporters.

Throughout this discussion, examples of each price quotation will be cited. The assumed costs common to all examples are as follows:

Value of shipment, including export packing,
    f.o.b. factory, St. Louis, Missouri $1,000.00
Railroad export freight to Philadelphia 150.00
Ocean steamship freight charges 235.50
Marine insurance 2.50
Freight forwarder, including fees 12.00
Import duties in the Netherlands 200.00

Note: If credit is granted on the transaction, interest costs would be added. If war risk insurance is desired, the cost of such insurance would be added.

Ex (Point of Origin) Price. The price quotation under which the exporter's liability for loss or damage, his duties, and the costs included in the export price are at a minimum is the ex (point of origin) price. This price is also referred to as ex factory, ex mill, ex mine, ex plantation, ex warehouse, etc. (named point of origin), in the revised American rules and in the rules of the International Chamber of Commerce. The latter also recognizes the term "ex works."

> *Example:* Price quoted is $1,000, ex factory, St. Louis, Missouri.

The seller's responsibility and costs end at his factory. Although the buyer literally is called upon to "pick up" his shipment, the seller does render assistance at the buyer's request. This assistance comprises the shipment of the merchandise from St. Louis and obtaining a clean bill of lading[4] covering same. The route to the seaboard is to be selected by the buyer who, again, may seek the seller's assistance.

---

[4]A clean bill of lading (shipping document) is one that bears no superimposed clauses expressly declaring a defective condition of the goods or packaging. *Uniform Customs and Practice for Documentary Commercial Credits,* Article 16.

Under the revised American rules, the seller "bears all costs and risks of the goods until such time as the buyer is obliged to take delivery thereof"; and to "render the buyer at the buyer's request and expense, assistance in obtaining the documents issued in the country of origin, which the buyer may require either for purposes of exportation, or of importation at destination." The buyer in turn must "take delivery of the goods as soon as they have been placed at his disposal at the agreed place on the date or within the period fixed; pay all export taxes, or other fees or charges, if any, levied because of exportation; bear all costs and risks of the goods from the time when he is obliged to take delivery thereof; and pay all costs and charges incurred in obtaining the documents issued in the country of origin, or of shipment, or of both, which may be required either for purposes of exportation, or of importation at destination."

F.o.b. (Free on Board) Prices. In international marketing a wide range of f.o.b. prices are quoted. Some of them require loading of the exported or imported wares on railroad cars, lighters, or other conveyances at the seaboard, and still others require delivery on board international carriers that may or may not be at the seaboard.

F.o.b. (Named Inland Carrier at Named Inland Point of Departure). One of the abbreviations recommended in the revised American rules referred to above is f.o.b. (named inland carrier at named inland point of departure). This quotation is similar to the f.o.r. (free on rail) and f.o.t. (free on truck) (named departure point) quotations defined by the International Chamber of Commerce, although its definition is not exactly the same as that of the revised American rules. The latter require the seller either to load the goods in freight car or other conveyance or to deliver them to the inland carrier for loading; to provide a clean bill of lading or other transportation receipt on a freight collect basis; to be responsible for loss or damage until the goods have been loaded into the car or other conveyance and a clean bill of lading or transportation receipt has been obtained; and to assist the buyer, at his request, in obtaining the documents needed for exportation or importation.

The buyer, under this price quotation, must be "responsible for all movement of the goods from inland point of loading and all transportation costs; pay export taxes, or other fees or charges, if any levied because of the exportation; be responsible for loss or damage, or both, incurred after loading at named inland point of departure; and pay all costs and charges incurred in obtaining the documents issued in the country of origin, or of shipment, or of both, which may be required for purposes of exportation, or of importation at destination.''

Example: Price quoted is $1,000, f.o.b. cars (truck, barge, plane), St. Louis, Missouri.

Here, the seller is *responsible* for placing the merchandise on the kind of carrier named and for providing a clean bill of lading. There may be a hauling charge or a heavy lift charge or a delay that might entail penalties (demurrage) before the merchandise is placed in the custody of the carrier. In such ways, this quotation would include more costs than in the case of the ex warehouse quotation, and the price would be increased to include such costs. Thus, the use of the f.o.b. price quotation does impose more responsibility on the seller than the ex (point of origin) price.

F.o.b. (Named Inland Carrier at Named Inland Point of Departure, Freight Prepaid or Allowed). The revised American definitions recognize two additional f.o.b. quotations under which the shipper's responsibilities do not extend beyond the inland point of departure. When quoting an f.o.b. (named inland carrier at named inland point of departure) freight prepaid to (named point of exportation) price, the seller's obligations are those referred to in connection with an f.o.b. (named inland carrier at named inland point of departure), except that he is required to provide a clean bill of lading or transportation receipt issued on the basis of freight prepaid to the port of export. The buyer's obligations also remain the same, except that he does not pay freight from the inland point to the port of export.

The seller, under an f.o.b. (named inland carrier at named inland point of departure), freight allowed to (named point) quotation, also retains the same obligations as those listed above, except that the transportation charges to the port of export are included in the price but are then deducted from his invoice. The buyer's obligations likewise remain unchanged, except that he pays the freight charges to the port of export which the seller had deducted from his invoice.

> *Example:* Price quoted is $1,150, f.o.b. cars St. Louis, Missouri, freight prepaid (or allowed) to Philadelphia, Pennsylvania.

The quotation is basically the same as the simple f.o.b. cars St. Louis, Missouri, quotation. The seller, however, prepays or allows for the freight to Philadelphia. He assumes no responsibility for the shipment from St. Louis to Philadelphia, only the cost of shipping. This is a valid and valuable distinction. Losses may occur enroute and even if they are fully compensated by the carrier, certain procedures and waiting are required in order to present a claim.

Under the "freight prepaid" version of this quotation, the railroad freight charges are included in the price, as witnessed by a prepaid clean bill of lading. In the case of the "freight allowed" version, the freight charges are also included in the price but they are paid by the buyer, who then deducts these charges when paying the invoice. Therefore, under "freight prepaid," the buyer's *net* price is $1,150, while under "freight allowed," it is $1,000 ($1,150 less allowance of $150).

F.o.b. (Named Inland Carrier at Named Point of Exportation). An f.o.b. price quotation going a step further is the f.o.b. (named inland carrier at named point of exportation) quotation defined in the revised American rules. It was formerly known as an f.o.b. cars (named point on seaboard) quotation, and is similar to the free (named port of shipment) quotation defined by the International Chamber of Commerce.

The revised American rules again require the shipper to load the goods into the railroad car or other conveyance or to deliver them to the inland carrier for loading, and to render the customary assistance to the buyer, upon his request, as to needed documents. He must also provide a clean bill of lading or transportation receipt from the inland carrier. In addition, however, he must pay all transportation costs to the port of export and be responsible for loss and damage until the goods arrive in the car or other inland conveyance at this port.

The buyer is responsible for all movement from the inland conveyance at the port and for loss and damage incurred after arrival of the goods in the inland conveyance at the port. He must also pay export taxes or other charges levied because of exportation and all costs and charges incurred in obtaining necessary documents.

> *Example:* Price quoted is $1,150, f.o.b. cars Philadelphia, for export.

In this quotation the seller not only includes the transportation costs from St. Louis to Philadelphia, but he also assumes the responsibility for this movement. Billing the shipment "for export" assures two things: (1) that the shipment will be delivered at the steamer pier or railroad lighterage point at no extra expense (although there could be) and (2) that the export freight rate will apply on the rail haul. This rate may be lower than the corresponding domestic rail rate.

F.o.b. Vessel (Named Port of Shipment). The last named f.o.b. quotation should in no case be confused with the f.o.b. vessel (named port of shipment) quotation provided for in the revised American rules or the f.o.b. (named port of shipment) quotation defined by the International Chamber of Commerce rules. Although these definitions are similar, use of the terminology of the latter in the United States may lead to misunderstandings unless the exact point at which the liability of the American exporter ends and that of the foreign importer begins is specified.

The f.o.b. vessel (named port of shipment) quotation as defined in the revised American rules requires the seller to "pay all charges incurred in placing goods actually on board the vessel designated and provided by, or for, the buyer on the date or within the period fixed; provide clean ship's receipt or on-board bill of lading; be responsible for any loss or damage, or both, until goods have been placed on board the vessel on the date or within the period fixed; and render the buyer, at the buyer's request and expense, assistance in obtaining the documents issued in the country of origin, or of shipment or of both, which the buyer may require either for purposes of exportation, or of importation at destination." In our analysis, the services of a foreign freight forwarder are used. Since this functionary arranges for the movement and transfer of cargo to ocean steamers, he is engaged by the seller, and the expense for his services is not included in the quoted price, but absorbed or added to charges on f.o.b. quotations.

The buyer is required to "give seller adequate notice of name, sailing date, loading berth of, and delivery time to, the vessel; bear the additional costs incurred and all risks of the goods from the time when the seller has placed them at his disposal if the vessel named by him fails to arrive or to load within the designated time; handle all subsequent movement of the goods to destination: (a) provide and pay for insurance; and (b) provide and pay for ocean and other transportation; pay export taxes, or other fees or charges, if any, levied because of exportation; be responsible for any loss or damage or both, after goods have been loaded on board the vessel; and pay all costs and charges incurred in obtaining the documents, other than clean ship's receipt or bill of lading, issued in the country of origin, or of both, which may be required either for purposes of exportation, or of importation at destination."

> *Example:* Price quoted is $1,150, f.o.b. vessel Philadelphia.

Here the seller pays the costs and assumes the responsibility for the shipment from his factory in St. Louis to a place on board a vessel in Philadelphia. The actual price quoted is the same as quoted for the f.o.b. cars Philadelphia, for export price quotation. This is on the basis of no extra costs from the cars to the place on board the vessel. There could be a difference in cost, however, if special loading (grain) or any heavy lift were required and charged for. There may also be a long and expensive interval between the arrival of freight cars at the port of Philadelphia for export and the loading on a vessel in Philadelphia. For example, a sudden waterfront strike could delay loading. The exporter (seller) is responsible for placing the merchandise on the vessel, regardless of delays at the port. Moreover, the $12.00 forwarder fee is added to the charges (or absorbed) but does not appear in the price quotation.

In bulk trades, such as grain and coal, the buyer generally furnishes the vessel. In ordinary business, the seller ships on any common carrier. If he is a contractor with a shipping conference operating in the trade in question, he is obliged to ship on one of the vessels of the member lines.

F.a.s. (Free Alongside) Price. Still another quotation that does not extend delivery beyond the port of export is the f.a.s. vessel (named port of shipment) quotation as defined in the revised American rules or the similar f.a.s. (named port of shipment) quotation included in the terms defined by the International Chamber of Commerce. This quotation includes delivery of the goods free alongside, but not on board, the vessel at the port of export.

Under the revised American definitions, the seller must "place goods alongside vessel or on dock designated and provided by, or for, buyer on the date or within the period fixed; pay any heavy lift charges, where necessary to this point; provide clean dock or ship's receipt; be responsible for any loss or damage or both, until goods have been delivered alongside the vessel on the dock," and render the usual assistance, at the buyer's request, in obtaining necessary documents.

The buyer is required to give adequate notice to the seller as to the vessel's name, sailing date, loading berth and delivery time, and he must "handle all subsequent movement of the goods from alongside the vessel," including providing or arranging payment for insurance, ocean and other transportation, demurrage or storage charges in warehouses or on the wharf, and heavy lift charges, if any, for loading on board vessel. He is responsible for loss and damage "while the goods are on a lighter or other conveyance alongside vessel within reach of its loading tackle, or on the dock awaiting loading, or until actually loaded on board the vessel, and subsequent thereto."

The buyer is also required to pay export taxes or other charges levied because of exportation and all charges incurred in obtaining necessary documents. Differences in practice, in some trades, caused the joint committee in charge of the revised definitions to urge the buyer and seller to have an understanding "as to whether the buyer will obtain the ocean freight space, and marine and war risk insurance, as is his obligation, or whether the seller agrees to do this for the buyer."

Example: Price quoted is $1,150, f.a.s. vessel Philadelphia.

This quotation differs from the f.o.b. vessel quotation since the time and cost of loading, if any, are not included in the f.a.s. price quotation. In ordinary trade, f.a.s. is equivalent to f.o.b. as far as costs are concerned, but there may be great differences otherwise. If the merchandise sits on a steamship pier waiting for a vessel on which to load it, this waiting may be expensive. Under f.o.b. price quotations, the seller pays for the waiting time; under f.a.s. terms, the buyer pays for it.

In bulk trades where a buyer charters and furnishes his own vessel, the differences can be very great. Vessel demurrage charges are expensive and idle time not chargeable to the vessel is paid by either the buyer or seller, depending upon the quotation.

C.i.f. (Cost, Insurance, and Freight) Price. In contrast with the above price quotations, there are several that carry delivery and costs beyond the port of exportation. The most commonly quoted of these is the c.i.f. (named point of destination) quotation, the feature letters representing cost, insurance, and freight. The revised American definition, which is similar to but somewhat different from that of the International Chamber of Commerce, requires the seller to provide and pay for transportation to the port of discharge, including inland transportation to the port of export, port handling charges at this port, and ocean freight to the foreign port of destination. He must also provide and pay for marine insurance and export taxes or other fees of charges levied because of exportation.

The seller is required to provide war risk insurance "as obtainable in seller's market at time of shipment at buyer's expense, unless seller has agreed that buyer provide for war risk coverage." He must obtain a clean bill of lading to the port of destination and an insurance policy or certificate and dispatch them promptly to the buyer or his agent. Where an "on-board" ocean bill of lading is required, the seller is held responsible for loss and damage until the goods are on board the vessel, and where a "received-for-shipment" ocean bill of lading may be tendered, his liability continues "until the goods have been delivered into the custody of the ocean carrier." The seller must also provide, at the buyer's request and expense, certificates of origin, consular invoices, or other documents that "the buyer may require for importation of the goods in the country of destination and where necessary, for their passage in transit through another country."

The buyer, in case of the c.i.f. quotation, is required to accept the bill of lading and insurance documents when presented; "receive the goods upon arrival, handle and pay for all subsequent movement of the goods, including taking delivery from vessel in accordance with bill of lading clauses and terms; pay all costs of landing, including any duties, taxes, and other expenses at named point of destination"; pay for war risk insurance provided by seller; and pay the cost of the certificate of origin, consular invoices, and similar required documents. The buyer's liability for loss and damage begins where, as defined above, that of the seller ends, namely, on board vessel or in custody of ocean carrier at port of exportation.

The joint committee, however, recognizes certain variations in practice and advises that sellers and buyers should agree in advance as to the disposition of miscellaneous expenses, such as weighing or inspection charges; cost of certificates of origin, consular invoices, etc.; interest charges that the revised American rules include in c.i.f. prices; war risk insurance, and whatever procedure is to be followed in case goods are shipped freight collect.

> *Example:* Price quoted is $1,400, c.i.f. Rotterdam.

This quotation includes practically all the costs from St. Louis, Missouri, via Philadelphia, Pennsylvania, to Rotterdam, Netherlands. The responsibility of the seller, however, ends at Philadelphia, either on board the vessel or alongside the vessel, depending on whether an on-board bill of lading or a received-for-shipment bill of lading is called for.

The costs included in the quotation are the f.a.s. or f.o.b. vessel Philadelphia costs plus ocean freight and marine insurance to Rotterdam. While the buyer is responsible for war risk insurance and fees for foreign government documents, these are commonly paid (advanced) by the seller and added into the calculation of the c.i.f. price.

If a vessel should sink with c.i.f. cargo on board, the buyer (not the seller) would be obliged to present claims. Sellers, however, may prefer to handle these claims if, according to the method of payment, title has been retained in the name of the seller or his bank.

Under certain circumstances, the buyer or the seller may prefer a c.&f. (named point of destination) quotation. As defined in the revised American definitions, this quotation differs from the c.i.f. (named point of destination) quotation in that it does not include the cost of marine insurance, and does not require the seller to provide marine insurance and dispatch a marine insurance certificate or policy to the buyer or the buyer's agent.

Miscellaneous Price Quotations. The revised American rules contain definitions of two additional price quotations, neither of which is used extensively in the export trade of the United States. Both carry the transaction beyond the points referred to in connection with previously mentioned quotations.

Ex Dock (Named Port of Importation). The so-called ex dock (named port of importation) quotation includes "the cost of the goods and all additional costs necessary to place the goods on the dock at the named port of importation, duty paid, if any."

It differs from a c.i.f. (named point of destination) quotation in that the seller is also required to pay for war risk insurance, unless otherwise agreed upon; pay the costs of certificates of origin, consular invoices, and similar documents; pay "all costs of landing, including wharfage, landing charges, and taxes, if any;" pay all costs of customs entry and also customs duties and other taxes applicable to imports; and be liable for loss and damage "until the expiration of the free time allowed on the dock at the named port of importation."

The buyer is required merely to take delivery on this dock within the free time period, and to "bear the cost and risk of the goods if delivery is not taken within the free time allowed." In the United States this quotation and modifications such as ex quay or ex pier are not commonly employed in export trade, but they are used in the import trade.

Example: Price quoted is $1,600, ex dock Rotterdam.

This quotation adds to the costs included in the c.i.f. quotation, the war risk insurance, foreign government documentary fees, import duties in the Netherlands, and unloading costs, if any, in the Netherlands. It also adds to the responsibility of the seller because he is now responsible until the expiration of free time on the dock in Rotterdam. In this particular example, war risk insurance was not requested and there are no government documentary fees.

Again, this quotation is important in the bulk trades where chartered ships are used and heavy wharfage, dockage, demurrage, and other fees occur. Such a quotation is probably never made in ordinary trade (general cargo) as distinguished from bulk trades, both dry and liquid.

F.o.b. (*Named Inland Point in Country of Importation*). Another price quotation is the f.o.b. (named inland point in country of importation) quotation that includes all transportation costs to the inland point abroad at which delivery is to be made. It also includes all the other costs included in the ex dock quotation. The seller's liability for loss and damage continues "until arrival of goods on conveyance at the named inland point in the country of importation." The buyer is required to take delivery promptly from the freight car or other conveyance at the inland destination, to bear any costs that may arise after arrival there, and to be responsible for loss and damage occurring after arrival.

Other Types of Price Quotations. Other types of export or import price quotations such as c.i.f.&c. (cost, insurance, freight, and commission), c.i.f.c.&i. (cost, insurance, freight, commission, and interest), and c.i.f. landed (cost, insurance, freight, landed) are sometimes quoted; but they are not defined in the revised American rules, and the joint committee discourages their use unless a definite understanding as to their meaning is arrived at in advance by both the seller and buyer. Additional miscellaneous prices not frequently quoted in the export trade are freight or carriage paid to (named point of destination), free or free delivered (named point of destination), and ex ship (named port), which are defined by the International Chamber of Commerce.[5]

Comparison of Price Quotations. As a clear means of comparing the different price quotations that have been described, Chart 21-1 shows succinctly the responsibility and the charges, as between seller and buyer, for each step in an international marketing transaction.

---

[5]*International Rules for the Interpretation of Trade Terms* (1936).

Chart 21-1

"REVISED AMERICAN FOREIGN TRADE DEFINITIONS—1941" WITH CERTAIN PRACTICAL ADDITIONS

BREAKDOWN DIVIDING RESPONSIBILITY AND CHARGES BETWEEN BUYER AND SELLER, AS PERTAINING TO THE AMERICAN EXPORT TRADE ON THE COMMONLY USED SERVICES

Service	Ex Point of Origin — Resp.	Ex Point of Origin — Chg.	F.o.b. Named Inland Carrier Named Inland Point of Departure — Resp.	Chg.	F.o.b. Named Inland Carrier Named Inland Point Freight Prepaid to Named Point of Exportation — Resp.	Chg.	F.o.b. Named Inland Carrier Named Inland Point Freight Allowed to Point of Exportation — Resp.	Chg.	F.o.b. Named Inland Carrier Named Point of Exportation — Resp.	Chg.	F.o.b. Vessel Named Port of Shipment — Resp.	Chg.	F.a.s. Named Port of Shipment — Resp.	Chg.	F.o.b. Named Inland Point in Country of Importation — Resp.	Chg.	C. & F. Named Point of Destination — Resp.	Chg.	C.i.f. Named Point of Destination — Resp.	Chg.
Warehouse storage charges	S	S	S	S	S	S	S	S	S	S	S	S	S	S	S	S	S	S	S	S
Warehouse labor charges	S	S	S	S	S	S	S	S	S	S	S	S	S	S	S	S	S	S	S	S
Export packing	*	*	*	*	*	*	*	*	*	*	*	*	*	*	*	*	*	*	*	*
Loading at origin	S	S	S	S	S	S	S	S	S	S	S	S	S	S	S	S	S	S	S	S
Inland freight	B	B	B	B	S	S	S	**	S	S	S	S	S	S	S	S	S	S	S	S
Transportation at port	B	B	B	B	B	B	B	B	S	S	S	S	S	S	S	S	S	S	S	S
Storage at port	B	B	B	B	B	B	B	B	S	S	S	S	S	S	S	S	S	S	S	S
Forwarder's fee	B	B	B	B	B	B	B	B	S	S	S	S	S	S	S	S	S	S	S	S
Consular fee*	B	B	B	B	B	B	B	B	B	B	B	B	B	B	S	S	S	S	S	S
Loading on ocean carrier	B	B	B	B	B	B	B	B	B	B	S	S	B	****	S	S	S	S	S	S
Oceanfreight	B	B	B	B	B	B	B	B	B	B	B	B	B	B	S	S	S	S	S	S
Marine insurance*	B	B	B	B	B	B	B	B	B	B	B	B	B	B	S	S	B	B	S	S
Charges in foreign port	B	B	B	B	B	B	B	B	B	B	B	B	B	B	S	****	S	S	S	S
Customs duties & taxes abroad	B	B	B	B	B	B	B	B	B	B	B	B	B	B	S	***	B	B	B	B

* Export packing, war risk insurance, and consular fees are sometimes controversial, depending on the contract of sale.

** Shipped "Collect" and deducted from the invoice amount.

*** Seller is also responsible for foreign inland freight.

**** Prior to delivery on dock subsequent charges for account of buyer.

ABBREVIATIONS

Resp.........Responsibility
Chg..........Charges
S............Seller
B............Buyer
F.o.b........Free on board
F.a.s........Free alongside ship
C. & F.......Cost and freight
C.i.f........Cost, insurance, and freight

Source: George W. Tomlinson, Pointers on Export Letters of Credit, The First National (now First Pennsylvania) Bank (Philadelphia, 1953).

This presentation patterned after the one used by Dr. Roland L. Kramer, Professor of Commerce and Transportation, Wharton School, University of Pennsylvania.

List and Net Prices

International marketing prices may be quoted either as net or as list prices. A *net price* indicates that a definite f.o.b., c.i.f., or other quotation not subject to trade or quantity discounts of any kind is made by the exporter. A *list price* is a general price published in a catalog, price list, or advertisement, or otherwise given out by the exporter as the basis for computing the actual or net price to which particular importers, or classes of buyers, or buyers in particular markets are entitled. The difference in the two kinds of prices is a matter of price policy of particular interest to exporters of finished manufactured products rather than to exporters of the great staple commodities of international marketing.

List Prices. List prices facilitate the publication of prices in catalogs or price lists because trade discounts and sometimes quantity discounts are used in connection with them. A catalog or published price schedule containing list prices can be used for a longer period of time than one quoting net prices because the varying requirements of different buyers and markets, and the changes necessitated by changing conditions may be taken into account to some extent in the accompanying discounts. The exporter may authorize a single flat trade discount or a series of trade discounts, such as 30 and 10 percent. The list price provides a price basis giving a general idea as to the exporter's price level. The proper trade discounts can then be applied if his policy is to sell at different prices to different types of buyers in a given market, such as foreign agents, wholesale importers, retailers, or consumers.

List prices also facilitate the use of the same catalog and price list in different markets, the trade discounts being applied so as to take into account net price variations. If conditions should change so as to necessitate a readjustment of prices, it may be possible to make the adjustment by means of the trade discounts without republishing catalogs or printed price lists. Should the exporter adopt a policy of varying prices with a view to attracting large orders, his list prices will also be subject either to a single quantity discount or to a series of quantity discounts varying with the size of the order.

The use of the same catalog and list prices in different markets, however, is complicated when list prices are quoted c.i.f. In this case it is necessary to publish either a separate list price for each port or a schedule of ocean freight rates and marine insurance premiums for use in connection with the exporter's trade discounts and f.o.b. vessel list prices.

Net Prices. An exporter of a manufactured product may transmit net prices direct to customers or he may publish them in catalogs or price lists. The latter may be comparatively short-lived during periods when exchange fluctuations or other conditions compel price readjustments, and the number of markets in which the same catalog and price list is used may be small. Net price quotations, however, have the advantage of simplicity and this is particularly in evidence when c.i.f. quotations are made.

Quantity, Quality, and Time Bases of Price Quotations

Quantity Bases. An international marketing price quotation may be based either on a specified unit or on the shipment as a whole. Unit prices are more prevalent, and it is essential that the unit of quantity be definite. When a price per automobile, tractor, grain binder, or other machine or appliance is quoted, the product itself constitutes a definite unit; but when prices of commodities are quoted in terms of a ton or hundredweight, a barrel or drum or case, a bushel or quarter of grain, a bale of cotton or wool, etc., definition or understanding is essential because quantity units are subject to different interpretations.

When prices are stated on a weight basis, there should be an understanding as to whether the basic weight is the gross weight of the commodity plus packing, or its net weight; whether the weight at shipping point, delivery point, or other agreed point should govern; and whether or not an agreed tare allowance and weight tolerance shall be applicable.

Quality Bases. The quality of the exported or imported wares may also be variously specified in a price quotation. The price quotation may definitely indicate particular grades,[6] standards, degrees of polarization (sugar), types, percentages of mineral content, numbers, or other understood trade designations, or it may indicate known brands or makes. As sales are, however, frequently based upon direct specifications, catalog descriptions, previous sales, etc., it is important that quality designation and determination be defined in the export and import contract.

---

[6]With reference to wheat, one executive in the wheat business declared that "the United States grade standards do not adequately describe the quality of our wheat . . . . Factors used in the grain standards describe only the physical characteristics, most of which have very little relationship to end-use performance." This conclusion was reached as a result of a worldwide sampling survey of the condition of wheat of all exporting countries. See *Journal of Commerce* (July 18, 1963).

Time Bases. One further distinction of importance has to do with the cash or credit terms on which price quotations are based. Cash prices presuppose settlement before shipment, at the time of delivery, or shortly thereafter. If a period of credit is granted on the basis of a cash price, the importer will usually be required to pay interest at the time of settlement of the sales contract.

The extension of credit, however, is so prevalent in international marketing that many export and import prices are quoted on the basis of a stated number of days in the future, and cash discounts may be granted in case settlement is made at an earlier date. When extended into the future, allowance must be made for interest and perhaps also for the increased risk assumed by the exporter. A quotation at "60 days net, 2 percent discount for cash," for example, indicates that the price is based upon a credit period of 60 days without cash discount at the end of that time, but that settlement on a cash basis will entitle the importer to a cash discount of 2 percent. A quotation such as "2 percent 10 days, 60 days net," definitely limits the cash discount to a period of 10 days. Sometimes a series of cash discounts is stated in connection with a credit price for the purpose of encouraging prompt payment. It is an important function of the exporter to decide whether his prices will be quoted on the cash or the credit basis, and to decide upon a policy with respect to interest charges or cash discounts.

Miscellaneous Bases. Price quotations vary also as to the precision with which they fix the price that is to be paid at the time of settlement. Definite or fixed prices are, of course, the most prevalent in international as well as in domestic marketing. The sales contract, however, may provide that the settlement basis shall be the price current in an agreed market for a specified grade or other quality designation at the time of delivery; or that the settlement price of cotton shall be based upon the prevailing price of future contracts on an agreed speculative cotton exchange at the time the cotton buyer exercises his "spinner's option"; or that average prices in a particular market at an agreed time shall govern; or that the basis for settlement shall be the cost of production plus a fixed percentage or "cost plus." Further confusion may arise when the price is based upon a basic grade or grades with permission to deliver other grades subject to agreed price adjustments, as in the case of speculative grain, cotton, or coffee future contracts.

Government Control of Market Prices[7]

Sometimes governments, in their efforts to strengthen the position of certain producers, institute price control in such a way as to bring the artificial level of domestic prices above the free level of international prices. If the products thus supported are also exported, the price at which they are sold is inevitably below the domestic price. Thus, governments engage in dumping when such practices occur. By its price support plan, the United States Government has been pegging the prices of certain agricultural products at artificially high levels. In order to preserve such prices, the United States Government, through the Commodity Credit Corporation, has purchased vast quantities of agricultural products and kept them off the market. The surpluses thus acquired remain in Government warehouses and are disposed of by free distribution for use by educational and hospital institutions at home or by free grants to or by barter transactions with foreign countries.

Under Public Law 480 some of these surpluses have been exported by the United States Government and payment is received in the national currency of the buying country. These transactions are supposed not to interfere with normal trading in the same agricultural commodities by other countries. However, the United States is often guilty of dumping.

Since the depression of the 1930's, efforts have been made by individual government plans or by agreement among a number of governments to improve price levels of agricultural and primary products moving in international trade. Even as early as the pre-World War I period, countries producing coffee, sugar, nitrates, and rubber attempted to control the export prices of these products.

The reasons for these attempts are found in declining prices due to surplus production. If a single country or a group of countries is successful in keeping the quantity that is offered for export sale at a level low enough to justify the artificial price, the plan is likely to be successful. The unexported surplus, however, may become burdensome to the controlling country or countries, and essential production controls may not always be successful. Sources of competition may arise or expand and alternate products may weaken or destroy the price control plan.

For example, the United States cotton price support plan, dating from 1933, resulted in expanded production in alternate countries. As a result, the share of the United States cotton crop that was exported

---

[7]See also Chapter 18.

(formerly known as "King Cotton") dropped from 60 percent prior to 1930 to 23 percent in 1954; but due to a large share of the cotton exported under government aid programs and therefore not priced and sold commercially, the percentage in 1962 had risen again to about 50. This plan represents an effort by a single country to assist its own producers of a product that moves in large volume in international marketing.

Summary

1. International marketing price quotations are different in many respects from price quotations in domestic marketing. Many additional steps and consequent costs are incurred in moving merchandise in international commerce.
2. The American standard quotations and their precise definitions are generally binding on all international marketing with the United States, and they should be thoroughly understood. There are a variety of f.o.b. quotations, starting with f.o.b. named inland carrier at named inland point of departure, for example; f.o.b. cars St. Louis, Missouri; to f.o.b. vessel, named port of exportation. A recognized but nonstandard quotation is f.o.b. named inland point in country of importation. Other varieties of quotations are f.a.s. (free alongside vessel, port of export) and c.i.f. (cost, insurance, freight, point of import in country of importation). On c.i.f. quotations, the exporter's responsibility ends on board or alongside the vessel at port of export, depending upon the agreement.
3. Export and import prices may, as in domestic trade, be quoted as list or net prices. If list prices are quoted, scales of discounts are generally used, depending upon the marketing level to which the quoted price applies.
4. Prices are not always stated in terms of United States dollars. If prices are quoted in foreign currencies, exchange problems are encountered by the exporter.
5. Prices as quoted may be for a single item or for a given measurement (weight). Price quotations also refer to specifically identified merchandise as to quality. Finally, price quotations may be for cash or may include a certain period of credit extension. Discounts for cash may also be offered.
6. Dumping results when goods for export are priced lower than the domestic price for the same goods. In price control schemes, governments may also dump in the export markets.

QUESTIONS

1. Why is it of paramount importance that exporters and importers come to a definite understanding as to the precise meaning of price quotations?
2. Define the meaning of the price quotation symbols f.o.b., f.a.s., and c.i.f.

3. In international marketing, how many f.o.b. quotations can you cite? Explain the precise meaning of each.
4. Under an export quotation "c.i.f. Rio de Janeiro" on a shipment through the port of New Orleans, Louisiana, precisely where does the exporter's responsibility end?
5. Under an import quotation "ex dock San Francisco, California," from Calcutta, India, precisely where does the importer's responsibility begin?
6. Compare list and net prices as to:
   (a) Their meaning.
   (b) Their adaptability to use in international marketing transactions.
7. From an export sales angle, what advantages do you perceive in the quotation of prices in the currency of the buyer's country?
8. Why would an exporter hesitate or refuse to quote prices in foreign currencies?
9. Give examples of the use of unit prices, per ton prices, per drum prices, per bale prices, and per ounce prices.
10. Define dumping. Explain why and how national governments indulge in dumping.

PROBLEMS

1. Calculate the net price for a shipment of goods with a list price of $1,000, and discounts of 40 percent, 20 percent, and 10 percent.
2. Calculate the c.i.f. price to be quoted from the following data:
   Shipment of 90,000 one-half inch galvanized elbows (pipe fittings), packed in barrels.
   Weights and measurements: 12 pounds per 100 pieces; 3,000 pieces per barrel; gross weight per barrel, 390 pounds (including weight of barrel 30 pounds); measurement of barrel 20″ x 20″ x 28″.
   Terms of sale: 60-day sight draft, documents on acceptance (allow 90 days for outstanding funds).
   Price at factory, $35 per 100 pieces plus 50 percent for galvanizing. Discount, 76 percent. Railroad freight allowance, 75 cents per 100 pounds.
   Actual railroad freight rate, l.c.l. $1.25 per 100 pounds.
   Ocean freight, $30 per ton W/M (2,240 pounds or 40 cubic feet). The ship has the option of charging either on the basis of weight or measurement and will use the basis that yields the larger revenue.
   Freight forwarder's fee, $12.00
   Foreign government fees, $3.50
   Marine insurance, .25/$100 value (insure for 110 percent of c.i.f. quotation).
   Interest, 6 percent per annum.
   Bank and collection charges, $\frac{1}{4}$ percent.

COLLATERAL READINGS

Collins, V. D. *World Marketing*. Philadelphia: J. B. Lippincott Company, 1935. Chapter 10.

Dartnell International Trade Handbook, The. Chicago: The Dartnell Corporation, 1963.

de Haas, J. A. *The Practice of Foreign Trade*. New York: McGraw-Hill Book Company, Inc., 1935. Chapter 10.

Exporters' Encyclopaedia. New York: Thomas Ashwell and Co., Inc., annual.

Heck, Harold J. *Foreign Commerce*. New York: McGraw-Hill Book Company, Inc., 1953. Chapter 10.

Horn, Paul V. *International Trade Principles and Practices*, Third Edition. New York: Prentice-Hall, Inc., 1951. Chapters 30 and 31.

MacDonald, Philip. *Practical Exporting*. New York: Ronald Press Company, 1949. Chapters 5 and 12.

Pratt, E. E. *Modern International Commerce*. New York: Allyn and Bacon, Inc., 1956. Chapter 5.

Roorbach, G. B. *Import Purchasing: Principles and Problems*. Chicago and New York: A. W. Shaw Company, 1927. Chapter 11 B.

Rosenthal, Morris. *Techniques of International Trade*. New York: McGraw-Hill Book Company, Inc., 1950. Part I.

Tosdal, H. R. *Problems in Export Sales Management*. New York: McGraw-Hill Book Company, Inc., 1922. Chapter 6.

Towle, Lawrence W. *International Trade and Commercial Policy*. New York and London: Harper & Brothers, 1956. Chapter 26.

CHAPTER 22

PACKING, SHIPPING, AND INSURANCE

Having examined the nature of international marketing price quotations, our analysis will now move to the matter of packing, shipping, and insuring the shipment that we have sold or purchased through the marketing channels described in Parts II and III. Since the contents of this chapter represent a technical subject, the best we can do here is to sketch the main points of which the international trader should be aware.

Packing

American exporters some years ago were widely criticized because of their poor packing, but now they quite generally recognize packing for shipment as a highly important marketing problem. The occasional criticisms now heard are spasmodic and, in general, the quality of American packing is superior to that of any other exporting nation.

The preparation of goods for shipment is clearly the responsibility of the exporter. When he exports directly to foreign customers, he realizes the connection between goodwill and the condition of merchandise upon arrival. He will, moreover, be concerned with complaints arising because of loss or damage resulting from improper packing, since he may become involved in a trade dispute. He may receive packing instructions from his foreign customer and he usually complies with them. If they involve special costs over and above his customary packing, he may arrive at an understanding with his customer as to the payment. If he exports through an American middleman, the manufacturer has a more remote interest in his foreign business and may look no further than the port of export. Unless the middleman intends to repack merchandise reaching him as a domestic shipment, he will supply packing instructions to the manufacturers from whom he purchases export commodities.

The general considerations influencing the packing of shipments destined for overseas markets differ so widely from those applicable in domestic commerce that customary domestic packing, in many instances, becomes quite unsuitable. When overseas export shipments are made by rail or motor from inland points to the seaboard, the container rules and specifications enforced by the railroads in their rate tariffs and in the Uniform Freight Classification are applicable; but it is frequently essential to go beyond these requirements so as to assure safe delivery abroad and to take into account other export packing factors.

The Port of New York Authority

Special loading facilities are employed to stow long railway cars in the hold of a ship. Here a locomotive is being hoisted aboard a vessel for overseas shipment.

Safety In Transportation and Port Handling. With the exception of air express and of shipments to Canada and Mexico via rail and motor lines, United States exports reach foreign destinations by steamship; and if the consignee is located at an interior point, there is a further movement of the shipment. These conditions present a packing problem far more difficult of solution than is experienced in preparing goods for shipment via rail lines in the United States.

It is a well-known fact that the greater the number of handlings to which goods are subjected, the greater becomes the liability to damage. After arrival at the port of export, the shipment is transferred to the vessel; in case the steamer is not available, the goods may be stored until its arrival. Since all ports of the United States are not equipped for the transfer of export shipments directly from freight cars to vessels, much freight must be transferred from cars to steamship pier or vessel on trucks, drays, lighters, or other conveyances. In all of these operations, the goods are subjected to additional handling.[1]

Ship Hazards. The shipment is loaded into the hold of the vessel, usually by means of the ship's machinery, unless the weight is so great that special facilities must be employed. The shipment is then stowed in the hold of the vessel as compactly as possible. Packages that are placed in such a position as to support a number of other packages are necessarily subjected to a severe strain. Moreover, a certain rolling motion of the vessel enhances this strain considerably.

It is not unusual for a ship to have a seven-second rolling period. That is, it goes from the upright position to the extreme angle of heel and back to the upright in just seven seconds. The pitching period for the same vessel could quite possibly be twelve to eighteen seconds. Cargo in the hold then must move exactly as the ship. First as a thrusting piston it reacts against adjacent and super-imposed cargo. Then, as a giant shock absorber, it must arrest the movement of other cargo upon it. Failure to do this work results in crushing, distortion and breakage. Thus, working against dunnage and other pieces in stow during a ten day voyage from sea buoy to sea buoy, a single item of cargo can easily be moved nearly 200 miles in horizontal and vertical planes — and all this without a single day of "boisterous" weather![2]

Unloading Hazards. Upon arrival of the vessel at the port of import, the shipment is subjected to further handling in unloading, passage through the customs, and final removal to its ultimate destination. At

---

[1]The Insurance Company of North America reports that breakage accounts for 19 percent of all of its cargo losses.

[2]Insurance Company of North America, *Export Packing* (Undated, unpaged).

the most important foreign ports, unloading facilities are usually adequate for the expeditious and safe handling of merchandise. This is not always the case, however, and at smaller and less frequented ports the facilities may be antiquated or almost totally lacking.

The West Coast of South America is cited as a conspicuous example of an entire coastal stretch where, because of the formation of the coast line, the direct discharge of cargoes at piers or wharves is the exception rather than the general rule. Vessels frequently lie in the open roadstead, riding at anchor, and the loading and unloading of merchandise is hazardous. When vessels are so situated in the open sea or in harbors without direct access to piers or wharves, they are dependent upon lighter service for unloading. At certain seasons of the year it is extremely hazardous to attempt to discharge, and vessels at some ports may be detained several weeks out in a roaring and rushing roadstead awaiting a favorable opportunity to draw nearer the shore for the purpose of unloading into lighters. It is true that navigation conditions on this coast are unusual, but the necessity of unloading cargo with the aid of lighters, barges, junks, sampans, and other craft is common at outports of other countries.

Interior Hazards. In case the goods are to be delivered at an interior point, further movement and consequent handling are encountered. In some countries, for example, Colombia, the consuming public is mainly located inland, requiring that a considerable quantity of imports be transported for some distance after arrival in the country. In other cases, countries are landlocked and can be reached only through a foreign port. Bolivia and Switzerland are examples of countries of this type.

If interior transportation conditions are adequately developed, no difficult problem is presented. Even then, however, additional handlings of the shipment occur. On the other hand, means of transit may be primitive and the shipment may be subjected to various and severe handlings. Railroads, improved highways, or waterways are not always available, and in their absence beasts of burden are most frequently used.

Main Objectives of Adequate Packing. The keynote of adequate packing designed to carry merchandise safely through transportation and shipping risks obviously is strength. The problem naturally varies according to the commodity, since the susceptibility of an article to damage is a determining factor. Locomotives may not be packed at all, and the same is true of raw materials handled in bulk.

In the first place, a container must be employed that will hold together during the entire trip. The packing used in domestic trade may be satisfactory, or it may require reinforcements by using heavier lumber, cleats, straps, etc., or it may be wholly inadequate. It is inadvisable to learn of the most effective methods of packing solely through experience. There are organizations whose business it is to devise and test the strength and other properties of different types of packing. Considerable progress has been made during recent years in designing wooden containers that are lighter, yet stronger, than those formerly used, and improved fiberboard cartons and plywood boxes that are sufficiently strong when packed with the commodities to which they are adapted.

In the second place, the various units in a packing box must be packed so that they will not damage one another. This may be accomplished by the use of fiber separations, excelsior, balsawood pads, bracing, rubber shock-mounts or rubberized animal hair, or any of the various methods employed in domestic trade. The difference existing in international marketing is the greater likelihood of damage since containers that are considered satisfactory in domestic trade are not necessarily adaptable to international marketing.

Recently, steel containers have been used in international shipping, following their use in domestic trade. With the use of such containers, miscellaneous products can be safely stowed in a strong container that, in some cases, moves from warehouse to warehouse, i.e., from the exporter's place of business to that of the importer. This is accomplished without opening the container.

Climatic Considerations. Climate, as a factor influencing packing, is especially important in the case of articles readily affected by heat and moisture. It is essential for the exporter not only to be cognizant of the climate of the country to which the shipment is destined but also to be informed as to the route which the shipment will take. Goods shipped to the south temperate zone, for example, will cross the equator and they must be protected from the heat and humidity encountered in this tropical belt in case they are susceptible to any injury thereby. Also, the temperature changes experienced by many voyages may cause heavy sweat to form either in the ships' holds or on metal surfaces of cargoes inside their containers. In tropical areas there is often a pronounced rainy season and the damage that goods may sustain, if not properly protected, is considerable. Moisture and heat cause fungoid growths, while rust and sweating are also sources of annoyance and loss.[3]

---

[3]The Insurance Company of North America reports that for a recent five-year period, fresh water and sweat damage accounted for 13 percent of all losses paid, with sea water and heavy weather contributing an additonal 5 percent. Quoted by permission of the company.

Congestion at Unloading Port. Climatic conditions also affect the packing problem in other ways. It sometimes happens that owing to the great accumulation of merchandise resulting from the simultaneous arrival of several vessels at a foreign port, or from even the arrival of one vessel, all goods cannot find immediate shelter. This may be due to the fact that the size or number of warehouses is insufficient to handle peak loads expeditiously. During such delays merchandise is left unprotected in the open and at the mercy of the elements.

Interior Shipment. The interior transportation of merchandise by means of pack animals is another condition that causes goods to remain exposed to the weather. Extremes of climatic conditions may be encountered from the tropics of the lowlands to the bleak plateaus swept by wind, sleet, and snow. Usually no effort is made by those in charge of the caravans to protect the merchandise they are carrying. In some cases, canvas is spread over the packages but this is seldom, if ever, likely to be in such condition as to provide adequate protection.

Means of Protection from Climatic Conditions. A packing case may be of adequate strength to withstand the jolts and handlings to which it is subjected, but the merchandise within may suffer damage because of sweat and rust or other climatic perils. Exporters, therefore, employ many methods to protect goods from the effects of heat or moisture. Each type of product presents its own problem. The proper protection of merchandise from such climatic conditions is predicated more upon the inside packing afforded the goods than upon the outside container.

One of the most common methods of protecting merchandise from the effects of climatic conditions is that of lining the case, box, or other container with waterproof paper. In some instances, additional protection may be obtained by placing the articles themselves in a waterproof wrapper, thus providing two layers of paper. Biscuits destined to tropical markets, for example, call for an exceptional degree of protection from moisture. Some exporters wrap oil paper around the packages of biscuits, then place the packages in cartons that are also wrapped in oil paper, and these are in turn packed in cases. Tin inner or retail containers of various types, packed in wooden or fiberboard boxes, have come into more general use during recent years. Chemical treatment of the packing material is also becoming successful.

Hardware is often well protected by wrapping each unit individually in waterproof paper, the pieces then being enclosed in cartons, and the cartons enclosed in cases lined with heavy, water-resisting paper.

Perhaps the greatest extreme in efforts to protect shipments from water and dampness is found in the use of metal-lined, hermetically sealed cases. In this type of container, either zinc or tin is generally used and absolute protection from moisture is assured. Alternatively, many items consisting wholly or partly of optics or critical metal surfaces with such close tolerances that a preservative cannot be safely applied are protected by case liners or wrappings of a moisture vaporproof material. A desiccant can be placed within the moisture vapor barrier to absorb any moisture trapped in the air within the wrappings.

Metal goods, particularly those with a polished surface, are subject to the dangers of rust and corrosion. In order to guard against this risk, it is customary to coat the surfaces thickly with a slushing oil. Such substances are required to be sufficiently heavy to coat thickly the surface on which they are to be applied and to remain thereon indefinitely; they must exclude moisture and air and be capable of easy removal when placed in use.

Pilfering as a Packing Factor.[4] In the shipment of certain goods, notably those of relatively small bulk and high value, pilferage is a source of annoyance and loss. There is a long interval between the relinquishment of a shipment by the exporter and its receipt by the buyer. When delays are experienced in making proper shipping connections, when congestion holds up the passage of the merchandise through the customs, or when rehandlings are called for because of the condition of interior transportation abroad, the likelihood of pilferage is increased. Shipments to certain parts of the world are more likely to suffer pilferage than consignments destined to other areas, and it seems from experience that the former are principally those countries at which facilities are inadequate or primitive. But pilferage may occur at any point along the route. Merchandise while on the vessel is readily available to the seamen, and the exporters of packing-house products have had interesting experiences in this connection. The problem is a continuous one from the time of shipment until the safe arrival of the goods. Indeed, pilferage is not confined to international marketing, by any means, as the freight claim agents of American railroads and trucking companies will testify.

Under the title "The Great Grain Robbery" an editorial in the *Philadelphia Inquirer* of July 18, 1963, commented on the amazing fact

---

[4]Does not include inside-the-plant dishonesty and thievery, said to cause 7 percent of all business failures. See *Journal of Commerce*, January 11, 1962. The Insurance Company of North America reports that 20 percent of all losses suffered by underwriters of marine cargo are caused by theft and pilferage.

that 24 million bushels of grain out of a shipment of 40 million bushels sent to Austria in a barter deal had mysteriously disappeared. Senator John J. Williams of Delaware was quoted as stating "No man can be so stupid or so incompetent as to lose completely 24 million bushels of grain without knowing it."

If packages can be opened, the goods extracted, the missing weight supplied by stones or metals, and the package closed again without leaving any visible trace of the theft, it is impossible to determine where the pilferage has taken place. Effective devices against this evil consist in rendering a package not only difficult to pilfer, thereby lengthening the time required to complete the job and increasing the possibility of detection, but also in constructing containers so that attempts at tampering may be readily detected.

The exporter can do much to prevent pilferage by concealing the identity of the contents of his packages. This can be accomplished by avoiding the use of his own name or that of the merchandise on the outside of the container. It has also been suggested that only bonded truckmen be employed, whenever possible, and also that bonded stevedoring and lighterage concerns be engaged in case these services are not performed by the transportation companies.

Many devices have been developed for preventing pilferage, some of which are manufactured by concerns holding patent rights. It would pay an exporter who has suffered pilferage losses to study these methods and discover if any is suitable for his purposes. The more common methods of rendering pilferage difficult, if not impossible, include the use of double cases, the boards of the inside container running at right angles to those in the outside case; tongued and grooved boards glued; flat iron straps, or wire drawn tightly around the middle of the package; cleats that render the removal of boards difficult; nails of a type that hold fast in wood and are difficult to withdraw without splintering the lumber; cement-coated nails, because of their resistance to extraction; screws that are countersunk and the holes sealed with wax; wire netting; or three-way corner-cleated plywood boxes.

Patented devices, some of which claim to render pilferage impossible, consist of automatic inside locks; various types of strapping machines; seals and sealing devices; patented cases, some of which are collapsible; and different types of clips.

Freight Rates And Export Packing. The space occupied by a shipment of goods is affected by the method of packing employed. Because the railroads quote freight rates on the basis of hundredweight, the fact should not be overlooked that the classes into which shipments are placed for rating purposes are determined, among many other factors, by the space occupied by the merchandise. This space varies according to whether the goods are shipped knocked-down or set-up or are otherwise disassembled or reduced in volume. On the other hand, because of the physical impossibility of adding to the carrying capacity of a given vessel, ocean freight rates are usually quoted "weight or measurement, ship's option"; and the basis that yields the larger revenue will be applied in each particular instance. Many ocean shipments are in fact charged on the basis of space occupied, for example, "$40 per ton W/M," in which the "W" is 2,240 pounds and the "M" is 40 cubic feet.

Savings in freight rates, both on land and on sea, may be made by giving careful attention to this feature of the packing problem. Bulky and irregularly shaped articles should, if possible, be reduced in bulk by

General Motors of Canada Limited

In packing automotive material for export, the parts are knocked down and packed in units of 24 so that upon receipt and assembly 24 automobiles are produced. A thin layer of oil is sprayed over the parts, which, with the tar paper lining of the box, prevents water damage and rust.

disassembly. Machinery of various descriptions and automobiles are conspicuous examples of articles that have been scientifically studied to reduce their great bulk. To assist materially in the assembly or setting-up of articles shipped in a knocked-down condition, it is advisable to include a packing list and complete assembly instructions with each shipment. Nesting of articles of uniform shape is widely practiced in foreign, as well as in domestic, trade; and the compression of merchandise to be shipped in bales is becoming more common as compression methods are improved.

In all of the efforts to reduce space, it should not be forgotten that the weight of the shipment is also to be considered because rates, if based on the weight of a shipment, apply to the gross weight of both the container and its contents. As far as the question of ocean freight rates is concerned, however, saving space is of first consideration in connection with a wide range of commodities.

Customs Duties as a Packing Factor. When the shipment reaches the customs officials who assess the import duty, the weight of the unit is usually of greatest importance.[5] The exporter has the opportunity of keeping to a minimum the charges against the goods, particularly when customs duties are levied on a basis of weight. If "gross weight" is applied as the basis for import duties, excessive weight becomes unnecessarily costly. When "net weight" is the basis, as is more often the case, heavy outside packing does not affect the import duty. This is only true, however, if the packing container is of no commercial value. Unusual types of containers, efficient though they may be, may be charged for in addition to their contents because they are deemed to be of commercial value.

Legal Net Weight. The immediate wrapping that surrounds the merchandise (paper, cardboard boxes, bottles, cans) is included in the weight used for duty assessment in those countries which recognize "legal weight." In such instances it may be more economical to ship the merchandise in bulk and make a separate shipment of the containers. Each will then be appraised for duty on its respective basis. In some countries, specific duties are assessed on "legal net weight," which is arrived at by deducting defined tares from the gross weights of shipments.

More Than One Article in One Package. A further difficulty in connection with customs duties arises in packing different articles, dutiable

---

[5]See also Chapter 23.

separately, in one container. In some countries, the whole shipment is assessed the duty applicable to the highest rated article in the container.[6]

Knocked-Down Duty. Another factor to be considered is the completeness of the article upon examination at customhouses. Many countries levy a lower rate of duty as the product in question comes farther from being complete. The practice of shipping an article knocked-down, therefore, will often result in a saving in import duties, as well as in shipping and handling charges. An exporter will avoid excessive charges by conforming to all of the customs requirements of the countries to which he ships merchandise. In this way he may guarantee to his customer the lowest charges that the foreign country will permit.

Customer's Requirements And Packing Expense. Perhaps there is no aspect of the packing problem that proves so irritating to importers as the deliberate alteration or disregard of instructions by the exporter. When an importer transmits in his order certain specific instructions regarding the routing, packing, marking, or assortment of the shipment, it is safe to assume that he has done so for some good reason. If kilo and half-kilo packages are ordered, it is because the importer's customers are unfamiliar with pounds and half-pounds; if scarlet colors are desired, then orange will not be satisfactory; if complete assortments are ordered for each case to be shipped, then breaking up these assortments to suit the whims of the packer will be irritating to the buyer; if a certain routing is specified, even if the map shows a crow's flight to be shorter, there is some practical reason for the route indicated.

Good salesmanship may involve the demonstration of new and better ideas but, once an order is received, it is safe to assume that such instructions as the customer is careful enough to transmit are of sufficient importance for the exporter to follow carefully. The customer is particularly favorably placed with respect to customer's requirements, climatic conditions, local freight handling methods, inland transportation services, and perhaps the pilferage hazard.

The exporter should also consider carefully the cost of export packing both with reference to his own interest and that of his customer. Shipments should necessarily be packed with reference to the transportation, climatic, and pilferage hazards, but it does not necessarily follow that

---

[6]When the new steel shipping containers are used, they move in bond from the destination port to the importer's warehouse. There they are opened and duties are assessed on the specific contents.

the safest possible containers will be used. Packing costs must also be considered. Much has been done in some trades to reduce packing and transportation costs without sacrificing the cardinal requirement of reasonably safe packing methods.

Reconciling the Packing Factors. With such an array of problems, the export packer has no easy task. The most difficult considerations to reconcile are safety and economy. In endeavoring to guarantee safety, weights may be increased and economy sacrificed. Excessive diligence in pursuit of economy may sacrifice safety. The task is to find a method at least equally as efficient and safe, and yet more economical; or more efficient and just as economical. Safety is the fixed factor and it is of primary importance. Freight rates and customs duties should not be reduced to the detriment of security from damage or pilferage.

In studying this problem, the exporter is not left entirely to his own resources. Although he may have expert packers in his employ, scientific research is worthy of his attention. The Forest Products Laboratory at Madison, Wisconsin, conducts investigations into, and tests of, containers of various types. The results of these experiments are available to American shippers. Extensive equipment is used to test the strength of packing devices and the properties of various kinds of materials. Studies of shipping containers are also undertaken by various private container-testing laboratories and container manufacturers. Advice can be obtained from associations of container manufacturers, from packing engineers, and from marine insurance companies. The United States Bureau of International Commerce has published several valuable studies of export packing. Finally, the International Cargo Handling Coordination Association is active in seeking to make ship-borne cargo more efficient. It operates through various national committees that conduct series of symposia on various cargo handling subjects, with special emphasis on containerization (unitizing, palletizing, fishy-back). The impetus for developments along this line has been the increasing cost of labor as well as the attempt to reduce losses from damage and pilferage.

Marking Export Shipments. Marking shipments for international commerce is important and deserves close attention. The hazards that affect the mode of packing exert an influence on the marking which, if blurred or obliterated, leads to endless trouble; and government requirements must also be met.

For practical reasons, as well as for legal requirements in some countries, all marks are preferably stenciled. Marks should be of such size as to be readily discernible so that packages may be quickly identified. The essential data that should appear on a packing case, bale, or any unit are (1) the consignee's name and/or mark; (2) the destination; and (3) the routing instructions. This information is essential for the handling and delivery of the shipment. In this respect, the same principles are followed as in addressing a letter. Such data should appear in the most conspicuous place and should be duplicated on another side of the package to guarantee delivery. The routing is especially important in case the destination is located at an interior point, and in such instances, the port of entry is also indicated.

Shipping Marks. As commonly practiced in international marketing, the consignee's name or mark, the destination, and the routing may be set forth. The purposes of this method of indicating the consignee and destination are the brevity attained in marking packages and in preparing documents; the ease of identifying packages; and some degree of secrecy. Shipping marks, such as a circle with the importer's initials within, are devised by the importer or buyer and, when supplied, they constitute part of the instructions and are to be followed literally.

Supplementary Marks. Supplementary data, often required by foreign countries and advisable in any case, call for the following additional marks: (1) weights — gross, net, legal (as required by the particular country); (2) serial numbers of individual units when a number of packages is shipped; and (3) cubical measurements.

The only additional marking that should generally be placed on foreign shipments is an indication of the country of origin. This should be inscribed on the article and on the labels, tags, and printed matter that may accompany it. Although not required by all foreign countries, it may be well for the United States exporter to place the legend "Made in U.S.A." on all articles that are exported. In this way the requirements, if existent, will ordinarily be met, and possibly the American reputation for quality will be of some merchandising advantage.

Discretionary Marks. Discretionary marks, such as are commonly used in domestic shipments, may be employed with doubtful success in international marketing. "This side up," "Fragile," and similar cautionary marks may or may not attract attention and result in care on the part of stevedores and longshoremen; but if written in a foreign language, this chance will doubtless be enhanced. Moreover, as discussed in connection with pilferage, the identity of the merchandise should be concealed, and marks conveying unnecessary information are to be avoided.

Shipping

Shipping is much more complicated in international marketing than in domestic trade. Having packed the merchandise according to the principles discussed in the preceding section, it is now necessary to start the shipment on the way to its destination.

Export or Import Traffic Department. A company may have a special department to handle traffic. If the built-in type of export or import department is employed, the traffic function is performed by the domestic traffic department, with advice from the manager of the export or import department.

This department arranges for the shipment of the merchandise. This may be done by dealing directly with the transportation agencies or, more commonly, by employing a foreign freight forwarder.

Foreign Freight Forwarder. The foreign freight forwarder is in business to handle export and import shipments. He takes care of all documentary requirements; follows the shipment to see that it moves on the required route; and arranges for switching, unloading at the port of export, repacking, and loading on vessel. The forwarder also handles the banking transactions that are involved, pays all fees assessed by the government of the country of export and the country of import, may take out the required marine insurance if the shipper does not have his own open cargo policy, and constantly takes care of the interests of his principal, whether he is an exporter or an importer.

For this array of services, the forwarder charges a fee that defies standardization. He also charges for the expenses he has paid and the fees he has advanced.

Forwarders are located almost exclusively at seaports where they can take shipments as they are about to leave or to enter the country. Here also are the facilities required for the efficient physical movement of international marketing transactions. They must be registered with the Federal Maritime Board.

Shipping Companies. Shipments of general cargo move on the vessels of shipping companies. Shipments of bulk cargo, both dry and liquid, more often move on chartered ships. In the first case, a given shipper requires the use of a portion of the hold of a vessel. In the second case, the shipper usually engages the entire vessel and expects to fill it with his shipment.

Shipping companies are common carriers, while the chartered vessels used by shippers are private carriers.[7] Shipping companies that serve the United States fly the flags of all maritime nations. They commonly band together in the various trades in which they operate. By a *trade* is meant a foreign area and generally a seaboard of the United States. When so banded together, they are known as steamship conferences. Under the Shipping Act of 1916, steamship conferences are exempt from the antitrust laws, but they are required to submit to the jurisdiction of the Federal Maritime Board. Examples of "trades" in which conferences operate are *North Atlantic United States–United Kingdom; North Atlantic United States–Continental Europe; Gulf United States–Mediterranean; United States Pacific Westbound* (to east Asian countries); and many more.

The steamship conferences set the rates, rules, and regulations governing shipments moving in the "trade" in which they operate; and all members of the conference abide by these. Therefore, all rates quoted by any member of the conference are set by means of conference agreement. Negotiations for changes in rates by shippers or receivers must then be considered by the conference as a group.

Freight Rate Quotations. Freight rate quotations can be obtained from a freight forwarder or from the office of a shipping company. Steamship tariffs or rate books are generally not available for public acquisition, but they are filed for public inspection with the Federal Maritime Board.

As pointed out earlier in this chapter, steamship rates are commonly quoted on a weight or a measurement basis, ship's option. In other words, the merchandise is weighed and also measured. If the rate is $40 a ton and the weight ton is 2,240 pounds and the measurement ton is 40 cubic feet, a simple calculation will determine the charges. A shipment weighing 4,000 pounds and measuring 100 cubic feet would obviously yield more revenue to the carrier on the basis of measurement, since there are 2½ tons of payable freight on a measurement basis and less than 2 payable tons on a weight basis.

While 2,240 pounds is cited as the weight ton, the Far Eastern trades generally use 2,000 pounds as a weight ton. In all trades, 40 cubic feet equal one measurement ton. Some commodities, for example, iron and steel, however, are quoted on a straight weight basis. Articles of high

---

[7]Shipping companies also charter ships and operate them in common carrier service.

value are sometimes quoted at a rate that is a percentage of value, such as 5 percent ad valorem.

Contract Rates. Many conferences observe two scales of rates: (1) the regular tariff rate and (2) a contract (lower) rate.

A contract rate is available to all shippers and receivers in a given trade by signing a "shipper's contract." Under this contract, tendered by the conference, the shipper or receiver agrees to use conference vessels exclusively. Failing to do so, he loses his status as a contract shipper, thus being required to pay the higher tariff rate and also perhaps subject to a financial penalty.

In a case involving the reestablishment of the contract rate system by the Japan-Atlantic and Gulf Freight Conference, the Supreme Court in the winter of 1958 overruled the Federal Maritime Board by declaring this system to be illegal. Thereupon, Congress, under Public Law 85–626, declared that all present contract rate arrangements of other conferences would be considered frozen until June 30, 1960, by which time Congress would reexamine the shipping acts and decide what should be done by means of legislation. The final legislation was an amended Section 14 (b) of the Shipping Act, under which the dual-rate system employed by most conferences may be continued subject to certain restrictions. Basic in these limitations is one that has always been in the Act, viz., that the system will not be unjustly discriminatory or unfair as between exporters, shippers, importers, or ports, or between exporters from the United States and their foreign competitors. Eight specific conditions are also in the revision.

Nonconference Shipping Companies. Some shipping companies refuse to join a conference while some belong to conferences in certain trades in which they operate but refuse to join conferences in other trades. Nonconference shipping companies sometimes, but not always, quote rates lower than the conference contract rates.

A shipper or receiver, therefore, must decide whether or not it is desirable for him to sign shipper's contracts with conferences. If he does not sign a contract, he may use any shipping company he desires; but if a conference line is used, he will pay the higher tariff rate on his shipments.

Shipping Documents. Shipping documents in international marketing embrace (1) commercial documents employed by shipping, forwarding, and insuring companies and (2) documents which are required by governments.

Commercial Documents. The most important commercial document issued by shipping companies is the *ocean bill of lading*, such as the one illustrated on page 426. A bill of lading is (1) a receipt for the shipment; (2) a contract for shipment; and (3) if negotiable (or "to order"), it is documentary and transferable evidence of title to the shipment. This last use is of paramount importance as will be shown in the discussion of financing foreign shipments in Chapters 30 and 31.

As stated in Chapter 21, a bill of lading that is "clean" has no qualifying clauses indicating deficiency in count, description, packing, or any other factor. A "clean" bill of lading is usually required in all cases where financing is used.

A bill of lading, as printed, states that the merchandise has been "received for shipment." To become an "on board" bill of lading, it must be stamped by the shipping company with the words "on board."

Freight forwarders sometimes issue receipts to serve until a bill of lading is available. They also employ an instruction sheet for the use of their customers in conveying explicit instructions to them. They also, of course, have an expense statement.

Since the terms of an ocean bill of lading contract relieve the shipping company of practically all liability, marine insurance companies sell this protection. Marine insurance is discussed later in the chapter.[8]

Government Documents. On export shipments from the United States a *shipper's export declaration*, such as the one illustrated on page 427, is required by the United States Government. Normally this document is essentially used for statistical purposes, but with the need for export licenses covering certain strategic shipments and also covering any shipments to certain countries, the export declaration is of prime importance in such cases. A violation of export license regulations could involve a charge of perjury, and it usually causes cancellation of license privileges of the guilty party for a certain period of time.

On import shipments into the United States, the basic document is an *import entry*. Imports are subject to customs duties, but exports from the United States are entirely free of duty and also free of sales taxes — national, state, and local. For example, the importers of cosmetics pay national, and often state and local, sales taxes. If exported, such taxes are not payable; and if they have been paid, they are refunded upon submission of proof of export. On imports exceeding $500 in value, a

---

[8]"Historically, each voyage of an ocean-going vessel is a joint venture of the shipowner and all of the cargo owners." American Institute of Marine Underwriters, *Exporter's Guide to Cargo Insurance* (undated).

special customs invoice (Form 5515) is required. This document is prepared by the foreign exporter and signed by him, and it does not require consular certification.

UNITED STATES LINES CO.

(SPACES IMMEDIATELY BELOW FOR SHIPPERS MEMORANDA—NOT PART OF BILL OF LADING)

FORWARDING AGENT—REFERENCES	EXPORT DEC. No.
None	48763

DELIVERING CARRIER TO STEAMER:	CAR NUMBER — REFERENCE
Pennsylvania Railroad	PRR 78643

BILL OF LADING

(SHORT FORM)

(NOT NEGOTIABLE UNLESS CONSIGNED "TO ORDER")

SHIP American Hunter	FLAG USA	PIER 80 South	PORT OF LOADING
PORT OF DISCHARGE FROM SHIP (Where goods are to be delivered to consignee or On-carrier) If goods to be transshipped beyond Port of Discharge, show destination Here ➡ To		THROUGH BILL OF LADING	PHILADELPHIA, PA.

SHIPPER ... Cleveland Packing Company

CONSIGNED TO: ORDER OF ... Cleveland Packing Company

ADDRESS ARRIVAL NOTICE TO Emile Deschamps & Cie, 27 Rue de Napoleon, Le Havre, France

PARTICULARS FURNISHED BY SHIPPER OF GOODS

MARKS AND NUMBERS	NO. OF PKGS.	DESCRIPTION OF PACKAGES AND GOODS	MEASUREMENT	GROSS WEIGHT IN POUNDS
E D C Le Havre 1-83 Made in USA	83	Lard, in tierces Refrigerated at 35 degrees or over	--	29,880

FREIGHT PAYABLE IN   Philadelphia

	@	PER 2240 LBS..$		
$1.56	@	PER 100·LBS..$	466	13
FT.	@	PER 40 CU. FT.$		
FT.	@	PER CU. FT...$		
			$	
			$	
			$	
			$	

TOTAL . . $ 466 | 13

(TERMS OF THIS BILL OF LADING CONTINUED FROM REVERSE SIDE HEREOF)

IN WITNESS WHEREOF, THE MASTER OR AGENT OF SAID VESSEL HAS SIGNED **3**

BILLS OF LADING, ALL OF THE SAME TENOR AND DATE, ONE OF WHICH BEING ACCOMPLISHED, THE OTHERS TO STAND VOID.

UNITED STATES LINES COMPANY

BY ... (Sgd. by company)

FOR THE MASTER

B/L No.   ISSUED AT PHILADELPHIA, PA.

(Date and number perforated here)

MO.   DAY   YEAR

REVISED 10-57

103932-25M PRINTED IN U.S.A.

Figure 22-A. Ocean Bill of Lading

Foreign governments also usually require *consular invoices* or *certificates of origin*. They may also impose an import license system and without such a license, shipment cannot safely be made.

Form No. 29—Printed and Sold by Unz & Co., Inc., 24 Beaver St., New York 4, N. Y.—U 33204

Form 7525-V (Rev. July 1952) (See Instructions on Reverse Side)	U. S. DEPARTMENT OF COMMERCE BUREAU OF THE CENSUS—BUREAU OF INTERNATIONAL PROGRAMS **SHIPPER'S EXPORT DECLARATION** OF SHIPMENTS FROM THE UNITED STATES Export Shipments Are Subject To U. S. Customs Inspection	Form approved. Budget Bureau No. 41-R397.5.

CONFIDENTIAL For use solely for official purposes authorized by the Secretary of Commerce. Use for unauthorized purposes is not permitted. (Title 15, Sec. 30.5 (b) C.F.R.; 50 U.S.C. App., 2026c.)

READ CAREFULLY THE INSTRUCTIONS ON BACK TO AVOID DELAY AT SHIPPING POINT
For shipments to foreign countries, the export declaration (a) must be presented to and authenticated by the Collector of Customs before the goods are placed on pier or dock or other place of loading for the purpose of exporting by water or air; (b) must be presented to and authenticated by the Collector prior to exportation where the goods are exported by other means.
Declarations Should Be Typewritten Or Prepared In Ink

Customs Authentication (For Customs use only.)

Do Not Use This Area	District	Port	Country (For customs use only)
	11	01	

FILE NO. (For Customs use only.)

1. FROM (*U. S. Port of Export*) South Philadelphia	2. METHOD OF TRANSPORTATION (*check one*): ☒ Vessel ☐ Air ☐ Other (*Specify*)

2a. EXPORTING CARRIER (*If vessel, give name of ship, flag and pier number. If air, give name of airline.*)
American Hunter - USA Pier 80

3. EXPORTER (*Principal or seller—licensee*) Cleveland Packing Co.	ADDRESS (*Number, street, place, state*) Cleveland, Ohio
4. AGENT OF EXPORTER (*Forwarding agent*) None	ADDRESS (*Number, street, place, state*)
5. ULTIMATE CONSIGNEE Emile Deschamps & Cie.	ADDRESS (*Place, country*) Le Havre, France
6. INTERMEDIATE CONSIGNEE	ADDRESS (*Place, country*)
7. FOREIGN PORT OF UNLOADING (*For vessel and air shipments only*) Le Havre, France	8. PLACE AND COUNTRY OF ULTIMATE DESTINATION (*Not place of transshipment.*) Le Havre, France

(9) MARKS AND NOS.	(10) NUMBER AND KIND OF PACKAGES, DESCRIPTION OF COMMODITIES, EXPORT LICENSE NUMBER, EXPIRATION DATE (OR GENERAL LICENSE SYMBOL) (Describe commodities in sufficient detail to permit verification of the Schedule B commodity numbers assigned. Do not use general terms. Insert required license information on line below description of each item)	(11) SHIPPING (Gross) WEIGHT IN POUNDS* (required for vessel and air shipments only)	(12) SPECIFY "D" OR "F"	(13) SCHEDULE B COMMODITY NO.	(14) NET QUANTITY IN SCHEDULE B UNITS (State unit)	(15) VALUE AT U. S. PORT OF EXPORT (Selling price or cost if not sold, including inland freight, insurance and other charges to U. S. port of export) (Nearest whole dollar; omit cents figures)
E D C						
Le Havre	83 tierces lard	29,880	D	00530	24,000 lbs	$3,581
1-83	General license GLSA					
Made in USA						

These commodities licensed by the U. S. for ultimate destination....................Diversion contrary to U. S. law prohibited.

16. WAYBILL OR MANIFEST NO. (*of Exporting Carrier*) 137	17. DATE OF EXPORTATION (*Not required for shipments by vessel*)

18. THE UNDERSIGNED HEREBY AUTHORIZES_____ TO ACT AS FORWARDING AGENT FOR EXPORT CONTROL AND CUSTOMS PURPOSES. (Name and address—Number, street, place, State) (DULY AUTHORIZED
EXPORTER_____BY OFFICER OR EMPLOYEE)_____

▶ 19. I CERTIFY THAT ALL STATEMENTS MADE AND ALL INFORMATION CONTAINED IN THIS EXPORT DECLARATION ARE TRUE AND CORRECT. I AM AWARE OF THE PENALTIES PROVIDED FOR FALSE REPRESENTATION. (*See Paragraphs I (c), (e), on reverse side.*)
Signature (Sgd. by officer of company) For Cleveland Packing Co.
(Duly authorized officer or employee of exporter or named forwarding agent) (Name of corporation or firm, and capacity of signer; e.g., secretary, export manager, etc.)
Address Cleveland, Ohio (Phila. manager)

▶ Declaration should be made by duly authorized officer or employee of exporter or of forwarding agent named by exporter.
*If shipping weight is not available for each Schedule B item listed in column (13) included in one or more packages, insert the approximate gross weight for each Schedule B item. The total of these estimated weights should equal the actual weight of the entire package or packages.
*Designate foreign merchandise (reexports) with an "F" and exports of domestic merchandise produced in the United States or changed in condition in the United States with a "D." (*See instructions on reverse side.*)
CARRIERS, FORWARDERS AND EXPORTERS ARE REMINDED THAT IF A DESTINATION CONTROL STATEMENT IS REQUIRED ON A SHIPPER'S EXPORT DECLARATION COVERING A GIVEN SHIPMENT, SUCH STATEMENT MUST ALSO APPEAR ON ALL COPIES OF THE BILL OF LADING AND COMMERCIAL INVOICE. (*See Comprehensive Export Schedule.*)

Do Not Use This Area

Figure 22-B. Shipper's Export Declaration

Marine Insurance[9]

Marine insurance companies and underwriting organizations are keenly interested in export packing methods, and they make recommendations based on their experience. One of the basic factors considered by an underwriter in quoting a marine insurance premium is the loss experience of each shipper. This is a tangible measure of the packing problems of every shipper, and it offers a reward to effect improvements in the loss and damage record.

Marine insurance to cover cargo risks is commonly placed on all shipments moving in international seaborne trade. The insurance may be placed by the exporter for his own account or for the account of the buyer; or it may be placed by the importer with his own chosen underwriter. This is not so simple as it may sound. For example, the importer may state that he will take care of the insurance. In this case, let us say that he is purchasing under a letter of credit. The letter of credit calls for furnishing an on-board bill of lading in order to collect under the credit. If a loss should occur between the time the goods leave the exporter's warehouse and before the on-board bill of lading is issued, the credit could not be used and the insurance taken out by the importer probably would not cover the loss. The exporter would be well advised, therefore, to provide protection against this kind of risk. This can be done by the issuance of an inland marine policy or by an endorsement on his open cargo policy to provide coverage for his own account until the bill of lading is issued.

There are certain advantages to the exporter who places his own marine insurance. For example, where the sale is f.o.b. steamer, Philadelphia, the importer's insurance may only become effective when the goods are loaded aboard the steamer; hence, any loss to the shipment between the exporter's warehouse and the steamer may not be covered. To protect against such a risk the exporter would need to purchase an inland marine policy or a special endorsement for his open cargo policy. Were the exporter to sell f.o.b. steamer, Philadelphia, with the stipulation that he would provide the marine insurance, he would have complete protection at the importer's expense.

Exporters who are unpaid for their shipments until delivery to destination or later are also in a more secure position with their own dollar marine insurance.

---

[9]Information furnished and checked through the courtesy of Henry W. Farnum, Vice-President, Insurance Company of North America.

Types of Risks. Marine insurance differs from many other forms of insurance in that the insured has a choice of a vast variety of risks against which insurance can be effected. In broad categories, the risks that are commonly insured against are:

1. Free of damage insurance. This is a very limited form of insurance and covers only *total* loss of the goods; partial losses are not covered.

2. Fire and sea perils. Under this coverage, F.P.A. insurance, claims are paid only in case the vessel is stranded, sunk, burned, on fire, or in collision; and only if the damage is caused by fire or sea perils.

3. Fire and sea perils with average. This is the same as No. 2 above, except that it is not necessary to show that the vessel has been stranded, sunk, burned, on fire, or in collision.

4. Named perils. This includes the fire and sea perils insurance as in No. 3 above and to which a number of additional perils may be added, such as fresh water damage, hook damage, fuel oil damage, theft, pilferage, nondelivery, or breakage.

5. All-risk insurance. This is the most complete coverage commonly written, but it is confined to losses from physical loss or damage from any *external* cause, exclusive of war, strikes, and riots. This coverage does not include loss due to the inherent nature of goods nor does it cover market losses due to delays in shipment, for example, missing the Christmas sales season. If insurance is desired to cover the excluded perils, under certain very limited circumstances they can be included in the insurance policy by endorsement except for war-risk insurance, which requires a separate policy.

All of these coverages include general average[10] and salvage charges. Marine insurance is one of the few kinds of insurance where it is permissible, in addition to insuring the value of the goods themselves, to insure profit. While the sales price of goods usually includes the exporter's profit, it does not include the import duties imposed by the country of importation nor the importer's anticipated profit. In practice, a common rule is to insure for an amount equal to all known costs plus 10 percent.

---

[10]The word "average" is derived from the French word "avarie," meaning damage; damage that is common or general to the entire venture — ship and cargo — is known as general average. "Particular average" refers to the single or individual shipment.

Losses Covered Under Marine Policies. Basically, there are two types of losses under marine insurance policies: (1) particular average and (2) general average.

Particular Average. Damage to the goods themselves is known as *particular average* and may be classified as follows:

1. Total loss. The amount stated in the insurance policy is paid.

2. Total loss of part of a shipment, for example, theft or pilferage. The policy pays the insured value of the part lost.

3. Reparable loss — fender of an automobile is crumpled; it is repaired in the country of importation. Loss paid is the amount of the repair bill.

4. Replaceable loss — fender must be replaced by a new one which must be shipped by the exporter. Loss paid is total costs of new fender, packing, freight, etc.

5. Loss due to depreciation of the value of the shipment. The amount of depreciation is worked out with the exporter or the goods are sold at auction. The percentage of depreciation thus arrived at is then applied to the insurance policy and this amount is paid. For example, if 25 percent depreciation is agreed upon, the insurance company pays 25 percent of the value stated in the insurance policy.

In all of these situations, the limit of liability, of course, is the face amount of the insurance policy.

General Average. Loss or damage common to the entire venture is known as *general average.* This involves liens of third parties. If a voluntary sacrifice is made in face of impending disaster, and that sacrifice is successful in preserving at least a part of the common venture, then all who survive (ship and cargo) contribute pro rata in accordance with the value saved in order to make up the value of whatever was sacrificed.

A classic example of general average loss is by jettison, or throwing overboard certain cargo to save the voyage. If 10 percent of the combined value of ship and cargo is thus sacrificed, all owners, including the owner of the jettisoned cargo, contribute 10 percent of their respective values to reimburse the loss for the cargo that was jettisoned.

More common today is a case of fire in which water is used to extinguish the fire. The common sacrifice here is damage to cargo by water; cargo damaged by fire or smoke is not damaged as a result of a voluntary sacrifice and therefore is not subject to general average adjustment.

Insurance Policies and Certificates. There are two ways that a risk can be declared to an insurance company. The first way is to send the company a copy of a certificate or a special policy, and the second is to use a short declaration insurance form.

The certificate or special policy is prepared according to circumstances, either in the exporter's office, occasionally in the office of an insurance broker, perhaps in the office of the freight forwarder, or maybe in one of the offices of the insurance company. This certificate or special policy is necessary *only* when the exporter is required to furnish evidence of insurance to some third party, such as a bank, a customer, or a third party to whom claims, if any, are to be paid. The certificates and special policies are both negotiable instruments and hence facilitate the settlement of claims in the country of the consignee.

In this situation, the exporter often takes out an open insurance policy that sets forth the risks for which there is insurance and the special policy completely reflects the open policy coverage. Every shipment that is made by the exporter under this open policy is certified to the insurance company, with complete descriptions, value, and all necessary details. With this information, the insurance company is in position to calculate a rate. By the use of an open policy, the exporter is protected on all of his shipments to the extent that he advises the insurance company of every transaction.

In the second way, if there is no necessity to evidence insurance to a third party and if claims are to be paid to the exporter only, a short declaration insurance form can be used.

If terms of sale or letters of credit call for an insurance policy, a policy must be provided; a certificate, which looks very much like a policy, will not do. Provision is usually made to accept certificates.

Summary

1. Packing shipments for international marketing is often more exacting than packing for domestic trade. Although additional or more severe handling at ports and on interior transportation often calls for stronger packing, costs cannot be ignored. Moreover, increased weight due to packing incurs higher shipping costs and possibly higher import duties in some countries.
2. Climate, particularly humidity, is a problem that must be considered in packing certain kinds of goods. Pilferage must also be protected against. Marking of export packages is important and must be done carefully.
3. Shipping may be handled by a freight forwarder or by an exporting firm itself. Steamship tariffs often provide for lower contract rates for shippers

who agree to tender all of their shipments to the members of a steamship conference. Full shiploads of cargo are handled by ship brokers who provide a ship for this purpose.

4. In shipments by steamship lines, the bill of lading is the title document. Governments also require certain documents such as export declarations, export licenses, consular invoices, and certificates of origin.

5. Marine insurance to cover cargo risks is commonly placed on all shipments moving in international seaborne trade. The insured chooses from a variety of risks and obtains the protection that his transaction requires. The most complete coverage commonly written is all-risk insurance, but even this will not cover losses caused by delay or due to the inherent characteristics of the goods being shipped.

6. Losses paid under marine insurance policies include a variety of so-called particular average losses and also general average losses. The former refer to damage specifically to the goods insured and the latter refer to loss or damage common to the entire venture.

7. Insurance policies and/or certificates are essential as part of the supporting documents for financing international marketing transactions.

QUESTIONS

1. Where does the responsibility lie for packing merchandise for international shipment? Explain.
2. Describe the hazards of sea transportation from the standpoint of safety of cargo.
3. How may cargo be protected from damage caused by (a) sea transport; (b) hot, humid atmosphere; (c) pilferage?
4. How may cargo be packed in order to save on (a) ocean freight rates; (b) customs duties?
5. Why should an exporter follow his customer's packing and routing instructions?
6. Define "shipping mark." What is its purpose?
7. How much information and what kind of information should be placed on the outside of a container moving in international trade?
8. Explain the functions of a foreign freight forwarder.
9. What is a steamship conference?
10. Explain the application of the following steamship freight quotations:
    (a) $30 per ton W/M.
    (b) $25 per ton W.
    (c) $75 per ton W/M plus 10 percent ad valorem.
11. Define "contract" rate quoted by members of a shipping conference.
12. Define and explain the uses of an ocean bill of lading.
13. Name several government documents required for use in international marketing transactions. Explain the purpose of each.
14. Why is marine insurance so important in international buying and selling?
15. Distinguish between particular average and general average coverage.

PROBLEMS

1. Obtain a copy of a current report on shipping conditions in various world ports. (The Insurance Company of North America, Philadelphia, Pennsylvania, publishes such a report from time to time.) Supplement this information by news items appearing in *Business Abroad and Export Trade*, *International Commerce*, and other trade journals.

   Prepare a report covering the shipping conditions prevailing at the ports in a geographical area of your choice, for example, Europe, Latin America, Asia, Africa, etc.

2. Visit the waterfront (if there is one) of the area where you are located. Watch the handling of export and import cargoes on and off ships or barges, through terminals, and on and off railroad cars and motor carriers.

   Prepare a report on the operations that you witness. If possible, illustrate your report with photographs.

COLLATERAL READINGS

Bonnell's Manual on Packing and Shipping. Plainfield, N. J.: Bonnell Publications, Inc.

Bureau of National Affairs, Inc. *Export Shipping Manual*. Washington, D.C.: annual.

Collins, V. D. *World Marketing*. Philadelphia: J. B. Lippincott Company, 1935. Chapters 12 and 13.

Dartnell International Trade Handbook, The. Chicago: The Dartnell Corporation, 1963.

de Haas, J. A. *The Practice of Foreign Trade*. New York: McGraw-Hill Book Company, Inc., 1935. Chapter 17.

Exporters' Encyclopaedia. New York: Thomas Ashwell and Co., Inc., annual.

Heck, Harold J. *Foreign Commerce*. New York: McGraw-Hill Book Company, Inc., 1953. Chapter 10.

Henning, Charles N. *International Finance*. New York: Harper & Brothers, 1958. Chapters 3 and 4.

Horn, Paul V. *International Trade Principles and Practices*, Third Edition. New York: Prentice-Hall, Inc., 1951. Chapters 15, 16, 30, and 31.

Insurance Company of North America. *Export Packing*. Philadelphia: undated.

Leeming, Joseph. *Modern Export Packing*. Washington, D.C.: Government Printing Office, 1940.

Leonard's Guide. New York: G. R. Leonard and Company.

MacDonald, Philip. *Practical Exporting*. New York: Ronald Press Company, 1949. Chapters 8, 9, and 15.

Pratt, E. E. *Modern International Commerce*. New York: Allyn and Bacon, Inc., 1956. Chapters 7 and 11.

Roorbach, G. B. *Import Purchasing: Principles and Problems.* Chicago and New York: A. W. Shaw Company, 1927. Chapters 1 and 13.

———————————. *Problems in Foreign Trade.* New York: McGraw-Hill Book Company, Inc., 1933. Part VI.

Rosenthal, Morris. *Techniques of International Trade.* New York: McGraw-Hill Book Company, Inc., 1950. Parts II, IV, V, and VIII.

Shaterian, William S. *Export-Import Banking,* Second Edition. New York: Ronald Press Company, 1956. Chapters 6–10.

CHAPTER 23

PROBLEMS PECULIAR TO IMPORTING IN THE UNITED STATES

The import business comprises the task of buying foreign products for sale or use in the home market. Whether foreign products will meet the needs of the home market must be determined by the importing firm.

Crude materials that are imported find a market with manufacturers that have use for such minerals. The state of the activity of such manufacturers will therefore determine the extent of the market for such products. Many of these manufacturers not only import crude materials themselves but may operate mines and processing plants abroad from which to meet their requirements.

Foodstuffs are imported in great volume to meet the tastes and the needs of the public. Manufacturers, packers, and numerous marketing functionaries participate in this business. The extent of the market is determined by the population and standard of living as well as by the tastes of the public.

Semimanufactures and manufactured products are imported by manufacturers and merchants, respectively. Here the market is determined by the extent of activity in which the semimanufactures are used, and, for manufactured products, by the actual or potential demand.

In all of these cases, the imports are acquired by private business firms for good and valid business reasons. The expectation they have is that a market will be found and a profit will be realized.

In addition to these marketing problems, the importer must come to grips with the import regulations of the home country.

At international marketing association meetings where exporters and importers are both present, exporters often complain audibly about the tariff, quota, exchange, sanitary and administrative regulations, and other obstacles imposed by countries in which they seek to market their products. On occasion, a seasoned importer at the meeting will say, "What are you fellows complaining about? Have you ever tried to import anything in *our* country? If you did, you would not be so critical of what other countries do."

Importers in the United States have the problem of meeting the import regulations of the United States, which are administered by the customs service of the Treasury Department. As shown in the following analysis, these regulations are complicated and exacting — so much so that one importer, whose import business goes back over one century, summarizes by saying that "importing is hazardous." He has since gone out of business because the United States Government took over the import trade in his product (vegetable oils), relegating his operation to that of mere paper work. And this occurred recently in the United States where private enterprise flourishes! Officially, the United States Government frowns upon other governments that take over private business; it looks askance at quota systems abroad but has some import quota systems of its own; it penalizes dumping in the United States by importers but dumps exports of agricultural surpluses in other countries.

The United States Government, as shown in Chapter 4, promotes the export trade of the United States; in this chapter, the obstacles to importing can scarcely be called promotion. Such are the inconsistencies in foreign commercial policies, and it is the sovereign right of every government to indulge them. It is, therefore, appropriate to inquire into the ramifications of the system employed in the United States with which importers must deal.

Organization and Operation of the United States Customs Service

The customs service of a country has to do with the administration of regulations governing the movement of persons, ships, vehicles, and merchandise across national frontiers.

The United States customs service is under the direction of the Secretary of the Treasury. Its activities extend also to such functions of other departments as the enforcement of laws governing the importation of foods and drugs (Department of Agriculture); admission of immigrants (Justice Department); and labeling of wool products (Federal Trade Commission).

The general duties and powers of customs officers, in addition to those mentioned, are set forth in the United States Tariff Act of 1930, as amended, and in the United States Customs Regulations.

The Customs Administrative Act of 1938 (amending the Tariff Act of 1930) serves to simplify and interpret the numerous legislative, legal, and administrative provisions relating to customs procedure.[1] These duties include documenting of American vessels; exclusion of unauthorized vessels from the coastwise trade; collection of tonnage duties; regulations governing international aircraft regarding their landing, clearance, documentary requirements, etc.; the entry, appraisement, and warehousing of imported merchandise; collection of duties on imports; payment of drawbacks; compilation of statistics of commerce and navigation; enforcement of laws for the detection and prevention of smuggling and other customs frauds; and execution of such regulations as the Secretary of the Treasury may establish under statutory laws.

As prescribed in the regulations of the Secretary of the Treasury, the Bureau of Customs prepares the decisions with respect to the administration and interpretation of the customs laws and drafts regulations governing customs officers; prescribes forms and records to be employed, and methods and rules to be followed in the collection of duties and payment of drawbacks, as well as in the appraisement of merchandise; determines the fact of depreciation of foreign currency; remits fines and other payments; enforces the law with respect to prohibited imports; and exercises general supervision over the field service.

Customs Agency Service. A customs agency service of the Bureau of Customs is the investigating arm of the customs service, investigating foreign values, drawbacks, smuggling, frauds, etc. It also supervises the Customs Information Exchange, including the Antidumping Unit at New York. The Exchange acts as a clearinghouse for information relating to the valuation and classification of similar merchandise imported at the several American ports, thereby providing some degree of uniformity. It also distributes the valuation and cost reports prepared by customs attachés abroad.

Customs Districts. The United States customs service is divided into 45 customs districts covering the entire country and including Alaska and also Puerto Rico and the Hawaiian Islands. The district of the Virgin

---

[1]Such was the intention of that act. The Customs Simplification Acts of 1954 and 1956 were passed in order further to "simplify" customs procedure.

Islands is not included as it has its own customs laws. Each district is placed under the charge of a collector located at a headquarters port. Comptrollers of customs examine the collectors' accounts and verify the assessment of duties and allowances for drawback. In case of disagreement with a collector, the comptrollers report the facts to the Secretary of the Treasury.

Entry of Vessels and Aircraft. When a vessel arrives at an American port from a foreign country, the master is required to report the fact of arrival within 24 hours to the nearest customhouse and within 48 hours to make formal entry of the vessel. International aircraft, whether landing at an airport of entry or not, must obtain prior customs permission. Scheduled airlines file a copy of their flying schedule at the first place of landing. Customs officers here arrange for the entry of merchandise on the aircraft.

Entry of Merchandise. The consignee "enters" the merchandise by filing these documents:

1. Special customs invoice, in case the shipment exceeds $500[2] in value and is dutiable ad valorem. If this invoice is unavailable, or if it is not required as in most shipments free of duty or charged a specific (not ad valorem) rate of duty, the commercial invoice or a pro forma invoice may be accepted.
2. Bill of lading.
3. Owner's declaration, under oath, that prices and all other data in the invoice are correct. All of these data are detailed on a form known as an *entry blank*. In case any of these three documents is missing, bonds are to be posted.

In the entry the consignee declares the value of the merchandise, indicates the rate of duty (if any) and tariff classification of the merchandise, and designates how he intends to dispose of the goods. If an imported shipment has been sold or quoted in foreign currency, the entry is to report the value in dollars by conversion in accordance with the daily values of foreign currencies published by the Federal Reserve Bank of New York as of the date of exportation. The *consumption entry* indicates a consignee's intention of disposing of the imported merchandise domestically. In case a shipment enters, say Philadelphia, and the con-

---

[2]Increased from $100 in Customs Simplification Act of 1954.

signee located at St. Louis desires to clear through the St. Louis custom-house, an *I.T. entry* (immediate transportation in bond) is made. A *warehouse entry* permits merchandise to be placed in a bonded warehouse.

When making a consumption entry, a deposit is made at the customhouse equal to the estimated duty, and when the duties are finally determined, or liquidated, a refund may be made or an additional payment may be required. If entry is not made within forty-eight hours, the merchandise is sent to a bonded warehouse or public store and is held as unclaimed until entry is made. This time limit may be extended by the collector, and in the case of such articles as perishables or those requiring immediate movement, special delivery permits may be obtained before making formal entry. Merchandise that remains in a warehouse for one year without being entered is considered abandoned.

Appraisal of Merchandise. The portion of a shipment that has been retained by customs is classified as to whether it is dutiable or free of duty; and, if dutiable ad valorem, it is appraised for determination of value for duty purposes. The appraiser also ascertains the quantities of merchandise and the accuracy of the invoice and describes "the merchandise in order that the collector may determine the dutiable classification thereof." At large ports, appraisers specialize in certain types of merchandise as silk and wool textiles, cotton, linen, embroideries, laces, hosiery, toys, woodenware, etc. In case a package contains several articles subject to different rates of duty, the assessment may possibly be at a rate applicable to the highest dutiable product in the package. By separating the different articles, this assessment is usually avoided.

Customs Values. The customs value to be determined for imported merchandise dutiable on an ad valorem basis is the foreign wholesale value. This is not so simple as it may sound, however, since the Tariff Act of 1930 provided several alternatives for determining this value. The alternatives have since been altered by the Customs Simplification Act of 1956, and the definitions now used are:

1. Export value.
2. United States value.
3. Constructed value.
4. American selling price (in certain cases only).

Export Value. The *export value* is the market value or price of the merchandise packed ready for shipment at the time of exportation to the

United States, "at which such or similar merchandise is freely sold or . . . offered for sale in the principal markets of the country of exportation, in the usual wholesale quantities and in the ordinary course of trade for exportation to the United States. . . ." [3]

In the Tariff Act of 1930, both export value and *foreign value* were provided for, the higher of the two values to govern. The Customs Simplification Act of 1956 provides for the virtual elimination of foreign value (sale for shipment to any place, not only to the United States). Foreign value will, however, still be applied to the articles contained in a list compiled by the Secretary of the Treasury. These are articles where the elimination of foreign value would cause a decrease of 5 percent or more in dutiable value, based on actual appraisements during the fiscal year 1954.

For example, an imported product sold in 1954 for $100 in the country of export, and this price was paid for products shipped to the United States. At the same time, the country of export sold the same goods for shipment to another country for $110. Under alternative export or foreign valuations, the higher to govern, dutiable value would be $110, not $100. In such a case, foreign value would still apply, since it exceeds export value by more than 5 percent. This valuation is no longer called foreign value; it is now referred to as *alternative value.*

United States Value. The *United States value* is "the price, at the time of exportation to the United States of . . . merchandise . . . at which such or similar merchandise is freely sold or . . . offered for sale in the principal market of the United States for domestic consumption, packed ready for delivery, in the usual wholesale quantities and in the ordinary course of trade, with allowances made for" [4] various expenses, such as commissions, transportation, insurance, customs duties, and taxes.

Constructed Value. The *constructed value* is the sum of (1) the cost of materials and fabrication at the time preceding the date of exportation which would ordinarily permit the production of that merchandise in the ordinary course of business; (2) an amount for general expenses and profits usually charged; and (3) the costs of containers and all other expenses incidental to making the merchandise ready for shipment to the United States.

American Selling Price. The American selling price is employed as a means of equalizing costs of production when the rates of duty (based

---

[3]Tariff Act of 1930, Section 402 as amended.
[4]*Ibid.*

on foreign wholesale value) that may be changed under the flexible provisions of Section 336 of the Tariff Act do not afford such equalization.
As defined, the *American selling price* of an article produced or manufactured in the United States is "the price, including the cost of all containers and coverings . . . and all other expenses incidental to placing the
article in condition packed ready for delivery, at which such article is
freely sold or . . . offered for sale for domestic consumption in the principal market of the United States, in the ordinary course of trade and in
the usual wholesale quantities, or the price that the manufacturer, producer, or owner would have received or was willing to receive for such
article when sold for domestic consumption in the ordinary course of
trade and in the usual wholesale quantities, at the time of exportation of
the imported article." [5]

The appraiser's authority with respect to valuation is absolute; but
with respect to tariff classification, it is merely advisory. He reports his
findings to the collector and liquidation (final determination of duties)
may now be made.

Flexible and Variable Provisions. Rates of duty may not actually
be as indicated in the tariff law, since provision is made in the various
administrative sections of the Tariff Act of 1930 for changes in the established bases. The United States Tariff Commission is directed to investigate differences in costs of producing articles in the United States and in
the principal competing country. In order to equalize such differences,
the President may, upon recommendation of the commission, increase
or decrease a rate of duty or change a classification in such way as to
cause an increase or decrease in duty amounting to not more than 50
percent. If differences in the costs of production are not equalized in
this manner, the altered duty may be levied on the American selling
price of the goods.

Under Section 338, provision is made for combating discriminations
by foreign countries against United States commerce. Under Section
337, unfair practices and methods of competition in the import trade,
such as are intended to injure an American industry or to prevent the
establishment of an American industry or to restrain or monopolize trade
in the United States, are met by exclusion of such merchandise from importation into this country. The United States Tariff Commission is
directed to assist the President in investigations leading to such findings.

---

[5] *Ibid.*

Antidumping Duties. Under the Antidumping Act of 1921, as retained in the Tariff Act of 1930, additional duties may be levied in the case of dumping, the amount of the additional duty being the difference between the foreign market value and the price at which the same goods are sold for exportation to the United States. Section 303 provides for the collection of "countervailing duties" equal to the net amount of grants or bounties paid by any foreign business concern or government for the production or exportation of any article that enters American import trade. They are levied in the case of dutiable articles only and are in addition to regular duties.

Import Quotas. The duty payable on certain imported products depends upon the operation of a quota provision according to which lower rates are usually assessed up to a stated quantity of imports (quota). After this volume of imports is reached, additional imports during a designated period of time would be assessed higher rates of duty. For example, butter is imported under trade agreement authority and Department of Agriculture license at a duty of 7 cents per pound on a quota of 50 million pounds imported during the period November 1 to March 31. Butter imports in excess of this quantity or outside of the designated time period are assessed a duty of 14 cents per pound.

Other quota provisions limit the absolute quantity of certain products to be imported during a given annual period of time, with no reductions in rates of duty related to such quantity. In the case of Philippine imports, certain products are under both tariff and quantity quotas. As the rate of duty increases progressively after 1955, the quota admitted duty free into the United States is reduced progressively.

"The quota status of a commodity subject to a tariff-rate quota cannot be determined in advance of the entry. . . . It is not unusual that several entries may have been filed at more than one port at the exact time when the quota fills. . . . Many of the commodities subject to absolute quotas are presented for entry in such volume that the quota is filled at the opening moment."[6]

Finally, rates of duty, as applied, may be lower than established originally in the tariff act by reason of reductions effected under the Trade Agreement Act of 1934 and its extensions.[7]

---

[6]U.S. Treasury Department, Bureau of Customs, *Customs Information for Exporters to the United States,* p. 61.

[7]The above-named flexible provisions are inoperative with respect to articles on which the United States has granted a concession in a reciprocal trade agreement.

Customs Penalties and Controversies. Additional duties may be incurred in case of undervaluation of merchandise dutiable ad valorem. If the final appraised value of such merchandise exceeds the declared value, one percent additional duty may be levied for each one percent of the excess, subject to a maximum penalty of 75 percent. Appeals are heard by the United States Customs Court[8] and if the Court holds the undervaluation to have been unintentional, a refund is made. If the appraised value is more than 100 percent in excess of the declared value, fraud is presumed and the merchandise is seized.

Controversies Over Valuation. Controversies over valuation, classification, and other customs matters are common. In case of disagreement over value, where the appraiser has absolute authority as against the collector, appeal for reappraisement may be filed with the United States Customs Court through the collector of customs within 30 days by an importer, or within 60 days by a collector. Further appeals may be made by either a collector or an importer within thirty days from the date this decision is filed with the collector. The application is assigned to a single judge and, on appeal, to a full division of three judges. The decision rendered (published in *Treasury Decisions*, a weekly) is final and conclusive "unless an appeal should be taken by either party to the Court of Customs and Patent Appeals[9] upon a question or questions of law only."

Controversies Over Rates of Duty, etc. Controversies also occur over decisions of a collector relating to the rate and amount of duties chargeable, drawback claims, exclusion of merchandise from entry or delivery, and liquidation or reliquidation. In questioning such decisions, an importer may file a protest with the collector, setting forth specifically the reasons for objecting. If the collector and the importer cannot agree, the case is sent by the collector to the United States Customs Court.

American manufacturers, producers, or wholesalers engaged in producing or handling a type of merchandise that is also imported may file complaint with the Secretary of the Treasury whenever they believe the classification, valuation, or duty assessed on imported merchandise is too low or is otherwise improper. If their contention is not sustained by the Secretary of the Treasury (or, in the case of valuation, by the appraiser),

---

[8]The United States Customs Court, with headquarters at New York, consists of nine judges appointed by the President. The court functions in three divisions of three judges each, and individual judges are assigned to decide many questions. Section 518 of the Tariff Act of 1930 gives to judges and to divisions the power of judges of United States District Courts with respect to calling witnesses, keeping records, preserving order, and punishing contempt.

[9]The Court of Customs and Patent Appeals, the name adopted on March 2, 1929, consists of five judges appointed by the President and maintains headquarters in Washington, D.C.

appeal may be carried to the customs courts as previously described. In such proceedings, the importers affected are to be informed and they may appear to defend their position.[10]

Smuggling and Customs Fraud. Smuggling, which is the failure to declare merchandise, and *customs fraud*, which is the use of false, forged or fraudulent invoices and importation of merchandise contrary to law, are punishable under the Tariff Act.

Customhouse Brokers. For the routine associated with entering merchandise as well as in controversies that may ensue, an importer may engage the services of technical experts. Customhouse brokers take over all details of customs procedure. They are required to be enrolled under the rules and regulations prescribed by the Secretary of the Treasury.

Bonded Warehouses

Consignees may not always desire to pay duty and take possession of imported merchandise immediately after arrival. Provision is, therefore, made for storage of dutiable imports in bonded warehouses.[11]

In certain bonded warehouses especially authorized for the purpose, importers may clean, sort, repack, or otherwise change the condition of merchandise. They may not engage in manufacturing in such warehouses. Certain other types of warehouses, however, subject to stricter customs supervision and more exacting regulations, are designated as *bonded manufacturing warehouses.*[12] Only a few exceptions are made to the general rule that manufacturing in bonded warehouses is to be exclusively for export.

Special provision is also made for *bonded smelting warehouses.* The plants of manufacturers engaged in smelting or refining ores or crude metals may, upon giving satisfactory bond, receive imported ores or crude metals and smelt or refine them "together with ores or crude metals of domestic or foreign production."[13]

In general, all bonded warehouses are under bond satisfactory to the Secretary of the Treasury. They are in charge of a customs officer, who, jointly with the proprietor, has custody of all stored merchandise, subject to detailed customs regulations. Imported merchandise may be

---

[10]Tariff Act of 1930, Section 516.
[11]Warehouses may also be open spaces such as yards for handling bulk minerals, etc.
[12]Tariff Act of 1930, Section 311.
[13]*Ibid.*, Section 312.

withdrawn from bonded warehouses (1) for consumption (upon payment of import duties and accrued charges); (2) for transportation and exportation; or (3) for transportation and warehousing at another port.[14]

Drawbacks

The exportation of imported merchandise on which duties have been paid does not result in a refund of the duties except when articles manufactured from dutiable imported materials are exported or when imports fail to conform to specifications. In such cases, 99 percent of the duties paid may be refunded as *drawback*. Export for benefit of drawback must be made within three years from the date of importation.

Under certain circumstances, such as the destruction of goods not entitled to admission or the use of goods by vessels and aircraft in certain trades, refund of 100 percent is authorized.

Moreover, Section 308 of the Tariff Act of 1930 provides that certain imported articles "when not imported for sale or for sale on approval" may be admitted into the United States without payment of import duties, under regulations and bond for their exportation. Articles to which this privilege is accorded are samples of merchandise for taking orders; models of women's wearing apparel; "machinery or other articles to be altered or repaired"; articles intended for experimental purposes; automobiles and other vehicles and craft, etc., brought temporarily by nonresidents for touring or to take part in races or other contests; containers for compressed gas; and several others.

Free Ports or Foreign-Trade Zones

The reexport trade of the United States has been greatly handicapped by the following: the inconvenience, expense, and delay in the drawback system as it applies to imports that have passed out of the custody or control of the United States Government; the expense and restrictions incident to the storage, repacking, cleaning, mixing, blending, and manufacturing of imported merchandise in bonded warehouses, and reshipment from such warehouses.

Free Ports in the United States. As a means of overcoming such handicaps, the establishment of free ports in the United States has been

---

[14]*Ibid.*, Section 557.

authorized by the Foreign-Trade Zones Act of June 18, 1934. A *free port*, or a *foreign-trade zone*, as permitted by this act, is an isolated, enclosed, and policed area, in or adjacent to a port of entry and operated as a public utility by a corporation under the supervision of a Foreign-Trade Zones Board.[15] According to the Act, "each port of entry shall be entitled to at least one zone." Applications for a grant are to be made by "public corporations." Thus far, six zones have been established: Stapleton, Staten Island; New Orleans, Louisiana; San Francisco, California; Seattle, Washington; Toledo, Ohio; and Mayaguez, Puerto Rico.

The foreign-trade zone is an area without resident population; furnished with facilities necessary for lading and unlading; for storing goods, both domestic and foreign; for subjecting the goods to specified manipulation and processing operations; and for reshipping them by land and water. Moreover, by amendment of June 17, 1950, the Foreign-Trade Zones Act permits manufacture and exhibition of merchandise in a foreign-trade zone.

If reshipped to foreign ports, merchandise may leave a foreign-trade zone without customs supervision; but if reshipped for domestic use, existing customs laws must be fully complied with. The area is subject equally with adjacent regions to all laws pertaining to public health, vessel inspection, postal service, immigration, and to the supervision of federal agencies having jurisdiction in ports of entry, including customs, to a limited extent.

Free Ports and Free Trade Ports Outside the United States. Free ports or foreign-trade zones are not to be confused with *free trade ports*, such as Hong Kong, Singapore, Aden, and several others, where merchandise may be brought in and redistributed to other countries without customs formality of consequence. These are distributing points or entrepôts that derive their commercial importance from their focal position on ocean trade routes.

Free ports generally are intended to facilitate the conduct of re-export trade. For this reason, they have been established mostly in countries close to neighbors embracing a protective tariff system. Such ports as Barcelona, Bremen and Bremerhaven, Copenhagen, Gothenburg, Hamburg and Cuxhaven, Naples, and Stockholm have derived their commercial importance partly from the facilities afforded their commerce by means of free port areas.

---

[15]The Board is composed of the Secretary of Commerce as Chairman, the Secretary of Treasury, and the Secretary of Army.

Services Permitted in United States Foreign-Trade Zones. The Foreign-Trade Zones Act of 1934 provides that foreign and domestic merchandise entering a zone "may be stored, broken up, repacked, assembled, distributed, sorted, graded, cleaned, mixed with foreign or domestic merchandise, or otherwise manipulated." Manufacturing and exhibition are permitted according to the June 17, 1950, revision of the Act. Large-scale manufacturing is not contemplated, but rather processing and relatively simple operations. Exhibition will permit display of imported goods for sale but not at retail. Other changes in the law permit the binding determination of import duties and also internal revenue taxes on imported merchandise as long as it remains in a zone, and as long as no change is made in the product causing a change in classification. With this assurance of the actual amount of import duties and internal revenue taxes to be incurred, delivered prices in United States customs territory can now be confidently quoted on imported merchandise.

Another important change in the Act permits merchandise moved to or located in foreign-trade zones to be considered as having been exported. This provision, with certain exceptions administered under the jurisdiction of the Board, offers considerable advantage.

> A producer using dutiable imported materials in his product may recover drawback, that is, 99 per cent of the duty paid on the imported materials, without waiting until he finds a foreign customer, or until his foreign customer is ready to receive delivery, or until the merchandise actually arrives abroad. Owners of domestic products stored in customs or internal-revenue bonded warehouses may transfer their goods to a zone for export and secure immediate cancellation of the bonds. If such products are subject to internal-revenue taxes, payment of such taxes may be obtained — thereby accelerating the date when the funds invested become available again to the business.[16]

Advantages of Foreign-Trade Zones. The advantages claimed for foreign-trade zones in the United States may be summarized as follows:

> 1. The foreign exporter bears none of the expense for bonds or customs inspectors for as long as imports are stored, sold, manipulated, exhibited, or manufactured in a foreign-trade zone. This applies whether the merchandise is dutiable or nondutiable.
> 2. Imports may remain in storage with no time limit until entry into United States customs territory is desired.

---

[16]*Foreign Commerce Weekly*, Vol. XXXIX, No. 13 (June 26, 1950), p. 4.

3. Ships, lighters, railroads, motor trucks, and parcel post make direct delivery to or from zones, insuring speedy, efficient, and frequent carrier service.

4. Foreign exporters or their agents utilizing foreign-trade zones place owners of merchandise in a position to obtain dollar bank loans in the United States on negotiable warehouse receipts, thereby releasing capital for other transactions.

5. Shipments arriving improperly marked may be remarked at the zone to meet customs requirements in the United States, thus avoiding penalties.

6. Commodities under quota restrictions may be received, as indicated previously, in any quantity in excess of the allotted quota; they may be held without customs liquidation awaiting the next quota period or periods.

7. At any time while imported goods remain in the zone, and without incurring any liability to make payment or having to post bond, importers can obtain a determination, based on the tariff-classification status of the goods, not only of the duties but also of the internal-revenue taxes to which the goods would be subject upon formal entry.

8. Domestic merchandise, or products of foreign origin that have already entered United States customs territory duty-paid or duty-free, may be taken into a foreign-trade zone and be considered as exported for the purpose of the drawback, warehousing, bonding, and other provisions of the tariff act and internal-revenue laws.

9. In all foreign-trade zones, the examining of foreign merchandise is permitted. Such examination not only is convenient but may also prevent costly transportation to interior points, and subsequent costly return, of damaged or defective merchandise. Moreover, examination prior to customs entry precludes the possibility of payment of duties on damaged or unsalable merchandise.

10. Foreign firms may erect their own structures within the zone to perform manipulating or manufacturing processes adapted to their needs.[17]

Summary

1. The United States Government imposes regulations on import trade that to importers are just as onerous as the regulations imposed by other countries on exports from the United States.
2. Exporters in any country are frequently unaware of obstacles that their buyers (importers) face from government regulations, unless it is a tariff rate or a monetary regulation rendering difficult the payment for imports.
3. Import regulations in the United States are administered by the Customs

---

[17]Thomas E. Lyons, Executive Secretary, Foreign-Trade Zones Board, in *Foreign Commerce Weekly*, Vol. XL, No. 6 (August 7, 1950), p. 6.

Service in the Treasury Department. These regulations refer to permission for goods to enter, the valuations, quantities, rates of duties, etc.

4. The United States is divided into 45 customs districts with a collector in charge of each district. The comptrollers of customs act as auditors.

5. Vessels, airplanes, and merchandise must be officially "entered" into the United States through customs offices. There are several types of entry for merchandise, such as for consumption, transportation, warehouse, etc.

6. For products dutiable ad valorem, several bases of valuation are used, namely, export value, United States value, constructed value, and American selling price. Each basis is technically defined and has its special use.

7. Tariff rates may be changed administratively by the President of the United States upon recommendation of the United States Tariff Commission. Discrimination and unfair practices in the import trade are penalized. Dumping is a special type of unfair practice and it is also penalized.

8. Some imports have a tariff quota that limits the quantity to be imported at the stated tariff rate.

9. Willful undervaluation of goods dutiable on value leads to penalties. Special customs courts function to consider controversies.

10. Customhouse brokers handle all the details of customs procedures for importers.

11. Dutiable goods may be stored in bonded warehouses and processed without payment of duty unless withdrawn for domestic consumption.

12. Free ports, or foreign-trade zones as they are called in the United States, are areas that are removed from customs supervision. In such areas, foreign goods can be processed and manufactured without payment of duties unless withdrawn for domestic consumption. Many advantages are cited for foreign-trade zones in the United States.

QUESTIONS

1. Point out and comment on the inconsistencies in the foreign commercial policy of the United States. Why do such inconsistencies exist?

2. Define the function of the customs agency service.

3. Describe the geographical dispersion of the customs service.

4. How does a vessel from abroad make formal entry in a United States port?

5. Name the documents required for entering merchandise imports and state the significance of each.

6. How is the dollar value of an ad valorem import to be determined when the merchandise in question was paid for in German marks?

7. In the case of goods subject to ad valorem duties, what alternative valuations are provided for under United States regulations?

8. What action may an American producer take if he believes that his domestic market is being harmed by imports and that the import duty is too low?

9. What happens to the imports from countries that discriminate against United States trade?

10. What can be done under United States laws regarding imports that are mislabeled in order to deceive American purchasers?
11. How much additional duty is levied on an import that sells in the country of exportation for $10 and is quoted to American buyers variously at $8, $9, $10, $11, and $12?
12. How does an import quota work? Give an example.
13. How does the granting of a trade agreement concession in the import duty on a product affect the applicability of the flexible provisions of the Tariff Act to that product?
14. Define willful undervaluation and state the penalty for conviction.
15. Outline the procedure for adjudicating customs controversy over valuation of imports.
16. Outline the procedure for adjudicating customs controversy over customs classification and rate of applicable duty.
17. Define the functions of customhouse brokers.
18. What is the purpose of a bonded warehouse?
19. Describe a drawback and explain how it may be claimed.
20. Why are free ports or foreign-trade zones authorized to be established in the United States?
21. Define the permissible functions that may be performed in foreign-trade zones in the United States.
22. Distinguish between a free trade port like Hong Kong and a foreign-trade zone in the United States.
23. Comment critically on the asserted advantages of foreign-trade zones.

PROBLEMS

1. If there is a customhouse nearby, arrange a visit to the appraiser's stores. Examine the imported merchandise located there and also the billing that accompanies each imported item. Prepare a report of what you have seen.
2. The tariff treatment on certain imported merchandise has "hit the headlines." Chief among such merchandise are watches, bicycles, clothes pins (spring pins), and petroleum. From reports of the United States Tariff Commission and news items in such papers as the *New York Times* and *Journal of Commerce*, prepare a report on any one of these imported products (or any other) and bring out the contentions and decisions pertaining to it.

COLLATERAL READINGS

Customs House Guide. New York: Budd, annual.

Dartnell International Trade Handbook, The. Chicago: The Dartnell Corporation, 1963.

Downings United States Customs Tariff. New York: current.

Horn, Paul V. *International Trade Principles and Practices,* Third Edition. New York: Prentice-Hall, Inc., 1951. Chapter 32.

Humphrey, Don D. *American Imports.* New York: Twentieth Century Fund, 1955.

Pratt, E. E. *Modern International Commerce.* New York: Allyn and Bacon, Inc., 1956. Chapter 12.

Roorbach, G. B. *Import Purchasing: Principles and Problems.* Chicago and New York: A. W. Shaw Company, 1927. Chapter 13.

——————————. *Problems in Foreign Trade.* New York: McGraw-Hill Book Company, Inc., 1933, Part VI.

Rosenthal, Morris. *Techniques of International Trade.* New York: McGraw-Hill Book Company, Inc., 1950. Part III.

United States. *Customs Administrative Act of 1938.* Washington, D.C.: Government Printing Office, 1938.

——————————. *Customs Simplification Act of 1955.* Washington, D.C.: Government Printing Office, 1955.

——————————. *Tariff Act of 1930.* Washington, D.C.: Government Printing Office, 1930.

——————————. *Trade Agreements Act of 1934* and amendments thereto. Washington, D.C.: Government Printing Office.

United States Commerce Department, Foreign Trade Zones Board. *Annual Report.* Washington, D.C.: Government Printing Office.

——————————. *Laws, Regulations, and Other Information Relating to Foreign Trade Zones in the United States.* Washington, D.C.: Government Printing Office, December, 1958.

United States Tariff Commission. Studies of various commodities and policies relating to international trade.

United States Treasury Department Bureau of Customs. *Exporting to the United States.* Washington, D.C.: Government Printing Office, 1959.

United States Treasury Department. *Customs Regulations of the United States.* Washington, D.C.: Government Printing Office, various dates.

——————————. *Treasury Decisions.* Washington, D.C.: Government Printing Office, weekly.

CHAPTER 24

LEGAL ASPECTS OF INTERNATIONAL MARKETING

The problem of adjusting private trade disputes, although not peculiar to international marketing, is especially important in this branch of commerce. Commercial disputes are more difficult to avoid in international marketing because foreign as well as American commercial customs and laws are instrumental, and because of the greater likelihood of damage in course of transportation and the somewhat more general dependence upon samples, grades, or descriptions as the basis for sales. When commercial disputes do occur in international trade, their adjustment is complicated by the greater distance between buyer and seller and frequently by the absence of direct representation on the part of the exporter, as well as by differing trade customs and laws.

Growing experience on the part of international marketing enterprises, more careful selection of foreign agents and distributors, more precise and carefully drawn agency contracts, the establishment of foreign branches, and closer acquaintance with price quotations and with the commodities of international commerce tend to reduce the number of trade disputes; but from the very nature of merchandise transactions, misunderstandings are at times bound to occur. Many, of course, are adjusted directly between buyer and seller, sometimes on an entirely equitable basis. At other times, however, either the exporter or the importer reluctantly accepts a loss or an unsatisfactory adjustment.

Moreover, when an international trader transacts business abroad, he finds himself subject to the laws of the countries in which he operates. Foreign law may also apply to business transactions in which the jurisdiction is not so clearly settled. The rights, privileges, requirements, immunities, etc., that foreign law stipulates are always of vital interest to international traders who have any commercial or financial contact, direct or indirect, with other countries.

Foreign law is in many respects different from the law with which the exporter or the importer is already familiar. It is the purpose of this chapter, therefore, to point out some of the differences that are to be found and to offer a means of appreciating the complexity of the subject as a whole.

What Law Governs?

Perhaps the first question to consider relates to the law governing a particular transaction between say, an American and an Argentine. Is the American or the Argentine law to govern? How is this to be determined? In case of dispute, it is apparent that two different jurisdictions are involved. One way definitely to settle this question beforehand is to agree in the sales or purchase contract, or in the agency agreement, or in the course of correspondence, as to what law is to apply. American exporters often declare in advance that all conditions are to be interpreted according to the law of some designated state of the United States.

Failing to come to such preliminary understanding, the question of jurisdiction may be decided by private international law. According to some authorities, the law of the place at which the contract was *entered into* governs. Thus, if an American contracts in Argentina to purchase Argentine linseed oil, the Argentine law governs the transaction. On the other hand, some authorities hold that the law of the place of contract *performance* is to govern, and this is often a different country from that in which the contract was entered into. Thus, an American salesman might visit an Argentine importer of machinery and receive an order in which the exporter undertakes to deliver the merchandise f.a.s. vessel New York. Contract *performance* would take place in New York while the place of contract would be in Argentina.

Still other authorities consider both factors in an endeavor to apply the principles that the parties are presumed to have had in mind. In such reasoning, the law of the place of contract might be made to apply to such matters as formalities attending the transaction and unforseen difficulties. The law of the place of performance would govern the nature and extent of the understanding and the ways in which the contract is to be carried out.

Applying Foreign Law to National Proceedings. Since there is no uniformity in private international law, any one of these principles might be invoked in case a dispute should arise. The practice of the particular country in which litigation is instituted might govern the selection of the law that is applicable. Thus, an Argentine court in which an American would bring suit against an Argentine firm might decide that United States (municipal) law applies in the case, and the court would then apply the appropriate United States legal principles.

The practice of invoking the laws of one country in the courts of another is common and is an indication of the honest efforts of tribunals to render justice. These principles are not effective, however, if a definite previous understanding as to the law governing a transaction has been mutually agreed upon.

Commercial Usage. Aside from the municipal law or international law that would be invoked in connection with international commercial transactions, there is also the question of commercial usage. This is common law in the making and it is recognized throughout the world. Courts of law take cognizance of those established principles of trade and commerce embraced within commercial usage and accept them as binding upon merchants.

In endeavoring to determine the intent of the parties nothing could be more justly presumed than commercial usage, for businessmen know the customs in the trade with which they are engaged. These customs or commercial usages are found in conjunction with particular products, with specific countries, and with the functional side of commerce. Thus a quality designation of "fair average quality of the season" is interpretable not by law but by usage; the right to inspect merchandise before accepting the draft is recognized in some countries by law but may be the ordinary practice or custom; and a ton of cargo carried by a vessel may be one of several definitions, all of which an international trader is expected to know.

Common Law and Code Law

The countries of the Free World on a juridical basis fall essentially into two groups: common law and code law.

Common or *community law* developed in England during the centuries following the Norman Conquest of 1066. The common law was a body of unwritten principles, based on customs and usages of the community, that was recognized and enforced by the courts. Common law applies in the United Kingdom and other countries that now or formerly have been associated with British legal thought by reason of colonial or empire relationships.

On the other hand, the remainder of the countries of the world generally adopt the principles of code law. *Code law*, as distinguished from common law, consists of compiled laws, assembled into groups of identical or similar subject matter, thus constituting a code; and, as indicating the main branches of jurisprudence, it is divided into civil, criminal, and commercial codes.

Although a decided advantage of code law is the assembly of all the laws relating to a particular subject, these laws may become antiquated before changes are made. Realizing that many features of commercial codes are out of date, many countries have set for themselves the task of revising or rewriting them. The common law, in spite of the uncertainty, possesses the merit of flexibility.

Napoleonic Code. The earliest of modern legal codes was that promulgated by Napoleon in 1807. The French "Code de Commerce" has been literally adopted or accepted with modifications by many other countries in the world. The German Code, adopted in 1897, has exerted a decided influence upon the laws of the Teutonic and Scandinavian countries, while certain other nations have based their laws partly on the French and partly on the German systems. The fundamental codes have undergone changes in the countries of their origin as well as modifications where they have been adopted.

Codification of Commercial Law. Although the fundamental basis of commercial law in Great Britain and British territory, as well as in the United States, is to be found in precedents of court decisions, there is a tendency toward the codification of commercial law. Progress in this direction is substantially impeded in the United States by reason of the diversity of state laws. Nevertheless, uniformity to a fair degree has been attained in the Negotiable Instruments Law, while still greater codification of the law merchant has occurred in England.

The Uniform Commercial Code is usually divided into a number of books. These deal with the status of merchants; with special contracts peculiar to commerce, such as agreements for the organization of companies, commercial agencies, sales of merchandise, bills and notes, and mercantile loans; with maritime law; and with bankruptcy, insolvency, and suspension of payments. Moreover, the Civil Code frequently contains general regulations governing commercial matters and is to be consulted in connection with the Commercial Code.

Trademarks, Designs, and Commercial Names

A striking illustration of the difference between common and code law is afforded by the law governing "industrial property," particularly trademarks. The same principles apply to the protection of distinctive labels, while commercial names are generally protected throughout the world without complying with set formality. Designs are considered in the same legal light as trademarks, except that registration of designs is usually required prior to any use made thereof. To illustrate the principle, the following discussion will pertain mostly to trademarks.

Trademark Law. In common-law countries, ownership of a trademark is predicated upon use; while in code-law countries, ownership is acquired by *registration*. There are registration laws in common-law countries, but registration is recognized only as prima facie evidence of ownership acquired by use. From the standpoint of international marketing, however, there is value in trademark registration in a common-law country. Many foreign countries will not register a mark for a citizen of the United States unless it is registered in the United States Patent Office.

Trademark registration in a code-law country is a comparatively simple matter for any person who will thereby acquire title, even though a trademark is used by someone else, but is unregistered. Such registration constitutes infringement.

Infringement. *Infringement* consists not only in appropriating a trademark owned by another, but also in adopting a mark so similar in appearance, phonetic qualities, or meaning as to constitute effective infringement. However, when the laws of certain countries permit any one by a mere act of registration to acquire for himself valuable rights properly belonging to another, a more appropriate term would be *piracy*.

An American manufacturer of hosiery was informed that an unauthorized person in Peru had adopted a label almost identical in design to that used by him for a number of years — with the result that many customers purchased an inferior product, believing it to be the genuine American article.

An automobile manufacturer failed to register his trademark in a foreign country — perhaps because he did not deem that the market warranted the expenditure of approximately $100. Later a market developed through the efforts of his agent in the particular foreign country, the agent having registered the name of this automobile. Matters proceeded satisfactorily until the American manufacturer decided to select a new agent and found that it would be necessary to market his automobile *under a new name*, or otherwise pay several thousand dollars to the agent for the transfer of a registration that could have been obtained, as stated above, for $100.

A well-known candy lozenge, which may be seen in almost every drugstore and hotel lobby, and which is sold in many countries of the world, is readily identified not only by its trademark but also by its distinctive label which varies in color according to the flavor of the lozenge. The manufacturer of this product registered his trademark, which is superimposed on the colored label, in a country of Latin America and obtained the required certificate from the trademark office. However, he failed to obtain sufficient protection because another person registered the label used by this manufacturer and inserted a trademark, which, while not confusingly similar to that of the well-known American brand, would hardly be noticed because the label was the outstanding feature. Little could be done about this, unfortunately, because the American manufacturer failed to obtain all the protection afforded under the law. He had left open to the unscrupulous person the opportunity to pirate the label.

Protection from Trademark Piracy. In countries of the common-law group, where registration is regarded as prima facie evidence of ownership, an application to register a trademark may be defeated through court proceedings by proving prior use of a mark by another. This action involves expense and worry, but it will avail even in the absence of registration.

In code-law countries, however, the problem is far more serious, since registration provides the sole basis of ownership. Applications for the registration of trademarks in these countries may be protected in case a rightful owner files opposition within a short period of time (often thirty days) allowed by law to oppose such registration.

Trademark and patent attorneys retained by American concerns watch for applications to register trademarks in certain foreign countries. It may be repeated in this connection, however, that unless the American trademark is registered in the United States Patent Office, there will be no basis for opposing an application for registration in many code-law countries. After a trademark is registered in a code-law country, there is generally no way, after the period of opposition has expired, to defeat the registration, unless fraud can be provided.[1]

---

[1]The Bureau of International Commerce publishes up-to-date information on the protection of industrial property rights in most foreign countries.

International Conventions and Agreements Relating to Industrial Property

In an endeavor to reconcile the differences that exist among the users of trademarks, designs, and commercial names, international conventions have been formed. In this section we shall examine the protection that is afforded by two such conventions.

International Union for the Protection of Industrial Property. The International Union for the Protection of Industrial Property was drafted at Paris in 1883 and was modified several times, the latest being in 1958 at Lisbon. The Union now embraces practically all of the commercially and industrially important countries of the world. The headquarters of the Convention are located at Berne, Switzerland.

Under this Convention, the signatory countries agree to:

1. Register and protect the trademarks of the citizens of other signatory states to the same extent that national trademarks are protected.

2. Register trademarks of citizens of other signatory states in the form in which they are registered in the country of origin.

3. Acknowledge the property rights residing in trade names without the formality of registration.

4. Grant a priority period of six months (twelve months for patents and utility models) from the date of application for registration in the country of origin for making application for registration in any signatory state. Application made within the time limit prescribed is considered as simultaneous with the application for deposit in the country of origin.

General Inter-American Convention for Trade-Mark and Commercial Protection of Washington. The General Inter-American Convention for Trade-Mark and Commercial Protection of Washington affords, among the signatory republics of the Western Hemisphere, protection similar to that available under the Convention Union. In addition, it grants the right of a trademark owner "to apply for and obtain the cancellation or annulment of the interfering mark upon proving . . . (1) that he enjoyed legal protection for his mark in another of the Contracting States prior to the date of the application for registration or deposit which he seeks to cancel" and either (2) that the present holder "had knowledge of the use, employment, registration or deposit in any of the Contracting States" or (3) that the rightful owner has used the mark in the country where registration has been made by an unauthorized party, prior to his filing application for such registration or prior to his adoption and use.

An International Bureau was established at Havana to provide for central registration. The United States denounced the protocol under which this Bureau operated and ceased to participate in its work on September 29, 1945.[2]

Patents. Patent laws of the various countries differ more widely than those relating to other industrial property.

> Many countries have a provision in their laws that a patent may not be applied for after the publication of the invention there or in any other country. Some countries provide that publication or public use anywhere prior to filing the application will be a bar to novelty. Even a foreign application neither printed nor published, but only laid open to public inspection in a single copy somewhere abroad, may be detrimental to novelty. In some countries publication even by word of mouth may be detrimental. There are some few countries where confirmation or importation patents may be obtained after the issuance of a patent in the home country if the invention has not become known in that particular country.[3]

There are wide variations between countries insofar as the issuance of patent is concerned. Some countries refuse to grant patents on certain products, e.g., chemical compounds. Others issue patents soon after application is made, but affording protection for various periods of times. Moreover, most countries require that local manufacture be undertaken so that a patent cannot be used to protect the position of a business firm. The Soviet is not a signatory to the International Patent Agreement.

Common Market Concept. Under the antitrust rules of the Common Market, paragraph 305 provides that the Common Market Commission, which is the governing body, may, upon being notified of certain agreements or concerted practices, rule that such actions, even if they may restrict competition, are still permissable if it can be shown that they are reasonable, do not result in monopoly, and promote rather than impede interstate commerce.

---

[2]United States Department of State, *Participation of the United States Government in International Conferences, 7/1/41 to 6/30/45,* p. 212.
[3]*International Commerce* (November 26, 1962), p. 22.

Merchants and Their Obligations

The body of commercial law applies to a special group of society known as traders. A *trader* is usually defined as one who is habitually engaged in commerce as a profession; all other persons are *nontraders*. It is essentially to establish the relations between these two groups as well as between traders that the commercial code has been separately instituted.

Commercial Register. One of the primary obligations imposed upon traders in code-law countries is to enroll in the commercial register of the city or locality in which their business is transacted. These registers are usually maintained by the commercial courts, although chambers of commerce occasionally have charge of them. The register is viewed in a sense as a reciprocal obligation on the part of the trader in exchange for the trust and confidence that he elicits from the public. The information to be entered in the appropriate commercial register usually includes:

1. The firm or individual name.
2. A statement as to the nature of the business to be engaged in.
3. The address or place of business.
4. The name of the manager or employee in charge of the business.
5. At times, the amount of capital subscribed in the business, together with the amount contributed by each member.

A second group of registrable items consists of commercial acts that relate to the activities of a firm. These include all documents evidencing modification or dissolution; powers of attorney granted to other persons to act in such capacity; declarations of bankruptcy or suspension of payments, and even documents relating to marital status and attendant property settlements of members of a firm. Deeds and titles to real and industrial property may also be recorded in the commercial register.

Notary Public. Most of these documents must be legalized by a notary public. This official occupies a decidedly more important position in code-law countries than he does under the less formal common-law jurisdictions. The notary frequently is versed in the law, is often a member of the bar, and is placed under bond. The notary maintains a file or protocol of the contracts and documents he has legalized, every act being carefully performed in strict accordance with the law.

Required Book of Account. A further obligation imposed by the commercial code upon traders consists of the maintenance of a minimum number of prescribed books of account. These usually include a journal, an inventory book, and a correspondence file. Additional records may be kept at the discretion of the merchant. Sometimes it is unlawful to keep accounts in any but the national language. At periodic intervals, usually annually, records are inspected by the commercial court, each page being marked and the number of pages in each book certified. This procedure is known as *rubrication*.

Penalties for Failure to Register. Failure to register incurs penalties that consist of a fine or, as is more often the case, of certain legal disabilities. In the event of litigation in which an unregistered firm may become involved, serious difficulties are likely to be encountered, as it might then be necessary to prove legal existence which theretofore had not been established. Indeed, recourse to law courts may be refused an unregistered foreign company; petitions of bankruptcy may be held up or refused; books of account may not be accepted as legal evidence; and other serious impediments are incurred in this failure to register.

Applicability to Foreign Companies. A foreign concern selling through established trade channels abroad is not required to comply with these regulations, but in case a branch is established or a separate company is created under foreign law, these requirements are as effective as in the case of national concerns. Moreover, when business is transacted through foreign agents, the principal may be considered as doing business in a foreign country and therefore be required to comply with the commercial law. In case a foreign business should be registered abroad, certain legal steps are usually necessary in addition to those mentioned in an earlier chapter.[4]

Types of Business Organizations

There are several types of business concerns that are recognized under foreign law, and in many respects they are counterparts of business organizations found in the United States. These forms differ in certain respects as to their relative importance and, in some instances,

---

[4]Foreign legal requirements governing the establishment of branches are outlined on page 282 of Chapter 14.

they are entirely unlike the types of business organizations to be found in the United States.

Partnerships. Most business organizations in foreign countries are smaller units than are generally found in the United States. For this reason, partnerships occupy a more important position. *General partnerships* are authorized by the laws of all countries in the Free World and the liability of members is the same as under English common law: joint and several responsibility of all partners for the debts of the association.

The name of the firm (*société en nom collectif* — French; *socidad colectiva* — Spanish; *offene handelsgesellschaft* — German) may contain only the names of the various partners, and if not all of the names are included, it is to be terminated with the words "and company."

The contract of partnership may be entered into privately or, as generally is the case under Spanish and Latin American law, it is to be formally drawn up, notarized, duly recorded in the commercial register, and published in the daily press of the locality.

Limited Partnerships. The unlimited liability feature of a general partnership has greatly restricted the use of this form of business organization, thus giving rise to the *limited partnership*. The limited partnership (*société en commandité* — French; S. en C. — *sociadad en comandita* — Spanish; *Kommanditgesellschaft* — German) combines two types of partners: first, those who possess the same joint and several responsibility as those of the general partnership, and second, those who have restricted their liability to a definite amount of capital, as witnessed in the articles of agreement. The "sleeping" partners of the second class possess only a financial interest in the enterprise; they exercise the administrative function and their names may not appear in the firm name.

The limited or *commanditair* partnership may be formed either in a simple manner as regards capital holdings, or the entire capital may be divided into shares (French — *société en commandité par actions*), in which case transfer of shares of capital to third parties does not prejudice the partnership organization.

Limited Liability Companies. A further departure from the general partnership organization occurs in *limited liability companies*. These are essentially partnerships on shares by reason of the fact that, while on a personal basis, the business is actually a partnership; but with respect to capital holdings, it partakes of the nature of a corporation. An extensive development of this type of concern is found in the German G.m.b.H. (*Gesellschaft mit beschraenkter Haftung*). Since limited liability companies, as well as their prototypes in other countries, are best considered in contrast with the business corporation, attention will first be paid to corporation law in foreign countries.

Corporations. The *business corporation*, as known in the United States, is found in all countries of the world. It is known in most British countries as a limited (liability) company (Ltd.), in French as *société anonyme* (S.A.), in Spanish as *sociadad anónima* (S.A.), and in German as *aktiengesellschaft* (A.G.). General corporation laws have been enacted in practically all countries.

As contrasted with the types of organization previously discussed, the corporation is an association of capital and not of persons; it possesses an independent identity and exists for a definite or indefinite period of time regardless of the life of the organizers and members. A corporation may usually be formed in foreign countries by agreement of a minimum of five but often seven persons and, together with the text of the articles of incorporation and the bylaws, all of the documents are notarized. Following this, the papers are registered in the commercial register and are published in the official gazette. In most respects, the general features of corporation law in foreign countries are similar to those of American corporation law.

Corporations v. Limited Liability Companies. Now, what differences exist between the corporations, as we know them in the United States, and the limited liability companies which are found in some foreign countries?

The corporation, as it is organized in code-law countries, is particularly well adapted to the demands of large business involving considerable amounts of capital, but it often is too unwieldy and rigid for a modest-sized concern. It should be remembered that business abroad is still on a much more personal basis than it is in this country and units are usually smaller. The limited liability company, moreover, can be formed by fewer organizers, each of whom may participate actively in the affairs of the company. Formal requirements for organization are simple and greater flexibility is afforded with regard to organization and operation.

A limited company, as compared with a corporation, is a private and not a public concern. In fact, it may be a "one man corporation." Shares are generally held privately, there being no widespread distribution as often in the case of a public corporation.

Laws Relating to Sales

In many British jurisdictions, the law relating to contracts is contained in the sale of goods acts of which the United States prototype is the Uniform Sales Act. Many other countries have enacted laws that are analogous to or identical with these provisions, but certain features indicating the scope of foreign law as it applies to the subject of contracts should be noted.

Agency Law. It should be again emphasized that specific provisions agreed upon in sales or purchase contracts between Americans and foreigners will obviate unforeseen difficulties that may arise by the application of unknown foreign law. Agency law varies in different countries.

Often a legal distinction exists between a factor or mandate and a commission agent, although this terminology is by no means uniform. Legally, a *factor* is a manager or administrator of a business in the name of another, and the term does not always represent the same function as it does in the United States. The factor in foreign countries may, therefore, bind the principal in all matters in which he has been granted authority and also to the extent that this relationship is presumed to confer authority. The *commission agent*, on the other hand, is decidedly limited in the powers he possesses with relation to the property of the principal.

Installment Sales. The law of conditional sales is of growing importance to American exporters because the installment plan of selling, so widespread in the United States, is becoming similarly popular and useful in foreign countries.

The *installment* or *conditional sales plan*, whereby title does not pass to the buyer until all payments have been completed, is not recognized in all code-law countries. It is often ruled that delivery of merchandise completes a transaction and that a seller has no right to interpose and repossess goods because of failure to meet certain payments. With the insistence of modern merchandising for some legal basis whereby this plan may be operated in foreign countries, revisions of sales laws have been made in most countries. The Venezuelan "law on sales with reservation of title" authorizes the preservation of title in the seller for goods sold on installment terms. The law also provides, however, that if the purchaser cannot meet his installment payments and the seller reclaims the goods, the would-be purchaser "must be reimbursed for the payments already made less an adequate compensation for the use of the article while it was in his possession, plus damages.[5]

Power of Attorney

The *power of attorney* is a document conferring authority upon the party named to perform, for the account of the grantor, such acts as are specified therein. It is required abroad to establish the precise authority granted to travelers, agents, and attorneys to transact business for a foreign concern. Meticulous care is called for in the preparation of powers of attorney for use in code-law countries, as the law is often strict with respect to form and authentication.

Powers of attorney are necessary in most countries and advisable in all for any foreign traveling representative whether he be owner, partner, officer, or employee. Particularly complicated requirements may arise in connection with powers of attorney carried by representatives of corporations. In such instances it may be necessary to establish not only the right of the representative to act but also the power of the corporation to confer such right.

In drawing up the power of attorney, care is also to be exercised in stating the precise authority to be conferred. General powers of attorney are acceptable in some countries, but in others nothing is recognized unless it is specifically set forth. Although a power of attorney may be acceptable if written in English, it rarely is admitted as legally binding unless translated into the language of the foreign country. Two or three witnesses may be required in order to guarantee the authenticity of a power of attorney.

The specific requirements of each country vary in detail and should be studied closely. The power of attorney, with its importance and technicalities, is among the outstanding phases of foreign commercial law.

Bankruptcy and Insolvency

The laws of the different countries as they relate to this important subject vary considerably. "In some countries the primary object of the bankruptcy law is to punish the debtor, and this was the rule in the ancient law until the introduction of the principle of *cessio bonarum* in Roman

---

[5]*Foreign Commerce Weekly* (June 6, 1955), p. 9.

law."[6] In other countries efforts are made to assist an unfortunate debtor to make a settlement of his obligations and to start anew in business. The laws of some countries are out of harmony with this modern principle, since they have not been changed sufficiently to keep pace with the altered viewpoint.

Moreover, "many legal systems afford inadequate protection to creditors, and the available security devices are either antiquated, cumbersome or illusory. Determine whether the law provides for either real or chattel mortgages and, if so, whether a foreign corporation may hold or enforce rights thereunder."[7]

Suspension of Payments. A modified form of bankruptcy, known as *suspension of payments*, is recognized in some code-law countries. This consists of a personal moratorium granted by the court in cases of voluntary application in which the debtor shows inadequate liquid resources, yet sufficient security, to meet a fixed proportion of his debts within a specified period of time. The consent of the creditors may be necessary to establish this status. Since a period of years is permitted for the continuance of this arrangement, it is open to abuse by debtors.

Rehabilitation of a Bankrupt. Due to the registration system abroad and the juridical position occupied by traders as a class, it is necessary for a bankrupt to be rehabilitated as well as discharged. *Rehabilitation* refers to his reestablishment to the status of merchant with the capacity to carry on business again, while the term *discharge*, as generally employed, refers merely to the settlement arranged with creditors.

The bankruptcy laws of many countries are more stringent than those applying in the United States, particularly with respect to the discharge of bankrupts. Full payment of debts or composition with creditors may be required to obtain discharge and, in case creditors fail to agree upon a composition, the debtor is at all times in the future liable for payment of his obligations. If bankruptcy has been tinged with fraudulent conduct of any description, a debtor is not rehabilitated in many countries until a period of years has passed. This does not refer to his discharge from bankruptcy, which may be accomplished by financial settlement of his debts.

---

[6]United States Bureau of International Commerce, *Trading under the Laws of Australia*, Trade Information Bulletin 412, p. 36.

[7]*Foreign Commerce Weekly* (June 11, 1962), p. 1038. One of a series entitled "A Management Checklist for Overseas Business."

Taxation

In general, a foreign concern whose business is handled by a local agent or dealer in his own name is not considered as "doing business" in the agent's or dealer's country and therefore is not taxable. When, however, branches are operated[8] or an agent or dealer is employed and he works in the name of the concern he represents,[9] or when local business firms are purchased wholly or in part, then the taxes of the foreign country are directly felt. These taxes are levied at national as well as state and local levels.

The tax problem may become serious where it is claimed that an exporting firm in the United States is "doing business" in a certain foreign country and accordingly is subject to taxation on its *whole* worldwide business. It will be recalled that foreign branches of American firms may consist of separate corporations, partly owing to the likelihood of double taxation.

Double Taxation. International double taxation is the concurrent taxation by two or more countries on the same income, whether derived from business or from investment.

Considerable difficulty has been experienced in wrestling with this problem and in the negotiation of bilateral agreements or treaties. Such "treaties must, in the first place, take into account the present differences in the economic development, commercial and financial position, and the structure of the respective taxing systems of the countries concerned. In the second place, they must assure reciprocity in the concessions by a country in order to assure an equitable and sound tax treatment for individuals and corporations under the jurisdiction of both countries."[10]

Two different principles are followed in the negotiation of these treaties. The Continent-Europe approach reflects an allocation of taxing jurisdiction over broad types of income and assets among the contracting countries, while the Anglo-American type grants tax credits by the taxpayer's home country for taxes paid in other countries, coupled with certain tax exemptions or reductions in these other countries. Under both systems, however, there are certain modifications to be found in specific treaties.

---

[8]The subject of taxation and its relation to the establishment of foreign branches is discussed on pages 282 and 283 of Chapter 14.

[9]The role of the agent is fully treated in Chapter 10, commencing on page 192.

[10]Paul Depron, *International Double Taxation* (New York: The Committee on International Economic Policy in cooperation with the Carnegie Endowment for International Peace, 1945), p. 2.

Under the Continent-Europe approach, the property and profits of a corporation are usually taxed by the country in which it maintains its center of management, while the power to levy personal taxes on dividend income and on the ownership of stock is granted to the country in which the stockholders reside. On the other hand, the Anglo-American type of tax convention is based on the domestic laws with special arrangements. In general, dividends are taxable primarily by the country of the recipient, and corporation income by the country in which the head office lies. When one country is permitted to withhold a tax on dividends, however, the other is required to allow full credit for it against its own tax. The United Kingdom goes even further by giving credit, for corporate income taxes, on the proportion of corporation income allocable to the dividend paid by the country in which the head office is located. The United States Revenue Act of 1962 has spurred action on the part of the United States "to build a complete world-wide network of 'modern' double taxation treaties." These treaties would replace the 22 United States Tax Conventions now in force, and the Organization for Economic Cooperation and Development (OECD) is drafting a prototype double taxation treaty that may be adopted by the United States as a means of bringing about uniformity in such treaties.[11]

The National Foreign Trade Convention annually has adopted resolutions urging further consideration of legislation designed to relieve the burden of international double taxation and thus to provide tax equality for United States private enterprises operating abroad, when compared with their foreign competitors.

Discriminatory Taxes. Generally speaking, taxes are imposed irrespective of nationality. At times, a law may impose a greater burden upon foreign than upon domestic concerns, and often where this has occurred in recent years, the effect has been to force foreigners to organize companies abroad and thus become fully nationalized. The alternative may be withdrawal from the market.

Summary

1. When engaged in international marketing, traders of the United States encounter the laws of the countries with which they transact business.
2. In international marketing, the law of the exporting or importing country may govern, depending upon the provisions of law. The parties may agree

---

[11]See *Journal of Commerce* (April 5, 1963).

on the law that is to govern. Commercial usage is very important in helping to decide controversies.

3. The legal systems of the free world are divided between common law and code law. The United States (and the United Kingdon generally) follow common law (precedents) and the rest of the free world follows code law (inscribed codes). There is, however, a tendency in common-law jurisdictions to codify certain elements of commercial law, for example, commercial instruments law.

4. Trademarks, designs, and commercial names are good examples of the differencies in common law and code law. Under common law, the first user has legal ownership; under code law, the first to legally register becomes the owner. International conventions have been negotiated to attempt some reconciliation of these differences.

5. Patent laws of the various countries differ more widely than those related to other industrial property. These laws must be watched closely by firms holding United States patents.

6. Merchants in code-law countries are required to register in a commercial court, setting forth certain information concerning their standing.

7. There are many more partnership arrangements in code-law countries, while corporations are more common in the common-law jurisdictions.

8. Sales laws are also different, as in the law of agencies, conditional (time-payment) sales, etc.

9. A power of attorney is essential to transact certain kinds of business abroad.

10. Bankruptcy and insolvency are more rigidly legislated in many code-law countries.

11. Taxation may involve double taxation — a subject that the United States Government is slowly trying to overcome by means of treaties.

QUESTIONS

1. In case of dispute between an American citizen and the citizen of another country, how is the governing law to be determined?

2. Define (a) commercial usage; (b) common law; and (c) code law.

3. Cite the law concerning trademarks and labels as an illustration of the basic difference between common law and code law.

4. How can United States international traders best protect their property rights in trademarks and labels for use in other countries?

5. Discuss the various provisions frequently embodied in patent laws.

6. Define the concept of merchant in a code-law country.

7. With what legal obligations must a merchant comply? What penalties does he suffer for failure to comply?

8. Define the role of a notary public in code-law countries.

9. What is the meaning of the letters "S.A." following many Spanish and Latin American business names?

10. What is the meaning of the suffix "Ltd." in British business names? of "A.G." in German business names?
11. Contrast the business corporation of the United States and the limited liability companies commonly operating in foreign countries.
12. Is it feasible to sell abroad on an installment sales basis, as is commonly done in the United States?
13. How does the power of attorney relate to the code-law concept? Explain.
14. Are foreign laws more, less, or just as severe as United States laws are concerning bankruptcy and insolvency? Explain.
15. (a) Define international double taxation.
    (b) What is the United States Government trying to do about this matter?

PROBLEM

The Esterbrook Pen Company of Camden, New Jersey, found that Japanese-made pens sold in the Philippines carried such trade names as "Easterbrook," "Easterlook," "Esterbook," etc. These pens sold at a lower price than the legitimate Esterbrook Pen.

The Esterbrook Pen Company has its trade name registered in the United States Patent Office and also in the Philippines. It also knows that a treaty exists between Japan and the United States which guarantees the reciprocal respect of each other's property rights.

As this has become a serious matter, what do you advise the company to do?

COLLATERAL READINGS

Dartnell International Trade Handbook, The. Chicago: The Dartnell Corporation, 1963.

de Haas, J. A. *The Practice of Foreign Trade.* New York: McGraw-Hill Book Company, Inc., 1935. Chapter 15.

Exporters' Encyclopaedia. New York: Thomas Ashwell and Co., Inc., annual.

Gibbons, William J. *Tax Factors in Basing International Business Abroad.* Cambridge: Harvard University Law School, 1957.

Harvard University, International Program in Taxation. *World Tax Series.* Cambridge: Harvard University Press. Each volume deals with a different country.

Horn, Paul V. *International Trade Principles and Practices,* Third Edition. New York: Prentice-Hall, Inc., 1951. Chapters 3 and 4.

Kramer, Victor N. "The Application of the Sherman Act to Foreign Commerce," *The Anti-Trust Bulletin* (July-August, 1958).

Michel, A. J. and Kelman, K. *Dictionary of Intellectual Property.* New York:

Research Patents and Trade-Marks, 1954.

Most, Kenneth S. "Company Law and Practice Abroad," *The Accountant* (January 2, 1960.)

Peaslee, A. J. *Constitution of Nations.* Concord, N. H.: Rumford Press, 1950.

Pinner, H. L. *World Copyright* (4 Parts). New York: H. H. Beutler, 1953.

Pratt, E. E. *Modern International Commerce.* New York: Allyn and Bacon, Inc., 1956. Chapter 14.

Scher, V. A. *Patents, Trade-Marks and Copyrights.* White Plains, N. Y.: A. J. Phiebig, 1954.

CHAPTER 25

SETTLEMENT OF COMMERCIAL DISPUTES

As a means of settling commercial disputes arising from international marketing, a body of arrangements has been developed for worldwide application. These arrangements include conciliation, mediation, and arbitration as "peaceful" methods of settling disputes, and litigation as a "belligerent" method of settlement.

Conciliation and Mediation[1]

When the parties to an export or import transaction are unable or unwilling to adjust a trade dispute by dealing directly with each other, an effort at conciliation or mediation is frequently made. This may imply merely an attempt to allay ill will and to bring the disputants together on a more friendly basis, or it may mean that a trade association executive, an individual businessman, a business firm, or an agency of some kind, acting on the request of one of the parties or upon the mediator's own initiative, will make an attempt to adjust the dispute. Foreign service officers of the United States Government sometimes act in this capacity without, however, having any power to compel an adjustment. Some of the many permanent organizations that provide facilities and rules governing commercial arbitration also encourage conciliation or mediation. The rules of the International Chamber of Commerce, for example, invite interested parties to seek its good offices and provide for the creation of a conciliation commission to facilitate the attainment of a settlement without resort to arbitration or litigation.

---

[1]In mid-1963, the World Bank was reported to be considering a proposal recommending that international investment disputes be settled through an arbitration and conciliation center. Such center would be sponsored by the Bank. See *Journal of Commerce* (July 3, 1963).

Trade disputes are sometimes adjusted directly between the parties concerned or through the medium of third parties, even after they have been submitted for arbitration or after they have been taken to court. Should the disputing parties agree upon a settlement during the course of an arbitration proceeding, they frequently request that the arbitrators give their mutual agreement the status of an award so that it will be binding in case either party later becomes dissatisfied. Often an arbitration tribunal accedes to such requests. Courts of law often suggest the direct settlement of a trade dispute that has become the basis of litigation.

Commercial Arbitration

Should the disputing parties fail to get together directly or through the good offices of a conciliator or mediator, the alternative is either litigation in the courts or arbitration.

Advantages of and Reasons for More Extensive Use. As commercial arbitration is generally voluntary, it is dependent upon the voluntary inclusion of an arbitration clause in contracts or, in the absence of such a clause, upon the voluntary submission of the dispute after it occurs. Arbitration is making headway largely because of the shortcomings of litigation in matters involving trade. Litigation is apt to be costly, to occasion long delays during which business capital is tied up and trade is at a standstill, and to disrupt business friendships. Juries, moreover, may be somewhat more inclined to compromise disputes, and both juries and judges may be poorly equipped to decide a trade dispute, a fair adjustment of which may depend upon complete understanding of a complicated business transaction.

Many trade disputes are not matters of law but of fact, and in many instances such questions of law as do arise in interpreting a business contract are of secondary importance. The tendency of commercial arbitration is in the direction of tribunals consisting of unbiased arbitrators who are experts in their line, or at least are businessmen who are familiar with the sort of facts and practices that arise in the course of a trade dispute. In comparison with court litigation, commercial arbitration lays claim to lower cost, speedier decisions, fewer instances of permanent loss of customers, and more intelligent understanding of the nonlegal points at issue in trade disputes.

The more extensive use of commercial arbitration is also due in part to higher business standards and better business ethics. Its use has undoubtedly been furthered by the enactment of improved arbitration statutes here and abroad, and by the organized efforts of commercial organizations. Many of these commercial organizations have conducted campaigns of education, published carefully devised arbitration rules, set up permanent arbitration machinery, and taken active measures to place their facilities at the disposal of exporters and importers as well as of businessmen engaged in domestic commerce.

Systems of Commercial Arbitration. There are today what might be described as four basic systems of commercial arbitration:

1. British System.
2. International Chamber of Commerce System.
3. Soviet Union System.
4. Western Hemisphere System.

We shall briefly look at each one of these systems and then examine a development that has furthered the use of commercial arbitration.[2]

British System

The London Court of Arbitration was founded in 1892 as a joint committee of the London City Corporation and the London Chamber of Commerce. It was organized to settle commercial cases, but today it handles the many different kinds of disputes that can be legally arbitrated in London. Its rules conform with English arbitration law which, in the main, provides that arbitration awards will be enforceable at law. Hence, those who take their cases to the London Court of Arbitration have assurance that the awards will be enforced by the courts.

In England there are also many trade and commodity associations such as the London Corn Trade Association, the Incorporated Oil Seed Association, the London Rubber Trade Association, the London Fur Trade Association, the London Spice Trade Association, the British Wool Federation, the Liverpool Seed, Cake and General Produce Association, and many others that deal with thousands of cases each year.

---

[2]Morris S. Rosenthal, "The Promotion of International Commercial Arbitration," *The Arbitration Journal*, Vol. 6, No. 4 (1951), pp. 225–228.

International Chamber of Commerce System

The International Chamber of Commerce, in which many countries throughout the world participate through their national committees, has its headquarters in Paris. The Chamber was organized in 1920 by business groups in a few countries who felt that businessmen could do much to help in expanding the flow of goods and services if they worked together in all phases of international trade.

More than forty countries today share in the work of its many commissions which devote themselves to the solution of economic and technical problems that arise in international trade. The Chamber has established a court of arbitration under whose rules arbitrations are conducted. Merchants and manufacturers in all parts of the world use the facilities of the International Chamber of Commerce in Paris for the settlement of their disputes.

Soviet Union System

The Soviet Union system of arbitration provides for the adjudication of disputes between the state agencies of the Soviet government and business firms in other countries with which they deal. Two of the arbitration tribunals of the Soviet Union are active in this field of international trade. They are the Maritime Arbitration Commission of the All-Union Chamber of Commerce which was established in 1930 and the Foreign Trade Arbitration Commission of the All-Union Chamber of Commerce which was established in 1932. Arbitrations are conducted in Moscow and the awards are enforceable under the code of civil procedure of the Soviet Republic.

Western Hemisphere System

The American Arbitration Association was organized in 1926 and the New York State law of 1920 and the Federal Act of 1925 both gave its growth great impetus. In the beginning it confined its activities to the settlement of disputes between parties in the United States, but it has grown greatly so that today it has arbitration panels throughout the United States of more than 12,000 arbitrators in more than 1,500 cities which handle cases in international trade, domestic trade, and labor management disputes. Its rules and regulations satisfy federal government legal requirements and the legal requirements of many different states.

During the 1930's, two additional arbitration tribunals were created in the Western Hemisphere which, with the American Arbitration Association, constitute the Western Hemisphere system. They are the Inter-American Commercial Arbitration Commission which conducts arbitrations in disagreements that businessmen in the Latin American Republics have with each other and with United States businessmen, and the Canadian-American Commercial Arbitration Commission which adjudicates disagreements between Canadian and United States parties.

Even though laws upholding arbitration awards are confined to comparatively few countries in the Western Hemisphere, the existence of the Western Hemisphere system has done much to bring about acceptance of arbitration awards by merchants and manufacturers in those countries where the law does not enforce arbitration awards but in which the force of public opinion causes the loser to accept gracefully a decision that has been made against her.

Voluntary International Arbitration Tribunals

One of the most recent developments which will do much toward furthering the use of arbitration and the creation of necessary arbitration tribunals everywhere is the proposed system of voluntary international arbitration tribunals that is being sponsored by the International Business Relations Council of the American Arbitration Association. The attempt to create additional voluntary arbitration tribunals grew out of the already successful effort to establish reciprocal arbitration agreements among arbitration tribunals that have been in existence and that have operated successfully for many years. For example, the International Chamber of Commerce, the London Court of Arbitration, the American Arbitration Association, and many other arbitration bodies now provide clauses that can be used in contracts as a result of which disagreements will be submitted to one or the other of two arbitration tribunals in the countries of the seller or buyer, depending upon their wishes either at the time of signing a sales contract or at the time of submission of a dispute to arbitration. These reciprocal clauses provide for the conduct of the arbitration by one of two specified arbitration tribunals with the application of the rules of procedure of the tribunal under whose auspices the case is conducted. Merchants and manufacturers have shown an increasing desire to accept these reciprocal arbitration clauses in their sales contracts.

Types of Commercial Arbitration Tribunals

Commercial arbitration tribunals for the adjustment of private trade disputes may, to facilitate description, be classified according to (1) their temporary or permanent character and the manner of their selection, and (2) the number and qualifications of the arbitrators.

Temporary Tribunals. The setting up of a temporary tribunal to arbitrate a particular dispute is a long-established practice, but one that has given way to some extent to the utilization of permanent machinery created in advance. When the business contract does not contain an arbitration clause, or when the arbitration clause does not specify a tribunal already in existence, the parties concerned may, of course, agree to create a temporary tribunal in accordance with their own wishes; or, in case they agree to arbitrate under the terms of an arbitration statute, so as to be assured of a binding award, they will bring about the appointment of a tribunal as provided for by law. They variously agree upon a single "umpire"; upon all of the members of a larger tribunal; or each may select an arbitrator, these to select a third member or umpire. They may utilize the arbitration panels maintained by various commercial organizations as a list from which they will select their arbitrators, and they may call upon the permanent arbitration committee or an executive of such an organization to make selections. They may also depend upon the panels provided by organizations such as the American Arbitration Association, Inter-American Commercial Arbitration Commission, or the International Chamber of Commerce.

When arbitration proceedings are to be conducted under the terms of an arbitration statute, a court of law, if it is legally authorized to do so, may appoint an arbitrator when for any reason the party fails to avail himself of his right of selection. The United States Arbitration Act of 1925, Section 5, for example, makes such provision.

Permanent Tribunals. The tendency of commercial arbitration, particularly in international marketing, is toward the greater use of the facilities provided by permanent commercial organizations or permanent arbitration tribunals. Organizations such as the International Chamber of Commerce, the London Court of Arbitration, the Chamber of Commerce of the State of New York, the Chamber of Commerce of the United States, and the American Arbitration Association are typical organizations that have adopted definite arbitration rules and that maintain committees or tribunals to facilitate the arbitration of trade disputes.

Many organizations with specialized interests also make provision for commercial arbitration in their particular fields. Grain, cotton, coffee, sugar, rubber, jute, and other organized commodity exchanges commonly provide for the arbitration of trade disputes arising out of exchange transactions. A large number of trade associations have also adopted rules and maintain facilities for the arbitration of disputes in their respective trades or industries. Various British trade associations are also active in the commercial arbitration movement and their services are at times utilized by American traders.

Permanent organizations of the types referred to variously assist the disputing parties in the selection of arbitrators, or undertake the actual appointment of arbitrators. They maintain the committees and executives necessary to accomplish this purpose and in some instances to supervise the arbitration proceedings.

Selection of Arbitrators. From what has already been said it is clear that there is no uniformity as to the number of arbitrators comprising an arbitration tribunal. There may be one arbitrator or umpire, or there may be two or more arbitrators, commonly three; and in the latter case all may serve on a common footing, or one of them may act as the deciding umpire.

There is, moreover, no uniform standard as to the qualifications of arbitrators. It has not been an uncommon practice to have each party appoint an arbitrator who would be his advocate, and to appoint a mutually satisfactory third arbitrator or umpire who would, in fact, decide the disputed issue. The tendency in the United States is strongly in the direction of arbitrators, all of whom are disinterested and unbiased. The more recently enacted arbitration statutes, in which the parties to a trade dispute are interested if they wish to be assured of the legal enforcement of the award, discourage the appointment of biased arbitrators. Business concerns that are willing to arbitrate "outside of the law," each depending upon the other's promise to accept the award, may, of course, continue to appoint arbitrators without reference to these statutes.

Should the trade dispute of an American business concern be arbitrated abroad, the selection of arbitrators may be governed by the laws of a foreign country. This will again depend upon the desire of the parties concerned to obtain an award enforceable at law. The laws of various foreign countries contain provisions as to the selection of the arbitrators which are binding in case awards are to be enforceable in courts of law. Aside from legal requirements, the tendency of commercial arbitration in Europe, as indicated by the rules of some of the principal European tribunals, is toward the appointment of unbiased arbitrators rather than partisans. The standard rules of the Inter-American Commercial Arbitration Commission also require the appointment of disinterested and unbiased arbitrators.

Commercial Arbitration Clauses

Definite clauses providing for the arbitration of trade disputes that may arise in the future are, to an increasing extent, being inserted into export sales and agency contracts. Experience has shown that better results can, as a rule, be obtained if arbitration is agreed to before a dispute arises, and the number of states and countries in which such clauses are legally valid and irrevocable is growing. The arbitration clauses found in some contracts are detailed, particularly when the future arbitration provided for is not subject to the rules of a permanent organization. The tendency, however, is toward compact and more or less standardized clauses.

The general arbitration clause of the American Arbitration Association is as follows:

> Any controversy or claim arising out of or relating to this contract or the breach thereof, shall be settled by arbitration, in accordance with the Rules of the American Arbitration Association, and judgment upon the award rendered by the Arbitrator(s) may be entered in any court having jurisdiction thereof.

The standard arbitration clause of the Inter-American Commercial Arbitration Commission is similar to the above but includes these words as to enforceability:

> This agreement shall be enforceable and judgment upon any award rendered by all or a majority of the arbitrators may be entered in any court having jurisdiction.[3]

It should be noted, however, that

> Arbitration clauses providing against future disputes are not specifically enforceable in a number of the Latin American Republics. This applies even to the standard clause of the Commission. Nevertheless, incorporation of a sound arbitration clause into all your contracts is strongly urged. . . . For we all have learned through first-hand experience that even where enforcement is not provided for, the good faith inherent in the use of such a clause predisposes parties to its observance in the vast majority of cases.[4]

Legal Aspects of Commercial Arbitration

Although commercial arbitration has been practiced for many years, both in domestic commerce and in international marketing, the progress that has been made during the past two decades is due in part

---

[3]Sidney Braufman, Executive Secretary, Inter-American Commercial Arbitration Commission, *The Arbitration Journal*, Vol. 6, No. 3 (1951), pp. 157–158.

[4]*Ibid.*

to the enactment of statutes that, subject to specific requirement, (1) provide a legal basis for the validity of contract clauses providing for arbitration of a future dispute, as well as of agreements to arbitrate an existing dispute, (2) stay action in courts of law during the life of the arbitration clause or agreement, and (3) provide a means for the enforcement of awards in courts of law.

United States and British Common Law. Under common law in the United States and Great Britain, an arbitration award in an existing dispute can, as a rule, be enforced in a court of law; but an arbitration clause in a contract providing for the arbitration of a trade dispute that may arise in the future is not legally binding, and agreements to arbitrate existing disputes also are revocable. Either party may refuse to appoint arbitrators, may revoke the authority of arbitrators who have been appointed, and may resort to court litigation. Arbitration under common-law rule, therefore, depends upon the integrity of the parties concerned.

New York Arbitration Statute. The handicap described in the preceding paragraph has been largely removed in the United States and in Great Britain by enacting arbitration statutes. In the United States prior to 1920, many states had enacted laws that facilitated the enforcement of awards but which did not materially change the common-law rule as to revocability. The New York State Arbitration Act of 1920[5] was the first definitely to remove the handicap. Article 2, Section 2, provides that "A provision in a written contract to settle by arbitration a controversy thereafter arising between the parties to the contract, or a submission hereafter entered into of an existing controversy to arbitration . . . shall be *valid, enforceable, and irrevocable,* save upon such grounds as exist at law or in equity for the revocation of any contract."

The Act further provides legal machinery to enforce the specific performance of arbitration clauses and agreements; makes provision for the appointment of arbitrators by the Supreme Court or a judge thereof, upon request of either party to an arbitration agreement in case the other party fails to name them; directs the court to stay court proceedings brought in violation of an arbitration agreement or submission; and authorizes either party to apply to the court for an order confirming the award and to obtain judgment for enforcement.

---

[5]*Laws of 1920,* Chapter 275; *Laws of 1923,* Chapter 341; *New York Civil Practice Act,* Article 84.

United States Arbitration Act. Similar state arbitration statutes have since been enacted in other states. The United States Arbitration Act of 1925 also follows the general trend of the New York State Act of 1920. It is "an act to make valid and enforceable written provisions or agreements for arbitration of disputes arising out of contracts, maritime transactions, or commerce among the states or territories or with foreign nations." Its weakness is that under the United States judicial code, the United States courts do not have jurisdiction to enforce the act unless the amount involved, exclusive of interest and costs, exceeds $3,000.

Arbitration Provisions in Other Countries. The legal status of commercial arbitration agreements and contract clauses as to their validity and irrevocability, and the enforcement of awards is, of course, complicated in international marketing because disputes in this branch of commerce involve citizens and laws of different countries. Many of the countries of continental Europe have fortunately enacted arbitration laws providing for the enforcement of arbitration awards rendered within those countries. England enacted such a statute as long ago as 1889. Some of these European countries enforce awards as court judgments and others as contracts. The legal enforcement abroad of arbitration awards rendered in the United States depends upon the laws of particular foreign countries. Many, although not all, European countries have enacted statutes under which awards arrived at abroad are enforced in their courts, subject to specific conditions varying in different countries.

In 1958, a treaty entitled "Convention on the Recognition and Enforcement of Foreign Arbitral Awards" was approved by a special conference in which representatives of 45 countries participated. The conference was sponsored by the International Chamber of Commerce under its consultative status with the United Nations Economic and Social Council. The convention provides for the enforcement of private arbitral awards granted in other countries that are parties to the convention. Before coming into effect, however, the convention must be ratified by the parliaments of the several countries. The United States abstained from voting on the convention.

Legal Procedure

In case litigation in foreign countries should become necessary, extreme care is called for in the steps to be taken. Indeed, the decision to carry a matter into the courts is in itself a weighty one. The admonition now generally accepted as to the wisdom of avoiding litigation, if possible, applies with added emphasis when foreign litigation is considered.

If a number of American firms are involved in the bankruptcy proceedings of the same foreign concern, it may be advisable to form a protective committee and to retain an attorney. The appointment of an attorney in foreign legal cases may be made from the American legal firms that specialize in foreign law, particularly the law of the jurisdiction in which a given case is to be tried; or a lawyer residing in the foreign country may be selected. In either case, a sufficiently comprehensive power of attorney is required in order to establish before the court the authority conferred upon the attorneys.

One experienced attorney expresses it this way: "I have had the experience abroad of watching several lawsuits firsthand and, although both of them ended in nominal victory, the costs, frustrating delays and extended aggravation which these cases involved were certainly more oppressive, by far, than any matters of comparable size I have watched in the United States."[6]

Summary

1. Apart from law, international marketing disputes may be settled by means of conciliation and mediation but chiefly by arbitration.
2. Arbitration usually is agreed upon in sales and purchase contracts. It is less expensive and faster than court proceedings. It deals, moreover, with factual matters that frequently are the basis of a commercial dispute.
3. There are several systems of commercial arbitration today:
   (a) The British system was established in 1892 and enjoys the backing of the courts in the enforcement of arbitral awards.
   (b) The International Chamber of Commerce system dates from 1920 and it is extensively used.
   (c) The Soviet Union system deals with commercial disputes between the Soviet business state agencies and business enterprises in other countries with which they deal.
   (d) The Western Hemisphere system, spearheaded by the American Arbitration Association, is used extensively although few countries in this area assure legal enforcement of arbitral awards.
4. Numerous commodity trades have devised their own arbitration rules and procedures.
5. In the selection of arbitrators, the tendency is to seek disinterested but informed arbitrators.

---

[6]Andrew W. Brainerd in *Export Trade* (June 12, 1961), p. 32.

6. In the United States, the federal Arbitration Act of 1925 provides legal means of enforcing arbitral awards, even those involving future, rather than past, disagreements.
7. Litigation in foreign countries is to be avoided, if at all possible.

QUESTIONS

1. In the event of an international marketing dispute, how could settlement be reached by means of mediation or conciliation?
2. Why is arbitration frequently more effective than litigation in settling commercial disputes?
3. Classify and identify the recognized commercial arbitration systems available in international marketing.
4. How may an arbitration panel be selected apart from using the facilities of established arbitration associations?
5. Comment on the number and qualifications of arbitrators to serve on an arbitration panel.
6. Outline and explain the essential elements of arbitration legislation.
7. What is the status of an arbitration clause in a contract with a business firm in a country that does not legally validate arbitration?
8. How is litigation conducted in code-law countries?

PROBLEM

You have been waiting for a remittance of $5,000 from a customer in another country. The merchandise has been delivered, but payment has not been made on the assertion that the merchandise shipped was not the same as that described in your firm's catalog. You have since learned that this customer has overbought and is therefore in financial difficulty. The customer offers to submit the dispute to arbitration. Will you accept this offer? If so, why? If not, why not?

COLLATERAL READINGS

American Arbitration Association. *The Arbitration Journal.* New York: quarterly.
———————————. *Arbitration News.* New York: periodically.
Chase, Stuart. *Roads to Agreement.* New York: Harper & Brothers, 1951.
de Haas, J. A. *The Practice of Foreign Trade.* New York: McGraw-Hill Book Company, Inc., 1935. Chapter 16.
Domke, Martin (ed.). *International Trade Arbitration — A Road to World-Wide Cooperation.* New York: American Arbitration Association, 1958.
Exporters' Encyclopaedia. New York: Thomas Ashwell and Co., Inc., annual.
Rosenthal, Morris. *Techniques of International Trade.* New York: McGraw-Hill Book Company, Inc., 1950. Chapter 3.

PART V

FINANCIAL FEATURES OF
INTERNATIONAL MARKETING

The financial features discussed in this part deal with those involved in international business transactions engaged in by business enterprisers. It is on the bases described here and the facilities analyzed that practically all of world trade is financed.

Part V begins with an analysis of the private and of the government financing facilities available in the international business field. Then follow two chapters dealing with international commercial payments. These are vitally important chapters because these methods are quite technical and exacting; and if an exporter is unable to collect for a shipment made abroad, what use is there in exporting? The matter of credit extension and analysis in international marketing is presented, followed by foreign collections, guarantees, and insurance. Part V concludes with a discussion of foreign exchange and the control thereof by government fiat.

All of the above presentation is from the standpoint of the business enterprise engaged in international marketing.

CHAPTER 26

INTERNATIONAL BANKING FACILITIES: PRIVATE (UNITED STATES)

One of the most important facilities for the conduct of international as well as domestic marketing is banking service. Until World War I, banks of the United States were engaged primarily in the development of the agricultural and industrial resources of the country. The United States was a borrowing nation, and it depended largely upon the banking facilities of other countries for the conduct of its international marketing. Overseas business was transacted largely in sterling; the dollar was little known abroad.

At this period in the development of American international business, private banking houses (usually partnerships), and not incorporated banks, largely performed international banking service. National banks were prevented from effectively engaging in international financial transactions by the law, and the laws of only a few states permitted the conduct of international banking. Private banking houses, on the other hand, were not subject to the restrictive measures applicable to national banks, and they were able to engage freely in the varied functions of international banking.

With the rapidly growing immigrant business toward the end of the nineteenth century, the attention of banks was attracted to this phase of foreign banking; and with the increasing number of American tourists traveling abroad and the expansion of American manufactured exports in the first half of the twentieth century, more interest in international banking was displayed.

The two World Wars added a new development in the international banking structure. Due to the need of vast sums to finance the first World War and to aid in the recovery of devastated countries, the United States Government itself established a type of banking facility. When this task was finished, the financing of international trade and investment reverted to the private banking institutions. In an effort to expand United States exports, as part of the recovery program induced by the Great Depression of the 1930's, the United States Government organized a special bank that is still in operation. Finally, World War II not only repeated the demands for large sums that World War I previously demonstrated but brought about two new conditions. These new conditions were the threat of communism and the challenge of the less developed nations. The breakup of the European and Japanese empires following World War II gave birth to many new sovereign states that struggled to progress with seemingly insuperable obstacles to impede them. These two new conditions gave urgency to the need for financial aid to discourage communist penetration and to raise the living standards of the less developed nations of the world.

The response to these conditions has been the establishment of both United States and multigovernmental banking facilities that have been added to the banking institutions serving international business.

This subject will be treated in two chapters. The present chapter will deal with the private international banking facilities and the succeeding chapter will discuss the United States Government banks and the multigovernmental or world banks.

Types of Private Banking Facilities

Marked development in American banking service came after the Federal Reserve Act had authorized national banks to establish foreign branches and Federal Reserve banks to discount acceptances.

Provisions of the Federal Reserve Act. Essential legislation in this connection was provided by Section 13 of the Federal Reserve Act whereby Federal Reserve banks are authorized to discount acceptances arising out of international trade, "which have maturity at the time of discount of not more than three months' sight . . . and which are endorsed by at least one member bank." Member banks are authorized to accept drafts drawn upon them that have not more than six months' sight to run.

By reason of this law, an American foreign trader may go to a bank (probably his own bank) now a member of the Federal Reserve System and dispose of his bills of exchange. Without this wide market for drafts, the foreign trader would be obliged to sell his documents to foreign banks, or to private banking houses; otherwise, as usually was the case, he waited for the maturity of his bills before he could receive his funds. This burden on his own financial resources militated strongly against granting credit in international marketing and placed him at a decided disadvantage as compared with European competitors who were adequately provided with markets for bills of exchange.

Foreign Branches. Section 25 of the Federal Reserve Act provided for the establishment of foreign branches of national banks under certain stipulations regarding capital, lending authority, etc. Further treatment of this subject will be deferred until later in this chapter.

Edge Law Banks. Under Section 25A of the Federal Reserve Act, provision is made for federal incorporation of concerns to engage solely in international or foreign banking or in other financial operations abroad. Incorporated banks now perform international financing functions parallel with those of private banking houses. The foreign investment (or long-term loan) field in which the private banker formerly held a prominent position by reason of long personal contact with foreign governments and other large borrowers is no longer available to the private banker as a commercial banker. Under the Banking Law of 1933, investment banking was divorced from commercial banking, and this step led to the formation of separate private as well as incorporated investment houses. Edge Law banks are discussed in greater detail later in this chapter.

Acceptance Houses. Acceptance houses and dealers act as brokers, buying and selling trade and bank acceptances arising in international commerce. Although comparatively few in number in the United States, these agencies perform an important function. Some of them discount bills of exchange without recourse to the drawer.

Foreign Bank Connections in the United States. Another private facility for financing United States international business is afforded by branches here or other direct connections of foreign banks. Large banking institutions of practically all of the international trading nations maintain connections in the United States by means of (1) a branch office, (2) an agency, or (3) ownership of an American bank.

Branch Office. The branch office maintains contact, straightens out bothersome matters, and promotes goodwill.

Agency. The agency is not engaged in general banking, but it does operate foreign exchange, collection, discount, letter of credit, and other departments; and it may act as paying agent for foreign securities payable in United States dollars. Agencies are licensed under the laws of the several states, which usually forbid them from accepting deposits from residents of the state (New York law), or else discourage such deposits. They do, however, accept deposits from abroad. Many foreign banks that operate agencies in this country confine their activities largely to the business of the home country; others are operated on a worldwide basis.

Ownership of an American Bank. American banks have been organized and established in a few instances by foreign banks. Since they are organized under the banking laws of the United States, they perform the same functions as other American incorporated banks.

Foreign Department of a Bank

With the growth of international business, banks organized special foreign departments, which not infrequently are headed by a vice-president of the bank, with assistants and managers as required. For smaller banks, the foreign department is usually supervised by a manager.

Services of Foreign Departments.

The foreign departments of banks perform functions that include every activity required to finance imports and exports. They make payments as requested by correspondents or branches and cash drafts drawn against them; handle inquiries received from correspondents or branches; provide foreign credit and business information; issue commercial letters of credit for imports into the United States and all other countries; handle export credits opened by foreign depositors for shipment of commodities from the United States; handle export drafts for collection or discount; issue travelers' letters of credit; purchase and sell drafts and cable transfers; make contracts for purchase and sale of foreign exchange payable at future dates; make loans on commodities stored in the United States for ultimate shipment abroad, generally against warehouse receipts; accept drafts for customers' accounts; accept drafts for foreign branches or correspondents to create dollar exchange; handle the purchase and the sale of acceptances drawn on banks and institutions payable in the United States; handle disposition of refused merchandise shipped under financial arrangements negotiated by branches, correspondents, or themselves; and generally seek to promote international marketing by undertaking market surveys, preparing trade reports and lists of prospective foreign agents, and rendering advice to American businessmen and to foreign businessmen coming to the United States.

Services of Interior Banks. Interior banks, while not located in the seaboard atmosphere of international marketing, may also engage in foreign commerce. Usually the foreign department of an interior bank is known as the Foreign Exchange Department, and its functions are principally the purchase and the sale of foreign exchange, negotiation of drafts, and issuance of letters of credit. A travel service is commonly offered to prepare itineraries and to sell traveler's checks. In a few cases, credit and collection service may also be offered.

Interior banks usually deal through seaboard institutions, and they may maintain (deposit) accounts in foreign banks. With such facilities they are in a position to render valuable service for inland exporters and importers. Some few interior banks have successfully specialized in this type of service.

Overseas Arrangements of American Banks

Overseas arrangements of banks are provided either by correspondent banks abroad or by foreign branches.

Correspondent Banks. In the case of correspondent banks, agreements are entered into for the reciprocal exchange of all business. This plan is analogous to the agency system of merchandising and it embodies many of the same comparative advantages and disadvantages. Foreign (national) banks offer familiarity with foreign conditions, clientele, language, and customs. These banks have their established business and they may be fully equipped to conduct overseas trade. Native correspondent banks are under no such legal restrictions as may be imposed upon foreign banks, for example, the facility of discounting bills of exchange with central banks. Further, they do not arouse the resentment that the establishment of a foreign branch might create, because of the competition it would offer. In some instances, however, national banks may be undesirable as correspondents, and then it is necessary to select banks or branches of banks of a third country or of the United States.

In operating overseas through correspondents, there is not always assurance that a correspondent will render completely satisfactory service. A foreign bank may, for example, be quite lenient in handling documents by permitting inspection of merchandise prior to acceptance or payment of a draft, irrespective of instructions to the contrary; or by holding a draft until arrival of shipment, likewise regardless of instructions. A foreign bank may not be impressed with the necessity of gathering complete information in connection with a refusal of acceptance or payment. In still other respects, such as the issuance of credit reports, foreign banks may fail to accord with the view of banking service as understood and practiced in the United States. Moreover, banks have been known to fail, taking with them all funds in their possession, including those collected for the account of foreign exporters.

It is important to note that an American bank is not considered to be responsible for the acts of its correspondents. Article 12 of Uniform Customs and Practice for Documentary Credits (1962) states:

> Banks utilizing the services of another bank for the purpose of giving effect to the instructions of the applicant for the credit do so for the account and at the risk of the latter.
>
> They assume no liability or responsibility should the instructions they transmit not be carried out, even if they have themselves taken the initiative in the choice of such other bank.
>
> The applicant for the credit shall be bound by and liable to indemnify the banks against all obligations and responsibilities imposed by foreign laws and usages.

The correspondent plan is utilized to a far greater extent than the branch system. One large New York bank, for example, has over 11,000 correspondents which indicates the impossibility of any bank providing, by means of branches, such extensive worldwide service. There are many places in the world where, regardless of theoretical advantages, a branch could not be profitably maintained.

"Banks that have or intend to develop substantial foreign business often supplement their correspondent relationships by establishing representative's offices in selected foreign cities. A representative's office is a means of establishing better relations with foreign markets and closer ties with local banks in those markets."[1]

Foreign Branches. The establishment of American banking facilities in foreign countries paralleled the growth and the direction of United

---

[1]*Federal Reserve Bulletin* (December, 1956), p. 1285.

States international business. Private banking houses (partnerships) were early engaged in international banking, with branches or affiliations in western European countries. A few trust companies also established branches in Europe, the earliest in 1887. In addition, foreign banking corporations, authorized under state laws to engage solely in banking abroad, were organized. The earliest of these, dating from 1902, was the International Banking Corporation, which operated in the Far East. It has since been acquired by the First National City Bank (New York).

Establishment of Foreign Branches. The removal of legal restrictions as far as national banks were concerned was accomplished by Section 25 of the Federal Reserve Act, which provides that any national bank possessing capital and surplus of $1 million or more may obtain permission from the Federal Reserve Board to establish branches abroad or to invest an amount not exceeding 10 percent of its paid-up capital and surplus in the stock of American banks engaged principally in international or foreign banking, either directly or through the control of a local banking institution. Under regulations of the Federal Reserve Board, an American bank that sought to invest in the stock of corporations engaged chiefly in international or foreign banking was required to enter into an agreement with the Board restricting and limiting the operations of such foreign financial corporation.

In response to these provisions and to the rapidly expanding international business of the United States, a rapid movement set in toward the establishment of foreign branches of American banks. Branches were established in foreign cities where business, either actual or prospective, was considered of sufficient volume. Between 1917 and 1922, eleven corporations were formed under Sections 25 and 25A of the Federal Reserve Act. All of these have been either liquidated or absorbed by other banks.

The organization of special foreign banking corporations was pronounced in 1920, when they constituted the most numerous type of operating banking offices abroad.[2] By 1926, however, only the American Express Company remained in existence. In that year the number of American banking institutions having offices abroad was 12, compared with 20 in 1920. By 1933 this number had declined still further to 8. In 1939 there were 10 banking institutions with overseas operation — 4

---

[2]These included the Continental Banking and Trust Co., Mercantile Bank of the Americas, American Foreign Banking Corporation, Asia Banking Corporation, Park-Union Foreign Banking Corporation, and the American Express Company.

national banks, 4 trust companies, 1 private banker, and 1 express company. The national banks had a total of 124 banking offices abroad. The trust companies had 12 offices abroad, and the single private banker had 2 offices abroad. The American Express Company had 36 offices abroad. The grand total of overseas offices was 174.

At the end of 1962, ten member banks had in active operation 145 branches in 39 foreign countries and overseas areas of the United States. Of these, 5 national banks operated 111 branches and 5 state member banks operated the other 34 branches. The geographical distribution of these branches was as follows:[3]

Latin America	66
Continental Europe	9
United Kingdom	14
Africa	3
Near East	3
Far East	27
United States Overseas and Trust Territories	23

In addition, the American Express Company had nearly 300 branches and offices overseas.

In 1962, Congress passed an amending law designed to enable United States banks with branches abroad to compete more effectively. These include powers, as interpreted by the Federal Reserve Board in Regulations M and H, (1) to issue guarantees up to 50 percent of the bank's capital and surplus, provided the combined total of unsecured obligations is not over 10 percent of the bank's capital and surplus; (2) to accept drafts or bills of exchange under the same provisions as apply to United States domestic banks (Section 13); (3) to invest in securities, including stock of central banks, clearing houses, and development banks of the country where the branch is situated, up to 1 percent of total deposits; (4) to underwrite and deal in obligations of the national government, not exceeding 10 percent of the capital and surplus of the branch; (5) take liens on foreign real estate in connection with credit extensions, and to perform certain minor functions.

Some banks and the Comptroller of the Currency believe that the Board has not fully carried out the will of Congress in this matter.[4]

Foreign Branches of Banks of All Nations. According to an analysis of the foreign branches of the banks of all nations, published in the *Federal*

---

[3]Federal Reserve Board, *Annual Report* (1962), p. 126.
[4]See *Journal of Commerce* (August 6, 1963).

Reserve Bulletin covering the year 1954, there were approximately 1,250 such branches (including agencies and offices). The figure given for the United States is 112, compared with 500 for the United Kingdom, 376 for Continental Europe, and 118 for Canada (exceeding the United States). The analysis contains the following comment:

> London remains the world center in which there is the largest concentration of offices of foreign banks, followed by New York and Paris. British banks maintain 40 percent of the number of foreign offices, although the trade of the United Kingdom and its dependencies is about 15 percent of the world today. To these may be added banks from other countries of the sterling area and Canada, which together maintain 15 percent of foreign offices compared to a similar share in world trade. . . . United States banks have less than 10 percent of the total number of foreign banking offices while this country contributes more than 15 percent of world trade.[5]

Advantages of Branch Operation. The advantages of foreign branches of American banks differ somewhat from those of the branch-house method of merchandising because, as frequently asserted, the operation of foreign branches by American banks is a matter of national interest. This may be true when, under the correspondent system, it is necessary to select a branch of a foreign bank with headquarters in a nation competing in world markets with the United States. Branches of foreign banking institutions are established in other countries primarily in the interest of their nationals and this may lead to aggressive methods of competition. This competition has been known to take the form of divulging trade secrets available through documents; copying invoices, bills of lading, etc., for use in aiding home manufacturers to compete more effectively; or deliberately quoting unfavorable dollar exchange rates. It does not follow, however, that such criticisms apply to all foreign (third country) banks or even to a majority of them.

As a corollary, it may be stated that an American branch bank is capable of managing business in the interest of American trade (and without any discrimination against foreign customers). The foreign branch is working directly for the customers of the home office. As expressed at the beginning of foreign branch banking of the United States, "They are thus all complete local banks, but in another aspect they are to be regarded as banking houses of one great international bank; the personnel and the policies of their organization are purposely kept homo-

---

[5]*Federal Reserve Bulletin* (April, 1955), p. 365.

geneous; they are not permitted to grow apart in the spirit of separateness they would necessarily feel if they were just foreign subsidiaries of some American institution. The American and foreign customers of the _____ Bank are thus all in one family, in a sense."[6]

This unity of interest is manifested in many ways. The branch gathers trade data useful for the extension and protection of the foreign business of its American clients (for they are clients of the branch as well as of the home office), investigates information bearing upon credit risks in a manner as nearly comparable with American methods as local conditions permit, and protects merchandise delivered in its care with a special interest in the rights of American exporters. Moreover, the home office stands fully back of the branch and can never disclaim responsibility for its acts.

Regulation of Branches. When American banks establish branches abroad, they become amenable to the laws of foreign countries. Many foreign nations place no onerous restrictions on the establishment of branches by alien banks, merely requiring them to conform to certain documentary formalities in addition to regulations in effect for domestic banks. In some countries, regulations are more stringent, imposing restrictions as to functions, capital requirements, the investment of capital funds and surplus, and other matters. Infrequently, strong nationalistic feeling may render it difficult for an American bank to procure a foothold in certain foreign countries. South Africa, Australia, New Zealand, and Canada are among the countries that will not permit branches of foreign banks to establish business; they must be chartered under the law of the country. In the summer of 1963, one American bank acquired one-half interest in a Canadian chartered bank that had been established in 1953 as a Canadian chartered corporation owned by Dutch capital.

Establishment of Foreign Banks. The organization of special foreign banking corporations (not branches) was pronounced in 1920, as stated above. Only a few of these banks, however, continue in operation.

As compared with a branch, a banking corporation has some disadvantages, such as smaller loan limits, but it also offers some advantages. A banking corporation may be more flexible than a branch in meeting particular or changing conditions in foreign markets. For instance, it can acquire controlling or minority interests in a foreign

---

[6]*Ibid.* (October, 1918), p. 942.

bank, thus holding shares jointly with local investors, which a foreign branch cannot do. A foreign financing corporation, on the other hand, may conduct abroad certain investment-type activities that are not permitted to a United States bank.[7]

Edge Law Banks

Another type of private banking facility for international business consists of banking institutions organized solely for the purpose of engaging in international financial transactions. To be mentioned in this connection are the so-called "Edge Law Banks." The Edge Law, which was enacted in December, 1919, as Section 25A of the Federal Reserve Act, provides for the federal incorporation of concerns to engage solely in international or foreign banking or in other types of foreign financial operations.

Provisions of the Edge Law. The Edge Law permits the incorporation of two distinct types of banks: first, commercial banks, performing functions relating to the exportation and importation of merchandise, such as issuance of drafts and letters of credit and dealing in foreign exchange and bullion; and second, investment banking houses, buying and selling foreign securities and issuing their own debentures secured by bonds, stocks, etc., of foreign corporations or governments. By this means, the investment bank is permitted to extend long-term credit to foreigners by accepting as security the stocks, bonds, and other valuable papers they may offer and, in turn, selling in the American market its own debentures, based upon these foreign securities. In no case is an Edge bank permitted to perform both the commercial functions and the investment banking functions.

The Federal Reserve Board exercises close supervision over Edge Law banking corporations, requiring that annual reports be filed and that permission of the Board be obtained for any variations from the legal stipulations. The life of these corporations is 20 years, renewable for similar periods. A minimum capital of $2 million is required, a majority of which must be held by American citizens or concerns. With minor exceptions, these banks are to engage only in business of an international character. If a commercial bank, it may generally receive deposits from outside of the United States only. If a debenture and investment business is transacted, the liabilities assumed when debentures are

---

[7]*Ibid.* (December, 1956), p. 1286.

issued are restricted to ten times the capital and surplus of the business. Moreover, investments in one foreign corporation may not exceed 10 percent of the capital and surplus of the Edge corporation, except in the case of investment in a banking institution, when the limit is 15 percent.

Operations Under the Edge Law. Before World War II, few banks had been completely organized under the Edge Law. The Edge corporation that has been longest in operation is the Chase Bank, New York, organized in 1930 as a commercial bank. In 1957, it was replaced by the Chase International Investment Corporation with authority to engage in the investment phase of Edge operation. Interest in Edge bank operation increased with the continued expansion of United States international business. In addition, facilities have been established for the extension of medium- and long-term credit in international trade; the appearance of the newly established countries as well as the challenge and opportunity of the less developed nations; the convertibility of major currencies; and, the economic outlook resulting from the European Economic Community all contributed to the increased interest in foreign banking on the part of United States banks.

As of 1962, there were 11 Edge banks in operation in addition to 5 "Agreement" Edge banks (state chartered) but operating under the supervision and authority of the Federal Reserve Board. As of mid-1963, there were 25 Edge banks and 5 "Agreement" banks in operation while several additional banks had been authorized to operate but had not begun.

In the summer of 1963, the Federal Reserve Board revised its regulations concerning Edge Law banks. Revised Regulation K provides, among other things, (1) permission to combine the banking and the investment business in one enterprise; (2) freedom to make investments up to specified limits without prior approval of the Federal Reserve Board; (3) the right to issue guarantees on the same basis as afforded foreign branches by revised Regulation M; and, (4) authority to establish any number of branches in any country where the Edge bank has an office.

These banks are in the business of providing capital for the financing of development and expansion of business outside the continental limits of the United States. They participate in financing operations with other banks and industrial concerns. By this means, medium- and long-term financing is provided — frequently with practically no recourse to the international marketing firm utilizing this service. The United States has come a long way in the field of international banking since the passage of the Federal Reserve Act in 1913. The chief benefit of the act was to open the banking system of the United States to trading in documents arising out of international marketing. This has literally brought international trade financing to every section of the United States.

The expansion of American banks overseas by means of both branches and, mainly, correspondents has widened the connections of United States banks to the ends of the earth. Renewed interest in Edge Law banks will provide additional facilities to participate in investments in other countries. This field has been largely assumed by several United States Government and multigovernmental banks that have come into being chiefly since the end of World War II. A description of the purposes and operation of these facilities will follow in the next chapter.

Summary

1. Prior to 1913 international banking facilities for the international marketing of the United States were largely in the hands of private bankers. The passage of the Federal Reserve Act in 1913 opened the banking system of the United States to international marketing financing and operation. Member banks are authorized to discount bills of exchange and to rediscount them at Federal Reserve banks. There are also acceptance dealers and branches of foreign banks in the United States.
2. The services performed by international financial institutions are numerous. For summary purposes, mention should be made chiefly of discounting bills of exchange, issuing letters of credit, confirming letters of credit, collecting accounts, and protecting the exporter's interests throughout the period of time from shipment to surrender of title documents to a bank abroad or to the importer.
3. United States banks have branches and (mostly) correspondents throughout the world. There are nearly 150 foreign branches of United States banks and thousands of foreign correspondents. Branches offer certain advantages to international marketers, such as one-bank control and continued interest in an American trader.
4. Foreign (correspondent) banks are not expected to have any special interest in United States business firms who are not their direct customers, but they are far more numerous than the number of foreign branch banks.
5. Special international marketing banks include so-called Edge Law banks. Certain conditions have aroused increased interest in these banks.

QUESTIONS

1. Why did the United States banks show so little interest in international marketing operations until around the period of World War I?
2. Explain the significance of Section 13 of the Federal Reserve Act to an international marketing firm.
3. Describe the functions of an acceptance house.
4. How do foreign banks operate in the United States?
5. Comment on the services offered by the foreign department of a bank. In your judgment, which of these services are peculiar to international marketing with no counterpart in domestic trade?
6. How can a bank in Kansas City, Missouri, offer international business services to its clients?
7. As to the use of foreign correspondents of United States banks,
   (a) Comment critically on the cited advantages.
   (b) Comment critically on the cited disadvantages.
8. Under what provisions are United States banks permitted to establish foreign branches?
9. Comment on the advantages of foreign branch operation by United States banks.
10. In what ways may foreign branches be regulated or controlled by foreign governments?
11. What is an Edge Law bank? Define its functions.
12. Comment on the activity thus far displayed in organizing Edge Law banks.

PROBLEMS

1. Select one country other than the United States and determine its legal requirements for the establishment of branches of nonnational banks.
2. Visit a bank in your locality that you believe offers international business services. Discuss the subject with the officer in charge and write a report of your inquiry.

COLLATERAL READINGS

American Management Association, International Management Division. "Sources and Methods of International Financing," *A.M.A. Management Report No. 59.* New York: American Management Association, 1961. Part 3.

Dartnell International Trade Handbook, The. Chicago: The Dartnell Corporation, 1963.

Heck, Harold J. *Foreign Commerce*. New York: McGraw-Hill Book Company, Inc., 1953. Chapter 6.

Henning, Charles N. *International Finance*. New York: Harper & Brothers, 1958. Chapter 10.

Horn, Paul V. *International Trade Principles and Practices*, Third Edition. New York: Prentice-Hall, Inc., 1951. Chapter 28.

Pratt, E. E. *Modern International Commerce*. New York: Allyn and Bacon, Inc., 1956. Chapter 9.

Roorbach, G. B. *Problems in Foreign Trade*. New York: McGraw-Hill Book Company, Inc., 1933. Part II C.

Shaterian, William S. *Export-Import Banking*, Second Edition. New York: Ronald Press Company, 1956. Chapters 1–4.

Stern, Siegfried. *The United States in International Banking*. New York: Columbia University Press, 1951.

CHAPTER 27

BANKING FACILITIES: UNITED STATES GOVERNMENT AND MULTIGOVERNMENTAL

International traders may not feel concerned with the matter of United States Government or multigovernmental financing because, in most instances, they do not come in direct functional contact with either. An exporter may sell equipment to a foreign customer, draw his drafts, and collect his funds without being aware of the fact that these funds came from a grant or a loan from the United States Government or a multigovernmental agency to the country in which his customer is located. Similarly, an importer of strategic or critical materials may be reimbursed from funds provided by a government agency. The role of government in the field of international finance is now extended to a global operation, along with the International Bank for Reconstruction and Development, the International Finance Corporation, and other international agencies.

United States Foreign Policy Regarding International Finance

Before describing the operation of specific governmental financial facilities and arrangements, a brief introduction dealing with United States foreign policy should be helpful. When any government participates in financial operations in foreign countries, these operations are an expression of the foreign policy that is being pursued.

In the United States, with its tradition of private enterprise, the Government was generally content with merely facilitating international marketing, namely, negotiation of treaties, international business promotion and protection, merchant marine policy, etc. With the coming of World War I, the United States Government became a source of finance by reason of the needs of our allies and of postwar reconstruction.

In view of its foreign policy to back the allies, then to prosecute the war successfully, and, finally, to aid in the rehabilitation of devastated areas, the Government provided funds necessary for these operations by taxes and loans. By this means, exporters of materials used for these purposes were financed from funds provided by the Government.

The same situation was repeated in connection with and in the aftermath of World War II. In contrast with the World War I period, the years and decades following World War II have introduced two new and long-lasting conditions. As mentioned in the preceding chapter, these are the communist threat and the pressing needs of the less developed nations. As a result of these new conditions, the United States Government and the multigovernmental or world financial agencies have expanded and continue unto the present time with no sign as to when they may discontinue their operations.

A significant change in the United States Government financing operations occurred in 1951 when the phraseology of recovery, economic cooperation, relief, etc., was swallowed up in the new phrase "mutual security." This term clearly reveals the relationship between international marketing and international politics. From that date until the present, the chief thrust of the United States Government financing in international matters has been mutual security — from communistic threat and from the threat also of the less developed nations that are caught up in the global expression of "rising expectations." We witness a kind of grim race between backward and politically inexperienced nations and the political road that they will travel—communism or democracy!

In support of our democratic road, the United States Government is laying out billions of dollars each year to help improve the lot of the peoples of the less developed nations. The multinational financial agencies, in large measure, are also bending every effort to bring about improved economic and social conditions in the less developed areas.

The reader is reminded that these Government and multigovernmental financial agencies are discussed in this chapter because of their direct relationship to international marketing. It bears repetition to state that the business firm engaged in international trading or operations depends in some measure on these financial agencies for a portion of his business and for the improved potential that may be seen as a result of the provision of economic and social advances. And this statement is true regardless of the nationality of the business firm; these measures are global in their impact.

An analysis of the United States Government and multinational financial agencies presently in operation will now be undertaken on a comparative basis. Each agency will be considered in its relation to the several analytical aspects that will be used.

United States Government Financial Agencies

The following discussion includes the Export-Import Bank of Washington and the Agency for International Development.

Export-Import Bank of Washington. Following our recognition of Soviet Russia in 1934, a special government bank was organized to finance anticipated trade with that country. Established on February 12, 1934, the Export-Import Bank of Washington never did participate in Soviet trade because of difficulties resulting from the adjustment of Russian debts owed United States citizens. A second bank was, therefore, established on March 12, 1934, to finance trade with Cuba but it soon engaged in wider operations and was liquidated in 1936. Since that time the (first) Export-Import Bank of Washington has filled an expanding role in the field of international finance. Its lending functions, however, differ from those of commercial banks because, in addition to questions of solvency, the banks' directors face such questions as these: How will the domestic economy of the United States be affected? Will a loan contribute to friendly relations with the foreign country concerned? How will the interest of private United States creditors of the foreign country be affected?

The Export-Import Bank is one of the financial expressions of the foreign policy of the United States. The "Good Neighbor Policy," now expressed by the Alliance for Progress, is basically the keynote of our Latin American relations, and loans from the bank to Latin American countries serve this policy. As United States policy was intensified due to World War II, the financial operations of the bank were also increased and expanded.

Agency for International Development (AID). Another United States Government agency engaged in financing international trade and investment is the Agency for International Development (AID). This agency is a lineal descendant of the Lend Lease Administration (1941), the Economic Cooperation Administration (ECA) (1948), the Mutual Security Program (1952), the Foreign Operations Administration (FOA) (1953), and the International Cooperation Administration (ICA) (1955).

AID was established in 1961 and is an organ of the United States Department of State. Its main purposes are (1) to assist in developing economic resources and productive capacity of less developed countries, (2) to further assist the development of less developed countries by expanding markets for United States agricultural products (so-called Cooley loans — P. L. 480), and (3) to encourage, facilitate, and increase the participation of private enterprise in furthering the economic and social development of less developed countries.

Multigovernmental Agencies

The multigovernmental agencies that are engaged in helping to finance international trade and investment are the International Monetary Fund (IMF) (1944), the International Bank for Reconstruction and Development (IBRD) (1946), the International Finance Corporation (IFC) (1956), the International Development Association (IDA) (1960), the Inter-American Development Bank (IDB) (1959), and the Inter-American Social Progress Trust Fund (1961).

The IMF will be described in Chapter 33 where it will be explained that the Fund operates in the area of foreign exchange. The IBRD, or World Bank, seeks to aid the development of productive facilities and resources of countries that are members of the Bank; in other words, to obtain any aid from the World Bank, a country must be a participant in the Bank and a member of the World Bank board. The IFC, on the other hand, seeks to further economic development by encouraging growth of productive private enterprise in *less developed member countries*; i.e., a country must be a member of the IFC, which is an affiliate of the World Bank, but it must also be less developed.

The IDA is designed to promote economic development in member countries by providing finance on terms which are not possible under the IBRD or IFC.

The IDB is strictly western hemisphere in its financing operations, with special emphasis on Latin America. Its function is to assist in accelerating the process of economic development in the member (Latin America) countries. The IDB also administers the Inter-American Social Progress Trust Fund which provides capital and technical assistance to support efforts of Latin American countries to achieve greater social progress and balanced economic growth.

International Bank for Reconstruction and Development. This organization came into being in 1946 as an international financing facility to function in both areas of reconstruction and of development. Membership in the Bank is limited to countries that first join the International Monetary Fund.

The scope of the Bank's functions is set forth in its articles:

> 1. To assist in the reconstruction and development of its member countries by facilitating the investment of capital for productive purposes, and thereby promote the long-range growth of international trade and the improvement of standards of living.
> 2. To make loans for productive purposes out of its own funds when private capital is not available on reasonable terms.
> 3. To promote private foreign investment by guarantees of, and participations in, loans and investments made by private investors.

The Bank is authorized to make loans for special projects chiefly, and these loans are to be made to governmental bodies in the borrowing countries or for government-guaranteed loans to private interests. Despite the word "Reconstruction" in its title, which indicates the 1946 expectation that the Bank would help to finance the reconstruction of war-torn areas, only less than $500 million has been loaned for this purpose. The explanation of this situation is that the Bank was spared the necessity of undertaking huge reconstruction loans because the European Recovery Program, otherwise known as the Marshall Plan, came into effect. Thereupon, in 1948 the Bank turned its attention to financing the development of its member countries.

In the Bank's financial statements, development loans are divided into several categories. Transportation heads the list with nearly 40 percent of the total loaned. Electric power is not far behind with 33 percent of the total. Industry accounts for about 18 percent of the amount loaned, agriculture and forestry for 10 percent, and loans for general development the small balance.

The IBRD's loans have gone chiefly to Asia and the Middle East (over one third), to Europe and the Western Hemisphere (nearly one fourth each), and the balance of one sixth to the rest of the world.

International Finance Corporation. A proposal for a new kind of international banking institution has been increasingly advanced by the so-called less developed countries. In 1953 the United Nations General Assembly requested the IBRD to study such a proposal. Early in 1955, the IBRD submitted the "Articles of Agreement of the International Finance Corporation" for submission to the various governments. The corporation came into existence on July 24, 1956.

This bank has the "essential function . . . to assist in the economic development of its member countries by promoting the growth of the private sector of their economies. It [the Charter] also makes plain that, in carrying out this function, the Corporation is to supplement and assist the investment of private capital and not to compete with such capital." It is "a developmental agency intended to operate particularly in the less developed areas;" and "is intended to finance only enterprises which are productive in the sense of contributing to the development of the economies of the member countries in which they operate."[1]

Members of the IBRD are eligible to become members of the International Finance Corporation, and the distribution of shares of stock is based on the same proportionate principle that governs membership of the IBRD.

The operations of the IFC show that three fourths of its financing has gone to Latin American countries, with most of the balance going to countries in Asia and the Middle East. European countries have received practically nothing.

International Development Association. The IDA is a third offshoot of the World Bank.

> The primary purpose underlying the establishment of IDA was the creation of a supplementary source of development capital for countries whose balance of payments prospects would not justify their incurring, or continuing to incur, external debt entirely on conventional terms. The financial terms attaching to IDA credits have, therefore, been designed with due regard to this purpose.
>
> IDA credits are repayable in foreign exchange, but on very lenient terms. In each of the credits so far made, a government has been the borrower; the credits are repayable over a period of 50 years, free of interest; there is a 10-year period of grace, following which 1 per cent per annum is payable over the next 10 years, and 3 per cent per annum over the final 30 years; to help meet IDA's administrative costs, a service charge of ¾ per cent is payable on amounts withdrawn and outstanding. Compared with conventional loans, these terms bring substantial alleviation to the repayment obligations of borrowing countries, and bear much less heavily on their balance of payments.[2]

Started in 1961, the IDA has made one third of its financing for India, another one third for Latin American countries, with the balance scattered in Africa and Asia.

---

[1] IBRD, "Articles of Agreement of the International Finance Corporation and Explanatory Memorandum" (April 11, 1955), pp. 31–32.
[2] IDA, *Annual Report* (1961–62), Washington, D.C. 1962.

Comparative Analysis of These Agencies

To facilitate the study and understanding of these various agencies, attention is called to pages 508–511. This summary lists the purposes and activities of these agencies. The subsequent outline of the subject is presented on a topical rather than an agency basis in the hope that the reader will better understand the differences which are represented by these agencies.

1. Assistance to private enterprise
   Under this heading, all of these agencies (in various degrees):
   a. Facilitate and/or conduct surveys or feasibility studies pertaining to plans for economic development
   b. Grant political and credit risk guarantees
   c. Provide equity investment (IFC only)
   d. Grant loans for trade and investment
      (1) Trade — Given transactions only — Export-Import Bank
      (2) Investment — All agencies
2. Factors influencing the financing of trade and investment
   a. Location of enterprise
      (1) AID — Less developed countries
      (2) IDA — Less developed *member* countries
      (3) IFC — Generally less developed, but some for developed countries
      (4) IBRD — Both, but mostly less developed
      (5) Eximbank — Both
      (6) IDB — Latin American countries only
   b. Type of transaction or project
      (1) Eximbank — A given transaction
      (2) AID — Finance commodity import programs
      (3) All others — Investment
   c. Procurement
      (1) AID and Eximbank — Tied to the United States
      (2) IDB and Social Progress Trust Fund — Tied to member countries — U.S.A. and Latin America
      (3) All others — Untied
   d. Type of financing required (local currency or foreign exchange)
      (1) Eximbank — U.S. dollars
      (2) IBRD — In currency loaned

      (3) IDA — In currency loaned but has never accepted local currency

      (4) IDB — Some local currency for lending but also foreign currency for local costs.

      (5) IFC — Both

      (6) AID — Both — Administers Cooley loans (P. L. 480) that cover local currency

  e. Residence of borrower

      (1) Eximbank — United States or foreign firm or friendly foreign government

      (2) IMF, IDA — Member governments

      (3) IBRD — Member governments and public or private enterprises guaranteed by member governments

      (4) IFC — Private firms in less developed member countries

      (5) IDB — Member governments, private local firms and public or private relending agencies

      (6) AID — U.S. and foreign companies and foreign governments

  f. Size of loan — Not important; each transaction or loan (investment) is worked out separately

  g. Terms and Conditions

      (1) Generally, for long periods of time; over 5 years

      (2) IFC generally requires some equity participation

      (3) IBRD requires government guarantee of private loans

  h. Private or public

      (1) Eximbank — Export trade financing — private

      (2) IFC — Private only

      (3) All others — Government or agencies for economic and social development

  i. Government only — Terms and conditions

      (1) Repayable in dollars or hard currency at interest for 5–25 years — Eximbank, IBRD, and IDB (ordinary resources "window")

      (2) Repayable in dollars or hard currency at *no* interest (only service fee) up to 50 years and long grace periods up to 10 years — IDA and AID

AGENCIES WHICH HELP FINANCE FOREIGN TRADE AND INVESTMENT

(Prepared in the Bureau of International Programs, Department of Commerce)

	EXPORT-IMPORT BANK	AGENCY FOR INTERNATIONAL DEVELOPMENT (AID)			INTERNATIONAL MONETARY FUND (IMF)²
	U.S. Dollars	U.S. Dollars¹	Foreign Currencies: Special Loans	Investment Guarantees	Currencies of Member Countries
Purpose	Aid in financing, and facilitate U.S. foreign trade.	Assist in developing economic resources and productive capabilities of less-developed countries and increase economic cooperation, trade and private investment.	Assist in development of less developed countries and expand markets for U.S. agricultural products.	Encourage, facilitate and increase the participation of private enterprise in furthering the economic and social development of the less-developed countries.	Promote international monetary cooperation and encourage stability by providing resources to meet short-term balance of payments problems and by other means.
Resources	$7 billion of which $1 billion capital stock subscribed by U.S. Treasury; $6 billion borrowing authority.	Annual appropriation (1.1 billion for FY 1962) supplemented by long term commitment authority ($7.2 billion for FY 1962–1966.)	Up to 25% of proceeds of sales of U.S. surplus agricultural commodities in each country.	Annual appropriation. Currently $1 billion for specific risks; $90 million for all risk, and $10 million for pilot housing in Latin America.	Resources consist of gold and holding of member currencies aggregating $14.85 billion. The U.S. quota is $4.125 billion.
Nature of Loans	1. Project loans. 2. Exporter credits. 3. Medium — term comprehensive guarantees or insurance. 4. Short-term comprehensive insurance.	1. Loans to foreign governments. 2. Loans to private U.S. and foreign firms. 3. Loans to intermediate financing institutions.	1. Loans to U.S. firms, their subsidiaries and affiliates abroad for business development and trade expansion. 2. To U.S. or foreign firms to expand foreign markets for U.S. agricultural products.	Guaranteed investments include equity, loans, licensing arrangements, contributions in kind or any combination of these.	Member's purchases from IMF of currencies of other members for an equivalent amount of the member's own currency. A member's purchase of currency from the IMF must be repaid by re-purchases.
Who Can Apply	1. U.S. or foreign firm, or friendly foreign government. 2. U.S. exporter. 3. U.S. banks; or exporter directly until cover becomes available at Foreign Credit Insurance Association (FCIA) 4. U.S. exporter at FCIA.	1. Foreign governments. 2. U.S. firms and firms in recipient countries. 3. Development banks, savings and loan associations and other relending institutions.	1. U.S. firms only. 2. U.S. and local firms.	U.S. citizens and firms, U.S.-chartered corporations "substantially, beneficially owned by U.S. citizens" and their wholly-owned subsidiaries on new investment in friendly less-developed countries with which the U.S. has an overall guaranty agreement.	Member governments.
Guarantees	1. May guarantee payments of project loan financed by private sources. 2. Not applicable. 3. Up to 85% of credit and political risks. 4. Up to 85% of credit risk; up to 95% of political risk.	Not applicable.	Not applicable.	1. Guarantees of new investment against specific risks (expropriation, inconvertibility, loss due to war, revolution or insurrection). 2. All risk guarantees. 3. Guarantees of investment in private pilot or demonstration housing projects in Latin	Not applicable.

	EXPORT-IMPORT BANK	AGENCY FOR INTERNATIONAL DEVELOPMENT (AID)			INTERNATIONAL MONETARY FUND (IMF)[2]
	U.S. Dollars	U.S. Dollars[1]	Foreign Currencies: Special Loans	Investment Guarantees	Currencies of Member Countries
Maturity	1. Eight to more than 20 years according to nature of project. 2. One to 5 years (exceptionally 7 years). 3. One to 5 years (exceptionally 7 years). 4. Up to 180 days. Special cases up to 1 year.	1. In general up to 40 years, including ten-year grace period; in special situations, substantially shorter terms. 2. Flexible; grace periods in some cases; economics of project a major consideration. 3. Flexible to permit revolving credits, including grace periods in some instances.	Based on nature of project but generally not exceeding 10 years.	Normally up to 20 years.	Members undertake to re-purchase within a period not exceeding 3 to 5 years.
Current Interest Rates or Fees	1. Minimum interest 5¾%. 2. Minimum interest 6%. 3. Fees vary by market and term of credit. 4. Fees vary by market and term of credit.	1. Generally ¾ of 1 per cent, ut varies under special circumstances. 2. Based on nature of project, generally 5¾ percent. 3. Based on local rates and nature of sub-loans.	1. Based on local rates and nature of project. 2. Based on local rates and nature of project.	1. Current rate is ½ of 1% on liability for each risk actively covered; on "standby" coverage, ¼ of 1%. 2. Under consideration, probably 2%. 3. (Same as 2 above.)	Service charge of ¼ of 1%, plus interest on purchases in excess of quota increasing with length of time purchase outstanding and amount purchased. Lowest rate is 2% per annum.
Currency of Repayment	U.S. dollar.	U.S. Dollars[1]	Foreign currency loaned.	Not applicable.	Gold or convertible currencies.
Where Proceeds Must Be Spent	In the United States.	Primary emphasis on U.S. procurement.	Locally.	Not applicable.	Not limited to U.S. procurement.
Relationship to Other Sources of Financing	Does not compete with private capital.	Must take into account whether financing obtainable on reasonable terms from free world sources.	None.	Not applicable.	Cooperates with and acts through member countries, treasuries, central banks, stabilization funds, or similar fiscal agencies
Decision Making Body	Board of Directors with advice of National Advisory Council on Int'l. Monetary and Fin. Problems (NAC).	Administrator of AID with advice of NAC.	Administrator of AID with advice of NAC.	Administrator of AID with advice of NAC.	Board of Governors or, as delegated, the Board of Directors; U.S. Director instructed by NAC.
Legal Authority	Export-Import Bank Act of 1945, as amended.	Act for International Development of 1961, Section 201.	PL 480, Sections 104(e) and (g).	Act for International Development of 1961, Sections 221-224.	Articles of Agreement; and Bretton Woods Agreement Acts.

[1] AID aso extends grant assistance for development and support of economies. In some circumstances Supporting Assistance may take the form of local currency repayable loans.

[2] IMF's contribution to economic development efforts, while important, is indirect rather than direct.

AGENCIES WHICH HELP FINANCE FOREIGN TRADE AND INVESTMENT

(Prepared in the Bureau of International Programs, Department of Commerce)

	INTERNATIONAL BANK (IBRD) *Currencies of Member Countries*	INTERNATIONAL FINANCE CORP. (IFC) *Dollars*	INTERNATIONAL DEVELOPMENT ASSOCIATION (IDA) *Currencies of Member Countries*	INTER-AMERICAN DEVELOPMENT BANK (IDB) *Currencies of Members (Principally Dollars)*	INTER-AMERICAN SOCIAL PROGRESS TRUST FUND *(IDB Administered Trust Fund) — Dollars*
Purpose	Aid the development of productive facilities and resources in member countries.	Further economic development by encouraging growth of productive private enterprise in less-developed member countries.	Promote economic development in member countries by providing finance on terms not possible under IBRD, of which IDA is an affiliate.	Contribute to accelerating process of economic development in member countries.	Provide capital and technical assistance to support efforts of Latin American countries to achieve greater social progress and balanced economic growth.
Resources	Capital subscriptions of member countries: $20.4 billion of which approximately $2 billion in and $18 billion callable. U.S. subscription is $6.35 billion of which $5.7 billion is callable, if required by the Bank to meet its obligations.	Capital subscription of member countries of $96.4 million, and proceeds of sale of investments.	Proposed initial subscription of $1 billion, of which $916 million subscribed, U.S. subscription is $320.3 million. Review of resources required every five years with a view to replenishment.	Authorized resources of $959.5 million (U.S. share $450 million) of which $813.2 million is for "Ordinary Operations" and $146.3 million is for "Fund for Special Operations"; $431.6 million of callable capital to meet defaults on Bank's securities of which U.S. share is $200 million.[a]	$394 million appropriated by the U.S.
Nature of Loans	Loans to member governments to other public or private entities if guaranteed by a member government.	Investment in productive private enterprises. May now subscribe to their capital stock. Guarantee of member governments not sought.	Credits to member governments or territories.	Loans to member governments or political sub-divisions of such members and to public and private entities in those countries from the Bank's resources for "Ordinary" and "Special" operations.	Loans in fields of land settlement and use, low income housing, community water and sanitation and, to a limited extent, higher education.
Who Can Apply	Member governments, public and private entities guaranteed by member government.	Private firms operating in less developed member countries on projects which contribute to the development of the private sector, offer promise of returns, and for which adequate financing from private sources is not available on reasonable terms.	Member countries, and their territories.	Member governments, their agencies and subdivisions; private local firms (or owned jointly by local interests); public or private re-lending agencies.	Governments, public institutions, private borrowers and cooperatives.
Guarantees	Full or partial guarantees of loans by private lenders for purposes noted above, if such loans are guaranteed by a member government. Guarantee authority has not been exercised.	Not applicable.	Not applicable.	May guarantee in whole or in part loans by private investors. Guarantee Authority has not been exercised.	Discretionary.

	INTERNATIONAL BANK (IBRD)	INTERNATIONAL FINANCE CORP. (IFC)	INTERNATIONAL DEVELOPMENT ASSOCIATION (IDA)	INTER-AMERICAN DEVELOPMENT BANK (IDB)	INTER-AMERICAN SOCIAL PROGRESS TRUST FUND
	Currencies of Member Countries	*Dollars*	*Currencies of Member Countries*	*Currencies of Members (Principally Dollars)*	*(IDB Administered Trust Fund) — Dollars*
Maturity	Generally 15-25 years.	Generally 5 to 15 years.	All credits so far extended for 50 years, with 10 years grace period and graduated authorization.	1. 10-20 years in "ordinary operations." 2. 10-50 years in "special operations."	Generally 15 to 30 years.
Current Interest Rates or Fees	5¾% currently — based on cost of money to Bank, plus 1% commission and ¼% for administrative expenses.	Currently about 7% for loans. No fixed interest on equity participation.	¾ of 1% service charge; no interest.	1. Currently 5¾% for "Ordinary Operations." 2. For "Special Operations," about 4% repayable in currency of borrower, higher in certain cases where funds are for relending.	Generally 1¼% to 2¾% payable in local currency plus a ¾ of 1% per annum service charge, payable in dollars.
Currency of Repayment	Currencies loaned.	Currencies invested — usually U.S. dollars.	Currency loaned, or other foreign exchange as appropriate. Has power to accept local currency but no indication power will be used.	1. For Ordinary Operations" in currency lent. 2. For "Special Operations," in whole or in part, in currency of borrower.	Largely in the currency of the borrowing country.
Where Proceeds Must Be Spent	Not limited to U.S. procurement.	Not limited to U.S. procurement.	Not limited to U.S. procurement.	Not limited to U.S. procurement.	Limited to procurement in U.S. and member countries.
Relationship to Other Sources of Financing	Cannot lend where private capital is available on reasonable terms.	Cannot lend where sufficient private capital is available on reasonable terms.	Cannot lend when private capital is available on reasonable terms.	Cooperates with other sources of financing. Takes into account the ability of borrower to obtain private loans on terms which the Bank considers reasonable.	Must take into account whether assistance can be obtained from national or international agencies or private sources on reasonable terms.
Decision Making Body	Board of Governors, or, as delegated, the Board of Directors; U.S. Director instructed by NAC.	Board of Governors, as delegated, the Board of Directors; U.S. Director instructed by NAC.	Board of Governors or, as delegated, the Board of Directors; U.S. Director instructed by NAC.	Board of Governors, as delegated, Board of Directors; U.S. Director instructed by NAC.	IDB as trustee; IDB Board of Directors, U.S. Director instructed by NAC.
Legal Authority	Articles of Agreement and Bretton Woods Agreement Act.	Articles of Agreement and International Finance Corporation Act.	Articles of Agreement; and International Development Association Act.	Agreement, establishing the Inter-American Development Bank; and the IDB Act (PL 86-147).	The Social Progress Trust Fund Agreement, and Act authorizing Inter-American Social and Economic Cooperation program.[6]

[3]On the basis of current membership. Authorized resources originally contemplated $1 billion which was reduced to $959.5 million when Cuba did not become a member of IDB.
[4]Excludes $100 million administered by AID for grants and for loans for health and education; and $6 million to the Organization for American States for technical assistance in public administration and other fields.
[5]Agreement signed on June 19, 1961 between the U.S. and IDB.
Source: Foreign Commerce Weekly (May 14, 1962), pp. 886-87.

(3) Between these two extremes (IDB "windows"):
Fund for Special Operations, up to 30 years at low interest, partly repayable in local currency; and Social Progress Trust Fund, social type development projects up to 30 years, very low interest, partly repayable in local currency

Discussion of Specific Agencies

The oldest of the United States Government or of the multigovernmental financial agencies still operating is the Export-Import Bank of Washington, D.C. This was established in 1934 at a time when there was a wave of liberalism in the field of international commercial relations, as far as the United States was concerned. The aim of the Export-Import Bank always has been and continues to be to promote the exportation of United States products. Initially, it made loans to American exporters on a "full recourse" basis. Later, in connection with exports of capital goods, certain transactions were financed on a partial "without recourse" basis. The period of loans originally ran to two and three years except in the case of financing agricultural exports, for which the *credit* period was shorter, but the period of loans was later extended.

In 1954, the Export-Import Bank extended its operations to include what was called "exporter credit lines" under which the bank undertook to cover 60 percent of the invoice amount of sale of American products *without* recourse on the exporter. Guarantees were also provided under which an exporter would absorb 25 percent of the risk and his own private bank, backed by the Export-Import Bank, would guarantee the other 75 percent. For these services a fee was charged.

With the appearance of export credit insurance through the Foreign Credit Insurance Association (FCIA), which the Export-Import Bank was instrumental in setting up and which the bank supports for political risk insurance, the former method of granting exporter credit lines was suspended.

The Inter-American Development Bank came into being in 1959 to promote the economic development of the Latin American republics. The bank is a result of the pressure exerted by the Latin American countries to provide a financing facility that would be less strict than the Export-Import Bank. What the Latin American countries actually sought was a bank that would lend dollars to be repaid in local national currency. As finally worked out, only 15 percent of the resources of the IDB are in the "soft" (local currency repayment) category; the other 85 percent are designated as "hard" loans, requiring repayment in United States dollars and carrying commercial terms. This is the difference between the two "windows" of the IDB.

The Inter-American Social Progress Trust Fund is administered by the IDB and is designed to provide capital and technical assistance to support efforts of Latin American countries to achieve greater social progress and balanced economic growth. As shown in the preceding summary, the United States Government has supplied all of the $394 million in this fund, which operates chiefly in the "soft" loan category.

The Agency for International Development is the latest name of a succession of agencies of the United States Government whose function is to dispense and administer the foreign aid appropriations made each year by Congress.

Magnitude of Operations

We shall now examine the data available as to the magnitude of the operations of the several agencies discussed in this chapter. The following tables will present the data for each agency, and observations will be made on the scope and magnitude revealed therein.

At the outset, it will be of interest to examine a statement covering the entire range of United States Government foreign assistance from the end of World War II (July 1, 1945) to December 31, 1961. Table 27-1 shows that the total amount involved has been nearly $97 billion, of which $5 billion went to pay the United States share in the several international financial institutions. The balance of over $91 billion is assistance, of which nearly $33 billion was for military and nearly $59 billion for nonmilitary assistance. The geographical breakdown of the $59 billion for nonmilitary assistance shows that Europe received over 40 percent; the Far East and Pacific received over 20 percent; the Near East received about 20 percent; the American Republics received over 7 percent; and the small balance was distributed over the remaining areas of the world.

We shall also examine the magnitude of the financing operations of the Export-Import Bank specifically. These data are included in the overall statistics presented in Table 27-1. This is also true of the funds utilized by AID and the predecessor aid agencies whose funds depend upon annual Congressional appropriations.

Table 27-1
MAJOR UNITED STATES GOVERNMENT FOREIGN ASSISTANCE
July 1, 1945 to December 31, 1963.
(In millions of $ U.S.)

Total — net...		96,671
International financial institutions................		5,304
IDB...	250	
IBRD..	635	
IDA...	259	
IFC...	35	
IMF..	4,125	
Assistance..		91,367
Military..	32,641	
Nonmilitary..	58,726	
Nonmilitary assistance		
Western Europe...........................	23,786	
Eastern Europe............................	1,587	
Near East...................................	11,946	
Africa..	1,554	
Far East and Pacific......................	13,285	
American Republics.......................	4,480	
Other Western Hemisphere................	33	
Other international organizations and unspecified areas..............................	2,057	

Source: U.S. Bureau of the Census, *Statistical Abstract of the United States: 1964* (85th ed.; Washington, D.C., 1964), Table 1216.

Geographically, the lending of the Export-Import Bank as shown in Table 27-2 has gone to Latin America, Europe, and Asia, in that order.

The magnitude of operations of the IBRD is covered in Table 27-3. These figures are net of cancellations and refunding and thus do not represent the entire amount that the IBRD has advanced. It will be noted that nearly $6.5 billion of the approximately $7 billion loaned by the IBRD has been for development purposes.

The geographical breakdown shows that Asia and the Western Hemisphere have been the largest recipients of these funds, with Europe close behind.

The purposes of these loans indicate that basic needs receive precedence. Electric power generation and distribution headed the list with $2,336 million, closely followed by transportation with $2,261; third was industry with $1,129. The other uses are small, being agriculture and forestry, $529; general development, $205; and communications, $27.

Concerning the IDB whose operations are shown in Table 27-4, it will be recalled that it deals exclusively with the inter-American area.

Table 27-2

EXPORT-IMPORT BANK OF WASHINGTON

Financing operations 1934 — December 31, 1963
(In millions of $ U.S.)

Area	Authorized	Disbursed or Shipped	Repaid	Outstanding
AFRICA				
Credits	497	300.7	152.5	148.2
Guarantees	39.1	11.8	2.0	9.8
Medium-Term Insurance	2.5	*	—	*
Short-Term Insurance		17.2	13.2	4.0
ASIA				
Credits	3,028.5	2,029.1	1,124.2	904.9
Guarantees	383.5	246.9	158.2	88.7
Medium-Term Insurance	8.9	2.5	.5	2.0
Short-Term Insurance		33.3	23.4	9.9
CANADA				
Credits	775.7			0
Guarantees	.4	.1	*	.1
Medium-Term Insurance	*			
Short-Term Insurance		3.7	3.0	.7
EUROPE				
Credits	4,408.3	3,052.4	2,493.9	558.5
Guarantees	78.4	20.3	7.7	12.6
Medium-Term Insurance	2.4	.7	.1	.6
Short-Term Insurance		169.7	125.1	44.6
LATIN AMERICA				
Credits	5,085.3	3,675.7	1,704.7	1,971.0
Guarantees	149.3	50.5	11.6	38.9
Medium-Term Insurance	37.6	7.1	1.0	6.1
Short-Term Insurance		229.3	164.0	65.3
OCEANIA				
Credits	54.2	21.7	16.7	5.0
Guarantees	8.8	2.0	.9	1.1
Medium-Term Insurance	.3	.2	—	.2
Short-Term Insurance		12.0	8.9	3.1
MISCELLANEOUS				
Credits	13.1	4.4	4.4	—

* Less than $100,000.

Source: Export-Import Bank of Washington, *Semi-Annual Report to Congress* (for the six months ending December 31, 1963), pp. 136–142.

Table 27-3

INTERNATIONAL BANK FOR RECONSTRUCTION AND DEVELOPMENT

Financial Operations as of June 30, 1963
Net of cancellations and refunding
(In millions of $ U.S.)

Total	6,983	
Reconstruction	497	
Development	6,486	
Geographical breakdown of development loans		$6,486
Asia	2,354	
Western Hemisphere	1,738	
Africa	917	
Australia	417	
Europe	1,057	

Source: IBRD Report, June 30, 1963.

Table 27-4

INTER-AMERICAN DEVELOPMENT BANK

Financial Operations as of September 30, 1962
(In millions of $ U.S.)

Ordinary Capital — Loans, Total	190.4	
Taken by participants	7.0	
Canceled	.5	
Outstanding		182.9
Fund for Special Operations — Total	76.2	
Canceled	.1	
Outstanding		76.1
Social Progress Trust Fund		256.9

Source: Inter-American Development Bank, Report, September 30, 1962.

Table 27-5

INTERNATIONAL DEVELOPMENT ASSOCIATION

Financial Operations as of June 30, 1962
(In millions of $ U.S.)

	Total	Disbursed	Undisbursed	Not Yet Effective
Grand Total	235.1	12.2	162.4	60.5
Asia	160.3	7.4	98.3	54.5
Western Hemisphere	59.0	3.0	50.0	6.0
Africa	15.8	1.6	14.1	

(Totals may not add due to rounding.)

Source: IBRD Report, June 30, 1962.

Table 27-6

INTERNATIONAL FINANCE CORPORATION

Financial Operations as of June 30, 1963

(In millions of $ U.S.)

	Total	Dis-bursed	Undis-bursed	Not Yet Effective	Canceled	Acquired by Others	Outstanding standby and underwriting committments
Grand Total	90.5	60.8	9.8	5.5	7.8	2.8	3.7
Asia	15.5	6.6	1.5	.9	2.3	.4	3.7
Western Hemisphere	58.9	43.2	3.5	4.3	5.4	2.4	
Africa	7.8	4.4	3.4				
Australia	.9	.9					
Europe	6.8	5.9	——	.9			

(Totals may not add due to rounding.)

Source: International Finance Corporation Report, June 30, 1963.

Summarizing these tables, the following points are pertinent:

1. The magnitude of the operations of the financial agencies covered in these tables is about $19 billion, counting from the time of their beginning to the various dates centering around June 30, 1962.
2. The magnitude of the United States Government foreign assistance operations alone far exceeds the total of all of these agencies; and the Export-Import Bank, which is one of the agencies, shows the largest amount of assistance financing and these figures are included in the overall United States Government data in Table 27-1.
3. As far as the specific agencies are concerned, the geographical distribution shows Latin America to be the largest recipient, followed by Europe and close behind by Asia. Africa trails and other areas practically do not show up at all.
4. Counting the total United States Government foreign assistance as in Table 27-1, deleting Export-Import Bank operations as in Table 27-2 (because those operations are already counted in Table 27-1), and then adding the data in Tables 27-3 to 27-6, we find that Asia (combining Far East and Near East when these appear separately) has been the largest recipient of foreign assistance with nearly $28 billion, followed by Europe with over $24 billion. Then follow Latin America with $4.6 billion and Africa with nearly $2.0 billion.

See next page for Summary of Chapter 27.

Summary

1. The United States Government has gone heavily into international finance for war, reconstruction, and economic development purposes.
2. Two fundamental conditions have influenced United States Government financial operations overseas since the close of World War II. These are the communist threat and the pressing needs of the less developed countries.
3. Both United States Government and multigovernment financial agencies provide funds that pay for exports of merchandise.
4. The Export-Import Bank has been in operation since 1934, and its function is to assist in financing exports from the United States that increase the productive capacity of the borrower (individual or political entity) and on terms not obtainable through private banking channels. Financing can be done on a nonrecourse basis to the exporter.
5. The Agency for International Development (AID) seeks to aid the less developed countries by improving their productive capacity. This effort is designed to encourage the participation of private enterprise in such development.
6. The IBRD is a multigovernmental financing agency engaged in aiding the development of productive facilities and resources of the countries that are members of the bank. Only governments or government-backed applicants are accepted.
7. The IFC is a subsidiary of the IBRD and operates in the less developed countries that are members of the IFC and the IBRD.
8. The IDA is also an IBRD subsidiary and functions only for members. It finances operations on less strict terms than those applying to IBRD and IFC operations.
9. The IDB is a Western Hemisphere financial agency, whose function is to facilitate the economic development of the Latin American countries. It also administers the Inter-American Social Progress Trust Fund that provides capital and technical assistance to promote these objectives.
10. All United States Government and multigovernment financial agencies help private enterprise by means of feasibility studies, guarantees against credit risks, providing equity capital (IFC), and financing trade and investment. The Export-Import Bank, in connection with trade financing, deals with specific export transactions.
11. Financing by United States Government agencies and the IDB requires the procurement of supplies from United States sources or from Latin American countries, respectively. There is no such restriction on the source of supplies paid for by the other agencies.
12. The Export-Import Bank is the only agency that deals only in United States dollars in connection with its financing operations.
13. Generally, loans are made for long periods of time. This indicates that these agencies do not compete, at least actively, with private banks and financial institutions.

14. The Export-Import Bank and the IFC deal essentially with private borrowers; all others deal with governments and government-sponsored agencies.
15. There is a wide variety of terms, interest, and currency among the several agencies.
16. The magnitude of the financial operations of these agencies from the beginning of their operations is in the amount of $19 billion, and including all of the United States Government assistance since the close of World War II, it is over $55 billion.
17. The largest recipients of foreign assistance are Latin America, Europe, and Asia; if all postwar assistance by the United States Government is included, Europe is far ahead, followed by Asia, with Latin America and other geographical areas far behind.

QUESTIONS

1. Explain the policy of the United States Government in the field of international finance. Do you agree with this policy? Explain.
2. Of what interest to private foreign traders is the subject of the United States Government in international finance?
3. Why was the Export-Import Bank established? Describe its financing operations.
4. Are credits extended to United States exporters by the Export-Import Bank without recourse?
5. May a borrower from the Export-Import Bank spend the loan anywhere he chooses? Explain.
6. Discuss the purposes of the Agency for International Development (AID).
7. Why was the IBRD established? How far has it gone in fulfilling its purposes?
8. Distinguish between the objectives of the IFC and the IDA.
9. Account for the establishment of the IDB. Has it satisfactorily served its purposes?
10. In what specific ways do these agencies extend assistance to private enterprise?
11. Is geographical location of the borrower or buyer a factor in determining eligibility for financing or loans? Explain.
12. Why are loans from these agencies generally for long periods of time and at low interest rates?
13. Why is the matter of the currency that is to be borrowed and the currency in which repayment is to be made of such importance?
14. Explain why Europe, Latin America, and Asia are the largest geographical recipients of loans and grants since the close of World War II.

PROBLEMS

1. From your library, obtain a copy of the latest report of any of the agencies discussed in this chapter. Study this report and prepare your own analytical review.
2. Examine any one of the reports of the IBRD dealing with the economic and financial situation in a given area. Determine the extent to which such a thorough analysis appears to be necessary in order to ascertain the desirability of extending a loan to the area concerned.

COLLATERAL READINGS

American Management Association, International Management Division. "Sources and Methods of International Financing," *AMA Management Report No. 59.* New York: American Management Association, 1961. Part 2.

Arey, Hawthorne. *History of the Operations and Policies of the Export-Import Bank of Washington.* Washington, D.C.: The Export-Import Bank, 1953.

Bankers Trust Company. *Washington Agencies that Help to Finance Foreign Trade.* New York: Bankers Trust Company, 1962.

Dartnell International Trade Handbook, The. Chicago: The Dartnell Corporation, 1963.

Export-Import Bank of Washington. *Semi-Annual Report to Congress.* Washington, D.C.

The International Bank for Reconstruction and Development. *Annual Report.* Washington, D.C.

International Finance Corporation. *Annual Report.* Washington, D.C.

International Development Association. *Annual Report.* Washington, D.C.

Loomis, John E. *Public Money Sources for Overseas Trade and Investment.* Washington, D.C.: BNA, Inc., 1963.

The World Bank, the IFC, and the IDA. *Policies and Operations.* Washington, D.C.: 1962.

CHAPTER 28

INTERNATIONAL COMMERCIAL PAYMENTS: CASH,
OPEN ACCOUNT, AND BILLS OF EXCHANGE

International commercial payments consummated in the conduct of
international marketing may be broadly grouped into the following
classes:

1. Cash.
2. Open account.
3. Bills of exchange.
4. Letters of credit.
5. Special terms of payment.

In this chapter we shall examine the nature and use of the first three
kinds of international commercial payments. Letters of credit and
several special terms of payment will be discussed in Chapter 29.

Cash

Cash is both a method of remittance and a term of payment, but as
a method of payment in international marketing it is rarely used.

A Method of Remittance. As a *method of remittance*, the international
marketing concern may use checks, as in domestic trade. If accounts are
maintained in banks in various countries and in various currencies,
checks may be drawn and paid in a variety of currencies. Or, cash may
be remitted by means of an international money order. The great volume
of funds moving between countries in the conduct of international trading, amounting to nearly $130 billion annually, is remitted through bank
channels.

Banks in the United States have deposit accounts abroad, and foreign banks have deposit accounts in United States banks. When funds are to be paid out of any of these accounts, they are generally used for purposes of financing trade. An exporter in the United States receives dollars for the merchandise that he sells, regardless of whether the price was stated in United States dollars or in some other currency. If, for example, the price were given in Italian lira, then the American bank's lira account in Italy is increased and the Italian bank's dollar account in the United States bank is reduced. The conversion of the lira into United States dollars is a foreign exchange transaction taken care of by banks — in this case, by the United States bank.

This is the way that cash is transferred between countries for all international transactions — trade, service, debts, tourists, interest, etc. The actual transfer (not just book transactions) of funds between countries occurs when balances must be replenished.[1]

A Term of Payment. In a more specific trade sense, cash is a *term of payment*. Cash may be called for with the order, or against certificates of manufacture as work on a complicated machine progresses, or at time of shipment, or at the time and place of export. One exporter declared that his terms of payment are perfect (in his case): "We have the best inducement in the world. Since we deal with a high-value item, we require deposit with the order. If full payment is not received when shipment is ready, the deposit is forfeited. Our terms are strictly cash upon delivery. While not desirable, it is necessary due to the nature of our product." This statement was made in 1958![2]

Unattractiveness to Buyer. Cash methods of payment, at best, are unattractive to a buyer. In the case of cash upon shipment, the buyer assumes the entire burden of financing the shipment; he is out of funds a considerable time before he receives the goods, incurring a loss in the use of working capital as well as a loss in interest; and he resents the possible imputation that he is unworthy of credit extension. Terms of cash with order are open to even more serious objection, as the buyer is, in this case, entirely dependent upon the honesty, solvency, and promptness of the exporter with whom he is dealing.

---

[1]See Chapter 32 for a discussion of foreign exchange.

[2]Quoted from Export Managers Club of New York, Inc., *Service Bulletin 2214* (August 7, 1958).

Conditions Favoring Use of Cash Method. It is to be anticipated that cash payment will be required by certain exporters of certain importers in certain territories and at certain times. Under the following conditions, the use of the cash method is favored:

1. If an exporter is shortsighted in his export policy, is financially weak, or is shipping goods abroad spasmodically, he may insist upon cash payment in one form or another.

2. If an importer is of unknown or of doubtful standing, he cannot expect (although he usually requests) the extension of credit.

3. When custom prevails, as in the case of remote parts of the world, or when internal conditions in a country are unsettled, thus casting a continual element of doubt upon the future paying ability of residents of that country, cash is the logical method of payment.

In the years following 1930, the fear of sudden and unpredictable imposition of exchange restrictions forced exporters to demand cash or guarantee payment for shipments to many countries. After restrictions had been in force, it was often possible again to extend normal credit within the permissible framework of these restrictions. Moreover, unusual conditions, such as the insatiable demand for merchandise following the close of global conflicts, may create a seller's market resulting in the competition of buyers to have orders filled, and at such time, prepayment of cash may be readily obtained.

4. On orders for merchandise requiring special construction, exporters are often justified in requiring the payment of cash against certificates of manufacture.

Partial Cash in Advance. A departure from the strict terms of cash with order occurs in the requirement of partial cash in advance. The amount of prepayment required in this instance is generally sufficient to reimburse the exporter for packing, freight, and all other transportation charges to and from the foreign destination, as well as insurance and all other expenses that the exporter would lose in case the shipment were refused by the importer and subsequently returned. Adequate protection may thereby be afforded the exporter; and the flexibility of this method, coupled with other means of payment for the balance, affords a desirable method of financing in some instances.

Open Account

The open-account method of payment for export shipments swings to the opposite extreme from the cash method. Under an open-account extension, goods are shipped to a consignee without documents calling for payment — the commercial invoice of the exporter indicating the liability. Payment for goods so shipped is usually stipulated as a certain number of days after date of shipment, or occasionally it may be left to the discretion of the buyer. Open-account payment is also provided under a consignment shipment, in which case reimbursement is to be made upon disposal of the merchandise. Manufacturers operating branches abroad may ship supplies to their branches under open account.

Nature of Open-Account Transactions. No documentary basis of obligation or of ownership is provided under the open-account method. This lack of security to the exporter presents the singular distinction between the open account and other credit methods of payment. In view of the fact that a documentary basis is absent, the open-account method presents obvious difficulties. Only unreliable means of safeguarding the interests of the exporter are available, and although under the law of one country he may be able to sustain his rights, he cannot do so in every country because of the divergence of law and custom throughout the world. Moreover, it is unusual for a bank to make advances to an exporter on the security of his accounts receivable.

Thus, the entire burden of financing the business rests upon the exporter. With the extended use of the open account, a greater amount of liquid capital is required by the exporter than under other forms of payment. When prices are quoted in foreign currency, the exchange risk is assumed by the exporter. Because of the indefinite maturity of the invoice, it may be impossible for an exporter to protect himself against exchange losses with any degree of accuracy.

Conditions Favoring Use of Open Account. Sales on open account can safely be made only to customers of the highest credit standing and then only when stable and favorable economic and political conditions prevail. Distance is also a factor influencing open-account payment. In the trade with Canada, for example, payment terms are substantially the same as in the United States domestic trade, and some of the business is conducted on open account. The same is true, in some lines, in the trade with Great Britain and Latin America.

The open account, as is also the case with cash payment, represents a method of payment that is inherently simple. In the open account, merely a book entry is made to evidence an obligation; and in cash terms, payment is taken care of in advance. There is no necessity of making banking arrangements, no drafts to draw, and no commissions or fees of any consequence to pay. Ease of operation, appreciated by both buyer and seller, is provided. These favorable conditions are, however, outweighed by the obvious difficulties in the general adoption of either of these methods of payment.

Bills of Exchange

We come now to the most common method of payment in international trade, under which the greater part of international commerce normally is financed. Bills of exchange, also known as drafts, provide a documentary evidence of obligation; and the entire financial burden is sustained by neither the exporter nor the importer.

$395.00 September 3, 19--
Sixty days after sight PAY TO THE
ORDER OF The Philadelphia National Bank
Three hundred ninety-five DOLLARS
VALUE RECEIVED AND CHARGE TO ACCOUNT OF
TO Jose Torres & Cia.
No. 1074 Lima, Peru
Arthur Wayne, Treasurer
Century Products

Figure 28–A. **Draft (Bill of Exchange)**

Drafts, or bills of exchange, are drawn by sellers of goods, calling upon buyers either to pay or to accept for payment a designated sum of money at a determinable future time. *Acceptance* consists of an acknowledgment to this effect written across the face of the draft and signed by the drawee (buyer), obligating him to provide payment of the amount stipulated within the period of time designated. When accepted, a draft becomes a *trade acceptance*. The two features provided by this method of payment and which are essential to satisfactory use in international marketing are: (1) the documentary evidence of obligation is readily transferable and (2) provision is made for a definite or determinate maturity of the obligation.

Types of Drafts. A draft drawn without collateral documents attached is known as a *clean draft*, while one with certain stipulated documents of shipment, insurance, etc., is known as a *documentary draft*. In international marketing, it is the documentary draft which is employed almost exclusively.

Parties to Draft Transactions. There are three parties to every draft transaction. These are:

1. The *drawer* — the person who executes the draft (exporter).

2. The *drawee* — the person on whom the draft is drawn and who is required to meet the terms of the document (importer).

3. The *payee* — the party to receive payment (exporter or exporter's bank).

The drawer is the person to whom payment is due and is therefore the seller or exporter. The drawee is the person who owes the payment — the buyer or importer. In international transactions the payee is usually the exporter (also the drawer), but it may often be a bank that is named as payee on behalf of the exporter.

Tenor or Usance. The time at which payment of a draft is to be made is known as *tenor* or *usance*. With respect to tenor, bills of exchange are of three kinds: (1) sight draft, (2) arrival draft, and (3) date draft.

Sight Draft. A *sight draft*, literally interpreted, calls upon the drawee to accept and pay the draft upon "sight" or presentation. This may mean that the draft will be payable before the goods arrive abroad, because the draft is dispatched through the mails and the goods generally move by freight lines. In some countries, it is an accepted custom for a bank to hold a draft to await the arrival of the goods for which the draft is drawn before presenting it to the drawee.

Arrival Draft. An *arrival draft*, which calls for payment upon the arrival of the merchandise, would seem to avoid the difficulties arising from the delivery of a sight draft before the receipt of the goods. The word "arrival" makes definite reference to the *shipment*, while in the sight draft the word "sight" refers to the *draft*. Inasmuch as drafts are usually drawn in duplicate and are sent through the mails, their arrival abroad is more certain than is the arrival of goods. For this reason, there is no precise due date of an arrival draft, since the merchandise may never actually arrive at its destination. The absence of a definite or ascertainable maturity date thus renders arrival drafts nonnegotiable in many foreign countries. In lieu of arrival drafts, it is better in general practice to employ sight drafts and to instruct the bank to defer presentation of the draft until the goods have arrived.

Date Draft. The *date draft* calls for payment on a specified date or, as usually is the case, at so many days after date. This type of draft is affected in no way by the movement of goods. The maturity is definite but rigid and inflexible.

Time Designations on Drafts. The time at which payment of a draft is to be made is indicated in the terms of sale agreed upon between the buyer and the seller. Ordinary periods of time for which drafts are written are 30, 60, and 90 days.

A 60-day sight draft, for example, calls upon the drawee to meet his obligation within 60 days after he has accepted the draft. Here again the time sight draft is generally employed because of its greater flexibility, although date drafts, in spite of their rigidity, are also widely used.

The maturity of a date draft is much more accurately set than is the case with a sight draft, for it is impossible to know exactly when a sight draft will be presented for acceptance and when the obligation will thus begin to run. In practice this date is determined approximately from the average length of time required to send a draft to a particular country for acceptance or payment. By adding this time to the tenor of the draft, a fairly accurate estimate of the maturity date is obtained. For example, in the case of most shipments to South America, about two weeks are allowed for a draft to reach its destination and to return. Thus, a 60-day sight draft can be expected to be honored by the drawee in about 75 days.

Mode of Transfer of Documents.[3] In addition to the time designation in a quotation involving the use of drafts, there is also a declaration of the mode of transfer of documents covering shipments. The fundamental commercial documents required in international marketing and called for in draft transactions are:

1. Ocean bills of lading (airmail receipt, air transportation waybill, inland railroad bill of lading, certificate of mailing, or consignment note or receipt), negotiable, made out to order,

---

[3]For a further discussion of the documents that cover international shipments, see Chapter 22.

and usually endorsed in blank. Although the number varies, one full set (three) of these papers is generally required.

2. Marine insurance certificate, or marine insurance policy, in duplicate.

3. Commercial invoice, in duplicate.

These are the minimum documents required, both as to number of copies and type. The importance of each of these documents is briefly presented below.

Negotiable Bill of Lading. A *negotiable bill of lading*, endorsed in blank, is (1) a receipt for goods, (2) a contract of carriage, and (3) evidence of title to property, the holder being the lawful owner. With the transfer of this document from hand to hand as legitimate owners supplant each other, full control of a shipment may be exercised. Unless the drawee pays or accepts the draft covering the shipment, possession of the bill of lading will be withheld by the bank; and without the bill of lading, the goods will not be delivered to him.

Marine Insurance Certificate. The *marine insurance certificate*, or *policy*, protects the shipment, and consequently the holders, for value against marine and other insurable perils, thus nullifying this element of risk.

Commercial Invoice and Other Documents. The *commercial invoice* indicates the types, quantities, prices, terms, and other matters which relate to the shipment.

Other documents that may normally be required or may be advisable at times are packing lists, inspection certificates for certain products, and consular invoices or certificates of origin, when required by foreign governments. The United States Government requires an export declaration for all export shipments, as well as export licenses for certain goods and certain destinations. Import licenses may also be required by the importer's country.

Since the possession of essential documents is so important, their transfer is an integral part of financing, and instructions as to their disposal are always included in the sales terms. The disposition of the documents may be made upon payment of the draft or upon acceptance of the draft, as indicated by the expressions "documents for (or against) payment" and "documents for (or against) acceptance," respectively.

Illustrations of Quotations. Combining the tenor of drafts and the mode of transfer of documents, we arrive at the forms of quotations widely employed in international marketing transactions. A few of these designations are given for illustration.

At Sight (S/D). The draft is payable upon presentation, and a complete statement would include "documents for payment" (D/P). This is essentially c.o.d.

Thirty Days After Sight (30 Days S/D-D/A). The draft is payable 30 days after presentation and acceptance, documents delivered upon acceptance.

Thirty Days After Date (30 Days D/D-[D/A or D/P]). The draft is payable 30 days after the date on which it is made out, documents delivered against acceptance of the draft, or against payment, as arranged.

On Arrival. The draft is payable upon arrival of the merchandise, which may be delayed or may never occur. The documents are delivered against payment of the draft.

Ninety Days After Sight (90 Days S/D-D/P). In the case of this time-sight draft, documents against payment, an anomaly appears to exist since the draft is payable 90 days after presentation and acceptance, but the documents are not to be delivered until the draft is paid. The significance of this type of payment appears in quotations to distant markets where it is customary to order merchandise in large lots. An Oriental importer of textiles, for example, might order a large quantity of piece goods to supply him for an entire season's trade. He may not be in a position, however, to pay for the entire lot at once; and under the terms now considered, he makes withdrawals and pays for each unit withdrawn, as he finds it convenient, receiving the documents that authorize possession as he pays for each lot of merchandise. The time designation of 90 days then means that the full amount of the draft is to be retired within this period after acceptance.

Disposition of Drafts. When trade bills or drafts are drawn in international trade, the exporter (drawer) may dispose of them by discounting, by borrowing, or by placing for collection.

Discounting or Borrowing. The drawer may discount or sell the draft to a bank or he may obtain an advance or loan from a bank, using the draft and collateral documents as security. It is not to be understood, however, that it is always ·possible to realize the first option, nor that a loan may always be obtained for the face amount of the draft in the second case. Inasmuch as recourse is always reserved against the drawer of a trade bill, unless other arrangements are made,[4] his standing has an important effect upon the salability of his drafts.

In case the drawer seeks a loan from his bank with the documents as collateral, he may be obliged to accept, say 90, 75, or 60 percent of the face of the draft. This may in no way be a reflection upon his integrity, but it may be determined by the marketability of the goods offered as security and by the interest of the banker in the business offered to him. Staple goods, for example, are more readily salable than are specialties, and generally command a larger loan.

In any event, the bank will deduct a discount from the amount advanced to the drawer. The amount of discount represents interest, usually at 6 percent, for the estimated length of time elapsing from the date of discounting or hypothecating the draft until funds are in possession of the bank again. This period of time is computed in the same manner as given above for estimating the maturity date of a sight or time-sight draft, plus the time required to receive payment by the lending bank. The exporter may pass this expense on to the importer by concealing it in his price or by charging the interest to him, as will be discussed at a later point.

Placing for Collection. If the exporter or drawer is not seeking to discount or to borrow on his draft, the draft and all documents attached are passed on to the bank with instructions to send them abroad for collection. Most drafts placed for collection are handled by the home bank (or bank in the United States) of the drawer. Some firms themselves, however, send the draft and collateral documents abroad to a bank for collection, claiming that this procedure is (1) faster, (2) less expensive, since there is only one bank collection charge, and (3) in accordance with the wishes of certain customers. Even for those who follow this procedure, there are instances in which it is more desirable to use the facilities of a bank in the home country.

In international marketing, drafts placed for collection are usually drawn in duplicate in order that delays or losses may be avoided as much as possible. If the first draft reads, "90 days after sight of this first of exchange (second unpaid)," the duplicate draft will read, "90 days after sight of this second of exchange (first unpaid)." The duplicate is then sent forward to the collecting bank on a mail steamer following the first

---

[4]Facilities are available for discounting drafts without recourse to the drawer. An extra charge is made for this accommodation. See also Chapter 31.

£840 July 15, 19-- No. 460

ninety days after sight of this
FIRST of Exchange (Second unpaid) pay to the Order of
THE PHILADELPHIA NATIONAL BANK
Eight hundred forty pounds sterling
Value received and charge the same to account of
To Martin Metals Ltd.
London
Jackson Mining Corp.
Walter Hill, President

£840 July 15, 19-- No. 460

ninety days after sight of this
SECOND of Exchange (First unpaid) pay to the Order of
THE PHILADELPHIA NATIONAL BANK
Eight hundred forty pounds sterling
Value received and charge the same to account of
To Martin Metals Ltd.
London
Jackson Mining Corp.
Walter Hill, President

Figure 28–B. **Drafts: First and Second of Exchange**

draft and is automatically valueless in case the first has arrived safely. The first draft is often sent by international airmail and the duplicate, by steamer mail.

Bank Instructions. The instructions that are given to a bank in connection with drafts placed for collection are decidedly important, the most significant points to be covered being:

1. Explicit identification of the drawee, particularly if his name is a common one.

2. Whether shipping documents are to be surrendered against acceptance of the draft or only against payment.

3. Whether acceptance or payment may or may not be deferred until the arrival of the goods in the event that the shipment has not arrived prior to the arrival of the draft.

4. Whether the drawee is to be given the privilege of inspection of the merchandise before accepting or paying the draft.

5. Whether the foreign bank shall "protest"[5] the draft in the event of nonacceptance or of nonpayment.

6. Whether the presenting bank is to cable in the event of the dishonor of the draft. It is usually important to have this done because prompt notice of rejection enables the drawer to take speedy action in reselling and salvaging the merchandise.

7. Whether interest and collection charges are to be borne by the drawee, and whether such charges are to be waived if payment of them is refused.

8. Full instruction as to the disposition of the goods (warehousing, insurance, etc.) in the event that the drafts are dishonored.

9. The giving of the name and address of the foreign representative or attorney with whom the bank should communicate in case of trouble, and a statement whether such party is empowered to act with full authority or only to serve in an advisory capacity.

Additional Cost Items in a Draft. Drafts may be drawn without naming the exact amount due. A number of small items must also be considered in drawing a draft in order that an exporter may recover the full amount to which he is entitled. Such items include interest, bank charges, and rates for money transfers. In case the cost of these items is to be borne by the drawee and is not included in the price, this fact may be indicated in the draft.

INTEREST AND BANK CHARGES. After naming the sum for which it is drawn, a draft may state: "plus all collection charges and interest at the rate of 6 percent per annum." Tact is required in placing such items in the body of a draft, however, since they usually prove irritating to a drawee. It is a much better practice to include small items in the price rather than to create resentment by displaying them separately. The insertion of such clauses, moreover, is not permissible everywhere because they tend to render the amount of a draft indefinite and therefore illegal.

---

[5]"Protest" consists of the entering of a formal legal notice of refusal on the part of the drawee to pay or to accept the draft as agreed. This step is necessary in most countries to sustain subsequent legal action resulting from such refusal. See Chapter 31.

TRANSFER OF FUNDS. A clause may be inserted in a draft to indicate the exchange rate at which payment is to be made. In the case of sight drafts, this may read: "payable at the collecting bank's selling rate on day of payment for sight drafts on New York." In the case of sterling bills drawn on overseas areas of the British Commonwealth, in settling the question of funds, it is customary to insert the colonial clause, "payable with exchange, English and colonial stamps added, at the current rate in London for negotiating bills on the colonies."

Risks Borne by the Exporter. The draft method of payment, as has been pointed out, places the final responsibility upon the exporter, as he is subject to recourse until the drawee has completely settled his obligation. The necessity for securing adequate credit data on the drawee is apparent. Indeed, one of the disadvantages of discounting drafts, rather than placing them for collection, lies in the possibility of considering them as closed transactions, whereas they can never be so considered until the drawee has remitted.

In addition, under the draft or trade bill method of credit extension, the exporter runs the risk of rejection of the merchandise by the importer. In this case, the importer probably will not accept the draft. The exporter is then faced with the problem of disposal of the refused shipment — whether by forced sale abroad, by storage, or by return to the United States or other market.

Operation of a Trade Bill Transaction. Following the lines on Chart 28-1, we shall now trace step by step a trade bill transaction in international marketing. In the present instance, it is a 60-day sight-draft transaction in United States dollars.

1. The American exporter makes shipment to a British importer, with the billing made out to the name of the exporter.

2. The exporter delivers the draft and shipping documents to the American bank, which sends the draft and shipping documents to the British bank.

3. The British bank notifies the importer that the documents have arrived and presents the draft to the importer for acceptance, payment in 60 days.

4. Upon accepting the bill of exchange, the shipping documents are surrendered to the importer and he can now claim the shipment.

5. The accepted bill of exchange is returned to the American bank by the British bank.

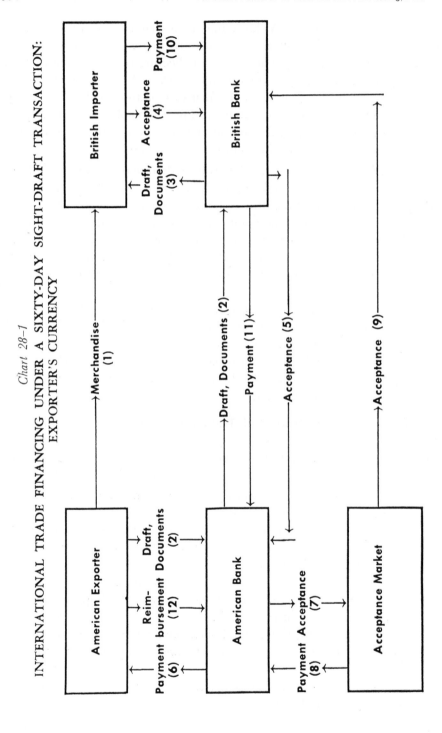

Chart 28–1

INTERNATIONAL TRADE FINANCING UNDER A SIXTY-DAY SIGHT-DRAFT TRANSACTION: EXPORTER'S CURRENCY

6. The exporter discounts the draft and receives advance payment.

7. The American bank, in turn, disposes of the bill of exchange in the acceptance market.

8. Upon receiving such funds, the American bank is now in a liquid position again, having discounted the draft in Step 7.

9. When the 60-day maturity approaches, the bill of exchange is sent to the British bank by some financial institution that had purchased it from the American bank. (In Step 7 the American bank had disposed of the bill of exchange in the acceptance market).

10. The British bank receives payment from the British importer in pounds sterling and the conversion of sterling to dollars is made by the British bank.

11. The funds are transmitted to the present holder of the trade acceptance (shown in Chart 28-1 as an American bank).

12. The American exporter settles with the American bank to complete the transaction.

Summary

1. International commercial payment terms are classified into cash, open account, bills of exchange, letters of credit, and special payment terms.
2. Cash is rarely used as a method of payment in international marketing.
3. The open-account method of payment is generally used only on shipments to an exporter's foreign subsidiaries and sometimes to nearby markets, such as United States export sales to Canada.
4. Bills of exchange, or drafts, are the most common means of effecting payment in international marketing.
5. A draft is drawn by an exporter on an importer, calling upon him to pay or agree to pay a certain sum at a definite or determinable future time. If drawn at sight, the draft is payable at sight. If drawn at so many days after sight or date or arrival, the draft is generally presented to the importer for acceptance. This is accomplished through a foreign banking correspondent or a branch of the exporter's bank.
6. Documentary drafts have supporting documents attached and are generally used in international marketing transactions.
7. Drafts may be discounted (sold), borrowed on, or placed for collection. Explicit instructions are given the bank that forwards a draft for collection.
8. Under the draft method of payment, the risk of nonacceptance or nonpayment is borne by the exporter.

QUESTIONS

1. Define *cash* as a means of international commercial payment.
2. Under what conditions would an exporter demand and expect payment in cash?
3. Why would an importer be willing to pay cash?
4. How does an open-account transaction function?
5. Why can open-account terms be safely extended in certain transactions?
6. From the exporter's standpoint, explain the disadvantages of quoting on open account?
7. Define *bill of exchange.*
8. Define *acceptance* and *trade acceptance.*
9. Distinguish between *clean* and *documentary* drafts.
10. Identify the parties to a draft transaction.
11. With respect to tenor, distinguish among (a) sight drafts, (b) arrival drafts, and (c) date drafts.
12. Explain the purposes of each of the essential documents used in a documentary draft transaction.
13. What choice does an exporter have in disposing of the documentary drafts he has drawn to cover his international transactions?

PROBLEMS

1. Visit the United States Post Office and request an application for an international money order. Examine the application and also that section of *The Postal Manual* which contains regulations governing the international mail service. Prepare a report on the operation of this means of making an international payment.
2. In a fashion similar to that of Chart 28-1 and the accompanying discussion in the text, prepare a chart in which you trace the steps followed in an open-account transaction. Then prepare an enumeration and definition of each one of these steps.

COLLATERAL READINGS

Dartnell International Trade Handbook, The. Chicago: The Dartnell Corporation, 1963.

de Haas, J. A. *The Practice of Foreign Trade.* New York: McGraw-Hill Book Company, Inc., 1935. Chapter 14.

Exporters Encyclopaedia. New York: Thomas Ashwell and Co., Inc., annual.

Fayerweather, John. *Management of International Operations,* Text and Cases. New York: McGraw-Hill Book Company, Inc., 1960. Chapter 7.

Heck, Harold J. *Foreign Commerce.* New York: McGraw-Hill Book Company, Inc., 1953. Chapters 8 and 9.

Henning, Charles N. *International Finance.* New York: Harper & Brothers, 1958. Chapters 3, 5–9, 11, 14, and 15.

Horn, Paul V. *International Trade Principles and Practices,* Third Edition. New York: Prentice-Hall, Inc., 1951. Chapter 28.

MacDonald, Philip. *Practical Exporting.* New York: Ronald Press Company, 1949. Chapter 13.

Pratt, E. E. *Modern International Commerce.* New York: Allyn and Bacon, Inc., 1956. Chapters 9 and 13.

Roorbach, G. B. *Import Purchasing: Principles and Problems.* Chicago and New York: A. W. Shaw Company, 1927. Chapter 12.

——————————. *Problems in Foreign Trade.* New York: McGraw-Hill Book Company, Inc., 1933. Part V.

Rosenthal, Morris. *Techniques of International Trade.* New York: McGraw-Hill Book Company, Inc., 1950. Part VI.

Shaterian, William S. *Export-Import Banking,* Second Edition. New York: Ronald Press, 1956. Chapters 12 to 15.

Wasserman, Max J., Charles W. Hultman, and Laszlo Zsoldos. *International Finance.* New York: Simmons-Boardman Publishing Corporation, 1963. Chapters 8 and 9.

CHAPTER 29

INTERNATIONAL COMMERCIAL PAYMENTS: LETTERS OF CREDIT

In the preceding chapter we examined the nature and use of three methods of international commercial payments — cash, open account, and bills of exchange. In this chapter we shall conclude our discussion with a description of commercial letters of credit and other special terms of payment.

Commercial Letters of Credit

In the letter of credit method of payment in international marketing, drafts are drawn upon a bank and not upon an importer, thus becoming *bank acceptances* rather than *trade acceptances*. Greater security therefore attaches to the transaction than in the case of trade bills. It is not to be presumed, however, that this security is to be realized in every instance, since the forms of letters of credit vary widely to fit many different purposes and conditions. Attempts at standardization have been made, however, as for example, the recommendations of the Commercial Credit Committee of the American Acceptance Council in 1922. The International Chamber of Commerce has also recommended uniform regulations governing documentary credits.[1] The revision effective July 1, 1963, was particularly notable because for the first time the British banks subscribed to these conditions, and it is anticipated that Canadian and other Commonwealth banks will also subscribe.

A *commercial letter of credit* is an instrument issued by a bank at the request of a buyer of merchandise whereby the bank itself undertakes to accept and/or pay drafts drawn upon the bank by the seller of the mer-

---

[1]See *Uniform Customs and Practice for Commercial Documentary Credits* (1933), revised 1962.

chandise concerned. The seller is governed by requirements set forth in the instrument. A letter of credit thus provides a means of substituting a bank credit for mercantile credit and affords the exporter security for payment.

Parties to a Letter of Credit. Three essential parties to a commercial letter of credit are:

1. The *opener, account,* or *importer* — the buyer who opens the credit.
2. The *issuer* — the bank that issues the letter of credit.
3. The *beneficiary* or *accreditee* — the seller in whose favor the credit is opened.

In practice, however, additional parties are introduced in order to perform certain necessary functions. For the sake of clarity it is well to note that in addition to the three parties already mentioned, only one other party to a letter of credit transaction creates a new credit relationship — the confirming bank. The *confirming bank* is a bank in the beneficiary's country, which, at the request of the beneficiary, is instructed by the issuer to confirm the undertaking of the issuer.

Additional parties usually to be found in a letter of credit transaction, but in no way affecting the credit relationship and financial responsibility already set up, are the advising bank; the paying, accepting, or drawee bank; and the negotiating bank.

The *advising bank* is located in the country of the beneficiary and notifies the beneficiary of the opening of the credit. In case the letter of credit is also confirmed, the advising and the confirming bank are the same.

The *paying, accepting,* or *drawee bank* is the one on which drafts are to be drawn, or, as known in banking parlance, the one "on whom drafts are available."

The *negotiating bank* or *negotiator,* also located in the country of the beneficiary, voluntarily (not by instruction of the issuer) pays the drafts of the beneficiary drawn under the letter of credit. This party usually is also the adviser — the adviser by appointment of the issuer, and the negotiator of the drafts on its own volition.

In a broader sense, any bank that pays or accepts drafts, whether or not on its own initiative, may be said to negotiate the drafts, and the term "negotiator" may sometimes be used interchangeably with the paying or accepting bank. Upon acceptance by a responsible bank, a

F.D. 12   **APPLICATION FOR COMMERCIAL LETTER OF CREDIT**

THE PHILADELPHIA NATIONAL BANK   _____ 19_____
     PHILADELPHIA 1, PA.

Gentlemen:

                              We hereby request you to issue by cable your irrevocable credit, as follows:
                                                                 mail

In favor of _____

For account of _____

Up to the aggregate amount of _____

Available by _____ drafts drawn, at your option on you or any of
                      (Please specify tenor)

your correspondents for _____percent invoice value.

Documents Required: (Please indicate by check)

☐ Commercial Invoice

☐ Consular Invoice

☐ Marine Insurance Policy or Certificate
   War

☐ Full set onboard ocean Bills of Lading issued to order of The Philadelphia National Bank,

   Philadelphia, Pa. Notify _____

   Bills of Lading to be dated not later than _____

☐ Other documents _____

   _____

Evidencing shipment of: _____
                         (Please mention commodity only, omitting details as to grade, quality, price, etc.)

   _____

   _____

   _____

For shipment to _____

Insurance to be effected by _____
                              (If insurance effected other than by shipper, give name of issuing Company)
Drafts must be drawn and negotiated not later than _____
                              OTHER CONDITIONS

We
 I will execute your usual form of obligation for credit when presented to us
                                                                             me.

                                                    _____

Figure 29–A. **Application for Commercial Letter of Credit**

bill of exchange becomes a *banker's acceptance*, which is recognized as prime paper for discount. A banking institution is attracted to negotiating drafts because of the interest and bank charges that are received for this service.

Types of Letters of Credit. Letters of credit are of various types to fit various conditions. It is always good policy to be fully informed regarding the terms of a particular document that may be employed in any transaction. The principal types of commercial letters of credit are described in the following paragraphs.

Revocable or Irrevocable. As to cancellation or duration, letters of credit may be classified as revocable or irrevocable. The privilege of revocability refers to the right of the issuing bank to revoke the undertaking to honor drafts drawn upon it. Revocable credits are not legally binding undertakings between banks and beneficiaries.[2] In actual practice, the term "letter of credit" is generally accepted in the literal sense that it logically conveys, and irrevocability is usually understood.

Confirmed or Unconfirmed. A letter of credit may be confirmed or unconfirmed. If the letter of credit is confirmed, the irrevocable obligation of the issuer is then guaranteed by a confirming (also advising) bank located in the beneficiary's country. This act is generally understood to impose upon a confirming bank the same responsibility as that which attaches to the endorser of a check. Confirmation is sought by a beneficiary in case of dissatisfaction with the security that is offered by the issuing bank, which is foreign to him. The beneficiary therefore desires, in addition, the guarantee of a bank in his own country.

The specific factors that firms in international marketing consider in determining whether to request confirmation of an irrevocable letter of credit include the following:

1. The foreign market — its foreign exchange and political conditions.

2. The buyer (importer).

3. The nature of the merchandise, for example, special manufacture must be confirmed.

4. The standing of the issuing bank.

5. The volume of the transaction.

6. Whether the issuer (the foreign bank), in some cases, tends to delay the return of funds or does not follow instructions transmitted to it with the documents.

7. The competitive situation and the need for the order.[3]

---

[2]International Chamber of Commerce, *Uniform Customs and Practice for Commercial Documentary Credits*, Article 2. The article further declares that revocable credits may be canceled or modified at any time and without notice to the beneficiary. When, however, the credit has been transmitted to a correspondent or to a branch bank, changes are effective only upon receipt of notification by the correspondent or branch, prior to payment or negotiation or the acceptance of drawings thereunder by such branch or bank.

[3]Export Managers Club of New York, Inc., *Service Bulletin 2118* (August 22, 1957). These points are made by members of the Club and not by the Club itself.

BANKING SINCE 1782

THE FIRST PENNSYLVANIA

CABLE ADDRESS
PENCO, PHILADELPHIA

INTERNATIONAL BANKING DEPARTMENT   **BANKING AND TRUST COMPANY**

PHILADELPHIA 1

IRREVOCABLE COMMERCIAL LETTER OF CREDIT

October 30, 19--

NO. 0000

Belgian Machine Company
Brussels
Belgium

GENTLEMEN

WE HEREBY AUTHORIZE YOU TO DRAW ON US

BY ORDER OF Philadelphia Machine Company, 500 Chestnut Street, Philadelphia 1, Pa.

AND FOR ACCOUNT OF   same
UP TO AN AGGREGATE AMOUNT OF Five Thousand and 00/100 Dollars U.S. Currency (U.S.$5,000.00)

AVAILABLE BY YOUR DRAFTS AT Sight for full invoice value
ACCOMPANIED BY   Commercial Invoice in Triplicate
                 Consular Invoice in Duplicate
                 Packing Lists
                 Full set, clean on board Ocean Bills of Lading, consigned to our
order, and marked, "Notify Philadelphia Machine Company, Philadelphia 1, Pennsylvania".

EVIDENCING SHIPMENT OF: Five Lathes @ $1,000.00 each
                         F.o.b. Vessel Antwerp to Philadelphia

Partial shipments prohibited.
Transshipment prohibited.
..We understand Insurance will be effected by the buyer.

DRAFTS MUST BE DRAWN AND NEGOTIATED NOT LATER THAN December 31, 19--

EACH DRAFT MUST STATE THAT IT IS "DRAWN UNDER LETTER OF CREDIT OF THE FIRST PENNSYLVANIA
BANKING AND TRUST COMPANY, NO. 0000   DATED October 30, 19--   ."

WE HEREBY AGREE WITH THE DRAWERS, ENDORSERS, AND BONA FIDE HOLDERS OF ALL DRAFTS
DRAWN UNDER AND IN COMPLIANCE WITH THE TERMS OF THIS CREDIT, THAT SUCH DRAFTS WILL BE
DULY HONORED UPON PRESENTATION TO THE DRAWEE.

THIS CREDIT IS SUBJECT TO THE UNIFORM CUSTOMS AND PRACTICE FOR DOCUMENTARY CREDITS
(1962 REVISION), INTERNATIONAL CHAMBER OF COMMERCE BROCHURE No. 222.

VERY TRULY YOURS,

B-813 Rev. 6/63   AUTHORIZED SIGNATURE

Figure 29–B. **Irrevocable and Confirmed Import Letter of Credit**

Finally, in the import trade of the United States, confirmation is the exception and not the rule. This is true because the beneficiary (in this case, an exporter in a foreign country) has as much faith in the United States bank that issues or opens the credit for the American importer as it has in the bank in its own country that would be confirming the credit.

Moreover, there are no exchange restrictions in the United States for normal trade operations.

Revocable and Unconfirmed. The revocable and unconfirmed type is not a desirable letter of credit, as it does not necessarily provide a substantial assurance of draft payment. Such assurance is directly waived by the words, "or unless sooner revoked," following the insertion of the expiration date of the credit. The lack of assurance of payment to a beneficiary and the differing views as to exercising the right of revocation have combined to place this document in disfavor. It essentially is merely a confirmation of order.

Irrevocable and Unconfirmed. In the irrevocable and unconfirmed type of letter of credit, the undertaking is not revocable by the issuer (unless the consent of the beneficiary is obtained) but it is not confirmed by an advising bank. In this case, a binding responsibility is placed solely upon the issuing bank.

Irrevocable and Confirmed. In the irrevocable and confirmed document, which is recognized as a legitimate letter of credit, there is a dual undertaking of two banks. The issuer agrees not to cancel or modify the credit without the permission of the beneficiary, and an advising bank confirms or guarantees the responsibility of the issuer.

While an irrevocable and confirmed letter of credit is a virtual guarantee of payment from the standpoint of the responsible banks, it is no such guarantee from the standpoint of fulfilling the conditions of the credit. For example, accidents, strikes, or government allocations of material may delay the production of an export order so that the expiration date of the credit cannot be met.

Assignment of a Letter of Credit. Some international marketing transactions are conducted by trading firms rather than by producers and manufacturers, and some manufacturers purchase expensive units to be used in the manufacture of products for which they have an export order. The price that the trading firm or the manufacturer pays for the merchandise to be exported as purchased or as incorporated in a product that is to be exported is less than the price at which it will be sold to the buyer abroad. Therefore, if the transaction is completed under a letter of credit, the exporter will be unable to receive payment until the order has been shipped. However, the trading firm or the manufacturer may wish to finance its purchase from the supplier of the merchandise that is

---

GIRARD TRUST CORN EXCHANGE BANK
PHILADELPHIA
INTERNATIONAL DIVISION   October 22, 1963

EXPORT ADVICE NO. E 5607/12345

Philadelphia Machine Export Company

204 Chestnut Street

Philadelphia 6, Pa.

COPY

NOT NEGOTIABLE

AT THE REQUEST OF Banco Chileno, Valparaiso, Chile

YOU ARE HEREBY NOTIFIED THAT THEY HAVE ISSUED IN YOUR FAVOR their irrevocable   LETTER OF

CREDIT FOR ACCOUNT OF Maquinaria Chilena Ltda., Valparaiso, Chile

AVAILABLE BY YOUR DRAFTS AT sight

ON ourselves

FOR ANY SUM OR SUMS NOT EXCEEDING IN ALL Eight Thousand Four Hundred and 00/100 Dollars * *
($8,400.00) U. S. Currency * * *

COVERING   4 Model M-432 Knitting Machines at $2,100.00 each, c. & f. Valparaiso,
to be shipped from Philadelphia, Pa., to Valparaiso, Chile

DRAFTS MUST BE ACCOMPANIED BY THE FOLLOWING DOCUMENTS (1) Commercial Invoice in sextuplicate,
(2) Full set clean on board ocean bills of lading, issued to order, blank endorsed,
(3) Expense notes in triplicate.

SHIPMENTS MUST BE COMPLETED AND DRAFTS NEGOTIATED ON OR BEFORE December 31, 1963

SPECIAL INSTRUCTIONS (1) Partial shipments permitted, (2) Bills of Lading to be
marked "Freight Prepaid", (3) Insurance to be covered by the buyer.

EXCEPT SO FAR AS OTHERWISE EXPRESSLY STATED, THIS CREDIT IS SUBJECT TO THE UNIFORM CUSTOMS AND PRACTICE FOR
DOCUMENTARY CREDITS (1962 REVISION), INTERNATIONAL CHAMBER OF COMMERCE BROCHURE NO. 222, FOR THE DEFINITIONS
OF CERTAIN EXPORT QUOTATIONS REFERENCE IS MADE TO THE GENERAL DESCRIPTIONS OF THOSE TERMS INCLUDED IN THE
"REVISED AMERICAN FOREIGN TRADE DEFINITIONS, 1941"

NO. E 5607/12345

We confirm this Credit and thereby undertake that all drafts drawn and presented
strictly in accordance with the terms hereof will be duly honored by us on presentation.

VERY TRULY YOURS,

GIRARD TRUST CORN EXCHANGE BANK
PHILADELPHIA

AUTHORIZED SIGNATURE

B.F. 34 a

Figure 29–C. Irrevocable and Confirmed Export Letter of Credit

to be exported later. To do so, the trading firm or the manufacturer may
use the letter of credit that it has received from the foreign buyer. This
arrangement is known as an *assignment* and to accomplish this, it is merely

necessary to add the words "and/or assignee" after the name of the beneficiary and after the approval of the foreign buyer who opened the credit originally.

In the assignment of a letter of credit, the foreign buyer is aware of the name of the supplier and also the price to be paid the supplier because this information appears in the invoice that is used to warrant payment under the letter of credit. If it is desirable to conceal this information from the foreign customer, a letter of assignment may be issued by the trading firm or the manufacturer, directing the paying bank to assign a specific sum of money to the supplier. By this means, the foreign customer will not be informed of the transaction. This may not be entirely possible, however, because revealing information may be exposed by some other document, such as a consular invoice.

Back-to-Back Credits. Sometimes this contingency can be overcome by using the already existing letter of credit as security for a loan of a lesser sum to the beneficiary. Under this arrangement, known as a *back-to-back credit*, a second credit is opened, independent of the first letter of credit, but based upon it as security. By this means, the trading firm or the manufacturer obtains the funds with which to pay the supplier.

The actual shipment and the procurement of the required documents is dependent, however, upon too many outside influences over which neither the trading firm (or manufacturer) or supplier has any control and tends to pose the question of whether or not payment will ever be effected under the letter of credit. It is also for this reason that back-to-back letters of credit are generally frowned upon by banks."[4] This comment is also applicable to the assignment of letters of credit.

Red Clause. The so-called *red clause*, which received its name from the practice of writing the clause in red ink on the letter of credit, is not used today as such.[5] The purpose of the red clause is to enable a beneficiary to receive funds *before* merchandise is ready for shipment. The trading company or the manufacturer, rather than use an assignment or a back-to-back letter of credit, might arrange with the paying (United States) bank to advance funds to pay for parcels of supplies or of parts of machinery that will not be exported until some time later. Thus, the

---

[4]George W. Tomlinson, *Pointers on Export Letters of Credit* (Philadelphia: The First Pennsylvania Banking and Trust Company, 1953), p. 46.

[5]The practice is said to have originated in the early China trade where goods would be collected from a variety of suppliers who required cash payment. The red clause authorized the bank in China (doubtless a foreign bank) to advance funds to the beneficiary against his draft drawings, with assurance that documents would be forthcoming later.

bank would be financing purchases without shipping documents and only with promises to pay, but with the letter of credit as collateral. The amount of such advances would, of course, be deducted from the amount for which the letter of credit has been opened.

Checking Export Letters of Credit. Exporters are seeking to encourage the issuance of letters of credit suitable to them by preparing guides for the use of banks issuing such credits. The guides are sent to buyers abroad when negotiating a contract of sale, and the terms and terminology of the credit are expected to follow the contract terms. For example, the contract may call for the purchase of specific products; the credit then specifies these particular products. Thus, if this procedure is followed, there can be no misunderstanding when the sales invoice and the letter of credit are compared.

As a guide to good practice in connection with the receipt of the advice of a letter of credit, George W. Tomlinson suggests that the following questions be considered by the beneficiary:[6]

1. Has the correct title been used in addressing you as beneficiary?

2. Has the correct title of the buyer been used?

3. Is the amount sufficient? Take into consideration the terms of the sale and possible addition of any charges.

4. Is the tenor of the drafts the same as your quotation to the buyer?

5. Is the credit available at the banking institution or in the locality requested by you?

6. Are the documents required in the credit in accordance with your arrangements with the buyer and can you furnish such documents?

7. Is the description of the merchandise correct? (Check unit price, trade definition, point of shipment, and destination.)

8. Do you agree with any special instructions which may appear in the credit?

9. Is the expiration date and place of expiration satisfactory?

10. Is the credit confirmed by a domestic bank, or is an unconfirmed credit satisfactory?

Checking Documents. Since the terms of a commercial letter of credit are so exacting and the payment under the credit depends upon meeting all of the requirements set forth therein, the beneficiary cannot

---

[6]Tomlinson, *op. cit.*, p. 11. Reproduced by permission of the First Pennsylvania Banking and Trust Company.

be too careful in checking every step in the transaction. The following pertinent questions may be asked at this stage in an endeavor to develop a procedure for checking documents.[7]

1. Are all the required documents presented, and have you the correct number of copies?
2. Do the marks and numbers and description identify the documents as covering the same shipment, or are other means of identification provided? (It is not uncommon for an exporter to make similar shipments under different letters of credit and mix up the documents).
3. This operation consists of checking each individual document, beginning with the draft.
   a. Is the credit unexpired?
   b. Do the figures and filling agree?
   c. Does the amount of the draft agree with the total of the invoice?
   d. Is the amount within the limits of the credit?
   e. Is the drawer the same as the beneficiary appearing on the letter of credit?
   f. Is the drawee correct?
   g. Does the draft indicate the number of the credit under which it is drawn?
4. Commercial Invoice:
   a. Is it the beneficiary's invoice?
   b. Is it addressed to the "account" party mentioned in the credit? Article 30 of the Uniform Customs and Practice for Commercial Documentary Credits states invoice should be addressed in the name of the applicant or others mentioned in the credit. (Hereafter reference to the Uniform Customs and Practice for Commercial Documentary Credits will be made only by giving the Article number).
   c. Does the description, quantity, price, and trade definition agree with the credit?
      Article 30 states description of goods on commercial invoice must correspond with description in the credit.
   d. Are there any additions not specifically mentioned in the invoice but which justify payment because of the conditions of the credit? This is where use is made of trade definitions.
   e. Is the calculation correct?
      Article 32 states where the word "about" is used it may be construed as permitting a difference of 10 percent more or less. This can apply to the amount of the credit, the quantity, or the unit price, but it must preface the one involved. Article 32 also permits a 3 percent leeway on the quantity

---

[7]*Ibid.*, pp. 17–25.   Revised by author to conform to July 1, 1963, revision of *Uniform Customs and Practice for Commercial Documentary Credits.*

specified, when the quantity is given by weight or measurement but does not apply to containers, units, or individual items. The object is to overcome the shipment of partially filled containers. Article 33 permits partial shipments, unless the credit stipulates otherwise. If more than one type of article is to be shipped, and the prices are not shown in the credit, it is advisable to consult the paying bank for their interpretation of the pro-rata amount. When a credit prohibits partial shipment, two bills of lading on the same steamer generally are permitted, provided they are both "on board" bills of lading.

Article 34 provides that if shipment by instalments within given periods is stipulated and any instalment is not shipped within the period allowed for that instalment, the credit ceases to be available for that or any subsequent instalment, unless otherwise specified in the credit.

5. Insurance
   a. What documents?
      Article 24 states that insurance documents issued by companies or their agents or by brokers or underwriters are acceptable; and must be as specifically described in the credit.
   b. Is the insurance issued in the same currency as the letter of credit?
      Article 26 states coverage should be so issued.
   c. Is the insured valuation not less than the c.i.f. value or not less than the amount of the draft or the amount of the commercial invoice, if the latter is greater?
      This is a requirement covered by Article 26. (When dealing with f.o.b. shipments, many banks prefer at least a ten percent coverage of the f.o.b. value).
   d. Are the risks covered as called for in the credit?
   e. If the policy or certificate is issued in original and duplicate, do you have both copies?
   f. Has the "loss payable party" provided his endorsement?
   g. Is the policy or certificate dated subsequent to the date of shipment?
      Article 25 gives banks the right to use their discretion in refusing or paying. (The object is to have insurance coverage at the commencement of the voyage).
6. Bills of Lading:
   a. Do you have a full set?
   b. Are the bills of lading "clean"?
      Article 16 explains that a clean shipping document is one that bears no superimposed clauses expressly declaring a defective condition of the goods or packaging. The appearance of any clauses on shipping documents is something which should be discussed with the paying bank beforehand.

    c. Do the bills of lading indicate an "on board" shipment?
Article 18 states an "on board" shipment can be evidenced by a statement signed or initialed on behalf of the carrier. This method is employed when a form of bill of lading other than the usual "on board" form is used.

    d. Are the bills of lading in negotiable or nonnegotiable form?

    e. Is the correct consignee and "notify party" used?

    f. Do the bills of lading require endorsement?

    g. Is the consignor satisfactory?
Article 21 gives banks the right to require the name of the beneficiary to appear on the bill of lading as shipper or endorser.

    h. Are the bills of lading signed by the carrier?

    i. Is the freight "prepaid" or "collect"?
Article 15 states the stamping of bills of lading with the words "freight paid" or "freight prepaid" or words of similar import will be considered sufficient proof of the payment of the freight, but the words "freight prepayable" or "freight to be prepaid" or words of similar import are not acceptable.

    j. Is the destination correct?

    k. Is transshipment permitted?

    l. On deck shipments evidenced by the bill of lading will not be accepted unless specifically authorized in the credit. Article 20.
Article 19 rules that banks may accept bills of lading permitting transshipment provided the same bill of lading covers the entire voyage, and provided the terms of the credit do not prohibit transshipment.

    m. Are the bills of lading stale dated?
Article 41 gives banks the right to refuse the documents if in their judgment they are presented to them with undue delay. (Generally speaking, this definition applies mostly to stale dated bills of lading. Many banks classify bills of lading as stale dated when it is impossible for the documents to reach the issuing bank on or before the arrival date of the carrying vessel).

7. Other Documents:
Article 7 gives banks the right to accept such documents as tendered without responsibility on their part, provided the letter of credit does not further define such documents except by name.

Authority to Pay. The *authority to pay* is a special form of authorizing payment that has been devised for international trade. By means of this instrument, an advising bank merely notifies the seller of the right to present, for payment or acceptance, drafts drawn on the advising bank, "subject to revocation or modification at any time without notice to" the seller. There is no undertaking to honor drafts on the part of either the issuing or the advising bank; it "is simply for your guidance in preparing and presenting drafts and documents." Although not synonymous with a revocable letter of credit, which is valid until revoked, the authority to pay is much clearer in its meaning and removes the confusion that may exist with a legitimate letter of credit.

Miscellaneous Types of Letters of Credit. When payment authorized by a letter of credit is designated in funds of the country of the beneficiary, the credit is said to be in *local currency*. The converse of this is *foreign currency*. Stipulation of currency is also made by naming the funds in which payment is authorized, as for example, payment in dollar credits or sterling credits.

Although usually made for a fixed sum of money, a letter of credit may be renewable, and it is then known as a *revolving letter of credit*. Some of the ways in which this may operate are:

1. The amount of the credit, when exhausted, may at once be available for further drawings.

2. As soon as shipments and collateral drawings are made that utilize a portion of the credit, the sum thus withdrawn may become again available, restoring the amount of the credit to the original sum.

3. Drawings may be limited to a stated sum for each period of time, as a month during the life of the credit; and in case the sum authorized for drawing in any one month is not utilized entirely, the balance is made available for subsequent drawings. This is known as a *cumulative letter of credit*.

4. The amount of credit, when exhausted, may become available for further drawings only after the buyer or opener has retired his obligations in favor of the issuing bank. In any case, the total amount of credit available and the period of time for which the credit is granted are limited.

Finally, in authorizing the type of draft to be drawn under a letter of credit, the letter may be either for cash payment or for payment at a definite or ascertainable future date. Using the terminology employed in connection with bills of exchange, applicable also to letters of credit, there may be sight or acceptance credits, respectively.

Under present trading conditions, a letter of credit is often used to finance international transactions as an assurance of the availability of United States dollars and as an indication of compliance by the buyer with his own government regulations which pertain to imports and payment therefor.

Operation of a Letter of Credit Transaction. To arrange in a logical manner the facts previously given and to observe several additional features of the operation of a letter of credit transaction not already explained, an illustration of international trade financing under an irrevocable, confirmed letter of credit, 60-day sight draft drawn in exporter's currency will be presented. This illustration is graphically depicted in Chart 29-1. It should be observed that the burden of arranging the letter of credit falls upon the importer.

1. A commercial letter of credit (say 60-days, irrevocable, confirmed) is mutually decided upon as the method of payment for a bill of goods ordered by a Brazilian importer, the price being quoted in the currency of the exporter's country.

2. The importer (opener) arranges the credit with a bank in his domicile and fills out a formal application. (This application may be forwarded by the bank to a correspondent, in case the former has no foreign connection).

3. If the application is accepted, the letter of credit is signed and the bank in the importer's domicile becomes the issuer. This contract protects the bank by guaranteeing payment of all sums expended by the bank under the credit, and security is required by the bank in accordance with the standing of the importer.

4. The preliminary steps now having been completed, the credit is made available by preparing the (import) letter of credit in favor of the exporter (beneficiary). Being irrevocable, it cannot be rescinded by the issuer without the consent of the beneficiary. The document is sent to the advising bank.

5. The advising bank informs the beneficiary by means of an *advice of letter of credit* (export credit). As the credit is to be confirmed, the adviser is instructed by the issuer to add its name to the obligation, guaranteeing the latter's undertaking. There is now available an irrevocable and confirmed letter of credit.

6. When the shipment is ready, and this is within the time

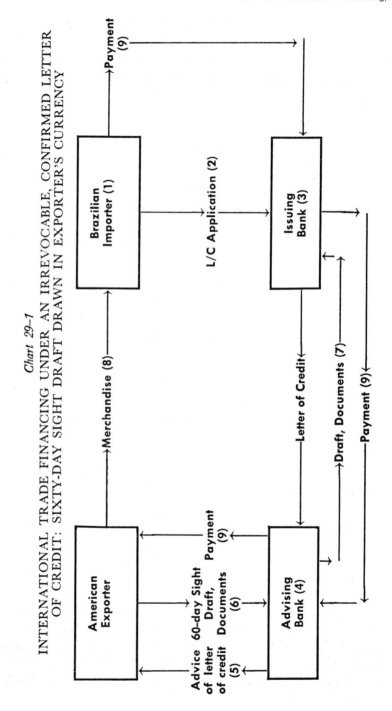

Chart 29–1

INTERNATIONAL TRADE FINANCING UNDER AN IRREVOCABLE, CONFIRMED LETTER OF CREDIT: SIXTY-DAY SIGHT DRAFT DRAWN IN EXPORTER'S CURRENCY

limit fixed by the letter of credit, the beneficiary draws a draft at 60 days' sight on the issuing bank and presents it with documents attached to the advising and confirming bank. The letter of credit may be "specially advised" and thus indicate the bank or banks that will honor the draft; otherwise, the exporter is obliged to locate a bank that will discount it. The advising and confirming bank is required to check carefully all of the documents presented and to determine the authenticity of the credit.[8] As the draft is drawn upon the issuing bank, the negotiator must look to it for reimbursement, and any discrepancies in the documents may be grounds for refusal of payment on the part of the issuing bank. (If the letter of credit is opened in a currency foreign to the beneficiary, it is often customary to draw the draft on the foreign correspondent of the issuing bank and the correspondent is then known as the paying or accepting bank).

7. The draft is now sent, with documents attached, to the issuing bank for payment or acceptance, depending on whether the letter of credit is for cash or acceptance. The case under consideration is an acceptance credit.

8. The merchandise is shipped to the importer in Brazil, but with the documents made to the order of the beneficiary, who endorses them either in blank, or to the confirming bank that, in turn, will endorse them to the issuing bank. The issuing bank accepts the draft and releases the merchandise to the importer, upon his signing a *trust receipt*. This document, widely used in the United States and Great Britain, is an acknowledgment by the importer that the ownership of the goods remains with the bank, possession only being transferred; and guarantees disposal of the merchandise solely as specified in the trust receipt. In most foreign countries a document known as a *warrant* is employed in lieu of a trust receipt. This is in the nature of a duplicate warehouse receipt (not indicated in Chart 29-1).

9. At the expiration of the 60-day period following acceptance of the draft by the issuing bank, payment is made by the

---

[8]Regarding the responsibility of a bank seeking to determine the authenticity of a credit, Article 9 of *Uniform Customs and Practice for Commercial Documentary Credits* states that there is no liability or responsibility "for the form, sufficiency, accuracy, genuineness, falsification, or legal effect of any documents, or for the general and/or particular conditions stipulated in the documents or superimposed thereon; nor do they assume any liability or responsibility for the description, quantity, weight, quality, condition, packing, delivery, value, or existence of goods represented thereby. . . ."

Brazilian importer and, in turn, by the issuing bank. Should the importer fail to meet his obligation, there would be no recourse upon the exporter as long as either the issuing or the confirming bank honors the draft. In this respect, the credit is a virtual guarantee of payment.

Since the transaction was a 60-day acceptance, the draft is probably returned to the advising bank as soon as it is accepted by the issuing bank. This would be done if the advising bank desired to rediscount the draft and place itself in a fully liquid position. In every event, the draft or bill of exchange will make a round trip from the advising bank to the issuing bank and, finally, back to the advising bank with the payment.

Advantages of Letters of Credit to Buyers. Although the burden of financing is placed upon the buyer under a letter of credit transaction, this method of payment affords certain attractions to him.

1. Perhaps the greatest practical benefit derived by the buyer is in the protection of setting a definite date by which the seller is required to ship the order. The buyer, accordingly, may figure on prompt delivery, as the credit will expire on the date set unless an extension is granted.

2. The buyer probably receives rock-bottom prices without any additions when he submits a letter of credit, since contingencies are so fully guarded against that an exporter finds it unnecessary to cover them in the price.

3. Advance orders, or orders running throughout a period of time, are also well protected by reason of the expiration date of the letter of credit as well as by the limitation of the sum of money for which it is drawn.

4. Finally, an attractive cash discount may be offered to importers for providing letter of credit payment.

Authority to Purchase

Another document employed in international marketing for the purpose of authorizing payment of drafts drawn by exporters is the *authority to purchase* (*A/P*). This instrument is in some respects similar to a letter of credit, but there are fundamental differences. The authority to purchase is used extensively in exports to Far Eastern countries, where the peculiar banking system makes it difficult to obtain satisfactory bank credit with which to finance purchases from abroad. The authority to purchase provides a basis for negotiating drafts drawn on an importer, but it does not provide bank credit; rather it provides a banking service.

The authority to purchase is an instrument addressed by an Oriental bank or branch of a foreign (American) bank to its agent, correspondent, or head office (in the United States) authorizing the latter to negotiate drafts of a designated American exporter when presented in accordance with the terms specified. The A/P is opened at the instance of the importer who binds himself, by agreement and not usually by depositing security, to accept or pay drafts drawn upon *him* and to reimburse the bank for banking charges.

There are forms of the A/P that correspond to the irrevocable and confirmed letter of credit; but when this type of bank credit is sought, a regular letter of credit should be used. The A/P should not be construed as a letter of credit in any accepted sense of the meaning, since the A/P is essentially a means of negotiating drafts on an importer — not on a bank. However, there are forms of the A/P that provide for no recourse on the drawer (exporter), and this arrangement may have been confirmed by a bank in the exporter's country. While an A/P provides no guarantee of payment of drafts drawn thereunder, it does provide a market for bills drawn and in some cases this is a decided advantage. For practical purposes, therefore, an A/P may be considered in much the same light as a favorable credit report on the importer.

Special Terms of Payment

Special terms of payment are arranged for certain transactions and under certain conditions that are singular in nature.

Loans and Government Grants. Shipments moving in connection with contract work abroad, for example, construction, may be paid for under a loan arrangement whereby banks or governmental agencies will advance funds. The exporter in this case may receive payment as though the transaction were domestic and the funds would arise from advances or from the sale of securities.

Export transactions financed under Export-Import Bank loans beginning in 1934, Lease-Lend operations beginning in 1941, ECA transactions beginning in 1948, and AID programs beginning in 1962 were paid for by the United States Treasury, constituting, as far as exporters are concerned, domestic transactions. Many purchases continue to be made under procurement contracts with United States Government agencies, the funds for such exported merchandise coming from Government channels.

Bonds. During financial stringency, exporters in some instances have been obliged or invited by foreign governments to accept bonds in satisfaction of claims for payment of export shipments. This has been done when funds have become "frozen" because of foreign exchange restrictions. Bonds have also occasionally been accepted by exporters in payment for current exports to certain countries.

Barter Transactions. Some international trade is financed by means of barter transactions. In such cases, the exporter may receive foreign currency for his merchandise and be permitted to utilize these funds for the purchase of designated foreign goods. He usually cannot, however, spend the funds freely. If unsuccessful or unwilling to sell this claim (at a discount) to an importer, the exporter would be obliged to purchase such wares in the hope of disposing of them himself. Outright barter is occasionally used — "Norway swaps 100,000 fox pelts for 6,000 tons United States prunes in barter deal by private enterprises."[9]

In 1963, United States Government agencies shifted the emphasis in barter transactions from strategic materials for stockpiling to offshore procurement to fill military and foreign assistance needs. In June, 1963, the United States announced a barter agreement with India involving $56 million. Up to 300,000 bales of cotton and possibly other surplus commodities valued at $40 million will be bartered for Indian ferromanganese, beryl ore, and mica.[10]

A type of barter occasionally occurs as a form of what may be termed "retaliation." Following the announcement of the plan of the United States Government to sell surplus cotton abroad at competitive prices (after more than two decades of export price control), the Mexican Government announced a "cotton compensation plan."[11] Under this plan, Mexican-grown cotton would be used to pay for certain imports. About ten groups of imports were initially selected to be affected by this

---

[9]*International Markets* (July, 1952), p. 119.
[10]See *Journal of Commerce* (June 6 and 28, 1963).
[11]*Foreign Commerce Weekly* (August 27, 1956), p. 8.

plan.[12] Later, it was declared that this was to be merely a temporary expedient to be followed until the current Mexican cotton crop had been sold.[13] In May, 1959, Mexico was reported to have stepped up this program, requiring cotton and other agricultural products to be exchanged for imported capital goods.[14]

The Soviet Union and some of the other communist countries frequently negotiate barter agreements with each other and with noncommunist countries, particularly those in the less developed stage. Presumably, these agreements are made because of the shortage or complete absence of foreign exchange with which to make international settlements. A recent (summer, 1963) agreement of this nature was announced by means of an AP dispatch from Dar es Salaam, Tanganyika. "Tanganyika and the Soviet Union have signed their first trade agreement. This nation will exchange sisal, cotton, hides, skins, tobacco and coffee for metal, tools, vehicles, road equipment, cameras, fishing boats, planes and other things."[15]

It is not difficult to see that when no value is placed on the amount of trade that is contemplated, as in the case of the Soviet-Tanganyika agreement, the transaction is little more than a refinement of the barter that takes place on the sandlots of America, when Bill swaps his jackknife for George's flashlight. This is as crude and unsophisticated as trade can be.

Summary

1. A letter of credit provides the financing basis on which bills of exchange are drawn. It is a supplement to — not a substitute for — a bill of exchange.
2. The commercial letter of credit shifts the responsibility of payment to a bank. The letter of credit is opened by a bank at an importer's request, and this undertaking may be confirmed by a bank in the exporter's country. If the letter of credit is irrevocable, the issuing bank cannot revoke; if it is also confirmed, the confirming bank in the exporter's country has assumed responsibility for payment.
3. There are many considerations involved in determining the desirability of confirming an irrevocable export letter of credit. In the case of United States import trade, irrevocable letters of credit are rarely confirmed.

---

[12]These groups were autos and trucks, assembled and unassembled; iron and stee pipe; firearms; watches; radio and television apparatus; whiskey, wine, and liquor; and complete machinery installations.

[13]*Foreign Commerce Weekly* (October 1, 1956), p. 24.

[14]*Journal of Commerce* (May 14, 1959), p. 11.

[15]*Philadelphia Inquirer*, August 16, 1963.

4. To facilitate payment to suppliers in the case of trading firms who purchase the merchandise that they export or of manufacturers who purchase expensive parts to be incorporated in machinery to be exported, a letter of credit may be made to be assignable. This is not always desirable, however, because the foreign buyer is often made aware of this arrangement, despite the attempt to conceal this information from him.

5. Back-to-back credits will overcome the obstacle to assignment, but it is not always possible to make such an arrangement with a bank.

6. A modern adaptation of the red clause permits a trading firm or a manufacturer to receive payment for supplies, using the letter of credit as collateral.

7. An exporter is well advised to check carefully the export letter of credit that has been opened on his behalf.

8. The same care is recommended to an exporter in checking his documents when the time comes to ship the order and to claim payment under the letter of credit. Many errors may easily occur at this stage of the transaction.

9. An authority to pay is a document that merely provides a financing mechanism that is not equal to even a revocable letter of credit.

10. An authority to purchase provides a basis for drawing bills of exchange, but it does not provide bank credit.

11. Special terms of payment include loans and government grants, bonds, and barter.

QUESTIONS

1. In what way does a commercial letter of credit provide a means of substituting a bank credit for mercantile credit?

2. (a) Name the three essential parties to a letter of credit.
   (b) What additional parties may be found in a letter of credit transaction?

3. Define the several types of letters of credit.

4. Why would an exporter be willing to accept a revocable letter of credit?

5. Why would an importer prefer to pay under an irrevocable and confirmed letter of credit?

6. Why are exporters cautious in utilizing a letter of credit payment?

7. Discuss the advantages gained by an exporter in obtaining a confirmation of an irrevocable letter of credit?

8. Of what value is the assignment of an irrevocable letter of credit?

9. How does a back-to-back credit operate?

10. What is the purpose and present-day use of the so-called red clause?

11. What should a beneficiary of an irrevocable letter of credit check when he receives an advice of the establishment of a letter of credit?

12. How important is the checking of the terms of a letter of credit and the documents when the time comes to receive payment under the credit? Cite several specific points to be checked.

13. Define an authority to purchase.
14. Describe three special terms of payment that are used in international marketing transactions.
15. Characterize barter as a means of conducting business.

PROBLEMS

1. Investigate and report on the payment terms customarily extended by United States exporters in any of the following lines:
   Automobiles, agricultural machinery, coal, explosives, grain, raw cotton, hardware, petroleum grease, writing instruments, and citrus fruit.
2. Investigate and report on the payment terms customarily received by United States importers of any of the following lines:
   Automobiles, cameras, coffee, sugar, pineapples, wearing apparel, rubber, jute, diamonds, and newsprint paper.

COLLATERAL READINGS

Dartnell International Trade Handbook, The. Chicago: The Dartnell Corporation, 1963.

Fayerweather, John. *Management of International Operations,* Text and Cases. New York: McGraw-Hill Book Company, Inc., 1960. Chapter 7.

Shaw, Ernest D. *Practical Aspects of Commercial Letters of Credit.* New York: Irving Trust Company, 1958.

Tomlinson, George W. *Pointers on Export Letters of Credit.* Philadelphia: The First Pennsylvania Banking and Trust Company, 1953.

Towers, Graham F. *Financing Foreign Trade.* Montreal: The Royal Bank of Canada, 1957.

Wasserman, Max J., Charles W. Hultman, and Laszlo Zsoldos. *International Finance.* New York: Simmons-Boardman Publishing Corporation, 1963, Chapter 10.

See also the list of readings given at the end of Chapter 28 on pages 536 and 537.

CHAPTER 30

CREDIT EXTENSION IN INTERNATIONAL MARKETING

One of the ever present problems in international marketing is the question of the extension of credit in export sales. The problem of credit extension rarely arises, however, in United States import trade because credit is seldom extended to American importers by their suppliers abroad. Moreover, a large part of the raw materials and foodstuffs imported into the United States is the product of American companies operating abroad. In great measure, they produce abroad in order to supply the American domestic market, and the business transactions consist essentially of taking money out of one pocket and putting it in the other.

Whenever international marketing groups assemble and the subject turns to marketing conditions in particular countries, the question inevitably is raised: "What terms do you grant?" The answers come back: "sight draft," "30 days," "60 days," "letter of credit," and so on. The difference in the terms is generally due to differences in the products for which the terms are cited. There are also differences due to the various ways in which conditions in a given market are appraised by the several exporting companies. Therefore, it would appear that the appraisal of the credit situation of a buyer in a particular market is determined by a number of factors. Before looking at these factors, however, it would be well to examine closely the meaning of credit.

The Meaning of Credit

Credit usually refers to the procedure of surrendering title to merchandise without assured payment. In other words, credit means trusting the buyer to pay for goods after he has obtained title to them. Under the various credit and payment terms described in Chapters 28 and 29, a buyer would receive credit under open account and under all draft transactions. Under a letter of credit, he actually does not receive credit because the exporter is assured of payment. Therefore, there is no credit risk; and without risk, there can be no actual credit.

Credit Needs of the Firm. There is another aspect of credit, however, that should also be considered. This is the credit — or better, the financial — needs of the firm that is engaged in exporting merchandise. This does not refer to the working capital that may be required to produce merchandise. It refers to that fact that under the terms of sale that are quoted, there is usually a period of time elapsing between the shipment of the order and the time that payment is received. As explained in Chapter 28, a payee of a draft may discount or borrow against the draft before its maturity but in so doing, he must pay interest for the period of time that the funds are advanced. Moreover, there is no assurance that the draft will be eventually paid by the drawee unless it is guaranteed, as will be described in Chapter 31, or unless it is drawn under a letter of credit. For this reason, the discounting of or borrowing against a draft remains a contingent liability on the part of the payee.

Nevertheless, banks stand ready to finance international shipments under the circumstances of the particular transaction.

Credit Line. The inference may easily be drawn that under all credit and payment terms except open account, a payee (exporter) has valuable documents that can be used to obtain immediate finances, if such finances are required. Such is not the case because banks will not discount or loan against drafts beyond a certain point, and this point is the *credit line* that the bank has set up for each individual customer. Therefore, the credit of an exporter or payee under a draft is involved because a limit is placed on the dollar value of discounting or borrowing that he will be permitted to receive.

Some writers refer to this situation as a matter of credit — and such it is because the credit standing of the exporting firm is involved. This type of credit, however, is much different from the usual meaning of credit, that is, the relinquishment of title to merchandise before receiving assured payment. For this reason, it appears to be preferable to refer to the credit line of an exporting firm as a financial arrangement to enable it to finance the exportation of merchandise on a credit basis.

Evolution of Export Credit by United States Firms

It is rather a time-honored criticism of American exporters that they are unwilling to grant the liberal credits in international marketing that are offered by some European competitors. If it is true that legitimate credit extension is predicated upon adequate information, then the general absence before World War I of foreign credit data in the United States may be cited as one reason for the failure of American exporters to extend liberal credit at that time.

European countries, particularly Great Britain, with an early start in overseas business, promptly developed the means of extending foreign credit. This was accomplished not only through sources of information but also by the creation of a banking system that would advance funds on trade documents. Until 1913, this facility was not generally available to American exporters, and this condition certainly did not encourage them to extend credit when it meant a personally sustained burden. Moreover, the United States was very active until the twentieth century, and was still fairly busy up to 1914, in developing her own resources and domestic business. Export trade was actively solicited only by exceptional concerns that at that time saw a limit to their domestic market. Export commission houses and merchants handled most of the business; and these, together with the manufacturers that were engaged directly in international marketing, granted credit in many instances. The manufacturers who took business as it came, and without solicitation, rarely granted credit as they were not forced to do so.

With the development of our interest in international marketing, together with the growth of sources of information and changes in banking methods, there is no longer any handicap on the part of American exporters in extending foreign credit. Perhaps it is true that Americans do not grant as liberal terms as do European competitors; and if such is the case, the answer would seem to be that they do not find it necessary to grant long credit because America's overseas business is enormous. It should be remembered that for certain reasons credit is essential to, and for certain other reasons it is desired by, foreign customers; and it is unlikely that sellers of merchandise will meet any more than the first group of circumstances, unless they are obliged to do so for competitive reasons.

Conditions Influencing Foreign Credit Extension

There are several conditions peculiar to international marketing that require an exporting firm to view credit extension in a light somewhat differently from domestic credit conditions. These conditions may be conveniently grouped under the captions:

1. Supply of banking capital.
2. Interest rates.
3. Diversification of production.
4. Time in transit and business turnover.
5. Exchange rate fluctuations.
6. Competition.
7. Custom.

At the outset, it is well to emphasize that the influence of these conditions varies from country to country. Indeed, in a market like Canada, the credit conditions are practically identical with those in the United States domestic market, except for the conditions of foreign exchange rates and tariff rates. When we move to our neighbor to the south, however, we find that all of the conditions influencing credit extension are applicable in Mexico.

Supply of Banking Capital. The working capital of a country comes from the savings that find their way into productive enterprises. The wealth that a country may possess in its mines, forests, wells, or fields contributes little to the supply of working capital while it is still locked in natural treasure vaults. Products must be produced and sold in the world's markets in order to provide the means of procuring the goods of other nations.

This condition of locked wealth exists in many of the underdeveloped or developing areas of the world, and there the supply of capital of a liquid or quickly usable nature is comparatively small. Moreover, production is conducted largely along agricultural, forestal, or mining lines and, particularly in the case of agriculture and of mining, there is a considerable period of waiting until returns are realized. Importers located in such areas have, therefore, depended upon foreign sellers to finance their purchases, whether they were shoes, automobiles, locomotives, or municipal improvements. Local bankers are unable to provide the financing, since the supply of capital flowing into their vaults is quite meager.

Interest Rates. When there is a serious lack of balance between the demand for and the supply of readily usable capital, an immediate result is the raising of the interest rate. In accordance with this imbalance and, of course, with the particular risks incurred, interest rates in nonindustrial areas usually are substantially higher than in industrial countries. In such circumstances, the wisdom of borrowing abroad at relatively low interest rates and lending the funds at home, where interest may be 7, 10, 15, or 20 percent, becomes apparent.[1]

In this connection, however, the question might well be raised as to whether or not this situation affords a proper need for credit. There is admittedly a difference between need and desire, and, whereas this unbalanced situation is generally considered as one requiring the extension of credit, it is obviously sound business sense on the part of foreign buyers to ask for credit. In the competition for world markets, the seller is often forced to yield to this demand for credit on the part of the buyer.

Diversification of Production. Lack of developed business activity and organization is another factor entering into the foreign credit situation. There is often a dearth of diversified business or trade in underdeveloped or developing areas of the world. Intensive specialization in commodity or functional lines may not be warranted, and the businessman may frequently find it necessary to combine several lines of activity in order to earn an adequate income. This imposes upon him a heavy financial responsibility, offering lucrative returns, perhaps, but at a slow rate of turnover.

A further factor accentuating this condition is the lack of diversified production. There is a greater dependence in many countries upon one or a few crops, such as coffee in Brazil, rubber in Malaysia, and sugar in Cuba. This means that the bulk of national productive activity in exportable products is engaged in one line with but few periods of harvest during the year. It is quite conceivable that a crop failure or a low price may cause an economic collapse. Growers may then be dependent for their livelihood not upon the returns from past efforts but upon anticipated earnings. Not only the grower, but also businessmen, bankers, and others may be placed in a precarious position. The gulf between today's purchases and tomorrow's income must be bridged. As the combination importer-exporter-wholesaler-banker-retailer cannot bridge it unassisted, the seller finds it necessary to do so if he is interested in building up trade.

---

[1]In 1963, interest rates in one South American country, racked with inflation, were $3\frac{1}{2}$ percent per month (42 percent per annum); and funds were not readily available at these rates.

Time in Transit and Business Turnover. The delay incurred in receiving imported goods is another condition influencing the extension of credit in international marketing. Because of the length of time elapsing between the date of shipment by the exporter and the time goods are received by the importer, there may be a considerable period during which, in the case of cash payment, the importer is without both funds and goods. If credit of sufficient duration is granted to enable the importer to obtain the goods before making payment, it is apparent that the exporter is the party who bears the financial burden of the import transaction; but the sluggishness of turnover may leave the goods on the hands of the buyer for a considerable additional period of time, during which the buyer's funds would also be tied up. This condition is of little significance in domestic trade where in a few weeks shipments may be made all over the country; but in international marketing it presents an important problem. It may require two or three months after shipment before the importer located at an inland destination receives his merchandise. Moreover, he finds it necessary to pay customs duties assessed against the goods before delivery, and there will also be transportation and other charges incident to his import shipments.

Distance and time, moreover, compel importers to place orders for goods at a considerable period before the selling season opens and for substantial quantities, sufficient to last a good part of the entire season. In such cases a severe loss would be suffered in the event of any delay in receiving goods in time for the opening of the season for which they were ordered; and any delay occasioned in receiving repeat shipments subsequently ordered for the same season would likewise cause loss.

Exchange Rate Fluctuations. Still another condition influencing credit extension in international marketing is the fluctuation in foreign exchange rates.

Whenever a buyer receives quotations and accepts prices in a currency foreign to his own, he assumes a speculative risk against which he may or may not be able to protect himself.[2] If he has agreed to pay for his purchases by sight draft, the latest he can postpone payment and receive possession of the goods is upon their arrival. This gives him no time to await a favorable turn of the exchange in case it is against him at the time the shipment arrives, and he may incur an exchange loss sufficiently great to eliminate his anticipated trade profit. Indeed, where the

---

[2]Further discussion of foreign exchange rates and the risks involved in international buying and selling is presented in Chapter 32.

arrival of vessels is not an occurrence of great frequency in a foreign port, it is likely that exchange rates, owing to the demands of importers at such time, will be higher when a vessel arrives and for several days thereafter. Importers, therefore, desire credit extension that will enable them to pay their drafts at a time when exchange seems to them to be favorable.[3]

Competition. Credit may also be extended for competitive reasons. As a means of promoting sales, especially in view of the intensity of competition in certain lines in certain markets, liberal credit terms may be offered.

Obviously, the granting of terms in excess of those that can safely be considered invites financial ruin. In the introduction of a new article or of a new brand of an established product, however, somewhat unusual credit terms may be granted with reason. Such a policy possesses the same expediency as temporary (price) dumping and may open a market that might otherwise be closed. In a competitive market, moreover, it may be difficult for an exporter to refuse credit terms at least as liberal as those customarily granted by rival exporters. As a general rule, however, American exporters have not adopted credit extension as a competitive method.

Custom. Finally, credit extension is influenced by the credit customs of the foreign market. Certain terms are often established in each market along commodity lines, and they are to be recognized by exporters selling in those markets.

Credit Data to Be Sought

In foreign, as in domestic credit work, it is desirable to extend credit where credit is due. The greater difficulty in ascertaining the foreign purchasers to whom credit is due is the peculiar problem of foreign credit work, as credit data are generally not so readily and authoritatively obtained as in domestic trade. The aim of all credit men is to keep losses at a minimum and, if humanly possible, to eliminate them altogether. To achieve this, the credit man obviously must be so informed as to make the approval of credit a matter of business judgment rather than guesswork. The search for credit information is continuous, since it is never

---

[3]Under conditions of exchange control, as described in Chapter 33, exchange rates are generally fixed, and the fluctuations in foreign exchange rates are not a condition influencing credit extension.

possible to gather too much or too recent data concerning either the general conditions affecting export credits or the individual credit standing of the exporter's customers.

The nature of the credit data to be sought may be treated under three headings:

1. Foreign market conditions.
2. Conditions or standing of the firm desiring credit.
3. Conditions influenced by the product.

Foreign Market Conditions. The credit standing of any particular importing firm cannot generally be considered apart from the credit conditions of the country in which the importer is located. These conditions relate to the financial, political, economic, social, and every other measurable condition that bears upon the paying ability of a country.

Conditions or Standing of the Firm Desiring Credit. The fundamental data relating to an individual's credit standing are embraced within the well-known triumvirate, or three "C's," of credit work: character, capital, and capacity.[4] The significance of these factors is generally accepted as in the order given. Few businessmen in foreign or domestic trade would relegate character to any other than premier position in this lineup. The general feeling prevails that, irrespective of the capital possessed, if the character of the firm is not satisfactory, the account is undesirable. In addition to the well-known triumvirate of credit, the nationality of the customer is sometimes of overriding importance.

Character. The organization and management of the concern is of prime importance in determining credit responsibility and it embraces both character and capacity. The years of continuity of business operation indicate the stability of a concern. A long-established house is not necessarily an honest one at any particular time, nor is the recently organized concern unreliable; but generally speaking, the longer a business firm has been established, the greater is the confidence that it can command. With age goes stability, and if, in spite of successive waves of prosperity and depression, a house continues in business, it is a fair indication of its business ability, or capacity. This does not exempt such concerns from investigation, however, as such an enviable record might be broken at any time. With this continuity of operation comes also a

---

[4]Two other "C's" may be mentioned, viz., country and commodity.

sense of character. Character is not synonymous with reputation, but these credit factors cannot forever remain far apart. And a house with a reputation firmly established, tested and tried, and with every indication of continued maintenance of such a cherished possession, is certain to possess character.

It is not to be presumed, contrariwise, that a young business cannot be trusted. Every individual or organization finds it necessary to begin sometime, and the small, recently established concern may possess qualities that in twenty or fifty years will place it in the position now occupied by older houses. The burden is on the credit man, in the case of a new business, to obtain a greater amount of information and to observe greater caution than when approving credit for old, established concerns.

Capacity. Although character is essential, credit cannot safely be granted to honest but careless or inexperienced customers. One of the most important matters for a merchant to handle intelligently is the maintenance of a proper balance between his commitments and his assets. Not only is it unwise for a businessman to overbuy, but it also creates a definite strain on his credit standing because his turnover will be slow, tying up part of his capital. Moreover, he runs chances of encountering unfavorable price or style changes before he disposes of his goods. The maintenance of such a balance was formerly considered to be the private affair of the merchant, but after some experiences of strained credit and of losses resulting from unwise purchases, this matter now receives close attention by the credit department. In this respect, the opinion of the credit department and the sales force of an exporter may differ, since a customer may overbuy because he has been oversold by a star salesman and, if so, the interests of the credit department have not been conserved.

By placing a limit on the credit to be extended safely, in the opinion of the credit man, to any one firm, a means of keeping a proper balance between purchases and assets is provided. This limit may be indicated in a credit report, for example: "We do not recommend that credit in excess of $500 be granted." It is advisable to determine a limit on the basis of known or estimated capital, turnover, number of sources from which purchases are made, and all of the credit factors that relate to the individual.

Capital. The financial condition and practices of the foreign firm are of importance in determining credit standing. Unfortunately, financial statements are still uncommon in many, although not all, foreign markets; and the amount of liquid capital may be difficult to determine.

Almost all credit reports show the capital authorized or employed in a business, but there is often no way of determining what liabilities are outstanding. A concern may possess cash of $50,000, real estate of $30,000, and merchandise, accounts receivable, etc., of $80,000; but there may exist commitments, actual or potential, that will exhaust all of these. Claims as to capital cannot, therefore, be accepted without closer investigation.

In this connection the significance of character is readily seen, as a business house with a high reputation would not be likely to conceal pertinent facts, even though they might indicate a poor financial condition. There is also to be noted the reticence on the part of many foreign businessmen to supply data relative to their financial standing. It is still unfortunately true that many business concerns construe requests for financial data as reflections on their standing and integrity. Until the full significance of the financial statement in business is grasped, this attitude is bound to persist. The policy of jealously guarding personal information is happily giving way to the modern idea practiced in the more advanced countries.

The financial practices of a customer would show his paying methods and his general ability to adopt and conduct a proper financial program. Investigation will usually show whether a concern is prompt or slow in payment or whether it is given to request for extensions or other special favors. An account that has never been known to default, but which is careless in meeting obligations at maturity, can hardly be considered a prime risk.

Nationality. The nationality of the concern is considered by all credit men because of the importance of racial and national characteristics as they relate to moral fiber, customs, background, and philosophy, all of which influence the credit risk. It is obvious that no one race or nationality is 100 percent honest or dishonest, but certain tendencies may be anticipated because of the accident of birth.

If a foreign customer should look on a contract as a means of protecting the buyer alone, the exporter gains nothing by arguing the relative merits and demerits, justice or injustice of the divergent points of view; but he is face-to-face with a potential loss under certain circumstances. Shrewdness is characteristic of some people as a group, and when shrewdness and trickery become entangled, losses again appear on the horizon. Such circumstances, however, are far from conclusive and may be entirely erroneous; but when they are encountered, it may be advisable to presume their existence and exert efforts to prove or disprove them.

Conditions Influenced by the Product. A final aspect of the credit data to be sought refers to the product itself. These conditions may be considered under the profit margin and the nature of the product.

Profit Margin. Both the exporter's and the importer's amount of profit has an effect upon the question of credits. If the seller is operating on a low margin of profit, it may be advisable for him to restrict credit terms as much as possible; and if the margin is high, he can afford to be more liberal. This is true not only because of the risks involved but also because of financial strain which may be greater when profits are small. The credit department is necessarily concerned with the exporter's own profits, turnover, financial needs, and ability.

Trade profits also influence the credit risk on the side of the importer. If he has not had the foresight or knowledge properly to figure the laid-down costs to him of goods quoted on terms of, say, f.o.b. vessel, Philadelphia, he may find that the cost to him compared with the market price he can command would eliminate his profit or even entail a loss. Even if he is alert, a loss may be incurred in case of a sudden decline in the market. The credit man should look into the lucrativeness of the business to the buyer because of the obvious connection this bears to the credit risk.

Nature of the Product. Credit considerations are also influenced by the product that is sold. This question is partly a sales problem and not wholly a credit problem, but the sales force in its zealousness may overlook the relationship. The importance of the product to the market is the same as the importance of buying in proportion to requirements is to the customer, and it may be viewed from two angles: (a) will the product take? and (b) can the market absorb?

The first query refers especially to new articles or new brands just entering the market. At such time, when credit extension may be necessary for market reasons, a decided risk is encountered in the unknown reception to be accorded the product. If it does not "take," the effect on credits can be readily deemed to be unfavorable. Even if an article should "take," however, there is a limit to the absorption power of a market; and although the importer probably considers this question carefully, the export sales force may by zealous persistence ignore it. It is, therefore, necessary for the credit man to consider the sales possibility of the product in view of the apparent effect upon credits. Overstocking as a result of market, not individual, conditions may ensue and credits may become "frozen" with unavoidable losses. The capacity of a market may be overestimated by the sales force, but such overestimation should never be the case with the credit man.

A further influence exerted by the product is the possibility of disposing of refused goods at a reasonable price. Staple products are more readily sold in an open market than are specialties, and the probable loss occasioned in the forced sale of staple lines is not great.

Foreign Credit Policy and Management

Whether or not credit will be extended on export sales is a matter that will be decided more by the policy of the exporting firm than by the foreign market, the foreign importing firm, or even product conditions. This is true because so many United States firms that engage in exporting or that might be interested in engaging in export are not prepared to adopt policies that might threaten to affect adversely the profitability of the undertaking.

If domestic credit terms are 2 percent cash discount in 10 days, 30 days net, a firm may be reluctant to consider any export credit terms that would prevent returns from reaching them for a period longer than 30 days. In international marketing, however, such a period may constitute no credit at all for the buyers, as previously explained. Therefore, foreign credit policy must be set by the management of an exporting firm, and within this limit credit can be extended in international marketing. This policy may establish standard credit terms with provision for deviation from these terms under proper examination and control. For this purpose, an export committee, such as that described on page 143, might be established, composed of an executive of the company (vice-president and director of exports), export manager, advertising manager, treasurer, and perhaps a trade manager concerned with the particular foreign market under consideration.

Foreign Credit Department. Any fairly large exporting concern finds a foreign credit department essential, the size of the department depending upon the demands of the business. There may and should be a foreign credit manager, whose qualifications may readily be ascertained from the functions that the department is called upon to perform.

These may be briefly summarized as follows:

1. Investigation of and passing on credit risks, which involve the assembly and filing of credit data and deciding the action to be taken in the case of each risk with respect to terms, amounts, and methods of credit extension.

2. Collection work, keeping after customers and building respect and goodwill.

3. Recommendation of the policies to be pursued with respect to matters such as exchange restrictions, exchange rate fluctuations, export credit insurance, trade disputes, and the refusal of shipments.

4. Cooperation with other departments as found necessary. For example, in the appointment of agents abroad, the credit department may collect for the use of the sales department all of the information available on prospective representatives, and work with the treasurer on all financial matters connected with international marketing.

Credit File and Standard Terms of Sale. The adoption of a definite credit extension policy is as logical and essential as the creation of a sales or any other business policy. In the work of approving credit risks, it is well to reduce motion to a minimum by providing automatic approval of reliable houses and the careful analysis of the factors determining all other risks. This policy may be worked out by means of a *credit file*, on which would appear, for each customer, the limit of credit that can safely and automatically be extended in view of the data received to date.

Another method of developing a credit extension policy is to adopt *standard terms of sale* for all reliable customers and place upon them the responsibility of submitting information intended to support more favorable terms. This plan is preferred by some exporters because it places upon the buyer the burden of establishing his credit rating and is likely to avoid exchanges of correspondence or cables in dickering over credit terms. Perhaps the greatest advantage of this method is the means thereby provided of serving notice on the sales department that terms will be granted only for the standard period of time stipulated. This tends to create in the sales force an interest in credit and collection work. The salesmen, knowing the automatic limitations thus set, would endeavor to assist the importer in establishing the right to more favorable terms.

Sources of Foreign Credit Information

In the performance of his work, the export credit manager must necessarily have at his command adequate sources of credit information. He will contact the references given in the orders received from foreign customers, and his firm's export salesmen, if any, may be requested to forward whatever credit information is at their disposal. If the firm maintains branch offices in particular foreign markets, the credit manager may receive valuable credit information from the branch-house managers, and a considerable degree of credit control may be transferred to the foreign branches. When an exporter sells through foreign agents or representatives, but retains responsibility for customer credits, the agents or representatives become a source of credit information. The foreign credit manager's own credit files may in fact contain complete and up-to-date information concerning some of the firm's regular foreign customers. But he must in many instances depend at least in part upon his contact with outside sources of credit information.

Mercantile Credit Agencies. The export credit manager may obtain credit reports from mercantile credit agencies whose primary activity consists of gathering and disseminating credit information. R. G. Dun and Company, which was established in 1841, and the Bradstreet Company, which commenced operations eight years later, were merged in 1933 and now operate as Dun & Bradstreet, Inc. The company now has over 200 offices abroad in probably every community of commercial importance.

Dun & Bradstreet, Inc., depends primarily upon its foreign connections, but the reports received from them are fortified by the results of investigation among American sources such as banks, manufacturers, and others having foreign connections and outlets. In the gathering of data, the reporters are somewhat handicapped, as are all others seeking foreign credit information, by the unwillingness of many foreign businessmen to provide the necessary information. The reports are as factual as possible, and they also contain opinions obtained from the local trading community. The company is gradually overcoming this prejudice, however, by means of correspondence and personal calls, showing businessmen that it is decidedly to their advantage to provide the information which is solicited.

Another mercantile agency is the Retail Credit Company of Atlanta, Georgia, which has facilities for reporting on individuals throughout the world. One of this company's major functions includes the making of character reports for use in determining credit status.

Mercantile credit agencies patterned after American companies are also operating in some foreign countries. Generally speaking, however, it is easier, more expeditious, and quite as satisfactory to confine attention to Dun & Bradstreet, Inc., here in the United States.

Various organizations engaged in the promotion of international marketing have also become sources of export credit information.

Banks. Many American banks, particularly those which specialize in foreign trade financing, have undertaken the gathering of export credit information for the use of their clients. Their export credit reports are prepared mainly on the basis of information received from foreign correspondent banks, from such branch banks as are maintained abroad by certain American banks, and from the information necessarily incident to the banks' foreign transactions. Thus, it can be seen that banks are less dependent upon trade opinion or commercial investigation.

The export credit reports are regarded as conservative and dependable as far as they go, but sometimes they are brief and formal and do not always contain all of the information desired by the exporter. The reports are found useful, however, by many of the clients of these banks. As banks customarily exchange foreign credit information, American banks not having foreign correspondents or branches are able to secure credit data for their clients from the banks that are regularly engaged in preparing export credit reports.

Exchange of Ledger Experience. Export credit information sources quite different from those referred to above are organizations that depend primarily or wholly upon an interchange of ledger experience on the part of the exporters themselves. Informal exchange of ledger experience has long been a means through which an export credit manager can obtain credit information by consulting other credit managers with whom he is acquainted or by communicating with the references given by foreign importers. Some exporters send printed forms on which credit data are requested, and they may offer to reciprocate in the informal interchange of credit experience. A more organized, but still informal, method of interchange occurs at the periodic gatherings of export men at the meetings of various local export or foreign traders' clubs.

More formal interchange of credit information and experience has, however, been organized and has become an outstanding feature of export credit work in the United States. Incorporation of the interchange of experience into a fully organized credit source is the plan of the Foreign Credit Interchange Bureau of the National Association of Credit Management. It is a nonprofit cooperative bureau, each member of which agrees to furnish to the bureau information as to the experience record of all of its foreign customers. All information relating to lists of customers or to the identity of each member is considered strictly confidential. Based upon the experience of approximately 36,000 members, the bureau is in a position to maintain a master file containing credit information on foreign firms and to provide its members with valuable individual credit reports, such as that shown in Figure 30-A.

In addition to the issuance of foreign credit interchange reports, the F.C.I.B. also conducts monthly round-table conferences covering current foreign credit, collection, and exchange problems; it operates a worldwide collection service to aid in collecting delinquent accounts; it issues a *Weekly Bulletin* in which are reported all current changes affecting foreign credits, collections, and exchange conditions; and it offers a consultation service for the benefit of members.

International Marketing Publications. Various international marketing publications offer an export credit service for the use of their advertisers. The sources of their credit information are not uniform. They variously depend upon correspondence with or questionnaires sent to overseas buyers, or reports received from American merchants and forwarding agents, overseas financial reporting agencies, overseas chambers of commerce and trade associations, foreign or domestic banks, or foreign correspondents.

United States Government. By including the United States Government as a source of foreign credit information, it is not to be inferred that the Government is in the credit-reporting business. Among its activities relating to the promotion of international marketing and coming within the scope of what is known as "commercial intelligence" is the provision of certain data for the benefit of American exporters. This information is procured through the Foreign Service representatives and is found in the World Trade Directory Reports prepared by the Bureau of International Commerce. These reports are mainly in the nature of sales information reports, but an examination of Figure 30-B will indicate that they contain valuable data having a bearing upon the credit standing of foreign customers.

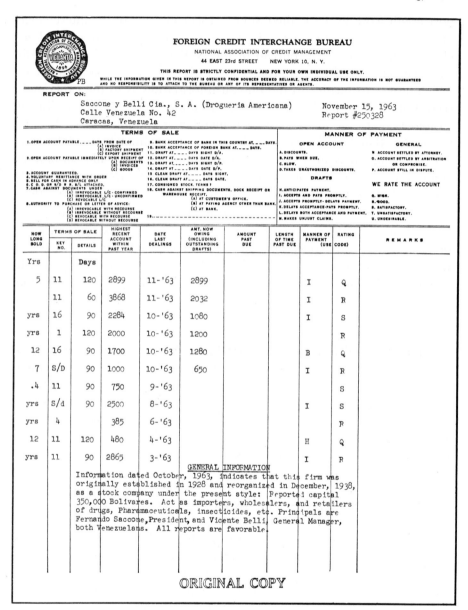

Figure 30–A. Foreign Credit Interchange Bureau Report

May .... Revised __X__
File Number _____

WORLD TRADE DIRECTORY REPORT

U. S. DEPARTMENT OF COMMERCE
Form 341—(3-5-54)

1. Name ___Ets. Doe___

2. Address ___11 Rue des Petites___ (Number) (Street) ___Pierre, Paris___ (City) ___France___ (Country)

3. (a) Importer of ___all kinds of hard and soft wood, timber and lumber___   (e) Wholesaler of ___---___

   (b) Retailer of ___---___   (f) Manufacturer of ___---___

   (c) Exporter of ___same as (a)___   (g) Commission merchant handling ___---___

   (d) Jobber or factor handling ___---___   (h) Sales or indent agent selling ___same as (a)___ (State qualifications on reverse)

4. Preferred language of correspondence ___French & English___

   Cable address ___KLEINWD___
   Codes used ___Bentley's___

5. Buys from following countries ___U.S.A., Sweden, Denmark, Norway, Germany___ (State proportions. If domestic, so state)

6. Organization ___Corporation___ (Corporation, partnership, etc.) ___1941___ (Year established) ___(reorganized 1946-1952)___ (Country where organized)

7. Head office ___Paris___ (Location)   Branch houses ___Le Havre, Bordeaux___ (Location)

8. Sales territory ___France and European countries___   Number of traveling salesmen employed ___2___

INFORMATION HEREIN IS FURNISHED U. S. TRADERS IN STRICT CONFIDENCE; SECONDARY DISTRIBUTION PROHIBITED

9. Representatives in United States ___Grove Trading Co., 2150 West 57th St., New York, N. Y.___ (Name) (Address) (If purchasing agent, so state)

10. Financial references ___Banque Francaise du Commerce Exterieur, Paris, France; Sixth National Bank of New York, New York City___

    Trade references ___See reverse___ (Give references in U. S. whenever possible and American references abroad)

11. Capital { Authorized ___Frs. 14,000,000___   Volume of business ___Frs. 250,000,000___ (Annual sales, state currency)   No. of employees ___12___
    Paid in ___Frs. 8,500,000___ (State currency; U. S. preferred)

12. Indicate relative size of concern (check) : Very large _____ Large _____ Medium __X__ Small _____ (Consider relative volume of business done by firm in its community)

13. Managers or partners (name, title, age, nationality) ___Jean Doe, President, 59 (French),___
    ___Harry Ferrand, Vice President, 50 (Belgian), Francois Meuble, General Manager,___
    ___56 (French)___

14. Capital stock controlled by ___the above___ (Name of persons most interested financially)

15. Selling agents for ___see reverse___ (State names of all firms; if exclusive, so state; use reverse side if necessary)

16. Indicate general reputation of concern ___Very good___ (See reverse side for additional comments)

17. Date of report ___March 1, 19--.___   Source of information ___John N. Brown, Second Secretary of Embassy___ (Name and post of preparing officer)

Use other side or separate sheet, if necessary, to give additional information

COMM-DC 38517

Figure 30—B. World Trade Directory Report

Summary

1. Credit is an ever-present problem in international marketing.
2. Credit may be defined as surrendering title to merchandise without having received assured payment.
3. Credit may also be defined as the financial burden sustained by the exporting firm from the time that shipment is made until the receipt of payment. This is better understood as financial burden. In this connection, the exporting firm receives a credit line from its bank under which documents will be discounted or purchased up to the limits of the credit line.
4. The conditions that influence foreign credit extensions are related to the supply of banking capital, interest rates, diversification of production, time in transit and business turnover, exchange rate fluctuations, competition, and custom.
5. The credit data that are sought fall under three headings: (a) foreign market conditions, (b) conditions or standing of the firm desiring credit, and (c) conditions influenced by the product.
6. United States exporters generally do not extend credits for longer than 90 days on ordinary commercial transactions. A foreign credit policy must be determined by every exporting establishment and, in some cases, the establishment of an export committee or a foreign credit department may be justified.
7. Sources of foreign credit information include references furnished by the buyer, mercantile credit agencies, international marketing organizations, credit reports from banks, the interchange of ledger experience, and international marketing publications. Helpful information is also provided by the World Trade Directory Reports of the Bureau of International Commerce.

QUESTIONS

1. Define the two meanings of credit and comment on these definitions.
2. What is a credit line and how does it function for an exporting firm?
3. Why were United States exporters so slow in developing export credit knowledge?
4. Why is credit so seldom extended in United States import trade?
5. In this chapter several conditions are mentioned that influence the extension of foreign credit in export sales. Explain and criticize each of these conditions.

6. How do foreign market conditions affect the credit standing of a business firm?
7. Discuss the relative importance of each of the three "C's" of export credit work.
8. Comment on the reliability, from a credit standpoint, of financial statements of foreign business concerns.
9. How does the profit margin of an exporter affect the amount of credit that he may grant?
10. How does the nature of products affect credit?
11. Outline the functions of an export credit department (or operation).
12. Of what use is an export credit file? Explain.
13. (a) Define the term "standard terms of sale."
    (b) How and by whom are these terms established?
    (c) How do such terms affect export sales potential?
14. Comment, in general, on the present availability of information for considering extension of credit by United States exporters.
15. (a) Compare the nature and scope of foreign credit reports received via banking channels with those received from mercantile credit agencies and international marketing organizations.
    (b) Compare each of these with the nature and scope of the interchange of ledger experience.
16. Examine Figure 30-B, which depicts the World Trade Directory Report of the Bureau of International Commerce. In what ways does this form fall short of what you now consider to be a completely satisfactory foreign credit report?

PROBLEM

The Foreign Credit Interchange Bureau of the National Association of Credit Management conducts regular round table meetings that deal with credit and collection experience in various foreign countries.

From copies of these reports or from the summaries that appear regularly in *Business Abroad and Export Trade*, prepare a report on the changing credit and collection conditions of the countries in a selected geographical area, for example, Latin America, Middle East, and Far East. For comparative purposes, you may wish to select a period of one year.

COLLATERAL READINGS

See the list of readings given at the end of Chapter 31 on pages 593 and 594.

FOREIGN COLLECTIONS, GUARANTEES, AND INSURANCE

After having examined the reasons for credit extension in international marketing, the credit data to be sought, the management of credit policy, and the various sources of foreign credit information, we shall now direct our attention to the objective of all international marketing — to receive payment for goods that have been sold. When payment is not forthcoming when due, steps must be taken to protect the interests of the creditor to as great an extent as possible. This chapter deals also with credit guarantees and insurance, whereby collections may be assured.

Making Foreign Collections

It is one thing to decide upon a policy to be employed in judging and granting credits but quite another to determine the most advisable course to be pursued in case of failure to make payment when it falls due. The collection policy begins as soon as negotiations with a customer have been completed. Tact is essential and collection letters of the type here considered should be written only by persons eminently fitted in this respect. In the acknowledgment of the order, the terms under which the sale is made are repeated and the assurance is expressed that the customer will meet the obligation he assumes. Such a tone of confidence, if aptly and tactfully employed in all correspondence, is a long step toward insuring collections. As the due date of the draft or the account approaches, the customer may be notified and the assurance may be expressed that he will meet his obligations.

Failure to Make Payment When Due. If payment is not made when due, prompt steps are to be taken. In case of draft transactions in which payment was not received within the time estimated, the bank is requested to ascertain the reason. Failure to make payment may be due to one of several reasons, and it is essential to know the status of a particular case before adopting a definite plan of action.

Claims Against the Exporter. The buyer may, for example, have fair or unfair claims against the exporter and for this reason fail to make payment. In such cases, the assumption is that after a reasonable adjustment has been made, the account will be paid. A thorough investigation is advisable in order to determine, if possible, the legitimacy of a claim and to place the responsibility. If the buyer is merely seeking to evade payment or is taking advantage of some technicality in his favor, the exporter may be forced to take steps to protect himself. Legitimate claims are, however, the general rule and if correspondence should prove unavailing, some form of conciliation or arbitration is highly advisable for making settlement.

Financial Embarrassment. Financial embarrassment is quite obviously a reason for failure to make payment, and here the collection policy, at least at the beginning, should be sympathetic and patient. Trying to rush such a case may cause entire loss, while friendly extensions and cooperation will probably secure the payment and, if not, will retain a customer. Such losses are at least partly compensated by the retention of goodwill on the part of those exporters who take the long-range view of the situation and help their delinquent customers back on their feet again.

Extended financial embarrassment may finally result in insolvency If this should be the case, the fortunate creditor is the one who insisted on and received his payment. Impending insolvency, however, can usually be discerned from up-to-date credit reports and, in such cases, the collection policy will aim to obtain funds before the crash comes. When insolvency occurs, it is highly desirable to place the case in the hands of a capable lawyer, or to instruct the bank to take the necessary steps, or in other ways to seek legal recourse. Laws relating to bankruptcy vary widely and the greatest care is essential.[1]

Exchange Restrictions. When payments are not made when due for reasons such as exchange restrictions, the credit, financial, sales, and executive officers of the exporting firm will, of course, decide upon a policy with respect to outstanding accounts and also upon the methods to be pursued in connection with future sales.

---

[1] A discussion of bankruptcy laws appears in Chapter 24.

Assistance in Making Collections. The exporter is not left entirely to his own resources in the matter of collections. Assistance can be obtained from organizations such as the Foreign Credit Interchange Bureau. Foreign collections are undertaken by various American and foreign collection agencies, and banks may press claims for payment. The foreign branches of American banks are especially valuable in this connection.

In draft transactions, the bank located abroad will, if so instructed, enter official protest in case of nonpayment of a draft, this step often being necessary to support subsequent court action.

Foreign Service Officers of the Department of State, while unable to assist directly in the collection of debts because of Foreign Service regulations, can use their good offices to aid in the adjustment of trade disputes. For example, a delinquent debtor abroad may be approached informally to determine whether a misunderstanding exists on his part. By such informal methods, solutions to delinquency problems are frequently to be found.

Litigation. Legal action may provide the necessary collection power, but, as is generally conceded, it should be employed only as a last resort. As a widely accepted policy, it is advisable to avoid litigation in foreign courts unless the amount involved is sufficiently large clearly to warrant this procedure. There are many objections to lawsuits in international trade, among the most significant being the delay and expense incurred, possible loopholes in foreign laws favorable to the delinquent, possible disastrous reaction to the exporter because of patriotic feelings abroad, possible political immunity of the defaulter, and general feelings of misgiving on the part of the exporter.

Credit Guarantees

Certainty of payment may at times be obtained by means of guarantees, provided, of course, the guarantor is thoroughly responsible. The several sources of credit guarantees may be grouped under the following headings:

1. Banks.
2. Sales agents.
3. Individuals.
4. Self-insurance of export credits.

Credit Guarantees by Banks. The oldest and most widely known method of shifting the credit burden by means of a guarantee is known as *del credere* — a term really synonymous with guarantee. *Del credere* transactions, in one sense, consist of discounting drafts drawn with the words "without recourse" placed under the signature of the drawer. The party (bank) that buys the paper thus becomes responsible under the bill and the drawer is entirely relieved. For this service a commission is charged that measures roughly the risk incurred in the guarantee.

Banking houses that deal in the discounting of such paper are known in the United States and abroad as *factors;* however, there are not many of them located in this country. Such factors are known to be able to obtain collection from countries that strictly control foreign exchange. In addition, certain special credit concerns that discount or make advances against drafts drawn on foreign customers without recourse, have been organized in the United States; and the Export-Import Bank in some instances does likewise.[2]

The payment of credits in international trade may also be assured by means of a bank acceptance. This may be provided by the irrevocable and confirmed letter of credit, under which, as explained in Chapter 29 the issuing and confirming banks are both responsible to the drawer of the drafts. Letters of credit, however, are not everywhere and at all times obtainable, and insistence upon this method of extending export credits by the exporter may, especially under competitive conditions, handicap his export sales efforts.

Credit Guarantees by Sales Agents. In another type of *del credere* arrangement, sales agents assume the risk. An exporter may employ the services of a commission sales agent abroad and the agent may assume the entire responsibility, including credit risks, to customers. In such an arrangement, the exporter generally extends credit to the customers but he looks to the agent for a part or all of the funds due under credit extensions, in case the customer fails to make payment. For this service the agent receives a *del credere* commission in addition to his usual salary and/ or commission.

Credit Guarantees by Individuals. Credit may also be guaranteed by individuals, but this practice has developed to a marked degree only in certain countries where the prevailing banking and commercial structures have failed to provide adequate protection of the rights of sellers.

[2]The functions of the Export-Import Bank are described in Chapter 27.

These individuals were called into existence because of the unusual conditions of native trade, and foreign houses generally refused to extend any credit without a binding guarantee. The responsibility of the guarantor is backed by cash, securities, and/or real estate of sufficient value to sustain adequately this position of trust. In addition to the credit guarantee, these individuals may perform merchandising and other functions. With the increased development of banking facilities in such countries, however, this system is declining; but until satisfactory means of obtaining adequate credit data on native merchants are available and until security of the rights of sellers is provided, some such form of credit guarantee may remain of importance.

Self-Insurance of Export Credits. *Self-insurance* takes the form of a reserve set aside for bad debts. This practice is followed in domestic as well as in international trade. The reserve is computed on the basis of past credit experience and is placed at an amount sufficient to offset prospective losses on accounts receivable, the assumption being that future losses will average the same as in the past. The failure of this statistical expectation to work out uniformly has wrecked many self-insurance plans, no matter what the subject matter covered.

The self-insurance plan of providing protection against foreign credit losses is perhaps more widely employed than any other. Exporters frequently feel that adequate protection is supplied by self-insurance, provided, of course, a conservative and wide-awake policy of credit extension is punctiliously observed. When credit is carefully granted, it is felt that losses will be small and that they may be readily assumed by the exporter. The amount set aside as a reserve for bad debt losses is a tax on the entire business — an expense of operation — and it is included in the selling price of the merchandise. If a sufficient reserve can be built up before a staggering loss is sustained, the plan may be quite satisfactory.

Export Credit Insurance

Insurance of foreign credits by means of an indemnifier who assumes the risk involved in consideration of a premium paid by the insured has attracted attention in the United States only since World War I. With the wholesale destruction and collapse due to this war, credit was severely strained and in some instances it completely disappeared.

In order to deal with this unprecedented situation, the American Manufacturers Foreign Credit Insurance Exchange was organized and began operating in 1919. In 1932, the Exchange discontinued its insuring function (continuing its rating and information services) due to the economic depression; but in 1934, it was replaced by the Export Credit Indemnity Exchange. This operation was discontinued in 1944.

The export credit insurance coverage included (1) insolvency of foreign customers and (2) uncollectibility of the obligation at law.

Exporters' Attitudes Toward Export Credit Insurance. Many American exporters have never been in favor of export credit insurance. The points usually stressed are (1) low average export credit losses, those of some exporters averaging, with the exercise of proper care, not over ½ of 1 percent or even less; (2) the existence of effective sources of export credit information; and (3) the employment of efficient export credit managers, some of whom feel that credit insurance is a reflection upon their knowledge and ability. It is admitted, however, that average credit losses vary by countries of destination and in many instances are substantially higher than estimates based upon the experience of some exporters, and that average credit losses may be influenced by the refusal of export credit when doubt exists or by insistence upon terms that are not acceptable to foreign importers who may in fact be good credit risks.

Some interest has been expressed in export credit insurance designed to cover long-term credits, particularly in the heavy industries. Some exporters are more interested in protection against losses resulting from exchange or other government restrictions and the catastrophe risk than in losses resulting from insolvency and uncollectibility at law.

Concepts of Export Credit Insurance Today. Export credit insurance today involves actually two concepts: (1) insurance of commercial credits and (2) insurance of "political" risks. These "political" risks are exchange transfer (inconvertibility) hazards that rarely can be anticipated by exporters. In recent years, responsible export opinion has expressed the need for United States Government help to meet these "political" risks; exporters, however, generally prefer to take care of the commercial credit risks themselves, through private credit facilities if such protection becomes necessary.

The subject becomes all the more involved because reports from foreign markets indicate that customers are increasingly being attracted from American suppliers by liberal credit terms offered by exporters of competing countries.[3] A brief review of export credit insurance practices in the United States and in other countries will be helpful in appraising this situation.

Export Credit Insurance in the United States. In the fall of 1954, the Export-Import Bank of Washington began an expanded program of exporter credits by financing up to 60 percent of the amount of specific or revolving credits and, in so doing, financed without recourse.[4] This program was slow in getting started, and by the end of the fiscal year 1956 (June 30) only $8.1 million in 65 exporter credit lines had been made, plus $3.9 million in 11 new exporter credit lines. The interest charged was 5 to 8 percent with maturities of 12 months to 12 years.

Exporters began to show greater interest in this means of financing capital exports, however, and the net amount of exporter credits as of December 31, 1957, was $180 million, and the same amount as of June 30, 1958.[5]

With the appearance of the Foreign Credit Insurance Association (FCIA) in 1962, this type of medium-term credit was essentially assumed by commercial banks through credit insurance and guarantees arranged through the FCIA and the Export-Import Bank.[6]

In early 1962, the Foreign Credit Insurance Association was established in collaboration with the Export-Import Bank. The Association is a voluntary group of private insurance companies that are interested in the insurance of foreign credits. The Association was a response to the invitation of the Export-Import Bank to participate with it in accordance with the directive of the President of the United States. Approximately 75 insurance companies are presently members of the Association.

Under this arrangement, the Export-Import Bank assumes 100 percent responsibility with respect to political risks, and the Export-Import Bank together with FCIA's member companies share the policy obligations with respect to commercial credit risks. Political risks are defined as inconvertibility of foreign currency to United States dollars, expropriation, confiscation, war, civil commotion or like disturbances, and cancellation or restriction of export or import licenses. Commercial credit

---

[3]Hubert Rousesllier, Director, French National Center of External Trade: "Many countries are granting terms exceeding the five-year limit spelled out by the Voluntary Berne Union Agreement." Quoted in *Journal of Commerce* (May 29, 1963).

[4]See Chapter 27 in which governmental activities in international finance are fully discussed.

[5]Export-Import Bank of Washington, *Semiannual Report to Congress* (June 30, 1958).

[6]*Ibid.* (December 31, 1962). See also Chapter 27.

risks are defined as insolvency of the buyer and his protracted default of any risk defined in the policy as a political risk.

Coverage. The insured under the FCIA policies bears 15 percent of the commercial credit risk and 5–15 percent of the political risk.

Two types of coverage have been offered. The first was a short-term policy, by which is meant a period up to 180 days. Later, on July 16, 1962, a medium-term policy was offered. This would cover a period over 181 days to 5 years.

As to the short-term policy, the insured must submit all of his export sales to the Association for coverage. The only exceptions are in case of shipments to Canada and also so-called secured (letter of credit) transactions. Moreover, the insured is required to have at least two credit reports in file in order to justify the extension of credit. When larger lines of credit are involved on behalf of special buyers, additional information may be requested. If the FCIA disapproves of the credit to any given buyer, this buyer's credit is excluded from coverage and the insured is not even required to report such sales.

The insured receives under the short-term policy a revolving form of coverage. Policies may be written in amounts from $1,000 to $15,000 to cover as many foreign buyers as the exporter may now have or subsequently acquire. By special application, buyers may be qualified for any reasonable amount in excess of $15,000. Since the coverage is revolving, the insured is advised not to take insurance for an amount above what he may reasonably estimate as the maximum that any buyer may owe him at any one time.

Policies are rated on terms of (1) cash against documents, (2) credit of up to 90 days, (3) credits up to 180 days, and (4) countries to which the exports are shipped. The Association states that an average premium on the short-term policy would be less than 1 percent of the gross value of the shipment.

Contract coverage is also available on a short-term policy. Under this endorsement, protection is afforded from the date of contract as contrasted with the date of shipment. The contract coverage is of special value to exporters who manufacture a product to special order and design where the buyer may become insolvent or merely cancel the contract. This means that losses occurring after the effective date of the contract of sale, but prior to actual shipment, may be insured for an additional premium, provided that the shipment is made within 180 days from the date of the contract.

Finally, discounts of up to 9 percent are available depending upon the size of the risk.

Medium-Term Policy. This policy runs from 181 days to 5 years. Installment payments are insured (guaranteed) rather than accounts receivable, and this includes interest on outstanding balances. The coverage on medium term for both commercial credit and political risks is 85 percent, although political coverage may be insured for as much as 90 percent.

In this kind of policy, insurance may be obtained on a case-to-case basis or on a revolving line of credit (repetitive sales) to one buyer or on a whole turnover basis. If the last named is used and a satisfactory spread is obtained, the political risk coverage is increased to 90 percent and a discount of premiums is allowed.

Premiums vary according to (1) term, (2) country, and (3) the financed portion (unpaid balance). Ordinarily, in medium-term insurance, FCIA requires a cash payment by the buyer of not less than 20 percent and the balance payable in equal installments or not less than six months. When the insurance applied for is over $100,000 and not over $200,000, the exporter is required to provide a guarantee of a commercial bank or other financial institution in the buyer's country satisfactory to the FCIA. If such guarantee is not offered, financial statements of the buyer for the most recent years are required. In all other cases, financial statements of the buyer for the most recent three years must be provided in addition to the previously stated requirements.

The exporter or insured has a 15 percent retention in each of the above installments. An example will clarify the subject.

SPECIAL TRANSACTION

Contract price....................	$100,000
Buyer's cash payment..............	20,000
Financed portion..................	$ 80,000
Exporter's 15% retention..........	12,000
Balance insured...................	$ 68,000

The buyer's debt to the exporter must be evidenced by a note approved by FCIA; it must be written in the English language; and it must be payable in United States dollars.

Contract coverage is also available in the medium-term policy where it is likely to be more in demand than for the short-term policy. The exporter is required to fill in an application that calls for a complete description of the entire transaction. This information is analyzed to determine the credit worthiness of the buyer. Interestingly enough, the Foreign Credit Insurance Association states that if the buyer is considered to be unworthy of credit insurance, "We would probably ask him (the exporter) to arrange for a bank guarantee."

Recent changes. Recognizing that foreign credit insurance in the United States is largely in the experimental stage, changes are bound to occur as experience is gained. Early in 1963, the FCIA announced that insurance policies on export transactions will be accepted to cover political risks only, for both short- and medium-term policies. At the same time, a lower rate schedule was announced. FCIA will also cover risks on the sale of technical services abroad by United States firms. These include architectural services, design, engineering studies and reports, and economic surveys. As reported in the *Journal of Commerce* of June 21, 1963, the FCIA in its sixteen months of operation has issued 1500 comprehensive policies, most of which were on a short-term basis. About one tenth of these were on behalf of new exporters. The aggregate amount of liability incurred was over one-half billion dollars.

In another report — *Journal of Commerce*, April 23, 1963 — it was shown that FCIA had 170 claims outstanding involving nearly $1,000,000. Of these, approximately 100 involve political risks for $700,000 and the balance was for commercial risks.

Side Benefits. "On the security of this insurance, the exporter may be much more active in competing with his foreign competitors on credit terms, when in his good judgment it is necessary and desirable for him to do so. This security also makes it much easier for him to obtain bank credit on the basis of the assignment of the proceeds of the policy. Further, this insurance will undoubtedly make it possible for exporters to expand their sales and it should also attract new firms into the export business, which is an objective very much desired by our Government in order to promote our general economy and to help correct our balance of payments problem."[7]

Attention is called to Chart 31-A that summarizes, in some detail, the facilities presently available to American exporters in terms of export credit insurance. The significant difference between short- and medium-term insurance is not the length of time for which the cover is written, but that under short-term insurance, consumer goods are covered and

---

[7]Foreign Credit Insurance Association, *Introducing Exporters, Bankers and Industry to Foreign Credit and Political Risk Insurance through FCIA* (undated pamphlet).

Char

U. S. EXPORT CREDIT INSURANCE
(Prepared in the Bureau of

	Short-term Insurance (Up to 180 days)[1]	
	Comprehensive (Political and Commercial) Coverage	**Political Risk Coverage Alone**
Purpose	To enable exporters to extend credit to buyers in friendly foreign countries by covering most of their risks through insurance, and by enlarging their potential capacity to borrow from banks and other financial institutions.	To enable exporters to extend credit to buyers in friendly foreign countries by covering most of the political risks through insurance.
Risks Covered[2]	(1) Commercial risks, i.e. insolvency and protracted default, and (2) political risks, i.e. currency inconvertibility, cancellation or restriction of import or export license, expropriation or confiscation, loss due to war, revolution or civil disturbance.	Political risks, i.e. currency inconvertibility, cancellation or restriction of import or export license, expropriation or confiscation, loss due to war, revolution or civil disturbance.
Type of Goods and Services[5]	U.S. produced merchandise sold abroad for dollars, generally consumer goods.	U.S. produced merchandise sold abroad for dollars, generally consumer goods.
Basis of Coverage	Whole turnover (all eligible exports), or reasonable spread of risks. (Option to exclude shipments to Canada and those covered by irrevocable bank letters of credit).	Whole turnover (all eligible exports), or reasonable spread of risks. (Option to exclude shipments to Canada and those covered by irrevocable bank letters of credit).
Amount of Coverage	85% of losses due to commercial risks; 95% for political risks. Policy subject to overall limit of liability and also to maximum amount of credit outstanding to each buyer.	90% of losses due to insured causes. Policy subject to overall limit of liability and also to maximum amount of coverage in certain countries.
Cash Payment Requirements	None	None
Repayment Period	Credit terms customary for the goods.	Credit terms customary for the goods.
Determination of Creditworthiness	Exporter shipping against discretionary limit specified in each policy must have in his files at least 2 satisfactory current credit reports from reliable sources. FCIA, at request of exporter, may arrange a special limit for a buyer in excess of discretionary limit.	None
Availability of Preshipment Coverage[6]	Yes	Yes
Availability of Advance Commitment	Generally not applicable.	Generally not applicable.
Cost	Variable, according to destination and terms of payment. Cost varies from 0.4% to 1.7%, averaging 0.75% of gross invoice value.[7]	Variable, according to destination and terms of payment. Rates about ⅔ of those for short-term comprehensive coverage.
Who Applies	Exporter	Exporter
Where to Apply	Through local insurance agent, broker, FCIA member company, or to FCIA itself.	Through local insurance agent, broker, FCIA member company, or to FCIA itself.
Administering Agency	Foreign Credit Insurance Assn. (FCIA), 110 William Street, New York 38, New York.	FCIA

[1]In special circumstances insurance will be provided up to 1 year under short-term policies.

[2]For large jet aircraft, 7 years.

[3]Both insurance and guarantees do not provide coverage when buyer refuses to accept goods, when a dispute exists between buyer and seller, or when exporter fails to live up to his contractual obligations.

[4]Early maturities are defined as first half of the installments of a 1 to 3 year credit or the first 18 months of a 3 to 5 year credit (excluding the 15% retained by the exporter). The later maturities include the remaining installments.

[5]Guarantees (comprehensive or political) are also available from Eximbank to U.S. suppliers for certain

Source: International Commerce (March 25, 1963), pp. 4–5.

31-A
AND GUARANTEE PROGRAMS
(International Commerce)

Medium-term Insurance (181 days to 5 years)²		Medium-term Guarantees to Commercial Banks (181 days to 5 years)²
Comprehensive (Political and Commercial) Coverage	Political Risk Coverage Alone	
To enable exporters to extend credit to buyers in friendly foreign countries by covering most of their risks through insurance, and by enlarging their potential capacity to borrow from banks and other financial institutions.	To enable exporters to extend credit to buyers in friendly foreign countries by covering most of the political risks through insurance.	To encourage banks to increase their nonrecourse financing to exporters. Also designed to facilitate the sale of export paper by commercial banks to other financial institutions.
(1) Commercial risks, i.e. insolvency and protracted default, and (2) political risks, i.e. currency inconvertibility, cancellation or restriction of import or export license, expropriation or confiscation, loss due to war, revolution or civil disturbance.	Political risks, i.e. currency inconvertibility, cancellation or restriction of import or export license, expropriation or confiscation, loss due to war, revolution or civil disturbance.	Eximbank guarantees political risks for early maturities and both commercial and political risks for later maturities. Commercial bank assumes credit risk on early maturities.⁴ Definition of commercial and political risks are same as given in other columns for insurance programs.
U.S. produced merchandise sold abroad for dollars, generally equipment and other durable goods.	U.S. produced merchandise sold abroad for dollars, generally equipment and other durable goods.	U. S. produced merchandise sold abroad for dollars, generally equipment and other durable goods.
(1) Case-by-case or revolving credit (repetitive sales) for one buyer; (2) whole turnover (all eligible exports) or reasonable spread of risks.	(1) Case-by-case or revolving credit (repetitive sales) for one buyer; (2) whole turnover (all eligible exports) or reasonable spread of risks.	Case-by-case or a revolving line of credit (repetitive sales) for one buyer.
85% of losses due to either commercial or political risks. (If on whole turnover or reasonable spread of risks basis, 90% of financed portion for political risks).	85% of losses due to insured causes. (90% if on whole turnover or reasonable spread of risks basis).	See "Risks Covered" entry above.
Foreign buyer provides 20% cash payment; exceptionally, 10% for good buyers in good markets. (Thus, financed portion normally 80% of contract price).	Foreign buyer provides 20% cash payment; exceptionally, 10% for good buyers in good markets. (Thus, financed portion normally 80% of contract price).	Foreign buyer provides 20% cash payment; exceptionally, 10% for good buyers in good market. (Thus, financed portion normally 80% of contract price).
Credit terms customary for the goods.	Credit terms customary for the goods.	Credit terms customary for the goods.
Exporter provides complete description of transaction(s) and credit information relative to buyer(s) and proposed guarantor(s).	None	Eximbank relies generally on credit judgment of commercial bank whose participation is required to be without recourse to exporter.
Yes, primarily for specially fabricated products, granted on merits of case.	Yes, primarily for specially fabricated products, granted on merits of case.	Yes, to exporters, primarily for specially fabricated products, granted on merits of case.
Yes	Yes	Yes
Variable, according to destination and terms of payment. Cost for case-by-case basis varies from 0.4% to 5.3% of invoice value.⁷	Variable, according to destination and terms of payment. Rates on case-by-case basis generally about ¾ of those for medium-term comprehensive coverage.	Variable, according to destination and terms of payment. Fees are roughly comparable to the insurance premiums under FCIA medium-term comprehensive policies. Charges notified only to banks.
Exporter	Exporter	Commercial bank or other financial institution.
Through local insurance agent, broker, FCIA member company, or to FCIA itself.	Through local insurance agent, broker, FCIA member company, or to FCIA itself.	Exporter applies to his commercial bank which deals with Export-Import Bank.
FCIA	FCIA	Export-Import Bank, Washington 25, D.C.

services (including architectural and design, engineering studies and economic surveys). Also political risk guarantees are available from Eximbank to U.S. suppliers for lease of equipment overseas or for consignment of goods awaiting sale, and goods abroad on exhibit at trade fairs, etc.

⁶Preshipment coverage is provided by FCIA through endorsement to policies. Basic FCIA policies provide insurance from time of shipment, whereas with contract coverage, protection is also provided while product is being manufactured. As of January 1963 preshipment coverage also became available to exporters for transactions covered by Eximbank guarantees to commercial banks.

⁷These rates, current as of March 1963, are subject to change.

practically the whole turnover must be submitted for insurance. The medium-term insurance covers chiefly durable goods, and it is conducted on a case-by-case or revolving credit basis. In no case is an exporter protected for 100 percent of his risk; he is obliged to take care of 15 percent of the commercial risk and 10–15 percent of the political risk. Moreover, under the medium-term insurance, buyers are required to advance 10–20 percent of the amount of the credit.

Export Credit Insurance in Other Countries. There are now 21 companies in European countries, Japan, and other areas offering foreign credit guarantee.

The Export Credit Insurance Organization represents the world's export credit insurance systems. It is known officially as the Berne (Switzerland) Union. FCIA was admitted to the Union in June, 1963. At the 20th Annual Meeting held in Taormina, Sicily, June 5–9, 1963, delegates from 22 credit insurance organizations representing 18 countries were present. Observers from the International Bank for Reconstruction and Development (IBRD), Inter-American Development Bank, Pakistan Insurance Corporation, and the Export Guarantee Fund of Finland were also present.[8]

Summary

1. Collections in international marketing call for patience and firmness. Every precaution is to be taken to protect the interests of the exporter.
2. Assistance in making collections abroad can be obtained from a number of agencies in the United States.
3. Credit guarantees may be obtained through letter of credit terms of payment or through personal guarantee by responsible individuals. Banks may discount bills of exchange without recourse; factors purchase export documents also without recourse.
4. Protection from credit losses can be provided by self-insurance and by guarantees under Export-Import Bank financing.
5. Export credit insurance is now available to American exporters through the FCIA, and with the backing of the Export-Import Bank.
6. Many foreign countries provide export credit insurance for their exporters. Political risks as well as insolvency are generally covered.

---

[8]*Export Trade* (June 24, 1963), p. 12.

QUESTIONS

1. Explain the meaning of the statement: "The collection policy begins as soon as negotiations with a customer have been completed."
2. Why is payment for international transactions sometimes delayed?
3. From what sources may an export credit manager secure assistance in making collections?
4. Outline all of the ways you can think of (not necessarily in this chapter) whereby export business can be conducted without suffering any export credit losses.
5. What is the nature of a *del credere* transaction?
6. What is the function of a *factor*?
7. Do American exporters now have the foreign credit insurance coverage that they desire? Explain.
8. Define the term "political risks."
9. Describe fully the self-insurance plan of providing protection against foreign credit losses. Do you believe it to be reliable?

PROBLEMS

1. (a) Outline an acceptable foreign collection policy, starting with the conclusion of an export sale on credit of 60-days' sight and developing the policy through the last step, payment by the buyer.
   (b) Assuming that the buyer in (a) does not pay as agreed, outline and explain the steps that you recommend be taken in a determined effort to make collection.
2. Select one foreign country in which you are interested and study the foreign credit insurance system, if any, that it has. Compare this system with that now available to American exporters and draw your conclusions.

COLLATERAL READINGS

Dartnell International Trade Handbook, The. Chicago: The Dartnell Corporation, 1963.

de Haas, J. A. *The Practice of Foreign Trade.* New York: McGraw-Hill Book Company, Inc., 1935. Chapters 9 and 14.

Fayerweather, John. *Management of International Operations,* Text and Cases. New York: McGraw-Hill Book Company, Inc., 1960. Chapter 7.

Heck, Harold J. *Foreign Commerce.* New York: McGraw-Hill Book Company, Inc., 1953. Chapters 8 and 9.

Henning, Charles N. *International Finance*. New York: Harper & Brothers, 1958. Chapter 5.

Horn, Paul V. *International Trade Principles and Practices*, Third Edition. New York: Prentice-Hall, Inc., 1951. Chapters 28 and 29.

MacDonald, Philip. *Practical Exporting*. New York: Ronald Press Company, 1949. Chapter 14.

Pratt, E. E. *Modern International Commerce*. New York: Allyn and Bacon, Inc., 1956. Chapters 10 and 13.

Roorbach, G. B. *Import Purchasing: Principles and Problems*. Chicago and New York: A. W. Shaw Company, 1927. Chapter 12.

——————————. *Problems in Foreign Trade*. New York: McGraw-Hill Book Company, Inc., 1933. Part V.

Rosenthal, Morris. *Techniques of International Trade*. New York: McGraw-Hill Book Company, Inc., 1950. Part VI, Chapter 37.

Tosdal, H. R. *Problems in Export Sales Management*. New York: McGraw-Hill Book Company, Inc., 1922. Chapter 10.

Wasserman, Max J., Charles W. Hultman, and Laszlo Zsoldos, *International Finance*. New York: Simmons-Boardman Publishing Corporation, 1963. Chapter 11.

Wyman, Walter F. *Export Merchandising*. New York: McGraw-Hill Book Company, Inc., 1922. Chapters 31–35.

CHAPTER 32

FOREIGN EXCHANGE

The discussion of foreign exchange rates will be limited to those phases of foreign exchange that are of direct interest to those concerned with international marketing. No effort will be made to cover the entire field of foreign exchange from the viewpoint of foreign exchange bankers, brokers and dealers, exchange speculators and arbitragers, security investors, and other interests, the activities of whom are also influenced by foreign exchange operations.[1]

Foreign Exchange Definitions

In international marketing the exporters and importers of any two countries think in terms of their own national currency. An American exporter, whether quoting prices in terms of the dollar or of the currency of a foreign country, expects eventually to receive dollars for his exported merchandise. The British exporter similarly expects to receive pounds sterling. The American importer may be called upon to settle on the basis of an agreed foreign currency, but he has in mind the number of dollars actually involved in his import transaction. As the prevailing foreign exchange rates between any two countries are the prices at which bills of exchange on one of these countries will sell in the currency of the other, they are, therefore, of direct importance to exporters and importers. The bills of exchange are expressed in terms of the price or rate at which the currency of one country is exchanged for that of another.

Gold Standard. When the currency of two countries was on a free gold standard, a definite "par" of exchange was computed on the basis

---

[1]See Chapter 26 for a discussion of international banking facilities.

of the weight of pure gold contained in the currency of the one country divided by the weight of pure gold contained in that of the other country. But this par was of importance primarily to the foreign exchange banker, for it was he, rather than the merchandise trader, who at times shipped gold instead of selling drafts or bills of exchange.

The merchandise exporter or importer is interested primarily in the actual rates of exchange between his country and specific foreign countries in which he is selling or buying goods. The exporter or importer, unless he has entered into an agreement that settlement shall be at par, is interested in the par of exchange only in that under normal conditions it limits exchange rate fluctuations. More specifically, when there is a free gold market in each of two countries, exchange rate limits are set by the cost of shipping gold, or so-called *gold points*. With a sterling exchange par of $4.8665 before the British pound was removed from the gold standard, the actual rates of exchange, for example, did not normally rise higher than this par of exchange plus the cost of shipping gold. They did not normally decline below par minus the cost of shipping gold. Wider fluctuations would cause foreign exchange bankers to ship gold rather than to sell drafts at rates of exchange beyond the gold points. The actual cost of shipping gold varies with the current cost of packing, cartage, insurance and freight, and current interest rates.

When, however, for any reason, there is not a free gold market in each of two countries between which an exchange rate is quoted, these gold point limits will not be operative, for under such conditions foreign exchange bankers may be unable to make gold shipments.

Gold and Inconvertible Paper Standards. When one of the two countries is on an inconvertible paper currency standard, there is no definite par of exchange. Gold cannot be shipped from the gold standard to the paper standard country as money, and the paper currency of the latter cannot enter the circulating medium of the gold standard country. There is nothing comparable to the gold points that fix the upper and lower limits between which the exchange rates of two gold standard countries fluctuate. In the paper money country, however, the upper limit of exchange must be related to the cost of purchasing gold with paper plus the cost of shipping the gold, but this does not in itself reduce exchange fluctuations to narrow limits.

When the amount of paper currency circulating in the paper standard country remains unchanged during a given period, the exchange rates between this country and a gold standard country will normally fluctuate in accordance with the supply of, and the demand for, exchange springing from the remittances being made between the two countries on account of the merchandise and invisible transactions requiring settlement. Exchange rates, even when the volume of paper currency remains steady, may fluctuate widely because of the absence of definite gold point limits. Should the currency of the paper standard country be inflated or deflated during a given period, it is obvious that further fluctuations may be caused by the very fact of inflation or deflation, for exchange rates currently reflect the relative values of the gold and paper currencies of the two countries.

During the post-World War I and II periods, for example, when many foreign countries were not on the gold standard, violent fluctuations in the exchange rates of the United States on several European countries were mainly due to, or were abetted by, the inflation of their paper currencies. Under such unstable monetary conditions, the current demand for, and the supply of, bills occasioned by merchandise exports and imports and other international business transactions did not primarily cause the wide fluctuations and appalling depreciation of exchange rates, and failed utterly to hold them within a narrow range.

In the absence of the gold standard in one of the countries, it does not, however, follow that exchange rates will fluctuate widely at all times. The several factors that influence exchange rates may either steady them or cause them to fluctuate violently. These factors, which will be defined more fully subsequently, also influence exchange rate fluctuations between two gold standard countries, both having a free gold market. The fluctuations in this case, however, will normally revolve around a par of exchange within limits set by the cost of shipping gold.

Inconvertible Paper Standards. When both countries concerned have abandoned the free gold standard and operate on the basis of inconvertible paper currencies, exchange rates will not of course fluctuate within the relatively narrow limits set by gold points. They will be influenced by the forces of supply and demand in the exchange market and may at times fluctuate widely and violently unless subjected to exchange control. This situation has become sufficiently widespread since the early 1930's to warrant more detailed discussion in Chapter 33.

Types of Exchange Rates. At any given time, in the absence of governmental control or restrictions, exchange rates on a particular country will vary according to the character of the bill of exchange — whether it is a banker's bill or a commercial bill and, if the latter, whether it is a clean or a documentary bill; whether a documentary bill is drawn for payment or for acceptance; and whether the collateral behind it is readily salable or not. In the case of commercial bills, the exchange rates paid currently will also vary according to the credit standings of the drawer and the drawee. The rates paid for commercial bills will further vary according to whether they run for long or short periods. Different rates of exchange are paid for bankers' bills, according to whether they are cable transfers, mail transfers, or checks; and different rates are paid for short as against long commercial bills.[2]

A distinction is also to be drawn between "spot" and "future" exchange. When an importer, for example, purchases *spot exchange*, he actually takes delivery for a definite amount of foreign exchange at the time of purchase for which he pays the rate then quoted for his particular bill of exchange. When he purchases a *future exchange* contract, he agrees to purchase a given amount of exchange on a fixed date in the future, or within a fixed period to pay for it at the rate specified in the future contract. This future rate may be higher or lower than the spot rate. The direction and extent of the deviation from the spot rate is largely governed by two factors: first, the supply and the demand for delivery of a given currency at a future time; second, the speculative opinion of the market concerning the future course of the rate of exchange of a given foreign currency. In practice the second element ordinarily determines whether the future rate will be at a premium or a discount under the spot rate, and the amount of discount or premium will be determined somewhat by the first factor.

Factors Influencing Exchange Rate Fluctuations

Free and uncontrolled foreign exchange rates fluctuate almost continuously, for they are constantly subject to influences, some of which tend to raise and others to lower them. Between gold standard countries the fluctuations are normally limited by the gold points previously defined, but between these limits constant fluctuations occur. In the absence of gold embargoes, paper currency inflation, or similar abnormal disturbing factors, these fluctuations are caused basically by the supply of and the demand for foreign exchange.

---

[2]See Chapters 28 and 29.

A maze of merchandise and other business transactions is conducted between the United States and foreign countries, and from these transactions are derived the remittances that influence the supply of and the demand for foreign exchange. These remittances vary constantly and are not the same between the United States and any two foreign countries. *Low exchange* (by which is meant a lower cost of purchasing foreign currencies) normally indicates a strong demand for United States dollars or a heavy offering of pounds sterling, francs, marks, lire, or other foreign money. *High exchange* conversely indicates a strong demand for foreign currency or a heavy offering of American dollars. The transactions comprising the credit items of the balance of payments between the United States and a foreign country tend to increase American holdings of foreign exchange and/or to reduce foreign holdings of dollar exchange; the debit items have, of course, the reverse effect. The influence of these supply and demand items upon current exchange rates has frequently been limited during recent years by governmental exchange control activities or restrictions, as will be examined in the following chapter.

Basic Transactions Affecting Supply of Foreign Exchange. The principal items normally constituting the supply of foreign exchange in the United States and, therefore, tending to reduce exchange rates, are American exports, American stocks and bonds sold abroad, foreign capital movements to the United States, interest and dividend payments on foreign securities held in the United States, foreign securities resold to foreigners, short-term loans made in the United States by foreigners, and payments due Americans for shipping, insurance, and other services. All of these items require remittances to this country and therefore result in a demand for dollars or a large volume of cash claims against foreign currencies.

Basic Transactions Affecting Demand for Foreign Exchange. The principal items normally constituting demand for foreign exchange and therefore tending to increase exchange rates are merchandise imports into the United States, foreign stocks and bonds sold in the United States (including all new American investments abroad and loans to foreigners), American securities bought back from foreigners, interest and dividends on American securities held abroad, United States tourist expenditures abroad, immigrant remittances, and payments to foreigners for services. All other miscellaneous transactions causing a demand for foreign exchange will add to the upward tendency of foreign exchange rates.

Abnormal Factors Affecting Exchange Rates. These various forces of supply and demand are now more numerous and complicated than in the past. For many years it was predicted that when merchandise exports exceeded merchandise imports, exchange would normally be low and that every widening of the gap would cause a downward movement. When the great service and capital movement items of the balance of payments appeared, this prediction became less accurate.

Foreign exchange rates, however, are not always dominated by these normal forces of supply and demand. Suspension of gold payments followed by inflation of paper currencies, enormous floating debts and appalling total public debts, industrial derangements, and in some instances, governmental instability, undoubtedly cause fluctuations and greatly depress exchange rates. A mere readjustment of merchandise exports and imports does not cure such abnormal exchange situations. Little is accomplished until steps are taken to bring about currency reform, balanced state budgets, debt funding, and general economic and governmental stability. Exchange rates are sensitive to any condition that shakes or destroys confidence.

Foreign Exchange Speculation. It should also be remembered that in a free exchange market there are foreign exchange speculators. While the wide fluctuations in exchange rates on some of the European countries during the postwar periods were not basically due to speculation in futures, speculative trading may at times have contributed to them. At other times, exchange speculation may have steadied exchange rates somewhat, for speculators who have sold future contracts may later appear as an important group of purchasers.

Money Rates (Interest) and Foreign Exchange. Exchange rates are normally also influenced by the money market in the United States and foreign countries, because money rates influence the flow of funds and, consequently, the supply of and demand for foreign exchange. Rising money rates in the United States normally tend to draw foreign bank funds to this country and bring home American bank balances held abroad,[3] and the effect is to depress exchange rates. Declining money rates in the United States tend to reverse this flow of bank funds and to raise exchange rates. Similarly, a rise in money rates in a foreign money market normally tends to draw foreign bank funds held in the

---

[3]This was the purpose of raising the rediscount rate by the Federal Reserve Board in July, 1963.

United States and available American bank balances to the foreign market, while a decline in money rates abroad tends to cause a reverse flow of bank funds. In the one case exchange rates tend to rise, and in the other, they tend to fall.

It does not follow that every fluctuation in the money market will promptly be reflected in foreign exchange rates, for other factors may retard or delay the flow of funds, and other factors are also constantly operative in the foreign exchange market. In the absence of exchange control or restriction plans, however, changing money rates frequently do cause fluctuations in foreign exchange. The exchange rates on long commercial bills, moreover, have frequently been influenced by discount rates.

The full effect of supply and demand forces upon current exchange rates has been curtailed in many countries by the exchange control and restriction plans that were adopted during the 1930's. These plans and the adoption of restrictions by additional countries after the beginning of World War II are discussed in the following chapter.

Effect of Exchange Fluctuations Upon Price Quotations or International Trade Profits

When the exporter quotes an export price or receives an offer in terms of foreign currency, he is concerned very directly with exchange rate fluctuations that may occur before he receives payment. When quoting foreign currency prices, the exporter has in mind a certain number of American dollars; but as his customer will pay in pounds sterling, marks, francs, pesos, or some other agreed foreign currency, the remittance in terms of dollars will depend upon the rate of exchange. The exporter accepts the risk of exchange fluctuation and, unless he takes steps to protect his expected profits, a decline in exchange may reduce them or even convert them into a loss. When he quotes his export prices in terms of American dollars, this direct risk is shifted to the foreign importer, who, unless he takes steps to protect himself against the risk of an unfavorable exchange fluctuation, may find himself obliged to pay a higher price on the basis of his own currency than he had anticipated.

Exporter's Means of Protection. When quoting prices in foreign currency, the American exporter may, in case he believes that exchange fluctuations will be slight or believes himself capable of judging the course of exchange, deliberately accept the exchange risk. He is speculating on his merchandise export transaction, for his profits will not be realized until payment has been received in United States dollars. He will be more inclined to do this if exchange rates have recently been quite stable, and if the character of his wares is such as to permit of rather wide price margins. He may be able to take the exchange risk into account in quoting his export prices, but in doing so limit the volume of his sales.

When exchange fluctuates within a comparatively narrow range, the exporter may be able to induce the foreign importer to agree upon a fixed or guaranteed rate of exchange, but arrangements such as these may be unobtainable at the very time when the exporter is most anxious to protect his profits. When the exchange risk is greatest because of wide fluctuations, the exporter who quotes foreign currency prices may find his only safeguard in the open exchange market where foreign currency bills for future delivery are bought and sold.

Hedging. Except in case of shipments to countries where there is no open exchange market for futures contracts, the exporter may hedge or protect his export profits in a large measure by selling futures contracts.

When he closes his export contract, the exporter may be able almost immediately to sell his foreign currency bill for future delivery to his banker. Later, when he has obtained his bill of lading, he will deliver his draft and receive payment on the basis of the rate at which it was sold for future delivery. Thus, the exporter has, in effect, availed himself of a fixed rate of exchange.

Or when he closes his export contract, the exporter whose bill of exchange is to be forwarded for collection may be able to sell an equivalent or nearly equivalent amount of foreign currency for delivery in the future at the time his bill matures. Should the exchange rate decline, meanwhile, he will in this case receive fewer American dollars on his merchandise transaction than he anticipated when closing his export contract, but he will be able to cover or buy back at a reduced rate the foreign currency that he had sold for future delivery. The profit derived from this future exchange transaction will about balance the amount of the reduction in the remittance on his export transaction, and he will again have assured himself of a fixed rate of exchange.

Another variation in the use of the exchange future arises when an exporter who anticipates heavy exports to be sold abroad in a steady volume, but without long-time advance contracts of sale, sells for future delivery over a long period his anticipated proceeds in foreign moneys.

As an example, let us say that an exporter in the United States sells a bill of goods worth $10,000, on 60 days' sight, to an Italian importer. The quotation is made in lira, at $.0016, or 6,250,000 lira. In order to hedge, the exporter sells a futures contract to deliver this number of lira, assuming there is such a market. Assume also that the price he obtains for his futures contract is the January 1 spot rate of $.0016 per lira. Thirty days are allowed for the transfer of documents between the United States and Italy.

As it will be seen in the following illustration, this is an ideal transaction, since the dates, rates, and amounts fitted exactly. They rarely, if ever, fit so nicely in everyday business.

	Merchandise Transaction	*Futures Transaction*	
Jan. 1	Sells order for 6,250,000 lira worth of goods. At $.0016 per lira, this equals......$10,000.00	Sells 90-day contract for 6,250,000 lira at $.0016..............	$ 10,000.00
April 1	Receives payment of 6,250,000 lira worth $.0016125... 10,078.13	Buys spot lira to cover at $.0016125.........	10,078.13
	Profit due to exchange..$ 78.13	Loss on futures contract.............. $ 78.13	

The cost of exchange hedging transactions to the exporter is small. The banker's profits, in general, result from a slight spread between his buying and selling rates. "For established customers of very high standing the contract may be entirely unprotected, regardless of the fluctuations of the rate in the period before delivery. In other cases, the customer may be asked to put up security if the rate goes against him during the period. In the usual case the customer signs a contract under which he obligates himself to cover fluctuations from his established contract price. And in some cases the customer provides collateral in advance at the time of making the contract, the amount of the collateral being based upon the probable maximum fluctuations during the life of the contract. This collateral will obviously vary with the stability of the currency. In any event, the seller or purchaser of a future makes very little outlay for his contract and in many cases none at all."[4]

Hazards of Hedging. The sale of futures contracts in many instances affords real protection to the exporter, but it does not always eliminate

[4]Ralph Dawson, "Protection Against Exchange Losses," *Report, Ninth Foreign Trade Convention,* p. 140.

the exchange risk entirely because he may be unable to close his export sales contract and sell his futures contract at exactly the same moment. He may also be unable to sell a futures contract exactly equal to his export transaction in the amount of exchange involved. Bankers, too, have at times withdrawn from future exchange operations in some currencies.

Importer's Means of Protection. When the exporter quotes his prices in terms of the American dollar, the exchange risk is shifted to his foreign customers, who may take steps to protect themselves against unfavorable exchange fluctuation. American importers, when buying foreign merchandise in terms of foreign currencies, similarly are faced by possible loss of profit resulting from unfavorable exchange fluctuations. The American importer, knowing that he will have to deliver a given amount of foreign currency at a future date, may purchase spot exchange when he orders his imported merchandise. This will eliminate the danger of a rise in the exchange on the importing country, but in doing so he ties up his funds until the merchandise is received by him. He may postpone his spot exchange purchase until the ordered goods have been shipped, but he will, nevertheless, be tying up funds for an appreciable period; and as exchange may rise during the period between dates of ordering and shipping, he no longer is certain of eliminating the entire exchange risk. He may purchase spot exchange from time to time without reference to goods actually ordered, so as to have on hand adequate exchange to meet future import commitments, the supposition being that he will buy exchange when, in his judgment, the exchange rate is favorable. His judgment may, however, be incorrect and, if so, he will become aware that he has been speculating in exchange.

When purchasing imports in terms of a foreign currency for which there is a market for future exchange, the American importer, therefore, may seek to hedge his import transactions by purchasing future exchange contracts at the time he obtains his import credit. He may not be required to tie up any funds whatever; and in case a deposit is required by the banker, the amount will be less than that involved in a purchase of spot exchange. Yet he may be assured that, when called upon to make payment for his imported wares, the necessary foreign currency will become available at a price determined at the time he purchased the futures contract.

Dollar Price Quotations and Exchange Risks. The most complete safeguard against unfavorable exchange fluctuations is, of course, enjoyed by American exporters and importers when settlement is to be made in United States dollars. They may, however, in such a case, retain a less direct interest in exchange fluctuations. Fluctuations following the closing of the sales contract may be so unfavorable that the foreign customer of the American exporter may, as a way out of his difficulty, refuse to accept delivery or, having accepted the goods, he may find himself unable or unwilling to meet his financial obligation. The foreign importer may have failed to take steps to protect himself against unfavorable exchange fluctuations and as a result finds himself under a serious handicap; or he may have engaged in unfortunate exchange speculation. Exchange rate fluctuations may in effect increase the exporter's credit and commercial risks. The exporter's interest may, of course, be influenced by the method of financing the export transaction that was agreed upon.

The American importer who has purchased foreign goods in terms of United States dollars may have an indirect interest in exchange rate fluctuations owing to the possibility that losses resulting from exchange fluctuations may induce the foreign exporter to delay shipment or fail to make delivery of the ordered merchandise. Although the American importer will not make payment and will not suffer a direct loss from exchange rate fluctuations, the orderly conduct of his import business is disrupted and, in case he has resold any of the ordered wares in advance of their receipt, he may be embarrassed. When purchasing abroad in terms of United States dollars, the importer is indirectly interested in having the foreign exporter take proper steps to safeguard himself against unfavorable exchange fluctuations.

Effect of Depreciated Foreign Exchange Upon Exports and Imports

Although the interest of American exporters and importers has at times centered chiefly in the risk incident to exchange rate fluctuations occurring after their export or import merchandise contracts have been closed, they have also been concerned with the influence exerted by depreciated exchange rates upon their current and future trading relations with particular countries. Does a severe decline in the exchange rates on certain countries, such as occurred during the postwar periods following the two World Wars, tend to handicap the American exporter and encourage imports from abroad? A serious problem is not apt to arise between gold standard countries because the gold points normally prevent severe depreciation in their exchange rates, and the flow of gold would eventually tend to readjust the commodity price levels. But it was amply demonstrated during these postwar periods that the exchange rates of the United States on a paper currency country may depreciate to an amazing extent. Prior to 1934, the United States dollar was on a convertible gold standard basis, but it was stated repeatedly that the American exporter was handicapped not only by violent exchange fluctuations but also by the very fact of depreciation, and that this depreciation conversely benefited the foreign exporter and the American importer.

Influence of Commodity Price Levels. If commodity price levels had promptly readjusted themselves as exchange rates depreciated and a so-called international purchasing power parity[5] had been maintained, depreciated exchange would have had little effect upon merchandise exports and imports. Such a readjustment, however, did not take place promptly.

Prices and exchange rates may in the long run gravitate to a common level, but price levels may move more slowly and a considerable lag may develop. In the absence of paper currency inflation or exchange control or restriction plans, the exchange rates on an inconvertible paper-currency country are governed mainly by the respective volume of remittances arising from merchandise exports and imports and the invisible items entering into the international balance of payments. Exchange rates may, therefore, depreciate very substantially, while the general commodity price level within the paper currency country, its volume of paper currency remaining unchanged, may fail to rise. Under such conditions exports from the United States to the paper currency country would be handicapped because their prices, if quoted on the basis of the current depreciated exchange rate and with a view to obtaining the number of dollars normally expected, would appear high to the foreign importer in comparison with the general level of the domestic prices prevailing in his country and higher than the import prices formerly paid by him.

---

[5]International purchasing power parity is a concept by which inconvertible currencies can be related. If at the beginning of a period the exchange rates of countries A and B had been at par, that is, 1 to 1, then an increase in the price level of A of 150 percent while an increase in the price level of B was 100 percent would reflect a relationship of 1.5 of country A's currency to 1.0 of country B's.

In essence, purchasing power parity poses this simple equation: if rent, shoes, food, tobacco, travel, insurance, and other costs of living (and/or doing business) in country A call for 50 percent more of A's currency than could be provided in country B with B's currency, then 1.5 units of A's currency would equal 1.0 units of B's currency.

If the American exporter, on the contrary, should quote his prices so as to keep them in line with the domestic price level of the paper-currency country, or if he should accept price offers from abroad on that basis, he would be receiving less in dollars than before the exchange rates depreciated. Imports received from the paper currency country, on the contrary, would be encouraged somewhat because the American importer could temporarily purchase merchandise at prices that in terms of United States dollars would be attractive. The resulting decline of exports and increase of imports would eventually tend to advance the exchange rates.

Internal Inflation and Exchange Rates. The exchange situation in many countries during the postwar periods, however, was complicated by currency inflation. An increasing volume of paper currency became the principal cause of severe exchange rate depreciation, and disturbing political and general economic conditions also exerted a depressing influence in some instances. In Germany, for example, after World War I commodity price levels did not rise as promptly as exchange rates declined; neither did the exceedingly severe exchange depreciation cause Germany to cease importing from the United States, and German exports to the United States did not flood the American market or other foreign markets to which American exports were shipped.[6] Imports from Germany increased substantially in 1922 and 1923, while exports to Germany from the United States declined somewhat, but the trade balance of the United States in our trade with Germany continued to be heavily on the side of exports. Export and import trade readjustments were entirely insufficient to overcome the serious exchange rate depreciation that then existed. The difficulty was overcome when the gold standard was reestablished in Germany as part of the Dawes plan in 1924.

Devaluation and Exchange Rates. During the early 1930's, when the United States dollar was still on a convertible gold standard basis and before it was devalued, but when the gold standard had been suspended in many foreign countries, there was further evidence of serious exchange rate depreciation with a depressing effect upon American exports to these countries and a stimulating effect upon imports received from them. As world trade was then affected by greatly reduced pur-

---

[6]While Germany during this period possessed an export sales advantage, this position was offset by the disadvantage of importing needed raw materials at high exchange rates. The export trade could not continue without these supplies of foreign raw materials.

chasing power and other evidences of acute business depression, as well as by exchange difficulties, it did not follow that exchange rate depreciation would be accompanied by an increase in imports into the United States or by a comparatively greater decline in exports.

Although during 1932, following the suspension of the gold standard in Britain in September, 1931, our exchange rates on Britain had declined seriously, imports from Britain declined greatly because purchasing power and the willingness to purchase merchandise within the United States, whether domestic or foreign, was undermined by the acute business depression. Our exports to Britain also declined, both because of the business depression in Britain and the depressing effect of exchange rate depreciation, but they declined relatively less in percentage than our imports from Britain. Nevertheless exchange rate depreciation, as a single trade factor, was handicapping American exporters and benefiting American importers. Under the conditions then prevailing, the export handicap and import advantage resulting from depreciated exchange were not overcome until after the United States dollar was removed from the convertible gold standard basis in March, 1933.

During the post-World War II period, destruction and severe trade dislocations seriously disturbed exchange rates and methods of financing trade. Germany did not, as after World War I, suffer exchange depreciation but Japan did. This was not a runaway inflation, however, because American financial assistance aided Japan in stabilizing exchange at a greatly depreciated level. Moreover, the influence of direct financial assistance from other countries in addition to new agencies, such as the International Monetary Fund, all introduced so many extraneous forces that exchange rate quotations by no means followed a natural course. These efforts after 1945 to prevent the kind of currency depreciation and chaos that followed 1918 were largely successful, despite the severe depreciation of certain European and Asiatic, as well as Latin American, currencies.

Summary

1. Foreign exchange is the act of purchasing the currency of another country, and the price that is paid is called the foreign exchange rate.
2. Under the old gold standard, each currency was expressed in terms of its gold content and it was an easy mathematical computation to calculate the par of exchange. Variations in rates from par are caused by supply and demand factors.
3. International marketing transactions that constitute supply factors, which tend to reduce exchange rates, are those which cause funds to flow into a given country (the United States). Such transactions are chiefly export sales, but they also include invisible items such as interest and dividends received on foreign investments and royalties received.
4. The demand factors tend to cause funds to flow from a country (the United States) and these are chiefly imports of merchandise, but they also include new foreign investments, government grants to foreign countries, and United States tourist travel abroad.
5. Exchange transactions can be for spot (immediate sale or purchase) or for future.
6. Exchange rates fluctuate frequently, usually within narrow limits. Exchange rates also depend on whether a given transaction involves a bank or a merchant, or whether it is secured or unsecured by documents, etc. Violent exchange fluctuations are caused by suspension of gold payments, currency inflation, government instability, and money rates.
7. Speculators operate under conditions of free exchange and tend to cause exchange rates to be stabilized.
8. Exporters and importers are greatly interested in foreign exchange rates. If an exporter quotes in foreign currency, his payment, when converted to his own currency, depends upon the exchange rate. The same is true of importers who purchase in foreign currencies. Even though prices are quoted in the currency of the United States exporter or the United States importer, their opposite numbers are affected by exchange rate changes.
9. Exporters may be able to hedge a transaction quoted in foreign currency by selling a futures contract for delivery of foreign exchange. Importers may also hedge by buying futures.
10. Exchange rate depreciation causes the prices quoted by the country with the depreciated rate to be lower to foreign purchasers. This will continue

as long as internal prices are not correspondingly raised. Exchange rate depreciation may provide an export price advantage to such a country.

11. With the existence of the International Monetary Fund, better worldwide control is provided to prevent exchange rates from fluctuating excessively.

QUESTIONS

1. Define foreign exchange. With what does it deal?
2. How many pesos of 10 grains of gold would another currency of 25 grains of gold purchase at par?
3. Would an American exporter expect United States dollars for his export transaction? Why would he not consider pesos acceptable?
4. Why would an American importer prefer to pay for his import transaction in United States dollars? Why in pesos?
5. Describe the relationship between the foreign exchange market and the balance of international payments.
6. Explain the two main factors that determine the quotation for foreign exchange to be delivered 60 days after the order for this future exchange has been placed.
7. How do exchange speculators influence foreign exchange rates?
8. Define hedging. How may an exporter hedge a transaction for which foreign currency is to be received? How may an importer hedge a transaction for which foreign currency is to be paid?
9. If American exporters sell and importers buy in United States dollars, is there any concern that they should feel for their customers and suppliers? Explain.
10. How does depreciated foreign exchange affect current transactions of exporters? importers?
11. How did United States trade with the United Kingdom react to the 1931 devaluation of pounds sterling? Why?
12. How did United States trade with Germany react during the post-World War I depreciation of the German mark? Why?

PROBLEMS

1. An American importer is purchasing Wedgwood ware from the United Kingdom. He is paying 2,000 pounds sterling and has 60 days in which to pay. The dollars he is hoping to pay (in order to preserve his profit) amount to $5,618.20 at a rate of $2.8091 per pound.
   (a) Determine the spot and the 60 and 90 days' futures quotations of sterling as of the time that you work out this problem.

(b) Calculate a hedging transaction to determine how adequately the importer would be able to protect against exchange losses.
2. You have been doing business with a firm in Brazil for 15 years. Your relations with this firm are close. There has never been any difficulty in obtaining payment, although delays have sometimes occurred. These have been due to the foreign exchange problems of the country of Brazil and not the buyer. During a recent period in which Brazil was in grave international financial trouble, the buyer courteously suggested that the next order be paid for in Brazilian cruzeiros. What do you advise the exporter to do?

COLLATERAL READINGS

Condliffe J. B. *The Reconstruction of World Trade.* New York: W. W. Norton & Company, Inc., 1940. Chapter 7.

Dartnell International Trade Handbook, The. Chicago: The Dartnell Corporation, 1963.

de Haas, J. A. *The Practice of Foreign Trade.* New York: McGraw-Hill Book Company, Inc., 1935. Chapter 14.

Heck, Harold J. *Foreign Commerce.* New York: McGraw-Hill Book Company, Inc., 1953. Chapter 14.

Henning, Charles N. *International Finance.* New York: Harper & Brothers, 1958. Chapters 12, 13, 15, and 16.

Horn, Paul V. *International Trade Principles and Practices,* Third Edition. New York: Prentice-Hall, Inc., 1951. Chapter 20.

Mikesell, Raymond F. *United States Economic Policy and International Relations.* New York: McGraw-Hill Book Company, Inc., 1952. Chapters 9 and 10.

—————————————. *Foreign Exchange in the Postwar World.* New York: Twentieth Century Fund, 1954.

National Foreign Trade Council. *Report — National Foreign Trade Convention.* New York: annual.

Pratt, E. E. *Modern International Commerce.* New York: Allyn and Bacon, Inc., 1956. Chapter 8.

Roorbach, G. B. *Import Purchasing: Principles and Problems.* Chicago and New York: A. W. Shaw Company, 1927. Chapter 12 B.

—————————————. *Problems in Foreign Trade.* New York: McGraw-Hill Book Company, Inc., 1933. Part V.

Shaterian, William S. *Export-Import Banking,* Second Edition. New York: Ronald Press Company, 1956. Chapter 11.

Towle, Lawrence W. *International Trade and Commercial Policy.* New York and London: Harper & Brothers, 1956. Chapters 3 and 5.

Wasserman, Max J., Charles W. Hultman, and Laszlo Zsoldos. *International Finance.* New York: Simmons-Boardman Publishing Corporation, 1963. Parts IV and V.

CHAPTER 33

FOREIGN EXCHANGE CONTROL

Before the depression years of the 1930's, governments acting through central banks or other authorities had on various occasions engaged in activities designed to influence foreign exchange rates. There have been instances of purchase and sale of gold exchange, monetary policy involving the devaluation of currencies or the limitation of currency circulation within prescribed limits, control of bank rates, and the seasonal purchase of foreign exchange. During World War I, moreover, British sterling exchange was pegged. "The New York banking house of J. P. Morgan and Company, acting on behalf of the British Treasury, undertook during the period between 1916 and 1919, to buy an unlimited amount of sterling at the fixed rate of 4.76 7/16. The funds for this purpose were supplied by the Treasury partly by means of gold shipments and the mobilization of British dollar securities, and partly by loan operations in the United States. From 1917 onwards, it was the United States government that provided the funds required by means of interallied loans to the British government."[1]

The primary objective in this chapter is to discuss certain phases of the various exchange controls that began during the early years of the business depression, particularly in 1931, and which have in many countries continued to affect foreign exchange.

Indirect Exchange Control

Since foreign exchange rates are influenced by the volume of international transactions, any governmental measures affecting the volume

---

[1]Paul Einzig, *Exchange Control*, p. 24.

of imports or exports may result in indirect control of exchange rates and the volume of available exchange. Trade restrictions or aids established for purposes quite aside from exchange control may actually influence exchange rates. The protective tariff rates, import quotas, license requirements, export subsidies, government price control plans, commercial treaties, and trade agreements involve a certain amount of exchange control. So also do import embargoes and embargoes on foreign loans.

There have been instances of private bartering transactions between individual traders that obviate the use of foreign exchange. Mention should also be made of bartering arrangements established by governments and governmental purchasing agreements. The former tend to avoid the use of foreign exchange and the latter to encourage or regulate trade between particular countries. Some of the purchase agreements are general in character while others make reference to specifically named commodities.[2]

Gold, Currency, and Equalization Fund Policies

Once the worldwide business depression became acute, the exchange control requirements of many countries were no longer met by indirect measures. Direct exchange control methods were adopted in many instances to influence exchange rates, correct dislocated balances of international payments, protect currencies, conserve the supply of gold, regulate the flow of international commerce, control the servicing of debt and interest payments, and related objectives. One type of direct exchange control took the form of exchange restrictions, which will be discussed later in this chapter. But exchange control measures, short of restrictions, were adopted in a number of instances.

Suspension of Gold Standard. Suspension of the gold standard was one of the steps taken by a number of countries. The first important move in this direction occurred in September, 1931, when the British gold standard was suspended. This was followed by a decline in dollar-pound sterling exchange rates from the old mint par of $4.8665, at the time of the suspension, to an average of $3.27 in December, 1932. American exporters frequently complained of an exchange rate handi-

---

[2]Henry Tasca, *World Trading Systems* (Paris: International Institute of Intellectual Cooperation, 1939), Chapter VIII, The Purchase Agreements (of the British Government).

cap in the British market, and British exporters had an exchange rate advantage in the American market even though, because of serious business depression, their exports to the United States did not advance.

As various other currencies related to the pound sterling followed the example of Great Britain, the situation soon became more serious. The exchange rate depreciation, moreover, probably because exports and imports were fundamentally retarded by the business depression, was not revised or readjusted automatically. Exchange rates did not again advance until the gold standard was suspended in the United States. This was done in March, 1933. As much was said at this time about the utilization of a gold policy for the purpose of advancing commodity prices in the United States, it may well be that exchange rate control was not the sole objective of the United States Government, but the effect of gold standard suspension upon exchange rates soon became apparent.

Revaluation of Gold. Gold and currency policy also included gold purchase, gold price, and gold export measures. Between March 6, 1933, when redemption in gold was suspended in the United States, and April 19, exchange rates remained fairly stable. When on April 20, however, the exportation of gold was prohibited, except as specifically authorized by the Treasury, the dollar depreciated rapidly in foreign exchange markets, for this gold-export policy indicated that the United States dollar was not to be maintained at its former par of exchange. Moreover, on October 25, 1933, the Government inaugurated a policy of purchasing gold at prices to be announced from time to time. The initial gold-purchasing price of $31.36 per ounce was gradually increased to $35 on January 31, 1934, when the dollar was officially devalued. The $35 gold price has remained since then.

Devaluation of Currency. Related to gold standard suspension was the formal devaluation of currencies in a number of countries. Gold standard suspension in the United States was followed in January, 1934, by the official devaluation of the dollar at 59.06 cents. The new dollar represented 13.71+ grains of fine gold or 59.06 percent of the 23.22 grains that the old dollar had contained. Exchange rates underwent further readjustments with reference to this official devaluation, but their major readjustment had already taken place after the gold standard had been suspended.

Exchange Equalization. The combined policy of gold standard suspension, gold-export control, dollar devaluation, and gold purchasing did much to overcome the exchange rate depreciation problem, but it did not assure exchange stability. It was, therefore, accompanied by the establishment of exchange-equalization accounts. The British Government had, in fact, established an account or fund of this character on April 25, 1932. The United States followed in January, 1934; Argentina, Canada, and Belgium in 1935; Czechoslovakia, France, Holland, Latvia, Romania, and Switzerland in 1937; Colombia in 1937; and Cuba in 1939. These funds represented a most direct effort to control exchange rates within limits deemed reasonable by the respective governments.

When exchange rates fluctuate excessively, an exchange-equalization account may be used to buy or sell foreign currencies in the open exchange markets so as to affect the forces of supply and demand. Exchange-equalization operations are related to gold policy, since a fund may also be authorized to buy and sell gold or to exchange foreign exchange for gold.

The operations of several equalization funds may be interrelated to some degree by international agreement. Thus on September 26, 1936, a "Tripartite Agreement" was entered into by the United States, Great Britain, and France, and this was further implemented on October 12, 1936, by a three-power pact under which the American, British, and French exchange-equalization accounts were granted reciprocal gold earmarking facilities.

Exchange Stabilization Arrangements. From time to time, countries make arrangements with other countries, whereby they will help each other to stabilize their respective exchange rates. This is done when war breaks out and great strains are placed on the monetary resources of belligerents.

When the balance of payments of the United States became adverse in the late 1950's, arrangements were made with a number of countries to provide a means to stabilize exchange in case it came under pressure. Under such an arrangement, each country will go to the rescue of another country when its exchange is under pressure. It will do this by going into the market and buying this exchange, thus creating an upward movement in the rate. The United States began in March, 1962, to make such arrangements with countries that enjoyed stable and exchangeable currencies. The first such "swap" arrangement was made with the Bank of France on March 1, 1962, and involved the sum of $100 million. By early 1963, ten more such agreements had been made with the United States. These are with the United Kingdom, Netherlands, Belgium, Canada, Switzerland, Germany, Austria, Italy, and Sweden; in addition, the Bank for International Settlements (Switzerland) signed an agreement. The total of the amounts that are thus available to help stabilize the United States dollar, if it weakens under pressure, is $1,100 million.[3]

In this general connection, the term *Eurodollar* is of interest. By definition, a Eurodollar is a dollar deposit originally made by a foreigner in the United States, or a deposit sold by an American to a foreigner, which is, in turn, lent or relent by financial institutions abroad. A typical transaction is as follows: A French bank borrows $2 million held to the credit of a London bank, paying 3¼ percent per annum for one month. It relends the money to a Paris commercial bank at 3⅜ percent, which in turn relends the money to an Italian bank at 3⅝ percent. The Italian bank lends the money to an Italian importer at 4 percent.[4]

Foreign Exchange Restrictions

Although the direct exchange control methods referred to have influenced very materially many exchange rates, particularly their current fluctuations, they do not fully serve the purpose of countries afflicted with a more than occasional or seasonal shortage of foreign exchange. Beginning in 1931, various countries adopted a form of exchange control known as *exchange restrictions*. Gradually the number of exchange restriction countries increased to well above thirty even before World War II began. Since then most of the countries that formerly had confined themselves to indirect control and direct exchange control short of restrictions have from time to time been added to the list.

An exchange restriction plan implies that the government of a nation, through a designated bank or other agency, undertakes to restrict the uses to which the available supply of exchange shall be put. Foreign exchange is allocated, in some instances in detail, as to its current use for the payment of import bills, interest on foreign loans, and other specific purposes.

---

[3]Federal Reserve Bank of New York, *Monthly Review of the FRB of New York* (March and August, 1963).

[4]Foreign Credit Interchange Bureau, *Foreign Credit Interchange Bureau Bulletin.*

Reasons for Exchange Restrictions. The basic reason for most exchange restriction measures is the absence of a volume of foreign exchange sufficient to meet freely all of the customary requirements of international marketing and finance. The exchange shortage is in some instances induced by a dislocation of foreign trade. The customary relationship between exports and imports of some countries is disrupted by the shrinkage of their export markets, by a disproportionate decline of the prices of some of their major raw materials or food export commodities, or by other circumstances. There is also a sharp decline in the movement of new foreign loans and investments to these countries. The destruction due to war so reduces productive capacity and creates demands for needed imports that a great shortage of desirable currencies, for example, the United States dollar, becomes a serious matter. The international balance of payments, therefore, is disrupted to such a degree that governments decide to determine how all or most of the available exchange should be used.

Objectives of Exchange Restrictions. More specifically, exchange restrictions are variously designed:

1. To provide the exchange necessary for the financing of essential imports.

2. To allocate or limit exchange for the servicing of external debts and investments.

3. To prevent the flight of capital.

4. To limit speculation.

5. To encourage lagging exports.

6. To encourage tourist travel.

It has also been discovered that exchange restrictions provide a bargaining basis in trade negotiations conducted with other countries, and that exchange restrictions can be made part and parcel of general economic planning by a government. When in the course of a planned economy political considerations become paramount, exchange restrictions can be utilized for the purpose of increasing, maintaining, or curbing trade with particular foreign countries.

In addition to these objectives, all of which are primarily related to a shortage of exchange, exchange restrictions also constitute a method of influencing or determining foreign exchange rates. When a government limits and prescribes the uses of all or most of the available exchange, it can and does fix the nation's official exchange rates and may also regulate any unofficial exchange rates permitted within its domains. The exchange rate-fixing power of some governments is further enhanced by import quotas, licensing plans, and other foreign trade control measures.

Administration of Exchange Restrictions. Exchange restriction measures are variously administered through a designated bank, exchange control commission, exchange control committee, export and import control, exchange control office, foreign exchange control board, or otherwise designated agency. Exporters in such countries are customarily required to receive payment in foreign currency and then to turn over to the exchange restriction authority all or such portion of their exchange as the current regulations require at an official buying rate. Importers and others requiring foreign exchange then purchase it, so far as the restrictions permit, at an official selling rate. The difference provides a basis for possible profit to the exchange control office or bank.

In some countries there is also a free exchange market in which exchange derived from certain exports or from other authorized services may be obtained, usually at higher cost to the importer. The rates in the free market may be subject to bidding, but the exchange authority may regulate them somewhat on the basis of percentage relationship to official rates or otherwise. Thus, in a single country there may be one or more pegged exchange rates for official exchange and also free market, curb, or otherwise designated rates applicable to exchange not allocated by the government. This is known as a system of *multiple exchange rates*.

Thus, on October 1, 1949, when Argentina announced depreciated exchange rates varying from 17 to 30.5 percent, but not changing the basic exchange quotation, the following scale of exchange rates was established:

Class of Exchange	Pesos per United States Dollar	
	Buying	Selling
Basic...	3.3582	6.0857
Preferential A..........	4.8321	3.7313
Preferential B..........	5.7286	5.3714
Special.	7.1964	...
Free.................	9.0000	9.0000

The application of the several rates depended upon the purpose for which the exchange was acquired or sold. Basic buying rates, for example, applied to meat, wheat, corn, linseed oil, and seed. Preferential A (buying) applied to edible oils, wool, and hides, while free (buying) applied to officially approved nontrade transactions, that is, tourists, services, and transfer of profits.

In 1950, the rates in Argentina were changed again, the basic selling rate increasing to 7.50, and the preferential selling rate, to 5.00. The respective basic and preferential buying rates were set at 5.00 and 7.50, respectively. The free rate (actually fixed by the Central Bank) was set at 14.00.

On October 28, 1955, Argentina "abolished" the multiple system of foreign exchange quotation and established a "single" official rate of 18 pesos per United States dollar, applicable to both export and import items. Articles on the official list of imports were paid for at 18; other articles imported were paid for at the free market rate, subject to a surcharge of 20 pesos (later changed to 40 pesos) to be paid by the importer; and, finally, other imports that were payable at the free market rate and not subject to surcharge.

The official rate of 18 pesos to the United States dollar remained in effect until Decree #11916 of December 31, 1958, canceled the rate and declared that there would be a single rate fluctuating according to supply and demand. (In December, 1958, the peso reached an all-time low in free trading at 76.80 pesos per United States dollar.)

> Argentina liberalized its foreign exchange control system in 1959. It opened a free market through which exchange transactions could be made and remittances abroad of profits, royalties, and capital effected.
>
> Argentina requires no import licenses. It regulates the flow of imports through the price mechanism, namely, through an import surcharge system. Exchange is made available on the free market where the rate is determined by supply and demand. Until April, 1962, the Central Bank entered the exchange market to prevent undue fluctuation in the exchange rate. Since then, the peso has been allowed to fluctuate freely and ranged mostly between 110 to 150 pesos to the dollar through December, 1962. In January, 1963, the rate settled at about 135.[5]

Exchange authorities have the further duties of distributing or allocating official exchange (1) between various exchange uses such as imported commodities and interest on foreign loans; (2) between par-

---

[5] U. S. Department of Commerce, *Basic Data on the Economy of Argentina* (Overseas Business Reports 63–84 [March, 1963]). Import commodities are classified into several lists with surcharges ranging up to 200 percent depending on the degree of protection accorded by the Government. Unlisted items carry a 150 percent surcharge.

ticular importers or other individuals or firms; (3) between particular classes of imported commodities; and (4) between particular foreign countries or sources of supply. They must also set up a plan for effective administration. Some authorities require import permits before imported products can be cleared through the customs, while others require import permits before import orders are placed.

Exchange authorities may also set time limits within which allocated exchange shall actually be used. There is usually a code of regulations that sets forth the general routine and basis for the allocation of the official exchange.

Blocked Accounts. As exchange restrictions largely determine the uses of available foreign exchange and most of them were adopted because of a shortage of exchange, one of the problems associated with them is the so-called *blocked accounts*. Blocked accounts represent national funds for which no official exchange is allocated or for which none is available. Some of them comprise import or other commercial payments, interest, and other financial payments that were owing before exchange restrictions were imposed. Others represent current import transactions in excess of allotted official exchange and for which no free market exchange is available, or other payments that cannot be transferred because of exchange shortage.

In exchange restriction countries such credits are held in blocked accounts by government authority. Their owners do not always have free use of them. The banks in which the accounts are held may be authorized to use them as the basis for loans, and the government may definitely restrict their uses and even direct their uses.

Germany, before World War II, and the United Kingdom, after World War II, afford classic examples of the ramifications of foreign exchange control.

Germany's Example. Germany, practically devoid of gold and foreign exchange, instituted a bewildering system of blocked mark accounts following the "standstill agreement" of 1933. While the official value of the mark was not changed, blocked mark accounts of various kinds and worth varying amounts in exchange were set up and shifted and changed constantly.

The "aski" mark — the most important international trading account — was acquired by exporting to Germany, payment being arranged under this system. The value of the aski mark and the German goods for which it was accepted varied frequently and widely, depending chiefly on the political and economic strength of each trading partner.

The United Kingdom's Example. The sterling area is a wartime and postwar development of the prewar sterling bloc dating from 1931. In that year, Great Britain devalued her currency by abandoning the gold standard. Thereupon, certain countries that kept their Central Bank reserves in the form of sterling rather than gold or foreign exchange of other kinds, and that also devalued, joined the United Kingdom in the formation of the sterling bloc. The countries included in this group included not only all parts of the British Commonwealth (except Canada and Newfoundland), but also Portugal, Egypt, Iraq, Thailand, Sweden, Norway, Finland, Denmark, Estonia, Iran, and Latvia. All of these countries conducted a high proportion of their trade with each other, and particularly with Great Britain.

> The prewar sterling area was the result of decisions by the individual nations. It was not based on any charter or agreements. . . . There was no exchange control and no pooling of dollars.[6]
>
> At the beginning of the war, the nations of the sterling area entered into an agreement to pool their resources of foreign exchange. Under this agreement all the nations undertook to do what in fact most of them had been doing before the war — namely, to sell their foreign exchange income to Britain, and thus to maintain the whole of their reserves in the form of sterling assets. They also agreed to be sparing in their use of dollars so as to reserve them for purchasing essential supplies from the United States. In return, Britain promised to supply from the pool the dollars and other currencies which the member countries required for their essential imports. . . . Each of the nations has remained responsible for its own import program.[7]

Another feature of the wartime (and postwar) sterling area is the piling up of credit balances in Britain for supplies furnished Great Britain by member countries during the war. At the end of the war, these balances amounted to the equivalent of something between $12 and $16 billion. Thus, during the war, the sterling area became a unit for exchange control purposes. Funds could move freely into the sterling area; a fence of exchange control stretched around the area. Moreover, most of the non-British nations left the area, only Iraq, Jordan, Iceland, and Ireland remaining.[8]

---

[6]British Information Services, *The Sterling Area* 1D627 (October, 1945), p. 3.

[7]*Ibid.*, p. 5.

[8]Egypt and Palestine withdrew from the sterling area in 1947 and 1948, respectively.

That the sterling area has been important to United States international marketing is seen from the fact "that more than two thirds of the items listed as net exports of the Overseas Sterling Area are net imports of the United States; almost four fifths of the net imports of the Overseas Sterling Area are net exports of the United States."[9] In terms of United States international marketing, the sterling area accounted for 12.5 percent of United States exports in 1957 and 15.5 percent of general imports; compared with 26.5 percent annual average 1934–1938 and 21.5 percent respectively.[10]

The exchange control system of the United Kingdom derived from the Exchange Control Act of 1947. It vested the operation of the system in "the Control," which operated through "authorized channels" (banks) in the purchase and sale of current foreign exchanges.

Exchange that was not current but was blocked comprised the large sterling balances accumulated against British accounts during and immediately after the war. Blocked sterling accounts were controlled by the Bank of England, and releases from blocked accounts to foreign exchange accounts required specific authority.

For current accounts, in which foreign traders are primarily interested because their current transactions are paid in this manner, the control divided up the world into several groups, depending upon the ease or difficulty of effecting transfers of foreign exchange to the respective groups. For example, early in 1957, there were four classes of exchange accounts: (1) American and Canadian account countries; (2) transferable account countries; (3) registered accounts; and (4) resident accounts — Scheduled Territories (formerly known as the sterling area).

Transfers from American and Canadian account countries, Group 1, to all groups were permitted without official approval.

Groups 2, transferable account countries, had unlimited transfer rights for remittances only to other countries in Group 2 and to resident accounts, Group 4.

Group 3, registered accounts, applied only to transactions in gold and could be opened in the name of persons resident in the transferable account countries, Group 2. Payments could be made from registered accounts, Group 3, for purchasing gold, United States or Canadian dollars, or for transfer to any other account.

---

[9]Economic Cooperation Administration, Special Mission to the United Kingdom, *The Sterling Area — An American Appraisal* (London: 1951), p. 31.

[10]*Ibid.*, pp. 114 and 116; United Nations, *Direction of International Trade* (May, 1958).

Group 4, resident accounts, *made* payments only to other resident accounts within the group but could *accept* payments from any source.

There was a shifting of countries in and out of groups, and from time to time a change in the groups themselves.[11]

The difficulties thus experienced with regard to sterling were a result of the inconvertibility of this widely-used currency. When the Anglo-American Financial Agreement was negotiated in 1945, one of the objectives was to bring about convertibility of sterling. The first drawings on the credit of $3¾ billion were available in July, 1946. Free convertibility was restored to a large part of currently earned sterling before the deadline (for providing for convertibility) of July 15, 1947, was reached. The rush to convert sterling was so strong that free convertibility was withdrawn on August 20, 1946, with only $400 million out of $3¾ billion of the loan remaining.

The year 1959 dawned auspiciously with the announcement on December 29, 1958, of the extended convertibility of the currencies of twelve European countries, including the United Kingdom. With this announcement, the first three groups of external sterling were merged into a single category called external account sterling, which is freely convertible into any other currency. The official exchange rates of $2.78–$2.82 are retained. The other sterling account, in effect, relates to residents who are still subject to exchange and trade control. Moreover, import quotas and licenses will still prevent the free use of sterling, even for those who hold external account sterling. Complete freedom of exchange will depend upon the availability of exchange, particularly United States and Canadian dollars. The steps thus taken, nevertheless, constitute a very decisive move toward complete convertibility.

European Payments Union (EPU) and European Monetary Agreement (EMA). An additional measure designed to assist in the recovery of Europe was an outgrowth of the integration implicit in the Organization for European Economic Cooperation (OEEC). The maze of foreign exchange and trade restrictions with which the world has been plagued was seriously interfering with the resumption of intra-European trade. In an effort to encourage this trade, an Intra-European Payments and Compensations Agreement was signed in the fall of 1948 with United States Government financial support through the Economic Cooperation

---

[11]The National City Bank of New York, *Foreign Information Service — Summary . . . Exchange and Foreign Trade Regulations,* as of January 1, 1957, pp. 33–41.

Administration (ECA). This initial effort was replaced in 1950 with the European Payments Union, also supported by means of United States Government finances. Each country in the Union was assigned both a debit and a credit limit. Obligations to pay or to receive funds coming within the limits were cleared, but requirements beyond the limits called for special arrangements. The Bank for International Settlements was the agent for the EPU.

Progress in the direction of self-help in the European area is evident from a comparison of data covering the initial agreement and data relating to the Union. With a gross intra-European deficit of $4 billion for 21 months (1948–1950) of the Agreement's duration to be settled, about one third ($1.4 billion) was taken care of by drawing rights (identical with the amount of United States Government financial aid), the other two thirds being covered by gold movements, new bilateral credit, etc., with only 2 percent being "compensated." On the other hand, during a period of 93 months of the EPU — to March 31, 1958 — the gross deficit was $17.2 billion for which "compensations" alone covered three fourths. Moreover, the $272 million of capital of the Union was intact and, in addition, gold and dollar holdings were $322 million.[12]

Since the beginning of EPU, France, followed by the United Kingdom, Italy, and Turkey, has been the largest debtor and Germany by far the largest creditor. In settlement of a cumulative debit of $5.6 billion, gold was used for over $3.6 billion, and credit for $1.0 billion.

Compensation is a means of settlement that at various times has had two meanings. Simple compensation is purely a mathematical calculation — an offsetting. Belgium sells to the Netherlands, whereby Belgium's credit balance is increased and the debit balance of the Netherlands is increased.

More complicated compensation — and the type generally used due to the usual absence of a perfect setup as in the first instance — is "a payment made by one country to another by utilizing the currency of a third country. A simple example would be the payment of a Norwegian debt to the Netherlands in sterling. It is evident that such a transaction

---

[12]Bank for International Settlement, *Twenty-eighth Annual Report* (1st, April 1957 — 31st, March 1958), pp. 198 and 204. See also earlier reports for greater detail. The dollar sign ($) in connection with EPU stands for United States dollars, or United States dollars' worth of gold, or EPU units of account (equivalent to United States dollars for accounting purposes).

involves a limited transferability of sterling; the Netherlands, creditor of both countries, has exchanged Norway as its debtor for the United Kingdom, to the extent that Norway's debt is repaid in sterling."[13]

It will be recalled that the EPU was a second major postwar step (in the European area) intended to facilitate a return to currency convertibility and thus promote an expansion in trade. It was simply a temporary device, which would terminate when the European Monetary Agreement came into force.

With the announcement on December 29, 1958, concerning the wider convertibility of the currencies of twelve European countries, EPU was replaced with the European Monetary Agreement (EMA). Under this arrangement, payments between European countries will be settled in gold in proportion to the amounts of the contributions of the several Contracting Parties; and interest and service charges are also to be paid in gold. A European Fund is established and units of account represent 0.88867088 grams of fine gold. A Multilateral System of Settlements is established "to facilitate the settlement of transactions in the currencies and between the monetary areas of the Contracting Parties by enabling them to obtain interim financing and the settlement of their claims, regularly, on terms laid down in advance."[14]

Each Contracting Party is to established buying and selling rates for gold, the United States dollar, or some other currency, and these rates are used as a basis for calculations and settlements in the System of Settlements. "The net claim or debt of each Contracting Party, at the end of each accounting period, shall be settled by a payment in United States dollars made by the Fund or made to the Fund, and the bilateral claims or debts of the Contracting Parties shall be settled accordingly."[15]

"Furthermore, the Organization for Economic Cooperation and Development (OECD) has taken over from the OEEC the two Codes for the Liberalization of Capital Movements and of Current Invisible Operations, the aims of which are to ensure the maximum degree of freedom for transfers and transactions between member countries in the fields of capital movements and services."[16]

---

[13]Bank for International Settlement, *Eighteenth Annual Report* (14 June 1948), p. 149.

[14]The Organization for Economic Cooperation and Development, *OECD* (Paris: OECD Publications, undated), pp. 88–89.

[15]*Ibid.*, Article 12(a).

[16]*Ibid.*, p. 24.

Foreign Exchange Agreements

Exchange restrictions and the shortage of foreign exchange have in many countries given rise to special agreements variously referred to as clearing, payments, clearing and payments, compensation, and exchange allocation agreements. These terms are frequently used in a somewhat loose fashion, for uniform terminology and definitions have not been attained in these agreements.

Clearing Agreement. The term foreign exchange *clearing agreement* usually refers to a bilateral agreement under which specified trade settlements are made *without* the transfer of foreign exchange between the two countries. Each country establishes a clearing account. Each account then receives in domestic currency the sums paid by its importers and makes payments to its exporters also in domestic currency. No exchange is transferred, and it is obviously impossible in this way to transact international marketing in excess of the amount in the clearing account of each country.

Clearing agreements constitute a means of enhancing trade somewhat beyond the volume sometimes possible under a system of drastic exchange restriction, and they themselves also constitute a form of exchange restriction. They may be compulsory so far as certain trade is concerned; they may contain definite provisions as to how balances shall be disposed of; they may provide that a stated percentage of the amounts remitted by importers shall be used for the payment of old or previously incurred commercial debts or to meet public or private financial debts.

Payments Agreement. The term *payments agreement* usually refers to a bilateral arrangement that governs the transfer of exchange between two nations. No clearing mechanism is provided because payments are made by the use of foreign exchange. An exchange restriction country and a country not pursuing a policy of exchange restrictions agree as to the use of exchange by the former within the limits set in the agreement. The exchange restriction country may agree that its importers will be authorized to make direct transfers of exchange to the exporters of the other country in payment of current commercial bills up to a specified percentage of the total volume of foreign exchange transferred to the exchange restriction country from the other country. Payments agreements may also provide that a specified percentage of the entire amount of the foreign exchange available for transfer in the exchange restriction country shall be used to pay old commercial debts or public and private debts of a financial character.

Clearing and Payments Agreement. The agreement known as a *clearing and payments agreement* is a combination of the two above types of exchange agreements. An arrangement of this type provides the necessary mechanism for the clearing of current commercial transactions without transfer of exchange. A country which has not adopted an exchange restriction plan may also agree that a specified percentage of the payments made by its importers will be set aside for the payment of old commercial debts and debts of a financial character. But the agreement may at the same time, in the case of the exchange restriction country, provide that old commercial debts shall be paid by importers by actual transfer of foreign exchange allocated to them for this purpose.

Compensation Agreement. The term *compensation agreement* is used so loosely that no definite meaning can well be assigned to it. In its broadest sense it may be applied to all of the various types of agreements referred to above. It is, however, applied in a narrower sense to agreements of a wide variety that call for the exchange between two nations of specified quantities or values of commodities and that provide a method of payment.

Compensation agreements are similar to the clearing agreements referred to previously in that they provide for the specific exchange of goods either on a direct barter basis or subject to payments provided for in the compensation agreement. Some of them are similar to clearing agreements in that payments are made by the importers of each country in domestic currency without transfer of exchange. But a compensation agreement may provide for a direct barter of specified quantities of other commodities; or for the barter of a specified quantity of a named commodity for a variety of other commodities; or for the purchase and sale of specified values of commodities with commitments on the part of the two governments that the necessary foreign exchange will be available.

Types of Import License and Exchange Restriction Systems.[17] The countries of the world, according to the restrictive systems they employ, may be divided into four categories, viz.:

---

[17]From *International Commerce* (July 1, 1963), pp. 16–18, supplemented by *ibid.*, (January 7, 1963), p. 11.

1. No import license or exchange restriction.

2. Import license on a limited number of items and no exchange restriction.

3. No import license *but* exchange restriction.

4. Import license and/or exchange license and restriction — import license may carry the right to acquire foreign exchange.

In the first category of no import license or exchange restriction, we find countries chiefly in the Middle East — Aden, Bahrain, Muscat, Oman, Qatar, Saudi Arabia, Trucial States, and Yemen. In addition, there are French Somoliland and, curiously, Yugoslavia for which the report states "an import license is not necessary but only licensed import firms are permitted to carry on import operations. An exchange permit is not required but the Government maintains strict control over foreign exchange allocations." Bolivia and Paraguay also appear in the select group. With respect to Paraguay "most imports are subject to prior deposit in local currency before shipment."

In the second category of an import license required for a limited number of items but no exchange license required, there are quite a number of countries — 34 out of 124 listed. Most of the European countries fit into this group, as well as 7 countries in Africa, 2 in Asia, and 9 in the Western Hemisphere (United States, Canada, Brazil, Jamaica, Costa Rica, Ecuador, Honduras, Panama, and Peru).

In the third category of no import license requirements but with exchange restrictions, there are 4 countries in Latin America — Argentina, Chile, Nicaragua, and Uruguay. Chile's regulations are quite complicated; no import license is required but a list of permitted imports is published and prior registration of such imports is required, with prior import guarantee deposits at the time of registration. Likewise, Uruguay requires no import license but almost all imports are subject to surcharges of from 20 to 300 percent of c.i.f. value. Argentina is also free of exchange restrictions but with exchange surcharges. In this group are also Ethiopia and the Philippine Republic which require an advance deposit on certain categories of imports.

In the fourth category of import and/or exchange licenses and restrictions, most of the countries of the world are listed, viz., 75 out of the 124 countries cited in the reports. Nearly all of the African countries are in this group, including the Union of South Africa, and most of the Asiatic nations, including Japan and the British colony of Hong Kong.

Some of the nations of the Western Hemisphere that fall in this category are those of the Caribbean islands, Colombia and Venezuela in South America, and Mexico. All of the communist states are included since they conduct their international trade as a government monopoly.

These countries change in their respective positions, depending upon their international trading and financial position. Of course, the communist states are not expected to liberalize their trading methods. It is clear, however, that restrictions on imports and exchange remittances are still widespread.

Effects of Exchange Restrictions and Agreements. Exchange restriction measures obviously cannot be considered without reference to the various types of exchange agreements that have been concluded by many foreign countries. Exchange restrictions, although intended to accomplish the objectives of the country enforcing them, have necessarily affected the international trading of the other trading nations throughout the entire world. As they are imposed primarily because certain countries are faced with a shortage of foreign exchange, it cannot in all instances be concluded that international trading as a whole has been curtailed. Their effect in this regard depends upon the policies variously pursued with reference to the allocation of exchange for current imports of merchandise as compared with exchange for commercial debts contracted in the past, for transfer of profits from enterprises operated, and for financial payments such as interest payments on public and private debts.

It should also be recalled that exchange restrictions are in many instances related to the quantitative restrictions on imports that so many foreign governments have considered necessary. But it is clear that exchange restrictions have:

1. Affected the importation of some classes of goods more adversely than others, the essential character of imports being considered in the allocation of exchange.

2. Affected the trade of some exporting countries more seriously than that of others.

3. Tended, particularly in connection with certain international agreements, to channelize trade bilaterally.

4. Been used by some countries for bargaining purposes.

5. Been utilized by some countries for the purpose of subsidizing particular exports.

6. Influenced domestic prices in some countries so as to handicap exports.

7. Complicated the routine work of importers and exporters.

Exchange restriction measures, however, also have certain desirable features under conditions of serious and more than seasonal or strictly temporary exchange shortage. Exchange restrictions have:

1. Stabilized exchange rates for both importers and exporters.

2. Aided various needy countries to obtain a larger supply of the commodities considered most necessary by their governments.

3. Enabled various debtor nations to safeguard their currency, control exchange rates in the national interest, protect their domestic economy to some extent against unfavorable commodity price changes, regulate interest and other financial payments, and otherwise protect themselves against threatening disturbances.

The International Monetary Fund (IMF)

The International Monetary Fund has been established to relieve exchange shortages and to provide some measure of control over the values of exchanges and variations in such values.

Purposes of IMF. The International Monetary Fund was established in 1944 for the following specific purposes:

1. To promote international monetary cooperation through a permanent institution which provides the machinery for consultation and collaboration on international monetary problems.

2. To facilitate the expansion and balanced growth of international trade, and to contribute thereby to the promotion and maintenance of high levels of employment and real income and to the development of the productive resources of all members as primary objectives of economic policy.

3. To promote exchange stability, to maintain orderly exchange arrangements among members, and to avoid competitive exchange depreciation.

4. To assist in the establishment of a multilateral system of payments in respect of current transactions between members and in the elimination of foreign exchange restrictions which hamper the growth of world trade.

5. To give confidence to members by making the Fund's resources available to them under adequate safeguards, thus providing them with opportunity to correct maladjustments in their balance of payments without resorting to measures destructive of national or international prosperity.

6. In accordance with the above, to shorten the duration and lessen the degree of disequilibrium in the international balances of payments of members.

Quotas. Each of the countries that is a member of the IMF is assigned a quota which amounts to a subscription. The United States was assigned the largest quota and it is now 27.7 percent.

The total subscriptions amount to $14.85 billion. Under the Articles of Agreement, individual subscribers were called upon to pay in gold initially the smaller of 25 percent of the quota or 10 percent of its net official holdings of gold and United States dollars. The balance was to be paid in local currency of the respective subscribers.

Exchange Rates. Par of exchange of the currency of each subscriber is required to be certified to the Fund. This must be expressed either in gold or in United States dollars. Fluctuations in par are to be no more than 1 percent for spot exchange and an unspecified margin, to be determined by the IMF, for other exchange transactions.

Changes of par value, not exceeding 10 percent, are considered routine. A second change of an amount not exceeding another 10 percent calls for an expression of the Fund's attitude. If the change is "necessary to correct a fundamental disequilibrium," the Fund must concur. Unauthorized changes in par value incur a penalty of ineligibility to use the Fund's resources.

Supplying Required Exchange. Basically, the function of the IMF is to supply a member, at its request, "with the currency of another member in exchange for gold or for the currency of the" purchaser. This is a simple foreign exchange transaction, namely, purchase sterling with United States dollars. The difficulty arises, however, when a British subject cannot purchase United States dollars with sterling because of a shortage of United States dollars at the disposal of the United Kingdom. Such a situation can be helped by the operation of the IMF from which the United Kingdom may purchase United States dollars with sterling. However, there is a limit. The transaction must not cause an increase in the Fund's holdings of the purchaser's currency (sterling) by more than 25 percent of its quota ($1.3 billion) per year, with a top limit of 100 percent, namely, 4 years at the maximum permitted.

As interpreted by the Executive Board of the IMF on August 24, 1955, this provision will permit transactions during a given *twelve-months' period* by which the holdings of a member's currency may amount to 200 percent of its quota. In no case, however, may the total purchases of such a member's currency exceed 25 percent of its quota.

Income. The IMF earns income by imposing service charges on foreign exchange transactions and handling charges on gold. The exchange charges increase as the amount of the overdraft increases.

Scarce Currencies. *Scarce currency* is a technical term by which the IMF characterizes a situation that existed after World War II with the "dollar shortage." When the IMF makes such a declaration, it is called upon to replenish its holdings of the scarce currency by borrowing or by purchasing for gold. The Fund may ration its own sales of such scarce currency. Countries are also authorized temporarily to impose restrictions on the use of such scarce currency.

Restrictions. Members are called upon also (1) to avoid exchange restrictions on current payments; and (2) to avoid discriminatory currency practices, including multiple exchange "except as authorized under this Agreement or approved by the Fund."[18]

Administration. A Board of Governors, with representation by each member country, has overall powers; and there are Executive Directors and a Managing Director. The number of votes for each member country is determined by the amount of its quota.

Operation. For the eighteen years 1944 to 1962, the Fund reported its transactions as follows: (1) currency purchased against member's own currency, $6.266 billion, of which $4.066 billion was in United

---

[18]Despite this provision, the Fund has used its authority to approve multiple exchange practices.

States dollars; (2) member's currency repurchased by member with convertible currency or gold, $4.098 billion, of which the United Kingdom, with $1.367 billion was the largest customer, followed by France with $.5 billion.[19]

General Agreement on Tariffs and Trade (GATT)

The reciprocal trade agreements program of the United States, beginning in 1934, and the General Agreement on Tariffs and Trade (GATT), beginning in 1947, also relate to the subject of exchange restrictions. All of these agreements seek to bring about nondiscrimination in commercial relations between the contracting parties. Under the terms of GATT, exchange policies, when used as a means of import control, are rigidly circumscribed.

Article XV of GATT deals with exchange arrangements and its provisions indicate the close tie, in this regard, with the International Monetary Fund (IMF). The preamble of Article XV declares it to be the policy of the GATT to cooperate with the IMF with a view to coordinating their policies within their respective fields of operation. No trade policy is to negate an exchange obligation under the IMF; and no IMF obligation is to vitiate any trade policy.

In all matters relating to monetary reserves, balance of payments position, or foreign exchange arrangements, the IMF is to be consulted and is to have the final word as to the facts in these matters. The IMF is also given authority to determine the actual conditions referred to in Article XII of GATT (concerning a decline in or a low level of monetary reserves, etc.). Any complaints by contracting parties as to inconsistencies by any party in the use of the provisions of this article are to be lodged with the IMF.

All contracting parties must either be a member of the IMF or enter into a special exchange agreement with the GATT parties. This special exchange agreement is to be about the same as set forth under the IMF.

Between GATT and the IMF there are now adequate international agreements to limit and control exchange rate discrimination that became so serious during the 1930's. This does not mean, however, that such discriminatory practices will cease entirely. As pointed out in the discussion of these agencies, considerable flexibility is provided under

---

[19]See *International Monetary Fund — Annual Report 1962.*

which unfair exchange practices are possible. In such cases, provision is made for "compensatory" adjustments, namely, self-defense on the part of countries that suffer injury. During the 1930's this reaction was termed "retaliatory."

Summary

1. Exchange control is exercised directly and indirectly by many countries and the free establishment of exchange rates is impeded or offset.
2. Policies that influence the extent and the value of international transactions indirectly affect exchange rates. The business depression of the 1930's caused exchange control to be widely practiced.
3. When gold was abandoned as a convertible basis for currencies and when it was revalued, exchange rates depreciated by means of devaluation.
4. Exchange stabilization agreements are made by means of bilateral arrangements between countries. By these agreements, any one country suffering from pressure on its exchange is assisted by the agreeing countries, which enter the market and create an artificial demand for the depressed currency, thus raising its rate. "Swap" arrangements is a popular name for such practice.
5. The term Eurodollar is basically a United States dollar bank account being sold to a foreigner (or any interest outside of the United States). Such foreign interest buys this account because he expects to earn a higher interest rate abroad. Such transactions involve what is known as short-term capital, sometimes called "hot" money.
6. Foreign exchange restrictions determine the purposes for which exchange may be used and the rate at which such uses may be satisfied. Usually, favorable exchange rates are quoted for the importation of essentials, and high rates or no exchange at all for so-called luxuries. Exports of certain products may be stimulated by attractive exchange rates and exports of readily marketable goods may be paid at less favorable rates.
7. Germany probably developed the most complex foreign exchange control system of all time in the decade preceding the outbreak of World War II.
8. The United Kingdom, center of the sterling area, represented the most complicated exchange control system in the post-World War II period up to 1959.
9. The European Payments Union was an arrangement under which exchange was transferred multilaterally within the Union as a means of stimulating trade and providing a payments mechanism. It has since been replaced by the European Monetary Agreement (EMA).
10. The European Monetary Agreement (EMA) seeks to provide exchange stabilization among the Contracting Parties. Settlements are made in terms of the United States dollar.
11. Convertibility of currencies is highly desirable in order to open worldwide markets and to end discriminations. Pound sterling has been the key currency for exchange convertibility in the Free World area.

12. Various agreements are negotiated between pairs of countries to conduct trade with or without financial payments. Pure barter may be provided or exchange payments may be made to liquidate outstanding balances.

13. An analysis of the import and exchange restrictions currently in effect indicates that most countries impose such restrictions.

14. Exchange restrictions do not necessarily curtail international trade as a whole. However, they have inevitably undesirable effects, and it is clear that the world economy would be much healthier if such restrictions were completely abolished.

15. The International Monetary Fund has supervision over exchange-rate policies of its members and it can provide exchange for countries that are in need of it.

16. The IMF is recognized by the parties to the General Agreement on Tariffs and Trade (GATT) as the authority for determining the foreign exchange status of countries who claim payments difficulties as a reason for discriminatory policies.

QUESTIONS

1. Define exchange control and explain its various meanings.
2. (a) How can a currency be pegged?
   (b) Why would a currency be pegged?
3. How does a customs tariff relate to the subject of exchange control?
4. Under the gold standard, certain gold points were recognized. What bearing did these gold points have on the subject of exchange control?
5. Why did a revaluation of gold by the United Kingdom and by the United States result in raising the exchange rates of these countries?
6. How is an exchange-equalization account related to exchange control?
7. Why do countries impose exchange restrictions?
8. What are the purposes of an exchange restriction plan? Comment on these purposes critically.
9. Describe a multiple exchange system and give examples of its use.
10. Comment on the freedom of "free" exchange markets in countries restricting exchange.
11. Define *blocked accounts*. How can they be liquidated?
12. Describe the concept of the sterling area.
13. How did the existence of the sterling area affect United States export and import trade? Explain.
14. Explain the purposes of the European Payments Union. In your opinion, how successful was this Union?
15. How does the EMA differ from the EPU?
16. Distinguish between a clearing agreement and a payments agreement.
17. Contrast the unfavorable and favorable effects of exchange restrictions.

18. Comment critically on the purposes of the International Monetary Fund.
19. Is there any limit to the amount of foreign exchange that any one country may purchase from the IMF? Explain.
20. Define the concept of scarce currencies. What policy implications are inherent in this concept as far as countries that suffer from such scarcity are concerned?
21. Explain the provisions of GATT concerning the use of discriminatory foreign exchange restrictions.

PROBLEM

Examine the most recent report of the International Monetary Fund on "Exchange Restrictions."

Prepare a report on the exchange control and restriction policy of any country of your choice; or, of the countries in any geographical area of your choice, such as Europe, British Commonwealth, Latin America, Asia, etc.

Supplement the information thus obtained by more recent information available from the foreign department of a bank located conveniently to you.

COLLATERAL READINGS

Bank for International Settlements. *Annual Report.* Basel, Switzerland.

Conan, A. R. *The Sterling Area.* London: Macmillan Co., Ltd., 1952.

Dartnell International Trade Handbook, The. Chicago: The Dartnell Corporation, 1963.

Dietrich, Ethel B. *World Trade.* New York: Henry Holt & Co., Inc., 1939. Chapter 6.

Einzig, Paul. *Exchange Control.* London: Macmillan Co., Ltd., 1934.

Ellsworth, Paul T. *International Economics.* New York: Macmillan Co., 1938. Chapter 21.

Heck, Harold J. *Foreign Commerce.* New York: McGraw-Hill Book Company, Inc., 1953. Chapter 14.

Henning, Charles N. *International Finance.* New York: Harper & Brothers, 1958. Chapters 16, 18, and 19.

Horn, Paul V. *International Trade Principles and Practices,* Third Edition. New York: Prentice-Hall, Inc., 1951. Chapter 20.

International Monetary Fund. *Annual Report.* Washington, D.C.: Government Printing Office.

————————. *Report on Exchange Restrictions.* Washington, D.C.: annual.

Mikesell, Raymond F. *United States Economic Policy and International Relations.* New York: McGraw-Hill Book Company, Inc., 1952. Chapter 10.
————————————. *Foreign Exchange in the Postwar World.* New York: Twentieth Century Fund, 1954.
Organization for European Economic Cooperation (OEEC). *Annual Report of the Managing Board of the European Payments Union.* Paris.
Pratt, E. E. *Modern International Commerce.* New York: Allyn and Bacon, Inc., 1956. Chapter 8.
Tarshis, Lorie. *Introduction to International Trade and Finance.* New York: John Wiley & Sons, Inc., 1955. Chapter 25.
Tasca, Henry J. *World Trading Systems: A Study of American and British Commercial Policies.* Paris: International Institute of Intellectual Cooperation, 1939.
Towle, Lawrence W. *International Trade and Commercial Policy.* New York and London: Harper & Brothers, 1956. Chapter 13.
Trued, M. N., and R. F. Mikesell. *Postwar Bilateral Payments Agreements.* Princeton: Princeton University Press, 1955.

INDEX

A